2 VOL. SET

THE DIARY OF
HUMFREY WANLEY
1715-1726

HUMFREY WANLEY

From a painting by Thomas Hill, 1722

THE DIARY OF
HUMFREY WANLEY

1715-1726

EDITED BY

C. E. WRIGHT

AND

RUTH C. WRIGHT

In two volumes

VOLUME I

1715-1723

LONDON

THE BIBLIOGRAPHICAL SOCIETY

1966

Oxford University Press, Ely House, London W. 1

GLASGOW NEW YORK TORONTO MELBOURNE WELLINGTON
CAPE TOWN SALISBURY IBADAN NAIROBI LUSAKA ADDIS ABABA
BOMBAY CALCUTTA MADRAS KARACHI LAHORE DACCA
KUALA LUMPUR HONG KONG

BIBLIOGRAPHICAL SOCIETY PUBLICATION
FOR THE YEARS 1961 AND 1962
PUBLISHED 1966

CONTENTS

PREFACE

THE late Mr. Seymour de Ricci in his *English Collectors of Books & Manuscripts (1530–1930)*, in the portion devoted to the collecting activities of Robert and Edward Harley, remarked, apropos of Wanley's Diary, 'it is a great pity that it has not been printed in full', and subsequently in a conversation in the spring of 1939 (after work on the present edition had already begun) Mr. de Ricci reaffirmed how important he felt such a work would be not only for the history of the Harleian Library but for the history of collecting in general in the early decades of the eighteenth century.[1] This was welcome encouragement for pursuing a task which was clearly going to be formidable since obviously nothing less than a fully annotated edition of the Diary would be sufficient. Further encouragement was forthcoming when the Bibliographical Society during the Secretaryship of Dr. R. B. McKerrow undertook with most encouraging readiness its publication; to the Society and to the continuing interest—and patience—of Sir Frank Francis, Dr. McKerrow's successor as Secretary, we are deeply indebted.

In view of the long period of time involved in the completion of this edition it may not be amiss to say something of the work entailed in its preparation. A complete transcript of the Diary (the MS. of which amounts to some 340 pages all written in Wanley's small, neat but closely packed handwriting) had been prepared by one of the editors by 1939 and concurrently a beginning had been made by the other on the individual examination of the MSS. in the Harleian Collection; World War II, however, brought the work to a complete standstill and this could not be resumed until 1946. In that year the MSS. were replaced on the shelves. The individual examination of the 7,660 MSS. in the Harleian Collection necessarily took a considerable time to complete in the limited free time available. Moreover, no beginning on the drafting of the footnotes could be made with any measure of completeness until a thorough examination had been made of ancillary material, more particularly that contained in the 'Wanleyana' preserved among the Harley Papers at Welbeck. We are most grateful to His Grace the Duke of Portland for his generosity in depositing them temporarily in the British Museum for our use in September 1947 and to his Librarian, Mr. Francis Needham, for making the necessary arrangements. The deposit of other Harley Papers by the Duke at intervals between 1947 and 1953 made further relevant material available too, which it was incumbent on us to examine. MS. material, some of it very considerable in bulk, relating to Wanley at every period of his life had also to be read through for any light it might throw on the background of the Diary and on the history of his early relations with Robert Harley and early years as Harley's Library-Keeper. This involved the examination of MSS. at several places outside London—in the Royal Library at Copenhagen and in the University Library at Uppsala as well as in the University Library at Cambridge, the Bodleian Library at Oxford, and the City Archives at Coventry. We should also like to express here our appreciation of the late Captain Bambridge's kindness in enabling us to see the Library and various papers at Wimpole Hall and of the generosity of the Academy of Sciences

---

[1] Mr. de Ricci also most generously placed at our disposal Wanley's own annotated copy of the first edition of Tanner's *Notitia Monastica* which was then in his possession (it is now BM Add. MS. 47842).

vii

at Moscow in sending us information and copies of material there relating to John Daniel Schumacher.

In conclusion we may observe that more than 600 persons make their appearance in the Diary, most of whom are identified with biographical notes in the Biographical Index, and approximately 2,000 manuscript items of those acquired during the period covered in its pages are identified in the footnotes and listed (with relevant details) in the Numerical Table. The text of Wanley's Memorandum Book for 1721–2 is printed in the Appendix in Volume II because of its relevance to those years in the Diary. In order to enable the reader to trace such subjects as sales, libraries, antiquities, &c., a Subject Index has also been prepared and is printed in Volume II immediately before the Numerical Table. An elaborate system of cross-referencing has been employed throughout in the footnotes in order to enable the reader to follow up individual transactions, which were often long drawn out and, being pursued at lengthy intervals, often liable to become entangled with other overlapping deals.

No edition of a work of this kind covering as it does so many different fields can be brought to completion without recourse to other scholars and our thanks are due to all those (whether specifically mentioned here or not) who responded to our appeals so readily.

We should particularly wish to acknowledge our gratitude to many members of the British Museum staff in a number of departments and would especially mention Mr. George Painter and Dr. Dennis Rhodes of the Department of Printed Books for their generous help in identifying editions of early printed books; Mr. T. C. Skeat, Keeper of Manuscripts, for advice on Biblical and Greek MSS.; Mr. Edward Croft Murray, Keeper of Prints and Drawings, for information on Andrew Hay and details in connexion with Sir James Thornhill's paintings at St. Paul's; Mr. R. L. S. Bruce Mitford, Keeper of British and Medieval Antiquities, and Mr. Peter Lasko, for assistance in identifying certain items in the Harleian collection of antiquities; Dr. D. R. Rosenwasser for help with Hebrew and other Oriental MSS. and Mr. E. D. Grinstead for assistance with Chinese MSS. and printed books; and Dr. Godfrey Davis and Messrs. Derek Turner, Richard Bancroft, and Donald Wilson for help of various kinds in various fields. At the Bodleian Library we would record our thanks to Dr. R. W. Hunt, Mr. L. W. Hanson, and Mr. D. G. Neill, and at the University Library, Cambridge, to Mr. J. C. T. Oates. In addition, Dr. William Beattie, Director of the National Library of Scotland, Mr. C. K. Adams, lately Director of the National Portrait Gallery, Mr. D. G. Ramage, University Librarian, Durham, Professor J. A. W. Bennett, Professor Francis Wormald, Director of the Institute of Historical Research, Dr. A. N. L. Munby, Librarian of King's College, Cambridge, Miss Joan Lancaster, formerly City Archivist at Coventry and now Assistant Keeper of the India Office Records, Mrs. Joan Varley, Archivist at Lincoln, and her former Assistant there, Mrs. Dorothy Owen, Mr. A. J. Farrington, formerly Assistant Archivist at Cheshire Record Office, Mr. T. S. Wragg, Keeper of the Collections at Chatsworth, Professor P. A. H. de Boer of the Peshitta Institute, Leiden, the Very Reverend Father Joachim Smet, O.Carm., at Rome, Mr. Anthony Wood, County Archivist at Warwick, and Miss Elizabeth Edmondson, Librarian of Sion College, all gave us useful information or assistance of many kinds.

We are specially grateful to Mr. Stanley Gillam, Librarian of the London Library who most generously made available to us his thesis and other material relating

Preface

to Arthur Charlett, and to Mr. A. G. Watson of the School of Librarianship and Archives, University of London, for so kindly giving us the results of his researches into the Harley and Cotton Charters.

We would also mention our indebtedness to the late Dr. Philip Corder, Assistant Secretary of the Society of Antiquaries, and to his successor, Mr. T. D. Tremlett, as also to the Society's Librarian, Mr. John Hopkins; to Professor Otto Pächt; the late Mr. Hugh Stanford London, Norfolk Herald Extraordinary; the Honourable David Erskine (for identifying a rare pamphlet for us); to Mrs. Saunders (née Cox Johnson), formerly Librarian in charge of the Local Collections at the St. Marylebone Central Public Library; Mr. H. M. Colvin, Fellow and Librarian of St. John's College, Oxford; Mr. N. S. E. Pugsley, City Librarian, Exeter; Mrs. Frances Vivian (for information about Consul Smith of Venice), and Dr. B. Jegers, of Newhaven, Connecticut, U.S.A. (for details of the 'Courland' Bible).

In conclusion we wish to record our gratitude to the Trustees of the British Museum for their permission to reproduce the portrait of Humfrey Wanley and a page from his Diary, and for allowing the printing of his Diary, Memorandum Book, and other material in their possession; also to the Society of Antiquaries for permission to quote from the Society's Minute Books and other papers. We should also like to thank the staff of the Oxford University Press for their co-operation and the care they have taken in the printing of a very complicated text.

C. E. WRIGHT
RUTH C. WRIGHT

London
1965

INTRODUCTION

HUMFREY WANLEY's Diary or Journal,[1] here printed for the first time in its entirety,[2] was kept by him while Library-Keeper in the service of Robert Harley, 1st Earl of Oxford, and Edward, his son, the 2nd Earl, and runs from 2 March 1714/15 to 23 June 1726, with, however, a considerable gap (except for one entry under 18 July 1716) between 22 August 1715 and 11 January 1719/20, when the Diary was resumed 'by my Lord Harley's Order'. It records the visits of, or to, booksellers and dealers, and negotiations with them; lists of manuscripts and printed books offered for sale, purchased, or received by gift; conversations with various people about library business; the visits of scholars and others to the Library, either as students there or as sightseers, and so on. It is in fact a record of the day-by-day business of a working librarian and is in no sense, therefore, a diary such as Pepys's or Evelyn's: apart from occasional references to his health, Wanley's allusions to personal affairs are few, for instance, a reference to the sudden death of his wife (on 3 January 1721/22)—'my late grievous Calamity' under the entry 15 January 1721/22—and to the death of his landlady (under 10 November 1724),[3] but a simple direct style,[4] happy choice of descriptive word and phrase,[5] skill in recounting an incident (such as the oft-quoted Warburton-Genoa Arms 'frolic' under 13 July 1720), a sarcastic, caustic tongue[6] and occasional use of 'asides' (as when he says that Mr. Hugh Thomas 'came to Study, as he think's' [cf. 11 May 1720, item 14]),[7] combined with the interest of the subject matter (at any rate to all those whose ways lie in the paths of librarianship) make it absorbing reading. The entry under 11 January 1719/20 suggests that when the Diary was begun in 1715 it was done so by Edward Harley's instructions and that it was, in a certain sense, intended to be an official record of his work as custodian of the Library. It is preserved in two quarto-size volumes in the Lansdowne Collection (nos. 771, 772) in the Department of MSS. in the British Museum,[8] the leaves of the volumes measuring 193 mm. × 157 mm., 230 mm. × 180 mm. respectively: it is

---

[1] It is referred to by Wanley himself as a 'journal' (cf., e.g., the entry under 11 Jan. 1719/20).

[2] Extracts from it were printed by John Nichols, *Literary Anecdotes of the Eighteenth Century*, i, 1812, pp. 85–94; J. A. Vincent, 'Wanley's Harleian Journal', *The Genealogist*, N.S., i (1884), pp. 114–17, 178–82, 256–61; W. R. Douthwaite, 'Humfrey Wanley and his Diary', *The Library Chronicle*, i (1884), pp. 87–94, 110–13; G. F. Barwick, 'Humfrey Wanley and the Harleian Library', *The Library*, N.S., iii (1902), pp. 24–35, 243–55. In 1918 Dr. M. R. James had a transcript of the diary made, his intention being to present an edition of the Diary to the Roxburghe Club but the work proved too considerable (Roxburghe Club Minutes III, 17 June 1918); a transcript, presented by Professor D. Nichol Smith, is now Bodleian Library, Oxford, MS. Eng. misc. e. 463 (see *Report of the Curators of the Bodl. Lib. 1958–1959*, p. 9).

[3] Wanley notes that he was 'desired and advised by divers to tarry within until her Funerall' (on 12 Nov.), and adds that as a result he made an allowance of 3 days time.

[4] As when he says of the Valetta Collection at Naples: 'Three Generations made it; and this Man, for Lucre of ready Money, sold it' (Diary, 25 July 1720, item 6).

[5] As when he describes Joseph Sparke coming 'again to teaze, and rub himself upon me' (see 27 Aug. 1720, item 16).

[6] Cf., e.g., entry under 27 Feb. 1724/5 about Mr. Walker.

[7] All these characteristics appear also in his letters: see especially a letter to Tudway, 5 Jan. 1715/16 (Harl. 3782, f. 162) relating to Dr. John Covel, Master of Christ's Coll., Cambridge, and Wanley's (almost brutal) outspokenness to Carte in a letter of 9 Mar. 1713/14 (Welbeck Wanleyana) about his efforts to obtain for the Library the Leicester Codex (which the Leicester Corporation had loaned to him Apr. 1712–Mar. 1713/14).

[8] For the reasons for its presence among the Lansdowne MSS. see C. E. Wright, 'Humfrey Wanley: Saxonist and Library-Keeper', *Proc. of the Brit. Acad.*, xlvi (1961), p. 99, Note.

written in Wanley's characteristic small, neat, clear handwriting[1] on a rather stiff good quality paper now very brittle at the edges; the first volume contains 89 folios, the second 90 folios, and both were paginated by Wanley himself, who also supplied each volume with an index. Each volume also contains supplementary notes on books and MSS. brought into the Library on specific dates (referred to in the present edition as 'Addenda'). It is obviously a fair copy,[2] made up in the evenings or as opportunity offered, probably from brief memoranda hastily scribbled on odd scraps of paper (including letters) that were readily to hand.[3] Moreover, the Diary is supplemented for the year 1721 (13 May–15 December) (with one entry for 1 January 1721/22) by a memorandum book, also preserved in the Lansdowne MSS. (no. 677), which is printed in Vol. II of the present work as an Appendix.[4]

The gap in the Diary from 1715 to the end of 1719 is most unfortunate and its discontinuance during these years is almost certainly due to circumstances connected with the collapse of Robert Harley's political career and its effect upon the Harley family fortunes. For, although there is evidence that from 1711 the day-by-day control of the Library (doubtless due to the pressure of political affairs) was in the hands of Edward Harley, it must never be forgotten that the true 'founder' of the Library was Robert Harley,[5] and although he might be praised by Thomas Tudway[6] after his loss of the Lord Treasurership in July 1714 for going 'vigourously on In furnishing his Library with ev'rything that is curious' and thereby showing the world that 'that great undertaking, does not depend upon ye Staff', nevertheless political events intervened and Robert Harley's committal to the Tower on 16 July 1715 (where he remained until 1 July 1717) made it difficult, if not impossible, for him to exercise any direct supervision of the Library. The amount of MS. material, however, that covers the gap in the Diary and at the same time supplements it or documents the period preceding it is very considerable; briefly described it is as follows: (i) correspondence between Edward Harley and Humfrey Wanley running from 22 February 1710/11 to 22 December 1724 preserved in the Welbeck Wanleyana; (ii) letters from various correspondents to Wanley divided between (*a*) those preserved in the Welbeck Wanleyana and (*b*) those in Harl. 3777–82; (iii) miscellaneous notes, memoranda, lists, and accompts preserved in the Welbeck Wanleyana, in the 'Welbeck Harley Papers',

[1] Wanley's handwriting was consistent in its characteristics of neatness and clarity: he was greatly troubled in 1700 that his handwriting had been affected by an illness, complaining in a letter to Charlett, 6 Dec. of that year (Bodl. Lib., Ballard MS. 13, f. 87) of 'the loss of that steadiness of my hand which I was once Master of'. Hickes found when the Cat. of Anglo-Saxon MSS. was being set up for his *Thesaurus* that 'three pages of your [i.e. Wanley's] Copie make a printed sheet' [of large folio size] (Hickes to H. W., 19 Sept. 1700, Harl. 3779, f. 152).

[2] That it was a fair copy is indicated by the fact that in one place (under 6 Mar. 1720/21, items 10 and 13) information is duplicated; by the correction of 'present' to 'late' in the entry under 4 Mar. 1720/21, item 4; by an error (corrected) in item 2 of 26 Jan. 1720/21 entry, due probably to homoioteleuton in copying from a rough note.

[3] A small autobiographical jotting appears at the foot of the first leaf of the draft (Harl. 7661) of his index to the Cat. of Printed Books at Wimpole (BM Lansdowne 816) and runs: 'Hindered [in preparing the index] by many persons coming to the library/Attending my Lord Oxford/The arrival of the Welbeck Library/Library-business with Mr. Noel, Mr. Tanner, Mr. Jones, &c.' Similar fragments of jottings, one dated 3 May 1718 and others ranging from 19 Nov. to 28 Dec. 1721, are preserved in Welbeck Wanleyana Misc. 48, 60, and (undated) 5, 80. An example of a letter utilized by Wanley for this purpose is that to him from Charlett, dated 10 Jan. 1710/11 (Welbeck Wanleyana).

[4] This is important because it contains, in addition to chronological entries, (1) a list of addresses; (2) a list of MSS., &c. in the hands of private persons and institutions 'proper for the Library'; and (3) under 13 May 1721, 'Notes relating to my Lords business, momentaneous'.

[5] Cf. Wanley's words in recording Robert Harley's death under 21 May 1724.

[6] Thomas Tudway to H. W., 10 Sept. 1714 (Harl. 3782, f. 29).

and in Harl. 7055; (iv) letters from Wanley to various recipients, of which the chief groups are those addressed to Sir Hans Sloane in BM Sloane 4037–40 (the last important because it contains (ff. 355–6) Wanley's account of John Bagford's collections); to John Anstis in BM Stowe 749; to John Covel, Master of Christ's College, Cambridge, in BM Add. 22910, 22911; to John Bagford, Harl. 4966; and to Arthur Charlett, Master of University College, Oxford (whose protégé Wanley was at Oxford), a long series from 1694 to 1721 (Charlett died the following year), preserved in Bodleian Library, Oxford, MS. Ballard 13;[1] and (v) correspondence with John Strype, the historian, preserved in the University Library at Cambridge and Harl. 3782.

These, with the Diary and Memorandum Book, are the main sources of material for the history of the Harleian Library from its earliest stages until Wanley's death in 1726.[2] They indicate also the wide range of Wanley's own circle of acquaintances and friends, a circle of great value to him as librarian, as was also the experience he had gained as a young man at the Bodleian Library (where he was an Assistant from 14 November 1695 to 1700), and as Assistant Secretary (1700–2) and subsequently Secretary (1702–8) of the S.P.C.K. To the latter he owed his experience of day-to-day administrative business and the useful enlargement of his circle of acquaintances; to the former and to his work on MSS. in various libraries at Oxford and Cambridge and in London preparing the Catalogue of Anglo-Saxon MSS. for the great *Thesaurus* of George Hickes (to whose notice he had been introduced by Charlett in 1695)[3] he owed his expertise in handling and describing MSS. and his palaeographical knowledge. It was these latter, of course, which stood most in his favour in his recommendation to Robert Harley in 1701; Hickes in his letter to Harley dated 23 April of that year specifically introduces Wanley as having 'the best skill in ancient hands and MSS. of any man not only of this, but, I believe, of any former age, and I wish for the sake of the public, that he might meet with the same encouragement here, that he would have met in France, Holland, or Sweden, had he been born in any of those countries'.[4]

So strong an impression had Wanley's palaeographical knowledge made on his contemporaries in the early years of the century that we find William Nicolson, Bishop of Carlisle, writing to him from Salkeld, 23 July 1702: 'I heartily agree with those worthy promoters of our English Antiquity, who press you to go on with your *Res Diplomatica*; and I am extremely well pleas'd to hear that you resolve to listen to their good Advice. You cannot do a more acceptable Service to the Commonwealth of Antiquaries: And, without flattery, you are the best qualified for the Undertaking.'[5]

Wanley had indeed shown a precocious interest in records and palaeography (perhaps fostered by his maternal grandfather, Humphrey Burton). While still at Coventry he had, in 1691, made facsimile copies of charters that were in the custody of James Fish of Warwick,[6] and even before attracting Bishop Lloyd's attention (apparently in 1694) his knowledge of hands and interest in MSS.

---

[1] Charlett's letters to H. W. are divided between Welbeck Wanleyana and Harl. 3778, ff. 29–65. One from Charlett to the Lord Almoner in Wanley's favour is in Welbeck Wanleyana, Misc. 64, and is dated 7 Apr. 1695.

[2] Perhaps reference should also be made to Stratford's letters to Edward Harley (printed *HMC Portland Papers*, vii, 1901).

[3] See Hickes to Charlett, 10 June 1695, Bodl. Lib., Oxford, Ballard MS. 12, f. 112.

[4] *HMC Portland Papers*, iv, p. 16.

[5] W. Nicolson to H. W., 23 July 1702 (Harl. 3780, f. 261).

[6] Harl. 7505, ff. 2b–19b *passim*.

and antiquities had led Sir John Dugdale to suggest that he should try to get employ-ment in the Tower records.[1] At an early date he began to compile a Book of Hands; from a reference by Hickes in a letter to Wanley of 28 January 1698/9[2] we know that this contained specimens of handwriting used in Domesday Book and the Red Book of the Exchequer and Hickes advised him to take it with him when he went to Cambridge in August 1699.[3] He showed too at an early age a keen interest in the whereabouts of MSS., an essential qualification in a future librarian.[4] It is not surprising then to find him in 1700 expressing a desire to go abroad and 'visit all the libraries of Europe'.[5]

It was but natural in view of this that one of the earliest productions Wanley prepared for publication should be devoted to the question of the dating of MSS.; this was entitled 'Part of a Letter, written to a Most Reverend Prelate, in answer to one written by his Grace, judging of the Age of MSS., the Style of Learned Authors, Painters, Musicians, &c. By Mr. Humfrey Wanley, dated 11 July 1701'.[6] There were, therefore, good grounds for Hickes's recommendation of him to Robert Harley, and what has been said will suffice to show how admirably fitted he was for the post he was subsequently to hold with Robert and Edward Harley and goes also a long way to explain the self-assurance and the range of knowledge that he was later to display in the pages of the Diary printed here.

As a cataloguer, too, he had had much experience long before he began the catalogue of Robert Harley's MSS. in 1708.[7] For the second volume of the great *Catalogi Manuscriptorum Angliae* that goes under Bernard's name and was published at Oxford in 1697 he contributed at least four catalogues, those, namely, of (1) the

---

[1] See letter from Charles King to H. W., 10 Sept. 1692, Harl. 3780, f. 38 (printed J. Nichols, *Literary Anecdotes*, 1812, p. 98). On Sir John see W. H. Godfrey, A. R. Wagner, and H. S. London, *The College of Arms*, p. 113.   [2] Harl. 3779, f. 82.
[3] Harl. 3779, f. 92. The book had been shown by Charlett to the Lord Chancellor (Lord Somers) in Aug. and to the Archbishop of Canterbury in Oct. 1697. (See letters from Charlett to H. W., 26 Aug. and 20 Oct. 1697 in Welbeck Wanleyana.) Much later—Aug. 1724—Wanley formed a project of 'taking Specimens of Greek MSS. with their Abbreviations' (see Wanleyana Misc. 10). A volume in Wanley's handwriting containing signs and abbreviations in Greek MSS. is still extant in the Welbeck Harley Papers (BM Loan 29/271). See also letter from H. W., 11 Aug. 1697, in Harl. 5911, f.1.
[4] See the remarkable letter written by him to Charlett, 15 Oct. 1694 (Bodl. Lib., Oxford, Ballard MS. 13, f. 55).
[5] See letter from Hickes to H. W., 23 May 1700 (Harl. 3779, f. 132).
[6] But not published until *Philosophical Transactions*, xxiv, 1706 (no. 300, June 1705), pp. 1993–2008. The 'Most Reverend Prelate' was Narcissus Marsh, Archbishop of Dublin, as appears from a remark made by Charlett in a letter to Wanley, dated 27 June 1701 (Welbeck Wanleyana): 'Your Answer to his Grace of Dublin I much desire to see, but would not have you intermitt your Businesse.' Wanley's printed *oeuvre*, perforce small, may be conveniently summarized at this point. It comprised the follow-ing: (1) Catalogues furnished by him to *CMA* (see pp. xv, xxviii, n. 1); (2) three contributions to the *Philo-sophical Transactions* of the Royal Society, of which he was elected Fellow in 1706 (see pp. xiv, xviii, n. 2, xxxviii, n. 2); (3) F. J. Ostervald, *The Grounds and Principles of the Christian Religion, explain'd in a Catechetical Discourse, for the Instruction of Young People. Rendred into English by Mr. Humfrey Wanley: and Revis'd by George Stanhope, D.D.* London, 1704; (4) the great catalogue of Anglo-Saxon manuscripts (referred to above, p. xiii), namely, *Catalogus Librorum Veterum Septentrionalium tam Manuscriptorum quam Impressorum* in G. Hickes, *Thesaurus Linguarum Veterum Septentrionalium*, ii, Oxford, 1705 (with a preface by Wan-ley addressed to Robert Harley, dated 28 Aug. 1704); (5) Accounts of the Cotton Library, the Bodleian, and other libraries at Oxford with those at Cambridge were supplied by Wanley to the 1704 edition of J. Chamberlayne's *Angliae Notitia* to judge from references in John Chamberlayne's letters to Wanley in Welbeck Wanleyana; Hearne states categorically (*Remarks and Collections of Thomas Hearne*, i, 1885, p. 130 under the date 16 Dec. 1705) that the account of the Bodleian Library in this edition was from Wan-ley's pen. Wanley also supplied materials for the account of the Harleian Library to the 2nd, 1714, edition of William Nicolson's *The English Historical Library*, pp. vi–viii (cf. Nicolson's letters of 8 June 1713 to H.W. in Harl. 3780, ff. 281–2 and of 6 May 1714, at f. 284: 'Inclos'd you have your own paper, thankfully returned; and such an Acc^t of my Lord's Library as I could suddenly compile out of this and some former notes of my own. You can readily (in an hour's time) correct its faults, & supply its defects' . . .).   [7] BM Add. 45701–7.

Free School at Coventry (*CMA* ii, pp. 33, 34 [nos. 1446–62]); (2) St. Mary's church at Warwick (*CMA* ii, pp. 203–6 [nos. 6683–6715]); (3) Basil Feilding, 4th Earl of Denbigh (*CMA* ii, 1697, pp. 35–39 [nos. 1463–1552];[1] and (4) John Ayres (*CMA* ii, 1697, p. 222 [nos. 7132–45].[2] So well were his catalogues made that Charlett could write to Wanley in 1694[3] of the catalogues supplied by him for *CMA* that 'those we receave from you, being taken with so much care and accuracy . . . they admit of no additions'. The skill shown in these doubtless led to Wanley being asked by Sir Hans Sloane in 1701 to prepare a catalogue of his own MSS. and printed books, of which the extant remains are preserved in BM Sloane 3972 B, C.[4]

It was his experience of cataloguing and his palaeographical knowledge that undoubtedly led to his being selected in May 1703 by the Trustees of the Cotton Library (one of whom was Robert Harley) to inspect and report on the collection with Matthew Hutton and John Anstis: the results of his work in this may be seen in several documents, one of which was the report itself which was drawn up by Wanley 22 June 1703.[5]

In view of his introduction to Robert Harley in 1701 and his frequent contact with him, it need cause us no surprise then to find, on the one hand, Wanley on 28 August 1704 addressing to Robert Harley the Preface of his Catalogue of Anglo-Saxon MSS., which was published in 1705, and, on the other, Robert Harley entrusting to him the negotiations which led up to Harley purchasing the library of Sir Simonds D'Ewes, which Wanley had inspected for him at the D'Ewes seat at Stowlangtoft in Suffolk in the October of 1703.

It is from this period, I think, that we must date Wanley's employment as Robert Harley's librarian, but probably only in a part-time capacity, since Wanley did not resign his Secretaryship of the S.P.C.K. until June 1708, though he had been entrusted earlier that year by Harley with the compilation of the 'Catalogus Brevior' of his MSS., the first volume of which (BM Add. 45701) bears the date 24 April 1708. This was the beginning of a long series of catalogues of their collections which Wanley was to prepare for Robert Harley and later for his son Edward and this is perhaps a convenient point at which to say something of these in more detail.

The first volume of the 'Catalogus Brevior' was finished 18 February 1709, and the second volume (BM Add. 45702) was completed 5 May 1710; the third (BM Add. 45703) was begun 6 May 1710 and completed 24 November 1711, the next volume—the fourth—(BM Add. 45704) being started two days later and completed 12 December 1712. No time was lost in continuing the work, the next volume—the fifth (BM Add. 45705)—being started the next day; this, however, was not completed until 12 July 1717. There is no evidence for the date of the beginning of volume six (BM Add. 45706) but it was completed 17 June 1721. He was not able

[1] See p. xxvii below where the letter from H. W. to the E. of Denbigh, 28 Nov. 1713 (Welbeck Wanleyana) is quoted: cf. also A. S. Turberville, *Hist. of Welbeck Abbey and its Owners*, i, 1938, p. 369.
[2] As early as 1691 he had made copies of a list of the MSS. given to Lincoln's Inn in 1676 by Sir Matthew Hale (Harl. 6030, ff. 10–10b) and of a Catalogue of Anglo-Saxon MSS. (Harl. 3317, ff. 20–29b).
[3] Charlett to H. W., 13 Dec. 1694 (Welbeck Wanleyana).
[4] A list of Sloane's MSS. had appeared in *CMA* ii, 1697, pp. 251–5 [nos. 8736–8999]. Wanley's other work made it difficult for him to carry out Sloane's request; on 12 Oct. 1701 he wrote to Sloane apologizing for the delay in beginning the catalogue (BM Sloane 4038, f. 252).
[5] On Wanley's work in this connexion see C. E. Wright, op. cit., pp. 107–8 and especially p. 108, n. 1. Robert Harley's copy of Smith's 1696 Catalogue of the Cotton Library with Wanley's report in his own autograph is now Oxford, Bodl. Lib., Add. MS. D. 82 (*S.C.* 30308).

to begin work on volume seven (BM Add. 45707) until 30 September 1724 and this was uncompleted at his death, the work breaking off with the description of article 10 in Harl. 2407 (originally MS. 100. D. 10).[1] It is this 'Catalogus Brevior' that supplied the text of the Catalogue of the Harleian MSS. published in two volumes in 1759, so that this, as far as the description of Harl. 2407, may be regarded as a posthumous addition to the small list of Wanley's published Works (see above, p. xiv, n. 6).[2]

This is but part of the cataloguing of the Library carried out by Wanley. Related to the main Catalogue of the MSS., the 'Catalogus Brevior', are two volumes (all that remain) of a 'Catalogus Maior' (BM Add. 45699, 45700), a projected work in which each MS. was to be described at great length, the MSS. being arranged in groups, such as 'Codices Manuscripti Hebraice', 'Codices Latini', and so on; this was a project utterly beyond the powers of a librarian with a multitude of calls upon his time and no assistant, even of one so competent and so hard working as Humfrey Wanley. In addition, Wanley left unfinished a subject index of the MSS. (BM Lansdowne 815), which was begun (see f. 1) on 9 January 1722/3 (a volume of 115 folios), and an 'Index in Chartas Antiquas' in the Harleian Collection (BM Add. 45711): this has no date at all. Primarily for his own use presumably was the small octavo volume (BM Add. 6052) of 61 pages containing classified notes on heraldic MSS. in the Harleian Collection; this too bears no date of compilation.[3]

As the Harleys' librarian he was, of course, concerned not only with their MSS. but also their printed books (as we can see from the Diary); these numbered 'upwards' of 12,000 at 10 September 1717 according to a letter from Edward Harley to Wanley written on that date. During the period of the Diary they were for the most part kept at Edward Harley's country seat at Wimpole and a catalogue of them was of course essential: 'You will be wanted at Wimpole, now the room for my books is finisht', wrote Edward Harley to Wanley in 1716,[4] 'to put them up and catalogue, this I shall desire very much to have done.' This task must have occupied Wanley during the greater part of his stay at Wimpole in 1716 and 1717. The catalogue he made is now preserved in BM Lansdowne 816. The books are press-marked I. A. 1 to XXVII. O. 32 and bear also running numbers (1–7040). It was begun 5 September 1716 and finished 14 June 1717. In a letter to Wanley at Wimpole dated 17 June 1717 Harley ordered him to return to London and to 'bring up what you have done of the catalogue of the Books at Wimpole', and on 13 August of the same year we find him writing to Wanley: 'I very much want to have the Index to my Catalogue made, and the catalogue bound up, it only spoils as it is loose and unbound, I cannot know what books I have.' The draft of the index was made in a very large folio volume, now Harl. 7661; in spite of Harley's expression of urgency it was not begun until 14 April 1718, but it was made in four days, the last page bearing the date 17 April 1718. The fair copy, 45 pages of four columns to the page, now bound at the end of the catalogue, Lansdowne 816, was finished 3 September 1718, and on 9 September Harley wrote from Wimpole: 'I have received the last Sheets of the Index and I like the whole very well, and thank you for your care in it. I belive [*sic*] few faults can be found with it.'

---

[1] It was of course severely criticized by Thomas Hearne (see his comments under 10 July 1726, *Remarks and Collections of Thomas Hearne*, ix, 1914, p. 161).

[2] For references made in the Diary to this 'Catalogus Brevior' see Subject Index under Catalogues, and for a full account of the subsequent cataloguing of the MSS. see pp. lxxx–lxxxiii below.

[3] It is probably the volume referred to in the Diary under 19 Oct. 1720.

[4] Edw. Harley to H. W., 4 July 1716 (Welbeck Wanleyana).

Pressure of other library work after 1718 obviously made it impossible for Wanley to continue the cataloguing of Harley's printed books on the scale of Lansdowne 816, but references occur in the Diary to two other volumes on printed books which Wanley found time to prepare and which are still extant. As to the first, under 6 June 1722 occurs the following entry: 'A letter sent to Mr. Elliot desiring him to come hither to Morrow to bind a New Sort of Catalogue of my Lords Printed Books which I finished here this Morning. . . .' This is now Harl. 3886. It was begun on 26 April and finished, as Wanley records in the Diary and in the MS. itself (f. 191), on 6 June 1722. It is described by Wanley in a letter to Harley, 12 June 1722 (in Welbeck Wanleyana): 'I [had] just begun a Book upon your going to Downe [Hall, in Essex]; it is Finished, and actually Bound. It is so contrived and ha's so many Additions and Observations touching Printers and Printing, (the whole, and every particular, relating to your own Library:) that I know your Lordship will approve it, and turn it over with Satisfaction; and cause me to make it at Wimpole still more complete.' The greater part of the book (ff. 1–146) is given up to an alphabetical author list of early printed books; it is followed, first (ff. 147–65), by an index of places with the names of the printers associated with each, and, secondly (ff. 166–81), by a 'Syllabus' of printers, the towns where each carried out his work, and the text was printed.[1] Miscellaneous notes (relating, for example, to books printed on vellum) occupy the last leaves; at f. 189^b is a list of printed books entered later under five dates of purchase ranging from 24 October 1722 to 18 January 1723/4; of those recorded, three (22 January 1722/3, 21 December 1723, and 13 July 1723) have no corresponding entry in the Diary, but the first and the last referred to above do occur, some of the items listed under the last date (18 January 1723/4) occurring in the list of 3 June 1723 in the Diary.

The second compilation is referred to in the Diary under 22 June 1721 (item 10) and again, after his return from Oxford, under 18 October 1721; under the first date Wanley writes: 'I finished the Copie of my Lords Catalogue of his old Latin Books.' The catalogue is now Harl. 7627 A, 7627 B, two thin duodecimo volumes; the former bears at the beginning the date 13 February 1720/1, the latter 20 June 1721: the second little volume therefore occupied three days' work. On his return from Oxford Wanley was evidently much distressed not to be able to find the two volumes and one, at least, was apparently still missing in December of 1721.[2]

Wanley's interest in printing was probably stimulated in large measure by his early friendship with John Bagford (dating back to 1695 at least) with whose collections he was well acquainted and of which he wrote an account for Sloane, 6 May 1707;[3] it will be recalled that he had catalogued Sloane's printed books in 1701. He had a particular interest in early printed Bibles, primers, &c., of which he made a collection of his own, a catalogue of which was imperfectly copied by Bagford (and is Harl. 5908, ff. 60–62^b) and was submitted to Robert Harley probably late in 1709.[4] The collection of Bibles was subsequently sold (possibly about 1710)[5] by him for the library at St. Paul's Cathedral, where the volumes—or many of them—are still preserved. His knowledge of English Bibles was at any

[1] One remarkable feature is the absence of any reference to Caxton or to works printed by him.
[2] In a letter to H. W., dated from Wimpole, 10 Dec. 1721, Harley says: 'You wrote two catalogues of the old [printed] books, one I have the other was left with you and is I suppose in your Desk or the Closet', and again, 12 Dec. 1721, '. . . if you have not found your catalogue of my old editions I will send you up y^t wch I have, if you remember Elliot bound them both at one time'.
[3] H. W. to Sloane, 6 May 1707, BM Sloane 4040, ff. 355–5^b. See also above, p. xv, n. 4.
[4] See Rob. Harley's reply, 31 Jan. 1709/10, in Welbeck Wanleyana.
[5] See letter from W. Hall to H. W., 6 Sept. 1710, in Welbeck Wanleyana.

rate sufficiently well known for him to be consulted by Charlett on the subject in 1716,[1] and his interest in the early history of printing led him to read a paper on the subject to the Royal Society on 27 October 1703.[2]

Few men in, or about, 1701 could therefore have been better equipped for the custody of the library which Robert Harley proposed to bring together and it is important in the first place to trace, as far as is possible, the progress of the collection during the period preceding the collapse of Harley's political career in 1715 and the beginning of the Diary.

The first block purchase of MSS. made by Robert Harley for his library was the collection of the 17th-century antiquary Sir Simonds D'Ewes (died 1650): this was bought for £450 on 4 October 1705,[3] and the negotiations were handled by Wanley who was responsible for handing over the money to the vendor, the 3rd Baronet, of the same christian name as his distinguished ancestor. The collection had been examined by Wanley in October 1703 at the family's seat at Stowlangtoft in Suffolk and he wrote to Robert Harley 20 November 1703[4] an interesting letter describing the library (printed books, MSS., prints and drawings, coins and pictures) and recommending its purchase. In this, as in future negotiations, Wanley obviously established happy personal relations with those with whom he had to negotiate; this appears clearly in the letters of Sir Simonds D'Ewes and his wife, Dela[rivière] D'Ewes, to Wanley, preserved mostly in Harl. 3778, ff. 176–206; the warmth on D'Ewes's side is unmistakable in the first letter, 13 October 1703 (the only one preserved in Welbeck Wanleyana): 'If [he writes] you met w$^{th.}$ anything here that made you amends for an uneasie Journey I shall be very much pleased, and when you let me know y$^{t.}$ you have some thoughts of performing the kind promise you made me of seeing Stow once more, I shall believe then you have forgott all the omissions, wch I now beg your pardon for; I hope we shall often meet at London and renew that Friendship, whose beginning pleas'd me so much. . . .' D'Ewes had been impelled to sell the library because of his sons' lack of interest and at first in a letter of 19 May 1704 had stipulated £500 as the lowest price; subsequently, after the sale, he offered Wanley in a letter of 12 November 1705 the portrait of Sir Robert Cotton which had belonged to his ancestor, the antiquary. The D'Ewes collection now runs from Harl. 1 to approximately Harl. 600 (with some exceptions and some outliers). It is an important collection containing many medieval MSS. in addition to the collections compiled by D'Ewes himself (including his parliamentary journals) and by antiquaries of the late 16th and 17th centuries (for example that of Ralph Starkey which he had purchased complete from Starkey's widow).[5]

[1] See Charlett's letter to H. W., 24 Jan. 1715/16, Harl. 3778, f. 33.

[2] This was subsequently printed in the *Philosophical Transactions*, xxiii, 1704 (no. 288, Dec. 1703, pp. 1507–16), under the title 'Some Observations concerning the Invention and Progress of Printing, to the year 1465. Occasioned by the Reverend Mr. Ellis's letter exhibited in Phil. Trans. No. 286. Pag. 1416'. It is printed anonymously but was identified as by Wanley by L. W. Hanson, Keeper of Printed Books, Bodleian Library, Oxford, on evidence in the Journal Book of the Royal Society under 27 Oct. 1703, the MS. of the first three pages being preserved in the Royal Society's archives headed 'Some Observations about the invention of printing by Mr. Humfrey Wanley. . . . Read Oct: 27: 1703.' See *Bodl. Lib. Record*, vi (1957–61), pp. 634–5.

[3] See C. E. Wright, op. cit., p. 110, n. 1. We may therefore ignore the silly story put out by William Oldys (see *A Literary Antiquary: Memoir of William Oldys, Esq.*, 1862, p. 38) and repeated by W. Y. Fletcher, *English Book Collectors*, 1902, pp. 104–5, that the price was said to be £6,000!

[4] See letter from H. W. to Robert Harley, 20 Nov. 1703, BM Lansdowne 841, ff. 62^b–63; and cf. also ff. 65–76.

[5] Several catalogues of the collection are extant. A printed one had appeared in Bernard, *CMA* ii, 1697, pp. 385–8 [nos. 9861–10072]; of manuscript cats. one compiled by Dugdale in the year preceding

The collection was certainly worth the £450 that Robert Harley paid for it and the task of arranging it appears to have been entrusted to Wanley at once, since we find Charlett in a letter written to Wanley in January 1706[1] saying: 'I am very much pleased to hear from Sᵣ Andrew Fountaine how agreeably you are imploy'd by Mr. Secretary Harley, in digesting the library of Sᵣ. Simonds D'Ewes.' Though the formal cataloguing of it did not begin until 24 April 1708 (BM Add. 45701) it is clear from other references in Charlett's letters to Wanley of 6 March and 30 December 1706 that Wanley was now in Harley's employ; in the first, Charlett writes: 'I am very glad you are imployed in so noble a Collection of MSS. and printed books' and in the second, refers to Harley as 'your Benefactor'.[2]

In the spring of 1707 the Library received a further considerable addition. The precise date of the new purchase is not known but we find Wanley on 22 April 1707 passing on to Charlett the news that Harley had '(for a considerable sum of money) bought the manuscripts in the library of the late Bp. Stillingfleet, wherein are many books of great value. And as the same honourable person does now appear the great patron of learning; so, his library is one of the most considerable, and in MSS., I believe, excels all private ones in the kingdom'.[3] This new acquisition was the manuscript portion of the library of Edward Stillingfleet (1635–99), Bishop of Worcester 1689–1699, who had formed a library famous in its time, which John Evelyn, on the Bishop's death, had been anxious that William III should purchase for the Royal Library.[4] The printed books were purchased by Narcissus Marsh (1638–1713), for the library that he established at St. Sepulchre's, Dublin. The MSS. acquired by Harley are now Harl. 665–904, 939–51, 964–1038 and were later described by Wanley in the third volume of his 'Catalogus Brevior' (BM Add. 45703) which was begun 6 May 1710 and completed 24 Nov. 1711.[5]

The next large block of MSS. acquired occupies Harl. 1585–1747 (with two out of sequence, Harl. 1811, 1812); it came into the Library at some indeterminable date but certainly before 13 December 1712 when Wanley began to catalogue it ('Catalogus Brevior', v, BM Add. 45705) and was a gift to Robert Harley from Colonel Henry Worsley, of the Worsley family of Appuldurcombe, Isle of Wight.[6] Unfortunately no deduction can be drawn with any safety from the position occupied by a group in a numerical series; on the basis of the numbers allotted to

D'Ewes's death is in Harl. 300, while also in the Harl. collection (no. 775) is a complete (but undated) cat. of the MSS., charters, and rolls. A copy of the *CMA* list with notes by Dugdale is in BM Add. 22917 and a transcript of a copy of the catalogue preserved in D'Ewes's library made in 1687 by 'R. H.' is in BM Add. 22918. But for these and other catalogues together with an account of the library see A. G. Watson, *The Library of Sir Simonds D'Ewes*, 1966. On D'Ewes's charters see A. G. Watson, 'Sir Simonds D'Ewes's Collection of Charters . . .', *Journal of the Soc. of Archivists*, ii, no. 6 (Oct. 1962), pp. 247–54.
[1] Charlett to H. W., 14 Jan. 1705/6 (Welbeck Wanleyana).
[2] Letters in Welbeck Wanleyana.
[3] H. W. to Charlett, 22 Apr. 1707 (Bodl. Lib., Oxford, Ballard MS. 13, f. 118). (Wanley also communicated the information to Strype in a letter of 1 May 1707: see below, p. xxi). Cf. the fragment of a letter of White Kennett's now preserved in BM Lansdowne 825, f. 81ᵇ, undated, but before 1711, in which Kennett says: 'In Mr. Harley's absence I have had access to his noble Collection of MSS. wᶜʰ is greater and of better Originals than I had imagined. He purchast all yᵉ Papers of Sᵣ Simonds D'ewes and Bp. Stillingfleet *and has had Agents to pick up what is valuable from all hands*' (editors' italics).
[4] See Evelyn's Diary under 29 Apr. and 3 May 1699 (Oxford Standard Authors ed., 1959, p. 1034).
[5] A list of Stillingfleet's MSS. with valuations by Wanley is Harl. 7055, ff. 73ᵇ–79; it is not dated. A catalogue of Stillingfleet's MSS. drawn up in 1685 is Harl. 7644 and another (undated) is Bodl. Lib. Rawl. D. 878, f. 63 (see W. D. Macray, *Cat. Cod. Mssorum. Bibl. Bodl.*, v, pt. 4, 1898, cols. 56–57). Notes on Stillingfleet's MSS. made by Tanner in 1699 are in BM Add. 6261, ff. 54–57ᵇ.
[6] He also, while Envoy Extraordinary at the Court of Portugal (1713–22), gave Harl. 1899, 1901, 1903–8. Harl. 2284 was given by another member of the family, Sir Robert Worsley, Bart. 'divers years since' [*sic. Harl. Cat.*]—presumably the 4th Bart. (1669–1747).

the MSS. an acquisition date *before* 1710 would be indicated, since we know that in that year Robert Harley purchased through Francis Gastrell, Bishop of Chester, the large collection of heraldic material that had been brought together by four generations of a family of herald painters in Chester, the last male survivor of whom, Randle Holme IV, had died in 1707;[1] the Randle Holme MSS. are Harl. 1920–2180, and 7568, 7569 but they were not described by Wanley until much later (certainly not before July 1717) in the sixth volume of the 'Catalogus Brevior' (BM Add. 45706).

Robert Harley's interests were strong in historical and heraldic material and it was probably in the period 1708–10 that the large collections of heraldic papers formed by a number of herald painters in the 17th century were acquired. These fall into three main groups, viz. (1) those acquired from 'Mr. Foresight an Apothecary' (cf. description in *Harl. Cat.* under Harl. 1402), who secured them as executor to a John Spicer. The descent of this group, if Wanley's note at the head of the description of Harl. 1402 is correct, seems to be clear, thus, Edmund Barwick, painter stainer, by sale → John Withie, of Fetter Lane, herald painter (Master of the Painter-Stainers Company, 1657) (d. ? c. 1678) [cf. description in *Harl. Cat.* under Harl. 1039, art. 1], by sale → John Saunders, Deputy of the Ward of St. Dunstans in the West and Master of the Painter-Stainers Company, 1680 (died c. 1687) [see Harl. 1040, art. 2] → John Spicer. This collection seems to run from Harl. 1039 (that is, following immediately on the last of the Stillingfleet block [Harl. 1038]) to 1057, 1067–1116, 1349–1487 (with the exception of Harl. 1419), a group which includes several of Nicholas Charles's heraldic MSS.[2] (e.g. 1353); (2) under Harl. 1172 Wanley writes: 'this Book is Written by divers Hands; namely by Henry Parker the Arms-Painter and others; but from fol 46 'tis almost all of the Handwriting of Robert Fisher the Arms–Painter, into whose Hands the Books of Mr. Sampson Lennard [Bluemantle Pursuivant 1616–33], Henry Parker, &c. came; the greatest Part of which, were bought of this Fisher's son by one Shires [of Southwark, cf. Harl. 1365] an Arms-painter, of whom I bought this Parcel for my Lord.' I think, though I cannot be positive, that the 'parcel' occupies Harl. 1133–96: certainly a Sampson Lennard volume is Harl. 1178 (though another, Harl. 1452, appears in the Foresight 'parcel'); and (3) those acquired from 'Mr. Comyns'[3] (see heading to description of Harl. 1530). This last group contained the papers of Richard Munday which had been acquired by Giles Campion, Painter-Stainer, whose collections in turn were acquired by Comyns. These seem to be Harl.

---

[1] On the Randle Holme family see J. P. Earwaker, 'The Four Randle Holmes of Chester, Antiquaries, Heralds and Genealogists, *c.* 1571–1707', *Journal of Chester Archaeological and Historic Soc.* (1891), and separately printed privately. The daughter of Randle Holme IV is said (apparently erroneously) to have married Francis Bassano, who secured many of the Randle Holme charters and rolls: as late as 4 Mar. 1720/21 Wanley writes in a letter to Lord Harley (Welbeck Wanleyana): 'Mr. Holme [IV] had a Pedegree of Thompson described in a Roll; but none of his Rolls came hither.' References are made several times in the Diary to attempts to secure Randle Holme's deeds: see Biographical Index under Boothe (Nathaniel) and Bassano (Francis).

[2] Nicholas Charles, Lancaster Herald, 1608–13: on him see A. R. Wagner, *Catalogue of English Mediaeval Rolls of Arms*, 1950, p. 140: his MSS. on his death were purchased by Camden.

[3] The catalogue of Comyns's parcel submitted to Robert Harley had apparently been drawn up by Robert Dale (d. 1722)—at the period postulated for this purchase, Suffolk Herald (later, 1721, Richmond Herald) and a Clerk in the Tower Records: see Edward Harley's letter to H. W., n.d. (unfortunately) (Welbeck Wanleyana): 'I spoke to my Father about the Heraldical MSS. in Comyns's Hands, and shewed him Dales Catalogue, He bid me tell you to agree for all you think fit and necessary to be in the library, and get them as cheap as you can, the sooner you agreed and got the books of this Fellows hands the better.' The price paid was £60 (see *HMC Portland Papers*, v, p. 516). See also an incident referred to in the Diary under 8 Feb. 1723/4, item 1, relating to 'Mr. Latton'.

1529–66, 1570, 1571, and 1577. (Harl. 1530 had been compiled by Campion in 1664.)

In 1708 and again in 1711 important 16th-century historical papers were acquired from John Strype, the historian.

Wanley's acquaintance with Strype had begun as early as 1706 and had arisen out of their common interest in the early editions of the English Bible, Wanley's collection of which must have been seen by Strype in 1706, since we find Wanley writing on 14 Jan. 1706/7 to Strype: 'I have augmented my Stock a little further since you saw it. . . .' and adding: 'and I expect to get more soon.'[1] Strype had, however, a further interest in Wanley, namely, in securing through him permission from Robert Harley to examine and transcribe papers in his library;[2] for in this same letter we find Wanley apologizing for not being able to submit Strype's request to Harley owing to the latter's being 'extremely hurried during this Parliament time,' but adding 'you may promise yourself from his Courtesie and Candour, all the Liberty you can desire in perusing and transcribing his old Papers, and you may be sure, I shall not forget you.' The desired permission was in fact communicated by Wanley to Strype in a letter of 26 May 1707.[3] On the first of the same month he had communicated to Strype the information that Harley had bought Stillingfleet's Library (cf. above, p. xix); 'Mr. Secretary Harley ha's bought the Manuscripts of the late Bp. Stillingfleet's Library, wherein are divers things, I believe, in your way. When you are desirous of perusing J. Stowe's books, &c. upon letting me know, I believe I can certainly procure you all the liberty you can desire.'

Naturally it was not long before a question arose of the purchase of some of Strype's MSS.; negotiations began in June 1708.[4] Harley on examining a catalogue of these (apparently ten books) offered £30 (notwithstanding that 'so great parts of them have been printed'), which Wanley considered 'a great sum of money for Ten Books, in this time of Scarcity'. After some haggling and a slight misunderstanding a deal was concluded (25 July) on Wanley's own responsibility at Strype's price of 40 guineas, the number of books, however, now being eleven not ten, and Wanley concluded his letter characteristically:[5] 'Since then that we are Agreed, I desire you to bring us the books [MSS., as is shown by Strype's endorsement] as soon as possible. I have reserved a Shelf for them, where I design to place them all together as soon as you shall deliver them.'[6] They were not received by Wanley until just before he left in July 1709 for Longleat[7] and are probably Harl. 416–26, which indeed occupy a new shelf, their original press-mark beginning at 39. B. 1; negotiations in 1711[8] led to the addition of a further batch of manuscripts from Strype, which might be those numbered 427–35, which would have completed

---

[1] Wanley's letters *to* Strype are in the Strype correspondence in the Baumgartner Papers (vols. i–x) in the Cambridge University Library. Copies of Wanley's letters made by William Cole, the 18th-century antiquary, are in BM Add. 5853. Wanley's letters *from* Strype are in Harl. 3781, ff. 121–37 *passim*.

[2] Strype to H. W., 2 Dec. 1706 (Harl. 3781, f. 121ᵇ).

[3] C.U.L., Strype Correspondence, iii, pt. iii, no. 296. The letter is of added interest in that it seems to confirm that Wanley was already acting officially as Robert Harley's library-keeper. It is in fact endorsed by Strype: 'Secretary Harley's leave to make use of his Library by his Library-Keeper'.

[4] Strype had left a cat. with Wanley: see Strype's letter to H. W., 7 June 1708 (Harl. 3781, f. 125).

[5] 'In all affairs wherein I happen to be concerned I love to come to a Point as soon as I may', Wanley was to write in a letter to [?John Cooper], 9 Dec. 1712 (Welbeck Wanleyana).

[6] H. W. to Strype, 25 July [1708], C.U.L., Strype Correspondence, iii, pt. iii, no. 336.

[7] See letter from H. W. to Strype, 14 Jan. 1709/10, C.U.L., Strype Correspondence, iii, pt. iii, no. 341. Wanley was at Longleat from 1 Aug. to 31 Oct. 1709 (see his letters to his wife in Welbeck Wanleyana).

[8] See Strype Correspondence, C.U.L., and Harl. 3781, ff. 126–7.

the shelf 39. B. (but for two blank spaces at the end, one of which was filled by Harl. 436, a gift from Hickes) but that they appear in a catalogue finished in 1710.[1]

The Strype papers were, of course, of great importance, containing as they do the papers of John Foxe the martyrologist and a portion of the Burghley papers, which Strype acquired (by borrowing or otherwise—'imparted to me' are Strype's words) in all probability from Sir William Hicks (2nd Bart., d. 1703), a grandson of Burghley's secretary, Sir Michael Hicks (d. 1612), whose family seat, Ruckholts, was in the parish of Low Leighton (Leyton, in Essex) of which Strype was Vicar from 1669.[2]

In 1720 a report in the newspapers that Strype was dead was noticed by Edward Harley who wrote at once[3] to Wanley: 'I desire you would take some care to secure his papers, or what he had that was valuable, and in my way.' This, however, was a false alarm, for Strype did not die until 1737, at the age of 94, in the latter part of his life living with his grandson-in-law, a Mr. Harris, an apothecary at Hackney, where he died.[4]

Two purchases of small groups of MSS. took place in 1712, both involving the Revd. Philip Stubbs,[5] who was employed in negotiations for the purchase of (1) papers of Sir Bulstrode Whitelocke, and (2) MSS. of Jean Aymon. The former were acquired from 'Mrs. Whitelocke' who according to Stubbs[6] had, 'after many traverses' . . . 'bought up all Sr Bulstrode's Autographa for sale, consisting of 25 MSS., most of y^m in Folio: she asks 100 Guineas'; Stubbs adds: 'As to my own part I have such a notion of y^{ir} Value, of His Diary, Swedish Embassy, Political Schemes, & Comments on all ye Texts in O. & N. Testaments relating to Governm^t. &c. that had I so much Money to spare as will compass them, I would take y^m off her Hands my self, & rejoyce under the purchase.' These are from the papers of Sir Bulstrode Whitelocke (1605–75), the Parliamentarian, contemptuously described in 1652 by Evelyn as 'one of their [the Rebels] unhappy Counselors, keeper of pretended *Liberties*' and most famous for his embassy to Sweden 1653–4. The MSS. now in the Harleian Collection endorsed by Wanley 'Bought of Mrs. Whitelocke' are 664, 1299, 1300, 1568, 1569, 1575, 1576, 1578, 1579, 1748, 1849; these curiously enough include none of the MSS. referred to by Stubbs, and the original MS. of his account of his embassy to Sweden, a book of his expenses there, and 28 volumes of historical, legal, and other papers collected by him are at Longleat in the possession of the Marquess of Bath,[7] while the autograph of 'Annals of his own Life' is BM Add. 37341–7.

[1] A 'stray' is Harl. 590, which was also bought of Strype.

[2] See *Biographia Britannica*, vi, pt. i (1763), p. 3847; Strype's Preface to his *Memorials of Abp. Cranmer*, 1694 (1840 ed., p. xiv); N. Salmon, *History and Antiquities of Essex*, 1740, p. 5; Preface to the *Catalogue of the Lansdowne MSS. in British Museum*; and cf. also intro. to HMC *Marquess of Bath MSS.*, Longleat, ii, 1907, p. v, relating to the Hicks papers that were taken to Longleat by Lady Elizabeth Bentinck (granddaughter of Edward Harley and eldest daughter of the 2nd Duke of Portland) who married in 1759 Thomas, Viscount Weymouth (afterwards Marquess of Bath); these too, presumably, had been in Strype's possession; did they also go to Robert Harley in 1711 with the Foxe papers?

[3] Edw. Harley to H. W., 27 Mar. 1720 (Welbeck Wanleyana).

[4] The great mass of Burghley papers, other than those at Hatfield and in the P.R.O., then passed not into Edward Harley's hands but into those of James West, at whose death they were purchased by William Petty, 1st Marquess of Lansdowne, and in turn in 1807 by the British Museum.

[5] See Biographical Index.

[6] Stubbs to H. W., 22 May 1712 (Welbeck Wanleyana).

[7] See HMC *3rd Report*, 1872, pp. xiii and 190–3. The Diary had been printed 1682 by Arthur, Earl of Anglesey, from the MS., *Memorials of English Affairs from the Beginning of the Reign of K. Charles I to the Restoration of K. Charles II* (new ed., 1732); the 'Swedish Embassy' was not published until 1772, *A Journal of the Swedish Embassy in the Years 1653 and 1654, . . .* based on MSS. in the British Museum (Add. 4991, &c.), under the editorship of Charles Morton.

The second commission entrusted to Stubbs was very much more important. This was the acquisition of a number of MSS. from Jean Aymon (1661–1734), who had fled to Holland in 1707 with MSS. stolen from the Royal Library in Paris.[1] A Report by Stubbs on the MSS. then at The Hague is contained in a letter written from Utrecht, dated 22 March 1712 (Welbeck Wanleyana); instructions (Welbeck Wanleyana, Misc. 37 (1)) to Stubbs, dated 2 July 1712, followed, listing the items to be bargained for in two 'parcels' in order of priority. By 20 September 1712 Stubbs had still not gone to Holland and reproaches and letters followed throughout October. By 20 November, however, he was at The Hague, as Wanley on that date addressed a letter to him there (ibid. 37 (3) (*f.*)) complaining of the excessive prices asked by Aymon for the MSS. A long memorandum (ibid. 37 (3) (*g*)), however, next follows, headed by Wanley, 'Brief Account of the Things lately Bought in Holland by the Revd Mr. Philip Stubs.' This lists 14 MS. items (in addition to 2 printed books in sheets) at a cost of 1625 guilders 'which amounteth not to 150 pounds sterling' and concludes with this curious note by Wanley: 'Now I considering their great Rarity, Antiquity, and other Matters of Curiosity pertaining unto them: as also, that by securing them, divers Weapons will be taken out of the Hands of Deists[2] & Papists: & much Additional Strength accrue to the Protestant Religion; do think them worth the said 1625 Guilders or even 100 Pounds Sterling more.' The memorandum is signed and dated by Wanley 3 Jan. 1712/13; a postscript added by Wanley is also important because of its bearing on a passage in the Diary (under the date 2 March 1714/15, item 4): it is as follows: 'Mr. Stubs saith that the Mons[r] not being willing (nor indeed able at this time) to sell the letters of Cardinal Visconti disclosing the Intrigues used in the Council of Trent; The Translation of the Works of Confucius with Chinese maps and other Books relating to the conduct of the Jesuits in China. The Persian Author treating of the Mahumetan Theology; he hath taken security for their being delivered safely unto Him or his Order Two Years next Ensuing; he then Paying for them 200 Guilders more.' This explains the reference in the Diary under the date referred to above to 'the MSS. still remaining in the Custody of Mons[r] Aymon in Holland, which were retrievable about 27th of November last', &c.[3]

The MSS. acquired by Harley in 1712 from Aymon are (the numbers in brackets are those of Wanley's 'Brief Account' referred to above): Harl. 1762 (no. 5), 1763 (no. 9), 1772 (no. 8), 1773 (no. 14), 1775 (no. 13), 1802 (no. 12), 1815 (no. 4), 1850–51 (no. 11), and 7016, ff. 1, 3–11, 14–18, 20, 22–37; and 7551, artt. 5–9 (nos. 1, 2, 6, and 7 of Wanley's list).[4] Of these the famous 'Codex Claromontanus', Harl. 1773, was returned by Edward Harley in 1729[5] and Harl. 7551, artt. 5–9, were returned by the Trustees of the British Museum in 1878 during the Principal Librarianship of Sir Edward Bond.[6]

---

[1] See L. Delisle, *Le Cabinet des manuscrits*, i, 1868, pp. 329–32.

[2] Was this a hit at Toland, the Deist, through whom Wanley had come to know of the Aymon MSS.?

[3] See Diary under the date referred to and footnote 4. But on these MSS. see Diary, 29 Nov. 1721, item 12, and footnote.

[4] Some of these MSS. were seen by Uffenbach when he visited The Hague in 1711; for their identification see Diary, footnote 4 to 2 Mar. 1714/15, item 4.

[5] The present Harl. 1773 now contains in fact the correspondence that passed (1727–30) on that occasion between Edward Harley and the Jacobite Earl of Middleton and the Abbé Jean Paul Bignon, the Royal Librarian, and Cardinal Fleury.

[6] In exchange for 242 volumes of transcripts of Loménie de Brienne State Papers, which had been made on the instructions of Colbert, Louis XIV's minister, and are now BM Add. 30525–766.

For the few years now remaining before the commencement of the Diary on 2 March 1715 we have but little material to document the development of the Library. There is, unfortunately, a break of over two years (23 June 1711 to 15 October 1713) in the series of letters from Edward Harley to Wanley, with but two letters from Wanley to Harley, only the second of which, 30 December 1713, has something to our purpose; in it Wanley reports the receipt of a parcel of papers from 'Mr. Paul' at 40 guineas, the presentation to the Library of three old deeds by himself as a New Year's gift and of MS. 94. A. 21 (*sic* for 22) [i.e. Harl. 1867] by Moses Williams. The papers of George Paul of Jesus College, Cambridge, are now widely scattered in the later Harleian MSS. (chiefly, for example, 6798, 7000–4, 7006, 7011, 7013–16 passim, 7018, &c.).[1]

The gift of a single MS. from Moses Williams reminds us that accessions to the Library also came by way of donations and though they were not at any time very numerous they were sufficiently so to make, cumulatively, a quite considerable addition to the Library in the pre-Diary period; some are dated, most are not. We may note among the dated ones that on 25 October 1707 George Hickes gave Harl. 436 (and on unspecified dates Harl. 414, 415 (two Oriental MSS.), 438, 440, 464, 586, 1129, 1764, 1804 ('una cum alijs nonnullis'), 1845); on 21 May 1709 Sir William Collier gave Harl. 935; on 15 July 1709 Robert Cunningham gave Harl. 467, 1215; on 28 April of the same year William Nicolson, Bishop of Carlisle, gave Harl. 662 and on 1 May 1713, Harl 1796; on 9 June 1710 Francis Aston gave Harl. 1419;[2] in 1712 Robert Nelson had presented Harl. 3985, a catalogue of MSS. of Grabe (to whom Robert Harley had rendered financial assistance) and in the same year John Bowack, writing-master at Westminster School, gave Harl. 1809. At unspecified dates (in addition to those presented by George Hickes noted above) Lord Bathurst gave Harl. 1512, 1513; Dr. William Stratford, Canon of Christ Church, Oxford, 90. C. 11+Harl. 1580–4;[3] Sir Gilbert Dolben, Harl. 1514–23; Matthew Hutton (whose own papers were subsequently bought), Harl. 410, 411 (?), 1232, 1834, 1835; and Sir Thomas Hoby, 3rd Bart., Harl. 1498;[4] Dr. John Beaumont, Harl. 1848, 1857; Peter Le Neve, Harl. 450, 452, 453, 1127; John Anstis, Harl. 1061–6, 1117–21, 1509–11, 1755, 1782, 1817; Robert Stephens, Harl. 1251; Francis Atterbury, Harl. 1758; George Holmes, Harl. 1760; Elizabeth Elstob, Harl. 1866 (a volume compiled by 'this Learned Virgin'); Hugh Todd, Prebendary of Carlisle, Harl. 1881; and White Kennett, Harl. 1231.

From several of the donors referred to above, and from others, individual MSS. were also bought: for example, from Peter Le Neve were purchased Harl. 391, 394, 395, 397, 398, 442, 444–9, 451, 454–61, 462(?), 463(?), 611, 930, 1128, 1132, 1278, 1288, 1799; from George Hickes, Harl. 439, 441; from Timothy Langley, Harl. 1327; from Alexander Cuningham, Junior, Harl. 1771 and 1814; from Thomas Tickell, Fellow of Queen's College, Oxford, Harl. 1865; from Richard Jones, Harl. 2251, 2336; and 'with other MSS. bought out of the late Duke of Shrews-bury's Library' Harl. 2317. So much is recorded by Wanley in the *Harleian Cata-logue* (i.e. up to Harl. 2407) or in the MSS. themselves, and most of these names

---

[1] With these, however, are also grouped items from another parcel of Paul's collections which were purchased from his landlady, the negotiations for the purchase of which are recorded in letters 1 July 1713–15 Jan. 1713/14 in Harl. 7007, ff. 1–7; cf. also Harl. 7008.

[2] A copy of the second part of the Inventory of the Wardrobe of Henry VIII, 1547, of which Part I is Soc. of Antiquaries MS. 129. Aston's letter accompanying the gift is in the Harl. MS. at f. 1*.

[3] Before the end of 1712 (cf. BM Add. 45704, finished 31 Dec. of that year).

[4] Probably in 1711 (cf. Edw. Harley to H. W., 23 June 1711 (Welbeck Wanleyana).

appear in Wanley's Memorandum of July 1715. To these must be added the quite considerable number bought of Wanley himself.[1]

One manuscript, Harl. 392, bought of John Bagford (whose collections were subsequently to be acquired), serves to remind us that Robert Harley was one of Bagford's biggest customers as we can see from Bagford's surviving account book for 1703–8 (Harl. 5998).[2]

Accounts for this earlier period (with the exception of that of Bagford) are unfortunately, however, wanting and for the prices of the larger block purchases we have to rely on Wanley's memorandum of 27 July 1715. For the period of the Diary, however, a considerable number of accounts and financial memoranda are preserved in the Welbeck Wanleyana.

From Edward Harley's letters which recommence on 15 October 1713 we can see what the chief preoccupations in Library affairs were in the two years immediately preceding the Diary's opening date.

Some of the negotiations or proceedings, as they frequently do in any librarian's life, proved abortive. The case of Moore's MSS. will serve as an example. On 31 July 1714 John Moore, Bishop of Ely, died; his library was well known to be a very considerable one. It is said to have contained a total of 30,755 volumes, the printed books amounting to 28,965 (comprising 6,725 folios, 8,200 quartos, and 14,040 octavos): the MSS. were 1,790 in number.[3] The library was kept at Ely Place off Holborn, the Bishop's London residence. In 1702, according to William Nicolson, Bishop of Carlisle, who dined with Bishop Moore on 19 January of that year, the library was contained in 'five rooms, besides closets' and included many valuable MSS.;[4] Nicolson refers especially to the famous 8th-century MS. of Bede's 'Historia Ecclesiastica' which Wanley was to describe in his Catalogue of Anglo-Saxon MSS. (Hickes, *Thesaurus*, ii, pp. 287–8) and which he claimed to have 'retrieved'.[5]

It is clear from a letter of Edward Harley to Wanley, dated 5 October 1714 (Welbeck Wanleyana), that he was interested. Wanley had presumably been to Ely Place (possibly in the summer) to look at the MSS. and had received a letter from Samuel Clarke, Moore's executor, dated 4 September 1714, on the subject of the disposal of the library:[6] the price stipulated in Clarke's letter was to be not less than £8,000. This Harley regarded as 'impracticable' and thought that it would

---

[1] These included Harl. 401, 585, 928, 1203, 1239, 1248, 1264–6, 1268, 1329, 1501, 1525, 1757, 1759, 1792, 1797, 1798, 1803, 1819, 1861–3, 1868, 1875, 1877–9, 1882–7, 1889, 1895–7, 1912, and 67. C. 11 (the Pierrepont Cartulary [=Davis no. 1308] removed from the Library and sent to Welbeck 'by Lady Oxford's Orders' 18 May 1749; it still bears the old press-mark and is still a Welbeck item [BM Loan 29/60].

[2] Others whose names occur frequently in this volume are John Moore, Bp. of Ely, Browne Willis, Hans Sloane, Walter Clavell, William George Pennington of Rotterdam, and Wanley: on 26 Aug. 1708 Bagford delivered to Wanley 'about 300 specements of ould MSS. @ 5s.' (f. 78ᵇ).

[3] See C. H. Hartshorne, *The Book Rarities in the University of Cambridge*, 1829, p. 23 (citing Baker); W. Y. Fletcher, *English Book Collectors*, 1902, pp. 125–9; S. de Ricci, *English Collectors*, 1930, pp. 34–35. A list of his MSS. appeared in Bernard *CMA*, ii (1697), pp. 361–78 (nos. 9187–860), and p. 390 (App., nos. 51–71) and 393–9 (App., nos. 675–827); a catalogue of those added to his library *after* 1697 was compiled by Thomas Tanner, who became his chaplain in 1698, and is now C.U.L. MS. Oo. 7. 50²; it contains 195 items, numbered 831–1025 in sequence from the last item in *CMA* (among these is the Moore MS. of Bede, which is no. 994). For the collation of MSS. with present shelf-marks in the University Library see H. R. Luard, *Catalogue of MSS. of the University of Cambridge*, vi (index), pp. 164–8. A list of incunabula and other early printed books belonging to Moore is in *CMA* ii, pp. 379–84.

[4] See *Trans. of the Cumberland and Westmorland Antiquarian and Archaeological Soc.*, N.S., i (1901), p. 39.

[5] See Wanley's letter to Benzelius, 28 May 1704 (printed R. C. Wright, 'Letters from Humfrey Wanley to Eric Benzelius and Peter the Great's Librarian', *Durham Univ. Journal*, i, no. 3, p. 191).

[6] Harl. 3778, f. 75; printed C. H. Hartshorne, op. cit., p. 20, n.

'be best to buy the MSS. first if possible and then to find some way to secure the choice printed books'. In a later letter, 16 November 1714 (Welbeck Wanleyana), Harley returned to the subject, writing to Wanley 'as to the Bp. of Elys library I do not think to give so much money for it as they ask: I think the best way is to let Bateman [i.e. Christopher Bateman, the bookseller] bye [*sic*] it or let it come to an auction and get the valuable books, and those that I have a mind for, without the trouble of all the rubish and Duplicates: this is my opinion but I would have you ask my Father what his Thoughts are.'[1] The library was as a matter of fact bought by George I for £6,450 and presented to the University of Cambridge 20 September 1715.[2]

Again, on 28 July 1714, Thomas Thynne, 1st Viscount Weymouth, died, when he was succeeded by his grand-nephew. It is not surprising to find Edward Harley therefore writing on 21 August 1714 to Wanley (Welbeck Wanleyana): 'Ld. Weymouth's MSS. will I hear come to be sold. pray when you have an opportunity inquire the truth of it.' Of this, too, nothing resulted, though reference is made in a letter from Edward Harley of 31 March 1715 to Lord Weymouth's cabinet.

For a brief period now—2 March 1714/15 to 22 August 1715—the history of the Library is documented by the Diary.

The Diary entries confirm most of the characteristics noted in the letters—the watchfulness on the part of both Edward Harley and Wanley for opportunities to acquire either whole collections or outstanding manuscripts that Wanley felt should properly find a place in the Library: thus, efforts were made to acquire the famous St. Chad's Gospels from the Dean and Chapter of Lichfield; the collections of Edward Lhwyd and especially the 'Red Book of Hergest' that belonged to Jesus College, Oxford; and the library of Sir Roger Twysden; and to bring to completion the troublesome business of the Aymon MSS.; the books and papers of Sir Matthew Hale 'not given to Lincoln's Inne' were to be kept in memory; some tentative plans were suggested to track down the 'Lauderdale Orosius'; Wanley also (26 March 1715) reminded Harley that Dr. Brewster of Hereford had 'some few old MSS. and among them, a Leiger Book of Malmesbury'—these had been listed in print in 1697[3] but went to the Bodleian Library (7 May 1715), shortly after Wanley spoke to Harley.

In spite of these failures, however, several collections were in fact added to the Library in this first period of the Diary (i.e. up to 22 August 1715), the most considerable being the collections of MSS. formed by Robert Bourscough, Archdeacon of Barnstaple, which were bought of his widow for £40 on 17 May 1715,[4] and two collections of papers, that of Thomas Baker, the non-juror, of St. John's College, Cambridge, now scattered through Harl. 6987–7018, which were received 14 March 1714/15,[5] and the collection of letters addressed to Gerard

---

[1] This may mean no more than that Wanley should seek a second person's views, in this case that of Robert Harley or it may have more significance and show that Robert Harley still exercised some say in Library affairs. Cf. the remark about the purchase of Comyns's heraldic MSS. in an undated letter (probably 1711) from Edward Harley to H. W. referred to above, p. xx, n. 3.

[2] See C. Sayle, *Annals of Cambridge University Library 1278–1900*, Cambridge, 1916, p. 92, and J. C. T. Oates, *A Catalogue of the Fifteenth Century Printed Books in the University Library Cambridge*, Cambridge, 1954, p. 14.

[3] Bernard, *CMA* ii, p. 356 (nos. 9067–71).

[4] These had been catalogued in Bernard, *CMA* ii (1697), pp. 232–5 (nos. 7620–710), 359–60 (nos. 9162–79). For identification of MSS. see Diary under 17 May 1715, n. 6. Wanley's own list of the MSS., compiled 15 Mar. 1714/15, is preserved in Welbeck Wanleyana.

[5] Baker's own MS. collections are Harl. 7028–50; on the acquisition of these see p. xxxvii below.

John Vossius (with some other MSS.) acquired from Richard Jones, the bookseller, on 15 August 1715, for £26. 17s. 6d.[1]

It was on the 16th July of this year that Robert Harley was committed to the Tower (where he remained until 1 July 1717) and one document that resulted from this critical moment in the Harley family fortunes gives us an opportunity of seeing what the Library consisted of at this stage in its history. It is a particularly appropriate date because the Diary breaks off a month later, 22 August, immediately preceding Wanley's first visit to Wimpole, Edward Harley's Cambridgeshire seat, which took place at the end of the month.[2] Wanley's visit to Wimpole and his staying there at intervals during the next few years are indicative of the difficulties that attended the fortunes of the Library at this time. Until January 1715 the Library had been housed at York Buildings in Duke Street off the Strand; in February 1715,[3] however, we find Robert Harley writing to Edward Harley from the Harley seat at Eywood (near Kington) in Herefordshire;[4] 'I desire you will speak to Mr. Thomas [the Steward] about Sir R. Davers' house and also that which was Earl Rivers' in Great Queen Street; there are two houses, and I know one is very fit for a Library. I hear Mons. Iberville is leaving it', and again in a letter to the Earl of Dartmouth, written on 1 March 1714/15 from Brampton Castle in Herefordshire, Robert Harley speaks of his having been under 'the necessity of removing my Library'.[5] The removal was made to Bath Court near St. James's Palace and there the Library remained until August 1717,[6] when it was transferred to the house acquired by Edward Harley in Dover Street, where it seems to have been placed, at least at first, in the Garden House;[7] and while the printed books were for the most part to be housed at Wimpole, this Dover Street house was at any rate to be the permanent home of the manuscript portion (with a few exceptions) of the Library. Arthur Collins in his *Historical Collections of the Noble Families of Cavendishe, Holles, Vere, Harley and Ogle*, published in 1752, observed (p. 213) that at that date Edward Harley's widow, although she herself spent most of her time at Welbeck, still retained the collection of manuscripts 'at her House in Dover Street' and it was from this address that the MSS. were removed at the end of 1754 or the beginning of 1755 when they became part of the national collections on the foundation of the British Museum.[8]

Some information about the size of the Library in 1713, two years before the Wanley memorandum of July 1715, is supplied *en passant* by Wanley in a letter of 28 November of that year addressed to Basil Feilding, 4th Earl of Denbigh, who died a few years later (1717).[9] 'I am the person', writes Wanley, 'whom your Lordship about twenty years ago, was pleased to Honor with your Permission of taking a Catalogue of your old Written Books, which was afterwards printed at

[1] For identification of MSS. in Harl. Collection see Diary under 15 Aug. 1715, nn. 2 and 3.
[2] See Edw. Harley to H. W., 25 and 28 Aug. 1715 (Welbeck Wanleyana).
[3] Robt. Harley to Edw. Harley, 6 Feb. 1715 (*HMC Portland Papers*, v, p. 506).
[4] The house was demolished in 1954: it was of 17th-century date and had been modernized in 1806. It was here that in 1812 the then Lady Oxford entertained Byron.
[5] Printed *HMC Earl of Dartmouth's MSS.*, 11th Report, App. V, pp. 321–2.
[6] See Thomas Tudway to H. W., 6 Sept. 1717 (Harl. 3782, f. 79): 'It is easy to suppose that my Ld. Oxford parting with his house in Bath Court has created you a great deal of trouble, in removing yᵉ Library. . . .'
[7] See Edw. Harley to H. W., 13 Aug. 1717 (Welbeck Wanleyana): 'There can no room in the House in Dover Street be allowed for the Library. the Garden House is the only room that can be spared, and if that will not do I cannot help it.'
[8] See BM Add. 6179, f. 72. And cf. p. lxxx below.
[9] H. W. to E. of Denbigh, 28 Nov. 1713 (Welbeck Wanleyana). Cf. also Harl. 7055, f. 17.

Oxford. . . .[1] Since then I have often thought of those books; and now having (for many years) had the Care and Custody of my Lord Treasurer's Library, wherein there are two thousand Books of the like kind (not to mention 1000 Rolls and 13000 Deeds) I not only study how to keep together what is already got but to Augment this great Collection as far as I am able: and I can truly say that my Success has in the main been answerable to my Industry. . . .'[2]

At 28 November 1713 then the Library contained 2,000 MSS., 1,000 rolls and 13,000 deeds.

According to his memorandum of 27 July 1715[3] the record then stood at 3,000 MSS., the rolls and deeds being the same as in 1713. In this memorandum Wanley characterizes the 'printed part' merely as 'numerous' but adds that the contents are 'excellent for their age, edition, use, richness, or rarity'; the valuation space is left blank, as is that for the MS. portion which is described immediately afterwards. The MSS. consist, writes Wanley, of 'books, charters or deeds, and rolls (not to insist upon the fragments of parchment and paper, which my noble Lord Oxford bought of me at £50) written in about twenty-six languages or dialects, and treating upon all sorts of learning and business'. The charters or deeds (about 13,000) 'are the most authentic testimonies or evidences as to families and estates, and the very seals of exceeding use. . . . This is the largest collection that is known to be anywhere'. The rolls amount to about 1,000.[4] Lastly, there are the unbound papers: 'The collection of letters and papers of state, of princes, nobles, scholars, etc., which are not yet bound up into books, being added to those in this Library which are already bound, makes the Harleian collection of papers much the best and most valuable and numerous of any now in England, excepting only that of Sir Robert Cotton.'

The primary purpose of the memorandum was, of course, to put, if possible, a valuation on the Library. This is shown by the spaces left for the insertion of figures in the part relating to printed books and manuscripts and by the paragraph of general observations which follows and which begins significantly with this sentence: 'It may be noted that old manuscripts do not fall, but rise in their price, so much so as to save the interest of the money laid out upon them', and by Wanley's statement in the paragraph referring to the rolls that he 'sold one single roll to my noble Lord for thirty guineas, a high price indeed, and yet I refused an hundred pounds of another person for it, because I resolved it should come into this Library'.

Then follows an estimate of the cost of the Library to date, which is totalled at £4,573; of this, £1,000 is said to have been spent by Robert Harley on his books *before* he made the purchase of Sir Simonds D'Ewes's 'study' which is reckoned at £550 (£500 plus incidental charges, though the receipt reveals that only £450 was paid);[5] Stillingfleet's MSS. cost £175; the heraldic MSS. bought of Foresight £85 and two other batches of heraldic MSS. bought of Shires and Comyns respectively £35 and £60 (see above, pp. xx–xxi); the price of the Aymon purchase

---

[1] A reference of course to Bernard's *CMA* of 1697, in which (ii, pp. 35–39 [nos. 1463–1552]) is the cat. of Denbigh's books; Wanley is thus disclosed for the first time as its compiler. See above, p. xv.

[2] Wanley then asks the Earl if he would be willing to give his MSS. to the Harleian Collection. Apparently the Earl was not, as the MSS. remained with the family until at least 1851, when many were acquired by the British Museum (Add. 18629–73).

[3] Printed *HMC Portland Papers*, v, pp. 514–16; see also for previous discussion of this document C. E. Wright, *The Book Collector*, xi, no. 2 (summer, 1962), pp. 159–61.

[4] At present the numbers are: Harley Charters, 10631; Harley Rolls, 916. See also pp. lvii–lxi below.

[5] On the purchase of D'Ewes's library and price paid see pp. xviii–xix above.

(when completed) is reckoned at £200 (see above, pp. xxii–xxiii); letters and papers bought of Baker (see above, p. xxvi), Paul (see above, p. xxiv) and of a Mrs. Shank amounted (with carriage) to about £102, while about £50 is reckoned for the drawings and prints, &c., bought of Kemp. £1,000 is allocated to books, charters, rolls, parchments bought of Wanley himself, Bagford, and others, and a round £1,000 is allocated to Wanley for library service and bookbinders. The MSS. bought of (Peter) Le Neve cost £30 and those of Strype £40 (see above, pp. xxi–xxii). To this is added £246 for furnishings (30 presses for books; 15 presses with pigeon holes for charters; and 3 deeper presses for 'very large MSS.'). Apart from acquisitions by purchase Wanley makes honourable mention of a number of benefactors, naming particularly, Colonel Henry Worseley, Dr. Hickes, Mr. Anstis, Dr. Stratford, Lord Harley, Mr. George Holmes, Sir Gilbert Dolben, Mr. John Kemp and Wanley himself, 'not to mention any of those who have given no more than a single book, excepting Sir Thomas Hobby'. Examples of donations from these and others we have already noticed (p. xxiv above).

This then was the state of the Library when, as a result of Robert Harley's committal to the Tower, the whole burden of administering it fell on his son, Edward.[1]

What sort of man then was the new master? At the risk of some repetition later we should say something of Edward Harley's character and personality here, as it is important to visualize what kind of man was directing affairs in the background of the Diary, which of course represents Wanley's point of view, though the frequent references to Harley in it never allow us to forget for long who was in fact controlling the Library's fortunes. Edward Harley was by character admirably fitted to inspire the expansion of the Library; from his early days at Oxford he had shown an interest in acquiring books, and from 1707 when he went up to Christ Church he began to run up considerable book bills[2] and this was the passion of course on which Wanley was to play during his Librarianship: it was this weakness doubtless that led Dr. Stratford, Edward Harley's Christ Church mentor, to say in 1720: 'You know I have often wished that you were bound prentice to Morley [Harley's agent] rather than to Wanley, with all due respect to Mr. Wanley's profession.'[3]

There was no sharp break at first in the interests that had guided his father in his collecting. In fact Edward Harley continued to enlarge the Library in the subjects which had been favourites with Robert: genealogy, heraldry, and historical and political material. We find him, for example, writing in 1717,[4] 'I shall be glad to make the collection of Heraldical MSS. as compleat as possible' and 'I shall be very sorry to miss any MSS. that relate to the History of our country'. Hence his desire to secure Johnson's and St. George's heraldic MSS., Strype's collections, and those of Matthew Hutton, and charters and cartularies. He shared his father's interest in theological and religious material, collecting particularly Bibles and Prayer Books in all their editions and in many languages, and in this he had a common interest with his Librarian. Books and pamphlets of political controversy also attracted his attention, the Library at its dispersal after his death being said to

---

[1] For the details of Edward Harley's life see Biographical Index, and for a study of him as collector see C. E. Wright, 'Portrait of a Bibliophile, VIII: Edward Harley, 2nd Earl of Oxford, 1689–1741', *The Book Collector*, xi, no. 2 (Summer, 1962), pp. 158–74. Reference should also be made to E. Goodwin's art. in *DNB* xxiv, 1890, pp. 394–6; G.E.C., *The Complete Peerage*, x, 1945, pp. 266–8; and A. S. Turberville, *A History of Welbeck Abbey*, i, 1938, pp. 291–387.

[2] *HMC Portland Papers*, vii, p. xviii.

[3] Stratford to Edw. Harley, 23 Mar. 1719/20 (*HMC Portland Papers*, vii, pp. 271–2).

[4] Edward Harley to H. W., 17 Nov. 1717 (Welbeck Wanleyana.)

have contained as many as 200,000 examples of such: a catalogue of 253 make-up volumes of tracts drawn up at an unspecified date is preserved among the Welbeck Harley Papers and from this vast collection of pamphlets were selected the contents of the *Harleian Miscellany*. These were interests that he and his father had undoubtedly inherited from their 17th-century Harley ancestors. With some subjects —such as alchemy and astrology—he had no patience at all.[1]

As time went on his bibliophilic pursuits were to develop rather on the lines of his own generation of bibliophiles: Coke of Norfolk, the Earl of Sunderland, Dr. Mead, and others, and were to be reflected in his devotion to early printed books— especially incunabula, early editions of the classics and books printed on vellum, and in his acquisition of fine illuminated MSS.—the Roman de la Rose and Froissart's Chronicles, and of others that today are of special palaeographical interest, such as the Codex Aureus from the Ménars Sale. He shared with Mead a strong interest in Greek MSS. and in 1724 we find him expressing to Wanley his disappointment that his collection of these was not larger;[2] it was probably his desire to increase the holdings of Greek MSS. that occasioned his persistence in the Covel purchase.

In addition he had, too, what was rare in his contemporaries, a quite remarkable interest in Oriental MSS.; as a result, the Library contains MSS. in Hebrew, Arabic, Persian (a Persian MS. was presented to him by Alexander Pope in 1723 [Harl. 5478]), Turkish, Armenian, Aramaic, Samaritan, and Syriac, with a few examples of the languages of South and South-East Asia such as Sanskrit, Gujarati, and Malayan with one even in Jaina-Prākrit (Harl. 415); from the Far East came one or two items in Chinese and Japanese.

Of course, like his contemporaries, he collected coins and medals: 'You know (he wrote to Wanley, 18 December 1715) that I am collecting coins, medals, &c that relate to England, Scotland and Ireland.' Of this and his acquisition of pictures and minatures more will be said later (see pp. lxiv–lxix below). His interest in antiquities was that of the dilettante and wide-ranging rather than discriminating: Greek and Roman inscriptions and statuary, and antiquities generally, Egyptian antiquities, material from the Middle Ages in England—from Queen Bertha's comb from the Arundel Collection to round stones used in the siege of Kenilworth Castle by Henry III, and the catalogue of the sale of his collections in 1742 supplies numerous examples of his appetite for curiosities—a Turkish General's truncheon, 'a cap of American feathers, presented to Queen Elizabeth, 1586', &c. Nevertheless, that he had a genuine concern for antiquities is shown by the records of the several tours he made through England, the journals of three of which were kept by Vertue,[3] and we find Harley, for instance, in a letter to Wanley of 15 September 1717 (in Welbeck Wanleyana) asking the latter while at Royston on his way to Wimpole to 'take down the old inscriptions that are in the church'.

Books, however, remained the dominating passion and he kept a keen watch on opportunities for acquiring these. On the death of George Hickes in 1715, he wrote to Wanley:[4] 'What is become of the books MSS. and papers, I wish you would enquire'; on hearing of Basil Kennett's death he wrote:[5] 'as to Basil Kennets study you will take care to lay your hands upon all the Books, prints & Drawings

---

[1] Cf. Diary, 15 Apr. 1724: Wanley's comment here probably reflects Harley's views.
[2] Edw. Harley to H. W., 29 Sept. 1724 (Welbeck Wanleyana).
[3] Harley's travel records are printed *HMC Portland Papers*, vi, pp. 64–66, 68–69, 74–181.
[4] Edw. Harley to H. W., 18 Dec. 1715 (Welbeck Wanleyana).
[5] Ibid., 22 Jan. 1715/16 (Welbeck Wanleyana).

that you shall like'; he instructed Wanley to encourage Noel to buy Dr. South's books;[1] a false report of Strype's death led him to ask Wanley to take care 'to secure his papers, or what he had that was valuable, and in my way'.[2]

As a result, the increase in the Library's size in MSS. and printed books (not to mention prints and drawings) became in a very few years under his control considerable. Thus he says in a letter of 1717[3] that he finds his printed books were now 12,000 in number and adds 'so as to them none should be bought but w[t] are very good & usefull':[4] at his death they numbered about 50,000. That he was well informed about the books in his collection is shown by several instances, especially in a correspondence with Thomas Hearne,[5] and he was generous in allowing it to be used by students of the history of printing, such as Maittaire who drew on its resources for his *Annales Typographici*, and Samuel Palmer when preparing his *The General History of Printing* (1732 or 1733) was invited to Wimpole to look at Bagford's Papers.[6] He was watchful of everything that concerned the Library, including the arrangement of its contents. In 1717 he told Wanley[7] that as to the Bibles he was to 'make the Shelves regular & let them fall as they happen except you had a mind to take all the Bibles out & lay them in another room w[ch] I think needless trouble'. He told Wanley also[8] to make the end of the study look well. Again, when the workmen were to work on 'the room within the Drawing Room' he gave Wanley precise instructions about the removal of the furniture.[9] He had a sharp eye for minutiae and a retentive memory: for example, he told Wanley in 1719 to 'put an *S.* in ever[y] MS. that came from L[d]. Sun[derland] & put them in a Box by themselves'.[10] 'Among the Whincops books in y[e] inner closet' (he wrote to Wanley in 1720) 'is a Polydore Virgil in 2 vol. with the Cecils arms on y[e] cover. send y[m] down.' He was not satisfied that all had been received that was due under Hugh Thomas's legacy of his papers;[11] he wants to know where Bowyer got the parcel of letters which had belonged to Prince Rupert and which he had presented to the Library—'how came he by them?' is the terse question.[12]

The relations between Edward Harley and Wanley were on the whole very good. Harley showed his appreciation of Wanley's efforts in several of his letters to him. He left the management of the Kemp affair entirely to Wanley.[13] With reference to the sale of Hickes's collection he wrote: 'I dont doubt but you will secure everything very well: your abilities no man can doubt, & I have no reason to doubt your endeavours to do me all the service you can.'[14] Of Covel Harley wrote: 'He acts a very cunning part but I do not doubt you will be even with him: I leave the matter entirely to your management.'[15] And many other examples could be cited. On the

---

[1] Edw. Harley to H. W., 1 Dec. 1717 (Welbeck Wanleyana).
[2] Ibid., 27 Mar. 1720 (Welbeck Wanleyana).
[3] Ibid., 10 Sept. 1717 (Welbeck Wanleyana).
[4] Cf. the injunction repeated 28 June 1718: 'I would have no printed Books bought but what [are] extreamly good & rare.'
[5] See, for example, his letter to Hearne, 25 Dec. 1731, printed in *Letters written by Eminent Persons*, ii, 1813, pt. i, pp. 82–89.
[6] See *HMC Portland Papers*, vi, 1901, p. 21 (Samuel Palmer to Harley, 15 April 1728).
[7] Edw. Harley to H. W., 13 Feb. 1716/17 (Welbeck Wanleyana).
[8] Ibid., 7 Mar. 1716/17 (Welbeck Wanleyana).
[9] Ibid., 11 Apr. 1717 (Welbeck Wanleyana).
[10] Ibid., 6 Sept. 1719 (Welbeck Wanleyana). See below, p. xliii.
[11] Ibid., 25 Oct. 1720 (Welbeck Wanleyana).
[12] Ibid., 30 Oct. 1720 (Welbeck Wanleyana).
[13] Ibid., 12 July 1714 (Welbeck Wanleyana).
[14] Ibid., 12 Jan. 1715/16 (Welbeck Wanleyana).
[15] Ibid., 25 Jan. 1715/16 (Welbeck Wanleyana).

other hand Edward Harley was not a man to be trifled with. In a letter of 14 October 1717 he tells Wanley that he has been looking over Wanley's recent letters and then sets out some particulars that had not been 'despatcht'. In 1720 he had occasion several times to rebuke Wanley: Wanley had let a cabinet go for polishing for which Harley had given no instructions and is told: 'I desire when I send for things they may be punctually sent down & not trifled off till an other time.' Complaint is made that paper had been dirtily and carelessly packed. And finally in December of that year Wanley received a scorching rebuke for reporting that the ship containing Harley's 'ritratti' obtained through Hay was to be discharged on 'the Eleventh Instant' which, unfortunately for Wanley, proved to be a Sunday, when no such business, of course, was done: 'this I take to be a banter,' wrote Harley, 'I am not so fond of the things to be pleased at being played the fool with. Mr. Hay should not have served me so, nor should you have wrote such gross Stuff to think I could be so imposed upon by it.'[1]

But Harley had a genuine interest in Wanley's welfare and health. When Wanley was dismissed from his housekeepership of the Hackney Coach Office in Surrey Street in December 1715, Harley allowed Wanley and his wife to take up their abode in the Harleys' St. James's Square house.[2] In 1724 he wrote expressing great concern at Wanley's having drunk some bad wine and went on: 'I desire earnestly you would take care of yourself, your Health is of great Value to me, you must remember you are got the wrong side of forty and cannot now be supposed to be able to struggle with indispositions as you was used to do, you have a good constitution and with care you may enjoy it many years, . . . I desire you will take what I have wrote as it is meant and as it proceeds from a true and sincere concern for you, I am not very forward to give my advice, but I assure you the true value I have for you has made me say so much.'[3] He urged Wanley to take more exercise and told him on one occasion not to meddle with Cambridge physicians but offered to get the advice of Sloane or Mead for him.[4] In 1716 he made Wanley a present of 'a Silver Pen' writing engagingly: 'I hope it will prove to your liking, there is a gold Nib and a silver nib one at each end, if you do not like them pray send them up to me again and I will have them altered, till they do please you.'

Harley was indeed a most generous patron. Notably among those who benefited from his patronage was James Gibbs, the architect, who worked for Harley at Wimpole and, as architect for the Cavendish-Harley estates in London, designed a new front for Harley's Dover St. house in 1737. It was Harley, too, who, pursuing the plan that the South transept of Westminster Abbey should be a pantheon of the poets, employed Gibbs between 1721 and 1724 to design the little cenotaph there to Ben Jonson.[5] Another protégé was the artist and engraver George Vertue, who makes frequent appearances in the Diary (see Biographical Index) and was at all times a welcome visitor to Dover St. and Wimpole: he was constantly employed to make drawings and engravings for Harley of objects in his collection.[6] At Har-

---

[1] Edw. Harley to H. W., 4 Dec. 1720 (Welbeck Wanleyana).
[2] Ibid., 11 and 18 Dec. 1715 (Welbeck Wanleyana).
[3] Ibid., 24 Sept. 1724 (Welbeck Wanleyana).
[4] Ibid., 27 Nov. 1716 (Welbeck Wanleyana).
[5] On Gibbs's relations with Harley see Bryan Little, *The Life and Works of James Gibbs, 1682–1754,*1955, *passim.* It was to Harley that Gibbs dedicated his *Rules for Drawing the several Parts of Architecture,* 1732: Harley had subscribed to his *Book of Architecture,* 1728, and is referred to in the Preface. Gibbs designed for Harley a monument to Wanley (see *Book of Architecture,* pl. 124).
[6] Many examples of this work are preserved in the Harley Collection of Prints in the possession of the Society of Antiquaries. See also bills in Edward Harley Papers, Misc. 3.

ley's death in 1741 Vertue was to describe his character in one of his notebooks: 'A Friend Noble—Generous—Good and amiable—to me—above all men a true Friend. The loss—not to be expressed.'[1] To Matthew Prior the poet (who died at Wimpole) Harley gave for his lifetime the Down Hall Estate in Essex.[2] To some authors he made gifts: Hearne received £50 from him in 1723;[3] he subscribed to their works.[4] He sent information to antiquaries and others about books and MSS. in his collections; he forwarded to Thomas Tanner in 1730 an account of his newly acquired Biddlesdon and Holm Cultram cartularies and in 1731 sent him notice that he had acquired a Register of Welbeck.[5] David Wilkins, who was preparing a new edition of Prideaux's *Marmora Oxoniensia*, sought the loan of the copy in the Library alleged to be corrected by Thomas Smith[6] and in 1732 begged admission to the Library to examine the catalogues of MSS. and records when preparing a new edition of his *Concilia*.[7] Francis Drake sought his support for *Eboracum*, his work on the antiquities of York.[8]

He made gifts to the libraries of others: to the Spalding Gentlemen's Society he presented in 1729 a set of the Greek Ecclesiastical Historians and some prints[9] and to the library of the Cathedral Church of Ripon he presented a number of books, selected from a list sent to him by the Dean, Heneage Dering,[10] which included Wharton's *Anglia Sacra* and Mabillon's *De Re Diplomatica*.

He numbered among his friends Prior,[11] Swift, Pope, Sir James Thornhill, Conyers Middleton, George Harbin, John Anstis, Sir Hans Sloane, Robert Freind, Headmaster of Westminster School, Zachary Grey, William Brome of Ewithington, Thomas Hearne, and Thomas Baker, and by his liberality established Wimpole in the eyes of artists and men of letters.[12]

This then is the man who was controlling the Library's development during the period of the Diary and who was Wanley's master.

For the history of the Library during the years immediately following Edward Harley's assumption of control but not covered by the Diary (i.e. August 1715–January 1720), we are fortunate in having a long series of letters from him to Wanley, memoranda, lists, bills, and receipts, preserved in the Welbeck Wanleyana, besides some evidence from a memorandum and account book of Nathaniel Noel.[13] Some of the negotiations for purchases in this period were protracted and complex and it is sometimes difficult to know when the purchase was concluded and indeed what was included in the purchase. The chief preoccupations of Harley and his librarian were the acquisition of Sir Henry St. George's MSS., the papers and MSS. of Dr. John Covel, books from the library of Dr. George Hickes, MSS., prints, and books from Basil Kennett's 'study', his own MS. collections from Thomas Baker, items from Lord Somers's library, John Bagford's collections and those of Matthew Hutton, the heraldic MSS. of John Johnson and books from Dr.

---

[1] Vertue's *Note Books*, vi (Walpole Society, xxx, 1955), p. 118.
[2] Which was the subject of Prior's ballad, 'Down-Hall', written in 1715.
[3] See Hearne's *Remarks and Collections*, viii, p. 143.
[4] References are frequent in the Diary to subscriptions being paid by Wanley on Harley's behalf. See Subject Index under Subscriptions.   [5] See *HMC Portland Papers*, vi, pp. 27, 39.
[6] David Wilkins to Edw. Harley, 24 Mar. 1725/6: *HMC Portland Papers*, vi, p. 19.
[7] Ibid., 30 Sept. 1732: *HMC Portland Papers*, vi, p. 43.
[8] Francis Drake to Edw. Harley, 25 Sept. 1732: *HMC Portland Papers*, vi, p. 43.
[9] See *HMC Portland Papers*, vi, p. 23.   [10] See 'Harley Letters and Papers, 1725–1740', f. 262.
[11] For his friendship with Prior see *HMC Marquess of Bath MSS*. iii (Prior Papers), 1908, pp. 448–508 *passim*.   [12] See Soame Jenyns's poem in Harl. 7318.
[13] G. F. Barwick, 'The Formation of the Harleian Library—Further Notes', *The Library*, 3rd ser. i (1910), pp. 166–71.

South's library, besides efforts to bring to a conclusion the Aymon affair, and work involved in absorbing into the Library the Holles Library from Welbeck.

First, as to the MSS. of Sir Henry St. George the younger, Garter King of Arms from 1703, who died in 1715. His father, Sir Henry St. George the elder (1581–1644), had also been Garter (1644) and his grandfather, Sir Richard St. George (d. 1635), the most notable member of the family, had been Norroy (1604) and then Clarenceux (1623) and had left large genealogical and heraldic collections, to which the later members of the family had made additions. Another son of Sir Henry St. George the elder, Sir Thomas St. George, who died in 1703, had also been Garter. The family was descended from Thomas St. George of Hatley St. George, a Cambridgeshire seat not far distant from Edward Harley's at Wimpole; it is interesting to note in passing that the Barnwell Register (Harl. 3601) purchased by Edward Harley 17 April 1724 in Cambridgeshire had belonged to Sir Richard St. George.[1] A list of Sir Henry St. George the younger's MSS. had appeared in *CMA* ii, 1697, p. 112 (nos. 4209–39). Harley showed at first only a mild interest in St. George's MSS., doubting if there was 'anything worth having';[2] it was left that Wanley should look over the collection and report further, Harley adding, possibly by way of warning, that 'the library is well stocked with Heraldical Books', implying perhaps that only if they were very good should they be negotiated for.[3] On 17 Nov. 1717 Harley wrote to Wanley rather more enthusiastically: 'I should be glad to have Sir Henry St. George's MSS. I desire you would endevor to buy them for me as cheap as you can. I shall be glad to make the collection of Heraldical MSS. as compleat as possible and I think that these are not to be neglected.'[4] It is difficult, however, to know if any were in fact acquired at this time; admittedly a number of Sir Richard St. George's MSS. are now in the Harleian Collection[5] but most of these were acquired before 1710 and probably came through other channels. Sir Henry St. George's collections were in fact sold, some to the Earl of Egmont, the rest in 1738.[6]

Much more prolonged and complex were the negotiations attending the purchase of the MSS. and papers of John Covel, the aged Master of Christ's College, Cambridge (see Biographical Index). Harley was desperately anxious to acquire these: 'Dr. Covels things will be worth all the Heraldical things over and over: I had rather loose all these things than the MSS.';[7] this was in the autumn of 1715, but Wanley, who had known Covel since 1699[8] when he had been entertained by him at Cambridge, had asked Covel for a catalogue of his MSS. as early as 1712.[9]

[1] See Diary, 1 June 1724, and footnote. The MS. bears Sir Richard's armorial bookstamp and *ex libris*.
[2] Edw. Harley to H. W., 13 Oct. 1715 (Welbeck Wanleyana).
[3] Ibid., 24 Oct. 1715 (Welbeck Wanleyana).   [4] Ibid., 17 Nov. 1717 (Welbeck Wanleyana).
[5] Harl. 41, 113, 173, 174, 177, 322, 329, 491, 504, 548, 562 all bear his inscription of ownership; 1437 is a volume of papers relating to the 1613 Visitation of Lancashire in his autograph but is a Withie book; pedigrees collected by him are in Harl. 6148 (acquired 23 Dec. 1738), and another of his collections (with an engraving of his coat of arms) is Harl. 5019. Harl. 6132 belonged to Sir Henry St. George the elder in 1644 and other MSS., possibly his, are Harl. 1368, 1439, 6131, and 6592. On St. George MS. material in D'Ewes's possession see A. G. Watson, 'Sir Simonds D'Ewes's Collection of Charters', *Journal of Soc. of Archivists*, ii, no. 6 (Oct. 1962), pp. 251–2. Sir Henry St. George, the elder, had been one of the Hatton-Dugdale circle (see *Sir Christopher Hatton's Book of Seals*, ed. L. C. Loyd and D. M. Stenton, 1950, pp. xxxiii–xxxvi).
[6] See A. R. Wagner, *Records and Collections of the College of Arms*, 1952, pp. 38–39, 71–73, and W. H. Godfrey, A. R. Wagner, and H. S. London, *The College of Arms*, pp. 50–51, 55–56, 86–87. Cf. also pp. lxxvii–lxxviii below, on these and the family.
[7] Edw. Harley to H. W., 24 Oct. 1715 (Welbeck Wanleyana).
[8] H. W. to Covel, 29 Sept. 1699 (BM Add. 22910, f. 488).
[9] Ibid., 30 Sept. 1712 (BM Add. 22911, f. 146).

But the Doctor was slow in responding, and Wanley's (and Harley's) impatience increased, so that we find Covel writing in May 1715:[1] 'My good friend, Be not in such haste, you shall hear from me effectually so soon as I have but my free-dome to recollect my thoughts. . . . I will review my Books again, before I set you positive price: it shall be as soon as I can. . . .' In September of the same year Wan-ley stayed with the Master at Christ's and subsequently mentioned in a letter to Covel Harley's desire to buy his MSS.[2] Eventually, a catalogue of MSS. was fur-nished by Covel enclosed with a letter to Wanley dated 13 Jan. 1715/16,[3] the prices being set against each item, prices so exorbitant in Wanley's view as to draw from him a sharp letter of protest.[4] Negotiations, however, were concluded on 27 Feb. 1715/16,[5] Covel certifying on that date that he had sold to Edward Harley 'All my written Books, Papers, & Parchments whatsoever; together wth my Wooden Clog Almanac'. And continues: 'And whereas, a Greek Manuscript containing certain of ye works, of Athanasius; a Smal Tract, containing Some Hymns of ye Greek Church; and my whole Collection of Original Letters from learned Men, Greek and others, are now either Mislaid, or not ready to come at; I promise, that I will make due, and Speedy Search for ye Same; and deliver them up to ye Said Lord Harley, as soon as I conveniently may, or they Shall come to my Hands.'

The amount paid was £300. The MSS. in Covel's catalogue comprise 12 Heb-rew (1–11^b), 39 Greek (12–50), and 38 Latin, Italian, &c. (separately numbered). Several of the Greek MSS. were important and the collection was a notable addition to the Library, but it is impossible to identify with certainty *all* the Covel MSS.; Wanley inserted on the flyleaf or first leaf of each volume acquired a roman number corresponding with that in Covel's Catalogue but others may be identified by notes in Covel's autograph or bearing his name.[6]

Nevertheless, Covel proved evasive and his papers were not forthcoming; in September 1717 he was apparently claiming that 'there was some misunderstand-ing but all should be set right'.[7] Some of the letters, however, appear to have been received much later, since we find Harley writing to Wanley in 1724,[8] 'I think to send up the smal parcel of Covels letters': perhaps this is the volume of letters to Covel, 1670–1710, now Harl. 6943. That continuous difficulties were encountered with Covel throughout is clear, however, from the letters written to Wanley by Thomas Tudway (see Biographical Index), who was employed as an intermediary

---

[1] Covel to H. W., 16 May 1715 (Welbeck Wanleyana).

[2] H. W. to Covel, 18 Sept. 1715 (BM Add. 22911, f. 171).

[3] Covel to H. W., 13 Jan. 1715/16 (draft in BM Add. 22911, ff. 183–4^b); the catalogue is BM Add. 22911, ff. 180–3.

[4] H. W. to Covel, 24 Jan. 1715/16 (BM Add. 22911, ff. 185–6).

[5] BM Add. 22911, f. 201.

[6] Harl. 2316 (labels on ff. i, ii appear to be in Covel's hand and extracts from the MS. are in BM Add. 22911, ff. 357–64^b), 2332, 2335 (f. 1*, 'John Colvyle, 1665'), 2366 (descr. in Covel's *autogr.*, f. 1*), 2378 (ff. 1–4 table by Covel, with *autogr.* note rel. to date, f. 4), 2558 (inscr.), 2811 (inscr. 1659, f. 1), 3348 (inscr. by Covel), 3570, ff. 74–399 (= VIII), 3831 (see note by H. W., f. 1), 3929 (addition in Covel's *autogr.*), ?4253–6, 5460, 5486 (f. 1, 'Giovanni Covelli. 1670'), 5521 (inscr., 1702), 5537 (notes by Covel, 1679, 1710), 5545 (= XLVII), 5548 (= XLVI), 5550 (= XLVIII), 5554 (= XLI), 5555 (= XL), 5557 (= XLIV), 5560 (= XLII), 5561 (= XLIII), 5563 (= XLV), 5570 (= XLIX), ?5573 (?Covel notes), 5575 (= XVIII), 5579 (= XIX), ?5596 (? Covel notes), 5598 (Covel notes), 5614 (= XXX), 5620 (= XXXI), 5626 (= XXXIII), 5630 (= XXIX), 5633 (= XXXII), ?5640 (? notes by Covel), 5643 (= XXVI), 5649 (= XX), 5650 (= XXI), 5653 (= XXII), 5688 (= XVI), ?5715 (note by Covel, f. 1), ?5720, 5721 (? titles by Covel), 5734 (= XXXVIII), 5739, 5740 (= XXXVII), 5742 (= XXXV), 5776 (= XXV), 5777 (= XXIV), 5778 (= XXVI), 5783 (= XXXVI), 6302 (= XXXIX). On 5773–5 see letter from Covel to H. W., 21 Mar. 1712/13 (in Harl. 3778, f. 105).

[7] Edw. Harley to H. W., 3 Sept. 1717 (Welbeck Wanleyana).

[8] Ibid., 29 Sept. 1724 (Welbeck Wanleyana).

with Covel to try to straighten things out, and in fact the bulk of Covel's papers and correspondence was never received in the Library: they are now BM Add. 22910–14 and were acquired by the Museum at the Dawson Turner sale in 1859.

Notwithstanding these difficulties Wanley was again at Christ's College in March 1716, when he made a catalogue of the whole of Covel's library of printed books;[1] it runs to 43 pages with two double pages giving an alphabetical index. In April Wanley tried to make a bargain with Covel,[2] writing that Harley is 'willing to purchase your whole library together, at a price reasonable between Man and Man. And he will also, whensoever you shall desire it, Lend you from hence any reasonable Number of those books, for any reasonable term of time. But this Favor he will grant to no other person whatsoever.' Covel, however, did not rise to this; in a letter of 17 Jan. 1722/3[3] reporting Covel's funeral Tudway says: 'I remember when you took a Catalogue of ye Masters books, you mentioned his Collection was a choice one', and the library (with Covel's coins and antiquities) was sold by auction by Christopher Cock 9 March 1723/4.[4]

On 18 December 1715 Harley wrote to Wanley: 'I see in the Prints which I am very sorry for that good Dr. Hickes is dead, what becomes of his books MSS. and papers, I wish you would enquire.' Dr. George Hickes the non-juror had died 15 December 1715: by a codicil to his will (which was published by Edmund Curll in 1716) he bequeathed all his 'MSS., Letters, and Written Papers, relating to any Controversies' he had been engaged in, to another non-juror, Hilkiah Bedford, together with copies of his own published works, and directed that his books should be sold 'for the best price' that could be got; in the purchase of these Noel was involved (having, according to his memorandum book, bought Dr. Hickes's Library and others on 17 December 1715: 129 folios at a guinea being £138. 13s. 6d. and 119 quartos and octavos being £335. 14s. 0d.) and offered[5] Harley first refusal of individual items. Harley was particularly anxious[6] that the whole collection of books relating to the 'Septentrional Nations' should be secured; 'I do not doubt' (he wrote later)[7] 'but all ye Book-buyers are about this collection, therefore I dont doubt but you will secure everything very well', adding: 'your Abilities no man can doubt, and I have no reason to doubt your endeavors to do me all the service you can.'[8]

Early in the year of Hickes's death, on 3 January 1715, had died Basil Kennett, brother of the more famous White Kennett, Bishop of Peterborough, but an interesting man in his own right.[9] From 1706 to 1713 he had been chaplain to the English merchants at Leghorn, where he is said to have been in some danger from the Inquisition, and on his return to England lingered on his journey through France, collecting books and visiting French scholars. He appears to have been a quiet scholarly man, who had in 1696 published *Romae Antiquae Notitia, or the Antiquities*

[1] It is dated 5 Mar. 1715/16 and is preserved in Welbeck Wanleyana, Misc. 16.
[2] H. W. to Covel, 3 Apr. 1716 (BM Add. 22911, f. 208).
[3] Tudway to H. W., 17 Jan. 1722/3 (Welbeck Wanleyana).
[4] Harley was also interested in his coins and medals, and a catalogue by Wanley of Covel's medals and coins (valued by Wanley at £45. 5s.) is in BM Add. 22911, ff. 265–80.
[5] Edw. Harley to H. W., 5 Jan. 1715/16 (Welbeck Wanleyana).
[6] Ibid., 8 Jan. 1715/16 (Welbeck Wanleyana).
[7] Ibid., 12 Jan. 1715/16 (Welbeck Wanleyana).
[8] Wanley's efforts won Harley's approval: 'you have taken true pains in this matter, which do deserve more yn bare thanks, and shall not go without an addition' (Edw. Harley to H. W., 15 Jan. 1715/16, Welbeck Wanleyana). Several MSS. had been given to the Library by Hickes (see p. xxiv).
[9] On him see G. V. Bennett, *White Kennett*, 1957, pp. 254–5; also *DNB*.

of Rome and was, for a brief moment on his return from Italy, President of Corpus Christi College, Oxford. When rumours of the dispersal of his collections[1] got about it was natural that Harley's thoughts should turn to the possibility of securing some of his things: 'As to Basil Kennett's study', he wrote to Wanley,[2] 'you will take care to lay your Hands upon all the Books, prints and Drawings yᵗ you shall like. It must certainly be a curious collection, He had good judgement, as well as great opportunities.' His library had been bought by Noel on 6 January 1716:[3] the 60 folios had cost £64. 10s. 0d., the 425 quartos and octavos £127. 10s. 0d., and by 3 February Noel had bought his prints and drawings for £60. 0s. 0d. That Harley secured something out of these purchases is proved by the fact that we find him writing from Wimpole 30 January 1715/16 to Wanley giving instructions for the dispatch of books, &c., of Basil Kennett.[4]

The year 1716 was to be a very busy one. From March onwards Wanley was negotiating with the antiquary Thomas Baker, Fellow of St. John's College, Cambridge (like Hickes a non-juror), about MSS. in his possession.[5] Harley thought, rightly, that Wanley would have 'better play with Mr. Baker than with the old Don' [i.e. Covel],[6] and agreement was reached at the end of the year, the deed of bargain and sale being drawn up and signed by Baker on 6 December 1716 (the witnesses being Wanley and John Billers), accompanied by an inventory; both documents (in Wanley's hand) are inserted (ff. 1 and 2) in Harl. 7028, the first of the 21 volumes comprised in the sale, a memorandum by Baker (dated 24 December 1719) being added (f. 3) in respect of two additional volumes for an extra guinea: the MSS. are now Harl. 7028–50.[7] The price paid was 20 guineas;[8] a condition of the sale was that Baker should retain the MSS. until his death.[9]

In May 1716 Harley was expressing the wish that 'Noel could buy Lord Somers' things, if Bateman buys them, I shall not have my choice'.[10] Lord Somers, the great Whig lawyer and statesman, had died on 26 April of that year but his estate fell to his two sisters, the younger of whom married Somers's friend, Sir Joseph Jekyll, Master of the Rolls (1717–38), into whose possession passed Somers's library. There are frequent references in the Diary to attempts to secure through Jekyll's clerk, Robert Sanderson, Somers's Saxon charters but without success.[11] Jekyll's

[1] On his death and the disposal of his books and effects see BM Lansdowne 1041, ff. 221–99 *passim*: a reference to things he had collected in Italy is made in a biographical notice by White Kennett in BM Lansdowne 987, f. 223.

[2] Edw. Harley to H. W., 22 Jan. 1715/16 (Welbeck Wanleyana).

[3] See his Memorandum Book (G. F. Barwick, op. cit.).

[4] Edw. Harley to H. W., 30 Jan. 1715/16 (Welbeck Wanleyana). A list of the remainder of Basil Kennett's books, &c., dated 22 Dec. 1717, is in Welbeck Wanleyana, Misc. 22. A list of biblical and liturgical books, dated 11 Jan. 1717/18, acquired from Basil Kennett's brother, White Kennett, is in Welbeck Wanleyana, Misc. 21; a receipt signed by White Kennett shows that he received £200 for the books.

[5] For MSS. purchased from him for £40 in 1715 see Diary under 24 July 1715 and footnotes, and above, p. xxvi.

[6] Edw. Harley to H. W., 13 Mar. 1715/16 (Welbeck Wanleyana).

[7] A *copy* of the deed of sale and the memo. relating to the two additional volumes (*without* the inventory) is preserved in Soc. of Antiquaries MS. 264, ff. 51ᵇ–52ᵇ.

[8] The receipt, signed by Baker and dated 31 Dec. 1716, and accompanying a letter from Baker to H. W., 28 Dec. 1716, is preserved in Welbeck Wanleyana.

[9] The catalogue of his MS. collections is printed in Robert Masters, *Memoirs of the Life and Writings of the late Rev. Thomas Baker*, 1784, *ad finem*, separately paginated, 42 MSS. in all, of which 1–23 are Harl. 7028–50, and 24–42 and A–D are Cambridge University Library MSS. Mm. 1. 35–Mm. 2. 25: see also *Catalogue of MSS. in the Library of the University of Cambridge*, v, 1867, pp. 193–567.

[10] Edw. Harley to H. W., 19 May 1716 (Welbeck Wanleyana).

[11] See Biographical Index under Sanderson. Somers's other sister married Charles Cocks, of Worcester, and their daughter married Philip Yorke, 1st Earl of Hardwicke, the Lord Chancellor; most of Somers's collection of original papers and letters were lost by a fire in the chambers of Charles Yorke, the 1st

library was sold 26 February 1739 and it was not until this last year that Harley apparently obtained any of Somers's MSS.[1]

The death of John Bagford in the Charterhouse on 15 May of the same year (1716) threw another collection on to the market. John Bagford had brought together a great collection of material, MS. and printed, relating to the history of printing[2] and Harley early expressed a wish to 'have the best of Bagford's things':[3] in June he wrote again to Wanley:[4] 'I should be glad to get Mr. Bagford's things, is there any one else about them.'[5] The intermediary in the purchase appears to have been not Noel but Christopher Bateman[6] and the transaction was completed by 27 November 1716: 'I have bought and got into my custody all J. Bagford's things', wrote Harley on 27 November 1716, and added, 'I have bought his picture of Mr. Howard, which he drew of him.'[7] The Bagford collections are now Harl. 5414, 5419, 5892–998 (except for 5955).

Under 27 June 1716 Noel notes in his Memorandum Book, 'Heraldical MSS. 86.0.0'; this must certainly refer to the acquisition by Harley of the heraldic MSS. of John Johnson, the arms painter,[8] who had been Master of the Painter-Stainers Company, 1696.[9] Efforts to obtain these in March and June of 1715 are recorded in entries in the Diary, from the last of which we learn that the price stipulated was £60 (plus a gratuity to the intermediary, a Mr. Howell). The collection must have been quite considerable: there survives (in Welbeck Wanleyana) a fragment (pp. 5–8) of a catalogue of them by Wanley headed: 'Continuation of the Short Catalogue of Mr. John Johnson's Heraldical MSS.' In addition to MSS. and Rolls the purchase contained printed books, as one section is headed: 'Printed books which I delivered unto Mr. Noel upon your Lordships accompt.' It is impossible to identify any Johnson group among the Harley MSS. now, but no. 6 of the MSS. in

Earl's younger son, in Lincoln's Inn, 27 June 1752. Perhaps the Anglo-Saxon charters, which cannot now be traced, perished then (see also p. lviii, n. 3). Papers in BM Add. 36116, ff. 172–203[b] disclose that a division of the library was made in 1729 between Yorke and Jekyll.

[1] Harl. 6298 and 6918 are endorsed by Edward Harley as from Lord Somers followed by the date 6 Jan. 1738/39; and Harl. 7333 and 7334 can be identified with nos. 3 and 2 respectively at f. 153 in the Catalogue of Somers's MSS. in Harl. 7191. Harl. 6315 may also be a Somers item. Cf. p. lxxvii below.

[2] On Bagford see T. F. Dibdin, *Bibliomania*, ii, 1811, pp. 430–7; *D.N.B.* ii, 1885, p. 396; W. Y. Fletcher, 'John Bagford and his Collections', *Trans. Bibl. Soc.*, iv (1898), pp. 185–201; W. Y. Fletcher, *English Book Collectors*, 1902, pp. 129–37; S. de Ricci, *English Collectors*, 1930, p. 34. Wanley's friendship with Bagford was of long standing, from 1695 at least (his letters to Bagford are in Harl. 4966); he was well acquainted with the Collections and had furnished Sloane with an account of them in 1707 (Sloane 4040, ff. 355[a]–355[b]), the substance of which appeared in print under the title 'An Account of M[r] Bagford's Collections for his History of Printing, by M[r] Humphrey Wanley, F.R.S.' (appended to Bagford's 'An Essay on the Invention of Printing'), *Philosophical Transactions*, xxv (1708) (no. 310, Apr.–June 1707), pp. 2407–10.

[3] Edw. Harley to H. W., 27 May 1716 (Welbeck Wanleyana).

[4] Ibid., 20 June 1716 (Welbeck Wanleyana).

[5] Thomas Hearne was interested; cf. *Remarks and Collections of Thomas Hearne*, vii, 1906, p. 287, under the date 20 Oct. 1721: 'Humphrey Wanley also said that he was the main Instrument in getting Mr. Bagford's Papers for L[d] Harley, and that he laboured hard for them, and had like, nevertheless, to have missd of them. This was Roguery. For they were most certainly design'd for me. . . . I told him, had the Papers come to me, I would have methodiz'd them, & published a Book from them, for the Service of the Publick, & the Honour of Mr. Bagford.' Baker had urged H. W. in a letter of 23 Nov. [1718] (Welbeck Wanleyana) to undertake a history of printing based on Bagford's collections and Wanley's own collections and observations.

[6] See Edw. Harley to H. W., 27 Oct. 1716 (Welbeck Wanleyana).

[7] An engraving of Howard's portrait of Bagford (formerly at Wimpole) was made by George Vertue in 1723; it is reproduced in T. F. Dibdin's *The Bibliographical Decameron*, iii, 1817, opposite p. 281.

[8] Cf. Edw. Harley to H. W., 4 July 1716 (Welbeck Wanleyana): 'I am glad you have bought the Heraldical MSS. of Johnson at last.'

[9] See Biographical Index.

quarto is probably Harl. 3375, a volume of St. Loe Kniveton's collections, and no. 26 may be Harl. 3674, a transcript of the Register of the Honour of Richmond, presumably made from Cotton Faustina B. vii.

Another purchase of 1716 was the MS. collection of Matthew Hutton, the antiquary, Wanley's colleague in the inspection of the Cotton Library in 1703 (and a great-grandson of Matthew Hutton, Archbishop of York), who had died in 1711. (Before his death Hutton had given a number of charters to the Library (Harl. Ch. 83. A. 21–83 C. 9.) and Harl. 410, 411, 1232, 1834, 1835 [see above, p. xxiv]). According to Hearne[1] Hutton's MS. collections were bought by Harley for £150;[2] they are now Harl. 6950–85, 7519–21. And Harley bought from Noel on 7 July 1716 an Ordinary of Arms (now Harl. 6092) that had belonged to Hutton. Harley was also interested in Hutton's printed books; in July he looked over Wanley's catalogue of these[3] and on 7 August, while acknowledging the receipt at Wimpole of Johnson's heraldic MSS., complains that he had not received 'all the printed books of Dr. Hutton'. This purchase was made presumably through Noel, since we find an entry in his Memorandum Book under 10 August for 22 folios at £23. 13s. 0d. and 209 quartos and octavos at £62. 14s. 0d.: 'From Dr. Hutton's Library and others'.

In a letter of 23 March 1716/17 from Edward Harley to Wanley we first hear of negotiations on foot to acquire the library of Dr. Robert South, the famous Court preacher, who had died on the 8 July 1716. The passage is interesting and worth quotation:

> I do not believe that he [Noel] is likely to get Dr. Souths books at least not yet, there is a most strange woman to deal with, she asks a great price for them, she once promised me that I should have the most valuable part of the collection (as I thought) with the collection of pamphlets with his observations on them, I was once to see them, after all though she had promised me and Dr. Stratford that I should have them, she went of from her promise, and there they be, I believe it must be another sort of man than Noel to manage though Noel will do well in one respect he will give her more money than any one Bookseller, and that is the God she adores; she asks 1000 ℔ for the collection which is worth about 200 ℔.—

Nevertheless, the books *were* bought by Noel: in February of 1718 Harley was urging Wanley[4] to encourage Noel to buy the books and in March an entry in Noel's Memorandum Book records a parcel from the library of Dr. South at £159. 12s. 0d.

Probably the most important event of 1717 or perhaps early 1718, however, was the acquisition of a large group of MSS. from the Continent through Noel (presumably from Noel's agent Suttie) which included a considerable number of MSS. from Cues on the Mosel. The only reference to this in Harley's letters is in one of the 17th November[5] in which he says: 'Are the Books come from Holland? Among which you make mention will come Cardinal Cusanus's MSS. Fusts Bible in 1462 and other Books of Antient Dates and all extream valuable, what is become of this mighty Cargo? I am affraid the 500 Galons of Rhenish wine has drunk them all up.' Perhaps this is the collection referred to in a letter from Wanley to Harley written nearly a year previously[6] when he reports Noel as saying

---

1 T. Hearne, *Remarks and Collections*, iii, 1889, p. 280.
2 'At a very dear rate' according to *Harl. Cat.* under Harl. 7520.
3 Edw. Harley to H. W., 22 July 1716 (Welbeck Wanleyana).
4 Ibid., Feb. 1717/18 (Welbeck Wanleyana).
5 Ibid., 17 Nov. 1717 (Welbeck Wanleyana).
6 H. W. to Edw. Harley, 23 Dec. 1716 (Welbeck Wanleyana).

'that he shall soon receive from beyond the sea, one of the finest Parcels of Books that ever came to England'. The collection was presumably the result of several years' tours in Germany, especially in the Rhineland, by Noel's agent Suttie, who makes one personal appearance early in the Diary (21 June 1715) as selling to Robert Harley a Persian MS. and two liturgical MSS. The latter are Harl. 2897 and 2967: the former belonged to John the Fearless, Duke of Burgundy (assassinated 1419) and the latter to Antoine, Bastard of Burgundy, son of Philip the Good (d. 1504), both apparently therefore 'strays' from the 'Librairie de Bourgogne', which may have been acquired by Suttie in journeys in the Low Countries (since we know that he had been working on the Continent at least since 1711). Whether, of course, the parcels of Wanley's letter of December 1716 and Harley's of November 1717 are in fact the same it is impossible to say; if they are different, that of December 1716 might contain the results of Suttie's tours of Germany made in the summer of 1716 though we have no confirmatory evidence of his being there then.[1] On the other hand (as we shall see in more detail later, p. xlviii below), he was working in the Rhineland throughout the late summer and autumn of 1717 and the parcel of Harley's November 1717 letter is more likely to have been the result of these journeys and the Cues MSS. now in the Harleian Collection (other than those acquired 18 January 1723/4) may very well have been part of this latter parcel.[2]

Unfortunately, no further reference is made in Harley's letters to this long-expected parcel from abroad, and further observations on MSS. that may have come from the Continent as a result of Suttie's journeys both now and later will more properly be made in discussing the sources on the Continent from which MSS. were being acquired not only by Noel but by others (see pp. xlvi–lii below).

What was probably the largest accession to the Library in 1718, at any rate in printed books, came as a result of the death of Lady Henrietta Harley's mother, the Duchess of Newcastle, which had taken place on 24 December 1716.[3] This led to the clearing of the 'Holles' library at Welbeck, the Newcastle seat in Nottinghamshire, which began under the direction of Isaac Hobart, presumably one of the upper servants,[4] in April 1718. The books were dispatched to London in five loads (the north side of the library being cleared first) on 18 and 25 April, and 3, 9, and 16 May, the loads containing 1,167, 457, 556, 893, and 1,554 books respectively, the grand total being 4,627 items. In addition, a separate box containing the works of Margaret, Duchess of Newcastle, and a number of rentals was sent off after 28 May, when Hobart wrote to Wanley: 'I think I may now tell you there is not a book left belonged to my Lord unless there should be any in three Trunckes in

---

[1] A number of MSS. are endorsed by Wanley as bought of Noel in 1716, namely, Harl. 2380, 2720, 2753, 2957, 3030, 3040, 3062, 3161, 3562, 3577 (ff. 159–231), 3673, 3773, 4982, 5004, 5463, 5511, 5833, 5872, 5883, 6071, but these are a very mixed bag: it is interesting, however, to note that one at least was of German provenance, namely, Harl. 5004, which came from St. Martin the Greater, at Cologne.

[2] They are now Harl. 2497, 2620, 2621, 2637, 2652, 2668, 2672, 2674, 2738, 3243, 3261, 3631, 3702, 3710, 3734, 3934, 3992, 5692. All came from the Hospital of St. Nicholas at Cues. See also P. Lehmann, 'Mitteilungen aus Handschriften II', *Sitzungsberichte der Bayerischen Akademie der Wissenschaften, Phil. Hist. Abteilung* (Jan. 1930), Hft. 2, pp. 21–27. Of course not all Cues MSS. had belonged to Cardinal Nicholas of Cues (1401–64): on these see B. L. Ullman, 'Manuscripts of Nicholas of Cues', *Speculum*, xiii (1938), pp. 194–7, and on the Cardinal himself see E. Vansteenberghe, *Le Cardinal Nicolas de Cues*, Paris, 1920. On the MSS. at Cues today and an account of the library see J. Marx, *Verzeichnis der HSS.— Sammlung des Hospitals zu Cues*, Trier, 1920.

[3] The marriage of Henrietta Cavendish Holles, the Newcastle heiress, to Edward Harley had taken place (31 Aug. 1713) against the Duchess's wish and some years of vexatious dispute and estrangement followed before a reconciliation was effected just before the Duchess's death (see A. S. Turberville, *A History of Welbeck Abbey and its Owners*, i, 1938, pp. 300–22).

[4] See letters from Isaac Hobart to H. W., 21 Apr.–15 July 1718 (Welbeck Wanleyana).

that room beyond the Library': the contents of these—pamphlets—repacked in two trunks were also later sent. Most of the MSS. were in one box—no. 29—which contained 460 items. Wanley naturally inquired if there were any deeds or cartularies relating to the former monastery, to which Hobart replied (16 July 1718) that he had made inquiries of 'Mr. Farr' (presumably the steward) whose answer was that 'there is a room over his, locked up, wherein are a great many writings relating to the Estate and amongst them such Deeds, and that the late Duchess had a schedule of them, which he thinks is now in the possession of my Lord Harley, wth the key of ye Room'; this room may have remained untouched until much later since presumably from it came the 'large parcel of old Deeds or Charters, lately brought-up from Welbeck' recorded in the Diary as sent in on 20 July 1725.[1] A Register of the monastery is Harl. 3640 (see above p. xxxiii).

The receipt of the library was reported by Wanley to Harley at Bath in a letter of 8 June 1718; while expressing his pleasure that the library had arrived safely and that it contained 'good books', Harley added the injunction: 'I desire nobody may see the Welbeck books.' Harley's intention was to dispose of the Welbeck library after taking such printed books as he wanted; the MSS., of course, were to be retained. Accordingly Wanley drew up a statement of numbers and volumes on 7 October 1718;[2] the price proposed by Harley was £600 but 'you must ask Noel more y^n this sum and you must make it a matter of great kindness that he has the books at that price'.[3] Wanley reckoned the books at 1,004 folios and 1,414 octavos, excluding imperfect volumes, and was prepared to set a first valuation of £1,000 on them in Harley's name, but as Noel was being offered the pre-emption a reduced price of £800 was settled for negotiation; as there were indications that Noel, however, would not rise to this figure Harley set £500 as his lowest price,[4] now adopting a more defensive line—Noel 'knows that I must sell because I would not be troubled with so many duplicates', he wrote. Wanley then prepared for a final battle with Noel, drawing up for the purpose on 18 October 1718 an *aide-mémoire*[5] which has passages of extraordinary interest both as to the kind of argument Wanley was prepared to use and also as to what it discloses of previous transactions between Harley and Noel. Wanley's reasoning was to be as follows: first, the books 'belonged to a very Noble Family', whose names appear still in many of them and if the Duke of Newcastle's arms are removed from the lesser and inferior books Noel has but to 'clap them upon others' and they will 'go off at a price much advanced'. Moreover, only £800 is being asked for them though Harley values them at £1,000. And again consider the great favours received from the Harley family: if reasonable offers are not made Noel would not be 'fit to be dealt with hereafter'. And Harley's forbearance is cited in his not having hindered Lord Dupplin from trading with him (Noel); the family could help him to Lord Somers's Books and 'as to the Cambridge duplicates you cannot have them without my Lord'. Then follows a retrospective passage of interest for the history of the Library: after saying that Harley had brought Noel into 'a Name and Repute' Wanley goes on: 'You know He gave you too much for Fowkes's Books, He has bought of you many Books of Hicks, Payne, Dorrington, &c. which would have

---

[1] For identifications of Harley and Cotton Charters endorsed by Wanley as from Welbeck see n. 1 to that date.
[2] Welbeck Wanleyana Misc. 72(a).
[3] Edw. Harley to H. W., 9 Oct. 1718 (Welbeck Wanleyana).
[4] Ibid., 12 Oct. 1718 (Welbeck Wanleyana).
[5] Welbeck Wanleyana Misc. 72(b).

been Shop-Keepers. By His influence you bought Lanes, Huttons, Souths, &c. from which he immediately took great quantities off your Hands. He ha's been and yet continues the best of all your Customers; and you have gotten clearly by him as much Money as he asks for this Collection.' Lastly, Harley is not asking for ready money but only that the sum agreed should be 'placed to Accompt'. In spite of all Wanley's arguments, however, Noel would make no advance on £450, according to a letter of Harley's;[1] nevertheless, in his Memorandum Book under 22 October 1718 we find Noel crediting Harley with £500 for 'a parcel of books which came from Welbeck'.

It is disappointing that the MSS. from Welbeck absorbed into the Library cannot be identified with the exception of a very small handful;[2] of these the only important one is Harl. 4955, the famous 'Newcastle' MS. of poems of Donne, Ben Jonson, and others, a volume which began life as an account book, the entries for July 1680–March 1681 being signed by Thomas Farr (see above, p. xli).

It is possible, however, to identify the MSS. from the original collection of Robert Harley which were absorbed into the Library and which should be mentioned here because, with the Welbeck Library, they represent the second of the two family libraries incorporated into the Harleian Library. This group of MSS., most of a political or legal character, can be identified either by the presence of Robert Harley's armorial bookplate bearing the inscription 'Robert Harley of Bramton Castle in the County of Hereford Esq' which appears in a large number of them[3] or by a facsimile signature, 'Ro: Harley', stamped on the title-page or a leaf near the beginning, usually gilt washed:[4] a few are in armorial bindings, 'Ro: Harley' being disposed symmetrically on each side of an oval cartouche enclosing the Harley coat of arms.[5]

Of the earlier family library little can have remained in the Castle in view of its destruction in the year following Brilliana Harley's defence of it in the late summer of 1643, but the subject matter, mostly political and theological (the predominant interests of the family), and the fact that very many are of early or mid 17th-century date indicate clearly enough that some of the MSS. are from the old family collection (e.g. Harl. 4068, a volume of political collectanea dated 8 August 1650; Harl. 6292 has several Harley names written on flyleaves). One MS. that had belonged to Sir Edward Harley (1624–1700), Robert Harley's father, is Harl. 402 which Sir Edward had acquired 'of Mrs. Downe at Bar[n]staple 1658'; Harl. 1275 ('w[th] others') had been bought by him from 'Dr. [Thomas] Warmestry';[6] and Harl. 3586 had also belonged to him (letters to him being bound in at ff. 146, 147). The initials 'E. H.' in Harl. 1786 may indicate that that had also been his. To Thomas

---

[1] Edw. Harley to H. W., 19 Oct. 1718 (Welbeck Wanleyana).
[2] Harl. 4008, 4771, 4945, 4955, and 7571 are endorsed by H. W. 'Welbeck'.
[3] Namely, Harl. 399, 412, 584, 952, 1058, 1198, 1208, 1209, 1218, 1220, 1222, 1224, 1225, 1250, 1275, 1282, 1308, 1309, 1313, 1315 (the basic MS. of Selden's Table Talk), 1323, 1325 (a Thomas Hobbes MS. of 1640), 1332, 1337, 1346, 1749, 1783, 1786, 1898, 4056, 4068, 4761, 4892, 5138, [5254], 5758, 6011, 6013, 6268, 6276, 6278, 6283, 6423, 6604–6, 6681, 6701, 7156, 7159–69, 7310, 7404, 7431. For a reproduction see W. Y. Fletcher, *English Book-Collectors*, 1902, p. 151.
[4] For example, Harl. 1217, 1218, 1225, 1309, 1325, 1346, 1749, 6604–6, 7156, 7160–9. Examples also exist of Harley's printed books so treated (for example, A. Schott, *Itinerarium Italiae*, n.d., from the Ham House Library, Sotheby's, 21 June 1938, lot 326; [A. Gavin], *The Frauds of the Romish Monks & Priests*, 1691, from the Castle Howard Library, Hodgson's, 20 July 1944, lot 249; Henry Wharton, *Anglia Sacra*, 1691, Bernard Quaritch's Catalogue no. 780, 1958, item 308; Sir G. Mackenzie, *The Institutions of the Law of Scotland*, 1684, Bernard Quaritch's Catalogue no. 672, 1949, item 12; and a copy of Bernard's *CMA* on loan to the Institute of Historical Research from the Public Record Office).
[5] Harl. 1217, 1218, 1225, 1308, 1309, 1325, 1346, 1749, 6604–6, 7159–69. For a reproduction see C. Davenport, *English Heraldic Book-Stamps*, 1909, p. 204.   [6] Dean of Worcester: d. 1665.

Harley, Robert Harley's uncle, belonged two MSS. in the Library: Harl. 4101, a volume of political papers, one item in which (that of bills of indictment for Kent (ff. 171–209)) bears the note (f. 171): 'This Book was given to me at Pluckley [i.e. Pluckley near Ashford in Kent] . . . March 1657.' (Can the donor whose name was erased have been a Dering of Surrenden, the Dering seat at Pluckley?); and Harl. 3986, a 14th-century volume of St. Bernard's Sermons, was acquired by him 10 May 1654.[1] In addition, four MSS. (Harl. 2659, 3257, 3326, and 3586, ff. 68–145) were brought up from Brampton Bryan in August 1722 by Edward Harley,[2] and some deeds relating to the Harley family or Wigmore at the same time.[3] After Robert Harley's death in 1724 Edward Harley was again at Brampton and on 16 October 1725 forty-two MSS. brought up from there were sent into the Library.[4] Thus what was probably the final clearance of the Brampton library took place in the same year as that of Welbeck.[5]

It will be necessary here to note one other acquisition made before the resumption of the Diary in January 1720.

In a letter from Harley to Wanley dated 6 September 1719 occurs this injunction: 'pray put an *S.* in ever[y] MS that came from Ld Sun. and put them in a Box by themselves'. This is a mysterious entry but 'Ld Sun.' must, presumably, be for 'Lord Sunderland': if so the reference is to Charles Spencer, 3rd Earl of Sunderland, the noted bibliophile and Edward Harley's keenest rival, the news of whose death on 19 April 1722 was to provoke Wanley to a passage of rejoicing in his Diary.[6] But no sale of Sunderland's books is recorded in 1719 and the allusion must have been to some private transaction, possibly through Noel who certainly was involved in buying books for Sunderland's library, as is clear from two entries in Wanley's Diary under 4 December 1721 and 12 July 1723 (in the latter of which Noel is reported as complaining that Sunderland's executors had still not paid him).[7] At any rate, whatever the explanation, it is a fact that in a number of Harley MSS. Wanley has written neatly the word 'SUND' on the flyleaves: the MSS. are 2561, 2589, 2632, 2660, 2694, 2712, and 3922. All are of continental provenance, chiefly Italian or German, with one (2712) of French origin from the Benedictine abbey of Chaise-Dieu.

Sunderland's chief interest, however, was in printed books, in incunabula and early editions of the classics particularly, though he did buy in 1720 (according to Wanley) a parcel of Greek MSS. for £1,500 from Joseph Smith of Venice.[8]

In 1719 also, with the death of Samuel Stebbing, Somerset Herald, on 21 August,

---

[1] Thomas Harley's name is written over the Harley coat (f. 3^b) in the 1661 copy of the 1594 Visitation of Shropshire in Harl. 1241; it is perhaps not without significance that the transcript was the work of Thomas Hanford of Wigmore, a Herefordshire township associated with the Harleys, from which Robert took the title of his Barony.

[2] See Diary under 1 Sept. 1722: Wanley's list of the MSS. is in the Addenda, Lansdowne 771, f. 78^b (see p. 200 and footnotes).

[3] See Diary under 3 Sept. and 10 Sept. 1721, item 2 (pp. 157, 161).

[4] For list and identifications see Diary under 20 Oct. 1725, item 7, and footnotes. Also absorbed into the Library were some of Robert Harley's office papers (e.g. Harl. 7405–505, 7639 A, B).

[5] See Diary under 20 July 1725: and cf. above, p. xli.

[6] Cf. Wanley's Diary under 4 Dec. 1721 for his comments on Sunderland's bids.

[7] Cf. also Diary, 22 Jan. 1719/20, item 11, when Noel reported to H. W. that he had been offered 200 guineas 'to lett the Earl of Sunderland have the Preference before all others, as to the buying of his old Books'. In addition Noel's Memorandum Book records the delivery of 3 parcels (mostly of fine editions of the Latin classics) to Sunderland for £610.

[8] On Sunderland see M. Kerney in B. Quaritch, *A Dictionary of English Book Collectors*, pt. ii, 1892; W. Y. Fletcher, *English Book Collectors*, 1902, pp. 165–9; S. de Ricci, *English Collectors*, 1930, pp. 38–40, 55 n. On a Sunderland auction at The Hague see below, p. liv, n. 1.

there arose the possibility of securing another collection of heraldic MSS.; Edward Harley was ready enough to have them,[1] but the matter still hung fire in January of the next year[2] and nothing further is heard of the MSS.

At the end of this year Wanley was at Wimpole and when the correspondence between him and Edward Harley begins again on 17 March 1720 (when Wanley is back in London) Harley's letters are no longer the primary source, which for the next six years is the Diary itself, although the letters supplement it usefully here and there.

The programme of acquisitions sketched above cost, of course (apart from the absorption of the Welbeck and Brampton Bryan Libraries), a great deal of money. At one point, August 1717, Edward Harley had betrayed anxiety in his letters to Wanley about the amounts going out:[3] 'I cannot imagine how I come to be so much in his [Noel's] Debt, when he has been paid a $\frac{lb}{1000}$ in money besides several Duplicates w^{c}h have been returned to him, I think it extreamly extravagant, and if it cannot be otherwise ordered that I can have books at easier rates, I shall leave all thoughts of buying any more Books.' It was perhaps as a result of this that Wanley drafted an agreement to be concluded between Noel and Harley.[4] This is undated but the reference in it to books from the libraries of Hickes, Kennett, and Dorrington 'now' at Wimpole (of these the Hickes and Kennett books had been supplied, as we have seen above, pp. xxxvi, xxxvii, between December 1715 and May 1716) suggests a date in the later part of 1717, a view confirmed by the appearance of a first account between Noel and Harley in the former's Memorandum Book under 30 January 1718. By the terms of the proposed agreement a fixed price is stipulated for all books to be bought of Noel, viz. 20s. per Folio, 6s. per Quarto, 3s. per Octavo, and 2s. for Duodecimo and less; and approximately these prices are in fact quoted in Noel's Memorandum Book for the Hickes, Basil Kennett, and Dorrington books, as well as for Matthew Hutton books. Further, Harley is to have the right to exchange with any books bought any duplicates, choosing for his own use the better copy and returning to Noel the rejected volume. As for MSS. Noel undertakes to 'discover the real and firm cost thereof' giving Harley also first offer or refusal of any parcel of MSS. he should acquire, Harley in turn to allow Noel a clear gain of 5 per cent. over and above all costs and charges. Thirdly, Harley was to have the liberty of examining any parcel or library bought, of laying aside any he wanted, and of drawing up catalogues if he so wished, 'before any Customer be permitted to see them'.[5] Again, Harley would have the right of returning any duplicates or books he did not like. The same covenant was to apply to Prints, Drawings, Pictures, 'and all other Rarities whatsoever, as for Manuscripts'. Lastly, certain stipulations were laid down about the settlement of the outstanding account.

It is not difficult to recognize Wanley's mind at work in drafting an agreement so advantageous to his master, a reason perhaps for its never having been carried beyond the draft stage; certainly no such covenant in a signed form exists among the surviving papers.

The sums paid to Noel were undoubtedly very large. According to Noel's Memorandum Book of 1715–28 the total amount paid by Harley to Noel was

---

[1] Edw. Harley to H. W., 10 Sept. 1719 (Welbeck Wanleyana).
[2] See Diary under 18 Jan. 1719/20, item 2. Some of Stebbing's papers are in Harl. 6944.
[3] Edw. Harley to H. W., 18 Aug. 1717 (Welbeck Wanleyana).
[4] Welbeck Wanleyana, Misc. 30.
[5] There was trouble with Woodman the bookseller over his failure to observe a similar stipulation (see p. liii below).

£10,814 in money and about £650 in books. The amounts due and payments made can be followed in the accounts preserved in the Welbeck Wanleyana, with some supplementary information from Noel's Memorandum Book. This, of course, leaves on one side the amounts being paid for privately negotiated purchases, such, for example, as those from Baker, Le Neve, and Strype, and for purchases from booksellers or dealers other than Noel, for which the record is very much less complete, though Davis and Woodman bills for the later period exist. Perhaps the Noel accounts are the most instructive. Thus, as early as 17 August 1715 he had been paid £162. 10s. 0d. A typical example of the confused state of the accounts is that for 17 July 1716 with its entries for amounts due and credits to be allowed.[1] The first statement of account in Noel's Memorandum Book between Harley and himself is dated 30 January 1718 and shows £2,451. 16s. 6d. due, of which Harley paid off £1,917. 11s. 0d., still leaving an unsettled balance of £534. 5s. 6d. Even more revealing are accounts in the Welbeck Wanleyana, especially that dated 17 January–23 March 1718/19, which shows that a total of £1,016. 3s. 6d. was due to Noel, towards which Harley paid no more than £100 on 2 March 1718/19: payments towards the balance of £916 were later made by Harley as follows: £310. 13s. 4d. on 15 July 1719; £300. 0s. 0d. on 1 March 1719/20; £200. 0s. 0d. on 11 June 1720—that is, a total of £810. 13s. 4d.—but instead of this almost clearing the debt we find, not altogether to our surprise perhaps, Wanley noting at this point that Harley still owed Noel £739. 5s. 2d. in view of additional purchases, with the result that at 8 June 1720 a total of £1,239. 5s. 2d. is due; towards this, £300. 0s. 0d. was paid by Harley 18 October 1720. Of course some credits were allowed by Noel (for example, £500 for the Welbeck books) but these are but drops in the ocean; when we learn from Noel's Memorandum Book that on 18 January 1724 alone there arrived two parcels for Harley—one for £1,450 and another for £108. 18s. and that purchases on 12 August 1724 were agreed at £600, we are not surprised to find that when accounts were balanced on 25 March 1725 Harley still owed Noel £2,000. Notwithstanding this, Harley agreed on 26 July 1728 to a purchase of MSS. at £1,800, and the last entry in Noel's book is revealing:

N.B. on July 12 1729, I settled accounts with the Earl of Oxford and there was due to me the sum of One Thousand pounds over and above the two Thousand for which I have received his Lordship's Bonds for a Thousand Pounds each. I likewise received on the settling this acct. another Bond of his Lordship for One Thousand Pounds.

At this date Wanley had been dead three years and in another eleven years Harley would be compelled to sell Wimpole to the Earl of Hardwicke for £86,740. Events had indeed justified the wisdom of Dr. Stratford's remark to Edward Harley in 1720 (referred to above, p. xxix).

But disbursements to other booksellers and individuals were also going out, though usually in smaller amounts, yet continuously. On 27 January 1717/18 £1. 11s. 6d. was paid to George Vertue, the engraver, for a number of books, and to William Hanbury went 8 guineas on 14 May 1718 also for books; a purchase from James Moetjens, the bookseller, on 3 February 1718/19, amounted to £14. 14s. 6d.; while in August and October of 1720 no less than £400 was paid to Robert Sanderson the antiquary and Clerk in the Rolls Chapel. In addition, various

[1] See C. E. Wright, 'Portrait of a Bibliophile, VIII: Edward Harley', *The Book Collector*, xi, no. 2 (Summer, 1962), pp. 162–3.

small sums went to several people by way of gratuities for services in connexion with the Library;[1] for example, Salomon Negri received £5. 7s. 6d. on 15 October 1717 and 5 guineas on 10 January 1717/18 for help presumably with Arabic MSS., Rabbi Aaron Moses received 3 guineas in October 1713 for writing 'some leaves in Hebrew' for Wanley, and 5 guineas went to Thomas O'Sullivan on 9 September 1720 possibly for help in connexion with Irish MSS. For the years 1720–6 evidence is also afforded by the Diary, to which (and the Subject Index, under Prices) I refer the reader: we may note as an example, that Harley paid to Gibson for 51 MSS. from Italy £200 in 1723 (see 4 April 1723, item 17, n. 8) and £279. 10s. 6d. in 1725 for 53 MSS. from Italy (see Diary, p. 341, no. 53 of list *ad finem*). There was too, a general rise in prices in the twenties, which has to be taken into account, due to a number of causes, not least increasing competition at home and abroad.[2]

As the Diary progresses and, as we shall see later, especially in the 1720's, the pattern of book-collecting is changing; the main initiative in the search for fresh material is passing out of the hands of Edward Harley and his Librarian into those of the booksellers and dealers and their agents operating abroad, though the Diary at the same time reveals no abatement in the keenness of Harley or Wanley to seize on any opportunity for adding to the collections that might present itself (see pp. lvi–lvii below). Noel still remains a prominent figure. The others are Andrew Hay and John Gibson, the last working through anonymous agents in Italy, the former on his own in France and Italy, his affairs in London being handled during his journeys by his brother, George Hay. This emphasizes, too, the change in the sources being tapped. Material is being sought and obtained no longer primarily in this country as in the first two decades of the century, when the typical collections acquired were those of Sir Simonds D'Ewes, Stillingfleet, the Randle Holmes, and on a smaller scale of Hickes and Hutton. The one exception is that of Archdeacon Batteley, one block of which had been bought 5 November 1723 and for a second group of which negotiations were continuing at the close of the Diary. This is in part a true picture of the London book trade itself. It is surely significant of this changing pattern to find, for example, the booksellers Woodman and Lyon securing cargoes from abroad for their auctions; thus they were to sell the Loménie de Brienne Library 28 April 1724, and those of Henri de la Bazonière 1 February 1724/5, of Valentin Esprit Fléchier, Bishop of Nîmes 24 January 1725/6, and Louis de la Chapelle 2 May 1726,[3] which were disposed of through the London market, as was the material from Italy[4] in the famous Fairbarne sale of December 1721, which was to cause such a stir in the bibliophilic circles of the time.[5]

By contrast, the sales of libraries of English origin were slight affairs: the Earl of Radnor's 2 May 1721, John Covel's 9 March 1723/4, that of the Chamberlaynes on 11 March of the same year, and that of John Bridges in February and March of 1725/6, the exception being the dispersal of the enormous library of Thomas Rawlinson, which began on 4 December 1721 and continued at intervals until 1733.

What we should wish particularly to know are the precise sources on the Continent from which the contents of the parcels were drawn and this is information normally denied to us, but there are in the Diary, however, some references in

---

[1] See Welbeck Wanleyana, Misc. 50.
[2] On this see C. E. Wright, *Humfrey Wanley*, pp. 116, 117.
[3] See footnotes to the Diary entries under 2 Apr. 1724 (item 12) and 12 Jan. 1725/6 (item 3).
[4] The title of the sale-cat. was 'A Small Parcel of scarce Valuable Books and MSS. lately imported from Italy'.   [5] See the Diary under 4 Dec. 1721.

general terms. Thus, it is stated under 4 September 1720 of three MSS. bought of Noel (Harl. 2433, 3162, 3171) that they were 'lately brought from Flanders', and certainly Harl. 3162 has an *ex libris* of 1340 of the Carthusian house of La Chapelle at Hérinnes near Enghien in Hainaut, Belgium. On 20 March 1720/21 Gibson told Wanley that he had sixteen good MSS. coming from Italy and Wanley 'found him sitting upon the Books' when he visited him on 17 June 1721; reference is made in the latter entry to Gibson's 'Agent in Italy'.[1] Of these MSS. some have unidentified coats of arms and one (Harl. 2780) was written in 1463 at Siena, but this of course is no certain indication of its whereabouts in 1721. Again, 7 November 1721, Wanley agreed with Gibson for eight MSS. 'lately arrived from Italy':[2] so 'lately' that Wanley refrained from dating them 'lest any inquisitive person coming in, should thereby perceive how lately they were bought'.

Under 1 May 1722, of the parcel of eleven MSS. later (5 May 1722) bought of Gibson we learn that they were 'lately come from Florence'.[3] Another parcel 'from Italy' was reported by Gibson 8 May 1722, and under 22 March 1722/3 (item 5) of a group of MSS. subsequently bought of him[4] we are told that 'They all came out of a Monastical Library Founded or Endowed by the Guicciardini'; of these, three do in fact have inscriptions associating them with members of the Guicciardini family (Harl. 3387, 3458, 3714). Of many of the MSS. in this block Wanley thought poorly, observing they 'had better been let alone', and added: 'In short they seem to shew, what I hear from others, that the Italian Monasteries do now begin to be pretty much drained of their old Printed books and MSS.'[5] On 12 January 1724/5 (and cf. 19 February 1724/5) Gibson was talking to Wanley about Greek MSS. in Florence, and the MSS. acquired 23 February 1724/5 certainly came from Italy, since they include many that must have been derived from the Zomino bequest in the Public Library at Pistoia.[6] Again, under 3 March 1724/5, in the course of conversation between Gibson and Wanley about fixing the prices of MSS. sent in by Gibson, the latter is said to have remarked 'that his Agent at Florence is gone to another part of Italy (which he would not name) in order to buy a choice parcel of books'.

Andrew Hay worked in both France and Italy. On 12 January 1719/20 he announced his intention of going in the spring to Italy 'by the way of France' and Wanley drew up accordingly a commission (a most interesting and instructive document) for him to make purchases on Harley's behalf;[7] the first fruit of this journey was the purchase in Paris of the library formerly belonging to the Chancellor Pierre Séguier (1588–1672), which was reported to Wanley by Andrew Hay's brother on 1 June 1720,[8] and was acquired by Harley in September. On 22

---

[1] For list and identifications of the MSS. see Diary, 17 June 1721, item 12, and footnotes.

[2] For list and identifications see Diary, 9 Nov. 1721, item 1, and footnotes.

[3] For list and identifications see 5 May 1722, item 1, and footnotes.

[4] Listed under 4 Apr. 1723, item 1.

[5] Other references by Gibson to MSS. from Italy occur in the Diary under 12 Feb. 1719/20; 18 Feb. 1719/20 (three very fine MSS. 'from Italy'), 17 Mar. 1719/20 (presumably referring to those of 18 Mar. 1719/20 and 23 Apr. 1720), and 7 Nov. 1720.

[6] See list of fifty-three MSS. (valued at £279. 10s. 0d.) under 23 Feb. 1724/5 and footnotes for identifications: see also Numerical Table under MSS. identified for Zomino da Pistoia items. Cf. also F. A. Zaccaria, *Bibliotheca Pistoriensis*, Turin, 1752 (see especially pp. 37–45 for inventory of his library taken in 1460 and preserved in the Pistoia archives).

[7] The commission was dated 26 Apr. 1720 and handed to Hay 3 May 1720: the original was sold at Sotheby's 29 Oct. 1962, lot 185 (part of). It was printed in the Preface to the 1759 *Cat. of the Harleian MSS.* and again in that to *A Catalogue of the Harleian MSS. in the British Museum*, i, 1808, pp. 6–7.

[8] See Diary under 1 June 1720, item 5, and for list of MSS. see footnote to 5 Sept. 1720.

September of the same year George Hay showed Wanley a list of printed books that Andrew Hay 'had lately bought in Italy' and from the entry under 28 April 1721 we learn that Andrew Hay was in Rome.[1]

Gibson's agent is nowhere named but Noel's agent on the Continent we know to have been George Suttie. Suttie's first appearance in the Diary was a personal one, when in 1715 he offered to Robert Harley a Persian MS. and two liturgical MSS. for which he was offered—and accepted—5 guineas.[2] Next, under 17 July 1716 in Wanley's accounts[3] we find an entry for £60 for 'A Parcel of Books and MSS. (Suttie's)': and that these came not from an English source but from abroad we learn from the corresponding entry in Noel's Memorandum Book under 16 June 1716: 'A Parcel of Books & MSS. delivered to Mr. Wanley by agreement from abroad. £60.0.0.' Suttie was accustomed to send to Noel letters giving details of his journeys and purchases and it is one of the greatest misfortunes of all for a study of the formation of the Harleian collection that these are no longer extant, except for the brief notes (and some extracts of lists) which Wanley was in the habit of making from these before returning them to Noel.[4] With three exceptions the Wanley–Suttie notes preserved in Welbeck Wanleyana bear dates that fall within the gap in the Diary between 1715 and 1720. Wanley has noted on his extracts the dates and places from which the letters were written. Accordingly some of Suttie's journeys can be plotted as follows: 1717: Trier, 12 August; Coblenz, 2 and 9 September; Cologne, 28 September and 12 October; Worms, 14 November; Mentz (=Mainz), 20 November; 1718: Cologne, 4 January; Strasbourg, 10 February,[5] 20 February, 7 March,[6] and 17 March; Mentz (=Mainz), 9 April; Würzburg, 14 July; Nuremberg, 30 July; Ingolstadt, 8 August; Frankfurt, 16 September; Metz, 3, 15 October; Trier, 2 November; Cologne, 26 November and 29 November;[7] Liège, 21 and 29 December; 1719: Liège, 13, 24 January and 6 February; 1720 (under 4 February in the Diary a letter had been received from Suttie from Châlons with the information that he was going on to Lyons [see

[1] Andrew Hay did not prove entirely satisfactory and he later surrendered his commission ('he having done nothing therein') to Wanley at the latter's request (see Diary under 17 Apr., item 6, and 20 Apr. 1722, item 6). Hay's interests of course lay primarily in antiquities (he bought the Valletta collection) and pictures.

[2] See above, p. xl; and Diary under 21 June 1715, item 10, and footnote.

[3] In Welbeck Wanleyana. Relevant passage is printed in C. E. Wright, art. cit., *The Book Collector*, xi, no. 2, p. 162.

[4] Some of these are preserved in Welbeck Wanleyana. A number of references occur in the Diary to letters and catalogues from Suttie (see Biographical Index under Suttie).

[5] Against this Wanley has written: 'The MS. Lat. Bible of Arenstein (wanting a leaf) will not come, under 20 Pistoles, I have testified against this Price. The Vitae Sanctorum (of Arenstein) in 4 very large Volls fol Velum written A.D. 1034 ending with the Life of Ludovicus Generosus Conversus, who was of the family of Nassau and the Founder. which Life is said not to be extant elsewhere 40 Pistoles asked for it. I have said the price is too great.' These, however, came into the Library with other Arnstein MSS. 16 Jan. 1720/1. See list and footnotes for identifications under that date, and cf. p. xlix below.

[6] Wanley has written the following against this: 'The Cardinal de Rhoan Abp. of Strasbourg [i.e. Armand Gaston Maximilien de Rohan, Cardinal, Bp. and Prince of Strasbourg, 1674–1749] hath bought Thuanus's Library [in 1706], & Employs Mr. la Fay to buy books for him; who procur'd the last year the fine Editions of Caesar and Lactantius, with some MSS. on Velum, which came dear from an Abbey on the other side of the Rhine. This la Fay sent the list mentioned in another Paper. He will go to Slested [Schlettstadt, now Sélestat, south of Strasbourg] to see the Library of Beatus Rhenanus [1485–1547], which is still entire in the Stadthouse, as is said. . . . Many of the books mentioned in this Lre have the Elector Palatins Arms, being plundered by the French upon their taking of Heidelberg' [in 1689 and again in 1693].

[7] Under Cologne for 29 Nov. Wanley has added a note: 'He ha's seen some MSS. which formerly belonged to the Carthusians at Kingston upon Hull. Among them, is a fine St. Cyprianus; and a Collection of Poems with Miniatures to the Memory of the Earl of Pembroke their Founder fol. but can't get them as yet.' At the end of a list of seven MSS. is written 'All these MSS. were of Cusanus'.

below]); Grenoble, 20 March; Lyons, 30 March.[1] There is a gap then in Wanley's references until 21 September 1722 when Suttie wrote from Piacenza, but in the Diary under 28 February 1720/21 it is noted that he was at that date in Italy. For the later years, until the last reference to him in the Diary under 26 May 1726, we can piece together from it some information: in January 1725 he was in Paris leading 'a vagrant and idle life' and in August he met Noel at Calais; in November, however, he was again (or still) in Paris and could not leave before paying off his gambling debts. However, in January 1726 he was going to Liège 'about Baron Crassier's' things[2] but was soon back in France with 'fine things' which he had lately bought there (cf. Diary under 16 March 1725/6).

Interesting as these details are in themselves—and they are indeed interesting, as revealing how an agent might journey to and fro on the continent of Europe in the early decades of the 18th century in search of MSS. and early printed books to supply the wealthy collectors of the English market, in much the same way as Dibdin was to make early in the next century the continental tour described in his book, *A Bibliographical Antiquarian and Picturesque Tour through France and Germany*, published in 1821, a tour which was undertaken primarily for the same purpose for the library of the great 19th-century bibliophile, Lord Spencer, at Althorp[3]—yet they would have a greater interest still for our study of the Harleian Library if we were able to relate precisely the places visited by Suttie either to MSS. subsequently in the Library or to Noel purchases recorded in the Diary or to both. Of course, some few MSS. can be so related. The Arnstein books referred to by Wanley in a marginal note against Suttie's Strasbourg visit of 10 February 1718, and rejected by him as too highly priced, were in fact purchased three years later (16 January 1720/21) and are Harl. 2798–2802. Other volumes bearing the Arnstein *ex libris* and acquired on that date are Harl. 3032, 3042, 3050, 3052–5, 3058, 3076, 3101, and 3114. Were Harl. 2782 and 3075 also from Arnstein? Possibly from one of the journeys undertaken by Suttie into Germany from Strasbourg derives Harl. 2594, a MS. from St. Martin's Abbey at Wiblingen near Ulm which was bought by Harley on 20 February 1719/20. From the Trier–Coblenz journey of 1717 and/or the Trier–Cologne one of 1718 must surely derive the great mass of Cues MSS. (discussed above at pp. xxxix–xl) most of which bear no date by Wanley,[4] and Harl. 2826, a 9th-century Gospels which was in use as late as the 17th century at Eller near Cochem on the Mosel, but a stone's throw from Cues. Included in the 20 January 1721/22 purchase from Noel were three MSS. from a church at Augsburg,[5] while in the same purchase and also of Augsburg provenance is the small group of MSS. (Harl. 2829, 2953, 3668, 3676) from the library of Conrad Peutinger (d. 1547) of that city. The absence of date inscriptions by Wanley leaves us completely in the dark as to how far several MSS. of German provenance may safely be associated with Suttie's journeys. Mr. Derek Turner has shown convincingly that the original home of the 12th-century Lectionary, Harl. 2889, was the Benedictine monastery of St. Michael at Siegburg, which is some fifteen miles south-east

---

[1] Wanley has written against this: 'The books wanting are at Coblentz, with the Ancient MSS. (He is going for the Danube.)'

[2] For Baron Crassier see footnotes to 16 Aug. 1725 in Diary.

[3] For a recent example see the late Dr. E. P. Goldschmidt's account in his paper, 'Austrian Monastic Libraries' (*The Library*, 4th ser., xxv (1944–5), pp. 46–65) of similar journeys undertaken by him between 1913 and 1917 in the area of the old Austro-Hungarian Empire for the *Gesamtkatalog der Wiegendrucke*.

[4] Cues MSS. dated by Wanley bear a much later date, viz. 18 Jan. 1723/4 (e.g. Harl. 2728).

[5] Harl. 2890, 2908, 2941—at any rate, liturgically so associated.

of Cologne,[1] but the MS. bears no date by Wanley and we have no information as to when it came into the Harleian Library; again, when (and how) did the three MSS. belonging to the Augustinian Friars of Helenenberg near 'Welschbilch' (Welschbillig) near Trier (Harl. 3290, 3597, 4091) come into the Library? Two MSS., Harl. 2803, 2804, contain *ex libris* inscriptions that show that they belonged to St. Mary's Church 'in suburbio' at Worms, presumably the Liebfrauen Kirche in the Wein Berg, and were placed by Wanley in the Library next to the Arnstein group, Harl. 2798–2802; were they a part of the 16 January 1720/21 purchase and if so did Wanley fail by an oversight to inscribe them accordingly, or was the evidence destroyed at the time of binding? Were they by chance acquired by Suttie on his visit to Worms on 14 November 1717? And the same queries are posed by Harl. 2910 which belonged at one time to the Dominicans at Mainz, one of the places visited by Suttie in 1717 and again in 1718, and by Harl. 2835, whose home, as its *ex libris* discloses, was the famous Benedictine house at Maria Laach, easily reached from Suttie's base at Coblenz. Two MSS. from the Monastery of St. Peter at Salzburg (Harl. 2485, 3849) did not reach the Library until 18 January 1723/4; we should have expected them to come into the Library at an earlier date, but did they emanate from the projected journey 'for the Danube' referred to by Wanley in an annotation against the Lyons entry? The explanation of such a time-lag, if such there was, might very well be that some of the MSS. purchased on the earlier journeys were gathered together and held at one place until circumstances financial or otherwise were favourable for their transport: such a place might well have been Coblenz (as is almost suggested in one of his notes by Wanley), which was exceptionally well placed at the junction of the Rhine and the Mosel as a gathering-place for material and also for subsequent onward shipment down the Rhine for Rotterdam and England.

So far as Italy is concerned we lack for Suttie any of the general information supplied in the Diary for Gibson, the chief agent for Italian acquisitions, but we do know (see above, p. xlix) that Suttie was at Piacenza in the autumn of 1722, and, presumably, he made more than a fleeting stay in North Italy then and in the following year. Some purchases of Italian provenance make their appearance, at any rate, in the large 18 January 1723/4 Noel block. Were the MSS. (Harl. 2556, 2579, 2707, 2730, 2744) from the Capilupi library at Mantua acquired on the spot from some impoverished member of the family (see below, p. lii)?

For France, too, any correlation of the MSS. bought of Noel with Suttie's movements there (which belong to 1720 and then the later years of the Diary) is impossible. In the 13 August 1724 purchase from Noel, which had 'lately come from beyond the sea', we may note at least eight manuscripts from French ecclesiastical establishments—Harl. 2510 from the Dominicans of Chartres; Harl. 3661 from (presumably) the Benedictine house of Ste. Trinité at Caen; Harl. 3712, a cartulary of the Cluniac priory at Domène; Harl. 7195 from the Franciscans of St. Omer; Harl. 2790, 2991, and 2992 from the Cathedral Church of St. Cyr at Nevers and Harl. 3661 from the Carmelites there. But how did manuscripts from the South, two MSS. from the Abbey of Fontfroide (near Narbonne) (Harl. 3958, 4952) and two from the Cathedral Church of St. Nazaire at Carcassonne (Harl. 3630, 4980) reach the Library? Or the MS. from St. Pierre at Jumièges (Harl. 3941)?

I am assuming that the MSS. were acquired on the spot or, at any rate, in the

---

[1] D. H. Turner, 'The Siegburg Lectionary', *Scriptorium*, xvi (1962), pp. 16–27, pll. 2, 3; cf. also *Siegburger Lektionar*, Siegburg, 1964.

neighbourhood of their former homes, and I think that this assumption is, generally speaking, a fair one where the continental libraries are concerned, in view of the considerable information that we have about the libraries and their contents about this time in the works of Jean Mabillon (in the citations in his *De Re Diplomatica* (Paris 1681: suppl. 1704; 2nd ed. 1709), and in his *Iter Germanicum* (Hamburg, 1717), which contains the fruits of his journeys made in 1683 with Michael Germanus) and of Bernard de Montfaucon (in his *Diarium Italicum* of 1702 and in his great work on Greek palaeography, the *Palaeographia Graeca* of 1708—not to mention his *Bibliotheca Bibliothecarum Manuscriptorum* of 1739, the French equivalent of the *Catalogi Manuscriptorum Angliae* of 1697), and in the records of the journeys of the two Maurists, Martène and Durand, undertaken from 1708 to 1713 and again in 1718 and 1719 throughout France and Flanders in pursuit of material for the projected revision of the *Gallia Christiana*, the results of which were published in 1717 and 1724 in their famous *Voyage Littéraire*. Unlike Mabillon and Montfaucon who wrote in Latin, Martène and Durand wrote in French, as did Jean-Baptiste Le Brun des Marettes who also made a tour through France about this time, not, however, a *voyage littéraire* but a *voyage liturgique*, the results of which were incorporated in his *Voyages liturgiques de France*, published at Paris in 1718, the purpose of which is clearly stated in its sub-title: *Recherches faites en diverses villes du Royaume, contenant plusiers particularitez touchant les Rits et les Usages des Églises,* &c. A similar tour to that of Martène and Durand was undertaken later for Switzerland by Augustin Calmet who published the results in his *Diarium Helveticum* in 1756; the places visited by Calmet included Einsiedeln, St. Gall, Murbach, Reichenau, Moury, and Rheinau, and under each place he lists the manuscripts he saw there. The late 9th-century Gospels, Harl. 2797, which was acquired by Harley in 1725 (not from Noel but from Woodman) and which bears on folio 1 an *ex libris* of the monastery of Ste. Geneviève in Paris, we know from a reference in the *Journal des Sçavans* for 1684 was in that house in that year. And libraries both private and monastic were still rich enough in the last years of the 17th century and the early ones of the 18th to supply Nicholas Joseph Foucault with material for the great library which he was able to amass in those years:[1] what he was able to secure from the monastic houses (anxious probably to obtain his favour in the regions over which he exercised control) is shown by the MSS. of monastic provenance from his library which went into the Harleian Library in 1720: for example, the two Harl. MSS. (3176, 4985) from the Jesuit College of La Flèche, the latter of which passed into Foucault's hands in 1706; the 10th-century Smaragdus MS. (Harl. 3078) from St. Pierre at Moissac; the 15th-century Psalter (Harl. 2949) from the penitents of St. Lô (either at Rouen or Manche in Normandy); and the 12th-century Rabanus Maurus MS. (Harl. 3104) from the monastery of St. Sauveur le Vicomte in Normandy. Circumstances in Germany generally (suffering from the Thirty Years War)[2] and in the Rhineland (suffering from the effects of French invasions) were particularly favourable to the acquisition of MSS. and early printed books, either direct from the monastic houses and private owners or through local dealers. The 'acquisitions' made by Graevius during his periods of study in the cathedral library and elsewhere at Cologne in 1657 are some indication of this. Again, no satisfactory explanation is forthcoming of the part played

---

[1] On Foucault and his collecting activities see L. Delisle, *Le Cabinet des Manuscrits*, i, 1868, pp. 374–9.
[2] Wanley notes in Suttie's letter of 14 July 1718 from Würzburg 'a Parcel of MSS. . . . found, which were buried in the Swedish War.'

by the Elector Palatine's librarian, Büchels, in the 'sales' from his master's library which he arranged with Zamboni in the 1720's. Material in the manuscript itself (a list of the Fraternity of the Rosary of our Lady at Eller) indicates that Harl. 2826 was in use there at least in the early part of the 17th century. The MSS. from the Hospital of St. Nicholas at Cues must surely have been obtained *in situ* since the larger part of the Hospital's library still remains at Cues.[1]

Again, in Italy the Capilupi library was in existence at Mantua as late as the end of the 18th century when it was the subject of the Jesuit Juan Andres' little volume, *Catalogo di' Codici Manoscritti della Famiglia Capilupi di Mantova* (Mantua, 1797). And the library of S. Giovanni in Verdara at Padua was still sufficiently well supplied in the early decades of the 18th century to furnish Sir Thomas Coke and Gibson's agents with a considerable enrichment to the Holkham and Harleian Libraries respectively; and the Zomino MSS. now in the Harleian Library were in all probability secured either at, or in the neighbourhood of, Pistoia.[2]

On the other hand, the French religious houses, it is true, suffered severely in the religious wars of the 16th century. Thus, it is known that MSS. at Ferrières were dispersed with the pillaging of the library there by the Calvinists in 1567. Nevertheless, it is interesting to note that the Cluniac house of La Charité-sur-Loire, for example, in spite of its having been 'brûlée & ruinée par les heretiques' still preserved 'un ancient manuscrit qui contient la regle et les sermons de Saint Columban' which the Prior was able to exhibit to the two Maurists at their visit in 1708.[3] A parallel indeed to what in some instances happened in England at the dissolution of the monasteries in the 1530's is supplied by Fleury: after the plundering of the Abbey of St. Benoît-sur-Loire by the soldiery in 1562 in the religious wars, part of the library passed into the hands of the Abbey's steward, Pierre Daniel of Orléans (d. 1603).[4] The French authorities, however, were watchful of attempts to export their more valuable MSS. One manuscript acquired by Suttie was seized by order of the French King and placed in the Royal Library; this is the purchase referred to by Wanley in the Diary under 7 August 1723, a Cardinal Du Perron Greek MS. obtained by Suttie from the community of St. Taurin at Évreux.[5] The Évreux MSS. certainly remained at St. Taurin's until the end of the century, when they were removed to the Bibliothèque de la Ville there. Much the most puzzling of the acquisitions from France is the large block of no less than seventy MSS. from the Jesuit College at Agen,[6] all undated by Wanley.

This use of dealers and agents such as Noel/Suttie, Gibson, and Andrew Hay

---

[1] See J. Marx, *Verzeichnis der HSS.-Sammlung des Hospitals zu Cues*, Trier, 1905. On the acquisition of the Cues MSS. see pp. xxxix–xl above.

[2] On the Zomino MSS. at Pistoia see above p. xlvii, n. 6, and below p. 474.

[3] *Voyage Littéraire*, i, pp. 36, 37. A late 12th-century Psalter written for La Charité-sur-Loire was acquired in the Noel purchase of 13 Aug. 1724 and is Harl. 2895 (for a reproduction of a page from it see Warner, *Reproductions from Illuminated Manuscripts*, i, pl. xix). A perusal of the *Voyage Littéraire* reveals indeed how much manuscript material was still in the libraries of the monastic houses (such as Clairvaux, Souvigny, St. Germain at Auxerre, Joüy, and many others, not to mention the houses at places such as Troyes and Bourges).

[4] See H. Hagen, *Catalogus Codicum Bernensium* (*Bibliotheca Bongarsiana*), Berne, 1875, pp. xi–xiv, and for MSS. owned by him see index of owners, p. 649; cf. also L. Delisle, *Le Cabinet des Manuscrits*, Paris, ii, 1874, pp. 364–6 and E. Pellegrini, 'Membra Disiecta Floriacensia', *Bibliothèque de l'École des Chartes*, cxvii (1959), pp. 5–56. But several early MSS. still at St. Benoît-sur-Loire in 1709 were seen in that year by Martène and Durand (see *Voyage Littéraire*, i, pp. 66–68).

[5] Cf. also Diary under 13 Sept. 1723; and see L. Delisle *Le Cabinet des Manuscrits*, i, 1868, p. 370, on the incident: according to Delisle the MS. was seized at Orléans.

[6] See H. Omont, on Scaliger and Agen in 'Notes sur les Manuscrits grecs du British Museum', *Bibliothèque de l'École des Chartes*, xlv, 1884, p. 323.

working on the Continent is one of the several well-defined categories into which the activities concerning MSS. and printed books fall within the major period of the Diary. The employment of these and of booksellers at home had become essential to feed what are now the main types of interest: finely illuminated MSS., Greek and Oriental MSS., incunabula and, especially, early editions of the classics, while on the other hand for cartularies and charters, heraldic MSS., and English historical papers the main channels are still primarily private ones. Thus, all the well-known booksellers of the period make an appearance in the pages of the Diary—Woodman and Lyon, Charles Davis, the famous Christopher Bateman, Daniel Browne, the Vaillants, and so on. Of these Charles Davis, who had begun about 1717 as an apprentice of Noel and was, in the period of the Diary, an associate of Woodman, makes frequent appearances throughout, his first being in connexion with Woodman's sale of the Earl of Radnor's MSS. on 2 May 1721. This sale is one good example of a consistent policy followed by Wanley, namely, of demanding that Harley should have first pick and pre-emption—thus, the Radnor MSS. were shown by Woodman to Wanley 24 March 1720/1, who ordered the MSS. to be laid aside until Harley should see them, but subsequent entries reveal that Woodman ignored this injunction and printed a catalogue of them, an action which involved Wanley and Davis in some sharp words on 29 April and 1 May, Wanley being mollified apparently when another intermediary reported that Woodman would offer the MSS. to Harley at a cheap price. This right of pre-emption appears to have been exercised too with the Woodman and Lyon sale of the Loménie de Brienne library of 28 April 1724, when Wanley on the day preceding the sale marked certain of the books for Harley's option and secured from Woodman and Lyon an assurance that all such books had been 'taken-out & locked-up securely for my Lord'. Again, when Varenne told Wanley (27 October 1722) that he was going to Paris he was asked, if he happened to light upon any rarities, to let Wanley see them first upon his return.

Charles Davis was, at any rate, in sufficient favour with Wanley to be sent by him on 29 December 1722 to Robert Harley, who wanted 'somebody to serve him in the way of out-of-course Books, as John Bagford used to do'.

The employment of the booksellers made it possible for Wanley to follow a pick-and-choose policy also when the libraries of English collectors came to auction, in a way that would not have been easy in private negotiations with individual owners; in this way Harley was given the chance of acquiring such of the Greek books printed at Jassy and Bucharest as he still required (to replace the damaged copies in the set bought of Sherard in 1723) by Charles Davis out of those bought by the latter at the Covel auction of 9 March 1723/4. Again, John Wyat, the bookseller of St. Paul's Churchyard, was 'fixed' by Wanley 'in my Lords Service' 22 May 1723 to secure 'without making a noise' John Strype's papers when Strype should die.

Sometimes it was necessary to transfer a transaction from one bookseller to another, as in the complex business of securing those of Archdeacon Batteley's MSS. which were not bought from the Archdeacon's nephew on 5 November 1723: although Bateman was the alleged purchaser in 1724 he was later displaced by Newton on Wanley's advice to Batteley.

The main source for the items from the large English collections was indeed quite clearly the booksellers as opposed to the earlier method of direct purchase; thus, to mention only those libraries referred to in the Diary, the Earl of Stamford's was handled by Ballard (16 January 1721), the Earl of Radnor's by Woodman (2 May 1721), John Covel's by Cock (9 March 1723/4) and the Chamberlaynes', father and son, by Daniel Browne (11 March 1723/4). Several foreign libraries too were sold on the London market, such as those of Loménie de Brienne, la Vallière, Fléchier, and la Bazonière (already referred to, p. xlvi) which were all handled by Woodman, while the Freebairne books from Italy were auctioned by Ballard. Little interest, however, was shown by Harley in auctions abroad; in the case of the Fredrik Rostgaard sale of 7 January 1726 at Copenhagen, of which Wanley sent Harley a copy of the sale catalogue, Harley refused to 'meddle at a Sale so far-off', though Sir Hans Sloane, be it noted, bought several MSS. at this sale. In 1715, however, Paul Vaillant had received a commission to make bids at the sale of the Bibliotheca Sarraziana at The Hague and the notable instance of a purchase from a foreign auction is, of course, the Codex Aureus (Harl. 2788), which was purchased at the Ménars Sale at The Hague in 1720, Vaillant again being the agent.[1] Attempts, however, were consistently made to acquire libraries built up abroad: at intervals in 1720 Noel was discussing with Wanley ways and means of buying the library of Baron Hohendorf, which was sold, however, *en bloc* to the Imperial Library at Vienna, when it was offered for sale at The Hague. Fruitless negotiations continued throughout 1720 and again over several years, 1722–6, in an attempt to obtain portions of the collection of MSS. made by Joseph Smith[2] of Venice, but greater success attended those conducted through Maittaire in 1724 and 1725 for the acquisition of MSS. (including those of Graevius) from the library of the Elector Palatine at Düsseldorf from Zamboni.

But others besides booksellers and their agents were to be used in the search for material further afield. Nothing indeed demonstrates more clearly the way in which the initiative for this search for such acquisitions for the Library had been taken in the earlier period by Wanley, than the several commissions drawn up by him that survive from the pre-1720 period, especially that to George Daniel, apparently drafted for him on his departure for Smyrna in 1712, instructing him to search for Greek manuscripts, some of which are particularized, and that addressed to Samuel Palmer, dated 22 June 1718, immediately preceding his proposed journey to Persia.[3] The former is but one example of the search for manuscripts in the Levant that was going on almost continuously throughout the latter half of the 17th century and the early part of the 18th, the post-1720 examples being furnished in the Diary itself by the activities of Lisle, Mould, and Sherard,[4] which were to supply the Library with many of its Greek and most of its Oriental manuscripts. The French were particularly active in the Levant, first during the minority of Louis XIV under the influence of Mazarin and Séguier and then later under the powerful initiative of Louis XIV's great minister Colbert, with the result that large collections of Greek and Oriental manuscripts from the area then controlled by the Ottoman Empire

---

[1] Vaillant was again the agent for purchases at 'the late Earl of Sunderland's auction' at The Hague probably in 1723, the bills for which, with lists of MSS. and printed books bought, are in Edw. Harley Papers, Misc. I. On Sunderland see above, p. xliii.

[2] For details and on Smith see Biographical Index.

[3] The commission to Daniel is in Harl. 7055, ff. 17–18: cf. also the commission in Welbeck Wanleyana, Misc. 40, dated 28 Sept. 1712 and 30 Sept. 1713. That to Palmer is in Welbeck Wanleyana, Misc. 71. Another commission from this period not to be overlooked is that addressed to Thomas Harley, Envoy Extraordinary at Hanover, 27 Apr. 1714, relating to Professor Lentz's Syriac manuscript (Harl. 7526, ff. 150–1).

[4] See Biographical Index under Lisle, Mould, and Sherard, and Subject Index under Greek and Oriental manuscripts.

were secured for the Royal Library at Paris; to achieve this aim the French either employed their diplomats, such as the ambassador at Constantinople (for example, the Marquis de Nointel (1670–9)), and consular agents, or dispatched special agents for the purpose, such as Antoine Galland,[1] one of Nointel's staff, who made journeys in the Near East in 1673 and later, Monceau and Laisné between 1667 and 1675, Vaillant, the numismatist, in 1674 and later, and especially the German Dominican, Johann Michael Wansleben (who had collaborated while in England in the preparation of Walton's Polyglot Bible), between 1671 and 1675.[2] Of all these activities Wanley must have been very well aware, more especially as several journeys of the same kind were being undertaken by French scholars on royal instructions in Wanley's own lifetime, such as those of Paul Lucas (1664–1737) at various dates between 1699 and 1724, his accounts of the earlier of which were published by him between 1705 and 1719.[3] With these and other published accounts of such journeys Wanley would be well acquainted.

In like manner therefore Wanley was to utilize to good purpose the services of the chaplains and consuls of the Turkey Company in the Levant and the Near East to obtain there Greek and Oriental manuscripts as well as antiquities for Edward Harley.

As a result, two Greek and one Arabic MS. collected by Samuel Lisle while chaplain to the Factory at Aleppo from 1710 to 1719 were acquired on his return to London in 1720. Not only were these men important as direct intermediaries for purchase but also for the information they gave Wanley about conditions on the spot and the MSS. to be found in various places: thus Lisle told Wanley (18 January 1719/20) of the Gospels at Nea Moni and of the Patriarch of Antioch's printing press at Aleppo. The information about the Greek MSS. at Nea Moni was not forgotten and ways and means of procuring them were discussed with Sherard (who had been Consul at Smyrna 1703–16) on 17 November 1720. In consequence, letters went to Bernard Mould, then chaplain at Smyrna, who agreed to go to Salonica and Scio (Chios) and also (on Sherard's advice) to Mount Athos (cf. 17 April 1721, item 8); as a result, Mould, on his return to London in 1725, brought back with him about 20 Greek and Hebrew MSS. and some antique inscriptions, together with 'an antique brasen head of a bearded man, found in Thyatira', having earlier—in 1722 (see 18 May)—sent to London to his sister for Harley five Turkish MSS. (see Diary, p. 146, n. 5). These contacts were of a particular value for Harley who showed a quite exceptional interest in Oriental MSS., an interest not unknown perhaps to his contemporaries, since the one MS. presented by Alexander Pope, the poet, in April 1723 was a Persian MS. (Harl. 5478) (see Diary, 3 July 1723).

Small collections of books were also acquired abroad by scholars in their travels and several of these or parts of them were subsequently purchased by Harley. Dr. Conyers Middleton, Chief Librarian of the University Library, Cambridge,

---

[1] The French Orientalist (1646–1715) best known to fame as the first to make known in Europe (1707–17 in twelve volumes) the stories of 'The Thousand and One Nights'.
[2] For an account of these and later similar activities on the part of the French and the extraordinarily interesting documents relating to them see Henri Omont, *Missions Archéologiques Français en Orient aux XVIIe et XVIIIe Siècles*, Paris, 1902, 2 vols. See also L. Delisle, *Cabinet des Manuscrits*, i, 1868, pp. 274–9, for the activities inspired by Colbert; the 'Remarques' drafted by Jean-Baptiste Cotelier are of particular interest (Delisle, op. cit., pp. 276–7) and should be compared with Wanley's commissions. For a brief note on the subject see Charles Astruc's 'Les Fonds Grecs du Cabinet des Manuscrits de la Bibliothèque Nationale' contributed to the catalogue of the *Byzance et la France Médiévale* exhibition at the Bibliothèque Nationale, 1958.
[3] On Lucas's journeys see Delisle, op. cit., i, pp. 332–3, 371.

who was travelling in Italy in 1724 and 1725, sold to Harley two parcels of MSS. acquired in the course of this journeying—11 December 1724 (18 MSS. and 2 printed books) and 25 February 1725 (29 MSS.); it was he who gave Wanley information about Domenico Passionei's MSS. in Rome (now in the Biblioteca Angelica there). The small parcel of 'Six MSS. lately come from Italy' offered in 1726 (cf. Diary, 25 January 1725/6) by John Wright, Lord Kinnoull's library-keeper, may also be the result of a foreign tour by Wright, who had previously sold to Harley (24 June 1723) a group of no less than 13 MSS., which included one MS. (Harl. 3746) from S. Andrea della Valle in Rome and no less than 5 MSS. from the library of the Aragonese Kings of Naples (Harl. 3046, 3481, 3482, 3485, 3699).

Everywhere in the Diary are examples to show that the watchfulness displayed in the pre-1720 period in the correspondence between Harley and Wanley for opportunities to make additions to the Library had in no way abated. Constant attempts were made by Wanley to persuade those who visited the Library, or had been shown favour in borrowing books from it, to assist in securing MSS. for it or to give or bequeath books and MSS. in their possession. When Nathaniel Boothe the lawyer came to consult Randle Holme MSS. on 23 January 1719/20 Wanley took the opportunity 'of reviving the Matter of the old Deeds which were in the possession of the said R. Holme' with the result that Boothe promised to make an effort to secure them from their present owner, without success as it proved, the owner, Francis Bassano, being 'obstinately bent not to part with them' (cf. Diary, 11 June 1722). Likewise, Roger Gale, after looking over a number of MSS. and charters on 25 January 1720/21 and borrowing three charters, promised to give the original letters written to his father by foreign scholars, at the prompting, we need not doubt, of Wanley, and the letters duly came into the Library in May of the following year. When Dr. Daniel Waterland (who had first visited the Library in May 1723) called on Wanley on 27 April of the next year Wanley raised with him the question of obtaining the Greek MSS. at Sion College, Waterland being a Fellow of the College by reason of his Rectorship of St. Augustine's in the City; to stimulate Waterland's efforts Wanley presented to the Doctor two printed books from his 'own poor study'. With Joseph Sparke he established good relations when Sparke came to collect subscriptions and materials for his *Scriptores* in 1722 and 1723 and thus obtained from him information about a number of private libraries in Northamptonshire (those of Lord Griffin at Dingley, of Sir Verney Cave at Stanford, and the Earl of Cardigan at Deene) and a promise to exchange some of his own old printed books. From Archdeacon Frank, who was the intermediary in Harley's acquisition of the Newnham Cartulary (Harl. 3656), Wanley sought information about two Bedfordshire libraries, that of the Osbornes at Chicksand Abbey and that of Sir John Napier at Luton Hoo (cf. Diary, 17 February 1719/20). When Stukeley called into the Library 27 May 1721 to look at one of Hugh Thomas's MSS. he promised upon Wanley's 'motion' to ask Dr. Richard Mead to exchange his Latin Gospels MS. for Harley's Avicenna MS. When Clayton was shown on 10 June 1725 MSS. he had not seen before he promised, on his return to Lancashire, to serve Harley especially with regard to old deeds and the Cartulary of Whalley Abbey. The heraldic interests of Joseph Barret the goldsmith (the purchaser in 1724 of Arthur Charlett's collection of coins), who made frequent visits to the Library to consult heraldic MSS., in addition to those he made on business, Wanley planned to exploit by allowing him to borrow four heraldic MSS. every week, hoping that Barret would be correspondingly grateful and thus doubly zealous in securing coins for Harley (cf. Diary, 29 January 1724/5). Foreign visitors to the Library were frequently asked, or volunteered, in return for the civilities they had received, to further Harley's interests abroad: a 'Monsieur Le Duke', a French physician, born in Constantinople, offered in 1723 to serve Harley on his return there; Schumacher, the Czar's Library-Keeper, who was shown the treasures of the libraries both at Dover St. and at Wimpole in 1722, was supplied, when he left England, with a formal commission to buy MSS. of Wolfius at Hamburg and the Fust and Schoeffer Prayer Book of 1457 belonging to Uffenbach; and the Duke of Saxe Gotha's librarian, one Leibe (or Lieve), offered to serve Wanley on his return through France.

Worth-while parcels of MSS. of English provenance were, however, still being acquired (though on a smaller scale) either through Noel, for example, from whom came MSS. of Dr. Peter Allix and Dr. Thomas Whincopp in 1720 and of Simon Harcourt of Penley in 1724, or through private individuals, either by gift as in the case of George Harbin the non-juror and William Hanbury (both of whom presented several collections of letters to the Library), or by purchase, the most notable of the latter being the large group of MSS. bought 6 July 1720 from John Warburton, Somerset Herald, most of which must have been picked up by Warburton, when in the north of England, from the Earl of Carlisle; they included a large number of Lord William Howard of Naworth items.

Throughout the period of the Diary, either in its pages or from evidence outside it, we can watch Wanley making persistent efforts to acquire for the Library 'plums' from elsewhere: in 1715 the St. Chad's Gospels from Lichfield, the Red Book of Hergest at Jesus College, Oxford, and the Lauderdale 'Orosius', from 1719 to 1721 the Benedictional of St. Ethelwold, in 1720 the Saxon Charters that had belonged to Lord Somers, and in 1725 the 'Blickling Homilies' and 'Blickling Psalter' from Pownall of Lincoln. When Sir George Wheler visited Wanley on 3 June 1723 and invited him to stay at Durham in the following summer, Wanley's first thought was that in this way he might be able to obtain the 'Books, Charters, & others things which will be more useful to the world in my Lords Library, than in that remote corner of the Kingdom'. Nothing escaped him. Being at Vaillant's on 19 April 1722 he saw a small paper MS. of Virgil and other Latin poets and immediately persuaded Vaillant to make a present of it and carried it away with him. With Conyers Middleton he discussed plans for obtaining duplicates from the University Library, Cambridge, of which there were very many as a result of the presentation by George I of Bishop Moore's library to the University. When John Bridges mentioned, during a visit to Wanley on 12 November 1722, that he was going to order in his will that his whole Library should be sold after his death, Wanley immediately asked that 'he would charge his Executors that my Lord may have the pre-emption of what he may then Want', &c.; and when Sanderson told Wanley on 14 November 1722 that he was examining Secretary Thurloe's papers then in the possession of Sir Joseph Jekyll, Wanley at once begged him to try to get them for Harley 'for an Equivalent'.

The Harleian Library, like the Cottonian Library founded by Sir Robert Cotton in the late 16th and early 17th century, is rich not only in codices and post-medieval historical and political papers but also in charters and rolls. The acquisition of charters and rolls was undoubtedly closely related to Robert Harley's own particular interest in British history and genealogy, for as Wanley remarked in his report on the collections in 1715: 'They are most authentic testimonies or evidences as to families and estates, and the very seals of exceeding use.'[1]

On this side of the Library's collections the Harleys were ably assisted by their Librarian, for Wanley, as was natural in one coming to librarianship from Anglo-Saxon studies[2] and the cataloguing of Anglo-Saxon material and, moreover, born in the great age of antiquarian scholarship—of Spelman, Dugdale, Dodsworth and Somner—had a proper understanding of the value and importance of charters. Hence, his persistent efforts in the Diary at intervals between 1720 and 1722 to trace and if possible to secure Lord Somers's Anglo-Saxon charters,[3] and, again, his request to Mr. White of Warwick, when he came to see the Library on 23 January 1720/1, that he would persuade 'Mr. Fish of Warwick to sell his old Deeds & Rolls to my Lord'; no one was better acquainted with the Fish charters than Wanley, who in his prentice days at Coventry had made beautiful facsimile copies of them (now preserved in Harl. 7505) as part of his early palaeographical studies.[4]

This early interest of Wanley's in charters had nearly upset his relations with Dr. Thomas Smith, the Cottonian Librarian, through his ill-advised request to borrow the great collection of Anglo-Saxon charters preserved in Cotton Augustus II.[5] Moreover, apropos of the Harleian Library it is interesting to note that among Wanley's few surviving letters to Robert Harley is a long one, dated 6 July 1703,[6] discussing Harley's famous spurious Edgar charter of 964 (now Harl. 7513).[7]

Wanley was therefore well fitted to look after a collection which by 1715, according to his report of 27 July of that year, contained 13,000 charters 'of all ages up to 900 years'—'the largest collection there is known to be anywhere', he added—and 1,000 rolls, the latter, be it noted, including not only the usual account and estate rolls, &c., but such precious items as the Guthlac Roll (Harl. Roll. Y. 6).[8] To house the charters fifteen presses with pigeon holes were required.

The present number of Harley Charters is 10,631 and of Rolls 916.

Two reasons may be advanced to explain part at least of the discrepancy between the present and the 18th-century figures. Some losses occurred in the move to Bath Court, St. James's, in 1715 as we know from a memorandum of Wanley's dated 8 January 1714/15.[9] Some at first missing, Wanley found; others he thought might be somewhere in their respective boxes and therefore findable 'for the Pigeonholes', writes Wanley, 'do not go to the Back as they should; whereby hundreds of charters slipped out of their places, as I found. Or else these Charters may be

---

[1] *HMC Portland Papers*, v, p. 515. On this report see above, p. xxviii.
[2] The prime importance of the 'Dissertatio Epistolaris' prefixed to Hickes's *Thesaurus Linguarum Veterum Septentrionalium* in which Hickes was very materially assisted by Wanley was 'in its treatment of Anglo-Saxon charters as a fundamental source of Anglo-Saxon history' (see D. C. Douglas, *English Scholars*, 1939, p. 112).
[3] See Subject Index under Charters. They had been described by Wanley in his catalogue of Anglo-Saxon MSS. in Hickes's *Thesaurus*, ii, pp. 301–3, and the texts were fortunately printed in John Smith's ed. of *Bædæ Historia Ecclesiastica Latine et Saxonice*, of 1722, pp. 764–82; they are no longer extant (see above, p. xxxvii, n. 11, and Biographical Index under Somers).
[4] See Diary under 23 Jan. 1720/1, and footnote to that date for fuller details of Wanley's knowledge of this collection of charters and rolls.
[5] See Smith's letter to H. W., 8 June 1697, printed Ellis, *Letters of Eminent Literary Men*, pp. 245–8.
[6] Preserved in Harl. 7526, ff. 148–9.
[7] The text had been printed in Henry Spelman's *Concilia*, i, 1639, p. 432. It is discussed in Hickes's 'Dissertatio Epistolaris' to his *Thesaurus*, pp. 86 and 152, and an engraved facsimile of it, dedicated to Robert Harley, is inserted at the end of the 'Dissertatio'. Printed by B. Thorpe, *Diplomatarium Anglicum Aevi Saxonici*, 1865, pp. 211–15; W. de Gray Birch, *Cartularium Saxonicum*, iii, 1893, no. 1135.
[8] See below, p. lxi.
[9] Welbeck Wanleyana, Misc. 43.

utterly lost, for in removing, all the Locks gave way, & every Box came open to me, & I myself saw several Deeds drop from them as the Boxes were brought in'.

Secondly, as Mr. Andrew Watson has recently shown,[1] at least 127 Harley charters *other than* those acquired from Sir Simonds D'Ewes in 1705 are in the Cotton Collection in which, in addition, are 293 D'Ewes charters and rolls which must belong to the Harley purchase; thus, out of the 1450 or so Cotton Charters no less than 420 are in fact Harley Charters.

The *locus classicus* for any discussion of the provenance of Harley's collection of charters is supplied by a passage in the Diary under the date 23 November 1722, item 14 (the year date being erroneously written by Wanley 1723). The information contained in this passage may be summarized as follows:

(1) From the Sir Simonds D'Ewes purchase came the charters in Boxes, 43, 44, 45, 46, 47, 48, 49, 50, 51, 52, 53, 54, 55, 56, 57, 58 (Mr. Watson reckons the charters and rolls in the D'Ewes collection as 7800 and 563 respectively);

(2) From Thomas Mansell, of Margam, Glamorganshire (created Baron Mansell of Margam in 1712) came the charters 75. A. 1–75. D. 25: presumably before 1712 to judge from the form of the wording 'The Right Honourable Thomas, now Lord Mansell' in the entry which suggests that Wanley had some donative note before him. It is of interest to observe in passing that all relate to the Cistercian Abbey of Margam. The gap between 58 and 75 is explained by the fact that there were no charter boxes 59–74 and the same is true of 81 and 82, &c. (see below);

(3) From 'the late Reverend Dr. Matthew Hutton' of Aynhoe, the antiquary (died 1711), came, by gift, charters 83. A. 21–83. C. 9;

(4) From John Anstis, the elder (1669–1744), came, also by gift, charters 83. C. 10–84. B. 61 (except for a few in 83. B. 8). As regards the gift of charters to the Library by Anstis it should be noted that under 18 July 1716 it is recorded in the Diary that 'Mr. Anstis gave a Second Parcel of old Deeds, about 363 in Number, which will all be Endorsed with the Date above' and deeds identified as so endorsed by Wanley are listed in the footnote to that date; a parcel of these was received by Wanley from Wimpole on 24 December 1722 and again from the same source came another parcel (including some of Robert Harley's as well) on 20 February 1722/3;

(5) Some, Wanley notes, came from Lord Harley. One so endorsed and dated 5 February 1719/20 is Harl. Ch. 111. B. 53, and for others see Diary 3 September 1722, item 3, and footnote to that date;

(6) The rest, in Boxes 84, 85, 86, 111, and 112, 'excepting some of Sir Simonds D'Ewes's abovementioned, which are very easily discerned and known', were bought from Wanley, according to his memory, 'if they be not Indorsed to the contrary'. A gift of 46 deeds and 3 rolls by Wanley is noted in the Diary under 21 November 1722, item 12 (for the identifications see footnote to that date). Three were given by Wanley on 30 December 1713 (Harl. Ch. 111. D. 27, G. 40, 41), as was 111. G. 50 on an unspecified date. In Box 111 the following—A. 6,

---

[1] A. G. Watson, 'Sir Simonds D'Ewes's Collection of Charters, and a Note on the Charters of Sir Robert Cotton,' *Journal of the Soc. of Archivists*, ii, no. 6 (Oct. 1962), pp. 247–54. Notes by Wanley on some Harley charters written on small loose pieces of paper are inserted as ff. 73–77 in the manuscript catalogue of the Harley rolls and charters begun in May 1787, BM Add. 43500. The fact that some *Cotton* rolls had been improperly assigned to the Harleian Collection was noted in 1855 by Sir Frederic Madden (Add. MS. 43500, f. 67). For a description of Add. MSS. 43500-2, the cat. of the charters and rolls in the British Museum by Samuel Ayscough and others, see *Catalogue of Additions to the Manuscripts, 1931–1935*, p. 162.

B. 4, 12, 13, D. 14—are endorsed as being bought of Wanley. The gap between 86 and 111 is explained by the fact that there were no presses for charters between those numbers. The last Harley Charter is 112. I. 67.

The further history of the charter collections has to be pieced together from references in the Diary or by endorsements on the Charters. The chief donors were James Hill, the Hereford antiquary, who, according to endorsements on the charters, gave on 30 March 1719 no less than twenty;[1] Robert Sanderson, Clerk in the Rolls Chapel, who gave on 14 December 1720 23 old Charters;[2] 'Mr. Bateman', at unspecified dates;[3] 'Mr. Hagley' (possibly William Hagley);[4] Dr. John Hudson, Bodley's Librarian from 1701 to 1719;[5] Thomas O'Sullivan, the Irish scholar, who makes frequent appearances in the Diary.[6] Further, Charles Mawson, Chester Herald, gave two, Harl. Ch. 111. C. 9 and 10, George Holmes one (Harl. Ch. 111. C. 15), a Mr. Pitcairn one (Harl. Ch. 112. A. 15), and Mr. Geo. Tilson also one (Harl. Ch. 112. B. 11). In addition to two given on 21 April 1722 (Harl. Ch. 111. B. 49 and C. 25), George Harbin gave also 111. C. 13 (the date in the endorsement is indecipherable), and, on 12 December 1722, 14 deeds were given by William Holman of Halstead.[7] In the Hugh Thomas bequest of MSS. to Robert Harley (see Diary under 20 October 1720) a number of charters were included (for identification see footnotes to date referred to).

Among the charters purchased are a number endorsed as having been bought of Nathaniel Noel,[8] the bookseller, two or perhaps three from John Strype,[9] several from Peter Le Neve,[10] and no less than thirty-three from George Paul of Cambridge.[11]

Lastly to be noted is the important batch received from Welbeck. Under 27 August 1720, is the first notice of a parcel of 'old Bulls & some other Deeds, mostly relating to Rufford Abbey' being received from Welbeck.[12] No further reference to charters from Welbeck occurs until 20 July 1725, when Wanley notes in the Diary that Harley 'sent in a large parcel of old Deeds or Charters, lately brought up from Welbeck';[13] this may represent the final clearance of the evidence room at Welbeck.

Of the rolls less can be said. Mr. Watson has shown that Harl. Rolls A. 1–Q. 4, with two outliers, Z. 25 and D. D. 4, belonged to D'Ewes.[14] Harl. Roll S. 16 is endorsed 'Given by H. W.' but without date, but the following, also given by

---

[1] Harl. Ch. 111. D. 18 (?), 35, E. 1, 18, 55, F. 59, H. 12; 112. A. 1, B. 13, 42 (?), 47, 57 (?), C. 1, 19, D. 12 (?), E. 2, 33, 34, 47.

[2] See Diary, 15 Dec. 1720, item 4, and footnote for identifications.

[3] Harl. Ch. 111. D. 1, 29, 34, G. 15, 19; 112. A. 22, 30, 62, B. 24, C. 32, D. 13, 52, F. 1, 9.

[4] See Biographical Index under Hagley. The following Harl. Charters are endorsed as given by him: 111. D. 42, E. 5, 19, 20, F. 22; 112. A. 17, 58, B. 18, 19, 38 (?), C. 35, D. 22, E. 20.

[5] Harl. Ch. 111. A. 21, 37; B. 46; C. 20, 30, 31, 32, 33, 34.

[6] See Biographical Index. He gave Harl. Ch. 111. E. 30 and 112. A. 37, the latter on 10 Mar. 1718/19.

[7] Of which seven have been found among the Cotton Charters: see footnote to 12 Dec. 1722.

[8] Harl. Ch. 111. A. 1, 39–43, B. 1, 2, 3, 5.

[9] Harl. Ch. 83. A. 15, 16 and possibly 83. A. 13.

[10] Harl. Ch. 83. A. 2, 3, 6, 7.

[11] On the purchase of MSS. from George Paul and his landlady see above, p. xxiv. The Harl. Charters bought of him are 111. A. 16, B. 7, 8, C. 19, 23, 29, 60, D. 4, 16, 22, 24, 45, 57, E. 41–43, 45; 112. A. 3, 52, 63, 64, B. 1, 14, C. 14, 41, 50, 53, D. 56, E. 12, F. 6, 14, 24, G. 29.

[12] These are endorsed by Wanley 17 Aug. 1720—the date under which the receipt of the parcel is entered in the Addenda to the Diary (see p. 197). For identifications of this group of Welbeck deeds see footnote to 27 Aug. 1720. For the bulls see H. I. Bell, 'A List of Original Papal Bulls and Briefs in the Dept. of MSS., British Museum', *E.H.R.* xxxvi (1921), pp. 393–419, 556–83.

[13] See above, p. xli, and generally for the removal of the 'Holles' library there, pp. xl–xlii. An isolated Rufford Abbey bull from Welbeck was sent in 17 Nov. 1725.

[14] See A. G. Watson, art. cit.; we have also to thank Mr. Watson for supplying us with notes about the other Harley Rolls.

Wanley according to the endorsements, bear dates as follows: S. 32, 1722; and T. 17, 1721/2. Y. 20 has the date 1705 and Z. 21 that of 1724.

The rolls are not exclusively account or estate rolls but include pedigrees and one precious item of the Harleian Collection, namely, the Guthlac Roll (Harl. Roll Y. 6), a late 12th-century vellum roll in which, in medallions, the life of St. Guthlac is pictured in eighteen outline drawings in ink with slight tinting.[1] The early history of this is obscure. Our starting-point for its 18th-century history is a record of its having been exhibited by Peter Le Neve at a meeting of the Society of Antiquaries at the Young Divel Tavern in Fleet Street on 23 January 1707/8; it is described in Wanley's minutes of the meeting as: 'An Imperfect Roll wherein were many Historical Drawings relating to the Life of St. Guthlac Abbot of Crowland, and the Endowment of that Monastery, done about the time of Ric. I.'[2] Its next appearance is as an accessory in Thomas Hill's 1711 portrait of Wanley now preserved in the rooms of the Society of Antiquaries; presumably, therefore, it was at that date in the Harleian Collection, since the Greek MS. which Wanley is holding is a Harley MS. and it is unlikely that non-Harleian accessories would have been used in a portrait of one who was already the Harleys' Library-Keeper.[3] Whether Le Neve himself owned it and whether if so it was bought from or given by him to the Library we cannot say.

If most of the material discussed in this Introduction relates to MSS. it is because most of the information about the Library comes to us through Wanley's Diary and letters and Wanley's interests and indeed responsibilities as Librarian were *primarily* related to the manuscripts in the collection. But Harley had a voracious appetite for printed books as the Osborne *Catalogus Bibliothecae Harleianae* of 1743–5 witnesses, with a strong bias towards incunabula and other early printed books (including those printed on vellum). This part of the Library's contents was used by Michael Maittaire for his *Annales Typographici*, the second volume of which, published in 1722, was dedicated to Edward Harley, and Samuel Palmer when preparing his *History of Printing* was invited by Harley to Wimpole to peruse Bagford's papers about printing, &c.[4] The printed portion of the Library, housed at Wimpole and therefore sometimes referred to as 'Bibliotheca Wimpoliana', was already extensive by the autumn of 1717, when it numbered, according to Harley himself, at least 12,000 volumes.[5] This number was steadily increased over the following years, reaching 50,000 by the time of Harley's death in 1741.

References to purchases of early printed books and books printed on vellum are frequent in the pages of the Diary. Large numbers of these came from Italy through Gibson. Under 27 April 1721 the Diary notes that Harley agreed to give £20 to Gibson for sixteen printed books, of which at least seven were incunabula including the 1478 Milan Cicero's De Officiis; on 7th June of the same year[6] Harley bought from the same agent another batch of early printed books, of which four were incunabula (Pliny, Virgil, Caesar, and Aristotle) while in May of the following year he bought from Gibson no less than 18 incunabula[7] with a further five in

[1] The roll was reproduced in facsimile with an introduction by Sir G. F. Warner for the Roxburghe Club in 1928.

[2] Harl. 7055, ff. 1ᵇ–2; Joan Evans, *A History of the Society of Antiquaries*, 1956, p. 37.

[3] The portrait is reproduced in *The Society of Antiquaries of London: Notes on its History and Possessions*, 1951, pl. iii (*b*) and J. Evans, op. cit., pl. iv.

[4] Cf. *HMC Portland Papers*, vi, p. 21.

[5] Edw. Harley to H. W., 10 Sept. 1717 (Welbeck Wanleyana). Only 7,040 volumes, however, appear in Wanley's catalogue of the Wimpole Library in BM Lansdowne MS. 816.

[6] Cf. Diary under 17 June 1721 (for list).   [7] Cf. Diary under 5 May 1722.

September.[1] In December Gibson sold yet others, including a 1495 Venice Plautus and a 1475 Suetonius. From Germany and France, too, came early printed books through Noel. Incunabula came also from other sources; among books purchased of William Akeman on 19 June 1721 was the Sweynheym and Pannartz Jerome's Epistles of 1470, and four incunabula were bought of Stephens on 13 July 1723.

Like other collectors of his time and later Harley had a strong interest in books printed on vellum and several references to them occur in the Diary: under the Noel list of 3 June 1723 thirteen are listed (of which one was Melchior Pfintzing's Tewrdannckh of 1517 and four were incunabula), while others referred to in the Diary are a Rouen Primer of 1503, a Verard Hours of 1504, a copy of the 1460 Clementines, and a 1472 Virgil.

But Harley's interest in printed material was wide-ranging: Wanley secured from Sherard early in 1720 a promise of obtaining for Harley a complete set of the Greek liturgical books printed at Venice 'if such a set can be gotten' and persistent efforts—eventually rewarded—were made to obtain a set of the books printed at Jassy and Bucharest. It is true that the most complete picture of Harley's interest in printed books is obtainable from Osborne's catalogue, a perusal of which throws up into sharp relief certain special interests. He had many annotated or grangerized copies: for example, Strype's own copies (with his notes) of his Lives of Whitgift, Parker, and Grindal (into the last of which had been inserted original letters of Grindal: Osborne, iii, no. 233); Dugdale's copy of Savile's Scriptores of 1596 with Dugdale's own notes (Osborne, iii, no. 1); Sir Simonds D'Ewes's copy of Godwin's Annals of 1611 with D'Ewes's notes and his armorial bookplate; a copy of Bale's *Catalogus Scriptorum* (Basel, 1557) with Bale's own notes which had belonged to Baker, and Davies of Kidwelly's *Rites and Monuments of the Church of Durham*, 1672, interleaved with MS. notes by James Mickleton (Osborne, iv, no. 11729), which had been bought by Harley from Roger Gale (cf. Diary, 18 May and 3 July 1721).

The good condition of the books was regarded as important: Hearne noted in his edition of Robert of Gloucester's *Chronicle* (p. 33) the fineness of Harley's copy of the very rare work, John Rastell's *Pastyme of People* (1529) (STC 20724) (presumably Osborne, iii, no. 253). The early books from the Library were therefore eagerly sought after by later bibliophiles such as James West, Sir Mark Masterman Sykes, Count MacCarthy, Lord Spencer, and Thomas Grenville; the library of the last-named was bequeathed by him to the British Museum at his death in 1846 and several incunabula from Harley's library in this way reached the Museum, among which we may mention especially the 1470 Rome edition of Cicero's Epistles to Atticus (G. 9381) which is still in its Harleian binding and had belonged at one time to a monastic house in Bamberg (probably Osborne, i, no. 5024). A vellum copy of the French version of Pope Pius II's *L'Histoire d'Eurialus et de Lucrèce* printed by Verard at Paris was preserved in the British Museum among the Harleian MSS. until 1867 and still bears the old Harleian MS. press-mark 128. A. 10 (now Printed Books Dept., press-mark C. 22. b. 1), as does also the incunable now press-marked 1 A* 2247, a Gratia Dei of Joannes Baptista printed in 1500, on which is still inscribed in Wanley's hand the Harleian press-mark 63. C. 36 (transferred from the MSS. Department in 1872). The British Museum copy of Pynson's 1506 Sarum Manual (C. 52. g. 2) has an autograph inscription by Harley dated '20 Mar. 1720' and is in a Harleian binding, as is a copy of the 1478 Milan

---

[1] Cf. Diary under 10 Sept. 1722.

Cicero Ad Familiares now in the Cambridge University Library which has the inscription 'Wimpole Sept. 23 1721'.[1] The British Museum copy (C. 11. c. 1) of Raoul Le Fevre's *The Recuyell of the Historyes of Troye*, printed by Caxton at Bruges in 1475 is also a Harleian Library volume and Wanley's efforts to obtain Caxton's second Bruges book of 1475, *The Game and Playe of the Chesse*, from Lord Somers's collection can be followed in the pages of the Diary;[2] Harley was certainly successful in securing a copy (Osborne, iii, no. 4048) and the Library was indeed famous for its collection of Caxtons, no less than six of which reappeared in the Ham House sale of 1938, having been bought by Lord Dysart at the Osborne sale. Edward Harley himself, in a letter to Thomas Hearne, 25 December 1731, wrote: 'I have a great number of books printed by Caxton, and in very good condition, except a very few. I think the number is forty-two.'[3] No Caxton is recorded in Wanley's 1717 catalogue of the Wimpole printed books and they were probably acquired in the late 20's, largely perhaps from the Thomas Rawlinson sales. As a gloss on Harley's remark about the condition of his Caxtons it is worth noting that he owned the only known perfect copy of one Caxton, *The Book of the Noble Histories of King Arthur*, printed in 1485, which was afterwards in the Earl of Jersey's library and subsequently in that of the American collector Robert Hoe. One of the Harley Caxtons had an interesting provenance; this was the copy of *The Book of Divers Ghostly Matters* printed by Caxton at Westminster in 1491 and perhaps Caxton's last printed work, which was lot 41 in the Ham House sale of 30 May 1938; it bore on its title-page in a late seventeenth-century hand the *ex libris* of the English Benedictine nuns of Our Lady of Good Hope in Paris, a community which had received generous support from Queen Henrietta Maria. It would be interesting to know where and when Harley acquired it. The Library was rich too in the works of Caxton's successor, Wynkyn de Worde, and of William Pynson,[4] besides containing such rare examples of English printing as the *Tractatus brevis & utilis de Originali Peccato* of Aegidius Columna, printed at Oxford in 1479,[5] which was Osborne, iii, no. 6674.

The Library was also rich in bibliographical tools, such as catalogues of foreign as well as English libraries and palaeographical works (such as those of Mabillon and Montfaucon).

Fine illustrated books also claimed Harley's attention, such as the *Hortus Eystettensis* published at Basel in 1613 (Osborne, v, no. 1771), to which reference is made by Wanley in the Diary under 1 September 1724, and Maria Sibylla Merian's work on the Surinam plants and insects published at Amsterdam in 1719—of which Harley acquired a copy for £3 in 1720 according to the Diary (under 16 January 1719/20). Books on numismatics were sought after, naturally in view of Harley's interest in coins, and occasional references to these too are made in the Diary; Sherard, for example, on 20 May 1723 was asked to search in Holland for a copy of Lastanosa's book on Spanish coins. Books on antiquities were well represented; where is the copy of Webb's *Antiquities of Stone-henge* of 1655 with manuscript notes by Philip, Earl of Pembroke, which was Osborne, v, no. 1714? Several

---

[1] J. C. T. Oates, *Cat. of XV Century Books in Cambridge Univ. Lib.*, Cambridge, 1954, no. 2265.7.
[2] See Biographical Index under Somers.
[3] T. F. Dibdin, *The Bibliographical Decameron*, iii, 1817, p. 299.
[4] A copy of Lady Margaret Beaufort's translation of Jacobus de Gruytrode's *The Mirroure of Golde*, printed by William Pynson on vellum about 1505, from the Harleian Library and in a Harleian binding was the subject of a special brochure issued by Bernard Quaritch Ltd. in 1958.
[5] See E. G. Duff, *Fifteenth Century English Books*, 1917, no. 3.

books from Wanley's own collection passed into the Library and of these a few can still be traced; his interleaved copy of Gibson's *Chronicon Saxonicum* of 1692 with Wanley's own collations is now BM Add. 44879 (Osborne, iii, no. 4096) and his annotated copy of the first edition (1695) of Tanner's *Notitia Monastica* is now BM Add. 47842 (Osborne, iv, no. 11924). In the search for printed books of exceptional interest Harley was ably assisted by Wanley, whose own knowledge was extensive and who had early made a collection of English Bibles, a subject on which he was consulted for instance by Charlett;[1] he had also written a paper on the early history of printing,[2] an interest that may have been fostered by his friendship with Bagford.

Other interests well represented were editions of classical authors, history, English and foreign biography, heraldry and genealogy, and works of theological and political controversy,[3] of the last of which Harley formed an enormous collection of tracts and pamphlets.[4]

Like many other bibliophiles of his day Harley was interested in collecting also antiquities and coins and medals; the latter were regarded by John Evelyn as a 'necessary adjunct' to a Library,[5] being as it were an extension of the portraits which were also deemed to be essential for a library of any pretensions.

As early as 18 December 1715 Harley had written to Wanley, 'you know that I am collecting coins, medals, &c. that relate to England, Scotland, & Ireland', and it was one of Wanley's duties as Librarian to feed this interest. There are many instances in the Diary of the way in which Wanley measured up to this responsibility; sometimes the acquisitions involved negotiations, as in the case of Charles Maddison's collection acquired through his executor Sanderson; John Kemp's; Arthur Charlett's (after his death) through Barret the goldsmith; and John Covel's, which came, after his decease, into the sale-room with his library on 4 March 1723/4 and which (see above, p. xxxvi) Wanley had catalogued some nine years earlier.[6] There were several competitors in this field—the Duke of Devonshire, Archbishop Wake, and notably, of course, the Earl of Pembroke, and some agents, such as Sherard, were supplying all of these.[7]

Wanley spared no efforts to see that Harley's collection should be as complete as possible; he noted, for example, in the Diary under 15 July 1724, that the set of King George's silver coins and medals was incomplete and took a list to Barret to fill in the gaps. The larger collections whether by gift or purchase involved listing and cataloguing, as in the case of the substantial block that Harley sent in from Anderson in 1724 (16 July). The collection was sufficiently notable to draw the attention of numismatists such as Genebrier, who came with Sherard to see the Roman gold coins and especially those of Carausius (cf. Diary, 24 July and 31 July 1724). And when the Society of Antiquaries projected a history of all coins relating to Great Britain from the earliest times, James Hill undertook to get a description of Harley's Saxon coins.[8] 'Finds' resulted also in individual additions,

[1] Charlett to H. W., 24 Jan. 1715/16 (Harl. 3778, f. 33).　　　　[2] See above, p. xviii, n. 2.
[3] Some of the works in this last field derived from Robert Harley's collection and represent his interests: a copy of [A. Gavin's] *The Frauds of the Romish Monks and Priests*, 1691, appeared in the Castle Howard sale at Hodgson's in 1944 (20 July, lot 249) bearing his facsimile signature gilt washed and his armorial bookplate.
[4] From these Osborne was to publish the selection entitled *The Harleian Miscellany*, 1745, in 8 volumes under the editorship of William Oldys.
[5] See Evelyn to Pepys, 1689 (printed in Evelyn's *Memoirs*, ed. Bray, 1827 ed., vol. iv).
[6] Probably 1715; catalogue in BM Add. 22911, ff. 265–80. Wanley valued the whole at £45. 5s. 0d.
[7] Cf. Diary, 19 Jan. 1720/1, item 9.　　　　[8] Soc. of Antiquaries Minute Book, 3 Jan. 1722.

such as two presented by John Reissen, both dug up at Bath, a brass coin of Nero (25 May 1725) and a silver coin of Gallienus (26 November 1724); coins found at Kingsland in Herefordshire were presented by Thomas Harley (20 August 1720) and others found at Colchester were included in a batch of antiquities left with Wanley by Mr. Great, apothecary of that town (16 November 1720). Nor did Wanley's knowledge in this field fail him; in 1720 (16 August) some battered Roman coins were offered for sale which he rejected 'believing some sharper to make them [his] first Essay'. To house part of his collection Harley acquired in 1720 (26 May) from Sir Andrew Fountaine a coin cabinet which had belonged to the great French Surintendant des Finances, Nicholas Foucquet (1615–80); this may be the cabinet that we hear of in 1725 as being in the 'Great Withdrawing Room' (presumably at Dover Street). After Harley's death the sale of the coins was sufficiently large to occupy six days (18–23 March 1741/2) at Cock's rooms in the Great Piazza, Covent Garden, and to merit a Preface to the Catalogue from George North, the antiquary. This sale included also medals, to which frequent allusions are likewise made in the Diary, one of the most famous being the marriage medal of Mary, Queen of Scots, and Lord Darnley of 1565, which Anderson the Scots antiquary claimed that 'he could never see before, neither in Scotland or elsewhere' (cf. Diary, 2 May 1724/5).[1] References occur also to Thomas Simon's death medal of Oliver Cromwell (1658), the medal commemorating the coronation of Charles II at Scone (1651), and others. Closely related were the gems, the most notable contemporary engraver of which was Charles Christian Reissen and many references occur to examples of his work executed for Harley. He was also consulted on one occasion (23 April 1725) by Wanley as to a seal which 'was pretended to be antique' and proved to be modern. Wanley's interest in seals was of long standing, for Robert Harley had been interested in these and his collection had been the subject of a report by Wanley as far back as 1708.[2] One matrix acquired by Wanley and noted as a great rarity was that of the seal of Dunfermline Abbey, which was given him by his nephew (16 February 1725/6). Yet an offer of 'dies' of about thirty medals of foreign princes was rejected by Wanley as being 'out of my Lords way of buying' (18 June 1722). Some ancient gems were acquired, as the 'Egyptian Scarabæus of Jasper, with Hieroglyphics engraven on the bottom' brought in by Hay (8 February 1720/1, item 3), and a reference to this Egyptian scarab is sufficient to remind us that in his interest in antiquities Harley included those from Egypt, an interest rare at this time. This led him to acquire, through Sherard, the Egyptian antiquities brought together at Cairo by Consul Farringdon (9 and 13 February 1721/2). The Egyptian antiquities were sufficiently noteworthy for people to come to see them, as Dr. Woodward did (27 February 1723/4), and Egyptian items appeared with the Greek, Roman, and Etruscan antiquities offered by Schroeder, which caused so much trouble in 1724 and 1725. But Harley's interest in antiquities was all embracing as can be seen from such individual items as a gold ring inscribed with runes found at Newbury and given to Harley by Lord Bathurst (16 February 1720/1, item 2), a Roman 'Locust of Brass studded with Silver' from Andrew Hay (16 March 1722/3), a Roman inkpot which Hay had concealed from Harley and which Wanley seized for him (4 May 1724),

[1] A drawing of Harley's specimen, made by Vertue, is now preserved in the Society of Antiquaries, Harley Collection of Prints (subsequently it was engraved by Vertue; for details see footnote to 13 May 1725).
[2] 31 Oct. 1708: see BM Lansdowne 841, ff. 72ᵇ, 73.

a Roman key of brass found in digging the foundations for a house at the west end of the Oxford Chapel in Vere St. (9 March 1724/5), cannon balls from Kenilworth Castle promised by Mr. White of Warwick (23 January 1720/1), a copper seal of the arms of Geoffrey FitzPiers from the same place, given by Wanley's nephew, George Browne (7 May 1726), 'two old keys' from Woodstock (7 May 1726), the 'old Gylyngham silver-Spoon' bought of Warner the goldsmith, besides—to come to more important items—two from the Arundel collection sold at Stafford House, an ivory cup and cover (11 May 1720), and the famous 'Queen Bertha's Comb' (4 May 1720); not to omit, as a last example, the Turkish silver inkhorn belonging to the Grand Vizier's secretary captured at the Battle of Belgrade (see 14 February 1721/2). Nor must we overlook the antique lamp from the Colbert Collection figured by Montfaucon and given to Harley by Matthew Prior, of which Harley had engravings prepared by Vertue from drawings by Grisoni, which he was in the habit of distributing to friends or specially favoured visitors to the Library; several references occur in the Diary to these prints of 'my Lord's Lamp'. The Grisoni drawings are preserved in the eight volumes of the Harley collection of prints in the Library of the Society of Antiquaries, which contain drawings of many of the antiquities referred to above (Queen Bertha's comb, the Roman key from Vere St., the Dunfermline Abbey seal matrix, &c.) in addition to others, among which may be singled out as of special note a drawing dated 1735 of the 'episcopal crosier of Brass Gilt with gold found some years ago hid & cramm'd in the Roof of an old House lately belonging to Sr Harry Pickering of Whaddon near Wimpole in Cambridgeshire', then belonging to Harley. But perhaps a sharper impression of Harley's magpie propensity is best given (apart from an examination of the sale catalogue of the collection in March 1742) by the contents of two boxes (to be sent down to Wimpole) listed by Wanley under 25 November 1721: namely, a Roman brick from Colchester, two stones with runic inscriptions, a stone with the Arms of Courtney 'found by Mr. Auditor Harley in the Church of —— in Northamptonshire, in an Heap of Rubbish', an old shirt of mail, the laced band of K. Charles I, the Shash [*sic*] of Archbishop Laud, and four little parcels of Casts from Sanderson and Sir Simonds D'Ewes. Nor must we overlook the 'Bird Ibis, being Embalmed by the old Egyptians', brought in 13 May 1721, or the 'piece of Amber including some water' which Sherard gave (16 March 1724/5). Such heterogeneous collecting ranks Harley with his contemporary, Sir Hans Sloane,[1] or later with Horace Walpole (whose 'curiosities' included Wolsey's red hat, the pipe which Van Tromp smoked during his last sea fight, the spurs King William struck into the flanks of Sorrel at the Battle of the Boyne, Turkish pipes, scimitars, and Chinese baskets);[2] it is but the end of a long tradition of collecting that goes back in England through the Museum of the Tradescants founded at Lambeth in 1629[3] and that of William Charlton seen by Evelyn in 1686, to the 'Wunderkammer' of the German princes of the Renaissance.[4] This side of Harley's character was to be repeated in his daughter, and heiress, Lady Margaret Harley, later Duchess of Portland, who formed at Bulstrode[5] a great Museum of natural and other curiosities (which was

[1] On Sloane's collections see G. R. de Beer, *Sir Hans Sloane and the British Museum*, 1953, pp. 108–13.

[2] See W. S. Lewis, *Horace Walpole*, 1961, p. 127. Walpole was outbid for Oliver Cromwell's nightcap.

[3] On the Tradescants see Mea Allan, *The Tradescants: Their Plants, Gardens and Museum, 1570–1662*, 1964.

[4] On the 'Wunderkammer' see F. H. Taylor, *The Taste of Angels*, 1948, Book iii.

[5] Bulstrode Park, near Gerrard's Cross, Bucks., was the chief seat of the Portland family from 1706 to 1810; in the latter year it was sold to the Duke of Somerset who pulled down the old house (see *V.C.H. Bucks.*, iii, 1925, p. 280).

to include the Barbarini (or Portland) Vase acquired for the Duchess from Sir William Hamilton) which was sold in a thirty-eight day sale in 1786.[1] This propensity in Harley himself may have been a reason for Woodward's saying that he would rather the natural curiosities which he had collected and bequeathed to the public should be housed in Harley's proposed new Library in Cavendish Square than 'in any other place' (17 May 1723), and to offer Harley his antiquities found in or near London, a promise not fulfilled. Nevertheless, Harley did secure some antiquities of more note, even if he lost the statues from the Valletta collection which went to the Earl of Pembroke and the Sigean boustrophedon inscription which he hoped to obtain; thus he acquired from what was probably the most important English collection dispersed in the period of the Diary, that of John Kemp in March 1721 (which had been the subject of a monograph by Robert Ainsworth in the preceding year), several inscriptions (cf. 2 May 1721), and from the Near East in 1725 from Bernard Mould[2] a fine bronze head of a man found at Thyatira (Ak Hissar, east of Smyrna) and from Sherard 'antique marbles' including the famous Hermogenes inscription.

The few references in the Diary to pictures convey no adequate idea of Harley's interest in acquiring paintings, but under 19 November 1725 Wanley lets slip the remark, with reference to the offer of two Spagnoletto paintings, that Harley 'wants now as much Room for his Pictures as he doth for his Books'. In fact, so far as the Diary is concerned, in addition to the two Spagnoletto paintings, only three others are specifically referred to, namely, 'Sacrifice to Ceres' by Rubens (25 October 1722), 'Our Saviors Head' by 'Carlo Dolce's master' (12 January 1724/5), and a 'Virgin and Child' by an unnamed artist (23 March 1724/5), besides two unidentified pictures acquired with books and antiquities from John Warburton on 16 July 1720.[3] But there is ample justification for Wanley's statement, since Edward Harley had been buying pictures for many years.[4] In addition to thirteen pictures bought at some unspecified date before 1724 from 'Mr. Gore', nineteen were purchased from Andrew Hay as early as February 1716, on the second of which month they were sent to Wimpole by James Gibbs the architect; and in the same year a further sixteen came from the same vendor. In 1719 sixteen more were bought from George Hay. In addition to a bequest of six paintings from Matthew Prior, who died at Wimpole 18 September 1721, Prior by his will, after specifying that his effects should be sold, stipulated that Harley should have the preference if he wished to purchase any of the pictures; as a result Harley acquired no less than 104 at the appraiser's valuation. In addition to paintings of the Flemish and Italian schools, there were included in this purchase Kneller's portrait of Dryden and Jervas's of Pope, with others of the English school. Further paintings were acquired from Andrew Hay in 1723 and 1724[5] (the former with some statuary at a cost of £50) and several were bought at Andrew Hay's sale at Cock's New Auction Room

[1] See the frontispiece to the sale-cat. of the Portland Museum, reproduced in W. Mankowitz, *The Portland Vase and the Wedgwood Copies*, 1952, pl. xxiv; D. E. L. Haynes, *The Portland Vase*, 1964, pl. xv; and from Horace Walpole's copy in W. S. Lewis, *The Duchess of Portland's Museum*, New York, Grolier Club, 1936.

[2] For the contents of a box of antiquities from Mould see also 8 Oct. 1722, item 13.

[3] Under 17 Jan. 1721/2 a reference is made to two Dutch paintings on copper being brought in by 'Vander-Meer', a landscape painter.

[4] See R. W. Goulding and C. K. Adams, *Catalogue of the Pictures belonging to His Grace the Duke of Portland*, Cambridge, 1936.

[5] And again on 21 Jan. 1724/5 Wanley records in the Diary that he went by Harley's order to see a number of pictures at Andrew Hay's.

in Poland St. on 19 February 1725/6.[1] There were, in addition, at several times individual purchases; for example, on 30 September 1726 Harley bought from James Sykes of Lincoln's Inn Fields for 5 guineas a picture of Chaucer,[2] and the cleaner he employed for his pictures, Henry Turner Broome of Westminster, supplied him in 1730 with a Holbein and offered him a Van de Velde, 'the Brower and the Philip Woverman'.[3] Most of the pictures that Harley brought together (309) were sold after his death by Cock at his 'house in the Great Piazza Covent Garden' in March of 1742, and from the contents of the catalogue of this sale we gain perhaps the clearest view of what Harley's collection consisted of, provided we bear in mind the fact that many items were retained by his widow; Vertue, who was employed to make a complete catalogue of the pictures, notes (BM Add. 23093, f. 26)[4] that 'All the family pictures. of the Cavendishes, Holles, Pierponts, Harleys, —etc. Noblemen Ladys and Gentlemen any wayes related. My Lady reserved for her own use not to be sold'.[5] Of people referred to in the Diary or known to be in Harley's circle of friends, we may note that his collection had contained portraits of Matthew Prior, Charles Bridgeman, the gardener, who laid out the Wimpole gardens (by Dahl), Humfrey Wanley (a portrait by Hill and a drawing), Thomas Baker of St. John's, Cambridge, Dr. Freind, George Harbin, James Gibbs, the architect, John Wootton, the painter, Andrew Hay, Sir John Thornhill, Alexander Pope (by Richardson), Robert Sanderson, Dean Swift (by Jervas), Dr. George Hickes, Dr. John Covel, John Bagford (by Hugh Howard), John Morley (by Kneller), Dr. Stratford, Salmon Negri, Dr. Tudway, and many others. Of antiquaries and poets whose portraits might be considered appropriate to a library, the collection contained those of Sir Robert Cotton (by Cornelius Johnson), Edmund Spenser, Shakespeare, Petrarch, John Selden, Samuel Butler (the author of 'Hudibras'), Abraham Cowley, William Camden, Sir Walter Raleigh (by Cornelius Johnson), Sir John Denham, Pepys, Chaucer ('in Kit-cat size'), Dryden (by Kneller), and so on. Of the famous masters the collection included paintings alleged to be by Veronese, Holbein, Van Dyck, Lely, Carlo Dolci, Poussin, Rembrandt, and Claude Lorraine. One painting included in the sale (fifth day's sale, item 3), 'A small Head of Renatus des Cartes, 1640', is probably the 'small picture' referred to in the Diary (under 14 April 1721) as being presented by James Hill, the Herefordshire antiquary. This reference to a small picture reminds us that nothing has been said of Harley's great collection of miniatures, the nucleus being portraits of members and connexions of the families of Cavendish and Holles, which were inherited by Lady Henrietta Harley. To this, Harley made considerable additions (for example, at the sale of the collection of L. Cross, the limner, 5 December 1722) and his interest in them is shown by the fact that many still retain on their backs the numbers and labels that he wrote in part or in whole.[6] In the Diary reference is made under 15 January 1723/4 to Sherard offering for 20 guineas a miniature of Charles II by Cooper, which was rejected (20 February 1723/4) because Harley had a finer, the finer example presumably being that still at Welbeck recorded by

[1] Title-page of this sale-cat. is reproduced as a frontispiece to W. T. Whiteley's *Artists and their Friends, 1700–1799*, 1928, i. The catalogue with prices and names of buyers is printed in *HMC Portland Papers*, vi, pp. 11–14. (Harley's name does not appear.)

[2] 'Harley Letters and Papers, 1725–40', f. 70.

[3] 'Harley Letters and Papers, 1725–40', letter of 8 Sept. 1730.

[4] Vertue's *Note Books*, vi (Walpole Soc., xxx (1955), p. 119.

[5] A catalogue of the *Countess's* pictures was compiled in 1747 on her instructions: it comprised 399 pictures (including 220 portraits).

[6] See R. W. Goulding, *The Welbeck Abbey Miniatures . . . a catalogue raisonné*, 1916.

Goulding, now no. 56; and another Cooper miniature, that of the Duchess of Cleveland, was offered 17 January 1722/3 by Du Mont, and also rejected.

This activity of Harley's was, however, peripheral to the Library proper and one with which Wanley had comparatively little to do, as the few references in the Diary quoted above show. Wanley's chief duties as Library-Keeper, in addition to those already described, and which are amply illustrated by the Diary, were the following.

(i) First, there was the preliminary examination and listing of MSS. and books offered, a task which frequently occupied Wanley for several days together; two days, 18 and 19 August 1720, were spent in taking a 'Short List' of Séguier's MSS. and 4 and 5 July of the same year in inspecting Mickleton's MSS., &c. Usually the lists are preserved in the Diary itself (e.g. the Paynell of Belaugh MSS. under 18 November 1721, Warburton's MSS. under 16 July 1720, the Gibson MSS. and printed books under 5 May and 10 September 1722, and the great Noel parcel under 3 June 1723), but occasionally they were catalogued in a loose paper kept among the Library papers (e.g. Wanley records under 16 March 1714/15 that he had taken a short list of Bourscough's MSS. (acquired later, 17 May 1715) and this list is in fact still preserved among the Welbeck Wanleyana Miscellanea), but of these catalogues normally very few remain.[1]

This preliminary work sometimes involved visits to the Custom House, as on one occasion (20 February 1719/20) when Wanley went there with Noel to see books inspected and cleared, made a selection for Harley, listed those selected, made a bargain with Noel, saw them packed up and supervised their removal to Dover Street; this must have represented a very full day's work. At other times he went to the booksellers' warehouses; on 21 December 1720, when he was in the City, he went to Bateman's and to Bowyer's warehouses. On 5 October 1722 he went with Gibson to Mr. Smith in Cornhill, brother of Consul Smith of Venice, and inspected 101 MSS. lately arrived, 'compared them with the Printed Catalogue:[2] and made proper Observations upon the Same, especially touching their Age, Hands, & Value, according to the present State of the Market'. In January 1720/1 (13 January) he was sent by Harley to Paul's Coffee House to look at the late Earl of Stamford's books and the listing of those kept out of the sale by the Countess occupied Wanley several days—fruitlessly as it turned out, since they were not bought by Harley. On another occasion he went to look at the Study of Samuel Hawes, Lord Winchilsea's chaplain, and bought on the spot three MSS. and an old English Primer printed on vellum. The arrival of parcels from abroad for Gibson and Noel proved in this way a heavy burden. The material had also to be reported on to Harley[3] with the prices fixed, about which very occasionally Wanley and the dealer or bookseller could not come to an agreement and the matter had to be remitted to Harley.[4] The examination of the booksellers' catalogues, too, must have been a time-consuming job, involving as it did the making of extracts for Harley's information;[5] conversely, he had also to check books marked by Harley in catalogues (as he did on 2 March 1723/4 at Charles Davis's, a job which occupied him in 'almost 2 hours Attendance').

---

[1] e.g. the list of Hay's MSS. is missing (cf. Diary, 13 July 1723, item 9).
[2] This printed catalogue had been given to Wanley by Harley 10 Sept. 1722. It appears to be unknown to the bibliographers of Consul Smith's catalogues.
[3] See, e.g. Diary under 21 Dec. 1722, item 4.
[4] See, e.g. Diary under 15 Nov. 1722, item 14.
[5] Cf. Diary, 7 Feb. 1723/4.

(ii) The greater part of the material acquired for the Library was received, it must be remembered, unbound, being conveyed in sacks[1] or packing cases. One of the first necessities was therefore, after noting the date of acquisition on the items,[2] to get them bound; in one instance the date was deliberately not inserted in eight MSS. received from Gibson on 7 November 1721 which were sent to the binder's the same day, the date being omitted 'on their first Pages, lest any inquisitive person coming in, should therby perceive how lately they were bought'. As a safeguard Wanley kept a delivery-list—what he called on one occasion (Diary, 21 May 1723) a 'check-note'. Title-labels also had to be written for the binder for each volume: a few of these survive today still loose in the volumes or partly bound in.[3] Occasionally the dates written by Wanley on the first pages have been lost, presumably through cropping by the binders,[4] and sometimes titles were mislaid.[5] When we consider the number of books sometimes sent to the binders at one time —20 to Chapman on 18 January 1720/1, 23 to Elliot on 24 January 1720/1—we can appreciate the amount of work involved in preparing them against binding.

Generally the binding was done in the binders' own workshops, but very occasionally on the Library premises:[6] the rebinding of the Codex Aureus by Elliot was begun by him on 27 June 1721 in the Library but later, 'having clothed the CODEX AUREUS in my Lords Marocco-Leather' (13 July 1721), he took it to his house to work on it 'with his Best Tools'. A proposal was discussed at one time of binding being carried on at Wimpole but the plan was not pursued.[7] Most of the books were bound in calf but for the more special ones morocco was used; the morocco skins required were obtained by Harley from Wanley's stepson-in-law, John Beaver, through Gibraltar, and were issued to the two binders as required.[8] Almost the whole of the binding work recorded in the Diary was carried out by Thomas Elliot and Christopher Chapman,[9] the former being responsible for the finer work, including the 'Harleian style' bindings. On return from the binders the books were carefully examined by Wanley and there are frequent complaints in the Diary about the way in which the work had been carried out: leaves transposed or loose, errors in titling,[10] inferior quality of leather and workmanship, omission of middle pieces or the use of ones too small in size.[11] As a result, books had frequently to be returned and sharp letters written.[12] On the other hand, technical

---

[1] Reference to 'sacks' is made in the Diary (e.g.) under 1 Aug. and 27 Dec. 1722 and 1 June 1723.

[2] Wanley sometimes put in the manuscript in the lower right-hand corner of the first page of the text or a flyleaf a number to correspond with that in the list under the date of acquisition in the Diary: e.g. in the list under 13 Aug. 1724 Harl. 3774 is no. 41 in the list and that number is neatly written in the lower right-hand corner of f. 2.

[3] e.g. in Harl. 2480, between ff. 1 and 2; in Harl. 3744, attached to f. 1 (reads thus, CANONIS/AVICENNÆ/ LIBRI/V, 11, & IV,/Calf./); in Harl. 2502 (VIRGILIUS./Calf.).

[4] See Diary, 29 Oct. 1722, item 2.

[5] By Elliot, e.g.; see Diary 19 and 21 Sept. 1722.

[6] e.g. Diary, 6 Apr. 1723 when Elliot did binding in the Closet: cf. also 6 and 7 June 1722.

[7] The proposal was made to Chapman 29 Oct. 1720 (Chapman's answer was received 1 Nov. 1720) and again 1 Dec. 1724; and to Elliot also 1 Dec. 1720 (cf. Diary also under 2 and 3 Dec. 1724).

[8] Sparingly (see Diary, 15 Oct. 1722, for instance).

[9] See Biographical Index: and also J. B. Oldham, *Shrewsbury School Bindings*, 1943, pp. 112–16 and pl. xxxiii for reproduction of a 'Harleian Binding'.

[10] What happened when Wanley's vigilant eye was not present to check bindings on return from the binders is illustrated by the slip in the original title label on the spine of Harl. 5005, which reads 'OPERA SANCTI APRIANI'—the last a mistake for CYPRIANI; this MS. was acquired 22 June 1726 and therefore came back from binding after Wanley's death.

[11] See Diary, 9 Apr. 1720, item 14; 8 June 1720, item 10; 14 Mar. 1721/2, item 5; 4 Mar. 1721/2 and 18 and 21 June 1722; 29 Sept. and 29 Oct. 1722; 12 Nov. 1722.

[12] On one occasion Harley himself made Elliot take back two books to amend their lettering (Diary, 9 July 1723).

problems occasionally arose and had to be discussed, especially with the Nevers Missal (Harl. 2991, 2992), 'so much of it is utterly perished, & a great part of what remains is so rotten that he think's he can save but little', reported of Elliot (Diary 3 November 1724) but Wanley encouraged him to do all he could; again on 9 January 1722/3 (item 10) Wanley had a long discussion with Elliot as to the 'best way of getting out the Cockles risen in my Lords Virgil, & Tullies Epistles, both Printed upon Vellum' (cf. Diary, 18 March 1722/3) and for his work on Isidore's 'Etymologiae' (probably Harl. 2686) Elliot is praised (Diary, 17 October 1724), it being 'with great labour repaired, & finely bound'.

(iii) In addition to the placing, cataloguing, binding, and repair of the books, Wanley was also responsible for the presses needed to house them in the Library. These were presumably unglazed presses with doors (cf. Diary, 23 March 1722/3). They appear to have required a good deal of attention; the presses being much swollen in January 1723/4 with 'this moist weather' Hazert the joiner had to ease all the doors, and in April of the preceding year 'a Door from each Box of the 3 Presses' had had to be removed for the same purpose.[1] In 1722, 1724, and 1725 new presses were ordered and delivered. The locks also gave trouble. Under 8 July 1721 (item 18) we learn of 'Mr. Abbot' reporting that he would come 'to Varnish & number some of the Presses'. (The press-marking was on the simple system of an arabic number for the press, capital letter of the alphabet for the shelf, followed by an arabic numeral for the book's place on the shelf: the printed books—if Wanley's catalogues of the printed books at Wimpole may be taken as evidence—had the number of the press in Roman numerals.) There are two references in the Diary to the presses being used as models for other libraries: on 2 July 1722 Humfrey Skelton the furniture maker came from Mr. Myddelton of Chirk Castle to inquire about 'the Manner of Disposition' of the presses as Myddelton proposed to build himself a library, and on 1 April 1723 Roberts the joiner came to look at the presses, as he was to make some for Lord Oxford (Robert Harley).[2]

(iv) In addition, Wanley's presence in the Library was required to cope with the flow of visitors. These fell roughly into four classes: (*a*) scholars desiring to consult or work on MSS. in furtherance of researches or in preparation for books of their own; (*b*) professional copyists or transcribers working for others; (*c*) callers who had some specific inquiry to make; and (*d*) what we may call casual visitors—distinguished or otherwise—who came to satisfy their curiosity and took up a great deal of Wanley's time in being entertained and shown the treasures of the Library. Among the first, (*a*), were Michael Maittaire, who looked over early printed books for his *Annales Typographici* (the second volume of which was dedicated to Edward Harley); William Stukeley, who was interested in ancient English dress; Richard Fiddes, who examined material for his Life of Wolsey; James Hill, who was searching for material on the antiquities of Herefordshire; Dr. John Freind, who called on several occasions in 1725 to look at medical MSS. in preparation for his *History of Physick*, and Richard Bentley, who inspected the Codex Aureus and other MSS. of the Gospels. Three professional copyists worked in the Library: William Rooke (Sanderson's clerk) for Robert Sanderson of the Rolls Office, William Slyford for John Bridges, the Northamptonshire historian, and a 'Mr. Proby' for Roger Gale, the antiquary. Among (*c*), the callers who had some specific inquiry to make, we may notice Francis Hutchinson, the Minister at Bury,

---

[1] Cf. Diary, 23 Apr. 1723.
[2] Wanley was also responsible for the library building as we can see from the Diary under 7 Dec. 1725.

who came (23 June 1720) to consult Bury cartularies in connexion with a local dispute about 'small Tithes' at Bury; and Dr. Antonio Cocchi, 'an Italian Physician, Learned & Curious', was brought to the Library 12 May 1725 and inquired after unprinted chronicles or annals of Italian affairs on behalf of Muratori, the famous Italian historian. By far the largest class was (*d*), the casual visitors, who came to see the Library as one of the sights of London, some introduced by members of the family—Lady Margaret Harley brought two of her cousins to see some fine books in 1721 and came again on her own account three times in 1723 to see some illuminated books, while two occasions are recorded when Edward Harley himself brought visitors to the Library; other relations of the family were 'young Mr. Vane my Lord's cousin' and Lord Foley. Such visits were frequently of some length: Count Simoneta of Milan was brought in by Gibson and was shown printed books and MSS. for above two hours, a visit from the Earl of Winchilsea lasted four hours, and the Library-Keeper of the Landgrave of Hesse-Darmstadt, Heinrich Gerdes, 'proving to be a Young Gentleman of Good Nature', was shown (25 June 1722) 'Rarities' for above three hours. Other visitors were Sir John Thornhill, Dr. John Woodward, Dr. Conyers Middleton, Sir Hans Sloane, Joseph Bowles (Bodley's Librarian), John Anstis, and Alexander Pope, to mention only a few. Nearly all were gratified by what they saw: one, Mr. Frietsch of Leipzig (introduced by Andrew Hay), on leaving, protested that 'he had not seen the like in any Library, hitherto, either in Germany, Italy or France': Bodley's Librarian was likewise astonished. One visitor, Nathaniel Tranter, Fellow of Corpus Christi College, Oxford, arrived obviously determined not to be impressed 'hugely extolling the MSS. kept in that College-Library, (all which I have formerly seen)' [says Wanley, adding] 'I soon made him throw-down the Cudgell, & yield the Precedency to my Lords, in all respects'. Some were not encouraged: for instance, a Mr. Justice, 'a young gentleman of but indifferent character'; and a Frenchman was waited on by Wanley downstairs, which the Frenchman took as 'a piece of Ceremony; but indeed, it was to see him out of the house without stealing something'. He was so unhelpful to Browne Willis that the latter left in great anger,[1] and for Arthur Collins he had no time whatever when Collins wanted Wanley's attendance about some of Cole's MSS. and Harley's pedigree, being summarily dismissed (Wanley records) as 'I was too busy to wait on him now, & gave him little encouragement to trouble himself (unasked) about my Lords Family'.[2]

(v) In addition, Wanley had to deal with requests for the loan of books from the Library, which were usually granted only with Harley's express permission (when Wanley was careful to get the borrower's 'note' or 'Cautionary Note' (cf. Diary, 21 June 1722)), though he occasionally acted on his own initiative, where the borrower (e.g. George Harbin) was known to be in Harley's favour, or had done Harley some service (e.g. John Beaver: cf. Diary, 13 March 1721/2, item 3).

Gratuities he always refused. His personal relations with scholars, other collectors (Sir Hans Sloane and Coke of Norfolk), booksellers (Noel, Browne, &c.) and dealers (Andrew and George Hay, and Gibson) were obviously very good, and he showed great skill in negotiation (as for instance in the Covel transactions), a skill to which Harley himself on several occasions in the course of the correspondence between himself and Wanley pays tribute. This skill and a happy gift of expression were notably employed in drafting the commissions which Wanley prepared as occasion demanded—for Andrew Hay going to Italy in 1720, for Sherard about to

[1] Diary, 13 Dec. 1725.   [2] Diary, 12 Feb. 1724/5.

go to France in 1721, for Samuel Palmer in 1720, for Schumacher on his return to Moscow in 1722. His palaeographical expertise was occasionally in demand for other than strictly Library business: he was consulted on two occasions by William Denison, Fellow of University College, Oxford, and the Duke of Beaufort's chaplain, first in 1721 as to the authenticity of two receipts[1] and secondly in 1723 about a deed of Henry III and its date (that was to be produced to the Attorney-General).[2] He was very considerably assisted by a good visual memory; he recognized in a MS. offered by Anthony Holbrook the handwriting of Ralph Starkey (the 17th-century antiquary whose collections had been acquired by Sir Simonds D'Ewes)[3] and in the Suidas MS. obtained for the Harleian Library from Durham he rightly identified the handwriting as that of the 'Leicester Codex' (though he misnamed the scribe).[4] This memory, a rare gift, enabled him also to recognize and reject MSS. that had sometimes been previously submitted to him,[5] one (a Koran MS.) as long as eight or nine years before.[6] All sorts of questions came to him for answer: once he was asked—by Erasmus Lewis—about the 'quantity of land comprehended in a Welsh Acre'.[7]

The family justifiably placed implicit trust in him. He held the keys of Harley's evidence room at Dover St. and at the time of Robert Harley's trial in 1717 Edward Harley wrote to him then at Wimpole: 'It is thought for my Lord Oxford's service that you should be in town at this time. . . . I send this messenger on purpose that you may be here in town on Wednesday [i.e. 19 June: the trial was due to begin on 24 June] at night; if you have any papers in wch you made collections out of the Cotton or Har Libraries, I desire that you would bring them up with you . . . pray before you come away give the necessary directions for the security of the House, Books, &c. to Cossens & Tribell.'[8]

Of course he was given also less responsible commissions by Harley, such as obtaining some of the best sealing wax and three or four pounds of the best tobacco[9] and ordering from Mr. Alberto of the Genoa Arms two hogsheads of Oporto wine.[10]

And most of this had to be accomplished in the period of his Library hours, which were from 8.0 to 11.0 in the morning and from 1.0 to 3.0 or 4.0 in the afternoon (according to the time of year), though we can have no doubt—and there is evidence to support the contention—that he gave up much of the evenings to Library business, or to offering hospitality to those who might be of use in this, as when (19 July 1722) he asked Lieve to sup with him in the evening.[11] In addition he was, we may be sure (and as numerous memoranda scattered throughout Welbeck Wanleyana show), reading widely to extend his knowledge in any direction that he thought might be useful to the Library and in meeting and talking with everyone (Sherard, Gibson, Noel, Schumacher, and others) who could keep him informed of what was going on in the library world abroad as well as in England.[12]

---

[1] Diary, 13 July 1721, item 4.   [2] Diary, 21 Oct. 1723.
[3] Diary, 9 Feb. 1725/6.   [4] Diary, 3 June 1723.
[5] See Diary, 28 June 1721, item 6; 1 June 1724.
[6] See Diary, 19 Oct. 1725. Cf. too the incident of the illuminated Psalter offered by Woodman 14 June 1723.   [7] Diary, 20 July 1723.
[8] Edw. Harley to H. W., 17 June 1717 (Welbeck Wanleyana).
[9] Ibid., 23 Aug. 1716 (Welbeck Wanleyana).
[10] Ibid., 15 Sept. 1717 (Welbeck Wanleyana); he was asked by Pope to perform a similar commission (see Pope's letters written to Wanley in 1725 in Harl. 3780, ff. 339, 341; printed in *Gentleman's Magazine*, lxxi, pt. 2 (July–Dec. 1801), p. 1067).
[11] Cf. also his inviting Dr. Woodward 'to eat a bit with me' (Diary, 7 June 1723).
[12] See Diary under 18 Feb. 1722/3, item 1, for Wanley's conversation with Sparke.

There is therefore ample justification for the remark of Thomas Bacon, Member of Parliament for Cambridgeshire, to Edward Harley after Wanley's death: 'You must never expect to find one equal to W[anley].'[1] With Wanley's death and the abrupt ending of the Diary—23 June 1726—a fortnight before, we lose our chief source of information for the history of the Library.

No permanent successor seems to have been appointed,[2] but fairly soon after Wanley's death Randall Minshull appears to have been acting as Library-Keeper; it was at any rate to him that William Oldys wrote on 9 January 1730 offering to the Library his collection of MSS.[3] and it was he who compiled the enormous subject-catalogue of Harley's printed books at Wimpole in twelve large folio volumes (now BM Add. 19746–57), possibly in 1729.[4] For a time William Oldys himself (1696–1761) seems to have been employed as secretary with some library duties, and to have received at any rate late in Harley's life an annual allowance of £200. Oldys, an inaccurate and gossipy writer, was a bibliographer and antiquary; he spent the years 1724 to 1730 in Yorkshire with the Earl of Malton and published a Life of Sir Francis Drake in 1736; from the year of Harley's death he worked as a bookseller's hack but in spite of his ignorance of heraldry was nevertheless appointed Norfolk Herald Extraordinary in April and Norroy King of Arms in May 1755.[5] We can be quite sure that Wanley would have regarded him with contempt; Minshull he had dismissed in the endorsement to a letter of Minshull's addressed to Noel, 2 March 1718/19, as 'the Catalogue-maker'.[6]

In addition, David Casley, who was Bentley's Deputy as Royal Librarian, appears to have been employed on the catalogue of the MSS. from about 1733.[7]

Nevertheless the Library continued to increase by gift and by purchase. The evidence is sometimes internal, sometimes external. Harley only occasionally wrote in the MSS. the date of acquisition, but sometimes he entered a more personal memorandum of some interest; thus, the Register of Kenilworth Priory (Harl. 3650) bears on its flyleaf (f. 1) the following in Harley's autograph:

This Book was given to me by my worthy and Learned friend James West esqʳ Janu. 28. 1736/7. This Gentleman told me this was the only MS. that was saved out of the Fire when his noble collection of MSS was burnt. Janu. 6. 1736/7 his chambers were quite burnt to the ground.[8]

[1] Thomas Bacon to Edward Harley, 22 July 1726 (Welbeck 'Harley Letters and Papers, 1725–40', f. 69: printed *HMC Portland Papers*, vi, p. 16).

[2] Bacon himself recommended in the letter to Harley already quoted Andrew Matte, amanuensis and Library-Keeper of John Bridges; Peter Le Neve recommended, 2 Apr. 1727, Thomas Allen who lived with John Thorpe at Rochester (*HMC Portland Papers*,'vi, p. 18); and Dr. Samuel Knight wrote 5 Aug. 1726 recommending one who appears to have been no less than Tom Martin of Palgrave (*HMC Portland Papers*, vi, p. 17).

[3] See 'Harley Letters and Papers, 1725–1740', ff. 184, 185.

[4] Cf. Harl. 7525, ff. 162–72. Additional evidence that Minshull was regarded as Library-Keeper is supplied by a statement made in the sale-cat. of James West's library in 1773 under lot 1909: 'Minshull's (Librarian to Lord Oxford) Proposals for Printing an Ample Account of Caxton's Books, etc.'

[5] See *A Literary Antiquary: Memoir of William Oldys, Esq.*, 1862; W. H. Godfrey, A. R. Wagner, and H. S. London, *The College of Arms*, pp. 115–16. Cf. *HMC Portland Papers*, vi, Index *sub* Oldys.

[6] Harl. 3780, f. 158.

[7] According to the 'Advertisement' prefixed to the original issue of the 1759 *Catalogue of the Harleian MSS.* the work on the Catalogue was 'laid aside; till about the year 1733; when it was resumed by the late Mr. Casley'. On the work of Casley and others on the *Catalogue* and the history of its publication see below, pp. lxxx–lxxxiii.

[8] This memorandum is reproduced in *The Book Collector*, xi, no. 2 (summer, 1962), pl. B (*a*). According to a note on the same fly-leaf written by West himself, the MS. had been acquired by him from Morgan Graves, the son of the antiquary Richard Graves (1677–1729) of Mickleton, Gloucestershire, 18 Feb. 1731. James West was an intimate friend and subsequently one of the executors of Edward

The most remarkable personal note, however, is that added by Harley on the first leaf of John Norden's 1620 Perambulation of Bromfield and Yale in Denbighshire (Harl. 3696), which was presented 16 February 1735/6 (through William Thomas, Harley's steward) by a Thomas Bowen, an act which drew from Harley the following:

> The present of this book to me from Mr. Bowen is a very uncommon proceeding, and much contrary to the usual way of acting in the world, I mean to remember favors or to show any gratitude to a Family, which it was not any way in their power to further oblige, this I say is much to Mr. Bowens Honour and accordingly by me set down. March 22 1735/6 Oxford and Mortimer.

Of interest too is Harley's memorandum in Harl. 4996 which records how the MS. was found: 'This Book is said to have been found in taking down the West Gate of Whitehall A.D. . . . between the Wainscot and the Wall and was given by Mr. Thomas Robe Sept. 1726.'[1]

Patrick Anderson, the son of James Anderson, the Scots antiquary, sent to Harley from Edinburgh, 11 July 1730, the Cartulary of the Cistercian Abbey of Coldstream (Harl. 6670) and the 'completest old Scots Bible I could meet with' together with two MS. registers of public deeds granted in Scotland; in a covering letter he expressed the hope that he would soon be able to send two other MS. registers which would complete the series to the accession of James VI to the English throne: he had, as he observes, previously given the cartulary of Melrose Abbey (Harl. 3960) and a MS. of Fordun.[2] On 15 July 1726 Henry Grey of Billingbear near Wokingham in Berkshire sent Harley a few letters written by the Duke of Tuscany to Grey's great-uncle Sir Henry Neville, together with the original letterbook of Neville while ambassador in France (Harl. 4715); Grey adds: 'I sincerely wish the few papers I have sent may entertain you. As fast as the disorder my Library is in will permit me I will not fail transmitting you more of them.'[3] Harl. 5311 is endorsed by Harley as having been given to him by 'the Worthy and Learned Mr. Brome of Ewithington Herefordshire 1732'.[4] Several endorsements have no date and the manuscripts may therefore have come in at an earlier date; such is Harl. 4119 which was given (see f. 1*) to Harley by Thomas Sharp, Archdeacon of Northumberland, the son of John Sharp, Archbishop of York (who had died in 1714); the cartulary of Ramsey Abbey (Harl. 5071) bears the endorsement (f. 1*b) 'This MS. I had from Mr. John Murray', presumably John Murray of Sacombe in Hertfordshire,[5] who also in all probability was the earlier owner of the famous

---

Harley: he died 1772. On his library, which was sold in 1773, see R. C. Lucas, 'Book Collecting in the 18th century: The Library of James West', *The Library*, 5th ser., iii (1949), pp. 265–78. Most of his MSS. were bought by Lord Shelburne (afterwards 1st Marquess of Lansdowne) and are now in the Lansdowne collection in the British Museum.

[1] There are several examples on record of similar finds, of which one of the most remarkable was the discovery of a Reading Abbey Cartulary in a bricked-up chamber in Lord Fingall's house at Shinfield in Berkshire in 1792 (now BM Egerton MS. 3031). Several liturgical MSS. have been found in churches or elsewhere apparently having been deliberately concealed there (e.g. a Sarum Missal in the John Rylands Library, Manchester, was found in a chimney of a Leicestershire farmhouse [see *Cat. of Exhibition of Mediaeval MSS., John Rylands Library*, 1939, p. 48]). Thomas Robe had in 1723 (7 Jan.) sent to Lady Henrietta Harley the copy of a play for her approval and patronage (*HMC Portland Papers*, v, p. 634).

[2] *HMC Portland Papers*, vi, p. 30. [3] Ibid., p. 16.

[4] See Biographical Index on Brome.

[5] On him see Biographical Index: he had a great interest in early printed books: a list of the Caxtons owned by him is in S. de Ricci, *A Census of Caxtons*, 1909, p. 174. Murray's library was sold 8 May 1749. For a brief note on him see W. Y. Fletcher, *English Book Collectors*, 1902, p. 159; and T. F. Dibdin, *Bibliomania*, ii, 1811, pp. 437–8, and *Bibliographical Decameron*, 1817, iii, p. 283. His portrait was engraved by his friend George Vertue, who says he was called the Philosopher (Vertue's *Note Books*, vi, p. 107).

Sir Thomas More MS. now Harl. 7368;[1] the Cartulary was acquired after 1719, in view of Harley's reference to Hearne's use of the MS. for his edition in that year of Sprott's Chronicle. And in 1735 John Murray sent Harley 'a hamper of Books and papers' for we find Murray writing to Harley on 10 February of that year: 'I have sent you a hamper of Books and papers which has bin the product of my whole Life and am Gladd att going out of ye world they will be so well reposited.'[2] One block of manuscripts about which we should like to know more is that of which the individual items bear in Harley's hand the note: 'This did belong to King James [II]. I had it from Coll. Grahme',[3] the 'Coll Grahme' in question being presumably Col. James Graham, who was an active Jacobite until 1696 and later Tory M.P. for Appleby 1701–7 and for Westmorland 1707–27. He had been Keeper of the Privy Purse to James II. The Register of the Benedictine Priory of Deeping St. James in Lincolnshire (Harl. 3658) was given to Harley in 1733 by Dr. Zachary Grey, who was held by Harley 'in great Esteem' and was later to write a memoir of him and his father;[4] a Durham Missal that had formerly belonged to Sir Thomas Tempest of Stella (Harl. 5289) was given to Harley in 1731 by Lord Widdrington;[5] an Alcoran MS. that had belonged to Foucault (Harl. 5695) was given in February 1729/30 by 'my worthy friend Mr. Bacon', the Thomas Bacon who makes frequent appearances in the Diary;[6] Harl. 6198 was given to Harley by his son-in-law, the Duke of Portland, 'at his House in Whitehall', 17 September 1739; a volume of Wolsey's letters to the English Ambassador in Rome (Harl. 6345) was given in 1737 by Lord De la Warr;[7] and Harl. 7352, the inventory of the goods of Charles I sold in 1649 (of which another copy, with additional matter, is Harl. 4898) was given by Vice-Chamberlain Thomas Cooke.[8]

So much for additions to the Library in this later period by way of gifts. In a number of MSS. Harley has entered merely a date and we cannot know therefore whether the MS. came by gift or purchase:[9] but four MSS. (Harl. 6148, 6238, 6240, 6250) which bear in Harley's hand the date 23 December 1738 we know from evidence contained in a letter from William Oldys to Harley, dated 19 December 1738,[10] were purchased with four other books from Thomas Osborne, the bookseller, for £16. 4s. 0d. (against Osborne's original price of £25. 19s. 0d.) as a

---

[1] See C. E. Wright, 'Portrait of a Bibliophile, VIII; Edward Harley . . .', *The Book Collector*, xi, no. 2 (Summer, 1962), p. 169.

[2] John Murray to Edw. Harley, 10 Feb. 1734/5 (Welbeck Harley Papers). Possibly from this 'hamper' came the Sir Thomas More sheets.

[3] Harl. 3964, 4655, 4746, 4752, 4753, 4760, 4801, 4847, 4885, 4989, 5417, 7365, 7504, 7506.

[4] See BM Add. 5834, f. 286—vol. 33 of the collections of the antiquary, William Cole, who visited Grey at Ampthill, 26 July 1765, and was lent the MS. of Grey's memoir.

[5] That is, William Widdrington, 4th Baron Widdrington, d. 1743, whose first wife, Jane, had been the heiress of Sir Thomas Tempest; on the Tempest MSS. and their connexion with Widdrington see Diary, 29 Oct. 1720, item 12 (p. 73, n. 4).

[6] See Biographical Index.

[7] i.e. John West, 1st Earl and 6th Baron de la Warr, 1693–1766: this MS. has the inscription 'Char. Mac Carty 1716', below which Harley has written 'This Lady was afterwards Lady Delawar'. The interest shown by Harley in his books is illustrated by his further note in the MS.: 'there are parts of this MS. copied & in several librarys but not compleat. the Cotton I have not yet examined Nor the Paper Office.'

[8] Inserted is a letter, n.d., from Cooke to Harley: an endorsement by George Vertue is on f. 2*. See also Vertue's *Note Books*, vi (Walpole Society, xxx, 1955), p. 149.

[9] The dates so entered are 2 Feb. 1726/7 (Harl. 5674, 5693), 17 Feb. 1726/7 (Harl. 5541), 28 Dec. 1728 (Harl. 4714), — Jan. 1728/9 (Harl. 3863, 3916, 4094, 7357), 1 May 1729 (Harl. 5605), 22 Jan. 1729/30 (Harl. 3869), — Jan. 1729/30 (Harl. 5415), 17 Feb. 1732/3 (Harl. 5768, 6467), 1733 (Harl. 4630), 1733/4 (Harl. 4928), May 1735 (Harl. 3660), 18 Oct. 1738 (Harl. 6257), 6 Dec. 1738 (Harl. 6082, 6168).

[10] *HMC Portland Papers*, vi, p. 69.

result of arguments on Oldys's part: 'I got near ten pounds "bated" . . . and am satisfied I could not bring them lower, I am yet in doubt whether I shall not hazard your Lordship's displeasure for consenting to give so much, though I am certain I have incurred the bookseller's, in making him descend so far below his expectations.' And in a letter to Harley of 1 February 1728/9 John Warburton[1] offers, allegedly as from someone else, a 'Leiger-book' of Holm Cultram in Cumberland and the Seal of Cottingham Priory in Yorkshire, the first being valued at twenty guineas, the latter at ten:[2] the receipt shows that Harley paid no more than ten guineas for both. The MS. is now Harl. 3911. One purchase resulted from one of Harley's tours—journals or journal-letters of a number of which are preserved in the Welbeck Papers. In December of 1737 and January of 1738 Harley made a tour with James West through East Anglia; on 30 December they were at Ipswich where they spent some time looking round the town and here on this occasion Harley bought a MS. of Chaucer's 'Canterbury Tales', now Harl. 7335.[3] Harl. 5684, an important 10th-century Greek Gospels MS., Harley owed to the intervention and generosity of Sir Hans Sloane, who stood aside that Harley might purchase it;[4] this was one of the two Greek MSS. belonging to Johann Christoph Wolf at Hamburg for which Schumacher was given by Wanley a commission to treat in 1722,[5] and which Wolf had then refused to part with 'for any price whatsoever'.

In MSS. purchased at sales Harley entered the date (sometimes) and the name of the owner of the library. At that of Thomas Jett's books in 1731 (11 May) Harley acquired a MS. containing Giraldus Cambrensis's 'Topographica Hibernica' and other works, which had belonged to William Cecil, Lord Burghley (now Harl. 4003).[6] At the sixteenth part of the Thomas Rawlinson sales, which was devoted largely to MSS. and took place 4 March 1734 (the first sale had taken place thirteen years before, on 4 December 1721), Harley bought seventeen MSS.,[7] including the Glastonbury Abbey Terrier (now Harl. 3961).

The four MSS. noted as being from Lord Somers's collection pose a problem: of the four, two (Harl. 6298, 6918) are endorsed by Harley 'Janu: 6: 1738/9 Ld. Somers', and two (Harl. 7333, 7334), which from external evidence[8] are also Somers items, are dated 'Dec. 1738'. The Somers/Jekyll sale, however, took place at Paul's Coffee House 26 February 1739: were these MSS. acquired by private treaty beforehand or at a pre-view? One of the last purchases from a public auction was made in the very year that Harley was forced to sell Wimpole; lot 284 in the sale of the library of Charles Montagu, 3rd Earl of Halifax, 11 March 1739/40, was acquired by Harley for 11s. 0d. and is now Harl. 6201 (see f. 1*b).

No hint reaches us of impending disaster. On 12 July 1739 we find Oldys writing to Harley, in reply to a query as to whether there were any good MSS. left of

---

[1] Who had sold Harley, 16 July 1720, a large parcel of MSS., with two pictures, as recorded in the Diary. On Warburton see Biographical Index.
[2] *HMC Portland Papers*, vi, p. 23. On this seal see Birch, *Cat. of Seals*, i, 1887, p. 523.
[3] On f. 1 is the following inscription by Harley: 'Oxford. BH. bought at Ipswi[c]h Dec. 30: 1737.' The journal of the tour is printed *HMC Portland Papers*, vi, pp. 168–72.
[4] See *HMC Portland Papers*, vi, p. 40.
[5] See Diary, 24 Apr. and 1 May 1722 and for details p. 140, n. 5.
[6] It is lot 7, p. 7 in the sale-cat. of Jett's MSS. of 11 May: in the Burghley sale-cat. of 1687 it was lot 94, p. 85 (sold to Earl of Stamford for £1. 13s. 0d.).
[7] Harl. 3862, 3961, 3991, [4012], 4015, 4016, 4107, 4108, 4120, 4124, 4135, 4137, 4635, 4690, 4692, 6426, 7371.
[8] That of the Cat. of Lord Somers's Library in Harl. 7191: the former is no. 3 on f. 153 against which is written in the MS. 'Ld. Ox^d' [= Lord Oxford] and the latter is no. 2 on the same folio and is similarly annotated. On an earlier effort to obtain Somers MSS. see p. xxxvii above.

Sir Henry St. George's collection, that he had made inquiries of Osborne the bookseller, whose reply was that he had about 150 volumes which the owner might part with for about £100; Oldys reports also at the same time a collection of original letters in 42 bundles at not less than £200 and a part of Walsingham's collection of state papers at five guineas, and hopes to have a catalogue of the Saxon MSS. lately belonging to Elizabeth Elstob.[1] The tours also continued, one of the last being one of Wiltshire, Gloucestershire, and Oxfordshire, in the autumn of 1740, of which a record is preserved by George Vertue, who accompanied Harley.[2] Vertue noted it as a part of Harley's character that 'to out ward appearance at all times publickly, showed the least concern about his affairs and distresses—put on a free air of mirth & conversation—even to the surprise of his nearest intimates—never to own his care about it'.[3] But Vertue was forced to admit that physically he changed greatly towards the end. However this may be, the burden of debt compelled him to dispose of Wimpole in 1740; and on 16 June of the following year he died in London at his Dover Street house.

With the disposal of Wimpole the library there was brought up to London and placed in the new mansion which Harley had just completed in Marylebone to house it, Harley's intention being 'to Establish it as a publick Library hereafter in or near London'; according to Vertue the library there filled twelve rooms and two galleries,[4] that at Dover St. being contained in 150 presses, the deeds and seals being preserved in addition in '25 wainscot presses double doors'.[5]

The MSS. at Dover Street remained for the moment untouched; the Harley family papers were removed to Welbeck; out of the pictures the Countess retained only those that were related to the family and its connexions, as we have seen above (p. lxviii). The rest of the collections—coins and medals, antiquities, prints, and printed books—was sold.

The first to go were the pictures, Greek and Roman antiquities and inscriptions, books of the prints and drawings of ecclesiastical vestments, &c., that had been brought together by Talman (who had discussed with Wanley 21 November 1721 his wish to sell them), 'the King of France's Cabinet complete' (to which several references are made in the Diary), engraved portraits of the 'most Eminent men in Europe' in 30 volumes, and curiosities from the Arundel Collection. To the paintings included in this sale reference has already been made. The eight volumes of prints and drawings of Greek and Roman antiquities, monuments, seals and coins (many of them engraved or drawn from examples in Harley's own collection) (Catalogue, p. 12, lot 25 under Bronzes, &c.) were bought by the Society of Antiquaries;[6] and the collection of Vertue's prints made by him for Harley (Catalogue, p. 16, lot 27) was sold to the Earl of Ailesbury for 50 guineas.[7] The sale of these was handled by Cock of Covent Garden, who was also responsible for the auction of the Greek, Roman, and English coins immediately after the sale of the antiquities, namely, 18–23 March 1741/2: for the catalogue of these a preface was written by George North the antiquary. Cock also disposed of further collections

---

[1] *HMC Portland Papers*, vi, pp. 71–72. On the St. George MSS. see above, p. xxxiv.
[2] Vertue's *Note Books*, iv (Walpole Society, xxiv, 1936), pp. 180 ff.
[3] Ibid., vi (Walpole Society, xxx, 1955), p. 117.
[4] Ibid., vi, p. 63.
[5] Ibid., vi, p. 119.
[6] See Society of Antiquaries Minute Book under 4 and 8 Mar. 1741/2: the amount paid was £28. 9s. 0d. and an index of them was compiled by Joseph Ames, the Secretary, in 1745.
[7] According to Vertue himself (see his *Note Books*, vi, p. 124).

of prints—Italian, Flemish, and French—from 17 February to 11 March 1745/6. In the meantime the library of printed books to the number of 50,000, together with 41,000 prints and pamphlets, had been sold to Osborne the bookseller for £13,000: on 4 October 1742 Osborne wrote in a letter to Dr. Thomas Birch: 'Haveing purchased the Library of the Earle of Oxford, a more valuable Collection than perhaps was ever in the hands of any Bookseller, I am desirous of consulting the Learned with regard to the disposal of it, and have therefore inclosed the Scheme of a Catalogue which I intend to publish in February.'[1] Osborne's Proposals for his Harleian Catalogue were printed in *The Gentleman's Magazine* for December 1742 (xii, pp. 636–9), but had been issued separately in folio form[2] on 1 November. The 'Proposals' contained 'An Account of the Harleian Library' written by Samuel Johnson,[3] to whom also has been attributed the Preface inserted in vol. iii of the Catalogue and who subsequently wrote the Introduction to the *Harleian Miscellany*. Johnson's Account as printed in the 'Proposals' and *The Gentleman's Magazine* was reprinted by Osborne in the first volume of his *Catalogus Bibliothecae Harleianae* published in 1743. This catalogue eventually reached five volumes: volumes i and ii (with a continuous pagination) appeared in 1743, the first, opening with a Latin Dedicatory Epistle addressed to Sir John Carteret (afterwards, 1744, Earl Granville), Secretary of State, followed by Johnson's Account, and the second with a brief Latin address to the reader by Michael Maittaire. The sale of the items in these 2 volumes was due to begin 7 April 1743 and was to continue 'till public Notice is given, in the News-Papers, of its Conclusion'. The sale of the items included in volumes iii and iv was scheduled to begin 'in the Library' [at Marylebone] on 14 February 1744. A final volume—the fifth—was published in 1745 and included books dispersed at Osborne's Gray's Inn address between 22 April and 1 July of that year: this in fact included items not sold in the earlier sales, without any indication of this fact, and it is often impossible, as De Ricci points out,[4] 'to tell if a given description in volume v refers, or not, to the actual copy of the same book described in volumes i or ii' and there is no doubt that Osborne had the greatest difficulty in disposing of this enormous collection. The books were described—most inadequately—by Oldys who was also responsible for making the selection of the tracts printed in *The Harleian Miscellany*, the Proposals for which—to be published six sheets every Saturday, at 1 shilling, to begin 24 March 1743/4—were inserted in volume iii of the Harleian Catalogue: the *Miscellany* appeared in eight volumes, the last in 1746, and the tracts and pamphlets which supplied its contents were sold by Osborne in five catalogues in 1747 and 1748 (2 March 1747 (?); 1 April, 2 June, and 1 October 1747; 1 February 1748).

The intention of the compilers of the Catalogue, wrote Johnson, was 'that the books shall be distributed into their distinct classes, and every class ranged with some regard to the age of the writers; that every book shall be accurately described; that the peculiarities of editions shall be remarked, and observations from the

---

[1] Printed H. Ellis, *Letters of Eminent Literary Men*, Camden Soc., 1843, p. 368.
[2] A facsimile of the folio Proposals, with a preface by R. W. Chapman, was issued by the Clarendon Press, 1926.
[3] See Boswell's *Life of Johnson*, ed. Birkbeck Hill and L. F. Powell, Oxford, 1934, i, pp. 153–4. It was reprinted in the second volume (1773) of Tom Davies's anthology of Johnson's writings, *Miscellaneous and Fugitive Pieces*; in the ninth volume of the first collected edition (1787) of Johnson's *Works*; and in the later editions (e.g. the two-volume edition of Jones published in 1825, where the Account is printed vol. ii, pp. 353–7).
[4] *English Collectors of Books and Manuscripts*, 1930, p. 36.

authors of literary history occasionally dispensed; that, by this catalogue, we may inform posterity of the excellence and value of this great collection, and promote the knowledge of scarce books, and elegant editions'. But the intentions far outran the accomplishment, the works being in fact most inadequately described; the greater part of Johnson's Account is devoted to a summary of the various classes of material in the Library and their value in the widest context of scholarship. How difficult the Catalogue may be to use a glance at the headings will show: the chief ones are Bibles, Vulgate versions and others, with sub-headings for Concordances, Commentaries, and Patristics, followed by Theological Controversies and Liturgies (including the editions of the Books of Common Prayer); next come Classical Authors (with a separate heading for Elzevir editions); then Greek and Roman Antiquities, with numismatics, followed by History, in which is included such headings as British antiquities; Biography is followed by Heraldry and Genealogy, Law, Periodicals, and, with a separate pagination at the end, 'Books of Prints'. A confusing repetition of headings appears in volumes iii and iv but with some extensions, such as the separate and valuable group of books listed under 'Theological and Mystical Works in English' in volume iii, which also contains a class of printed books much sought after by collectors, namely, a list of books printed upon vellum. Nevertheless, the hope expressed by Johnson that the Catalogue would 'be purchased as a record of this great collection, and preserved as one of the memorials of learning' has been fulfilled and certainly in view of the dispersal of the printed books—'filtered through the base ingredients of Tom Osborne's Warehouse' to use Dibdin's words[1]—'as a record of this great collection' the catalogue, in spite of its imperfections, is of inestimable value.

'I allways wished', wrote Roger Gale in a letter to Stukeley in 1741,[2] 'poor Lord Oxford's most noble collection might have been kept entire together, but such is the vicissitude of human affairs. The title is gone from the principal branch of the family; the estate greatly impoverished; & the library, which was the delight & pride of both father & son, to be dispersed, no body knows where.' There was, however, one exception to this pessimistic and on the whole truthful picture of what happened after Harley's death. The MSS. were not sold to Osborne but were still untouched in the Dover Street house in 1753, when, in the debate in the House of Commons on the Bill dealing with Sir Hans Sloane's bequest of his collections to the nation, 'Mr. Pelham and the Speaker both spoke in great commendation of the Harleian manuscripts and seemed to express a desire that the publick might have them for 10,000 l'. So wrote James West to the Dowager Countess of Oxford on 19 March 1753.[3] Thus it came about that as a result of the suggestion of Pelham and Onslow the manuscripts were acquired for £10,000 by the nation (by the Act 26 Geo. II, c. 22, s. 3) and now form part of the manuscript collections in the British Museum, to which (then Montagu House) they were transferred at the end of 1754 or beginning of 1755.[4]

In conclusion, something must be said about the cataloguing of the manuscripts which was interrupted in the middle of article 10 in 100. D. 10 (Harl. 2408) by Wanley's death on 6 July 1726. This interruption appears to have continued until about 1733 when (according to the 'Advertisement' prefixed to the first volume of

---

[1] T. F. Dibdin, *The Bibliographical Decameron*, iii, 1817, pp. 299–300.
[2] See W. Stukeley, *Diaries and Letters*, ed. W. C. Lukis, i, 1882, pp. 327–8.
[3] For West's letter and the exchange of letters of the Dowager Countess and the Duchess of Portland that followed see *HMC Bath (Longleat) Papers*, ii, 1907, pp. 182–3.
[4] See BM Add. 6179, f. 72; also E. Edwards, *Lives of the Founders of the British Museum*, p. 325 (plan).

the 1759 published catalogue)[1] the cataloguing was resumed by David Casley, who was Deputy to Richard Bentley and other Keepers of the Cotton and Royal Libraries and who was free in that year to undertake the work on the Harleian MSS. presumably on the completion of his *Catalogue of the Manuscripts of the King's Library*, which was to appear in 1734.[2] Casley described MSS. 2408–5709 between 1733 and 1736. In 1741 Edward Harley died and some time afterwards his Trustees ordered the Catalogue to be taken up again, the work being entrusted this time to William Hocker, who had been Librarian to Richard Mead and was Deputy Keeper of the Records in the Tower; Hocker carried the work well towards completion, taking it up to Harl. 7355—in two years, according to the 'Advertisement'.[3] Of the work of Casley and Hocker the 'Advertisement' disarmingly remarks:

> It is proper to observe, in justice to Mr. Casley and Mr. Hocker that the circumstances under which they drew up their respective Parts, did not allow them the time necessary to complete the Catalogue upon so extensive a Plan as that of Mr. Wanley's: whose Part of the Work contains an abstract of most of the historical Manuscripts and a critical account of many of the rest.

After the transfer of the MSS. to the British Museum in 1754 or 1755 (when the MSS. were given the running numbers by which they are referred to today) those MSS. that remained to be dealt with were catalogued by the officers of the Department of Manuscripts, the Reverend Andrew Gifford, the Assistant Keeper (1756–84), cataloguing Harl. 7356–511 and the Keeper, Dr. Charles Morton (on whom see footnote 1 below), Harl. 7512–605; Morton had also supplied descriptions of some of the earlier Harley MSS. and made additions to that of Harl. 6295.

The history of the publication of the first Catalogue of the Harleian MSS. is a confused one. The title-page of the work issued in two volumes is as follows:

> *A Catalogue of the Harleian Collection of Manuscripts, purchased by Authority of Parliament for the Use of the Publick; and preserved in the British Museum. Published by Order of the Trustees.* London: Printed by Dryden Leach, And Sold by L. Davis and C. Reymers, opposite Grays-Inn, Holborn. MDCCLIX.

The printing appears to have begun in 1757 when the care of seeing the *Catalogue* through the press was entrusted to William Norris, Secretary of the Society of Antiquaries, who for several years was corrector of the press to Baskett, King's Printer; the delay in printing off the Catalogue was due to 'ill choice of Printer (Moore and Leach) the former of whom broke in the course of the work' and it thus took two years getting through the press.[4] If copies were indeed available to the public in 1759 they comprised only the descriptions of the MSS., preceded in volume i by an 'Advertisement' and a table showing the correspondence of the numbers of the MSS. to the original press-marks.[5] Subsequently, however, an

---

[1] A draft of the 'Advertisement' is inserted in vol. x of the 'Catalogus Brevior' (BM Add. 45710). The draft is in the hand of Dr. Charles Morton, the first Keeper of Manuscripts (1756–76) and subsequently (1776–99) Principal Librarian; some annotations on it are in the handwriting of Sir Frederic Madden, Keeper of Manuscripts from 1837 to 1866.

[2] Casley makes several appearances in the Diary (see Biographical Index).

[3] Hocker died in 1759 (see *The Gentleman's Magazine*, 1759, p. 551).

[4] See Norris's letter to the Trustees of the British Museum, dated 27 Feb. 1761, in Soc. of Antiquaries MS. 71 (ff. 1–3). On Norris see *DNB*, xli, p. 146.

[5] Some copies in this form must have come on to the market. (The editors of the present work possess just such a copy.) This is the Catalogue referred to throughout this edition of the Diary under the abbreviation '*Harl. Cat.* (1759)'.

Index and a Preface were added in addition to portraits of Robert and Edward Harley, the whole being complete for publication in 1763; this date is derived from particulars preserved in Dr. Charles Morton's official diary (BM Add. MS. 45871) and a letter of James West to the Duchess of Portland. The latter may be taken first: it is dated 20 February 1763[1] and in it West writes to the Duchess as follows:

> The catalogue of the Harleian Manuscripts is now printed and near publication in two large folio volumes, and the Trustees of the British Museum think it would be a very great embellishment to that work if the prints of the two Earls of Oxford, the great Collectors of that invaluable treasure, were prefixed to the book, as these were engraven by Mr. Vertue at Lady Oxford's expense for the book she ordered to be compiled of your Grace's family. If your Grace would permit some impressions to be taken off, the plates would be returned to your Grace with the thanks of the Trustees and of the public. I flatter myself your Grace will forgive an old friend of your Father's for this importunity.

That the Duchess gave her consent is clear from the presence of such portraits in some copies of the complete edition of the catalogue and from Morton's diary, which notes (f. 18[b]) under 27 May 1763 that there were received from the Duchess of Portland 476 prints of Robert Harley and 475 of Edward 'which [writes Morton] have been distributed among the copies of the Catalogues in the Museum, & these delivered to Mr. Davies [the bookseller]: and thus there being a deficiency in the number of prints delivered, which according to Mr. West's information was directed by the Duchess to be 500 of each, Mr. Davis has 20 copies of the Index &c. without the copperplate prints'. Morton's notes and arithmetic are most confused but it seems safe to deduce that the number of copies printed of this Catalogue was 500. The Preface bears the date 24 December 1762 and must also have been in print by this time. In addition, an index separately printed off in sheets was also ready; this index was prepared by Thomas Astle, antiquary and palaeographer and subsequently (1783) Keeper of the Records in the Tower.[2] And the complete work appears to have been received from the printers shortly before 10 June 1763, the precise number of copies according to Morton being: of the Catalogue, 99 large paper, 397 small paper, and of the Index and Preface 101 large paper and 393 small paper.

Accordingly in 1763 the public had available a Catalogue of the MSS. in two volumes comprising a Preface (including the original 'Advertisement'), a concordance Table, descriptions of the MSS., and an Index. The Preface is important because in it an attempt was made to indicate the various main divisions of the subject matter of the collection and to signalize in each group the most noteworthy items.[3] This Preface is in fact a very good one, notwithstanding the formal 18th-century flavour of its style, and still conveys an excellent view of the collection, besides printing usefully the Andrew Hay commission of 1720; indeed, when a

---

[1] *HMC Bath (Longleat) Papers*, ii, 1907, p. 185.

[2] Morton in his diary records (ff. 206–26) that in May of 1761 Astle had expressed a desire to undertake the index (in collaboration with 'a Mr. Gibbs', who subsequently dropped out) and produced a specimen; this was apparently approved and Astle formally undertook the work on 19 June 1761, at the rate of 7 guineas per sheet. The work itself and the revision of it appear to have been completed by 11 July 1762, when the index was ready for the press (Morton's diary, f. 23). The original intention had been that Morton should prepare an index as the sheets came from the press (see Soc. of Antiquaries MS. 71).

[3] It would be impossible to give any indication of the great wealth of the Harleian Collection of MSS. by following a similar practice here, but the reader may be referred to the brief selection of the more notable items given by Arundell Esdaile, *The British Museum Library*, 1946, pp. 234–7.

new edition of the Catalogue was prepared at the instance of the Commissioners for the Arrangement and Preservation of the Public Records early in the 19th century this Preface was reprinted (except for the last few paragraphs) and the Second Preface that was then added (signed and dated by Robert Nares February 1809) did little beyond amplifying the subject headings and adding to the number of noteworthy items signalized in the earlier Preface. The revised catalogue in 4 volumes, which is that in current use, was published between 1808 and 1812. The revision of the Catalogue from Harl. 3100 onwards was entrusted by the Trustees to the Reverend Robert Nares (Keeper of Manuscripts 1799–1807) who was so occupied until May 1806 when the beginning of volume iii was sent to the press. In 1807 Nares's successor, Francis Douce, took over, and volume i appeared in 1808; also published in 1808 were volumes ii and iii. The work of publication of volume ii did not proceed smoothly, however, since after the printing of volume iii had begun, it was discovered that the descriptions of nos. 2408–3100 (?Harl. 3099) required revision and 'many Additions, to make them at all Uniform with either the first or last part of the work': the necessary research was taken up voluntarily by Nares who worked on it until his retirement in the summer of 1807, by which time he had got to no. 2700. What remained was completed by Douce,[1] and some additions to this part of volume ii were made by Joseph Planta, who was Nares's predecessor in the Keepership (1776–99) and subsequently became (1799) Principal Librarian. In addition, from the beginning of 1801 to the summer of 1802 (in which year he died) Stebbing Shaw, the antiquary and historian of Stafford-shire, was employed to revise the topographical, genealogical, and heraldic MSS. The revision (which considerably extended the bulk of the descriptive material) related, it will be noted, from what is said above and from an examination of the two editions of the Catalogue, entirely to *post-Wanley* work. In addition, an index of persons, places, and matters was compiled by Thomas Hartwell Horne (1780–1862), the bibliographer and biblical scholar, who was employed by the Commissioners on the Public Records for that purpose; this was published in 1812 as volume iv, the Preface to which was signed by Horne on 1 January of that year.[2]

After 150 years the time is now admittedly ripe for a third revised edition of a catalogue which was originally begun by Wanley as long ago as 1708 and is still that in use by students.

[1] Page proofs of the descriptions of Harl. 2701–3099 (i.e. the concluding part of vol. ii) with correc-tions by Douce and others are preserved among Douce's papers in BM Add. 42574, ff. 72–91; this volume also contains (ff. 57–71) draft descriptions of many Harl. MSS. between nos. 2746 and 3105, the greater number by Douce himself. At ff. 1–56 are papers relating to Douce's work on the ordering and cata-loguing of the Lansdowne MSS. (included are drafts of his letter of resignation to the Trustees, in which allusion is made (ff. 22, 22b) to his work on the Harl. Cat.).

[2] The task of printing the work was entrusted to the King's Printers, George Eyre and Andrew Stra-han; on the latter see J. A. Cochrane, *Dr. Johnson's Printer: The Life of William Strahan*, 1964, especially pp. 126–7, 207, 211.

SELECT BIBLIOGRAPHY

A. CHIEF MANUSCRIPT SOURCES

(Humfrey Wanley is referred to throughout this section as H. W. to avoid needless repetition)

Welbeck Abbey, His Grace the Duke of Portland, K.G.: Miscellaneous Harley Papers (including Welbeck Wanleyana), deposited on indefinite loan in the British Museum (Loan 29).

British Museum:

Lansdowne 677. Memorandum Book of H. W., 1721–2 (for text see Appendix to vol. ii of the present work).

Lansdowne 771, 772. Diary of H. W., 1715–26 (the text of which is printed in the present work).

Lansdowne 814, *passim*. Miscellaneous papers of H. W., including list of original letters purchased of George Paul and H. W. himself.

Lansdowne 815. Subject index of Harl. MSS. compiled by H. W., 1723.

Lansdowne 816. Catalogue by H. W. of printed books at Wimpole Hall, 1716–18.

Lansdowne 841, ff. 62–67ᵇ. Letters from H. W. to [Robt.] Harley, 1703, n.d., rel. to Sir Simonds D'Ewes's collections.

Lansdowne 846, *passim*. Papers of H. W. relating to the Cotton Library, 1703, &c.

Harley 3777–82. Letters from various correspondents to H. W., 1692–1726.

„ 3886. Catalogue by H. W. of early editions of printed books, 1722–4.

„ 4966, *passim*. Letters from H. W. to John Bagford, 1695–1701.

„ 6030, 6388, 6402, 6863. Miscellaneous collections of H. W. relating to Coventry, &c.

„ 6430. Letters of Nathaniel Wanley (H. W.'s father), 1657–74, and H. W., 1695–6, n.d.

„ 7055, 7190. Miscellaneous papers of H. W. relating to the Society of Antiquaries, S.P.C.K., catalogues of Anglo-Saxon MSS., &c., [?1696]–1720.

„ 7505. Facsimile copies of Warwick deeds by H. W., 1690–2.

„ 7627. A, B. Catalogue by H. W. of Edward Harley's old Latin printed books, 1721.

„ 7661. Index of authors of printed books at Wimpole Hall by H. W., 1718 (the *draft* of the index in Lansdowne 816, ff. 135–7).

Additional 6052. Catalogue by H. W. of heraldic MSS. in the Harleian Collection, n.d.

„ 18238–48. Papers relating to the Harley Marylebone estates, 1720–54.

„ 22910, 22911. Correspondence and papers of John Covel, 1655–1748.

„ 45699, 45700. H. W.'s 'Catalogus Maior' of the Harleian MSS., n.d.

„ 45701–7. H. W.'s 'Catalogus Brevior' of the Harleian MSS., 7 vols., 1708–[26].

„ 47842. H. W.'s annotated copy of Tanner's *Notitia Monastica*, 1695.

Sloane 4037–9, *passim*; 4040, f. 355; 4044, f. 178; 4047, ff. 145, 153; 4061, ff. 264–78ᵇ. Letters from H. W. to Sir Hans Sloane, 1698–1724, n.d.

Stowe 749, *passim*. Letters from H. W., to John Anstis, 1715–25.

London, Society of Antiquaries: Minute Books, and Harley Collection of Prints.

Oxford, Bodleian Library:

Ballard 13 (*SC* 10799). Letters from H. W. to Arthur Charlett, 1694–1721.

Rawlinson letters 116–38 (*SC* 15004–26). Correspondence and papers of J. J. Zamboni, 1707–51.

Select Bibliography

Cambridge, University Library:

Additional 3773–83. Baumgartner Papers, vols. i–x (Strype Correspondence).

Coventry, City Muniments: Treasurer's Book of Receipts and Accounts, 1699–1733, and Council Minute Books.

Linköping Public Library, Sweden: Letters from H. W. to Eric Benzelius the Younger, 1700–4. (Rotographs in the University Library, Uppsala.)

Moscow, Archives of the Academy of Sciences: Letters from H. W. to John Daniel Schumacher, 1722.

B. PRINTED BOOKS

The following select bibliography covers only the chief printed books and articles used in the preparation of this edition: standard works of reference such as the Dictionary of National Biography, G. E. C. Complete Peerage, Alumni Oxonienses, Jöcher, Zedler, &c., *are excluded from it.*

AINSWORTH, R., *Monumenta vetustatis Kempiana, 1719–20*, 1720.

ANDRÉS, J., *Catalogo de' Codici Manoscritti della Famiglia Capilupi di Mantova*, Mantua, 1797.

ASTLE, T., *The Origin and Progress of Writing*, 1784.

BARTHOLOMEW, A. T., and GORDON, C., 'On the Library at King Edward VI School, Bury St. Edmunds', *The Library: A Quarterly Review of Bibliography & Library Lore*, 3rd ser., i (1910), pp. 1–27, 329–31.

BARWICK, G. F., 'Humfrey Wanley and the Harleian Library', *The Library: A Quarterly Review of Bibliography & Library Lore*, N.S., iii (1902), pp. 24–35, 243–55.

—— 'The Formation of the Harleian Library—Further Notes', *The Library: A Quarterly Review of Bibliography & Library Lore*, 3rd ser., i (1910), pp. 166–71.

BENNETT, G. V., *White Kennett 1660–1728: Bishop of Peterborough. A Study in the Political and Ecclesiastical History of the Early Eighteenth Century*, 1957.

BENNETT, J. A. W., 'Hickes's "Thesaurus": A Study in Oxford Book-Production', *English Studies*, N.S. i (1948), pp. 28–45.

BERNARD, E., *Catalogi Manuscriptorum Angliae et Hiberniae*, Oxford, 1697.

BIELER, L., 'Irish MSS. in Medieval Germania', *The Irish Ecclesiastical Record*, 5th ser., 87 (1957), pp. 161–9.

—— *Ireland, Harbinger of the Middle Ages*, 1963.

BIRLEY, R., 'The Library of Louis-Henri de Loménie, Comte de Brienne, and the Bindings of the Abbé Du Seuil', *The Library*, 5th ser., xvii (1962), pp. 105–31.

BLISS, P., *Reliquiae Hearnianae: The Remains of Thomas Hearne, M.A.*, 3 vols. 1869.

Bodleian Library at Oxford, A Summary Catalogue of Western MSS. in the, ed. F. Madan, &c. 8 vols. Oxford, 1895–1953.

British Museum: *A Catalogue of the Harleian Collection of Manuscripts . . . preserved in the British Museum.* [Commenced by H. Wanley, and successively continued by D. Casley, W. Hocker, & C. Morton, with an Index by T. Astle.] (With engraved portraits of Robert and Edward Harley as frontispieces.) 2 vols. 1759 [–63]. [The Preface (dated 24 Dec. 1762) and the Index were originally published separately 1763, the short Preface that preceded in the 1759 Cat. the descriptions being omitted.]

—— *A Catalogue of the Harleian Collection of Manuscripts . . . preserved in the British Museum.* [Revised by R. Nares, S. Shaw, and F. Douce.] With indexes of persons, places, and matters [by T. H. Horne]. The 1762 Preface to the first ed. being reprinted, followed by a second (and new) Preface by R. Nares, 4 vols. 1808–12.

British Museum: *A Catalogue of the Lansdowne Manuscripts in the British Museum.* With indexes of persons, places, and matters. [By Sir H. Ellis & F. Douce.] 2 pts. 1819.

—— *Index to the Sloane Manuscripts in the British Museum*, by E. J. L. Scott. With a Preface by Sir G. F. Warner. 1904.

—— *Catalogue of the Stowe Manuscripts in the British Museum.* With a Preface by E. J. L. Scott. 2 vols. (Vol. i, Text; Vol. ii, Index). 1895–6.

—— *Catalogue of Books printed in the 15th century now in the British Museum.* 9 pts. 1908–62.

—— *Short-Title Catalogue of Books printed in Italy and Italian Books printed in other Countries from 1465 to 1600 now in the British Museum.* Ed. A. F. Johnson, V. Scholderer & D. A. Clarke. 1958.

BROGLIE, C. P. E. DE, *La Société de l'Abbaye de Saint-Germain des Prés au dixhuitième siècle. Bernard de Montfaucon et les Bernardins 1715–50.* 2 vols. Paris, 1891.

BROOKS, E. ST. JOHN, *Sir Hans Sloane: The Great Collector and his Circle*, 1954.

BURMANN, P. (the Elder), *Sylloges epistolarum a viris illustribus scriptarum.* 5 vols. Leiden, 1727.

CHAMBERLAYNE, J., *Magnae Britanniae Notitia: or, the Present State of Great Britain with Divers Remarks upon the Antient State thereof*, 1708, &c.

[CHARRON, J. J., MARQUIS DE MÉNARS], *Bibliotheca Menarsiana*, The Hague, 1720.

CHISHULL, E., *Antiquitates Asiaticae Christianam Æram Antecedentes*, 1728.

Christ's College, Cambridge: Biographical Register, ed. J. Peile, 1910, 2 vols. [art. on Covel].

CLARK, A. C., 'The Library of J. G. Graevius', *The Classical Review*, v (1891), pp. 365–72.

—— L. G., *Collectors and Owners of Incunabula in the British Museum*, 1962.

CLARKE, W., *Repertorium Bibliographicum*, 1819.

C[OKAYNE], G. E., 'Mawson's Obits, &c. (July 1720–December 1729)', *The Genealogist*, N.S., ii (1885), pp. 143–7, 190–2; iii (1886), pp. 80–85, 139–45, 246–52; iv (1887), pp. 25–34, 165–9; vi (1890), pp. 19–27, 101–7, 181–3, 208–13; vii (1891), pp. 39–47, 105–12, 155–60, 221–4; viii (1892), pp. 129–32, 164–73.

COLLINS, A., *Historical Collections of the Noble Families of Cavendishe, Holles, Vere, Harley and Ogle . . .*, 1752.

COLVIN, H. M., *A Biographical Dictionary of English Architects, 1660–1840*, 1954.

COPINGER, W. A., *Supplement to Hain's Repertorium Bibliographicum*, 2 parts. 1895–1902.

CORMACK, J. M. R., *Notes on the History of the Inscribed Monuments of Aphrodisias*, Reading, 1955.

COURTNEY, W. P., art. 'Humfrey Wanley', in *Dictionary of National Biography*, lix, 1899, pp. 287–9.

CROSSLEY, J., 'Humfrey Wanley: Autograph Notices of his Family', *Notes and Queries*, 5th ser., v (1870), pp. 142–3.

DARLOW, T. H., & MOULE, H. F., *Historical Catalogue of the Printed Editions of Holy Scripture in the Library of the British and Foreign Bible Society.* 2 vols. 1903, 1911.

DAVENPORT, C., *Heraldic Bookstamps*, 1909.

DAVIS, G. R. C., *Medieval Cartularies of Great Britain*, 1958.

DE BEER, G. R., *Sir Hans Sloane and the British Museum*, 1953.

DELISLE, L. V., *Le Cabinet des Manuscrits de la Bibliothèque Nationale.* 4 vols. Paris, 1868–81.

DE RICCI, S., *A Census of Caxtons*, Bibliographical Soc., Illustrated Monograph no. 15, 1909.

—— *English Collectors of Books and Manuscripts, 1530–1930*, Cambridge, 1930.

—— *Handlist of MSS. in the Library of the Earl of Leicester at Holkham*, Supplement to the Bibliographical Soc. Transactions, no. 7, 1932.

DIBDIN, T. F., *Bibliomania.* 2 vols. 1811.

DIBDIN, T. F., *The Bibliographical Decameron.* 3 vols. 1817.

The Dictionary of Welsh Biography down to 1940, ed. Sir J. E. Lloyd, R. T. Jenkins, &c., 1959.

DOBSON, A., 'The Bibliotheca Meadiana', *Bibliographica*, i (1895), pp. 404–18.

—— 'Dr. Mead's Library', *Eighteenth Century Vignettes* (World's Classics ed.), iii, pp. 29–50.

DOREZ, L., 'La Bibliothèque di Giovanni Marcanova', *Mélanges G. B. de Rossi*, French School at Rome, vol. xii, Supplément, 1892, pp. 113–26.

DOUGLAS, D. C., *English Scholars, 1660–1730*, 1939; 2nd ed., 1951.

DOUTHWAITE, W. R., 'Humfrey Wanley and His Diary', *The Library Chronicle*, i (1884), pp. 87–94, 110–13.

DUFF, E. G., *Fifteenth-Century English Books*, Bibliographical Soc., Illustrated Monograph no. 18, 1917.

EARWAKER, J. P., 'The Four Randle Holmes of Chester, antiquaries, heralds and genealogists, c. 1571–1707', *Journal of Chester Archaeological and Historic Soc.*, 1891 (private reprint 1892).

EDWARDS, E., *Lives of the Founders of the British Museum with Notices of its Chief Augmentors and other Benefactors, 1570–1870*, 1870.

ELGER, T. W., *Catalogue of the Circulating and Reference Libraries and of the Old Library founded in 1700*, Bedford, 1892.

ELLIS, SIR H., *Letters of Eminent Literary Men*, Camden Soc., no. xxiii, 1843.

ELTON, C. I., and ELTON, M.A., *The Great Book-Collectors*, 1893.

ENGLEFIELD, W. A. D., *The History of the Painter-Stainers Company of London*, 1923.

ESDAILE, A. J. K., *The British Museum Library*, 1946.

EVANS, J., *A History of the Society of Antiquaries*, 1956.

[FLEETWOOD, W.], *Bibliotheca Monastica Fletewodiana. A Catalogue of rare Books and Tracts . . . including the Antient Conventual Library of Missenden Abbey . . . together with some choice Remains of . . . William Fletewode Esq.*, 1774.

FLETCHER, W. Y., 'John Bagford and his collections', *Transactions of the Bibliographical Society*, iv (1898), pp. 185–201.

—— *English Book-Collectors*, 1902.

FLOWER, R. E. W., *Catalogue of Irish MSS. in the British Museum*, iii, 1953.

FRATI, C., and SORBELLI, A., *Dizionario Bio-Bibliografico dei Bibliotecari e Bibliofili Italiani dal sec. XIV al XIX*, Florence, 1934.

Gesamtkatalog der Wiegendrucke, Bd. i– , Leipzig, 1926– .

GILLAM, S. G., 'The Thomason Tracts', *Bodleian Library Record*, ii (1941–9), pp. 221–5.

—— 'Arthur Charlett's Letters and Manuscripts', *Bodleian Library Record*, iv (1952–3), pp. 105–14.

GODFREY, W. H., Wagner, A. R., London, H. S., *The College of Arms*, London Survey, vol. xvi, 1963.

GORDON, A., art. 'Nathaniel Wanley', in *Dictionary of National Biography*, lix, 1899, pp. 289–90.

GOULDING, R. W., *The Welbeck Abbey Miniatures belonging to his Grace the Duke of Portland, K.G., G.C.V.O., A Catalogue Raisonné*, Oxford, 1916.

—— 'Henrietta Countess of Oxford', *Transactions of the Thoroton Society*, xxvii (1923), pp. 1–41.

—— (and ADAMS, C. K.), *Catalogue of the Pictures belonging to His Grace the Duke of Portland, K.G., at Welbeck Abbey, 17 Hill Street, London, and Langwell House*, Cambridge, 1936.

GRAEVIUS, J. G., *Catalogus Bibliothecae Luculentissimae . . . qua usus est dum viveret vir summus Jo. Georgius Graevius*, Utrecht, [1703].

GUIGARD, J., *Nouvel Armorial du Bibliophile: Guide de l'Amateur des Livres Armoriés*, 2 vols. Paris, 1890.

GUNNIS, R., *Dictionary of British Sculptors, 1660–1851*, 1953.

GUNTHER, R. T., *Life and Letters of Edward Lhwyd*, Early Science in Oxford, xiv, 1945.

GWYNN, A., 'Some Notes on the History of the Irish and Scottish Benedictine Monasteries in Germany', *Innes Review*, v (1954), pp. 5–27.

HAIN, L., *Repertorium Bibliographicum*. 2 vols. (4 pts.). Stuttgart, 1826–38.

—— See also COPINGER, W. A.

[HARLEY, EDWARD, 2ND EARL OF OXFORD]: *A Catalogue of the Collection of . . . Several Capital Pictures by the most Eminent Italian, French, and Flemish Masters, great Variety of Greek and Roman Antiquities . . .* Cock, Covent Garden, 8–13 March 1742.

HART, A., *William Lloyd, 1627–1717: Bishop, Politician, Author and Prophet*, 1952.

HARTSHORNE, C. H., *The Book Rarities in the University of Cambridge*, 1829.

HASSALL, W. O., *A Catalogue of the Library of Sir Edward Coke*, Yale Law Library Publications, no. 12, 1950.

Hearne, Thomas, *Remarks and Collections of*, ed. C. E. Doble, D. W. Rannie, and H. E. Salter, Oxford Historical Society, 1885–1921.

HICKES, G., *Linguarum Veterum Septentrionalium Thesaurus*. 3 vols. Oxford, 1703–5. [Vol. ii, Cat. of Anglo-Saxon MSS. by H. Wanley.]

Historical Manuscripts Commission. *Manuscripts of the Duke of Portland at Welbeck*, vols. iii–vi (Harley Papers, vols. i–iv), 1894–1901.

—— *Manuscripts of the Duke of Portland at Welbeck*, vol. vii (Letters of W. Stratford to Edw. Harley), 1901.

—— *Manuscripts of the Marquess of Bath at Longleat*, vols. ii (Harley Papers), iii (Prior Papers), 1907, 1908.

HOWE, E., *A List of London Bookbinders, 1648–1815*, Bibliographical Soc., 1950.

HUNT, R. W., 'William Pownall Antiquarian', *Lincs. Architectural and Archaeological Soc. Reports and Papers*, vol. ix, pt. 2 (1962), pp. 158–63.

HUNTER, J., *Catalogue of the Library of Lincoln's Inn*, 1838.

HUSSEY, C., 'Wimpole Hall, Cambridgeshire', *Country Life*, 21 and 28 May 1927.

JAMES, F. G., *North Country Bishop: A Biography of William Nicolson*, Yale Univ. Press, 1956.

JENKINS, J. G., *The Dragon of Whaddon: Life of Browne Willis*, High Wycombe, 1953.

JOHNSON, S., 'An Account of the Harleian Library' in T. Osborne's *Catalogus Bibliothecae Harleianae*, i, 1743, and Preface, ibid. iii, 1744.

KER, N. R., *Medieval Libraries of Great Britain*, Royal Historical Society, Guides and Handbooks no. 3, 1941; revised ed. 1964.

—— 'English MSS. owned by Johannes Vlimmerius & Cornelius Duyn', *The Library*, 4th ser., xxii (1941–2), pp. 205–6.

—— *Catalogue of Manuscripts containing Anglo-Saxon*, Oxford, 1957.

KÖNIG, E., 'Peutinger-Studien', in H. Grauert's *Studien und Darstellungen aus dem Gebiete der Geschichte*, Bd. ix, Hft. i and 2, 1914.

LATHBURY, T., *A History of the Nonjurors*, 1845.

LEES-MILNE, J., *Earls of Creation: Five Great Patrons of Eighteenth-Century Art*, 1962.

LEHMANN, P., 'Mitteilungen aus Handschriften II' [on Cues MSS., *inter alia*], *Sitzungsberichte der Bayerischen Akademie der Wissenschaften*, Phil.-hist. Abt., Jahrg. 1930, Hft. 2, Munich, 1930.

LITTLE, B., *The Life and Works of James Gibbs, 1682–1754*, 1955.

LOEFFLER, C., *Kölnische Bibliotheksgeschichte im Umriß*, Cologne, 1923.

Select Bibliography

Lowe, E. A., *Codices Latini Antiquiores*, 10 vols. 1934–63.

Mabillon, J., *Iter Germanicum*, Hamburg, 1717.

Macray, W. D., *Annals of the Bodleian Library*, 1868; 2nd ed., 1890.

Maittaire, M., *Annales Typographici*. 5 vols. 1719–41.

Mandarini, E., *I Codici Manoscritti della Biblioteca Oratoriana di Napoli*, Naples, 1897.

Martène, E., and Durand, U., *Voyage Littéraire de deux Religieux Bénédictins de la Congrégation de Saint-Maur*. 2 vols. Paris, 1717, 1724.

Marx, J., *Verzeichnis der HSS.-Sammlung des Hospitals zu Cues*, Trier, 1905.

Masters, R., *Memoirs of the Life and Writings of the late Rev. Thomas Baker, B.D.*, 1784.

Mathew, H. D., 'The Library at Naworth', *For Hilaire Belloc*, ed. Douglas Woodruff, 1942, pp. 117–30.

Mattingley, H., Burnett, I. A. K., Pollard, A. W., *List of Catalogues of English Book Sales 1676–1900 now in the British Museum*, 1915.

Mayor, J. E. B., *Cambridge under Queen Anne*, Cambridge 1911.

Michaelis, A., *Ancient Marbles in Great Britain*, Cambridge, 1882.

Milman, W. H., 'Some Account of Sion College and its Library', *Transactions of the London & Middlesex Archaeological Society*, vi (1883), pp. 53–122.

Montfaucon, B. de, *Diarium Italicum, sive Monumentorum veterum, Bibliothecarum, Musaeorum, &c. . . .* Paris, 1702.

—— *Bibliotheca Bibliothecarum Manuscriptorum Nova*, 1739.

Moule, T., *Bibliotheca Heraldica Magnae Britanniae*, 1822.

Nichols, J., *Biographical and Literary Anecdotes of William Bowyer*, 1782.

—— *Literary Anecdotes of the Eighteenth Century*. 9 vols. 1812–15.

Nicolson, W., Correspondence of. 2 vols. 1809.

Nixon, H. M., 'A Harleian Binding by Thomas Elliot, 1721', *The Book Collector*, vol. xiii (1964), p. 194.

Oates, J. C. T., *A Catalogue of the Fifteenth-Century Printed Books in the University Library, Cambridge*, Cambridge, 1954.

Oldham, J. B., *Shrewsbury School Library Bindings: Catalogue Raisonné*. Oxford, 1943.

Omont, H., 'Notes sur les manuscrits grecs du British Museum', *Bibliothèque de l'École des Chartes*, xlv (1884), pp. 314–50.

Osborne, T., *Catalogus Bibliothecae Harleianae*. 5 vols. 1743–5.

Overton, J. H., *The Non-Jurors*, 1902.

Oxford Dictionary of the Christian Church, The, ed. F. L. Cross, 1957.

Pearce, E. H., *Sion College and Library*, Cambridge, 1913.

Pearson, J., *Biographical Sketch of the Chaplains to the Levant Company*, 1883.

Petheram, J., *An Historical Sketch of the Progress and Present State of Anglo-Saxon Literature in England*, 1840.

Piggott, S., *William Stukeley*, 1950.

Plomer, H. R., *A Dictionary of the Printers and Booksellers who were at work in England, Scotland and Ireland from 1688 to 1725*, Bibliographical Soc., 1922.

—— (& Bushnell, G. H., & Dix, E. R. McC.), *A Dictionary of the Printers and Booksellers who were at work in England, Scotland and Ireland from 1726 to 1775*, Bibliographical Soc., 1932.

Pollard, A. W., & Redgrave, G. R., *A Short-Title Catalogue of Books printed in England, Scotland & Ireland . . . 1475–1640*, Bibliographical Soc., 1926; photo-offset reprint, 1956.

[*Portland Museum*]; *A Catalogue of the Portland Museum lately the Property of the Duchess Dowager of Portland deceased*, 1786.

PROCTOR, R., *The Printing of Greek in the Fifteenth Century*, Bibliographical Soc., Illustrated Monograph no. 8, 1900.

QUARITCH, B., *Contributions towards a Dictionary of English Book-Collectors*, 1892–1921.

READING, W., *Bibliothecae Cleri Londinensis in Collegio Sionensi Catalogus*, 1724.

ROSCOE, E. S., *Robert Harley, Earl of Oxford, Prime Minister 1710–1714, A Study of Politics and Letters in the Age of Anne*, 1902.

SABBADINI, R., *Le Scoperte dei codici latini e greci ne' secoli XIV e XV*. 2 vols. Florence, 1905, 1914.

SANDYS, E., *A Short History of Classical Scholarship*, Cambridge, 1915.

SCRIVENER, F. H. A., *Introduction to the Criticism of the New Testament*, 4th rev. ed., 1894.

SECRETAN, C. F., *Memoirs of the Life and Times of the Pious Robert Nelson*, 1860.

SISAM, K., *Studies in the History of Old English Literature*, Oxford, 1953.

SMITH, T., *Catalogus Librorum Manuscriptorum Bibliothecae Cottonianae*, Oxford, 1696.

SMITH, T., *Topographical and Historical Account of the Parish of St. Mary-le-Bone*, 1833.

STILLWELL, M. B., *Incunabula in American Libraries. A Second Census of Fifteenth-Century Books owned in the United States, Mexico and America*, The Bibliographical Soc. of America, New York, 1940.

TANNER, T., *Notitia Monastica*, Oxford, 1695.

TAYLOR, A., *Book Catalogues*, Chicago, 1957.

TAYLOR, F. H., *The Taste of Angels. A History of Art Collecting from Rameses to Napoleon*, 1948.

THOMPSON, J. W., *The Medieval Library*, 1939; reprint 1957.

THORNTON, J. L., *The Chronology of Librarianship*, 1941.

TOMASINI, J. P., *Bibliothecae Patavinae manuscriptae publicae et privatae quibus diversi scriptores hactenus incogniti recensentur ac illustrantur*, Udine, 1639.

TURBERVILLE, A. S., *A History of Welbeck Abbey and its Owners*. 2 vols. 1938.

ULLMAN, B. L., 'Manuscripts of Nicholas of Cues', *Speculum*, xiii (1938), pp. 194–7.

VERTUE, G., *Note Books*, Walpole Soc., xviii (1929–30) [vol. i], xx (1931–2) [vol. ii], xxii (1933–4) [vol. iii], xxiv (1935–6) [vol. iv], xxvi (1937–8) [vol. v], xxix (1940–2) [Index to vols. i–v], xxx (1951–2) [vol. vi].

VINCENT, J. A. C., 'Wanley's Harleian Journal', *The Genealogist*, N.S., i (1884), pp. 114–17, 178–82, 256–61.

VOCHT, H. DE, *Jerome de Busleyden: Founder of the Louvain Collegium Trilingue. His Life and Writings*. (Humanistica Lovaniensia, Ø 9.) Turnhout, 1950.

WAGNER, A. R., *Records and Collections of the College of Arms*, 1952.

—— *Catalogue of English Mediaeval Rolls of Arms*, 1950.

WAKEMAN, G., 'Humfrey Wanley on Erecting a Library', *The Private Library*, vi, no. 4 (Oct. 1965), pp. 80–84.

[WALKER, J.], *Letters written by Eminent Persons from Originals in the Bodleian Library*, Oxford, 1813. 3 vols.

WANLEY, H., Catalogue of Anglo-Saxon MSS.: see Hickes, G., *supra*.

WATSON, A. G., 'Sir Simonds D'Ewes's Collection of Charters, and a Note on the Charters of Sir Robert Cotton', *Journal of the Society of Archivists*, vol. ii, no. 6 (Oct. 1962), pp. 247–54.

—— *The Library of Sir Simonds D'Ewes*, 1966.

WEISS, R., *Humanism in England during the Fifteenth Century*, Oxford, 1941; 2nd ed. 1957.

Select Bibliography

WHEATLEY, H. B., 'Johnson as a Bibliographer', *Trans. of the Bibliographical Soc.*, viii (1907), pp. 39–61.

WHINNEY, M., *Sculpture in Britain 1530–1830* (The Pelican History of Art), 1964.

—— (and MILLAR, O.), *English Art 1625–1714* (Oxford History of English Art, vol. vii), 1957.

WHITLEY, W. T., *Artists and their Friends in England, 1700–1799.* 2 vols. 1928.

WILLIAMS, G., *The Orthodox Church of the East in the Eighteenth Century, being the Correspondence between the Eastern Patriarchs and the Nonjuring Bishops*, 1868.

WING, D., *Short-Title Catalogue of Books printed in England, Scotland, Ireland, Wales, and British America and of English Books printed in other Countries, 1641–1700.* Index Society, New York, 3 vols. 1945–51.

Wormald, F., and Wright, C. E., *The English Library before 1700*, 1958.

WRIGHT, C. E., 'Humfrey Wanley: Saxonist and Library Keeper' (Brit. Acad., Gollancz Memorial Lecture 1960), *Proceedings of the British Academy*, xlvi, 1961, pp. 99–129.

—— 'Edward Harley, 2nd Earl of Oxford, 1689–1741' (Portrait of a Bibliophile, VIII), *The Book Collector*, vol. xi (1962), pp. 158–74.

WRIGHT, RUTH C., 'Letters from Humfrey Wanley to Eric Benzelius and Peter the Great's Librarian', *The Durham University Journal*, N.S., i (1940), pp. 185–97.

YEOWELL, J., *A Literary Antiquary: William Oldys*, 1862.

ZACCARIA, F. A., *Bibliotheca Pistoriensis*, Turin, 1752.

Note added in proof

Since this work was completed the memorandum- and account-book of Nathaniel Noel, only known to the editors from the extracts printed by G. F. Barwick in 1910 and cited therefrom in the Introduction above *passim*, has appeared in the sale-room (Christie's, 9 Dec. 1965, lot 204) and is now BM. Egerton 3777.

NOTE TO THE READER

THE *text* of the Diary (including the descriptions in Greek and Latin of MSS. and printed books) has been given with Wanley's own spelling, abbreviations, &c., and only occasionally have words been expanded or missing letters supplied (in square brackets or italics) in the interests of clarification. No attempt has been made to normalize or make consistent the spelling of proper names in which Wanley was extremely erratic. Where Wanley has quoted (in Greek letters) the price paid for individual items in lists of MSS. or printed books the equivalent figures have been added in square brackets.

The *footnotes* to the text of the Diary are primarily of a bibliographical nature, their purpose being to identify the MSS. referred to (whether now in the Harleian Collection in the British Museum or elsewhere), to enable the reader to follow the course of the negotiations recorded and particularly to direct him to the significant date in them (usually that of their termination or of the acquisition of the items under discussion), and to indicate the present whereabouts of such letters or memoranda as are referred to by Wanley (where such are still extant and can be traced) or are otherwise relevant. In many cases cross-references are required merely to show when a book borrowed was returned: in such cases 'cf.' is used instead of 'see' which is reserved to direct the reader to a date or footnote containing information of substance or significance.

It should be noted that 'Welbeck Wanleyana' refers to the box-cases of Wanley material in the possession of His Grace the Duke of Portland and now on indefinite loan in the MSS. Department of the British Museum and that *Portland Papers* refers to those of the Duke of Portland's papers printed by the Historical Manuscripts Commission, in which the 'Harley Papers' occupy volumes iii–vii (1894–1901), the last volume being devoted to the letters written (1710–29) by Dr. William Stratford to Edward Harley. Where reference is made to the *originals* of the Harley Papers (occasionally necessitated by the fact that the *HMC* sometimes printed only extracts from or summaries of the letters) it is made thus (for example) 'Welbeck Harley Papers' and this covers both the bound volumes and the box-cases of the miscellaneous material; these papers also belong to the Duke of Portland and are on indefinite loan at the British Museum.

For details of persons referred to by Wanley in the Diary (whether booksellers or agents, visitors to the Library, or scholars working there) the reader should consult the *Biographical Index*.

All MSS. in the Harleian Collection (other than the charters or deeds) whose acquisition is covered within the Diary and which are identified in the footnotes, are listed in their numerical order in the *Numerical Table* printed in Volume II, pp. 473–518. For other MSS. referred to (for example, 'St. Chad's Gospels') reference should be made to the *Subject Index* (Volume II, pp. 468–72).

Owing to the dispersal of the *printed books* in the Harleian Library as a result of the sales of that part of the Library conducted by Thomas Osborne in the years 1743 to 1745, no systematic attempt could be made to identify the present whereabouts of the Harleian copies of the early printed books (incunabula, &c.) listed by Wanley as purchased from booksellers or agents, but in the case of incunabula the particular edition of the work referred to has been identified wherever possible, and references given to the identifying numbers in such standard works as Stillwell, BMC, and Hain (see List of Abbreviations for explanation of these references). Information, however, is supplied in the footnotes about the contemporary publications referred to in the text.

All the *manuscripts* identified and cited in the footnotes are in the Harleian Collection in the British Museum *unless otherwise stated* and are cited thus 'Harl. 61'.

In *cross referencing* in the footnotes, the references are usually gathered together in the footnote under the main date-entry, viz. either under the initial date if subsequent entries are merely allusive and no transaction is finalized, or under the terminal date where a transaction *is* finalized; where a list of acquisitions is given by Wanley it *normally* appears under the terminal date. Wanley's item numbers under each date in the Diary are cited in footnote references only where the date entry is a lengthy one or contains a number of such items, or where exceptionally the entries under any one date have been continued overleaf in the text to result in two items bearing the same number.

ABBREVIATIONS

BLQR	*The Bodleian [Library] Quarterly Record.* Vols. i–viii. 1914–38.
BLR	*The Bodleian Library Record,* 1938– .
BMC	*Catalogue of Books printed in the XV cent. now in the British Museum,* Pts. i–ix, 1908–62.
BMQ	*British Museum Quarterly.*
Bohatta (1924)	H. Bohatta, *Bibliographie der Livres d'Heures-Horae B.M.V.-Officia, Hortuli Animae, Coronae B.M.V., Rosaria und Cursus B.M.V. des XV und XVI Jahrhunderts.* Vienna, 1924 ed.
Bohatta (1937)	H. Bohatta, *Bibliographie der Breviere, 1501–1850.* Leipzig, 1937.
CLA	E. A. Lowe, *Codices Latini Antiquiores.* Vols. i–x. 1934–63.
CMA	E. Bernard, *Catalogi Manuscriptorum Angliae et Hiberniae.* Oxford, 1697.
CSC	*List of Catalogues of English Book Sales 1676–1900 now in the British Museum.* Ed. H. Mattingley, I. A. K. Burnett, and A. W. Pollard. 1915.
DACL	*Dictionnaire d'archéologie chrétienne et de liturgie.* Ed. F. Cabrol and H. Leclerq. Vols. 1– . 1907– .
Darlow and Moule	T. H. Darlow and H. F. Moule, *Historical Catalogue of the Printed Editions of Holy Scripture in the Library of the British and Foreign Bible Society.* 2 vols. 1903, 1911.
Davis	G. R. C. Davis, *Medieval Cartularies of Great Britain.* 1958.
De Ricci	Seymour de Ricci, *English Collectors of Books and Manuscripts (1530–1930).* Cambridge, 1930.
De Ricci, *Census*	Seymour de Ricci, *A Census of Caxtons.* Bibliographical Soc., Illustrated Monograph, no. 15, 1909.
DNB	*Dictionary of National Biography.* Ed. S. Lee, &c. Vols. i–lxiii, and Supplement. 1885–1901.
Duff	E. Gordon Duff, *Fifteenth Century English Books.* Bibliographical Soc., Illustrated Monographs, no. 18, 1917.
DUJ	*Durham University Journal.*
Fletcher	W. Y. Fletcher, *English Book Collectors,* 1902.
GW	*Gesamtkatalog der Wiegendrucke,* Bd. 1– , 1925– .
Hain	L. Hain, *Repertorium Bibliographicum.* Stuttgart, 1826–38. 2 vols. (4 pts.).
Hain-Copinger	W. A. Copinger, *Supplement to Hain's Repertorium Bibliographicum.* 2 pts. 1895–1902.
Harl. Cat. (1759)	*A Catalogue of the Harleian Collection of Manuscripts in the British Museum.* 2 vols. 1759.
Harl. Cat. (1808–12)	*A Catalogue of the Harleian Manuscripts in the British Museum.* 4 vols. 1808–12.
HMC	Reports of the Royal Commission on Historical Manuscripts. 1870– .
Macray	W. D. Macray, *Annals of the Bodleian Library,* A.D. *1598*–A.D. *1867.* All references are to the revised ed. 1890.

Abbreviations

Osborne	Thomas Osborne, *Catalogus Bibliothecae Harleianae.* 5 vols. 1743–5.
RCHM	Reports of the Royal Commission on Historical Monuments.
SC	*A Summary Catalogue of Western MSS. in the Bodleian Library at Oxford.* Ed. F. Madan, &c. 1895–1953.
STC	A. W. Pollard and G. R. Redgrave, *A Short-Title Catalogue of Books Printed in England, Scotland & Ireland and of English Books Printed Abroad, 1475–1640.* Bibliographical Society, 1926. (Photo-offset reprint, 1956.)
Stillwell	M. B. Stillwell, *Incunabula in American Libraries. A Second Census of Fifteenth-Century Books owned in the United States, Mexico and America.* The Bibliographical Society of America, New York, 1940.
Wing	D. Wing, *Short-Title Catalogue of Books Printed in England, Scotland, Ireland, Wales, and British America and of English Books Printed in Other Countries, 1641–1700.* Index Society, New York. 3 vols. 1945–51.

VOLUME I (*Lansdowne 771*), 1715–23

Al. Sig. [*deleted*] Andrea Hay 'a Casa sua sopra la Fonte Baboina in Roma.' (f. 1a)
[^ *deleted*]

Thomas [as *deleted*] Hesketh Esq, 'at Mr Wymes's a Surgeon in Brewer street near
Broad Street.' [^ *deleted*]

Rev^d M^r [*blank space*] Creake at Mr Doughtie's next to the Surgeons Armes in
King-street, Soho.

Henry [ry *deleted*] Fleetwood Esq. 'at Mr Chetwynds in Golding Square. (or at
John's Street near it)' [^ *deleted*]

Sig^r Haym in Wardour-street over against the Black horse, in old Soho. (the
Δ.Σ.Θ.Χ.Ρ. five or Six Words shewing each of these Lt͞res).

Mr Henry March at Mr Dunsters in Love-Lane near the Weigh-house in East-
cheap.

Consul William Faringdon, at a Packers, next door but one to the Gate-way or
Arch, going into Austin-Friers, in Broad-street.

A Mon^r. [*deleted*] Monsr. Sherard chez [*deleted*] Monsr. [*deleted*] Vaillant, au Jardin
Royal au Fauxbourg St Victor, a Paris. chez [*deleted*] Monsr. [*deleted*] Boerhaue
Professeur à Leide.

M^rs. Davies at M^rs. Walkers in Eagle-street near Red Lion-square, against Fishers
Court.

Mr John Gibson at M^r. Wrights house, the upper End of Scrope's Court in Low
Holbourne.

Mr Elliot at the Bible next the Blew-posts-Tavern, in Portugal-street, near Lincolns
Inne Back-gate.

Mr William Stirling Merchant, at his House in Billeters Square, London. Or at the
Blue-Coat-Coffeehouse in Sweetings Alley, near the Royal Exchange.

Mr Joseph Sparkes 'at M^rs. Ingrams in Water-lane, Fleet street, next door to the
Bay horse.' [^ *deleted and*] Mr Harrisons the Upper End of Wine-Office-
Court in Fleet-street [*substituted*].

Mr Thomas O Sullevane at Howell's Coffee-house in Wild-Street.

Mr Peter Hasert at the Hen & Chickens in Great Queen Street; a Glass-Shop.

2 March 1714/5.

p. I
(f. 2a)

Present, my Lord Harley; my Self.

1. This being S^t. Chad's day, I acquainted his Lordship, that I did, the last Somer,
write to Mr Kimberley Dean of Lichfield, desiring him to induce the Chapter
of that Cathedral, to part with their old Book called *Textus S. Ceaddæ*[1] to my
Lord of Oxford, his Lordship therefore giving them Money or Books to a
greater Value: but that I had never received any Answer. Also, that it had
appeared to me, that Mr Dean was absent from Lichfield at the time I wrote my
Letter, & long after: so that it might probably have missed him.

Order'd that this matter be kept in Remembrance, untill the meeting of
Convocation; and that Mr Dean Kimberley be then applied unto.

[1] St. Chad's Gospels: this famous 8th-cent. MS. is still in the possession of the Dean and Chapter of
Lichfield. (For description and relevant literature see *CLA* ii, no. 159.) See also 16 and 26 Mar. 1714/15.
It was subsequently on loan to Bentley, who left it with Wanley for Edward Harley to see (see 5 July 1721).

2. I reporting that D[r]. Lancaster is out of Town, and not expected up until about Easter: my Lord Order'd me to write to him about the MSS. of the late Arch-Deacon Bourscough, in order to the making a Bargain for them.[1]

3. I acquainting my Lord that the late M[r] Edward Lhwyd of Oxford left a large Parcel of antient MSS. Welsh & Irish, together with his own Collections, Papers, Stones, Medals, &c. which are seized by the University, for Debt, and may be retrieved for about 80 pounds.[2] Order'd that mention be made of this affair in the letter to D[r]. Lancaster, & that it be enquired how one of the chiefest of M[r] Lhwyds MSS. in Welsh, got (after his Decease) into Jesus-College Library, & what right that College hath unto it.[3]

4. His Lordship speaking of the MSS. still remaining in the Custody of Mons[r]. Aymon in Holland, which were retrievable about the 27th. of November last; and desiring to know why they are not delivered up? I acquainted his Lordship that M[r] Stubs (who was loth to take another Winters Voiage) had written to M[r] Ayhurst Secretary to the Earl of / Strafford to pay the remaining £20, and send the Books & Papers over; but not having seen M[r] Stubs lately, I know not what M[r] Ayhurst hath done herein.[4]—Ordered that I do write to M[r] Stubs by the Penny-post, to know how this affair stands.

p. 2
(f. 2b)

5. Upon occasion of mentioning the Things in M[r]. Aymon's hands, I acquainted his Lordship, that Myn Heer Vossius, (the Nephew of M[r] Isaac Vossius, & now living at Vourbourg near the Haghe) hath still in his Custody The Vossian Study, wherein are many Manuscripts Greek, Latin, &c. of extraordinary Value, The Original Epistles of all learned Men to the Vossij, & the Draughts

---

[1] See 17 May 1715 and footnote (for list).

[2] See also 14 Mar. (item 2), 16 Mar. (item 3), and 26 Mar. (item 4) 1714/15; 7 Apr. (item 2), 16, 19-21, 26, and 30 Apr. 1715; 2, 3, and 10 May 1715. Notwithstanding the statement under the last date and Wanley's assertion that the refusal of Lhwyd's MSS. 'was absolutely promised by Mr. Vice-Chancellor [of Oxford] to my Lord Oxford' (BM Stowe 749, f. 18), Lhwyd's colls. were not obtained for the Harleian Library; the subject was still being pursued later (see Lancaster's letters, 3 Apr. and 19 May 1716, in Harl. 3780, ff. 74, 76). Edward Lhwyd's colls. were widely dispersed (see De Ricci, p. 67); a portion of the MSS. appeared (with the Twysden library) in the Sebright sale, 6 Apr. 1807 (on which see *Gentleman's Magazine*, lxxvii (1807), pp. 419-21). See also next footnote.

[3] A ref. to the 14th/15th-cent. MS., entitled 'The Red Book of Hergest' (Llyfr Coch o Hergest) (cf. 16 Apr. 1715), still preserved in the library of Jesus College, Oxford (MS. cxi: see *Catalogus Codicum MSS. qui in Collegiis Aulisque Oxoniensibus hodie adservantur*, ed. H. O. Coxe, pt. ii, 1852, pp. 36-39, and *HMC Report on MSS. in the Welsh Language*, ed. J. Gwenogvryn Evans, vol. ii, pt. I, 1902, pp. 1-29); it had been presented to the College in 1701 by Thomas Wilkins, the younger, of Llanblethian, Glamorganshire, and a memorandum by him, dated 26 Mar. 1714 (occasioned probably by the events referred to by Wanley in connexion with Lhwyd), is inserted in the MS. (See also C. L. Wrenn, 'Curiosities in a Medieval Manuscript', *Essays and Studies by Members of the English Association*, xxv (1939), pp. 101-15 *passim*.) See previous footnote for other refs. in the Diary.

[4] See also 14 Mar. (item 3) and 21 Mar. (item 4) 1714/15. On Jean Aymon and his MSS. see L. Delisle, *Le Cabinet des manuscrits*, i (1863), pp. 329-32; iii (1881), p. 369. For Stubbs's earlier journey to Holland to buy the Aymon MSS. see *Welbeck Wanleyana*, Misc. no. 37, which contains the instructions to Stubbs (dated 2 July 1712), a list of the MSS. Harley wished to acquire, extracts from Aymon's cat., a brief account of what was actually bought, with prices (3 Jan. 1712/13), &c. Notes of MSS. bought from Aymon are in BM Add. 32096, ff. 355, 356. Reference should also be made to Wanley's description of Harl. 1802 in *Harl. Cat.* (1759) (cf. R. Flower, *Cat. of Irish MSS.*, ii (1926), pp. 428-32). An account of Aymon's MSS. as seen by Uffenbach at The Hague in 1711 is in Uffenbach's *Reisen*: the relevant part in English translation by Stegman of Berlin made in 1760 is in BM Add. 5338 and is printed by C. N. in *Gentleman's Magazine*, cii (1832), pp. 30-32. The MSS. listed are identified thus: 1. 12 leaves (i.e. part of Codex Claromontanus [*CLA* v, no. 521]) = MS. (formerly Harl. 1773) returned by Harley to Paris in 1729; 2, 3. = Harl. 7551, arts. 5-8; 4. = Harl. 1772; 5. = Harl. 1802; 6. = Harl. 1775; 7. = Harl. 3479; 15. = Harl. 1815; 16. = Harl. 1850-2. Item 7 (and one other MS. (Harl. 4355) not mentioned in this list) was acquired through Sherard; for identification see footnote to 29 Nov. 1721, item 12. (See also 18 May 1721, items 11 and 14, and footnotes.) Letters from Aymon to Stubbs and Drummond in 1716 are Harl. 3777, ff. 38, 40.

of theirs also; with other remarkable Papers, which may now be bought while Vossius (who is grown very old) be yet Living.[1]

6. Also, that Mons[r]. Cramer (Counsellor to the King of Prussia, in the Heeren Logement at Amsterdam,) hath the Apocryphal Gospel of S[t]. Barnabas, in Arabic & Italian. The book is written on old Paper, in 8[vo]. & hath Arabic Binding: but that it being a Liber Singularis, Cramer holdeth it at an excessive high price.[2]

7. Order'd that the two last Minutes be taken into Consideration, when M[r] Stubs' his Answer shall be received, & endeavors actually used for getting the Things out of Mons[r]. Aymons hands.

8. His Lordship enquiring what is become of Sir Roger Twisden's Library? I answered that it is bought by Sir Thomas Sebright: but that I cannot as yet learn whether Sir Thomas did buy the MSS. together with the Printed Books. Order'd that D[r] Thorpe be desired to write to his Friend, that we may know what was done.[3]

9. His Lordship being certified by me, that M[r] James Mickleton of Furnivals Inne, had told me that he knew a Roman-Catholic Gentleman in Town, who hath a great number of antient MSS. (amounting to about 300:) all which he had seen. That he had observed among them, an Heraldical Roll, with Rollers, almost as thick as a Mans middle, antiently painted: a Chartulary of Reading-Abbey bound up in old / Velvet, with a large Silver Cross on the outside- p. 3 Cover; with many other Curiosities. That the owner sett's no great Value (f. 3*a*) upon them. That if he could have bought them for a small sum, (as the owner had promised him that he should) he would only have taken what he liked; and I should come in for the remainder of the parcel. That the Owner having by the decease of a relation, received a supply of Money, would not part with his Books; and that being many times requested by me to tell the Name of the Gentleman, M[r] Mickleton always refused so to do; saying that I should never know it, untill he had gotten all that he liked of that parcel into his Chambers; and that then he would bring me to the Gentleman, that I might (if I pleased) buy the rest. My Lord considering this Relation; was pleased to say, that he would desire M[r] Pocklington, (who is very intimate with this M[r] Mickleton,) to try if he cannot, some way or other, gett out the Gentleman's Name & Place of Abode from him.[4]

[1] Isaac Vossius, the classical scholar and originator (with his father, Gerard John Vossius, d. 1649) of the collection, died 1689; his library was sold to the University of Leiden in 1710. See 21 Mar. 1714/15, item 4; 3 May 1722, item 5. 'Vourbourg', i.e. Voorburg, a few miles east of The Hague, in the 17th cent. the home of Spinoza and Huygens. A coll. of letters addressed to Gerard John Vossius was acquired for Harley (see 15 Aug. 1715 and footnotes 2 and 3). Several vols. of Isaac Vossius's correspondence are preserved in the Bodleian Library, Oxford, in the Rawlinson and D'Orville Colls.

[2] The Gospel of Barnabas referred to is a forgery of the 15th cent. at earliest, written in Italian by a renegade from Christianity to Islam (see L. and L. Ragg, *The Gospel of Barnabas*, 1907, and M. R. James, *The Apocryphal New Testament*, 1924, p. 22). Wanley's knowledge of this was derived probably from John Toland, who referred to it in *Nazarenus*, 1718, chap. v and preface; the MS. was acquired by Johan Friedrich Cramer in Amsterdam and lent by him to Toland in 1709. In 1713 Cramer presented it to Prince Eugène of Savoy, whose library in 1738 became part of the Imperial Library at Vienna (Ragg, op. cit., p. x). Cf. 21 Mar. 1714/15, item 4.

[3] The Twysden library, sold by Sir William Twysden, 3rd Bart. (see 14 Mar. 1714/15, item 4), remained in the possession of the Sebright family until its dispersal by Sir John Saunders Sebright, 7th Bart., 6 Apr. 1807. See also 11 Jan. (item 6) and 13 Jan. 1719/20; 5 Jan. 1725/6.

[4] i.e. 'Mr. Ainsworth of Southwark' (see 26 Mar. 1714/15, items 2 and 11). The items specified by Wanley have not been identified.

10. His Lordship appointed Monday-morning next, for conferring on these matters.

Monday 7 March, 1714/5.

His Lordship being busied, respited the business of this day, until to morrow.

Tuesday 8 March, 1714/5.

His Lordship was this morning also busied.

NB. I having been seized the next morning by a fit of the Stone-Cholic; nothing was done the remaining part of the week. /

p. 4
(f. 3b)

14. March 1714/5.
Present my Lord Harley.

1. The Secretary produced a Letter from D^r. Lancaster, who is willing that my Lord should have M^r. A. D. Bourscough's MSS. which the Widow valueth at £100. The same Letter also sheweth that Mr Grisdale the Doctors Curate hath Orders to suffer the said MSS to be inspected, & a Catalogue of them to be taken, if desired. The Secretary hereupon added, that he had been with Mr Grisdale, who owneth his having received such Orders from Doctor Lancaster, and hath promised to attend to morrow morning in Order to the Secretaries taking a List of them. Order'd that the Secretary do begin the Catalogue to morrow morning, and finish the same as soon as may be.[1]

2. D^r. Lancaster further sett forth in his said Letter that Mr Edward Lhwyds things are Sequestred by the University for Debt, & not yet bought: that the Catalogue of the same, now in the Vice-Chancellors hands, was made by Mr Parry, who had an opportunity of imbezeling what he pleased from the Parcel. That he will send up a Copie thereof, and enquire after the MS in Jesus College, if desired. Order'd that this be consider'd at the next Meeting.[2]

3. The Secretary produced a Letter from Mr Stubs, certifying that Mr Ayerst is now at Cambridge; that he will write to him forthwith; and will send his Answer, as also his own Opinion touching the state of my Lord Oxfords business with Monsieur Aymon.[3]

4. The Secretary produced a Letter from D^r. Thorpe; who writes, that he is acquainted by the Rev^d. Mr Boraston (who menaged the sale of S^r. William Twisdens Books) that Sir Thomas Sebright did buy the MSS, with the Printed books: the Said MSS. being by Mr Boraston deemed to be of no great Value. Order'd, that this be taken into consideration at next Meeting.[4]

5. The Secretary acquainted his Lordship, that he had received a Letter & a small Parcel from Mr Baker of Cambridge; wherein was the Original Letter of Erasmus, & some other Papers: and that Mr Baker write's that he hath, now, sent up everything that / belongeth to my Lord Oxford, except D^r. Beaumonts Determinations, which will come up about a month hence.[5]

p. 5
(f. 4a)

[1] See 17 May 1715 and footnote. Lancaster's letter (cf. 2 Mar. 1714/15, item 2) has not been traced.
[2] See 2 Mar. 1714/15, item 3, and footnote.
[3] See 2 Mar. 1714/15, item 4, and footnote. Stubbs's letter has not been traced.
[4] See 2 Mar. 1714/15, item 8. Thorpe's letter has not been traced. No further discussion of this subject is recorded.
[5] The letter from Erasmus (to R. Pace, 1521) is now Harl. 6989, f. 5 (it is endorsed 'Bought of Mr Baker'). The *letters* bought of Baker are scattered now in Harl. 6987-7018; his 23 vols. of *Collections* are

Wednesday 16 March 1714/5.

Present, my Lord Harley.

1. Order'd that Mr Dean Kimberley, be applied unto about the Textus S. Ceaddæ.[1]

2. My Lord said he had not yet spoken to Mr Pocklington, in pursuance of the 9th. Minute of the 2^d. of March; but would soon do it.

3. The Secretary related, that he did yesterday morning go to D^r. Lancasters, and that he did take a short List of Mr A. D. B[o]urscough's MSS. there; among which he found divers very good things. And that his Opinion is, that the Parcel will come cheap, if it may be procured for £.50; or 60. Ordered, that he do write to D^r. Lancaster upon this Matter, and offer £40 for the said Parcel:[2] and also desire a List of the things left by Mr Edw. Lhwyd, now under Sequestration, in Order to the coming to a Bargain for the Same.[3]

4. The Secretary produced a Draught of a Letter to Doctor Lancaster, upon the business above-mentioned, which was read; and being approved by his Lordship, was Order'd to be sent.

5. Order'd that the 5th. & 6th. Minutes of the 2^d. of March be considered, when Mr Stubs's next Letter shall come to hand.

6. My Lord asking what is become of the MSS. of Mr Johnson the late Armes-Painter? the Secretary replied that he shall have an Opportunity of talking with Mr Howel about that Parcel this afternoon.[4]

7. My Lord said, he heard that the MSS. & Papers formerly belonging to the late Lord Chief Justice Hale, and not given to Lincoln's Inne, might possibly be retrieved; & therefore Order'd this notice to be now taken thereof, that it may be considered another time. /[5]

Monday 21 March 1714/5.

Present my Lord Harley.

p. 6
(f. 4b)

1. My Lord Harley brought in a little Russian MS. bought of Mr Bagford.[6]

2. The Secretary related that the Rev^d. & Learned Mr Elstob deceased some time since; and that he having seen M^{rs}. Elstob his Sister, and making mention of the two MSS. which Mr Elstob had borrowed from the Library, (being 34.A.16. & 42.A.12:) she said she would take all due Care to see them safely restored.[7]

3. My Lord Harley expressing some Compassion upon the unexpected Decease of Mr Urry of Christ-church: the Secretary shewed that two MSS. borrowed for his use by the present Bishop of Rochester, while Dean of Christ-church,

---

Harl. 7028–50. See letters from Baker in Harl. 3777, ff. 76, 78. See also 21 Mar. 1714/15, item 5; 8 Apr. 1715; 16, 20, and 24 July 1715. The *Determinations* were probably still on loan to 'Mr Waren' (see Baker to Wanley, 30 Jan. 1714/15, Harl. 3778, f. 76). *See also* Biographical Index *under* Baker.

[1] See 2 Mar. 1714/15, item 1, and footnote.

[2] See 17 May 1715 and footnote. Wanley's short list is preserved in Welbeck Wanleyana.

[3] See 2 Mar. 1714/15, item 3, and footnote.

[4] See 26 Mar. 1714/15, item 5; 30 May 1715.

[5] See 26 Mar. 1714/15, item 6. On Hale's MSS. see *DNB* xxiv. 21 ff., and more fully on Hale MSS. at Lincoln's Inn, J. Hunter, *Catalogue of the Library of Lincoln's Inn*, 1838.

[6] Not certainly identified.

[7] William Elstob died 18 Mar. 1714/15; the 2 MSS. are Harl. 55 and 636 respectively. They were returned to the Library 9 May 1715.

are not yet Restored; and that he hath a note under the Bishops Hand for the same. My Lord undertook to menage this matter.¹

4. The Secretary related that he hath seen Mr Stubs and also Mr Ayhurst; who saith that he did speak unto Mr Aymon & Mr Johnson in Holland touching the delivering up the remaining part of the MSS. bought of the former: and that they only said, that not having received any Subscriptions from England, their Project of Printing some of them is yet at a Stand. Also, that Mr Stubs had hinted somewhat, as if he was willing, in the Somer-Season, to go again to Holland, & fetch the things over.² Hereupon, the Secretary (in pursuance of the 5th. Minute of Wednesday last,) did put his Lordship in Mind of the 5th. & 6th. Minutes of the Second Instant; and observed, that supposing Mr Stubs should go to Holland purposely to fetch away the things from Monsieur Aymon, yet (through want of Experience) he is not capable of buying Mynheer Vossius's things, which ought to be done at once; without giving him time to find out, for whom they are bought, or otherways to consider by what means he may enhance the price; and that he is no more capable of bidding for such a book as that of Monsr. Cramer; so that he can do but half my Lords business: He, the Secretary, offered his Service to go to Holland (as soon as his business in the National Lottery shall be ended) and to dispatch the whole without further trouble to Mr Stubs. My Lord said that this matter deserving good delibera-tion, he would Consider thereof against this day Sevenight.³

5. Order'd that the Secretary do put my Lord of Oxford (upon his coming up to Town) in mind of Mr Baker of Cambridge.⁴

6. My Lord deliver'd into the Library a very small MS. written in English-Short-hand.⁵

7. The Secretary related that Dr. Smith of Durham is come to Town. /

p. 7
(f. 5a)

Wednesday 23 March 1714/5.

My Lord brought in a Paper MS. in fol. consisting of divers Tracts; the first is, the Confession of Faith of Sr. Francis Bacon.⁶

Saturday 26 March 1714/5.

1. Order'd that Mr Dean Kimberley be applied unto, about the Textus S. Ceaddæ.⁷

2. My Lord was pleased to say that he had spoken to Mr Pocklington who readily promised to serve his Lordship in the affair with Mr Mickleton.⁸

4 [sic]. My Lord was further pleased to say that he had seen Dr. Lancaster, who owned the receipt of the Secretaries last Letter;⁹ and did promise to use his best

---

¹ John Urry died 3 Mar. 1714/15; the 'Bishop of Rochester' referred to is Francis Atterbury (Dean of Christ Church, Oxford, 1712–13). William Thomas (who was later responsible for the posthumous publication of Urry's *Chaucer* (1721)) borrowed in 1720 Harl. 78, 1239, 1758, and an unnumbered MS. (see 17 Aug. (item 7) and 14 Oct. (item 12) 1720). The MSS. borrowed by Urry may have been two of these. See 26 Mar. 1714/15, item 7; 7 Apr. 1715, item 3.
² Cf. 2 Mar. 1715, item 4, and footnote.
³ See 2 Mar. 1714/15, items 5 and 6, for Vossius and Cramer business. Wanley never went to Holland.
⁴ See 14 Mar. 1714/15, item 5.
⁵ Not certainly identifiable but possibly the shorthand miniature Psalter (Harl. 5307) noted by Wanley (f. 1*) as 'brought by Mr Bagford to my Lord Harley'.
⁶ Harl. 1893.　　　　　　　　　　　　　　　　　⁷ See 2 Mar. 1714/15, item 1.
⁸ See 2 Mar. 1714/15, item 9.　　　　　　　　⁹ See 16 Mar. 1714/15, items 3 and 4.

ɹndeavors to serve my Lord not only with relation to M^{rs}. Bourscough, but with the University about Mr Lhwyds things. Only he can do nothing until his return to Oxford.

5. The Secretary related that he had seen old Mr Howel; who said that Mr Johnson the Arms-painters relations are removed from Little Britain, but whither he cannot tell. That he had, in hopes of a Gratuity, promised his Service in procuring this parcel of Books. But the Secretary, finding him extremely broken since the last Year, and that His Memory & Apprehension are almost gone, believeth him capable of performing little.[1]

6. Order'd that the Books & Papers of the late Lord Chief Justice Hale, not given to Lincolns Inne, be kept in memory.[2]

7. My Lord was pleased to say that he had written to D^r. Terry the Sub-dean of Christ-church, to take proper Care to Secure the two MSS. borrowed out of the Library for Mr Urries use.[3]

8. The Secretary related, that he had been to visit D^r. Smith of Durham, who was absent. That in his Lodgings he saw a fine old MS. of part of Bede's Historical Works in Latin, borrowed of a Gentleman of Graies Inne: as also an Imperfect MS. of the Ecclesiastical History, in Saxon, a very antient Copie, borrowed of Doctor Tanner Chancellor of Norwich.[4]

9. Hereupon the Secretary further shewed that, besides Bedes Ecclesiastical History above-mentioned, there are two other valuable Saxon MSS. still in Private Hands. namely, / King Ælfɲeð's Translation of Orosius de Ormesta mundi, **p. 8** which formerly belonged to D^r. Dee, & lately to the Duke of Lauderdale: in **(f. 5b)** obtaining which, Mr Brome of Ewillington [*sic for* Ewithington] set on by D^r. Hickes, may do good Service.[5] That the other, is an antient & valuable Copie of Ælfricks Grammar, with some Saxon Homilies at the end, which he saw in Mr Anstis his Study; who hath also, the Psalterium Gallicanum of S^t. Hierom with the ⁜ & ÷ written about the time of the last King Æthe[l]dred, with the Litany & some prayers, being one of the most beautiful books that can be seen. but that Mr Anstis, although he hath put his own Numbers & Marks upon them, & placeth them among his other books, yet saith that they are not his own.[6]

---

[1] See 16 Mar. 1714/15, item 6.

[2] See 16 Mar. 1714/15, item 7.　　　　　　　　　　　　[3] Cf. 21 Mar. 1714/15, item 3, and footnote.

[4] The presence of Bede MSS. in Dr. [John] Smith's lodgings at this time is due to the fact that he was preparing an edition of the Historia Ecclesiastica which was published (posthumously) at Cambridge in 1722 under the supervision of his son, George Smith. The imperfect MS. of the Anglo-Saxon version of the Historia Ecclesiastica is now Bodleian Library, Oxford, Tanner MS. 10 (a 10th-cent. MS. from Thorney); the MS. of Bede's Historical Works borrowed of a Gentleman of Gray's Inn has not been identified.

[5] i.e. the late-9th-cent. MS. of the Anglo-Saxon translation of Orosius attributed to King Alfred, commonly called the Lauderdale (or Helmingham Hall) Orosius, now BM Add. 47967. Wanley in saying that it belonged to 'Dr Dee' (i.e John Dee, the Elizabethan astrologer, &c., 1527–1608) was apparently repeating a tradition, as Dee's signature is not now in the MS. The Duke of Lauderdale referred to is John Maitland, cr. 1672 Duke of Lauderdale, the politician (1616–82). The presumption that Hickes might have influence in this direction may be due to the fact that Hickes had been chaplain to the Duke 1677–82. This MS. had been recorded by Wanley (without examination) in his Cat. of Anglo-Saxon MSS., Hickes's *Thesaurus*, ii (1705), p. 303 and Preface, b 1; and had been previously noted by Hickes himself in his 'Catalogus Veterum Librorum Septentrionalium' in R. Jonas, *Grammaticae Islandicae Rudimenta*, Oxford, 1688, 1689, p. 167; to Hickes is probably due the tradition that it belonged to Dee, 'Hic Cod. olim fuit peculium Johannis Dee M.D.' (For a description of the MS. see N. R. Ker, *Catalogue of Manuscripts containing Anglo-Saxon*, Oxford, 1957, no. 133.)

[6] Neither of the items referred to appears in the Anstis sale cat. of 12 Dec. 1768.

10. The Secretary further said, that D^r. Brewster of Hereford hath some few old MSS. & among them, a Leiger-book of Malmesbury.[1]

11. After so much business done, & his Lordships departure; he returned, & said that he had just spoken to Mr Pocklington, who said that Mr Mickleton had told him that Mr Ainsworth of Southwark is the person who hath the MSS. mentioned in the 9th. Minute of the 2^d. of March. /

p. 9
(f. 6a)

4 April 1715.

1. My Lord Harley sent into the Library an antient Copie of Speculum Humanæ Salvationis, adorned with Illuminations in each page; whereof many are now decayed. The book is bound up in Crimson-Velvet, & hath the Arms of the old Kings of England at the bottom of the first Leaf.[2] The other book is a fine old Primer formerly belonging to Edward Lord North, whose Armes are frequently painted therein.[3] Both books cost 20 Guineas.

5 April. 1715.

My Lord Harley brought into the Library a thin MS. in fol. relating to the Earles of Essex Northampton Somerset, &c. temp. Jac. I. bought of Mr Bagford.[4]

7 April. 1715.

1. My Lord Order'd that that part of the 4th. Minute of 21 March last, relating to the Secretaries going to Holland; shall be kept in Mind.

2. The Secretary produced a Letter from the Vice-Chancellor of Oxford for D^r. Lancaster; the purport whereof is, that upon a report made by D^r. Hudson, the University had declined the buying of A. D. Bourscough's MSS.[5] and giving the Titles of some of the Welsh & Cornish MSS & papers now remaining among Mr Lhwyds things. Hereupon, his Lordship Ordered the Secretary to find out Mr Hugh Thomas, and to take a Certificate from him touching that Welsh MS which belonged to Mr Lhwyd, & since his decease came into Jesus-College-Library: and that he do deliver such Certificate to D^r. Lancaster, that it may be sent to the said Vice-Chancellor, in Order to reclaiming the said Book.[6]

3. His Lordship was pleased to relate, that D^r. Terry had certified him, that M^r. Urry of Christ-churches Closet is Sealed up; & will continue so until the arrival of his Relations from Scotland. /[7]

p. 10
(f. 6b)

8 April. 1715.

1. The Secretary brought in 2 Vol's of D^r. Beaumonts Determinations; being sent up by Mr Baker.[8]

---

[1] Five MSS., including the Leiger-book of Malmesbury, were given 7 May 1715 by Brewster to the Bodleian Library, Oxford. (Cf. Macray, p. 195; SC 27641-6.)

[2] Harl. 2838; this is no longer in crimson velvet binding but in one of 19th-cent. date (possibly as late as 1881). The old royal arms are (as Wanley says) on f. 1. The MS. is slightly damaged by damp. It has no date of acquisition by Wanley and the old press-mark is not in Wanley's autograph.

[3] Harl. 3000. Belonged to Edward North, 1st Baron North (1496?-1564); the arms mentioned by Wanley are on ff. 271, 276^b, and 277. No date of acquisition has been written in it by Wanley.

[4] Harl. 4302. The MS. is endorsed on fly-leaf by Wanley, '5 April. 1715. My Lord Harley.'

[5] See 17 May 1715 and footnote.   [6] See 2 Mar. 1714/15, item 3, and footnotes.

[7] See 21 Mar. 1714/15, item 3, and footnote.   [8] See 14 Mar. 1714/15, item 5, and footnote.

[—] April 1715.

2. The Secretary related that Mr Fiddis had given a smal parcel of Letters & Papers; which he had Endorsed as given by Him; and distributed into their proper places.[1]

3. The Secretary also related that he Himself had lately procured an Original Letter of Erasmus; and that he Gave the same, & placed it in the Library accordingly.[2]

16 April 1715.

4. The B^p. of Carlile came to the Library, & brought with him a Catalogue of the Welsh & Cornish MSS. belonging to Mr Edward Lhwyd deceased. Among them, appear certain Transcripts from the Old MS. called *Y Lhyvyr kôch o Hergest*, (which is the book meant pag. 1. §. 3.) owned in the said Catalogue to be now kept in Jesus-College-Library. The Titles of All the said M^r. Lhwyds Irish MSS. are omitted.[3]

19 April. 1715.

5. The Secretary went to Mr Alban Thomas, who formerly Lived with Mr Edw. Lhwyd, who gave him a Certificate Signed by his Hand, importing that *Y Lhyvyr kôch o Hergest*, did belong to Mr Lhwyd aforesaid, and was in his Possession at the Time of his Decease. And that above a year afterwards He the same Mr Thomas did see the same Stand among Mr Lhwyds MSS. in the Musæum.[4]

20 April. 1715.

6. The Secretary shewed the Certificate above-mentioned to D^r. Lancaster, and promised, that after he had taken a Copie of the same, he would leave it with him to be sent to Oxford, in Order to a Reclaim of the Book of Hergest.[5]

7. D^r. Lancaster saying that he had not yet heard from Mr Ayres, touching M^rs. Bourscough; the Secretary undertook to procure Her Direction, that She may be written unto from hence. /[6]

21 April 1715.

p. 11
(f. 7*a*)

1. The Secretary related, that by D^r. Lancasters advice, he had drawn up a Letter to the Vicechancellor of Oxford, in Order to the reclaiming Y Lhyvyr kôch o Hergest from Jesus College, & procuring all Mr Edw. Lhwyds Books & Papers to be Sold by the University to my Lord Oxford. Which Letter being Read, was Approved & Order'd to be sent.[7]

26. April 1715.

2. The Secretary produced a Letter from the Vice-chancellor of Oxford, shewing that he had Order'd one of Mr Lhwyds Welsh MSS. to be delivered to the

---

[1] The letters, &c., given by Fiddes are dispersed now in Harl. 7001 (ff. 93, 101, 104, 112, 113, 115–19, 125, 129, 133, 137, 143, 145); 7003 (ff. 168, 170, 331, 333–63); 7004 (f. 120); 7006 (ff. 249, 254).
[2] Now Harl. 6989, f. 9: a letter from Erasmus to Fisher, 1522, endorsed by Wanley (f. 10^b), 'Given by Humf. Wanley.'
[3] 'The Bp. of Carlisle' is William Nicolson. See 2 Mar. 1714/15, item 3, and footnotes.
[4] See 2 Mar. 1714/15, item 3, and footnotes; 'the Musæum' is the Ashmolean Museum, Oxford.
[5] See 19 Apr. 1715, and footnote.
[6] See 26 Mar. 1714/15, item 4, and footnote.   [7] See 2 Mar. 1714/15, item 3, and footnotes.

Principal of Jesus-College[1] for the Library there, he averring that it did really belong unto it. But that he would, er'e long, make a thorough Enquiry into that matter. That my Lord Bp. of Carlile & my Lord Mansell are Bidders for Mr Lhwyds things, but that they should not be disposed of, without my Lords Privity. The Secretary was Order'd to write again to the Vicechancellor about the Lhyvyr kôch o Hergest; to shew that neither of the Lords abovementioned have any intention of buying those things; to offer £.6. for the Irish MSS. alone; & to specifie my Lords intention of buying the whole parcell.[2]

30. April 1715.

3. The Secretary produced another Letter from the Vice-chancellor of Oxford; shewing that the Bp. of St. Asaph now Principal of Jesus-College, own's that the Book which he had received out of Mr Lhwyd's Collection, is the Lhyvyr kôch o Hergest; but that He should think himself obliged to make the Colleges Title to it good, because that on his Demand, He the Vice-Chancellor had parted with it. But that he should shortly have a Letter from the person who put it into Mr Lhwyds hands, & know's best where the Right lies. Mr [sic, for My] Lord shewed a desire that this matter may be searched to the bottom.[3]

4. His Lordship brought in an Imperfect MS. of Postils or Sermons, written in old English upon Parchment, in small 4to. /[4]

p. 12
(f. 7b)

2 May 1715.

1. The Secretary related that Mr Hugh Thomas did, this day, say, that Mr Edward Lhwyd of Oxford (in communication with him, about the Lhyvyr kôch o Hergest) several times owned that it was but lent unto him: in which times the book was in bad condition, without any cover, and the leaves transposed. That, afterwards Mr Lhwyd put the Leaves into their proper places, & Paged them with his own hand, & caused them to be finely bound up in Red Turkey Leather; and did declare to the said Mr Hugh Thomas, that he did so, because the book would never be demanded of him again.[5]

3 May 1715.

2. The Secretary produced a Letter from Dr. Lancaster, specifying that the Widow Bourscough will take £.40. for her MSS. and that the Principal of Jesus will undertake to prove that the Red book of Hergest belong's to His College. The Secretary was Order'd to write an Answer to Dr. Lancaster, desiring him to Order the said MSS. to be delivered up; and that the £40. shall be paid to him upon his Return to Town.[6]

3. The Secretary Related that the fine Prayer-book, which the late Lord Weymouth bought at the Price of £100; is now come into the Possession of Sir Robert Worseley; who (having been asked) is willing to sell it to my Lord at the same price.[7]

---

[1] i.e. John Wynne.   [2] See 2 Mar. 1714/15, item 3, and footnotes.
[3] See 2 Mar. 1714/15, item 3, and footnotes. 'The person' was Thomas Wilkins (see p. 2, footnote 3).
[4] Harl. 2420 (+2417).
[5] See 2 Mar. 1714/15, item 3, and footnotes.
[6] For Bourscough business see 17 May 1715 and footnote; for Lhwyd and 'Red Book of Hergest' affair see 2 Mar. 1714/15, item 3 and footnotes. Lancaster's letter has not been traced.
[7] See 4 and 6 May 1715.

4 May 1715.

4. M[r]. Harbyn brought the fine Primer in the Minute last above-mentioned, & delivered the same to my Lord Harley that it might be shewn to my Lord of Oxford, 'Who may have it at the price of One Hundred Pounds; which Sum my Lord Weymouth gave for it.' [' ' *deleted in MS.*]

5 May, 1715.

5. My Lord Harley brought in a little MS. Primer, or Horae B.V.M.[1]

6. May, 1715.

6. My Lord Harley was pleased to Order that the Primer above-mentioned be redilivered to M[r] Harbyn for Sir Robert Worseley; it being judged too dear at £.100. and his Lordship having another book, yet finer than this, in his View.[2]

9 May, 1715.

7. The Secretary brought from M[rs]. Elstob, the two MSS. Lent to her deceased Brother.[3]

10. May, 1715.

8. The Secretary produced a Letter from D[r] Lancaster, shewing that A. D. Bourscoughs MSS. may be fetched away from his house, & the Money paid to Mr Grisdale his Curate.[4] And that the University Delegates / are willing that p. 13 my Lord Oxford should have Mr Lhwyds MSS; also, that they will Inspect (f. 8a) the Accompts of Jesus College, to know whether that College paid for the Binding of Lhyvyr kôch o Hergest or not.[5]

17 May 1715.

1. My Lord Harley đđ £.40. to the Secretary for A. D. Bourscough's MSS. which he saw brought-in the same day; & began to put the present Date upon each of them; that thereby they may be distinguished from those which belong to other parcells.[6]

[1] Harl. 3180.
[2] But it was bought for £100, 14 Dec. 1717 (Welbeck Wanleyana, Misc. no. 50) and is perhaps now BM Add. 18850. [3] See 21 Mar. 1714/15, item 2, and footnote.
[4] See 17 May 1715, and footnote. [5] See 2 Mar. 1714/15, item 3, and footnotes.
[6] Cf. 2 Mar. (item 2), 14 Mar. (item 1), 16 Mar. (item 3), 26 Mar. (item 4) 1714/15; 7 Apr. (item 2), 20 Apr. and 3 May 1715. Bourscough's MSS. had already been listed in *CMA* nos. 7620–7710, 9162–79. The brief list in Wanley's autogr. (mentioned 16 Mar. 1714/15, item 3) is preserved in Welbeck Wanleyana. The Harl. MSS. bearing this day's date in Wanley's hand are: 1913–15, 1917–19, 2257, 2258, 2265, 2269–72, 2274, 2277, 2280, 2297, 2307, 2333, 2341, 2342, 2344–8, 2350, 2352, 2355, 2357, 2359–61, 2364, 2365, 2367, 2369, 2383, 2399, 2401, 2404, (?)2409, (?)2410, 2411, 2415, 2418, 2427, 2432, 2435–7, 2439, (?)2650, 2691, (?)2693, 2715, 2729, 2766, (?)2806, (?)2809, 2825, 2845, 2849, 2856, 2874, (?)2961, 2984, 3044, 3094, 3133, 3140, 3205, 3221, 3231, 3291, 3294, 3295, 3300, 3304, 3316, 3334, 3363, (?)3369, 3371, 3378, 3383, 3388, 3407, 3426, 3433, 3447, 3524, 3528, (?)3535, 3537, 3542, 3594, 3596, 3603, 3665, 3686, 3719, 3733, 3747, 3760, 3768, 3770, 3817–19, 3823, 3835, 3850, 4092, 4143, 4260, 4278, 4324, 4347, 4383, 4390, 4766, 4975, 4997, 5108 (ff. 145–52), (?)5118, 5130, (?)5225, 5233, 5235, 5244, (?)5250, 5345, 5958 (f. 87). Harl. Ch. 111. A. 19 and 111. C. 16 are also endorsed by Wanley with this date. The MSS. queried in the above list bear in Wanley's hand the date '7 May 1715', a slip for '17 May 1715'; some have been identified in the *CMA* list, as have Harl. 1916, 3554, ff. 255–92 (which bears *no* date by Wanley); Harl. 2266, 3366 endorsed by Wanley '17 May 1724/5' have been identified as Bourscough MSS. from the *CMA* list. For identifications with *CMA* list see Numerical Table. In Harl. 7526, f. 161, is a letter from Sam. Whalley, from Totnes, to John Anstis relating to the disposal of Bourscough's MSS. by his widow, dated 3 Apr. 1713.

19 May 1715.

2. My Lord Harley brought in three small MSS.[1]

30 May 1715.

3. The Secretary related, that Mr Howel had found out the Persons who own Mr Johnsons Heraldical MSS. that they say they will abate nothing of £60. for that parcel; and that Mr Howell expect's to be gratified for his trouble Whether they be bought, or not. The Secretary was Ordered to pursue this affair, upon the present foundation.[2]

2 June 1715.

4. My Lord Harley brought in two Warants under the Sign Manual of King Charles I. being bought of Mr Bagford.[3]

9 June 1715.

5. The Secretary brought in a Letter with the Sign Manual of K. Henry VII. and the Lords Prayer in the Hungarian Language, with a Latin Version; both given by Mr Granger.[4]

10 June 1715.

6. My noble Lord Oxford was pleased to bring in an Original Letter of the Elector Palatin to Qu. Anne: and an Extract from a letter of the late Emperor of Morocco to her Majestie, in Arabic; with an English Version.[5]

14 June 1715.

7. My Noble Lord Oxford was pleased to send in an Original Letter of Louise Princess of Holstein to Queen Anne.[6]

15, June 1715.

8. My Noble Lord Oxford was pleased to send in an Original Lre of Victor Amedeo the present King of Sicily, to himself.[7]

18. June 1715.

9. My said Noble Lord was pleased to send in an Original Lre of Queen Anne, to the Duke of Wirtemberg.[8]

[1] Harl. 5315, 5363, 7393.
[2] See 16 Mar. 1714/15, item 6, and footnote.
[3] Harl. 6988, ff. 164–165^b, 174–175^b.
[4] Harl. 6986, f. 7 ('K. Henry VII' should read 'K. Henry VIII') and Harl. 7013, f. 133; both are endorsed by Wanley as being given by Thomas Granger, of the East India House, with the date 8 June 1715.
[5] The letter of the Elector Palatine is Harl. 7016, f. 53. The Emperor of Morocco item has not been traced.
[6] Harl. 7016, f. 57.
[7] Not identified.
[8] ? BM Lansdowne 1236, ff. 240–241 b (Q. Anne to Duke of Württemberg, 24 July 1707). (Several items from the Harleian Library found their way into the Lansdowne Coll. via James West.)

21 June 1715.

10. The Secretary brought in the fine Persian MS.[1] with the two Liturgical MSS.[2] for which my Noble Lord Oxford had / offered five Guineas: The man, p. 14 Mr Suttie, having been with him, & grown willing to accept the same; which (f. 8b) Money, the Secretary paid out of his own purse. (and ha's been long since repaid.)

26 June 1715.

1. My Lord Harley brought in, a very small Theological MS. in old English; bought of Mr Bagford.[3]

16 July 1715.[4]

2. The Secretary produced a Letter from Mr Baker of Cambridge (in Answer to one written unto him by my Lord Harley's Order,) touching the £40 due to him for the books & Papers formerly bought of him: which £40, he desires may be paid to his Brother now in Town.[5]

20 July 1715.

3. The Secretary produced Mr Baker the brother's Receipt for the £40 above-mentioned.[6]

21 July 1715.

4. The Secretary produced a Letter from Dr. Smith of Durham now at Cambridge, who desires that my Lord will give a complete Sett of Dacier's Spicilegium, in lieu of the Greek MS of Suidas which was presented by the Dean & Chapter of Durham.[7]

24 July 1715.

5. The Secretary produced a Letter from Mr Baker of Cambridge, owning the Receipt of the £40 paid to his brother by his Order.[8]

2 August 1715.

6. The Secretary produced a Receipt under the Hand of Dr. Smith of Durham (dated 19 July 1715) for the Sett of Daciers Spicilegium abovementioned.[9]

6 August 1715.

7. The Secretary brought in 4 thick octavo books, partly written & partly printed, relating (chiefly) to our Common Law. Those three which are in Covers of Velvet, &c. are supposed to be of the Hand of the Lord Chief Justice Sir

---

[1] Not identified.

[2] Harl. 2897, 2967 (the latter is dated by Wanley; the former bears no Wanley inscription but was identified by Madden in a note in the MS. of the Diary).

[3] Harl. 2343.

[4] This day Robert Harley, 1st Earl of Oxford, was committed to the Tower (where he remained until 1 July 1717). It is significant that it was shortly after this (on 27 July 1715) that Wanley drew up the memorandum on the Harleian Library printed *HMC Portland Papers*, v, pp. 514–16.

[5] See 14 Mar. 1714/15, item 5, and footnote. Baker's letter has not been traced.

[6] See 14 Mar. 1714/15, item 5, and footnote.

[7] Smith's letter has not been traced. The 'Dacier's Spicilegium' is the famous *Spicilegium* of Jean Luc D'Achéry (d. 1685). The Suidas MS. is Harl. 3100 (which has no note by Wanley). See 3 June 1723, item 19, footnote 3.

[8] See 14 Mar. 1714/15, item 5, and footnote.   [9] See 21 July 1715, and footnote.

Edward Coke; and that the notes of the other, being in Parchment-Cover, are written by Sir William Stroud, Father to Madam Thynne, who gave them all four to the Library. /[1]

15 August 1715.

1. The Secretary having bought the following Parcel of MSS. of M[r] Richard Jones Bookseller at 26[lib]. 17[s]. 6[d]. brought in the books & his Receipt for the money. They are

   Original Epistles of Learned Men, &c. to Gerard-John Vossius.[2]
   Original Draughts of Gerard-John Vossius.[3]
   A very antient & fair Hebrew MS. Liturgical. in fol. Membr.[4]
   A Paper MS. in fol. written in the Spanish Rabbinical Letter, with many rude Pictures.[5]
   A Register-book of Will. Holloweye Prior of Bath & John Clark B[p]. of Bath & Welles.[6]
   An Antient MS in Velum; seeming to be a good Copie of S[t]. Ambrose's Epistles.[7]
   Original Process against Cranmer, Ridley, & Latimer at Oxford signed by the Public Notary. fol. membr.[8]
   Psalterium cum precibus & Illuminatt. vetust. membr. 8vo.[9]
   Liber pusillus, membr. in quo varia: scil. Liber metricus de Susanna, &c. per Fratrem Mårmaducŭcum [sic] de Melsa Magistrum de Beverlaco:— Legendariæ narrationes—Mirabilia Britanniæ—Missa Gulonis, i.e. Potatorum.—&c.[10]
   A Russian MS. in 4to-pap being a Chronicle of that Countrey, down to the decease of the false Demetrius; said to have been compiled by the Abbot of S[t]. Suria & his Brethren.[11]

19 August 1715.

2. The Secretary brought in the Original Greek Letter sent by the Deputies & Clergy of the Church of Alexandria in Egypt, to the Reverend M[r] Philip Stubs Rector of Garlick-hyth-Church, & Lodging at Sion-College. Which he desired the said M[r] Stubs to deposit into the Library at his gift. (NB. M[r]. Stubs afterwards said that He only Lent it, & desiring to have it back, it was restored to him.)[12]

22. August 1715.

3. The Secretary brought in a small Parcel of MSS. at 10 Guineas price; which were paid him instantly.

[1] Now Harl. 6686 and 6687 A–D. The former (Law Precedents, 33 Eliz.–5 Jas. I) appears in the cat. of Sir Edward Coke's books, compiled shortly before his death (3 Sept. 1634), now preserved at Holkham, under the number 293, the first item in the section of 'the books of the lawes of England', the latter (an annotated copy of Littleton) under the number 369 (see *A Catalogue of the Library of Sir Edward Coke*, ed. W. O. Hassall (Yale Law Library Publications, no. 12, 1950), pp. 22, 29). The velvet bindings are no longer extant.
[2] and [3] Harl. 7004, f. 118; 7011, ff. 5, 44, 46, 55, 64, 69, 71, 74, 93, 94–96, 103–6, 110, 113, 122–39; 7012; 7013, ff. 1, 152, 154–74, 185–9, 205–41; 7016, ff. 39, 41, 45, 47, 49, 51.
[4] Harl. 5701.   [5] Harl. 5794 (+ 5794*).   [6] Harl. 3970(= Davis no. 26).   [7] Harl. 3083.
[8] Harl. 3642.   [9] Harl. 2356.   [10] Harl. 2851.   [11] Harl. 3519.
[12] The letter to Stubbs has not been traced. It was possibly written to represent the circumstances of the Greek Church in Alexandria under the Turkish rule and is probably to be related to the mission of Arsenius in 1712, on which see T. Lathbury, *A History of the Nonjurors*, 1845, chap. viii, and G. Williams, *The Orthodox Church of the East in the Eighteenth Century*, 1868.

A Greek Nomo-canon written here by old Gennadius the Archimandrite & the younger Gennadius the Deacon his Nephew.[1]

An Antient & fine Psalter, &c. in old Norman-French.[2]

Thomæ Cantipratensis Bonum Universale.[3]

A Collection of Drawings for Garden-knots.[4]

4. My Lord Harley authorised the Secretary to give Commission to Mr Vaillant the Bookseller, to buy certain books to be sold at the approach[ing] Auction of Bibliotheca Sarraziana in Holland. /[5]

18 July 1716.

p. 16
(f. 9b)

M[r] Anstis gave a Second Parcel of old Deeds; about 363 in Number, which will all be Endorsed with the Date above. /[6]

11th. January 1719 This Journal resumed by my Lord Harley's Order.[7]

p. 17
(f. 10a)

20.

1. I acquainted my Lord, that m[r] Jonah Bowyer the Bookseller will secure such books as my Lord hath marked in his Printed Catalogue, at the approaching Auction;[8] or at least, such of them as may be had at reasonable Prices.

2. Also, that He hath a Number of Papers Printed & Written, relating to very many of the Ecclesiastical Benefices of England; at present, belonging to another Person. Certain of them I left with His Lordship.[9]

3. Also, that He is in Hopes of Buying the whole Library of the late D[r]. Batteley A.D. of Canterbury.[10]

---

[1] Not identified (Harl. 5556 was written by Gennadius the Deacon in London in 1714, but is not a Nomocanon).

[2] Harl. 3978. [3] Harl. 3832. [4] Harl. 5308.

[5] See *Bibliotheca Sarraziana, distrahenda per Abr. de Hondt et H. Scheurleer . . . ad diem 16 Sept. 1715, &c.* The Hague, 1715. A letter from Edward Harley to Wanley of 6 Oct. 1715 in Welbeck Wanleyana refers to the books purchased by Vaillant at this auction of the Library of G. L. de la Sarra.

[6] See 23 Nov. 1722, item 14, where Wanley states that most of the deeds that came from Anstis are within Harl. Ch. 83. C. 10–84. B. 61, but others were brought in 24 Dec. 1722 and 20 Feb. 1722/3. (The items in this parcel were apparently not endorsed with the date 18 July 1716 until 24 Dec. 1722.) Harl. Charters endorsed by Wanley '18 July 1716' are: 112. F. 26–44, 46–53, 55–58, 60–63; 112. G. 1–26, 28–42, 45–64; 112. H. 1–6, [7. n.d.], 8–21, [22 n.d.], 23–67; 112. I. 1–62. Cotton Charters endorsed with the same date by Wanley are: XXVI. 31, 35; XXVII. 146–51, 166, 167, 175, 176, 182, 188, 203; XXVIII. 5, 6, 8, 17, 22–24, 36, 43, 44, 48, 49, 53, 71, 76, 80, 84, 88, 91–94, 96, 99, 101, 102; XXIX. 1, 4, 5, 7, 12, 16. In a letter of 22 July 1716 to Wanley (in Welbeck Wanleyana) Harley says enigmatically: 'I think you did well to oblige Mr. Anstis with the Deeds &c.'

[7] Information about the library business that took place in this period of the gap in the Diary (viz. between 22 Aug. 1715 and 11 Jan. 1719/20 (except for the one entry under 18 July 1716)) is preserved in part in the correspondence between Edward Harley and Wanley in Welbeck Wanleyana. Letters therein from Harley dated 25 and 28 Aug. 1715 show that it was at this period that Wanley made his first visit to Wimpole, where he was engaged intermittently over the next year or two in cataloguing the printed books there (e.g. BM Lansdowne 816).

[8] No auction sale identified between 11 and 20 Jan. 1719/20. See also 20 Jan. (item 1) and 28 Jan. (item 1) 1719/20.

[9] See 19 Feb. 1719/20, item 6, and footnote.

[10] John Batteley, Archdeacon of Canterbury, had died 10 Oct. 1708. For progress of these long-drawn-out negotiations (which were conducted with his nephew, John Batteley, Master of the Court of Augmentations, through a number of booksellers—Bowyer, Noel, Bateman, and Newton) cf. 13 Apr. (item 2), 2 May (item 14), 20 May (item 15), 21 May (item 17), 25 May (item 9), 1 Nov. (item 2), 8 Nov. (item 8) 1720; 11 Jan. 1720/1, item 9; 16 May 1722, item 2; 2 Mar. 1722/3, item 8; 28 Mar. (item 24), 5 Nov. (list in footnote to this date), and 6 Nov. (item 11) 1723; 2 Mar. 1723/4, item 17; 20 May (items 9 and 10), 6 Oct. and 7 Dec. 1724; 16 July, 19 Nov. (item 2), 22 Nov. (item 7) 1725.

4. Also, that he hath a very fine Tully printed by the old Aldus; which He will bring to his Lordship.[1]

5. Moreover, I left with his Lordship some of Mr Sutties Letters & Catalogues which He sent to Mr Noel.[2]

6. Also, I reported from Mr Noel, that the Duplicates he hath Received from Sr Thomas Sebright, and the Books of the late D^r. Wyncupp & Mr Wase, lie ready for His Lordships Inspection.[3]

7. Further, that He hath a Prospect of Buying the whole Library of the late Baron Hohendorff, consisting of 9000 fine Printed Books, and a very great Number of Valuable Manuscripts.[4]

8. Likewise, that Mr Moetjens the Bookseller hath Madam Scotti's fine Book of the Surinam-Plants, &c. lately Printed, which he value's at about 4 Guineas.[5]

9. Lastly, that the two old Greek MSS. which M^r. Lisle late Chaplain to the Factory at Aleppo brought with Him from Turkey, are in Town, & Himself also.[6]

10. M^r. Britain late Professor of the Oriental Languages at Hall in Saxony, brought certain Rabbinical Books, & among them the Zohar in 3 Volumes, to sell; all which I rejected. He also left Cocceij Lexicon cum Supplement. Joh. Hen. Maij. *Franc.* 1714. fol. at the Price of One Guinea.[7]

11. Mr Christ. Bateman the Bookseller called here; but brought no News.

12. Mr Talman came and Offered to Sell his Collection of Drawings, (excepting those relating to Church-Matters,) to my Lord Harley, at reasonable price.[8] His Direction is at M^rs. Talman's in Great Trinity-Lane, 2 Doors on this Side the Swedish Church. /

[1] But see 13 Feb. 1719/20, item 8, and footnote.

[2] The Suttie Cats. are for the most part not traceable, having been returned to Noel. Wanley took extracts occasionally and these are in Welbeck Wanleyana, Miscellanea. Cf. 19 Jan. 1719/20, item 5.

[3] See also 13 Jan., 14 Jan. (item 4), 16 Jan. (item 9), 21 Jan. (item 8), 22 Jan. (item 10) and 17 Mar. (item 3) 1719/20; 9 Apr. (item 13), 30 Apr. (item 8), 6 June (item 2), 7 June (item 6) and 15 June 1720. On the Sebright Library see also 2 Mar. 1714/15, item 8, and footnote.

[4] Baron Georg Wilhelm von Hohendorf's library was offered at The Hague by Abraham de Hondt: *Bibliotheca Hohendorfiana; ou Catalogue de la Bibliothèque de feu Mons. George Guillaume Baron de Hohendorf*, 1720. It was acquired for the Imperial Library at Vienna for 100,000 Kaiser-Gulden. On Hohendorf see Zedler's *Universal Lexicon*, 1739, xiii, cols. 575–6, and also C. G. Jöcher, *Algemeines Gelehrten-Lexicon*, 1751, ii, cols. 1669–70. See 11 May (item 18), 13 May (item 1), 25 May (item 10), 27 July (item 8), 31 Aug. (item 1) and 20 Oct. (item 4) 1720; 13 Jan. 1720/1, item 11.

[5] 'Madam Scotti's... Surinam Plants' must refer to a copy in her possession of Maria Sibilla Merian's *Dissertatio de generatione et metamorphosibus insectorum Surinamensium: in qua, praeter vermes et erucas Surinamenses, ... plantae, flores et fructus, quibus vescuntur, et in quibus fuerunt inventae exhibentur ...* (J. Oosterwyk, Amsterdam, 1719, fol.). Harley's copy at Wimpole is entered in Minshull's Cat. (BM Add. 19750, f. 54); and was presumably the copy sold by Osborne (v, no. 1782).
See also 16 Jan. 1719/20, item 11.

[6] i.e. Harl. 5619 and 5689. See 18 Jan. 1719/20, item 5, and footnotes.

[7] See 14 Jan. (item 6) and 15 Jan. (item 7) 1719/20. The book is *Johannis Cocceij ... Lexicon et commentarium sermonis hebraici et chaldaici*. Editio novissima ... opere et studio Johannis Henrici Maji, &c. Frankfurt and Leipzig, 1714.

[8] See 14 Jan. (item 2), 23 Jan. (items 3 and 4), and 1 Feb. (item 10) 1719/20; 21 Nov. 1721. On John Talman's colls. of drawings (including those of ecclesiastical vestments) see H. M. Colvin, *A Biographical Dictionary of English Architects, 1660–1840*, 1954, pp. 589–91. The sale of his colls. appears to have taken place in Apr. 1727. That Harley acquired subsequently his drawings of ecclesiastical vestments, &c., is shown by the appearance of 2 vols. of such drawings in the sale cat. of Edward Harley's pictures, &c. under the 2nd day, 9 Mar. 1741/2, p. 6, lot 9.

12 January 1719
———
20.

1. The last Night I saw Mr Andrew Hay, lately returned from France; who related that He had seen Bernard Montfaucon, and his Collection of Antiquities, which is but small, & of no great Value. That he had no opportunity of Inspecting the Manuscripts; but however, perceived that they are no large Parcel. That he is of Opinion, the other will part with nothing while he Lives.[1]

2. Mr Hay further said, that the next Spring he shall set forward for Italy, by the Way of France & will faithfully execute any Commissions he shall receive from my Lord.[2]

3. My Lord gave me Leave to write to my Lord Oxford, about Lending the 3 Original Charters of Conan Duke of Britain & Earl of Richmond (now in this Library) to the Society of Antiquaries meeting at the Mitre Tavern in Fleet-street, who are about Printing the Cottonian MS. relating to the Honor of Richmond.[3]

4. Mr Paul Vaillant came, and gave me B. Montfaucon's Proposals touching his New Edition of S^t. Chrysostom's Works: of which, the two first Volumes are already come over, & valued at 50^s. a Volume on the large Paper. The two next Volumes, he said, will be ready by Easter next.[4]

13 January 1719
———
20.

5. My Lord Harley went to Mr Noel's, where we looked over the Library of the late D^r. Wyncupp, with many Books which formerly belonged to Mr Christofer Wase, & some Duplicates sent by S^r. Tho. Sebright. And His Lordship selected divers Books from them, which Mr Noel promised to send hither to Morrow.[5]

14. January 1719
———
20.

6. Mr Breton came about his Book;[6] and will send into Germany for the Grammar & Dictionary to the Vulgar Greek tongue lately printed there, & some other curious Books. He likewise gave Relatio Historica ad Epistolam Syriacam a Maha Thome, per Car. Schaaf. *Lug. Bat.* 1714. 4to. /[7]

1. Mr Talman came in the Name of the Society of Antiquaries, desiring the Loan of the 3 Charters of Conan Duke of Britain & Earl of Richmond.[8]

---

[1] On Montfaucon and his coll. of antiquities and its fate, see H. Leclerq in *DACL*, xi, pt. 2 (1934), cols. 2641–3 and works cited.   [2] See 26 Apr. 1720 and footnote.
[3] The 3 charters are Harl. Ch. 48. G. 40, 42, 43. The Cotton MS. relating to the Honour of Richmond is BM Cotton Faustina B. vii, ff. 72–135; it was printed by Roger Gale, *Registrum Honoris de Richmond*, 1772. The Society of Antiquaries, revived in 1707, was formally refounded in 1717; its early meetings were at the Mitre Tavern: the earliest minutes are in Wanley's autogr. (Harl. 7055, ff. 1–2). (On the early history of the Society cf. Joan Evans, *A History of the Society of Antiquaries*, 1956, pp. 33–44.) The request on behalf of the antiquaries was made by Talman, the Society's first Director (see 14 Jan. 1719/20, item 1). See also 19 Jan. (item 7), 25 Jan. and 27 Jan. (item 5) 1720/1.
[4] Bernard de Montfaucon's ed. of St. Chrysostom's Works was pubd. Paris, 1718–38.
[5] See 11 Jan. 1719/20, item 6, and footnote.   [6] See 11 Jan. 1719/20, item 10, and footnote.
[7] This is *Relatio Historica ad Epistolam Syriacam a Maha Thome, id est Magno Thom. . . . Episcopo . . . scriptam ad Ignatium, Patriarcham Antiochenum . . .* ed. Carl Schaaf, Leiden, 1714.
[8] See 12 Jan. 1719/20, item 3, and footnote.

2. He also made offer of his Historical & other Drawings, (not being Ecclesiastical) as my Lord shal like, at a reasonable price.[1]

3. Mr Mattaire came.

4. Mr Noel sent the Books which my Lord laid aside yesterday at his House.[2]

15 January 1719/20.

5. Doctor Fiddis came & communicated to me his Intention of Writing the Life of Cardinal Wolsey at Large; and desired me to transcribe for Him all such Materials in this Library, as I should find for His Purpose. I shewed him divers Things Here; & gave him Notice of many others in the Cottonian Library, &c. but as to Transcribing for Him, beg'd his Excuse, &c.[3]

6. Mr William Thomas came.

7. Mr Breton came, & I paid him one Guinea for Cocceij Lexicon.[4] He Live's at the Black Boy & Still near the Union-Stairs in Wapping.

8. My Lord brought in a Primer according to the Use of Rouen, Printed upon Velum at Paris, (A.D. 1503.) in 8vo. which he bought of Mr Vaillant for 10^s. 6^d.[5]

16 January 1719/20.

9. My Lord sent in a great Number of His Duplicate Books, in Order to be first Inspected, & then Delivered to Mr Noel.[6]

10. A Letter was sent to Mr Greene Blew-Mantel Poursuivant at Armes, Desiring him to bring a Sketch of my Lords Supporters on Monday Morning.[7]

11. M^r. Moetjens brought in His Bill; to which he added 3 pounds for the Book of the Surinam Plants & Insects, which he promised to send in forthwith. /[8]

18 January 1719, 20.

p. 20
(f. 11b) 1. Mr Greene brought a Trick of my Lords Supporters; for which, & for other Service heretofore done, my Lord gave him a Guinea & an Half, and I took his Receipt for the Money.[9]

2. M^r. Green related that there is, as yet, no Administration of Mr Stebbings Effects;[10] but that he will have a Constant Eie upon all proceedings, & give Notice, as Occasion shall require.

---

[1] See 11 Jan. 1719/20, item 12, and footnote. [2] Cf. 13 Jan. 1719/20, and footnote.
[3] Richard Fiddes, *The Life of Cardinal Wolsey*, was pubd. 1724. For his subsequent visits to collect materials see 12 May (item 20) and 16 Aug. (item 4) 1720; 14 Jan. and 11 Mar. 1720/1; 29 Mar. 1721; 17 Dec. 1722, item 16. Fiddes acknowledged (op. cit., p. xi) his indebtedness to the Harleian Library.
[4] See 11 Jan. 1719/20, item 10, and footnote.
[5] Unidentifiable; might be any one of Bohatta (1924), nos. 1337–40, assuming that by 'Primer' Wanley means 'Horae'.
[6] See 18 Feb. 1719/20, item 13, and footnote.
[7] i.e. the Harley armorial supporters, viz. 2 angels proper habited and wings displayed or. See 18 Jan. 1719/20, item 1.
[8] See 11 Jan. 1719/20, item 8, and footnote.
[9] See 16 Jan. 1719/20, item 10, and footnote. 'A Trick' is a drawing in which the tinctures are indicated by initial letters (e.g. 'a' for 'azure') and not painted.
[10] No further ref. is made to 'Mr Stebbings Effects'. He had died unmarried 21 Aug. 1719: some of his papers are in Harl. 6944.

3. Also, that young Grant old Mʳ Pinks Nephew ha's not as yet redeemed the Heraldical & other Books he pawned; but that He will have a constant regard to this Affair too.[1]

4. Dʳ. Sherard & Mʳ L'Isle came; and amongst other Things Dʳ. Sherard related how Dʳ. Covel came to him in Town, & desired him with Mʳ Edgecombe & Mʳ Chicheley to sett a Valuation upon his Coins & other Rarities: but the [*sic MS. for* that] He de[c]lined the doing it.[2] That the Metropolite of Smyrna is dead.[3] That Mʳ Chishul of Waltham-stow hath two fine Greek MSS. one very antient, being a Catena Patrum, which the late Lord Paget designed to have printed;[4] the other lately written in the Modern Greek, giving a learned & exact Account of the Faith of the present Greeks in the most Material Points; which book being fortified by proper Testimonials & Original Letters (since the design of Printing 500 Copies in the Original Language is laid aside) will be Printed by Dʳ. Chishull in English.[5] The Dʳ. also putt me in mind of the Old Deeds & Rolls, &c. remaining still in the Abbey of Missenden.[6] Certified that His Grace the Duke of Devonshire think's himself bound not to part with Sᵗ. Athelwold's book,[7] because Given him by General Compton, although he hath no great Value for it. That Mʳ Smith of Venice, write's that the Giustiniani will not part with their Greek MSS.[8] and that he will not Venture to send any of his own Books to England, as yet.[9] Upon my shewing them, the Parcel of different Hands & Languages in Letters & other Papers, He promised to add to the Collection; and that if my Lord Pleaseth, He will procure him a Sett of all the books which the Greeks have lately printed, at Jassi, Buchorest, &c.[10]

[1] No further ref. is made to this business.

[2] Wanley's cat. of Covel's coins is BM Add. 22911,ff. 265–79ᵇ; his valuation (£45. 5s.) is on f. 280. Cf. also 9 Mar. 1719/20, item 6; 30 Nov. 1720; 26 Feb. (item 2) and 6 and 8 Mar. 1722/3; 23 Oct. 1723, item 13; 22 and 28 Apr. 1724; 19 Jan. 1724/5, item 1. For Zacharias von Uffenbach's comments on Covel's coins, antiquities, and MSS. on 2 Aug. 1710, see J. E. B. Mayor's *Cambridge under Queen Anne*, 1911, pp. 146–52, 470–3.

[3] Le Quien (*Oriens Christianus*, 1740, i, cols. 745–6) identifies no one about this time until Ananias 1721.

[4] i.e. Harl. 5791 (not an ancient MS. as stated here but one written by Nicetas Serron in 1682). See 21 Mar. 1719/20; 27 Apr. (item 20), 28 Apr. and 23 June (item 9) 1720. Cf. also 12 Oct. 1724, item 2, and 8 Apr. 1725, item 5, which show that it was still only borrowed from Chishull. 'The late Lord Paget' was William Paget, 7th Lord Paget of Beaudesert, b. 1678, d. 1713; he had been Ambassador to Turkey, 1693–1702.

[5] i.e. Harl. 5729. See 21 Mar. 1719/20, when it was presented. The MS. was subsequently shown to Jenkyn Thomas Philipps, who was looking for something to print (see 4 July 1721, item 7, and 20 Apr. 1723), and was borrowed by him 21 June 1723 (item 13) and returned 10 Aug. 1723. Edmund Chishull's project of printing an account of the Faith of the Greeks and Catena Patrum was not carried out. (For an account of Chishull cf. his *Travels in Turkey and back to England*, with Preface by Richard Mead, 1747.)

[6] The Seat of the Fleetwood family. William Fleetwood, Recorder of London, the antiquary (d. 1594: cf. *DNB* xix (1889), pp. 268, 269) was settled at Great Missenden Manor, Bucks., at his death. At the date of the Diary the Manor belonged to John Fleetwood, who had succeeded his father (also John) in 1691 and died in 1745 (see *VCH Bucks*. ii (1908), pp. 348–9): the site of the Abbey had become absorbed in the Manor of Great Missenden. The sale of the library did not take place until 5–24 Dec. 1774: the cat. bears the title *Bibliotheca Monastica Fleetewodiana. A Catalogue of rare Books and Tracts . . . including the Ancient Conventual Library of Missenden Abbey . . . together with some choice Remains of . . . William Fleetewode Esq. . . .* sold by Samuel Paterson. The MSS. were lots 3588–3641. See also 23 June 1721.

[7] i.e. Benedictional of St. Ethelwold, until 1957 in the possession of the Dukes of Devonshire at Chatsworth, and now BM Add. 49598. For further efforts to secure this MS. see 2 May (item 13), 23 June (item 9), 29 Nov. (item 15), and 5 Dec. (item 6) 1720; 18 May 1721, item 11. Cf. *BMQ* xxvii (1963), pp. 3–5.

[8] The Giustiniani MSS. were sold to Thomas Coke (see 18 May 1721, item 12, and footnote).

[9] But see 7 Nov. 1720 and footnote.

[10] See 26 Jan. 1719/20, item 4; 23 June (item 9), 5 Nov. and 17 Dec. 1720; 20 May (item 6), 24 May (item 1) 1723 (when 7 folios and 2 quartos were sent); Wanley's Addenda, Lansdowne 772, f. 73 (under 24 May 1723) (at p. 416 of the present work). For price asked see 15 Jan. 1723/4. Another set of such

5. Mᵣ L'Isle said that the Hebrew Roll of which Mᵣ Samuel Palmer had made so much mention to me, seemed not to him to be very antient; nor is he sure that it ever was in the form of a Roll, it being written on both Sides. That its Price being Sett at 60ˡⁱ Sterling, he could not afford to purchase it. But if my Lord hath a Mind to it, he will write for it; and perhaps it may now come much

p. 21
(f. 12a)

cheaper, the Jewish Owner, / being lately reduced to great Poverty.[1] That the Gospels at the Monastery of Νημηνία in Scio, is a very fine and very antient Book in small folio, written all in Capitals, and (as he Remember's) without Accents.—And that it is an ᾽Εναγγέλιον, beginning with Sᵗ. John's Gospel on Easter-day.[2] That, as to his own books, he hath no more Manuscripts than two in Greek; the one containing Sᵗ. Chrysostom on Timothy, with Sᵗ. Sᵗ. [*sic MS.*] Basil περὶ ἁγνειας at the End:[3] the other containing only Sᵗ. John Damascen's Book of Barlaam & Josaphat.[4] With two Arabic MSS. the one a fine Alcoran;[5] the other being in 4 Volumes, is the Arabic Lexicon *Camus*.[6] That he will send them all hither to morrow, and refer's them to be Valued by Me, between my Lord & Him. He said further, that the Patriarch of Antioch hath a private Press at Aleppo, and there Prints Liturgical Books.[7] Mᵣ L'Isle lodge's with Mᵣ Ben. Cowse the Bookseller at the Rose & Crown in Sᵗ. Paul's Church-yard.

1. Mᵣ Lisle sent the MSS. above mentioned, together with the Camûs as he call's it, which is not the Manuscript Lexicon that I meant, but is Antonij Giggeij Thesaurus Linguæ Arabicæ. Mediolani, 1632. fol. 4 Voll.[8]

19 January 1719
20.

2. I brought to my Lord Mᵣ Anstis's Specimen of his intended History of the Knights of the Garter.[9]

3. Mᵣ Bogdani brought 7 Gold Medals to be sold: the Price set is 12 Guineas.[10]

4. I putt into the Closet two small for-worn Copper Coins one of Postvmvs, the other of Valens, which my Lord delivered unto me for that purpose.

5. Mᵣ Noel the Bookseller came, & received from me those Letters & Catalogues of Mᵣ G. Suttie, which I had of him to shew to my Lord.[11]

books belonged to Covel and was bought by Davis, of which Harley was offered the picking (see 22 Apr. 1724). On the presses at Jassy and Bucharest see L. C. Wharton in *Printing: a Short History of the Art*, ed. R. A. Peddie, 1927, pp. 286–7, and N. Hodos and I. C. Bianu, *Bibliografia Românéscă, 1508–1830*, 1903, vol. i (1508–1716), *passim* and especially tables at pp. 553–7.

[1] No further reference is made to this Hebrew Roll.

[2] For action by Sherard with reference to MSS. at Nemenia (i.e. the Monastery of Nea Moni on Chios (Scio)) see 5 Nov. 1720 and footnote 6. Cf. also 17 Apr. 1721, item 8, for further reference to this MS.

[3] Harl. 5689. See next entry, numbered 1.

[4] Harl. 5619. See next entry, numbered 1.

[5] Harl. 5477. See next entry, numbered 1.

[6] But see next entry, numbered 1.

[7] Although the Patriarch of Antioch at this date was Cyril III (1686–1724), another Patriarch, Athanasius IV, had been intruded and ruled 1700–28: about 1710 the latter had withdrawn to Aleppo (Cyril continuing to rule at Damascus). On Athanasius and Cyril see J. M. Neale, *A History of the Holy Eastern Church: The Patriarchate of Antioch*, ed. G. Williams, 1873, pp. 183–5: cf. also Le Quien, *Oriens Christianus*, 1740, ii, cols. 774–6.

[8] i.e. Antonius Giggeius, *Thesaurus Linguae Arabicae ex monumentis Arabum Manuscriptis et Impressis Bibliothecae Ambrosianae eruit . . . Latini juris fecit*, &c. Milan, 1632, 4 vols.

[9] Pubd. in 1724 under the title, *The Register of the Order of the Garter*, with introduction and notes by Anstis.   [10] See 22 Jan. 1719/20, item 9.   [11] See 11 Jan. 1719/20, item 5.

6. Mr Breton came, and I apprised him of my Lords pleasure to lay out some money with Him.[1]

7. My Lord sent a Foreigner to me, who brought a small Catalogue of the finest books in the world, as he boasted. But their Titles making but a mean Appearance, & their Prices being very high; I dismissed him.

8. My Lord Order'd me to write a Letter to Dr. Sherard, & invite Him & Mr. Lisle to Dine with Him the next Monday. /

20 January 1719
——
20.

1. My Lord Order'd me to write to Mr Bowyer to buy & send forthwith Crawfords Peerage of Scotland:[2] and to send hither such Books as he had bought for his Lordship at the late Auction.[3]

2. Mr Chapman & Mr Elliot the Bookbinders came; & my Lord gave Mr Chapman two Books to Bind, & to be brought back by this day Sennight.

3. Mr John Gibson came, & said that he ha's a small parcel of MSS. lately come from Italy, as also a parcel of fine printed books. I desired him to send in the MSS. & the Augustin de Civitate Dei presently.[4]

4. Mr Gibson sent in 23 MSS. the St. Augustine & a Latin Bible.[5]

5. Mr Bird the Carver promised me that my Lord shall freely command any book he hath; and he will also assist my Lord in buying Mr Austins antique Bustos,[6] when a proper time shall come.

21 January 1719
——
20.

6. I went to Mr Gibson's, saw his Parcel of old Printed Books, & brought with me His MS. of Lucius Florus.[7]

7. Mr Andrew Hay, upon some discourse, told me that he believed that Mr Cook of Norfolk might be induced to part with his MSS. to my Lord, in Excha[n]ge for other things.[8] This day I shewed Mr Hay the Library, to his great Satisfaction.

8. My Lord having sent in a great parcel of Duplicate Printed Books to be Sold to Mr Noel, I put the same in Order this day.[9]

---

[1] See 1 Feb. (item 11), 29 Feb. (item 8), 2 Mar. (item 16), 7 Mar. (item 16), and 9 Mar. (item 3) 1719/20 for his subsequent employment in cataloguing, &c.

[2] George Crawford, *The Peerage of Scotland: containing an historical and genealogical account of the Nobility of that Kingdom*, &c., Edinburgh, 1716.

[3] See 11 Jan. 1719/20, item 1, and footnote.   [4] See next item, and footnote.

[5] The St. Augustine and Latin Bible were printed books; a further MS. (Lucius Florus) was bought from Gibson 21 Jan. 1719/20, item 6. For the list and identification of the 23 MSS., the Lucius Florus and the 2 printed books see Wanley's Addenda, Lansdowne 771, ff. 76–77, and footnotes thereto (at pp. 194–5 of the present work). See also 2 Feb. (item 6) and 12 Feb. (item 1) 1719/20.

[6] No further ref. is made to this.

[7] See 20 Jan. 1719/20, items 3 and 4, and footnote. The Lucius Florus is Harl. 2557.

[8] See 23 June 1720, item 9; 17 Apr. (item 11), 21 Apr. (item 16) 1721. These MSS. were for the most part collected on his French and Italian journeys in 1712–18 by 'Mr Cook', i.e. Thomas Coke, later 1st Earl of Leicester (1697–1759), who was responsible for the greater part of the coll. of MSS. at Holkham Hall, Norfolk. (On Coke and the Holkham Library see S. de Ricci's intro. to the *Handlist of MSS. in the Library of the Earl of Leicester at Holkham*, Suppl. to the Bibl. Soc. Trans., no. 7, 1932.) Wanley was shown the MSS. by Coke (introduced by Mr. Downes) on 18 May 1721 (item 12).

[9] See 18 Feb. 1719/20, item 13, and footnote.

22 January 1719
20.

9. Mr Bogdani came and received from me the 7 Gold Medals he left here; they being to[o] dear, but not all genuine.[1] He talked of bringing some Silver Medals; but I told him it was needless, for they would (like former parcels) be too highly prized; and besides I did not find my Lord disposed to buy old Coins in such little parcels.

10. Mr Noel came & looked over the Duplicates; but my Lord having said that he would send in more this Day; I did not treat with Him.[2]

11. He Visited me in the Afternoon, & (among other Things) declared that Mr Alex. Cuningham had offered him 200 Guineas, to lett the Earl of Sunderland have the Preference before all others, as to the Buying of his old Books.[3]

12. Also, that the Earl of Pembroke had lately sent Mr Mattaire to him, for many old Books of great Value. /[4]

p. 23
(f. 13a)

23 January 1719
20.

1. Mr Brydges of Lincolne's Inne came hither, & tarried very long; talking about Printing Benedictus Petroburgensis, and the Chronicon Dunstapliæ, of both which I told him my Lord hath a Copie written by my Hand.[5] He desired to see the Chronicon de Bermundeseye,[6] & some other books, in this Library. I[n] discourse he said that his fine Greek Manuscript of part of Lucian's works cost him in Holland 300 Gilders, that is 30 pounds Sterling, and seemed not averse against pleasuring my Lord with it, in Exchange, or for Money.[7]

2. Mr Paul Christian Breton came.

3. Mr Talman came, whom I acquainted that I did believe my Lord might come & see his Drawings some time the next Week; & if so, I would give him previous Notice.[8]

4. He had much talk with me about Printing some of His Designs of the Ecclesiastical Habits, Vessels, Utensils, &c. used in the Greek & Roman Churches Engraven upon very large Copper Plates, by way of Subscription.[9]

---

[1] See 19 Jan. 1719/20, item 3. [2] See 21 Jan. 1719/20, item 8.
[3] Cf. what Wanley says of Sunderland under 4 Dec. 1721, and at the time of his death 19 Apr. 1722, item 3 (though Wanley unaccountably calls him Robert Spencer (i.e. 2nd Earl) instead of Charles Spencer, 3rd Earl, the bibliophile).
[4] i.e. Thomas Herbert, 8th Earl of Pembroke, 1656–1733, virtuoso and collector. Cf. 19 Jan. 1720/1, item 9, for ref. to Pembroke buying part of Abp. of Canterbury's coll. of coins, and 15 July 1720, item 5, for his interest in antiquities.
[5] Wanley's transcript of Benedict of Peterborough is Harl. 3666 and of the Chronicle of Dunstable, Harl. 4886; the former was copied from the original in BM Cotton Julius A. xi, art. 4 and Vitellius E. xvii, art. 3 (the transcript is dated 10 Apr. 1713 on f. 4), and the latter from BM Cotton Tiberius A. x (the transcript is dated 10 Oct. 1713, on f. 1). This work on Wanley's part may have been connected with a scheme for publishing a series of English historical works which was discussed with Robert Harley in 1707 (? 21 and 24 June) (see Memorandum by Wanley in BM Lansdowne 825, f. 77).
[6] Harl. 231.
[7] John Bridges's library was sold at his chambers, no. 6, Lincoln's Inn, 7 Feb.–21 Mar. 1725/6. Cf. under 5 Feb., 8 Feb. (item 7), 9 Feb. (item 10), 11 Feb. and 15 Feb. 1725/6; 1, 5, 9, 16, 21, 23, and 24 Mar. 1725/6 for the purchasing manœuvres before the sale. For details and identification of the 3 *manuscripti insignissimi* (of which the Lucian was one) eventually included in the sale of Bridges's library see footnote to 24 Mar. 1725/6. [8] See 11 Jan. 1719/20, item 12, and footnote.
[9] These were the drawings excluded from the coll. offered to Harley on 14 Jan. 1719/20, item 2 (and see footnote to 11 Jan. 1719/20, item 12).

5. Mr Booth the Lawyer came to consult some of the Manuscripts of the late Randle Holme of Chester,[1] the Copies of the Cartæ Antiquæ of the Tower, &c.[2] I took this Opportunity of reviving the Matter of the Old Deeds which were in the Possession of the said R. Holme, and were not bought with his Books, in such effectual manner, as that He promised me to write to His Friend in Chester, by the next Post, to buy them for him, & he will deliver them to my Lord at the same price, His Lordship paying the Carriage, &c. And hope's to perform this piece of service in little more than 3 weeks time.[3]

6. My Lord Order'd me to look over Mr Elliot the Bookbinders last Bill.

25 January 1719/20.

7. Yesterday, by Command, I sent a Letter to D^r. Sherard, desiring him to bring Mr Lisle to dine with my Lord next Tuesday.

8. This day having Inspected Mr Elliots Bill, I found him exceedingly dear in all the Work of Marocco-Turkey- & Russia-Leather: besides that of Velvet.

9. One Evening the last week, in Discourse between Mr Noel & Me, who advised him to Sell his Rabbinical Books to Mr P. C. Breton, Mr Noel declined it, & said that he would reserve them to another Opportunity, as likewise his Oriental MSS. so that my Lord is now quitted of any Obligation of buying them. /[4]

26 January 1719/20.

p. 24
(f. 13b)

1. I brought with me the two Copper-Plates of the late French Kings Entry into Utrecht A.D. 1672, presented to my Lord by Mr Noel.[5]

2. Mr Breton came.

3. M^r. Noel came, desiring my Lord to return the Balæus de Scriptoribus lately had of Him.[6]

[1] 'The late Randle Holme of Chester' was Randle Holme IV, who died 1707. The Randle Holme heraldic MSS. had been bought by Robert Harley through the agency of Francis Gastrell, Bp. of Chester, in 1710 and are Harl. 1920–2184. (On the Randle Holmes and their colls. see J. P. Earwaker, 'The Four Randle Holmes of Chester, antiquaries, heralds and genealogists, c. 1571–1707', *Journal of Chester Archaeological and Historic Soc.*, 1891.)

[2] Copies of the 'Chartae Antiquae' then preserved in the Tower of London (made, e.g., for Sir Simonds D'Ewes) may be found in Harl. 84 and 85. On the 'Chartae Antiquae' in the Tower see Joseph Ayloffe, *Calendars of the Ancient Charters . . . now remaining in the Tower of London.* 1774.

[3] From the entry under 11 June 1722, item 13, it appears that these deeds were held by one, 'Bassano, an herald-painter' (i.e. Francis Bassano, d. 1747). Boothe's further promises of help are recorded under 25 Mar. (item 17), 26 Apr. (item 4) 1721; 28 Feb. 1721/2; 11 June (item 13), 1 Dec. (item 8) 1722; 9 Jan. 1722/3, item 9; but the transactions came to nothing (see 11 June 1722, item 13).

[4] But cf. Wanley's note in Addenda, Lansdowne 771, f. 77, under 23 Feb. 1719/20 (at p. 196 of the present work), stating that Noel 'also delivered his oriental and other MSS' (see footnote thereto for identifications). See also 17 Feb. (item 11), 18 Feb. (item 13), 20 Feb. (item 9), and 23 Feb. (item 10) 1719/20.

[5] See 27 Jan. 1719/20, item 6, for their return. The print is that of Louis XIV's advance on and entry into Utrecht, 5 July 1672, engraved by R. de Hooghe. There is a copy in the 'History of the Netherlands' rooms at the Rijksmuseum, Amsterdam.

[6] See 27 Jan. 1719/20, item 6. The reference is to John Bale, *Illustrium Maioris Britanniae de Scriptoribus, hoc est, Angliae, Cambriae, ac Scotiae Summarium . . . ad annum M.D.XLVIII*, first pubd. 1548 under false imprint 'Gippeswici, per J. Overton' for D. van den Straten, Wesel (*STC* 1295).

4. D^r. Sherard & Mr Lisle came. The Doctor promised to procure for my Lord not only the Books printed by the Greeks at Jassi & Buchorest, &c.[1] but also a complete Sett of the Greek Liturgical Books printed at Venice, if such a Sett can be gotten.[2]

5. D^r. Adams Provost of Kings College came. He promised to write for a Greek MS. of the Octateuch now at Smyrna, that my Lord may have the buying of it.[3]

27 January 1719
20.

6. My Lord consented that Mr Noel may have the Balæus abovementioned.[4] And sent back by M^r. Chapman the Bookbinder, the two Copper-plates, Mr Noel would have presented.[5]

7. My Lord sent in a fair Copie of the Romant de la Rose, in French Verse.[6]

8. Mr William Thomas came; & borrowed the fragment of Piers Plowman, inscribed 62.B.16.[7]

28 January 1719
20.

9. My Lord Harley having before declared unto me his Intention of Buying the late Mr John Kemp's Collection of Medals, Marbles, & other pieces of Antiquity Greek, Roman & Egyptian, for divers Reasons; was further informed this day, that Will. Kemp the present Possessor of them, is grown greatly in Debt; so that, in probability, he must part with them in a short time.[8]

10. Mr Elliot the Bookbinder came; to whom I produced the Observations I made upon his last Bill, Shewing him, that (without catching at every little Matter) my Lord might have had the same Work done as well, and cheaper by above £31. He said, that He could have saved above 8 pounds in the fine Books, & yet they should have looked well. That he now cannot do them so cheap as he rated them at: that no man can do so well as Himself: or near the Rates I sett against His. But upon the whole, said He would write to my Lord, upon the Subject of this our Conference. /

p. 25
(f. 14a)

1. Mr Bowyer came (having before sent to my Lord the Books bought in the late Auction,)[9] with his Bill, as required by my Lord.

[1] See 18 Jan. 1719/20, item 4, and footnote 10.

[2] For the chief printers engaged in the printing of Greek liturgical works at Venice no special bibliography appears to exist, but the following may be consulted, viz. Robert Proctor, *The Printing of Greek in the Fifteenth Century* (Bibl. Soc., Illustrated Monograph no. 8, 1900), *passim*; the *General Cat. of Printed Books in B.M.* under the heading 'Liturgies', cols. 1–47; and Bohatta's bibliographies.

[3] Adams died 3 days later, but cf. 4 May 1721, item 16 and footnote.

[4] See 26 Jan. 1719/20, item 3.

[5] See 26 Jan. 1719/20, item 1.

[6] This MS. was subsequently returned to the owner: see Wanley's note in Addenda to Lansdowne 771, f. 76 (at p. 194 of the present work). See also 17 Feb. 1719/20, item 10.

[7] Harl. 875. Returned 23 Feb. 1719/20.

[8] Cf. 30 Mar. 1720, item 7; 16 Mar. 1720/1, item 18; 27 Mar. 1721; 2 May, 3 May (item 13), 4 May (items 14 and 17), 23 May (item 5), and 9 Nov. (item 7) 1721; cf. also Wanley's note in Addenda to Lansdowne 771, f. 78, under 4 May 1721 (at p. 198 of the present work). John Kemp's museum of antiquities (described in Robert Ainsworth, *Monumenta vetustatis Kempiana*, 1719–20, 1720, &c.) was auctioned at the Phoenix Tavern, Pall Mall, 23, 24, 25, 27 Mar. 1721 in 293 lots for £1,090. 8s. 6d. (cf. DNB). On a volume of prints and drawings bought of Kemp, cf. 6 Oct. 1720, item 2, and footnote. Harl. 1526, 1527 had also belonged to Kemp (who had bought them from John Innys in 1711).

[9] See 11 Jan. 1719/20, item 1, and footnote.

2. He also left a List of Musical Books to be Sold, being now in the Hands of the Rev^d. M^r. Estwick Minister of Great S^t. Hellen's. These books, I suspect, to be the Collection of Mr George Llewellyn late Chaplain of Christ-church; for the most part correctly written by his own Hand.[1]

3. Mr Bowyer further said, that the Boxfull of Papers he now hath by Him, relating to many of our English Parsonages, may now be had at about 20 Guineas; though it had cost above £100.[2]

4. Mr Sanderson of the Rolls came; and said that having (as I desired) enquired of S^r. Joseph Jekyll now Master of the Rolls about the 24 Saxon Charters which were in the Possession of of [sic] the late Lord Somers; S^r. Joseph affirmed that He had them not, and that His Lordship had disposed of them in his Lifetime.[3]

5. Mr Sanderson further said, that the Late Rev^d. Mr Matterson had made him his sole Executor; and that he having left a Collection of Medals, & other pieces of Antiquity behind him, my Lord should have the first View of them.[4]

1 February 1719/20.

6. I reported that I had been with Mr Bowyer, & inspected the Collection of Papers relating to the present State of our English Benefices; for which he ask's 20 Guineas; but may perhaps be induced to take less.[5]

7. Also, that I could not find Mr Estwick.

8. Also, that Mr Tanner had sent his Lordship by me, one Golden piece of Mary Queen of Scots: wch I delivered.

9. Mr Bogdani came to me with a Catalogue of Medals, which a Gentleman desires to sell; but that upon perusal of the same, I rejected them, as not being for my Lords purpose.

10. Mr Talman came, & desired to know my Lords Pleasure, with regard to his Prints & Drawings,[6] He being soon to return into the Countrey.

11. Mr Breton came. I desired him to send to Hall in Saxony for the Greek Bible said to be lately printed there. /[7]

---

[1] See also 30 Mar. (item 8) and 25 May (item 9) 1720. Estwick's library was not sold until 3 Dec. 1739.
[2] See 19 Feb. 1719/20, item 6 (for purchase) and footnote.
[3] 'The late Lord Somers' (viz. John Somers, Baron Somers of Evesham) died 1716; his coll. of Anglo-Saxon charters had been described by Wanley in his cat. of Anglo-Saxon MSS. in Hickes's *Thesaurus*, ii (1705), pp. 301–3, and the texts were to be printed in John Smith's ed. of *Bædæ Historia Ecclesiastica Latine et Saxonice*, Cambridge, 1722, pp. 764–82, where they are described as 'lately' (nuper) in the possession of Somers. Cf. 18 Feb. 1719/20, item 2; 11 Apr. 1720, item 19; 27 June 1722. They were probably destroyed in a fire at Lincoln's Inn in 1752 (see Biographical Index *under* Somers).
[4] Cf. 18 Feb. 1719/20, item 2; 22 Apr. (item 9), 27 Apr. (item 19), and 28 Apr. (item 1) 1720 (which shows that Matterson = Maddison); 3, 4, 5, 6, 7, 11, 18, 20, 25, and 26 May 1720 (when they were actually bought); 16 June 1720 and entry under 26 May 1720 in Addenda, Lansdowne 771, f. 77^b (at p. 197 of the present work). Maddison's tract on English coins is Harl. 6941, ff. 31–35.
[5] See 19 Feb. 1719/20, item 6 (for purchase), and footnote.
[6] See 11 Jan. 1719/20, item 12, and footnote.
[7] This must be a ref. to the 12° Greek New Testament printed at Orphan House, Halle, in 1710, 'Η Καινὴ Διαθήκη (the only recent Halle printing recorded by Darlow and Moule, *Historical Cat. of Printed Editions of Holy Scripture in the Library of the British and Foreign Bible Society*, no. 4961), a diglot ed. in which the Modern Greek version is a revision of that of Maximus.

p. 26
(f. 14*b*)

2 February 1719
––––
20.

1. A Letter was sent to Mr Cook the Painter, desiring him to procure two Copies of Mr Priors Poems, of the last small Edition, & to send the same to my Lord speedily.[1]

2. My Lord commanded me to look over a Catalogue of Books which are to be sold by Auction in Amsterdam, on the 13 of March next N.S.[2] & then to deliver the same to Mr William Thomas.

3. Captn [*blank space*] Hay (of the Errol-Family) came from M^rs. Kennet, desiring that I would go to Her to see a parcel of Books lately D^r. How's. I desired to see the Catalogue here.[3]

4. He left with me to Shew to my Lord a Silver Watch, which formerly belonged to King James I, & was by him given to Mr Hay's fathers Great Unkle.

5. He said further that he ha's about 900 old Books coming from Scotland; among which, some are said to be very curious: and that when they are come, I shall see a Catalogue of them.[4]

6. Mr John Gibson came and viewed the Books lately sent in by Him, & gave a short List of them, with his Prices, except of two, which he Leave's to my Lords own Valuation.[5] And he desire's my Lord to look upon those few which he ha's at his Lodging, on Friday-morning next; or to send word to the Contrary.

3 February 1719
––––
20.

7. Mr Brindley came to know if my Lord had any work for him; & say's that his Lordship lately gave him a Book to Bind. I referred him to his Lordship.

8. Mr Cook came with one of Mr Priors Poems lately printed in Holland, saying he can get more from thence.[6]

9. Mr Greenwood came with Mr Cook, desiring to see his interleaved printed Grammar, which he putt into D^r. Hickes's hands, for the benefit of His Remarks. I answer'd that that book is at Wympole.[7]

10. Mr Mountagu the Bookseller sent a MS. Primer, formerly a folio; but now, by Cutting into the Illuminations, reduced to a 4to. & bound in two Volumes. The lowest Price was said to be 8 Guineas. I having turned over both the Volumes, answered that the Price was, by much, too high; and besides, y^t my Lords [*sic*] had many Copies of the same vastly superior to it.

11. M^r O Sullivan came. I shewed him the MS. of Sicco Polentinus: which after a long perusal, he highly esteemed.[8]

---

[1] This must refer to the 8° ed. of Matthew Prior, *Poems on Several Occasions*, pubd. at The Hague, 1720, for T. Johnson, London. Cf. 3 Feb. 1719/20, item 8.   [2] Sale-cat. not identified.
[3] Nothing further heard of this matter.   [4] No further ref. to this cat.
[5] See 20 Jan. 1719/20, items 3 and 4, and footnote; see list (and footnotes for identification) in Addenda, Lansdowne 771, ff. 76^b–77 (at pp. 194–5 of the present work).
[6] See 2 Feb. 1719/20, item 1, and footnote.
[7] James Greenwood, *Essay towards a Practical English Grammar*, 1711. Two copies (one interleaved) were at Wimpole (see Wanley's cat. of printed books at Wimpole, nos. 157, 5678: BM Lansdowne 816, ff. 8, 111^b).   [8] Harl. 4769.

12. Mʳ Bell brought a piece of Gold, being that of the Coronation of K. Charles II at Scone, A.D. 1651. for my Lord to buy: he say's it belong's to one Mʳ Humble. I Shewed him why I suspect it to have been Cast, and not Stricken. /[1]

4 February 1719
―――
20.

p. 27
(f. 15a)

1. Mʳ Noel came, & certified me that he had heard that his 4 Cases are come down from Germany to within 15 Miles of Amsterdam: that they will be sent to Rot[t]erdam, & from thence Shipped off for England.[2]

2. He hath received a Letter from G. Suttey, dated from Châlons; with a Catalogue of Books lately Bought, wherein I could find few or none for my Lords purpose.[3] Mʳ Suttie is going for Lions; & complains that divers enriched by the Missisippi-Stock, hinder him in buying of Books.[4]

3. Mʳ Noel hope's to shew me his Bill of Loading here on Tuesday-next; & desires that all my Lords Duplicates may be ready by that time.[5]

4. Mʳ. Vertue the Engraver came.

5. The Lord Bᴘ. of Chester came, and desired me to peruse His Case, when printed.[6]

6. Mʳ. Auditor Harley desired that I might look him out the Copie of the Foundation of Winchester College, in Case it be in this Library.[7]

5 February 1719
―――
20.

7. Mʳ Humble came about the Gold Medal Mʳ Bell left with me, & ask's 4 or 5 Guineas for it.[8]

8. My Lord Harley sent in an Exemplification of an old Fine, under the Great Seal of K. Edw. III. Bearing Teste, anno regni 32.[9]

8. February 1719
―――
20.

9. Mʳ Chapman brought back the Books he had to Bind.

10. Mʳ Humble came, whom I paid for his piece of Gold.[10]

9 February 1719
―――
20.

11. I being very much Indisposed by a violent Cold, went Home.

---

[1] See 5 Feb. (item 7) and 8 Feb. (item 10) 1719/20. (Cf. BM *Guide to the Exhibition of Historical Medals*, 1924, p. 43, fig. 40.)

[2] For titles of 6 MSS. bought with printed books see Addenda, Lansdowne 771, f. 77, under 23 Feb. 1719/20 (at p. 195 of the present work); the MSS. were sent in 20 Feb. 1719/20 (item 8).

[3] See footnote to 11 Jan. 1719/20, item 5.

[4] i.e. the 'Mississippi Scheme' of John Law (1671–1729), Controller-General of French Finances (see *DNB* xxii. 230).   [5] See 18 Feb. 1719/20, item 13, and footnote.

[6] i.e. [Francis Gastrell's] *The Bishop of Chester's Case, with relation to the Wardenship of Manchester, etc.* Cambridge, 1721.   [7] For foundation charter of Winchester College see Harl. 1343.

[8] Cf. 3 Feb. 1719/20, item 12, and footnote.

[9] Harl. Ch. III. B. 53. Wanley's '32' should be '39'.

[10] Cf. 3 Feb. 1719/20, item 12, and footnote.

12. February 17<u>19</u>
20.

12. I returned; bringing with me a Printed book entituled *Tragica*, which Mr Noel bought for my Lord at the late Auction. /¹

p. 28
(f. 15*b*)

1. Mr John Gibson, & I agreed with Him (by my Lords Command) for the Parcel of Books he left here.²

2. I sent a Letter to Mr Chapman, to come hither to morrow.

3. Mr Bateman sent in a small Parcel of Books my Lord bought of him.³

4. My Lord Order'd me to peruse part of a Printed Catalogue of Books, which he had of Mr Vaillant.⁴

13 February 17<u>19</u>
20.

5. M^r O Sullivan came, to assist me in interpreting some Irish Sentences.

6. Mr Elliott came about his Accompt.

7. Mr Chapman came for a Parcel to Bind.

8. Mr Bowyer brought a clean Victorius's Tully, in 4 Volls, bound in Red Turkey, with the Leaves Gilded, to shew my Lord. I told him my Lord had the same book at Wympole.⁵

16 February 17<u>19</u>
20.

8 [*sic*]. Being at Home & Indisposed, I concluded a Bargain with A. D. Frank of Cranfield, about the Chartulary of Newenham, so long borrowed from the Bedford-Library, thus: The said Chartulary is to be my Lords; and he is to present to that Library St. Chrysostom's Works in Greek & Latin, Printed at Paris, for which his Lordship shall be Registred as a Benefactor to the said Library.⁶ Moreover, Mr Archdeacon will send up a List of his out-of-course

---

¹ 'Late auction' unidentified. 'Tragica', i.e. *Tragica historia de miseranda et abominosa illa laniena, anno a partu Virginis Mariae salutifero 1572, die xxiiij Augusti in regia metropoli urbe Parisina post nuptiarum navarreicarum ibi celebratarum, festivitatem, aliisque urbibus edita, reddita carmine heroico per F.R.E.F.* [Fresen] No date, but according to Brunet 1573: reprinted 1584 (copy of this ed. in BM). The author of this poem in Latin verse against the Massacre of St. Bartholomew was Rembertus Fresen.

² See 20 Jan. 1719/20, items 3 and 4, and footnotes.

³ Items unidentified.

⁴ Not identified.

⁵ 'Victorius's Tully', i.e. Cicero's works printed 1536–7 at Venice by Giunta under the editorship of Petrus Victorius the Florentine scholar (1499–1585).

⁶ The Cartulary of Newnham is Harl. 3656 (= Davis, no. 692). The Bedford Library was founded in 1700; at first kept in the vestry of St. John's church but c. 1708–48 in a building on the S. side of St. Paul's churchyard. A cat. of books in the library was pubd. in 1706 (see T. W. Elger, *Catalogue of the Circulating and Reference Libraries and of the Old Library founded in 1700*, Bedford, 1892, pp. iii–v). The cartulary is included among the books referred to in the Deed of Settlement of 20 Oct. 1704 (on which see T. Fisher, *Gentleman's Magazine*, lxxxvii (1817), pt. 2, pp. 135–7, 578). Cf. 18 Feb. (items 12 and 1), 8 Mar. (item 1), 18 Mar. (item 9) and 24 Mar. (item 3) 1719/20. The bargain here made was later challenged (see 12 Sept. (item 23), 19 Sept. (item 11), 23 Oct. (item 15), 24 and 25 Oct. and 30 Nov. 1723, and correspondence with Archdeacon Frank in Welbeck Wanleyana and Harl. 3778). The challenger was a Mr. Bromsal (see Welbeck Wanleyana, letter from Frank, 29 Nov. 1723). The Works of Chrysostom is the 12 vol. ed. pubd. Paris, 1636 (nos. 57–67 in cat. of old library, cf. Elger, op. cit. p. 237). The accession of the Cartulary of Newnham to the Harleian Library is duly noted by Wanley in his own copy of the 1695 ed. of Tanner's *Notitia Monastica*, p. 10 (BM Add. 47842).

Books, out of which my Lord may pick & choose out any Twenty of them Gratis.

17. February 1719/20.

9. I am also to advertise my Lord, that Mr A. D. Frank is heartily willing & ready to serve his Lordship, in any Library matters: and particularly with Mr Wale of Bedford, Sir . . . Naper of Luton-ho, and . . . Osborne of Chicksand-Abbey, (where most part of the old Monastical Library is said yet to remain) when a proper Opportunity shall happen.[1]

10. Mr George Hay came, inquiring for the MS. of the Romant de la Rose.[2]

11. Mr Noel came, & unsaid all that he had before promised me about his Oriental MS[S]; which he is willing to give in Exchange for the Duplicates now here; or otherwise, doe's not care to medle with them.[3]

18 February 1719/20.

12. My Lord declared himself willing to exchange his Paris-Chrysostom, for the Chartulary of Newenham.[4]

13. His Lordship condescended to Exchange his Duplicates with Mr Noel, for his Oriental MSS. /[5]

1. I wrote to Mr A. D. Frank, in pursuance of the two last Minutes.   p. 29 (f. 16*a*)

2. Mr Sanderson came to Study: gave the tatter'd MS. he before left here;[6] promised his utmost Service in retrieving the 24 Saxon Charters lately in the Possession of the Lord Somers;[7] and is willing to part with any of the late Mr Matterson's Rarities to my Lord.[8]

3. Mr Gibson came, & said he ha's 3 very fine MSS. lately come from Italy.[9]

19 February 1719/20.

4. Mr Beaver came to Study in the Library.

5. Mr Rooke, Clerke to Mr Sanderson, came to Transcribe some Papers for Him.

---

[1] 'Sir . . . Naper of Luton Ho.' Sir Theophilus Napier, Bart., of Luton Hoo, Bedfordshire, had died without issue 1719 and was succeeded by his nephew Sir John Napier, who died unmarried 1747, when the baronetcy became extinct. Chicksand Abbey, surrendered 22 Oct. 1538, was granted to R. Snow, from whose family it was purchased c. 1600 by Sir John Osborne; the Osborne referred to by Wanley is Sir John Osborne, 2nd Bart., who died 28 Apr. 1720. See also 6 May 1720, items 10 and 11, and footnote.

[2] Possibly 'Romant de la Rose' MS. referred to under 27 Jan. 1719/20, item 7; the MS., however, had been returned 4 Feb. 1719/20.

[3] See 18 Feb. 1719/20, item 13, and footnote.   [4] See 16 Feb. 1719/20, and footnote.

[5] For previous steps leading to this exchange see 16 Jan. (item 9), 21 Jan. (item 8), 25 Jan. (item 9), 4 Feb. (item 3), and 17 Feb. (item 11) 1719/20. See also 20 Feb. (item 9), 23 Feb. (item 10) 1719/20, and footnote to 23 Feb. 1719/20 in Addenda, Lansdowne 771, f. 77 (at p. 196 of the present work), where 'Oriental MSS.' are cited.

[6] Harl. 2391 (cf. Wanley's Addenda, Lansdowne 771, f. 77, under 18 Feb. 1719/20 (at p. 195 of the present work)). The date on which it was left is not recorded.

[7] See 28 Jan. 1719/20, item 4, and footnote.   [8] See 28 Jan. 1719/20, item 5, and footnote.

[9] See 26 Feb. (item 3), 17 Mar. (item 5) and 18 Mar. (item 8) 1719/20, for MSS. received by Gibson from Italy about this time. A list of what Harley actually bought from Gibson in this period is given under Wanley's Addenda, Lansdowne 771, f. 77^b, under 23 Apr. 1720 (at p. 196 of the present work).

6. Mr Bowyer brought a [his *originally written and deleted*] Collection of Papers relating to many Rectories & Vicarages in all the Counties of England, which my Lord bought of Him.[1]

7. Mr James Hill came.

20. February 1719
20.

8. This & some following days I was busied with Mr Noel the Bookseller, in se[e]ing his Books Inspected & cleared from the Custom-house; in Separating those that seemed for my Lords turn from the rest; in taking a List of them; in bargaining with Mr Noel for those which my Lord liked; & in putting them up, & seeing them brought hither.[2]

9. With them came also the Oriental MSS. (mentioned pag. 28, 11 & 13.) and likewise the remainder of the late D^r. Alixes MSS. which he allowed my Lord in Exchange for an Aldus's Horace.[3]

23. February 1719
20.

10. Mr Noel took away the Duplicates abovementioned except one book which was missing.[4]

11. M^r. Will. Thomas returned the MS. 62.B.16. which he had borrowed.[5]

24 February 1719
20.

12. M^r. O Sullivan came; as before.
Mr Harbyn Came.

25. February 1719
20.

13. Mr Beaver came to Study.

14. Mr Pocklington came, & promised to [take] care care [*sic*], about the Disposal of Mr Mickletons MSS. in proper time. /[6]

p. 30
(f. 16*b*)

26. February 1719
20.

1. I bought the Autographon of K. Edw. VI.'s Latin Catechism[7] of the Dutchman, by Mr Beaver's means.

---

[1] See 11 Jan. (item 2), 28 Jan. (item 3), and 1 Feb. (item 6) 1719/20.
[2] See 4 Feb. 1719/20, item 1, and footnote.
[3] See 18 Feb. 1719/20, item 13, and footnote relating to the Oriental MSS. and the duplicates. For 'Dr. Alixes MSS.' cf. Wanley's Addenda, Lansdowne 771, f. 77, under 23 Feb. 1719/20, and footnote (at p. 196 of the present work). The 'Dr. Alix' is Dr. Peter Allix who died in 1717.
[4] See 18 Feb. 1719/20, item 13, and footnote.
[5] Harl. 875. Cf. 27 Jan. 1719/20, item 8.
[6] Cf. 6 May (item 9), 10 May (item 13), 30 June (item 5), and footnote, 4, 5, 7, and 8 July, 3, 5, and 11 Aug. 1720; and 7 and 19 Jan. 1720/1; but see 7 Feb. 1720/1, item 14, where it is noted that Mickleton's MSS. had been sold to Spearman (on these see *The Durham Philobiblon*, ed. D. G. Ramage, i (1949–55), p. 40). [7] Harl. 3927.

2. Mr Beaver came to Study; & ha's promised his Endeavors to induce Dr Andrew's of the Commons to present his pieces of Roman Antiquity found at Trumpington, to my Lord.[1]

3. Mr Gibson came, desiring my Lord to call & see his Things, & saying that he ha's some more books lately come from abroad.[2]

27. February 1719/20.

4. Mr Beaver came to Study.

5. Mr Tanner the Goldsmith came, with OLIVER's Death's Medal of Gold by Simons, &c.[3]

29 February, 1719/20.

6. Mr Beaver came to Study.

7. Mr Bateman came (with a Strange Gentleman) desiring to see the Books which my Lord bought lately of M^r. Noel.[4] I answer'd that my Lord had laid a particular Charge on me, to lett nobody see them.

8. Mr Bretton came, & declared his sad Condition, & late Losses. I told him I believed my Lord would use his Service in Cataloguing some Hebrew MSS. lately come in, & gratifie him for the same.[5]

9. Mr Chapman the Binder came, brought home the Books last deliver'd unto him; was paid in full; & rec^d another parcel, to be brought back the next 4th. of April.

10. M^r O Sullevan brought me the Remarks he had made upon my Dissertation, upon the MS. 93.C.29. written in the 5th. Volume of the shorter Catalogue.[6]

1 March 1719/20.

11. I sent a Letter to Mr Chapman, desiring him to hasten my Lords Cowley's Poems.

12. M^r O Sullivan came; and promised to give an Account of the MS. 39.B.17.[7]

13. Mr Bowyer came, and shewed me a recent MS. Copie of S^r. Henry Spelmans Archaismus Graphicus; which I would not meddle with, my Lord having a better Copie of the same already.[8]

---

[1] No further ref. in Diary.
[2] See 18 Feb. 1719/20, item 3, and footnote.
[3] This was the medal struck in gold and copper by Thomas Simon to commemorate Oliver Cromwell's death, 1658 (see BM *Guide to the Exhibition of Historical Medals*, 1924, p. 45, fig. 42).
[4] See 4 Feb. 1719/20, item 1, and footnote.
[5] See 2 Mar. (item 16), 3 Mar. (item 5), 4 Mar. (item 9), 7 Mar. (item 16), 9 Mar. (item 3), and 10 Mar. (item 10) 1719/20 for further employment of Breton.
[6] The MS. is Harl. 1802 (cf. also 4 Mar. (item 11), 10 Mar. (item 11), and 15 Mar. (item 18) 1719/20). The 5th vol. of Wanley's 'Catalogus Brevior' is now BM Add. 45705, and Wanley's 'Dissertation' is at ff. 183–212. (Cf. also *Harl. Cat.* (1759) under Harl. 1802, where the 'Dissertation' covers 31 cols.)
[7] Harl. 432. O'Sullivan's account (apparently not produced until 18 June 1723) is inserted in 2nd vol. of Wanley's 'Catalogus Brevior', BM Add. 45702, f. 128^b. (Cf. also *Harl. Cat.* (1759) under Harl. 432, where part of it is printed with Wanley's commendation of O'Sullivan.)
[8] Harl. 6353, ff. 121–150^b: the copy was made 15 Feb. 1643–4.

2 March 1719
$\overline{20.}$

14. Mr Beaver came to Study.

15. I brought two small Books, which Mr Noel bought for my Lord at the late Auction of Dr Brooks books.[1]

16. Mr Breton came to give me the Titles of some Hebrew MSS.[2]

17. M^r. William Thomas came. /

p. 31
(f. 17*a*)

3 March 1719
$\overline{20.}$

1. Mr Rooke came to Transcribe for Mr Sanderson.

2. Mr John Le Neve came to transcribe an Act of Starre-chamber, relating to A.B^p. Sands.[3]

3. M^r O Sullivan came to Study.

4. Mr Beaver came to Study.

5. Mr Breton came to finish with the Hebrew MSS.[4]

4 March 1719
$\overline{20.}$

6. Mr Beaver came to Transcribe for himself.

7. Mr John Le Neve came to Transcribe for himself.

8. Mr Rooke came to Transcribe for Mr Sanderson.

9. Mr Breton came; and then we amended the Titles he putt upon some of the Hebrew MSS.[5]

10. D^r. Stukeley came to Study.

11. M^r. O Sullevan, came to look into the Irish MS. 37.B.17.[6] He desired me to let him have the Papers he lately brought to me, that he might somewhat correct the same, and add the necessary Quotations to them: I did so, he promising to bring them to me on Monday next.[7]

5 March. 1719
$\overline{20.}$

12. Mr Beaver came to Transcribe for himself.

13. M^r Le Neve came to Transcribe, for himself.

---

[1] Perhaps a ref. to the anonymous sale of 29 Feb. 1720 at D. Browne's, recorded *CSC* (BM press-mark S.-C. 466 (8)).

[2] Cf. 29 Feb. 1719/20, item 8, and footnote.

[3] The 'Act of Starre-chamber' is in Harl. 6265, ff. 89–92; it is a *copy* dated 8 May 1583 and relates to Edwin Sandys, Abp. of York 1576–88.

[4] Cf. 2 Mar. 1719/20, item 16.

[5] Cf. 2 Mar. 1719/20, item 16.

[6] 37. B. 17 is a slip on Wanley's part for 39. B. 17 (= Harl. 432): cf. 1 Mar. 1719/20, item 12.

[7] 'The Papers' referred to relate, however, to Harl. 1802 (cf. 29 Feb. 1719/20, item 10); see 10 Mar. 1719/20, item 11.

7 March 1719
—
20.

14. Mʳ Beaver came to Transcribe for himself.

15. Mʳ Le Neve came to Transcribe for himself.

16. Mʳ Breton came, whom I desired to write (for my Lord) a Sett of the Hebrew Alphabets, as well as he can, particularly of that which the Jews use in Writing of their Letters.[1]

17. I wrote a Letter to Dʳ. Sherard by my Lords Order. /

8 March 1719
—
20.

p. 32
(f. 17b)

1. I wrote to Mʳ A.D. Frank about the Paris-Chrysostom;[2] and to Dr. Tudway of Cambridge.

2. Mʳ Beaver came to Transcribe.

9 March 1719
—
20.

3. Mʳ Breton came, and brought me his Paper of Hebrew Alphabets.[3]

4. Mʳ Beaver came to Transcribe.

5. Mʳ Casley came to enquire after John Wycliffes workes here.

6. Dʳ Sherard & Mʳ Lisle came, and were paid off. My Lord order'd me to shew Dʳ. Sherard Dʳ. Covel's Catalogue of his Rarities.[4]

10 March 1719
—
20.

7. I went to Mʳ Corbet the Bookseller, about his Buck & Daniels Bible.[5]

8. I went to Mʳ Bacon, about the Collection of Greek & Roman Coins left by the late Mʳ Chancellor L[l]oyd.[6]

9. Mʳ Beaver came to transcribe.

10. Mʳ Breton came & deliver'd to me the Sett of Hebrew Alphabets he had written.[7]

11. Mʳ O Sullivan came, & said that he had much enlarged his Notes made upon the MS. 93.C.29. & would bring hither the same complete on Saturday, or on Monday next.[8]

---

[1] This set of Hebrew alphabets is Harl. 6841, ff. 31ᵇ–33ᵇ, and is dated by Wanley 10 Mar. 1719/20. Cf. 29 Feb. (item 8), 9 Mar. (item 3), and 10 Mar. (item 10) 1719/20.

[2] See 16 Feb. 1719/20 and footnote.

[3] See 7 Mar. 1719/20, item 16.

[4] See 18 Jan. 1719/20, item 4, and footnote 2.

[5] i.e. that pubd. by Buck and Daniel, Cambridge, 1638, fol.

[6] No further ref. is made to Lloyd's coll. of Greek and Roman coins.

[7] See 7 Mar. 1719/20, item 16, and footnote (for identification).

[8] Cf. 29 Feb. 1719/20, item 10, and footnote.

12. Mr Moetjens the Bookseller came, & brought part of the Catalogue of the fine Collection of Books & MSS. soon to be sold by Auction at the Hague; & being to be there himself, is willing to serve my Lord in any Commission.[1]

13. A Letter written to Mr Green the Pursuyvant, to come hither about a Pedegree my Lord would have him Copy.[2]

14. Mr William Thomas came, and borrowed 94.A.22. out of the Library.[3]

12 March 1719
20.

15. Mr. William Thomas came to Study.

14. March 1719
20.

16. Mr Beaver came to transcribe.

15 March, 1719
20.

17. Mr Beaver came to transcribe.

18. Mr O Sullevane came & deliver'd his Papers to me, much augmented.[4]/

p. 33
(f. 18a)

1. Mr Garwood came & borrowed Dr. Beaumonts Determinations.[5]

17 March 1719
20.

2. Mr Beaver came to transcribe.

3. Mr Noel came bluttering [*sic*] about one of Dr Whincopps books; but relinquished his Demand.[6]

4. Mr Rooke came to transcribe for Mr Sanderson.

5. Mr Gibson came, & acquainted me that he ha's lately recd from Italy a few MSS.[7]

18 March, 1719
20.

6. Mr Beaver came to transcribe.

7. Mr O Sullevane came to peruse the MS. 39.B.18.[8]

8. I was this morning at Mr Gibsons Lodgings, where I saw some old Printed books, & among them a Lactantius of Ven. 1478, in fol.[9] with 9 MSS. among

---

[1] Apparently Moetjens was not used in any commission; if the ref. here is to the Ménars sale of 10 June 1720 at The Hague, Vaillant was the agent (cf. 11 Apr. (item 18), 14 May and 17 May 1720).
[2] Cf. 9 Apr. (item 12) and 22 Apr. (item 6) 1720 and footnote. The transcript was finished by 30 Apr. 1720, see item 10.
[3] Harl. 1867.   [4] Cf. 10 Mar. 1719/20, item 11.
[5] Presumably the copy sent in by Thomas Baker, 8 Apr. 1715. Returned by Garwood 12 May 1720.
[6] See 11 Jan. 1719/20, item 6 and footnote.   [7] See 18 Mar. 1719/20, item 8.
[8] A slip by Wanley for the *Irish* MS. 39. B. 17 (= Harl. 432); cf. 1 Mar. 1719/20, item 12, and footnote. (39. B. 18 (= Harl. 433) is a Register of Letters Patent that probably belonged to Lord Burghley.)
[9] This could be Lactantius's *Opera* printed Venice, 1478 (for 1479), by Andreas de Paltasichis catarensis (Cattaro in Dalmatia) (Hain 9813; *BMC* v. 251) or that printed by Johannes de Colonia and Johannes Manthen, Venice, 1478 (Hain 9814; *BMC* v. 233).

them is a Breviarium Romanum, lately bought in the Monastery of S. Pietro d'Arena in Genoa, finely written;[1] a Seneca's Tragedies, fine,[2] both upon Velum. Non[i]us Marcellus,[3] some pieces of Tully,[4] an imperfect Virgil,[5] all upon Paper. Ovids Metamorphoses upon Velum;[6] &c. He said he will leave the Prices of these MSS. to my Lord & Me.[7]

9. I had a Letter from A.D. Frank, desiring that my Lords Chrysostom may be sent to Potton in Order to be putt into the Bedford-Library, in lieu of the Chartulary of Newenham.[8]

19 March, 1719/20.

10. Mr Beaver came to transcribe.
11. Mr Christian came; & said that Mr Andrew Hay will be in Town speedily.

21 March 1719/20.

11 [*sic*]. Yesterday I visited D^r. Sherard, and offer'd a Price (in my Lords Name) for Mr Chishul's Greek MS. of the Catena upon the Psalms & Scripture-Songs collected by Nicetas of Heraclæa & Serron.[9] The Doctor deliver'd to me the Gr. MS. of Elias Meniati late Bishop of Cernica & Calavrita in the Morea, upon the Original & Occasion of the Schism between the Eastern & Western Churches, as a present to my Lord.[10] He also shewed me divers Printed Books, in my Lords way.

12. Mr Will. Thomas came.

22 March 1719/20./

23 March, 1719/20.

p. 34 (f. 18b)

1. Mr Bowyer came, & brought a parchm^t. MS. in fol. containing a brief chronicle of England to A.D. 1366. with a Succession of the Popes to Benedict XII. & some Monkish Tracts, which I agreed with him for, at 20^s.[11] He also left a new Pamphlet for my Lord.

---

[1] Harl. 2986. On f. 1 is the inscription in Wanley's autogr.: 'Hic Codex olim fuit Monasterio Sancti Petri de Arena, in Civitate Januensi' (i.e. Genoa). The MS. has been rebound in 'Harleian Binding' and old fly-leaves and binding which might have provided confirmatory evidence are wanting.
[2] Harl. 2669.   [3] Harl. 2451.   [4] Harl. 2469.
[5] Harl. 2502.   [6] Harl. 2769.
[7] For Wanley's list of these MSS. see Addenda, Lansdowne 771, f. 77^b under 23 Apr. 1720 (at pp. 196–7 of the present work) and footnotes thereto for identifications. The MSS. were kept for Harley to inspect and were finally bought on 23 Apr. 1720. Cf. also 13 Apr. (item 3), 22 Apr. (item 8), and 23 Apr. (item 12), 1720.
[8] See 16 Feb. 1719/20, and footnote: i.e. Potton, near Bedford. See letter from Archdeacon Frank, dated 15 Mar. 1719/20, Harl. 3778, f. 234.
[9] Now Harl. 5791. See also 18 Jan. 1719/20, item 4, and footnote 4.
[10] Now Harl. 5729. See also 18 Jan. 1719/20, item 4, and footnote 5.
[11] Not identified.

24 March, 1719
20.

2. I having recd a letter from Dr Charlet lately, wrote to him today about his book.[1]

3. I wrote to A. D. Frank, in pursuance of my Lords Order, that the Chrysostom is sent according to his direction.[2]

28 March, 1720.

4. Mr Winnington jun. brought another Gentleman to see the Library.

30 March 1720.

5. I went to Mr Ben. Cowse, and disposed him to trade with my Lord for his Printed Antiquitates Britannicæ with MS. Additions;[3] his Box of Old Papers; his MS. of Nordens Survey of Cornwall, now printing; &c.[4]

6. I went to Mr Wiat the Bookseller, & engaged him to watch upon Mr Strype (who is above 76 years old, & ha's lately had an Apoplectic fit;) telling him, that if he would buy, in time, Mr Strypes, Manuscript Books, Papers & Parchments, my Lord will buy the same of him & allow him reasonable profit. To which he Agreed.[5]

7. I went to Mr Tanner; who told me that at present Will. Kemp will take no less than £3000, for his brothers Collection of Antiquities.[6]

8. Mr Bowyer came about the late Mr Llewellyn's Collection of Music, now about to be sold by Mr Estwick.[7]

31 March. 1720.

1 April 1720.

9. Mr Casley came to look into the MS. 93.D.2.[8] and talked as if Dr. Bentley had a Mind to borrow my Lords Manuscripts of the Greek Testament.[9]

10. Mr Bowyer sent a Latin MS. Prayer-book for my Lord to see.[10]

[1] Wanley's letter of this date is in Bodl. Lib., Ballard 13; Charlett's accepting the gift of Bayle's Dictionary, dated 11 Apr. 1720, is in Welbeck Wanleyana. This book was Peter Bayle, *Dictionary Historical and Critical* (pubd. London, 1710). (Cf. 9 Apr. (item 16) and 16 Apr. (item 15) 1720.) For refs. to a box of books to be dispatched to Charlett cf. 21 Apr. (items 21 and 1), 22 Apr. (item 7), and 3 May (item 16) 1720; Charlett's letter dated 9 May 1720, acknowledging such a box and pictures, including ones of Matthew Prior and Wanley himself, is in Welbeck Wanleyana.

[2] Cf. 18 Mar. 1719/20, item 9, and footnote. Frank did not acknowledge its receipt until 20 May 1720 (see Welbeck Wanleyana).

[3] Unidentified.

[4] John Norden's *Speculum Britanniae pars Cornwall* was pubd. 1728. The MS. is Harl. 6252.

[5] Cf. 24 Apr. (item 11), 25 Apr. (item 15), 3 and 4 May 1722; and 22 May 1723, item 12. Although Strype did not die until 1737 some of his colls. had found their way into the Harleian Library about 1708 (viz. Harl. 416-35 and Harl. Ch. (83. A. 15, 16). Wyat was used subsequently as the go-between when Harley desired to borrow some of Strype's papers (see refs. under Strype in Biographical Index). A letter of 27 Mar. 1720 from Harley to Wanley (Welbeck Wanleyana) may well have been the occasion of Wanley's visit to Wyat.

[6] Cf. 28 Jan. 1719/20, item 9, and footnote.

[7] Cf. 28 Jan. 1719/20, item 2, and footnote.

[8] Harl. 1806.

[9] Bentley did borrow a number of MSS. subsequently from the Library (cf. e.g. 6 May 1721, item 4, but see Biographical Index for full refs.).

[10] Harl. 2894. Cf. 5 Apr. 1720, item 6.

2 April 1720.

11. Mr Noel came & was spoken to, to lay aside a parcel of Classical books printed by Colinæus & Seb. Gryphius.[1]

12. Mr. O Sullevane came to peruse the Irish MS. as before.[2]

4 April 1720.

13. Mr Chapman the Binder brought the Parcel last dd to him; was paid; & recd another Parcel.

14. Mr James Hill came, & promised me to watch Mr Sam. Gale & see whether he ha's Dr Sherards Greek Inscription, (beginning with *ΕΡΜΟΓΕΝΗΣ ΧΡΥΣΙΠΠΟΥ*) or not. /[3]

5 April 1720.

p. 35
(f. 19a)

1. Mr Beaver came to Study.

2. Mr Vaillant sent in a MS. of Justinian's Code in fol;[4] having before sent to my Lord a MS. Q. Curtius.[5]

3. Mr Bridgewater the Cabinet maker came.

4. Mr Gibson came to look into some Scots Papers.

5. Mr Rooke came to Transcribe for Mr Sanderson.

6. Mr Bowyer came & I agreed with him for the MS. mentioned at p. 34, 10.

6. April 1720.

7. Mr Rooke came to Transcribe for Mr Sanderson.

7. April 1720.

8. Mr Rooke came to Transcribe for Mr Sanderson.

8 April 1720.

9. Mr O Sullevane came to peruse the old Irish MS. as before.[6]

10. I sent a Letter to Mr Greene the Poursuivant to come hither about my Lords Business.

11. Mr Harbyn the Clergy-man came; & seemed desirous to Collate my Lords old MS. of Tully de Oratore for himself.[7]

9 April 1720.

12. Mr Greene came & I shewed him the Pedegree my Lord would have him Copie, & the Book into which it is to be Entred.[8]

---

[1] 'Colinæus' = Simon de Colines, who took over Henri Estienne's business in Paris 1520–6 and continued subsequently independently as printer there. 'Seb. Gryphius' = Sebastian Greyff (1491–1566), one of the eminent printers of Lyons (from c. 1520).

[2] See 1 Mar. 1719/20, item 12, and footnote.

[3] See 3 June 1720, item 2. For Harley's purchase of Greek inscriptions from Smyrna through Sherard see 3 Feb. 1724/5 and footnotes and 16 Mar. 1724/5.

[4] Harl. 3758 (endorsed on the fly-leaf by Wanley, '11 Aprilis 1720'; cf. under that date, item 18).

[5] Harl. 2727 (endorsed on f. 1* by Wanley, '11 Aprilis 1720'; cf. under that date, item 18).

[6] See 1 Mar. 1719/20, item 12, and footnote.

[7] Probably Harl. 2736, which is the only 'old' MS. of Cicero's De Oratore in the Harl. Coll.; it is of 9th-cent. date. It had just been bought—23 Feb. 1719/20 (cf. p. 195 below).

[8] Cf. 10 Mar. 1719/20, item 13. For the identification of the Pedegree and the Book, cf. 22 Apr. 1720, item 6, and footnote.

13. Mr Noel came to see some Duplicates he is to have: & to know when my Lord will set aside those Books of Dr Whincopp's (sent in by Mr Noel) which he shall think fit to buy. Mr Noel finding that Whincopps single Pamphlets will take up more time in looking over than they are worth; gave them to my Lord.[1]

14. Mr Chapman the Binder sent home the antient MS. of the Latin Gospels, a leafe of which was transpos'd.

15. Mr James Hill came & perused some old Charters relating to the old Earls of Hereford.[2]

16. I wrote to Dr Charlett, desiring to specifie whether he would have Bayles Dictionary in French, or in English, for his Book.[3]

11. April 1720.

17. Mr James Hill came to Transcribe for Himself.

18. I agreed with Mr Vaillant for his MSS. of Q. Curtius & Justiniani Codex;[4] and directed him to send into Holland for a Specimen of the Character of the Latin Gospels written all with Golden Letters, which will be sold next June in the Auction of Menars's Books.[5]

19. Mr Sanderson told me that the Saxon Charters late in the Possession of the Lord Somers, cannot as yet be found: but he believe's that the Person who was his Lordships Secretary may know where they are. /[6]

p. 36
(f. 19*b*)

1. Mr Downe the Herald & Vice-Chamberlayne in the Exchequer came, to Enquire after a Persian Paper lent to Mr Mickleton deceased. And to know if my Lord will suffer one Mr Bridges of Grayes-Inne to take a Copie of S^r. Simonds Dewes's Abstract of Domesday-book relating to Herefordshire only.[7]

13 April 1720.

2. Mr Bowyer came, & said he ha's hopes of buying the late Archdeacon Batteley's books.[8]

---

[1] Cf. 11 Jan. 1719/20, item 6, and footnote.

[2] See 14 Apr. (item 13), 21 Apr. (items 3 and 5), 27 Apr. (item 22), 9 May (item 9) 1720, and 14 Apr. 1721 (item 5). These visits were probably made by Hill in connexion with his proposed history of the City of Hereford. (Cf. also *Vertue Note Books* (Walpole Soc.), i, p. 49, and Thomas Hearne, *Remarks and Collections* (Ox. Hist. Soc.), viii (1907), p. 103, under 2 Aug. 1723.)

[3] See 24 Mar. 1719/20, item 2, and footnote.

[4] For identification of the two MSS. see 5 Apr. 1720, item 2, and footnotes.

[5] i.e. the Codex Aureus (now Harl. 2788), which was lot 9 in the sale of the library of Jean Jacques Charron, Marquis de Ménars, announced for 10 June 1720 (see *Bibliotheca Menarsiana*, The Hague, 1720). In the priced cat. in BM (press-mark 271. b. 35) the price written against it is 1100 (i.e. Dutch guilders). It is described in the sale-cat. thus:

> '9. Quatuor Euangelia, Latinè. *MS. sur Vélin, écrit en Lettres Majuscules d'Or, très ancien, ayant plus de neuf siècles, enrichi d'Ornemens antiques; ce Manuscrit qui est d'une Beauté, d'une Antiquité, & d'une Conservation sans pareille, est très considérable.*'

The cat. has no plates; cf. footnote to 14 May 1720, item 4. For subsequent references to this MS., its purchase, &c., cf. 14 May (item 4), 17 May (item 5), 4 June (item 4) (report of purchase), 5 June, 6 June (item 1) (paid for), 21 June (item 6), 27 June (item 11) (delivered to Wanley), 28 June (item 1), 29 June (item 2) (placed in the Library), and 20 Aug. (item 14) 1720. For its binding by Elliot cf. 27 June and 13 July 1721.

[6] See 28 Jan. 1719/20, item 4, and footnote.

[7] The result of this application by Mr. Bridges is not known.

[8] See 11 Jan. 1719/20, item 3, and footnote.

3. Mr Gibson came, & desired that my Lord would call upon him, he keeping his Books for my Lords View.[1]

4. Mr Andrew Hay came, & agreed to execute my Lords Commissions in Italy, at a reasonable Allowance.[2] He also left with me a Purse wherein is a great Number of Coins, Scotch, English, & Foreign, to shew to my Lord.

5. Mr Moetjens came & left with me a large Book lately Printed in Holland, to shew my Lord.[3]

6. Mr Morgan my Lords Gentleman came.

7. My Lord sent me with a Stone Engraven with Persian Letters to Mr Salomon Negri.

14 April 1720.

8. Mr Beaver came to Study & Transcribe.

9. Mr O Sullevane came to peruse the Irish MS.[4]

10. I wrote to Mr Bowyer to send a Bayles Dictionary in English to my Lord.[5]

11. Mr Bowyer came & brought the Catalogue abovementioned,[6] with two [other deleted in MS.] Pamphlets, one a present to my Lord.

12. Mr Warburton came, & said his old Inscriptions are yet unsold.[7] He say's he ha's some Lieger-Books of Abbeys at his Lodgings with Mr Vander-Guchts the Engraver in Queen-street near the New Church in Bloomsbury.[8]

13. Mr. James Hill brought Mr Vertue to look upon the Bohun's Charters.[9]

14. Dr. Friend of Westminster came, & saw some MSS.

16 April 1720.

15. My Lord sent in Bayles Dictionary in English, for Dr. Charlett.[10]

16. Mr Moetjens came, was paid off; & took away his great Book.[11]

17. Yesterday I saw a choice parcel of MSS. with Mr Warburton: who is lately arrived from Northumberland.[12]

18 April 1720.

[1] See 18 Mar. 1719/20, item 8, and footnote. Harley inspected and bought them 23 Apr. 1720.
[2] See 26 Apr. 1720, item 18, and footnote.
[3] See 16 Apr. 1720, item 16.
[4] See 1 Mar. 1719/20, item 12, and footnote.
[5] This was for Charlett: cf. 24 Mar. 1719/20, item 2, and footnote.
[6] Perhaps of 'Mr. Llewellyn's musical MSS.', which was returned on 25 May 1720 (item 9) (cf. 30 Mar. 1720, item 8).
[7] This is the first ref. to Warburton's 'old Inscriptions', which appear to be identifiable with 'his Roman Altars' alluded to under 6 July 1720, but see also entries under 15 and 22 July, and 1 Aug. 1720, item 2 (cf. also Wanley's Addenda, Lansdowne 771, f. 77ᵇ under 16 July 1720 (at p. 197 of the present work). Further antiquities are referred to 3 Aug. 1720, item 3.
[8] These and other MSS. were the subject of protracted negotiations, cf. 16 Apr. (item 17), 17 May (item 7), 21 June (item 6), 27 June (item 10), 6 July and 7 July (item 3), 13 July, 14 July, 15 July (item 5), 16 July (item 6, for list and footnote for probable source of some of the MSS. and their connexion with Naworth) and 22, 25, and 30 July, 1 and 3 Aug. 1720; 30 Jan. and 3 Feb. (item 7) 1721/2.
[9] See 9 Apr. 1720, item 15, and footnote.
[10] Cf. 24 Mar. 1719/20, item 2, and footnote.
[11] Cf. 13 Apr. 1720, item 5.
[12] See 14 Apr. 1720, item 12, and footnote.

19 April 1720.

18. Mr Bridgewater came, & said that one Mr Bolton who lodges at a Comb-makers against St. Clement-Danes Church, makes Cards to hold Coins the best of any in London.

19. The Ld. Bishop of Chester & Dr Friend of Westminster came, & looked into some Books.

20 April 1720.

21 April 1720.

20. A Letter was sent to Mr Greene the Poursuivant to Attend my Lord.

21. Mr Gregory came & took Measure of the Parcel to be sent to Dr Charlet. /[1]

p. 37
(f. 20a)

1. A Letter was written to Dr. Charlet for directions how to send the said Parcel to him.[1]

2. Dr Stukeley came desiring to Copie some Figures of antient English Habits from the Manuscripts. I shewed him some; but told him it would be handsome to apply to my Lord for Leave first, in this Case. My Lord came after & gave him Leave.[2]

3. My Lord gave Leave that Mr James Hill may have Copies from the Seales of Herefordshire-Deeds for his Book.[3]

4. Mr Greene came, & received my Lords Commands.

5. Mr James Hill brought Mr Vertue to copie some of the Seales abovementioned.[3]

22 April 1720.

6. Mr Greene came & began to insert a Pedigree of Corbet into Withies book of Shropshire for my Lord.[4]

7. Mr Gregory brought a Box for the Books to be sent to Dr Charlet.[5]

8. Mr Gibson came, & my Lord said he would call on him & see his Books.[6]

9. I shewed my Lord some Coins & Medals of Gold & Silver, received from Mr Sanderson.[7]

10. Mr O Sullevane came to peruse the Irish Manuscript.[8]

23 April 1720.

11. Mr Greene came to transcribe for my Lord.

12. Mr Gibson sent in a Parcel of Manuscripts & Printed books, which my Lord bought of him yesterday.[9]

[1] Cf. 24 Mar. 1719/20, item 2, and footnote.
[2] Presumably in connexion with his projected 'history of the ancient Celts, particularly the first inhabitants of Great Britain' referred to in the preface to his *Itinerarium Curiosum*, 26 Dec. 1724. (On this side of Stukeley's work see Stuart Piggott, *William Stukeley*, 1950, chap. iv.)
[3] See 9 Apr. 1720, item 15, and footnote.
[4] Cf. 9 Apr. 1720, item 12, and footnote. 'Withies book of Shropshire' is Harl. 1396; the Corbet genealogical material entered by Greene is at ff. 53ᵇ–61.
[5] See 24 Mar. 1719/20, item 2, and footnote.
[6] See 18 Mar. 1719/20, item 8, and footnote; and cf. item 12 below.
[7] These were from Matterson's (i.e. Maddison's) coll. of medals, &c. (See 28 Jan. 1719/20, item 5, and footnote, and cf. 28 Apr. 1720, item 1.)
[8] See 1 Mar. 1719/20, item 12, and footnote.   [9] See 18 Mar. 1719/20, item 8, and footnotes.

25. April 1720.

13. M[r] Greene came to transcribe for my Lord.

14. M[r] Gibson came, & my Lord paid off his whole Accompt.

15. I sent a Letter to D[r]. Sherard, in answer to that which I last received of him.[1]

16. M[r] Dale brought M[r] Bulstrode with him to see the Library, & search into some Heraldical MSS.

26 April 1720.

17. M[r] Greene came to transcribe for my Lord.

18. My Lord Order'd me to Draw up a Commission for M[r] Andrew Hay, to buy MSS. in France & Italy.[2]

27 April 1720.

19. A Letter was sent to M[r] Sanderson, about my Inspecting his Coins to morrow.[3]

20. A Letter was written to D[r]. Sherard, about his Foreign Acorns & Seeds; & about M[r] Chishuls Greek MS. being a Catena upon the Psalms & sacred Odes collected by Nicetas Heracleensis.[4]

21. M[r] Greene came to transcribe for my Lord.

22. M[r] Vertue came to delineate some Seals for M[r] James Hill. /[5]

28 April 1720.

p. 38
(f. 20b)

1. I inspected the Collection of Coins Medals & Antiquities lately belonging to the Reverend M[r] Maddison deceased, & now in the Possession or Custody of M[r] Sanderson.[6]

2. D[r] Sherard sent the Acorns Seeds & Greek MS. yesterday.[7]

29 April 1720.

3. M[r] O Sullevane brought a MS. Primer to sell for his Friend; but it being not worth the buying, I rejected it.

30 April 1720.

4. A young man unknown brought 3 MSS. to sell, but would not declare whose they are, or how he came by them, or who he is, or to whom he belong's: Only that they come out of the Countrey, & he shall be paid for bringing them

---

[1] Wanley's letter must have been in answer to Sherard's of 23 Apr. 1720 in Harl. 3781, f. 52, which offers Harley a gift of acorns (from Italy) and mentions Chishull and the 'Catena in Psalmos'. (Cf. item 20 below.)

[2] Wanley's draft of this Commission, dated 26 Apr. 1720, was preserved in the West papers at Alscot Park and sold Sotheby's, 29 Oct. 1962, lot 185 (part of); it was printed with some inaccuracies in *Harl. Cat.* (1759), i, p. 5, n. 1, and reprinted in *Harl. Cat.* (1808–12), i, p. 6, n. 1. The original draft is endorsed in James West's hand, 'given me by Mr. Noel June 12 1744'. See 12 Jan. 1719/20, item 2; 13 Apr. (item 4), 3 May (item 17), 7 May (item 6), 1 June (item 5) and 22 Dec. (item 8) 1720; and 28 Apr. 1721, item 9. Wanley demanded the return of the Commission 17 Apr. 1722 and it was returned 20 Apr. 1722. For other refs. to Hay consult Biographical Index.

[3] Cf. 22 Apr. 1720, item 9, and footnote.

[4] Now Harl. 5791, cf. 18 Jan. 1719/20, item 4, and footnote 4.

[5] Cf. 9 Apr. 1720, item 15, and footnote.   [6] Cf. 28 Jan. 1719/20, item 5, and footnote.

[7] i.e. Harl. 5791, cf. above, 27 Apr. 1720, item 20.

from Little Britain. They were The works of Josephus in Latin, a large folio, above 500 years old. Constantini Monachi Cassinensis Liber qui dicitur Pantegni. fol. membr. Richard Hampoles Stimulus Conscientiæ, a Theological Poem in old English. 4to. membr. He asked Ten Guineas for them. But I finding the Owner was desirous of being conceald, & the Messenger in several Stories, would make no Bargain about them.

5. A Letter was sent to Mr Sanderson desiring him to meet me soon, that we may Treat about his Things.[1]

6. Another to D^r. Sherard, desiring him to call here, some day.

7. Another to D^r. Charlet of Oxford; again desiring him to direct Me how to send down the Box.[2]

8. Mr Noel came to enquire after the Duplicates of D^r. Whincop's book.[3]

9. Mr Robert Cuningham's 3 Sons came to see the Library.

10. Mr Greene came, having finished his copie of the Pedegree.[4]

11. Dr Fiddis came.

2 May 1720.

12. M^r O Sullevane came to peruse the Irish MS.[5]

13. Dr Sherard came, & promised to use his best Endeavors for procuring the Duke of Devonshires old MS. for my Lord.[6]

14. Mr Bowyer the Bookseller came, & desired me to go with him to see the late A.D. Batteleys MSS. which I did; but one of the owners being Sick, we could not be admitted to inspect them.[7]

3 May 1720.

15. I went to Mr Sanderson, & saw many Stones antient & Modern, with Petrifactions, Shells, & other Natural Curiosities; but would not medle about them, they belonging not to Mr Sanderson, but to Mr Maddison's Heir. Mr Sanderson promised to let me have his Demand for his Things, quickly.[8]

16. I had a Letter from D^r. Charlet, giving some Direction how his Books may be sent to his Carrier; & I sent the Box away accordingly.[9]

17. Mr Andrew Hay came, to whom I delivered My Lords Commission for buying up MSS. in France & Italy, being dated / 26 April 1720. I explain'd every thing so to him, that He understand's it very well, and say's he shall sett out for France the 11th. Instant.[10]

1. Mr Myddletone came.

p. 39
(f. 21a)

---

[1] Cf. 28 Apr. 1720, item 1, and see 28 Jan. 1719/20, item 5, and footnote.

[2] Cf. 21 Apr. 1720, item 1, and footnote.

[3] Cf. 9 Apr. 1720, item 13, and footnote.

[4] Cf. 9 Apr. 1720, item 12, and footnote. On 6 May he was paid 2 guineas for this (Welbeck Wanleyana, Misc. no. 49).

[5] See 1 Mar. 1719/20, item 12.

[6] i.e. The Benedictional of St. Ethelwold. See 18 Jan. 1719/20, item 4, and footnote 7.

[7] See 11 Jan. 1719/20, item 3, and footnote.

[8] See 28 Jan. 1719/20, item 5, and footnote.

[9] See 24 Mar. 1719/20, item 2, and footnote. Charlett's letter dated 1 May 1720 is preserved in Welbeck Wanleyana.

[10] See 26 Apr. 1720, and footnote. For first-fruits of his Commission in France cf. 1 June 1720, item 5.

4 May 1720.

2. I went to Stafford-house, upon information that there are two very fine MSS which will be sold at the Sale of the late Earl of Stafford's things, which Commence's to morrow. I found the one to be a sort of Breviary, the other to be a kind of Diurnal, both very finely Illuminated.[1]

3. A Letter was Sent to Mr Tanner, desiring him to attend my Lord this day by two of the clock. (in Order to receive my Lord's Commissions for Buying at the Sale abovementioned[)].

4. Mr Sanderson sent me a Letter, with the Price he putt's upon his Things; which price I think too dear, because very many of them His Lordship doth not want, or intend's to buy; many other's he hath already; and the remainder not considerable enough to induce him to part with so much as Mr Sanderson ask's.[2]

5. I went to Mr Warner the Goldsmith, desiring him to execute my Lords Commission for buying the MSS. abovementioned, and some other things at Stafford-house, which he readily undertook.[3] I also bought of him the old *Gylyngham*-Silver-Spoon for my Lord.[4]

5 May 1720.

6. A Letter sent to Mr Sanderson, to know upon what Grounds he put's so great a Value upon his Things.[5]

6 May 1720.

7. A Letter received from Mr Sanderson, insisting upon his Price; & desiring to know my Lords Resolution speedily, he having Chapmen ready who (he think's) will give more than he ask's my Lord.[5]

8. Sir James Thornhill brought two Setts of the Prints taken from his Paintings in St. Paul's Cathedral, for my Lord.[6]

9. Mr. Pocklington came, & informed me that Mr Mickleton's Things will be Sold about a Fortnight hence; and that several persons are concerned in the Sale.[7]

[1] The colls. of Henry Stafford-Howard, 10th Earl of Stafford, d.s.p. 27 Apr. 1719, were part of the old Arundel Coll.; Wanley refers under 7 May 1720, item 12, to Charles Howard being the owner. This was Henry Charles Howard of Greystoke, who (see *Vertue Note Books* (Walpole Soc.), v, p. 31) was the 10th Earl's executor: cf. also E. Edwards, *Lives of the Founders of the British Museum*, 1870, pp. 198–201, on Stafford House Sale. Cf. also items 3 and 5 below, and 7 May (items 3, 5, and 8), 14 May (item 5) 1720, and Wanley's statement that they were bought, in Addenda, Lansdowne 771, f. 77[b] under 7 May 1720 (at p. 197 of the present work). See 16 May 1720, item 4, for visit by Cunningham to see 'the 2 MSS. lately bought at Stafford-house' and 25 May 1720, item 10, for Noel's request to see what are apparently the same two. Cf. also 18 May 1720, item 11, for Bacon's visit to see 'the fine Prayerbook' and his comments.
[2] Sanderson's letter, dated 4 May 1720 (in Welbeck Wanleyana), offered his coll. of gold and other medals for 500 guineas. Cf. 28 Jan. 1719/20, item 5, and footnote.
[3] Cf. 4 May 1720, item 2, and footnote.
[4] For 1 guinea (see Welbeck Wanleyana, Misc. no. 49).
[5] See 4 May 1720, item 4, and footnote. Sanderson's reply, dated 5 May 1720, is in Welbeck Wanleyana.
[6] Sir James Thornhill's paintings of the dome of St. Paul's Cathedral were executed between 1714 and 1717; for them he received £4,000. There are 8 subjects of which engravings were made (possibly, in Mr. Croft Murray's view, from a series of small copies in monochrome) by Charles Du Bose, N. D. Beauvais, Bernard Baron, Gerard van der Gucht (4 subjects), and Charles Simoneau. None is dated and this entry by Wanley provides the missing information: it is worth noting that, according to Vertue (*Note Books* (Walpole Soc.), i, p. 65), Thornhill had presented a set of these engravings to the King on 2 May 1720. (We are indebted to Mr. Croft Murray for much of this information.)
[7] See 25 Feb. 1719/20, item 14, and footnote.

10. Mr Greene came & acquainted me that Sr. John Osbourne of Chicksand-Abbey is dead; that the Heir is a boy about 5 years old, and that Sir George Byng is Executor.[1]

11. A Letter written to Mr A.D. Frank, desiring an Account of the Old Books & Writings yet remaining in that Abbey; & his Advice how, most easily, to come at them.[1]

7 May 1720.

12. A Letter was sent to Mr Charles Howard (who is Owner of the Things now Selling at Stafford-house,) desiring him to appoint a Time when I may wait upon him.[2]

13. Another, to Mr Sanderson; desiring him to permitt none to see his Collection, till my Lord has viewed it. /[3]

p. 40
(f. 21b)

1. Mr Warner came to conferre with me about the Things now selling at Stafford-house.[4]

2. Mr Baron Scrope (who gave the fine Printed Missal, which was found in the Aquapulco Ship)[5] was brought here by Mr Rob. Cuningham; & promised to give a MS. to the Library shortly.[6]

3. Mr Warner came again, & said that the two fine MSS. at Stafford-house will be Sold to day, My Lord desired him to go thither again & buy them.[7]

4. Mr Hugh Thomas came about his own business.

5. Mr Howard desire's to see me at 5 this Afternoon.[8]

6. Mr Andrew Hay came, & conferred with me again about serving my Lord abroad.

7. Mr Christian came to take off Impressions from my Ladies fine Seals.

8. Mr Warner brought the two fine MSS. bought this day at Stafford house.[9]

9 May, 1720.

9. Mr James Hill brought Mr Dobbins of Herefordshire to see the Library.

10. Mr Chapman the Binder, brought the Books last Bound; was paid-off; & received another Parcell.

11. My Lord Order'd me to draw up a List of Books for him to see at Oxford.[10]

10 May 1720.

12. My Lord bade me enlarge that List.[10]

13. Mr Pocklington came & gave me hopes of Mr Mickletons things.[11]

---

[1] Cf. 17 Feb. 1719/20, item 9, and footnote. Frank's reply, dated 20 May 1720 (in Welbeck Wanleyana), deals (after acknowledging the gift of the Chrysostom) with Wanley's query about the books in Osborne's library; 'the Heir' was Sir Danvers Osborne, 3rd Bart.

[2] See 4 May 1720, item 2, and footnote.   [3] Cf. 4 May 1720, item 4, and footnote.

[4] See 4 May 1720, item 2, and footnote.   [5] i.e. from Acapulco in Mexico.

[6] No such gift is recorded.   [7] Cf. 4 May 1720, item 2, and footnote.

[8] Cf. item 12 above under this date.   [9] See 4 May 1720, item 2, and footnote.

[10] A memorandum (undated), headed by Wanley, 'At Oxford, your Lordship may please to see', comprising a list of MSS. and early printed books, is in Harl. 7055, f. 45. (An earlier memorandum in Wanley's autogr., dated 11 Apr. 1718, apparently addressed to Harley, relating to things to be seen at Salisbury, Oxford, &c., is also in Harl. 7055, ff. 48, 48b.)

[11] Cf. 6 May 1720, item 9, and footnote.

11 May, 1720.

14. M[r] Hugh Thomas came to Study, as he think's.

15. M[r] O Sullevane came to peruse the old Irish MS.[1]

16. I went, (by my Lords Order) to M[r] Charles Howard, about the Old Ivory Cup & Cover, (formerly part of the Arundellian Collection) & found him very civil, but throughly inclined to Sell it, as all his other things, at the dearest Rate. He ha's promised me a Sight of the Catalogue of the Books that are to be Sold at Stafford-house, if I call on him next Saturday.[2]

17. I went to M[r] Sanderson with my Lords Message; he say's he can have 1000 Guineas for his Collection; and ha's been offered an high Value to suffer a Gentleman to pick out 100 coins.[3]

18. I went to the Genoa-Armes, where M[r] Noel came & brought the first part of the Catalogue of Baron Hohe[n]dorf's Library, which he lent me, being the only book in England & brought expressly to him, as to the first Buyer. He declare's himself willing to be faithful to my Lord, & to suffer him to pick & chuse, but is obliged to desire my Lord to support him in the Purchase of the whole Library which the owner value's at 12000 pounds.[4]

12 May 1720.

19. I wrote to my Lord about M[r] Howard, M[r] Sanderson, M[r]. Noel, & A. D. Frank.[5]

20. D[r]. Fiddis came to talk & look about Cardinal Wolsey & his Legantine [*sic*]-powers.[6]

21. M[r] Garwood restored the two Volumes of D[r]. Beaumonts Determinations he had borrowed. /[7]

13 May 1720.

p. 41
(f. 22a)

1. Yesterday in the Evening M[r] Noel Visited me, & we had a long Conversation about the late Baron Hohendorfs Collection; which, he say's, consist's of Printed Books, MSS. Medals & other Pieces of Antiquity, for all which, he say's the present Owner now demands £12000. As to the Medals, &c. He propose's to Sell them to my Lord; The MSS. he say's, do now furnish a whole Room, and are valued at £1500, by the Widow, and shall be all Sold to my Lord according as I shall Value them. As to the Printed Books (which, indeed, are very Curious,) my Lord shall have the Liberty of picking out all he wants; and (for a moderate Consideration,) the Exchanging all his inferior Copies

---

[1] Cf. 1 Mar. 1719/20, item 12, and footnote.
[2] Cf. 4 May 1720, item 2, and footnote. This 'Old Ivory Cup & Cover' is presumably that described under lot 4145 in the sale of the Duchess of Portland's Museum 7 June 1786 (when it was bought by Tyson for £19. 8s. 6d.). In Bodl. MS. Gough Maps 43, nos. 91–94, and in Harley Coll. of Prints at Soc. of Ant., vol. ii, ff. 76–78, are drawings of an ivory tankard with cover made at Wimpole, Sept. 1724, by Vertue, who had exhibited to the Soc. of Antiquaries (see Minute Book) a similar tankard 30 Nov. 1720.
[3] Cf. 7 May 1720, item 13, and footnote.
[4] Cf. 11 Jan. 1719/20, item 7, and footnote.
[5] Presumably about the business mentioned under 11 May (items 16, 17, 18) and 6 May (items 10, 11) 1720.
[6] Probably in preparation for his *Life of Cardinal Wolsey*, pubd. 1724. Cf. 15 Jan. 1719/20, item 5, and footnote.
[7] Borrowed 15 Mar. 1719/20.

against such of Hohendorfs, as shall be Superior, in respect of the Larger Paper, finer Covers, &c. But then, in Consideration of these Concessions, He hope's that my Lord will support Him with a good Sum; the Purchase being of so great a Value, and the whole Money to be paid down, at once, upon delivery of the Things.[1]

2. Mr Beaver gave me a Printed Tract about Gibraltar, & the importance of that place to us; which he drew up for the late Admiral Cornwal's Information; and which, being somewhat mangled & disguised, was since privately published by the Admirals Secretary, under the false Appellation of *a Turkey-Merchant.* To this Copie Mr Beaver ha's made many remarks.[2]

3. Mr Mattaire came to see my Lords last parcel of fine Printed books. I attended him a very long while.[3]

14 May 1720.

4. Yesterday Mr Vaillant brought me a Specimen of the Character of that Latin MS of the Gospels, which is to be sold at the approaching Auction of Menars's Books at the Hague. These Char[a]cters are all Uncials, gilded over with Gold, and appear to be formed in very elegant Manner. Among them I observe A. G. V. M & E, so shaped, which is not commonly seen in the Body or Text of old MSS. although frequent in the Title, or Rubrics. In my Opinion, this most antient & valuable Book should be purchased, at any rate.[4]

5. This morning I went to Mr Charles Howard, for his Catalogue of the Books now about to be sold at Stafford house, which I received, & promised to return this Evening. Mr Howard said that a certain Gentleman of a considerable Estate had read the Inscription upon Queen Bertha's Comb, & that he would bid for it, as would several others, and among them his own Lady. Upon this, I prevailed with him to take-off Mrs. Howard; & went after Mr Pownhall to see if he was come to Town, & to direct him a little; which I did accordingly. /5

---

[1] Cf. 11 Jan. 1719/20, item 7, and footnote.

[2] The tract is: 'A letter to the lords commissioners for trade and plantation, concerning the advantage of Gibraltar to the trade of Great Britain, with some proposals to render that place more useful. By a Turkey Merchant. To which is prefixed, a chart to the Mediterranean Sea. Printed anno 1720.' It is no. 2 in the list of Gibraltar pamphlets in Appendix II to *The Propriety of Retaining Gibraltar Impartially Considered*, London, 1783 (BM press-mark 103. e. 8), where the traditional history of the origin of the pamphlet is given on p. 39, viz. that in 1717 John Beaver supplied to Admiral Cornwall (who was then at Gibraltar) a written statement about the advantages of Gibraltar (at the Admiral's request), that the Admiral died at Lisbon, and that his papers fell into the hands of his secretary, who published it under the fictitious name of 'A Turkey Merchant'. We are indebted for this identification to the Hon. David Erskine.

[3] Presumably those in the purchase from Gibson referred to under 23 Apr. 1720, item 12. Probably in connexion with Maittaire's work, *Annales Typographici*, pubd. 1719–41, in which he referred to many of Harley's early printed books.

[4] This was in accordance with the direction to Vaillant given on 11 Apr. 1720 (item 18) (cf. that date and footnote). It was afterwards found that this Specimen 'was injudiciously done' (cf. 20 Aug. 1720, item 14); it must have been specially executed as no plate is contained in the Ménars sale-cat.

[5] Cf. 4 May 1720, item 2, and footnote. 'Queen Bertha's Comb' is now in the British Museum, Dept. of British and Mediaeval Antiquities (under the reference 1916, 4–3, 1), to which it was presented by Maurice Rosenheim, F.S.A. After Edward Harley's death it was in the possession of his daughter and heiress the Duchess of Portland and was lot 23 in the Supplementary Coll. of Cameos which took place on the 39th day of the Portland Museum sale, 8 June 1786; it was bought by Kirkgate for 18s. (disguised in the printed list of prices under 'Cash'). It was subsequently in Horace Walpole's possession and appeared in the Strawberry Hill sale, 23rd day (20 May 1842), lot 12 (when it was bought for £3. 13s. 6d.). The comb bears an inscription that it was a gift from Pope Gregory to Queen Bertha. The comb is discussed by Sir Hercules Read, *Proc. Society of Antiquaries*, 2nd ser., xxviii (1915–16), pp. 168–71, and a drawing is in Harl. Coll. of Prints at Soc. of Ant., vol. ii, f. 49.

1. Mr Gibson came, and desired to know what my Lord will [give] for a fair p. 42
   Copie of the Latin Bible printed by the Maximi's at Rome A.D. 1470, in two (f. 22b)
   large Folio's. I would name no particular price; but said my Lord would easily
   determine, when he shall see the Books, which are now in Florence.[1]

2. Mr Bridges came to see my Lords fine Books lately bound; but I putt him off
   til Monday. He said also that Mr Bateman ha's an Heraldical MS. for which He
   demands Ten Guineas.[2]

16 May 1720.

3. Mr Bridges came to see my Lords fine Printed Books, & was attended by Me
   very long.

4. Mr Robert Cuningham came to see the 2 MSS. lately bought at Stafford-
   house.[3]

17 May 1720.

5. My Lord seeing a Specimen of the Character of the Latin MS. of the Gospels
   said to be all over written with Letters of Gold, gave Order for its being bought
   at Menars's approaching Auction, at the Hague, & sent over hither as soon as
   may be. The Commission to be given to Mr Vaillant.[4]

6. My Lord Order'd [me] to look over a parcel of antique Medals, offer'd to be
   sold.

7. Mr Warburton came to look upon some MSS. here; & say's he ha's gotten up
   some more of his old MSS. from the Countrey, which he desire's me to come
   to him & see.[5]

8. By my Lords Order I went to Mr Vaillant, & gave him Comission to buy the
   Golden Book of the Gospels above mentioned, with all Secresie & Prudence.[6]

18 May 1720.

9. Mr Mattaire came to make some further Observations upon certain of my
   Lords fine Printed Books.[7]

10. A Letter was sent to Mr Sanderson, acquainting him that my Lord will call &
    see his Collection, on Friday-morning next.[8]

11. Mr Bacon came & desired to see my Lords fine Prayer-book; which he himself
    bad £75 for, and would willingly have bought at £100, if my Lord should
    not buy it.[9] He desired also to see the fine Printed Books lately come from
    Binding.

12. M^r O Sullevane came to peruse the old Irish MS.[10]

[1] A ref. presumably to the 'Biblia Latina' printed by Sweynheim and Pannartz at Rome in 1471 (see *BMC* iv. 12). No copy of this Bible appears in the lists of printed books subsequently brought in from Italy by Gibson; one group of these is specified as having come from Florence. The Massimi brothers were not printers, but it was in their house that the printers Sweynheim and Pannartz set up their press in Nov. 1467.
[2] The 'Heraldical MS.' is possibly the first of the MSS. bought from Bateman and sent in 26 May 1720; viz. Harl. 4205.   [3] See 4 May 1720, item 2, and footnote.
[4] This is the 'Specimen' (supplied by Vaillant) under 14 May 1720 (item 4). For Codex Aureus negotiations see 11 Apr. 1720, item 18, and footnote.
[5] See 14 Apr. 1720, item 12, and footnote.   [6] See item 5 above.
[7] Cf. 13 May 1720, item 3, and footnote.   [8] See below 20 May 1720, item 14, and footnote.
[9] Probably a ref. to the 'Diurnal' bought at the Stafford House sale (cf. 4 May 1720, item 2, and footnote).   [10] Cf. 1 Mar. 1719/20, item 12, and footnote.

20. May, 1720.

13. My Lord redelivered the MS. 36.B.2.[1] which had been sent to M[r] Hearne of Oxford.

14. His Lordship went to M[r] Sanderson & saw his Collection.[2]

15. I had a Note from M[r] Bowyer, desiring me to meet him to morrow, in Order to see the remainder of the late A.D. Batteleys books.[3]

16. The Hon[ble]. M[r] Thomas Harley came to see some of my Lords fine Books.

21 May 1720.

17. I met M[r] Bowyer, & went with him to see the remainder of A.D. Batteley's Books which I found in Confusion, & most of the MSS. in very ill Condition. M[r] Bowyer promised me, that if he buie's these MSS. my Lord shall have the Old MSS. & Charters at 20 Guineas; & the Picking out of the Printed books before they come to Auction. /[3]

p. 43 (f. 23a)

23 May 1720.

1. M[r] Dockwra came, & I shewed him the fine Books.

2. M[r] Hill the Painter came to see my Lords fine-painted Book.

3. My Lord sent in some Prints to be presented to M[r] Topham & M[r] G. Holme; & I to send a L̃re with them.

4. M[r] O Sullevane came to peruse the Irish MS.[4]

5. M[r]. Bateman came to see my Lords fine MSS. & is willing to serve my Lord as to M[r] Williams the Printers MSS.[5]

24 May 1720.

6. My Lord took me to M[r] Bateman's, where he bought some Printed Books, & MSS.[6]

7. M[r] Nutting came.

25 May 1720

8. My Lord owned that he ha's the Six Go[l]d & Silver Coins lent by M[r] Sanderson, in his own Custody. And Order'd me to go to him this day, & Treat with him about the Price of the Whole Collection.[7]

9. M[r] Bowyer came, & received back the Catalogue of M[r] Llewellyns Musical MSS.[8] He said further, that he ha's not, as yet, agreed for M[r] A.D. Batteleys

---

[1] = Harl. 200. This was one of the MSS. of Robert of Avesbury (whose chronicle occupies ff. 79[b]–139[b]) used by Thomas Hearne for his *Roberti de Avesburi Historia de Mirabilibus Gestis Eduardi III*, Oxford, 1720: it is referred to and described by Hearne in his Preface (pp. xii ff.). Robert and Edward Harley each subscribed to the publication (see List of Subscribers, pp. li and liv).

[2] Cf. 28 Jan. 1719/20, item 5, and footnote.

[3] See 11 Jan. 1719/20, item 3, and footnote.

[4] Cf. 1 Mar. 1719/20, item 12, and footnote.

[5] Cf. 4 May (item 11), 7 May (item 5), 26 June (item 8), 1 Aug., 11, 12, and 13 Sept. and 27 Dec. 1722 (for list). Subsequently this business was transacted through Noel (not Bateman): see above dates and footnotes.

[6] See 26 May 1720, item 15 (for list).   [7] Cf. 28 Jan. 1719/20, item 5, and footnote.

[8] Cf. 28 Jan. 1719/20, item 2, and footnote. Bowyer had brought the cat. 14 Apr. 1720 (item 11).

Books.[1] That the MS of Horace, which was lent to D[r]. Bentley, is now in the Library of Trinity-College in Cambridge;[2] and that the Charters I saw did not belong to the Deceased, but to the Church of Westminster.[3]

10. M[r] Noel came with the first part of the Catalogue of Baron Hohendorff's Library to shew my Lord; & desired to see my Lords two fine MSS. He say's that his Emissary went yesterday for Brussels, in Order to bring over the remaining parts of the same Catalogue, & the lowest price of the Whole Collection.[4]

11. My Lord taking into Consideration M[r] Sanderson's Collection of Coins, Medals, &c. afresh: Order'd me to go to him again this Afternoon, to propose some abatements, & know his Lowest Price. And I went accordingly.[5]

26 May 1720.

12. I attended his Lordship and acquainted him with the Abatements agreed to by M[r] Sanderson, & his lowest Price: My Lord Agreeing to this Price, sent me to him to receive the Things & bring them away. I went, & brought away all that I could conveniently stow in a Coach with my Self; leaving some heavy things for M[r] Sanderson to send with his first Leasure.[5]

13. M[r] Joy came to see the Library, and was very well pleased.

14. My Lord bought of S[r]. Andrew Fountaine a Cabinet with Drawers (or Cards) for Medals; it will hold 1944 several Medals, & ha's besides two deeper Drawers at the Bottom. It formerly belonged to Mons[r]. Fouquet Surintendant of y[e] Finances of France.[6]

15. M[r] Bateman sent in the Printed Books & MSS. my Lord lately bought of him.[7] The MSS. are,
   1. Pictures of our Kings; of Knights of several Counties Tilting & Tourneying; & of Knights Banerets; all in their Sur-coats. fol.[8]
   2. Statuta Universitatis Cantabrigiensis; cum Decretis, &c. fol.[9]
   3. Statuta Collegij Christi Cantabr. cum allijs, 4[to].[10]

28 May 1720.

p. 44
(f. 23*b*)

1. M[r] O Sullevane came to peruse the old Irish MS.[11]

30. May 1720.

2. M[r] Morgan came.

---

[1] Cf. 21 May 1720, item 17, and footnote.

[2] This Horace MS. is Trinity College, Cambridge, MS. R. 3. 57 (M. R. James, *Cat. of Western MSS. in the Library of Trinity College, Cambridge*, ii (1901), no. 629); the MS. contains the following note: 'This belongs to Dr. John Batteley, Archdeacon of Canterbury.' It was given to the Library at Trinity 14 May 1712. It is a 12th-cent. MS. probably from Christ Church, Canterbury.

[3] Cf. 21 May 1720, item 17.

[4] For the Hohendorf sale see 11 Jan. 1719/20, item 7, and footnote. The 'two fine MSS.' were probably those bought at Stafford House; see 4 May 1720, item 2, and footnote.

[5] Cf. item 8 above and footnote. The 'heavy things' left were sent in 16 June 1720.

[6] Sir Andrew Fountaine was a notable collector of coins, &c.; he had contributed the section on Anglo-Saxon coins to Hickes's *Thesaurus*, 1705; nothing is known of this cabinet. For a ref. to Fountaine's antiquities see 10 Sept. 1720 and footnote.

[7] Cf. 24 May 1720, item 6. The 3 following MSS. bear in Wanley's hand the date 27 May 1720 and are given under that date in Addenda, Lansdowne 771, f. 77[b] (at p. 197 of the present work).

[8] Harl. 4205.   [9] Harl. 4821.

[10] Harl. 3848.   [11] Cf. 1 Mar. 1719/20, item 12, and footnote.

31. May, 1720.

3. Mr Noel came, & desired the Balæi Centurie, Poliphile, & Horace which came up from Wimple for him; & I deliver'd the same unto him accordingly.

1 June 1720.

4. Mr Gibson sent in a small, but Curious, Parcel of Books, which my Lord bought of him yesterday.[1] The MSS. are,
 1. M. Fabij Victorini Commentum super Ciceronis Rhetoricam primam.
  Glossulæ super Tullium de Amicitia.
  Glossulæ super Tullium de Senectute.
  Epistolæ quædam Georg. Trapezuntij & Poggij. chart. fol.[2]
 2. Lactantij Institutiones. chart. fol. min.[3]
 3. Terentius, Eleganter scriptus manu Italica rotundiore, A.D. 1471. 4to. membr. illum.[4]
 4. Hippocratis, &c. Epistolæ, Latine, per Rinucium Verdensem, chart. 4to. ten.[5]
 5. Propertius, cum brevibus Scholijs. chart. 4to.[6]
 6. Jul. Solinus de Situ Orbis, &c. chart. 4to.[7]
 7. Tullius de Officijs; manu Italica rotund. 8vo. membr. illum.[8]

5. Mr George Hay came & shewed me a Letter from his Brother Mr Andrew Hay written at Paris, importing that he ha's bought the Chancelier Seguier's Library, which is very Curious, & of which he transmitted a short Catalogue;[9] in looking over which I particularly observed
 Ovidius de Tristibus; Horatius de Arte Poetica, et Sermones. MS. antiq. perg. 12mo.[10]
 T. Livij Decades. MSS. perg. illum. fol.[11]
 Valerius Maximus. 4to. cum Notis.[12]
 Aristotelis Ethica. Seneca de 4 Virtutibus. MS. perg. 4to.[13]
 Eutropius, Vitruvius, Ælianus de instruendis aciebus, &c. MS. fol. chart.[14]
 Lucanus, cum Comment. MS. fol. perg.[15]
 Virgilius, cum Notis. MS. fol. chart.[16]
 Joan. Germanus Cabilonensis Episcopus de Virtutibus Philippi Burgundiæ Ducis. MS. 4to. chart.[17]
 Aymoini [sic] Monachi Floriacensis Historia Francorum. MS. fol. perg.[18]
 Andreae Ep̄i Magorin Gubernaculum Conciliorum; cum alijs Tractatibus, De Squaloribus Curiæ Romanæ, de Potestate Generalium Conciliorum, de Concilio Basileensi [sic], &c.[19]

---

[1] For subsequent refs. to this and another parcel cf. 6 June (item 4), 7 June (item 5), 8 June (item 9) 1720. For price settled on see 25 Aug. 1720, item 10. [2] Harl. 2679.
[3] Harl. 3147.   [4] Harl. 2527 (the date 1471 appears in colophon, f. 161).
[5] Harl. 3527.   [6] Harl. 2550.   [7] Harl. 2583.   [8] Harl. 3924.
[9] Pierre Séguier was the great French collector, d. 1672. See 5 Sept. 1720 and footnote for list of Harl. MSS. from the Séguier Coll. Cf. also 8 and 25 July 1720. They were seen by Wanley 15 Aug. 1720. Cf. also 17, 18, 19, and 31 Aug. 1720. This appears to have been Andrew Hay's first transaction undertaken under Harley's Commission (see 26 Apr. 1720, item 18, and footnote). Hay was scheduled to leave for France 11 May 1720.
[10] Harl. 2699.   [11] Cf. 5 Sept. 1720: the MS. was never sent in.
[12] Harl. 2759.   [13] Harl. 3396.   [14] Harl. 2508.
[15] Harl. 2477.   [16] Harl. 2503.   [17] Harl. 3539.
[18] Harl. 3974.   [19] Harl. 3767.

Playdoyers entre la Duchesse D'Angoulême Mere du Roy François I, et le Duc de Bourbon, pour le Duché de / Bourbonne, &c. MS.[1]

Divers traittes concernans les Droits des Roys de France sur diuers Royaumes. MS. fol.[2]

Martyrologium. Regula S. Benedicti. MS. fol. perg.[3]

Glossarium. Item, Glossarium S. Benedicti Lat. Gr. MS. perg. 4to. mag. antiq.[4]

Guido Aretinus de Musica.—Et de Infantia χρι 2 MSS. 12º. perg.[5]

Canon Avicennæ Latine, per Gerardum Cremonensem. MS. fol. mag. perg. illum.[6]

Recueil d'Ordonnances sur le fait des Finances du Royaume fait A.D. 1443.— Origo Regum Franciæ ab anno 374, ad Ludovicum XII. MS. fol. perg.[7]

Formulæ Instrumentorum in Cancellaria Romana. MS. fol. perg.[8]

Histoire Genealogique de la Famille de Seguier. fol. Original MS.[9]

Here are also Many MSS. relating to the Civil Law, Law of France, Miscellaneous Negotiations, Travails, Arrêts, &c.[10]

Histoire Generale du Schisme in l'Eglise depuis l'an 1378, jusqu'an 1428. MS.[11]

Mariage d'Elizabeth de France au Philippe II Roy d'Espagne. MS.[12]

Rotulus omnium Civitatum, Baroniarum, Castrorum, et Feudorum Regni Siciliæ. MS. Original. tres-curieux.[13]

Le tiers Volume de la Chronique Françoise, en Vers Françoise. MS. fol.[14]

Histoire de François I, et de la Prise de Milan. MS. fol. min.[15]

Annales de Metz, au l'an 1484. MS. fol. curieux.[16]

Recueil des Sceaux des Roys de France, par Auguste Galand. MS. fol. oblong. ten.[17]

Original Letters of K. Henry IV, &c.[18]

2 June 1720.

1. My Lord sent in a Parcel of Printed Books.

3 June 1720.

2. Mr James Hill came. He said that he had been at Hamstead to see Mr Sam. Gale; but could by no means gain Admittance into his Chamber to see his Things.[19] He said likewise that Colonel Dansey has many old Deeds, wherein divers of the Family of Harley are mentioned.[20]

4 June 1720.

3. Mr O Sullevane came to Study in the Old Irish MS.[21]

---

[1] Not identified.   [2] Harl. 4405.   [3] Harl. 3251.
[4] Harl. 2735.   [5] Harl. 3199 (the items quoted by Wanley are arts. 4 and 5).
[6] Harl. 3799–3809.
[7] Harl. 4362 (the items cited by Wanley are at ff. 20–97b, 98–124).
[8] Harl. 3664. (Wanley's description as 'Formulae Instrumentorum' is derived from the title on the spine.)
[9] Harl. 4938.   [10] e.g. Harl. 3705, pt. 2; 3834; 3857.   [11] Harl. 4365.
[12] Harl. 4462.   [13] Not identified among the Harley Rolls or MSS.
[14] Harl. 4498.   [15] Not identified.   [16] Harl. 4400.
[17] Not identified. (The only Auguste Galland MS. in Harl. Coll. is Harl. 4448, which does not answer to Wanley's description but appears to be a Séguier MS.)
[18] Cf. 5 Sept. 1720: never sent in.   [19] For purpose see 4 Apr. 1720, item 14.
[20] No further ref. to Col. Dansey and his 'old Deeds'
[21] Cf. 1 Mar. 1719/20, item 12, and footnote.

4. M[r]. Vaillant sent my Lord a Letter informing him that the Antient MS. of the Latin Gospels all written with Capital Letters of Gold, is actually bought in Holland for his Lordship.[1]

5 June 1720.

5. I wrote to M[r] Vaillant to know the Price of the Golden Manuscript, & to desire it may come to my Lord as soon as possible; & I had an Answer from him to Satisfaction. /[1]

p. 46
(f. 24b)

6 June 1720.

1. M[r] Vaillant waited on my Lord, to apprise him of the short Time within which the Codex Aureus may be expected: and my Lord then paid him the Price of it.[1]

2. M[r] Noel came to look upon the Books which my Lord send's off from the Whincopians.[2]

3. M[r] Chapman the Binder came, & brought the Parcel I last deliver'd to him. But he having blunder'd in Titling one of them: I sent him off with it, and did neither pay him, nor give him any more Work; but on Thursday-morning he is to bring the book again, amended; & then to be paid, & to have another parcel of Work.

4. M[r] Gibson came, and we talked much about the Parcel of MSS. & Printed Books, which he sent in the 1st. Instant; we could not agree about the Price this day; but I am to be at his Lodgings betime to morrow, & to pick out some more of his Books, that we may, so, agree.[3]

7 June 1720.

5. I called upon M[r] Gibson, and selected a small but choice parcel of Printed books for my Lord to see, & so to agree upon a Price for both parcels: & M[r] Gibson sent them in soon after.[3]

6. I sent a Letter to M[r] Noel & acquainted him that my Lord will keep of Whincop's books Folios 14, Quartos 67, Octavo's, &c. 104. and that the remainder shall be sent unto him in a few days.[4]

7. M[r] Harbin brought two Original Letters of the Queen of Bohemia, & Copies of Two Petitions of the Lady Arabella, & gave them to the Library.[5]

8 June 1720.

8. M[r] O Sullevane came to Study in the old Irish MS.[6]

9. M[r] Gibson came, but I told him my Lord ha's not yet made choice of the books he will keep of the last parcel.[7]

---

[1] See 11 Apr. 1720, item 18, and footnote.   [2] Cf. 9 Apr. 1720, item 13, and footnote.
[3] For list of MSS. and identifications see 1 June 1720, item 4; and footnote thereto for subsequent refs. to *both* parcels. The prices were agreed on 25 Aug. 1720 (item 10).
[4] Cf. 9 Apr. 1720, item 13, and footnote. Those kept were valued at £49. 14s. (Welbeck Wanleyana, Misc. no. 51).
[5] The letters of the Queen of Bohemia are Harl. 6988, ff. 113, 115; the Lady Arabella petitions are Harl. 7003, ff. 57, 58. All are endorsed by Wanley 'Given by the Rev[d]. M[r] Harbin, 7 June 1720'.
[6] Cf. 1 Mar. 1719/20, item 12, and footnote.
[7] Cf. 7 June 1720, item 5, and footnote.

10. Mr Chapman came, & was bidden to take the Rufinus's Eusebius he lately bound, back with him, & find the first Leaf (which was loose) & fix it to its proper place. And I further d̃d̃ him another Parcel to Bind.

11 June 1720.

11. Mr Chapman came with the Eusebius, he having found the lost Leaf & fixed it in it's place.

12. Mr Bateman sent in a small parcel of Books which my Lord bought of him lately.[1]

13 June 1720.

13. Mr Mattaire brought Mr Bowyer the Printer to inspect the Printing of the Tewrdank.[2]

14. Mr David Thomas came, & want's me to lend him books out of the Library; which I have flatly refused.

15 June 1720.

15. Mr Noel sent his Man for Whincops books & the others borrowed of him. I deliver[e]d them, & paid for their Carriage back.[3]

16. June 1720.

16. Mr Sanderson sent in the heavy pieces of Antiquity, being the Remainder of Mr Maddison's Collection.[4]

17 June 1720.

17. Mr Bateman sent in his Bill of the Value of the Parcel of Books my Lord bought last of him. /[5]

18 June 1720.

p. 47
(f. 25a)

1. I returned the Books of Medals I borrowed of Mr Vaillant; & send [sic] back to Mr Sanderson his Hamper, Blanket, & Napkin.

2. Mr James Hill came to Study in the Library.

20 June 1720.

3. Mr Bogdani came, & acquainted me that of the Foreign Bibles which I had desired him to get for my Lord, some are lost through Misfortune; but that the Liflandish (or Livonian) Bible, with the Courland-Bible is come safe to Coningsbergh, & will be brought hither in the first Ship Which comes from thence.[6] He also say's that he hath a very fine & large Saphire, proper to be used as a Seal.

---

[1] Cf. 17 June 1720.
[2] i.e. Melchior Pfintzing, *Die geuerlicheiten und einsteils der geschichten des loblichen streytparen und hochberümbten helds und Ritters herr Tewrdannckhs* [i.e. Maximilian I, Emperor of Germany], printed Hans Schönsperger, Nuremberg, [1517]. Harley acquired a copy of this printed on vellum 18 Jan. 1723/4 (cf. p. 245 of the present work).
[3] Cf. 7 June 1720, item 6.
[4] See 26 May 1720, item 12, and cf. 28 Jan. 1719/20, item 5, and footnote.
[5] Cf. 11 June 1720, item 12.
[6] He was paid £2. 15s. 6d. for these Bibles on 26 Feb. 1720/1 (Welbeck Wanleyana, Misc. no. 50).

4. M^r O Sullevan came to Study.

5. Mr James Hill came to Study.

21 June 1720.

6. I went to Mr Warburton, & took a List of his MSS. which I sent by the Post to my Lord;[1] together with the acceptable News that the Ship which bring's the Codex Aureus, is arrived on the Coast of England.[2]

7. Mr James Hill came to Study in the Library.

23 June 1720.

8. Mr Hutchinson, one of the Ministers of Bury S^t. Edmund came to consult some of the Leiger-books of that Monastery,[3] upon a Pretension the Ministers have upon certain small Tithes there. He also brought the MS. I desired to borrow out of the Library there,[4] which prove's not to be Coptic, as Mr Professor Ockley assured me.

9. D^r. Sherard came, and told me that the Duke of Devonshire will not part with his S^t. Æthelwold's MS. although he seem's not to Value it.[5] That he ha's a very fair Copie of Tullies Epistles ad Atticum, Printed by the Maximi at Rome A.D. 1470, which my Lord proposed to give in Exchange for the MS.[6] That He will treat with Mr Chishull about his Greek MS. Catena on the Psalms, sent in hither.[7] He will also have yet one more touch with His Grace for the said MS. He will send to the Patriarch of Constantinople for a Sett of all the Books Printed by the Greeks at Jassi & Buchorest:[8] and procure me a Sight of Mr Cook of Norfolks MSS. although Dr Hubard be absent.[9]

27 June 1720.

10. I went to Mr Warburton, & offer'd him 100 Guineas for his old MSS., &c. he having left the Price of all to me. He flew back from his Word, as many others

[1] Cf. 14 Apr. 1720, item 12, and footnote. For list of MSS. actually bought see 16 July 1720.

[2] Cf. 11 Apr. 1720, item 18, and footnote.

[3] The 'Leiger-Books' or Cartularies of the Abbey of Bury St. Edmunds in the library at this date were numerous and included at least the following: Harl. MSS. 27 ('Croftis' register, 230 (a fragment only, at ff. 176–87), 638 (ff. 119–38, 'Werketone' register), 645 ('Kempe' register), 743 ('Lakynghethe' register), 1005 (ff. 223–72, 'Liber Albus'); Sir Simonds D'Ewes had made extracts, &c. from several of these and other Bury Cartularies while they were in his or other ownership and these vols. of extracts, &c. are also in the Harl. Coll. For a full list of the abbey cartularies cf. Davis, nos. 95–134. Roger Gale was also interested in these Bury Cartularies (cf. footnote to 1 Mar. 1720/1, item 6).

[4] Cf. 31 Oct. 1720, which shows that it was the 'schole-library of Bury', presumably therefore that of the King Edward VI Grammar School there. On this library see A. T. Bartholomew and C. Gordon, 'On the Library at King Edward VI School, Bury St. Edmunds', *The Library*, 3rd ser., i (1910), pp. 1–27, 329–31. [5] Cf. 18 Jan. 1719/20, item 4, and footnote.

[6] This is the *editio princeps* of Cicero's Letters to Atticus, having been printed at Rome in 1470 by Sweynheim and Pannartz. Harley's copy, referred to here, is now in the British Museum, to which it came with the Grenville Library in 1846 and is G. 9381 (BM. IB. 17153) (for a description of it see *BMC* iv. 10). A note by Thomas Grenville on the fly-leaf reads: 'This is the Harleian copy sold again at Sir M. Sykes's sale [1824] and purchased by me.' It is still in its 'Harleian Binding' and came from a monastic house at Bamberg. It is not recorded by Wanley in his cat. of the printed books in the library at Wimpole (compiled 1716–18); it is presumably Osborne, i, no. 5024. The Duke of Devonshire's copy at Chatsworth, to which reference is made by Sherard, is presumably that recorded by Sir J. P. Lacaita, *Catalogue of the Library at Chatsworth*, 1879, i, p. 392. The Duke of Devonshire in 1720—the time of the proposed exchange—was William, the 2nd Duke.

[7] Cf. 18 Jan. 1719/20, item 4, and footnote 4. This had been sent in 28 Apr. 1720.

[8] Cf. 18 Jan. 1719/20, item 4, and footnote 10.

[9] Wanley had already discussed with Andrew Hay the question of Coke's parting with his MSS. (cf. 21 Jan. 1719/20, item 7). 'Dr. Hubard' is Dr. Thomas Hobart (see Biographical Index).

have done, & protested that two of the Books cost him almost that Sum; that he could never Expect to be Master of Such Books again; and that therefore he would not part with them under 300 Guineas: a price, in my poor Opinion, by much too horribly exorbitant to be complied with.[1]

11. This day the CODEX AVREVS LATINVS was cleared out of the Kings Warehouse, and delivered into my Custody. /[2]

28 June, 1720.

p. 48
(f. 25b)

1. This day, by my Lords Order, I drew up a short account of the said CODEX AVREVS, and sent it, by the Post, to his Lordship at Welbeck.[3]

29 June, 1720.

2. This day, I brought the CODEX AVREVS with me, & placed it in the Library.[4]

3. Mr Beaver came to see some of my Lords fine Books.

4. Mr James Hill came to Study.

30 June 1720.

5. Mr Pocklington came, & acquainted me that Mr Kitchin a friend of the present Owner of the late Mr. Mickleton's Collection, of MSS. & Antiquities; is willing that I shall inspect the same on the 4th. of the next Month.[5]

6. The Reverend Mr Bridges (brother to Mr Bridges late Comr. of the Customes) came to peruse some of the MSS. Mr Slyford came with him, bringing me a Letter from Mr Bridges, desiring liberty of transcribing all matters relating to Northampton-shire, from Dr. Hutton's Papers. I promised to write to my Lord about it.[6]

1 July 1720.

7. Mr Bateman's Servant came & told me that his Master ha's bought the Library of Dr. Green late of the old Jury, wherein he believe's there may be some Books for my Lords turn.[7] I promised to call there to morrow-morning; & then hope also to see Mr Cowse & Mr Wiat.

2 July 1720.

8. I went to Mr Bateman, & laid by a Parcel of Books for my Lords Inspection, at his Return.[7] I also called upon Mr Wyat, & at Mr Cowses, &c.

[1] Cf. 14 Apr. 1720, item 12, and footnote. For list see 16 July 1720.
[2] Cf. 11 Apr. 1720, item 18, and footnote.
[3] Cf. item 11 above. Harley's 'Order' was conveyed to Wanley in a letter from Welbeck dated 23 June 1720 (in Welbeck Wanleyana).
[4] Cf. item 11 above. It was given the press-mark 105. A. 4.
[5] Cf. 25 Feb. 1719/20, item 14, and footnote. See unfinished letter from Pocklington 'about June 1720' (see Wanley's endorsement) and cf. also letter from John Basset, 2 July 1720, postponing this visit (both in Welbeck Wanleyana), which did take place, however, on the 4th. 'The present Owner' is identified in 7 July 1720, item 2, as Mr. Cuthberts.
[6] [John] Bridges's purpose in obtaining permission to transcribe from Hutton's Colls. in the Library (viz. Harl. 6950-85, 7519-21) and Harl. Ch. 83. A. 21-83. C. 9 inclusive (cf. Diary 23 Nov. 1722, item 14) was to obtain materials for his projected History of Northamptonshire (pubd. posthumously 1762-91): Bridges died 1724. 'Mr. Slyford' was Bridges's amanuensis (cf. 18 July (item 1), 27 July (item 9), 29 July, and 1 and 4 Aug. 1720).
[7] This Library (except for items disposed of privately) was subsequently put up for auction at W. Mears's at The Lamb without Temple Bar 19 Jan. 1720/1.

4 July 1720.

9. I spent the greatest part of the day in Inspecting part of the late Mr Mickletons Collection of MSS. &c.[1]

5 July 1720.

10. I went again to Grayes Inne, & finished there as to Mr Mickletons things; and afterwards saw Mr Sanderson, who kindly promised his Assistance to my Lord in procuring them.[1]

6. July 1720.

11. I had a Letter from Mr Warburton, pretending that a Person of Honor desire's to buy his MSS. and that he had rather Sell them to my Lord, &c. Upon Deliberation hereupon, and taking this Motion of his Person of Honor to be a mere Sham; and his Resolution to part with his Roman Altars, to be at Ten times their Value, if he can get it; besides finding him to be extremely greedy, fickle, & apt to go from his Word: I thought it would be for the best not to be too forward in Sending him any Answer, but to lett him Send or Come again to me. /[2]

7 July 1720.

p. 49
(f. 26a)

1. Mr James Hill came to Study.

2. I met Mr Sanderson, at the Genoa-Armes, who told me that Mr Cuthberts, the Proprietor of the late Mr Mickleton's Collection of MSS. &c. is now in Town; & will lett him have the same, at the Price which another shall bid for them, and Advised me to bid no more than £.80 for them.[3]

3. Mr Warburton found me out there, & besought me to resume his Affair, which he would again putt into my Hands; and take what I would allow: but earnestly beg'd of me to get him more Money of my Lord, than what I before brought him. I look'd Cool, made no promise, but that I would write to my Lord.[4]

8 July, 1720.

4. I wrote to Mr Pocklington, bidding him offerr [sic] Mr Kitching (Mr Cuthbert's Agent) 80 pounds for Mr Mickleton's Collection of MSS.[5]

5. Mr James Hill came to Study.

6. I heard that the Ship with Mr Andrew Hays books is arrived in the River, but not yet Entred.[6]

7. Mr Cuthbert being come up to Town, Mr Kitching apprised him of Mr Pocklington's Proposal; and he told Mr Sanderson of the same, who also offer'd him the same Sum. Mr Cuthbert hath hereupon written to the Relations of Mr Mickleton in Durham, & also to the Dean & Chapter there, who

---

[1] Cf. 30 June 1720, item 5, and footnote. Wanley's list of these MSS. is Welbeck Wanleyana, Misc. no. 23.

[2] See 14 Apr. 1720, item 12, and footnote. The letter from Warburton dated 7 July 1720 relating to this business is in Welbeck Wanleyana.

[3] Cf. 30 June 1720, item 5, and footnote.

[4] Cf. 6 July 1720, and footnote.

[5] Cf. 30 June 1720, item 5, and footnote.

[6] See 1 June 1720, item 5, and footnote. These books (from the Séguier Library) were seen by Wanley 15 Aug. 1720.

desire to purchase many of the Things relating to their Church: and hopes to procure the same, at the price above, to Mr Sanderson, who is both an old friend & a near Relation.[1]

9 July 1720.

8. Mr James Hill came to Study.

11 July 1720.

9. Mr James Hill came to Study.

12 July 1720.

10. I brought with me the little Parcel I bought the last Friday;[2] whereof the MSS. are.
    1. Selected Praiers & Devotions for severall Occasions; & for all the Yeare. 8vo. temp. R. Caroli II.[3]
    2. Manuale Precum; tegmine cæruleo. Codex probe scriptus & Illuminatus, in membranis. volumine pusillo.[4]
    3. Manuale Precum; tegmine rubro: Volumen perexiguum in membr.[5]
    4. Psalterium cum Canticis Sacris, et precibus; in Membranis, volumine parvo & acephalo. (This cost nothing.)[6]
11. Mr James Hill brought Mr Peters the Painter, & Mr Witherston of the Temple, to see some of my Lords fine Books & Pictures. /

13 July 1720.

p. 50
(f. 26b)

1. Mr Warburton came to me at the Genoa-Armes, & then took me to another Tavern, & kept me up all the Night, thinking to Muddle me & so to gain upon me in Selling his MSS. &c. But the Contrary happened, & he induced to Agree to accept of the Sum he offered at the first, without the Advancement of a single Farthing: and he promised to bring them to me, on the Fourteenth by Six a Clock.[7]

14 July 1720.

2. Mr Warburton wrote to me that he was so disorder'd by OUR late Frolic (which, by the way, was all his Own) that he could not bring the Things till the Fifteenth by Six a Clock.[8]

15 July 1720.

3. Mr Hesket Windsor-Herald came with Mr Ashton of Lancashire, & look'd into many of the Heraldical MSS. Mr Hesket gave a Copie of the Emperor

---

[1] Cf. 30 June 1720, item 5, and footnote.
[2] i.e. 5 July, when there is no ref. to any purchase: possibly a ref. to the Bateman books seen on 2 July 1720.
[3] Harl. 4149.
[4] Harl. 2859. (Still in 'dark blue [morocco] binding'—*tegmine cæruleo.*)
[5] Harl. 2862. (Still in 'red [morocco] binding'—*tegmine rubro*: almost a 'minature book', measuring no more than 2⅜" × 2", hence *perexiguus*, 'very small'.)
[6] Harl. 2842. (A Psalter, imperfect at the beginning.)
[7] Cf. 14 Apr. (item 12, and footnote) and 16 July 1720 (for list).
[8] Cf. 13 July 1720: Warburton's letter (in Welbeck Wanleyana) is endorsed by Wanley: 'N.B. The frolick was his own: not of my seeking. I gave my Lord a particular account of it.'

of China's Sheet Printed in the Chinese, Mogul-Tartar, & Latin Tongues, about the Messengers he sent into Europe; of which, I had before given another finer Copie to the Library.[1]

4. Mr James Hill came to Study.

5. This Evening Mr Warburton came to my Lodgings & brought with him his MSS. & the two Pictures; & I paid him 100 Guineas in full for them, & some Brass-pieces of Antiquitie which were carried to be shewn to the Earl of Pembroke. A Sufficient List of his MSS. was taken the 21 of June last, & sent to my Lord; however, I will again describe them more briefly, that these individual books may be thereafter the better known.[2]

16 July 1720.

6. My Porter actually brought the said MSS. & Pictures hither;[3] being,

1. Nomina Villarum, &c. per varios Angliæ Comitatus. Exemplar Codicis Cottoniani de Honore Richemondiæ. Tricks of the Seals of many of our old Nobility, &c. wel[l] done.[4]	chart. fol. ampl. ten.
2. Speculum Religiosorum D. Edmundi de Pontiniaco. S^r. John Gowers English Poem's, Illum. & Adorned with the Armes of divers Families.[5]	membr. fol.
3. Stemmata quarundam Angliæ Familiarum. Collectanea e diversis, de Rebus Angliæ Chronicis.[6]	chart. fol. perhaps, by John Bale.

   4. Year-book of K. Edward II. imperfect at both Ends. membr. fol.[7]
   5. Nomina Villarum, &c. per diversos Angliæ Comitatus. chart. fol.[8]

---

[1] Hesketh (who was *Lancaster* Herald at this date) was introduced by Anstis as 'a neighbour and friend' (cf. letter of [July 1720] in Welbeck Wanleyana). The copy of 'the Emperor of China's Sheet' given by Wanley to the Library is Harl. 7013, ff. 50, 51; it is endorsed by Wanley 'Given by Humfrey Wanley, 28 Febr. 1718/19'. The letter from the Emperor K'ang Hsi (in Manchu, Chinese, and Latin) was dated 31 Oct. 1716 (on the background see A. H. Rowbotham, *Missionary and Mandarin*, 1942).

[2] Cf. 13 July 1720 (for *conclusion* of negotiations) and 14 Apr. 1720 and footnote (for full story and refs.); and 16 July 1720 (for list). For Thomas Herbert, 8th Earl of Pembroke's interest in early printed books cf. 22 Jan. 1719/20, item 12 (and footnote) and in coins cf. 19 Jan. 1720/1, item 9 (and footnote). In this year (1720) the Earl acquired 1300 busts and other sculptures from the Giustiniani Palace in Rome, &c. (see F. H. Taylor, *Taste of Angels*, 1948, pp. 313, 314, and A. Michaelis, *Ancient Marbles in Great Britain*, 1882, and Preface to Christie's sale-cat. 3 July 1961).

[3] Cf. 15 July 1720, item 5. It is clear from the identification of several of the MSS. purchased by Harley from Warburton with those in the cat. of the MSS. at Naworth of Charles Howard, 3rd Earl of Carlisle (1669–1738), dated 1692, printed in *CMA*, that Warburton must have obtained many of them from the latter; he had been in the North about this time, for under 16 Apr. 1720 Wanley notes that Warburton 'is lately arrived from Northumberland'. Several have the added interest that they had belonged to the Earl's famous ancestor Lord William Howard of Naworth (1563–1640); the Howard lion and Lord William's autogr. inscription, or notes by him, are (e.g.) in Harl. 3724, 3776, and in Harl. 3836 which bears no date by Wanley. Harl. 3911, a Register of Holm Cultram, which is in a binding similar to that of several in the list below and has list of contents in Warburton's hand, was not bought from Warburton until 1 Feb. 1728/9 (see *HMC Portland Papers*, vi. 23); it was reported by Warburton to Soc. of Ant. (Minute Book), 18 Dec. 1722.

[4] Harl. 4219.

[5] Harl. 3490 (belonged to Lord William Howard of Naworth; = *CMA* ii, no. 611).

[6] Harl. 2188 (the handwriting is not that of John Bale; Wanley subsequently (see BM. Add. 45707, f. 6 and *Harl. Cat.* (1759)) identified the hand from f. 50 onwards as that of Thomas Talbot, the antiquary).   [7] Harl. 3639.   [8] Harl. 2195.

6. S. Jeronymus super Danielem
S. Origenes de Susanna
Vita S. Nicholai.
Vita S. Botulfi Abbatis, &c.
Translatio Sanctorum Thornensium.
Vita S. Guthlaci.
S. Ambrosij tractatus varij. / ¹ } membr.
fol.
min.
manu
antiqua.

7. Vita Venerabilis Haroldi quondam Anglorum Regis. p. 51
De Regibus Knouto, Hardeknouto, & Haroldo; ut habetur in Cronicis (f. 27ᵃ
de Waltham.
Reliquiæ ab Haroldo, dicto Monasterio collatæ.
Reliquiæ ab Alijs dono-datæ.
Miracula, in eodem Monasterio facta.
Nomina Abbatum: &c.
Tractatus de Inventione S. Crucis in Monte acuto, & Deductione ejus-
dem apud Waltham cum alijs Historicis ad idem Monasterium pertinen-
tibus.
Chronicon a Conquestu, ad A.D. 1296.
De S. Brandano & alijs mirabilibus.
Henricus de Saltereia de Purgatorio S. Patricij.
Vita Tungalij Epī Casselensis.
Meditationes Bonaventuræ.
Marti[ro]logium Sanctorum in Anglia, Wallia, & alijs locis finitimis
natorum, et aliorum ibidem florentium & fructificantium. 4ᵗᵒ. ampl.
membr. varijs manibus.²

8. Vita S. Thomæ Beketti, Metris Gallicis vetustioribus.
Historia Guidonis Comitis Warwicensis, Versibus itidem Gallicis.
Imperf.
Versus facti ad complanandam Summan [*sic*] Decreti.
Annales a Xp̄o Nato, usque ad A.D. 1266. varijs manibus.
Bedæ Compendium de Gestis Anglorum.
Vita S. Roberti Heremitæ, per Ric. Stodlay, Imperf.
Chronicle of London, from 1 Rich. I. to the 8ᵗʰ. of K. Henr. VI.
Chronicon Monasterij de S. Albano, ab anno 1421, usque ad Annum
10, R. Henr. VI. cum alijs ad idem pertinentibus. John Stow used this.
Fragment of an old French Poem, about Esau, Jacob, &c.
Galfridi Anglici (de Vino salvo) Poema, cujus Initium, *Papa Stupor
Mundi.* 4ᵗᵒ. manibus diversis. membr.³

9. Epitaphium Petri Comestoris.
Versus Theologici
S. Aldelmus de Laudibus Virginitatis.
Epistola Alexandri Papæ III, ad Rogerum Eboꝛ Archiepiscopum.
4ᵗᵒ. manu eleganti. membr.⁴

10. A Divine Poem in Old English, Imperfect. *Init.* God made þe World, so
seyþ holy Wryt. 4ᵗᵒ. membr.⁵

¹ Harl. 3097 (perhaps belonged to Lord William Howard of Naworth; = *CMA* ii, no. 628).
² Harl. 3776 (belonged to Lord William Howard of Naworth; = *CMA* ii, no. 632; for the remaining
part of this MS. (now Harl. 3766) see 30 Jan. 1721/2 and footnote).
³ Harl. 3775 (? = *CMA* ii, no. 660).   ⁴ Harl. 3013 (? = *CMA* ii, no. 675).
⁵ Harl. 2377 (? = *CMA* ii, no. 670).

11. Chronicon, uti videtur, Ordinis Fratrum Prædicatorum, a Primordio temporis, us*que* ad Frēm Thomam de Lentino Priorem Provincialem Tusciæ, c. A.D. 1254. 4to. membr.[1]

12. Prosa Magr̄i Girobaldi Whitwhibanensis [*sic*] Archidiaconi.
    Oratio R. Manasse in Carcere.
    Narratio de 7 Dormientibus.
    De S. Petro Martire, *Carmen*.
    Topographia Hiberniæ, per Giraldum Cambrensem. /

p. 52
(f. 27*b*)

    De Cujusdam Claustralis Moribus et Vita.
    Quod Negligentijs seu Defectibus contingentibus circa Sacramentum Altaris, est occurrendum.
    Ep̄la Adriani Papæ ad Regem Anglorum.
    Symbolum Apostolorum, lingua Anglicana vetustiori.
    Pater Noster in Anglico *metro*.
    Fridericus Imperator ad Papam, &c. *versibus Latinis*.
    Epistola Valerij ad Ruphinum de non ducenda uxore. 4to. membr.[2]

13. Passio D.N.I.C. sec. Marcum, Lucam, & Johannem.
    Oratio S. Gregorij Papae Urbis Romae.
    Orationes S. A[u]gustini in Sanctis Sollemnitatibus.
    Oratio ad SS. Trinitatem.
    Pro dolore Oculorum.
    Termini Agelluli, quem apud Wintoniam possidebat Ealhswith; Anglo-Saxonicè.
    Confessionis & Absolutionis formula.
    　Codex, maximam partem, videtur exaratus ante Mille annos. 4to. membr.[3]

14. Historia de S. Norberto, de*que* Initijs & Incrementis Præmonstratensium.
    Expositio Regulæ S. Patris nostri Augustini, de Vita Clericorum.
    Hugo de S. Victore de XII Abusionibus.
    Sermo de tribus amicis.　　　　4to. membr.[4]

15. Vita S. Anselmi per Eadmerum.
    Vita Davidis Scotorum Regis, per Ailredum Rievallensem.
    Narratio de Regibus Anglorum ab Alfredo ad R. Stephanum.
    Vita S. Oswaldi Regis.

    Relatio cujusdam Sapientis de Purgatorio S. Patricij. ⎤ These seem
    Chronicon Joannis de Taxt.　. . . . . . . ⎬ to be of
    　　　　　　　　　　　　　　　　　　　　　⎦ John Bales
    　　　　　　　　　　　　　　　　　　　　　　　Hand.
    　　　　　　　　　　　　　　　4to chart.[5]

16. Chronicon Regum Anglorum a Bruto, us*que* ad R. Henricum VI. 4to. partim membr. partim chart.[6]

---

[1] Harl. 3723 (perhaps belonged to Lord William Howard of Naworth; = *CMA* ii, no. 646).
[2] Harl. 3724 (belonged to Lord William Howard of Naworth; = *CMA* ii, no. 641).
[3] Harl. 2965. This agrees with W. de Gray Birch's identification and is certainly correct (cf. his *An Ancient Manuscript*, 1889, pp. 18–20). The MS. is known as 'The Book of Nunnaminster' (for the most recent notice of this MS. cf. *CLA* ii, no. 199). It is of 8th/9th-cent. date, and belonged at one time to Nicholas Roscarrock (Roscarrock arms are on f. 37^b) and is therefore probably a MS. of Howard of Naworth, to whom Roscarrock was chaplain.
[4] Harl. 3935 (perhaps belonged to Lord William Howard of Naworth; = *CMA* ii, no. 666).
[5] Harl. 3846 (belonged to Lord William Howard of Naworth, in whose hand are notes throughout; = *CMA* ii, no. 651).　　　　[6] Harl. 4344 (? Lord William Howard of Naworth).

17. Registrum Chartarum Domûs Fratrum Carmelitarum de Hulum in
Foresta de Alnewyke.
Catalogus Codicum MSS., vestimentorum, &c. in Bibliotheca ibidem
conservatorum. 8vo. membr.[1]
18. Vita S^{tæ}. Mildrythæ Virginis, cum Lectionibus, Homelia, Missa, &c.
(per Eadmerum?)
Textus Translationis & Institutionis Monasterij B. Mildrethæ, cum mira-
culorum attestatione.
Versus (*Canonici*) de Bridelyngton facti A.D. 1327. 8vo.[2]
19. Devotions, &c. Collected by Anna Cromwell, A.D. 1656. (Oliver's
daughter Lady Claypole) [( ) *deleted in MS.*] 8vo.[3]
20. Astrological Discourse, in Old English; from Bartholomæus. ⎫ membr.
Astrological Poem in old English.   ⎬ 12mo.
The Maner of makyng Laws, in old English. /[4]   ⎭
21. Manuale Precum. membr. 16to.[5]
22. Manuale Precum; cui præfigitur Calendarium. 16to.[6]

p. 53
(f. 28a)

18 July 1720.

1. Mr Bridges came to see the CODEX AVREVS:[7] and then wanted to see D^r.
Hutton's Papers, which (after much Importunity, and Allegations of his having
a Generall Order, for seeing all things in this Library) I brought out to him;
and now he wants them to be Looked over & Abstracted by his Servant
M^r. Slyford.[8]

2. Mr Chapman the Book-binder came with the Parcel last Deliver'd unto Him;
& I paid him off.

19. July 1720.

3. Mr Noel brought Mr Holland the Stationer to see some of my Lords fine
Books.

20 July 1720.

4. Mr Chapman the Binder came; & I deliver'd to him a fresh Parcel to Bind.

22 July 1720.

5. I sent a Letter to Mr Warburton, putting him in Mind of sending the Antiquities hither, which were bought of him.[9]

25 July 1720.

6. I went to Mr George Hay and (to my great Surprise) learned that the Ship with
Seguiers MSS. ha's not been heard of since she was laden at Roan; all other
Reports of her being false.[10] And I saw the Collection of Statuas [*sic*] & Bustos,
Basso-Relievos, &c. now arrived from Italy, and proposed to be soon sold by
Auction. This, with what Mr Andrew Hay brought from thence about 2 years

---

[1] Harl. 3897 (=Davis, no. 11).   [2] Harl. 3908.
[3] Harl. 2311; Warburton had exhibited this to Soc. of Antiquaries (Minute Book) 20 Jan. 1720.
[4] Harl. 2320.   [5] Harl. 2880.   [6] Harl. 2885 (the calendar occupies ff. 7–12^b).
[7] i.e. Harl. 2788.   [8] Cf. 30 June 1720, item 6, and footnote.
[9] Cf. 6 and 15 July (item 5) 1720; they were sent in 1 Aug. 1720.
[10] See 1 June 1720, item 5, and footnote. Cf. also 8 July 1720, item 6, when she had been reported as
'arrived in the river'.

ago, was the Entire Collection of the Hon[ble]. Family of Valetta in Naples. Three Generations made it; and this Man, for Lucre of ready Money, sold it.[1]

7. Not hearing from M[r] Warburton, I sent him another Letter.[2]

27 July 1720.

8. M[r] Noel came, & said that Baron Hohendorffs Widow is gone from Brussels to take the Waters; & ha's already sold off her Goods, excepting the Books & other Curiosities belonging to the Library. His Messenger return's back in 2 or 3 days.[3]

9. M[r] Slyford came from M[r] Bridges, to make Extracts for him from D[r]. Hutton's Collections.[4]

10. M[r] Robert Cuningham came.

29. July 1720.

11. M[r]. Slyford came for M[r] Bridges.

30 July 1720.

12. I sent Letters to M[r] Warburton & M[r] Pownhall, to hasten them.

13. M[r] Bateman the Bookseller came. /

p. 54
(f. 28*b*)

1 August 1720.

1. M[r] Slyford came to transcribe for M[r] Bridges.

2. M[r] Warburton sent the Antiquities to me.[5]

3. August 1720.

3. I sent a Letter to M[r] Warburton, about seeing his MSS. & Antiquities lately come up to Town.[6]

4. I sent another appointing M[r] Pocklington time & place to meet M[r] Sanderson & Me; in Order to consult of the surest way of buying M[r] Mickletons MSS. &c. M[r] Pocklington came hither soon after.[7]

4 August 1720.

5. M[r] Hill the Painter came & I shewed him several of my Lords fine Pictures & other Things; and he being to go soon to M[r] Strangways in Dorsetshire, I

[1] This is a ref. to the Giuseppe Valletta Coll. in Naples. Of the statues, &c. referred to by Wanley a considerable number were acquired by the Earl of Pembroke (see A. Michaelis, *Ancient Marbles in Great Britain*, 1882). From this library Thomas Coke of Holkham had bought many books and MSS. between 1712 and 1718 (cf. De Ricci, p. 43); the rest of the library went in 1726 to the Oratorians of Naples (see E. Mandarini, *I Codici Manoscritti della Biblioteca Oratoriana di Napoli*, 1897, p. xi and *passim*). Cf. also 31 Aug. and 2 Sept. 1720.   [2] Cf. 22 July 1720.
    [3] Cf. 11 Jan. 1719/20, item 7, and footnote.
    [4] Cf. 30 June 1720, item 6, and footnote.
    [5] Cf. 22 July 1720, and footnote. They were sent with a covering letter, dated 1 Aug. 1720 (now in Welbeck Wanleyana).
    [6] i.e. a new Warburton Coll. of MSS. and antiquities: cf. 20 Aug. (item 15), 23 Aug., 15 Sept. (item 3), 22 Sept. (item 14), 1, 4, and 6 Oct. 1720; 25 Jan. 1720/1; 30 Jan. 1721/2; 2 and 9 Feb. 1725/6.
    [7] Cf. 25 Feb. 1719/20, item 14, and footnote.

The Diary of Humfrey Wanley 1720

instructed him to move that Gentleman to give some of his old Books & Deeds to this Library.[1]

6. Mr Slyford came to transcribe for Mr Bridges.

5 August 1720.

7. This Evening Mr Sanderson & Mr Pocklington met me, & we consulted together of the easiest way of obtaining Mr Mickletons MSS.[2]

6 August 1720.

8. I brought in the Breviarium Prædicatorum, Paris 1655, 4to. with Manuscript Corrections; which I lately bought for my Lord.[3]

8 August 1720.

9. Mr. Chapman brought in the Parcel I last dd him to Bind.

10 August 1720.

10. Mr O Sullevane brought his Copie of the old Irish Poem, about the 12 Apostles, extant in the MS. 93. C. 29. fol. 9, b, with a double Latin Version of the same, one in Verse, being stricter to the Original; the other in Prose, being looser & more explanatory.[4]

11. Mr O Sullevane likewise acquainted me, that the Library of those Learned men who went from Ireland with Marianus Scotus A.D. 1058. is yet remaining in some Church at Ratisbon & ha's been lately seen there.[5]

11 August 1720.

12. This day I accidentally met Mr Kitchin, who said that the late Mr Mickleton's MSS. are valued at £.200.[6]

12 August 1720.

13. I brought in a Spanish book, being a Description of the Escurial printed at Madrid, 1681. given to my Lord by Mr Geo. Hay.[7]

[1] Hill did go down to Melbury (see his letter to Wanley, dated 10 Sept. 1720 (in Welbeck Wanleyana), describing his reception and treatment there). The ref. is to Melbury House (Melbury Sampford, Dorset), the seat then of Thomas Strangways (d. 1726) (now the seat of the Earl of Ilchester). On Melbury House see RCHM Dorset, i (1952), pp. 164-7.
[2] Cf. 3 Aug. 1720, item 4. Sanderson wrote to Wanley, 6 Aug. 1720, to say he would be glad to have money in connexion with the matter discussed as he was much pressed for money (in Welbeck Wanleyana).
[3] This is probably Bohatta (1937), no. 1699.
[4] i.e. Harl. 1802. (On the MS., which contains the Four Gospels in the Vulgate Version with other material in Irish, see R. Flower, Cat. of Irish MSS. in the British Museum, ii (1926), pp. 428-32.) O'Sullivan's prose and verse Latin translation has not been traced; it came too late for insertion by Wanley in his long description of the MS. in his 'Catalogus Brevior' of the Harl. MSS., the relevant vol. of which had been completed by the summer of 1717.
[5] On the Irish foundations at Ratisbon see A. Gwynn in Innes Review, v (1954), pp. 5-27, and cf. L. Bieler in Irish Ecclesiastical Record, 5th Ser., 87 (1957), pp. 167-9, and idem, Ireland, 1963, pp. 138-41. But cf. 16 May (item 1), 29 May (item 2), and 1 June (item 8) 1722, when he claimed that this coll. was in fact in the Cathedral Library at Meissen, near Prague. (O'Sullivan came to study a MS. history of the Irish monastery at Ratisbon on 21 Feb. 1721/2: see the footnote to item 16 for details of this MS.)
[6] Cf. 8 July 1722, items 4 and 7, and footnote.
[7] Descripcion del Real Monasterio de San Lorenzo del Escorial, Madrid, 1681. (See A. Palau y Dulcet, Manual del Librero Hispano-Americano, Barcelona, 1951, vol. iv, no. 70765.)

14. A person left a MS. of the Lives & Miracles of St. Edmund & St. Fremund by John Lidgate; being the Present book to King Henry VI, whose Effigies & Armes are extant therein. The Stories are adorned with 111 Pictures.[1]

15 August 1720.

15. By my Lords Order, Letters were sent to Mr Bowyer & Mr Chapman.

16. I went to Mr George Hay, & saw the MSS. lately bought in France by Mr Andrew Hay, being the Remainder of the Chancelier / de Seguiers Library; & saw all that I noted at pag. 44,5. Except the MS. Livy, & the Letters of K. Henry IV, which yet may be there for ought I know. The Original Letters are disposed into many Volumes. And the Collection is much more Numerous & Curious, than I expected.[2]

p. 55
(f. 29a)

16 August 1720.

1. The person mentioned in pag. 54, 14. came again for it. He say's it belong's to one Mr [*blank space*] Colston. I dd the same to him.[3]

2. Mr O Sullevane came to Study in the old Irish MS.[4]

3. Mr Roswell [*substituted for* A Person, *deleted in MS.*] came offering a few batter'd Roman Coins to be Sold. I rejected them, believing some Sharper to make this first Essay.

4. Dr. Fiddis came enquiring after particular Letters of Cardinal Wolsey; which he can find at length elsewhere.[5]

5. Mr Colston's Porter brought the MS (abovementioned at no. 1.) back again at my Lords price. I bad him come to morrow for the Money.[6]

17 August, 1720.

6. Mr Sanderson came to see the CODEX AVREVS.[7]

7. Mr William Thomas borrowed (for a few days) 4 MSS. wherein are pieces of Chaucers Works; being 34.B.18. 67.C.3. 93.B.2. and one unmarked, of Troilus & Creseide.[8]

8. Mr Cols[t]ons Porter brought his Receipt, and was paid for the MS. above-mentioned.[9]

9. Dr. Smith (brother to Dr. Smith of Durham deceased) brought an Achate-Cameo, seeming to be the Head of Libera, & Antique. He say's it belong's to a Physician, who will part with it at a reasonable price.[10]

10. My Lord went to Mr Hay and saw the MSS. of the Chancelier Seguier.[11]

---

[1] Now Harl. 2278. Cf. 16 Aug. (items 1 and 5) and 17 Aug. (item 8) 1720.

[2] See 1 June 1720, item 5, and footnote. [3] Cf. 12 Aug. 1720, item 14.

[4] Cf. 1 Mar. 1719/20, item 12, and footnote. [5] Cf. 15 Jan. 1719/20, item 5, and footnote.

[6] Cf. 12 Aug. 1720, item 14, and footnote. [7] i.e. Harl. 2788.

[8] The MSS. of Chaucer's works are Harl. 78, 1239, 1758 respectively; the Troilus and Criseyde MS. cannot be identified with certainty. All were returned on 14 Oct. 1720 (item 12), except for Harl. 1758 (returned 3 June 1721) (item 2). Two of the 4 borrowed were used for John Urry's ed. of the works of Chaucer pubd. posthumously in 1721, under William Thomas's supervision, viz. 93. B. 2 (= Harl. 1758) and 67. C. 3 (= Harl. 1239) (see Preface, K) (cf. also 21 Mar. (item 3 and footnote) and 26 Mar. (item 7) 1714/15). Papers relating to Urry's Chaucer are in Harl. 6895.

[9] Cf. 12 Aug. 1720, item 14, and footnote. Its price was £31. 10s. 0d. (see Welbeck Wanleyana, Misc. no. 49).

[10] Cf. 1 Sept. (item 5), and 8 Sept. (item 15) 1720. [11] Cf. 15 Aug. 1720, item 16, and footnote.

18 August, 1720.

11. I went to M^r. Hay by my Lords Order & began to take a Short List of Seguier's MSS.¹

19 August 1720.

12. I finished the List of Seguiers MSS.¹
Mr Bateman brought to my Lord two Parchment-Rolls, as to be Sold.²

20 August 1720.

13. Mr Green brought to my Lord certain Leaves of Velum loose, wherein are Copies of Deeds, &c. illustrating the Descent of Chasteleine, & others, with Historical Notes & observations: being Fragments of a large Work begun by S^r. Simonds D'Ewes for the Instruction of his Posterity, who thereby might see their Descent traced from many antient Families. Note many of the Original Deeds here Copied; & many Papers conducing towards this Work of Sir Simonds's own hand are yet extant in this Library.³

14. Mr Vaillant was sent by my Lord to see how the CODEX AVREVS itself agree's with the Specimen taken from it in Holland before it was bought. And upon Sight, he own'd that it was injudiciously done.⁴

15. A Letter was sent to Mr Warburton, desiring him to appoint a Time & Place for my seeing his MSS. &c.⁵

16. Mr Thomas Harley gave my Lord 2 small parcels of old Coins of Brass, all worn, & of the Lower Empire (except an old French Counter) said to have been found in Hereford-shire; I think, about Kingsland. /

22 August 1720.   p. 56
                                                                              (f. 29*b*)

1. My Lord sent in a fine MS. given him the 20th. Instant by Mr Vaillant; the Title whereof. is Francisci Patritij Pontificis Cajetani de Institutione Rei Politicæ Libri IX. (Scripti A.D. 1512.)⁶

2. Mr Greene came to know my Lords pleasure about the Parchments he brought 2 days ago. He say's that Mr Anstis had bidden 2 Guineas for them; & I sayd my Lord would give no more.⁷

---

¹ Cf. 15 Aug. 1720, item 16, and footnote.
² Not to be confused with the parchments returned to 'Esqr Bateman' under 8 Sept. 1720, item 14 (see Wanley's own Index for confirmation that these are two different people).
³ These fragmentary leaves belonged to 'Esqr Bateman' and were returned to him 8 Sept. 1720, item 14. Cf. also ref. under 22 Aug. 1720, item 2. A pedigree of the Chastelaine family followed by *facsimile* transcripts of relevant charters from the Clopton muniments, on 11 large vellum folios bearing the title 'The Historicall Descent of the Familie of Chastelaine', is preserved in Harl. 6152: it is followed (ff. 12, 13) by unfinished similar material relating to the family of 'Basset of Welledone' (on f. 12 is the date 1632). This material was executed to Sir Simonds d'Ewes's order by his clerk. The original (17th-cent.) page numbers show that the leaves in Harl. 6152 are completely disordered and that several items are missing; 2 leaves in a volume of fragments among the Welbeck Papers and probably belonging to this vol. (numbered 26 and 27) dealing with the family of Peiton (a family related to that of Chastelaine) are probably the 2 leaves referred to by Wanley below under 10 June 1725 as being in Mr. Le Neve's possession. The papers by D'Ewes himself and by his clerk relating to Chastelaine are in (e.g.) Harl. 380, 381, 593, which came into the Harleian Library with D'Ewes's Coll. in 1705.
⁴ Cf. 14 May 1720, item 4 (for ref. to Specimen). The MS. is Harl. 2788.
⁵ Cf. 3 Aug. 1720, item 3, and footnote.
⁶ Harl. 3491. (For date 1512 see colophon, f. 187^b.)
⁷ Cf. 20 Aug. (item 13) and 8 Sept. (item 14) 1720.

3. Mr William Thomas came.

4. Mr Oliver Marton came.

5. I visited Mr Warbu[rton] [*This item is deleted.*]

24 [4 *written over* 3] August 1720.

5 [*written over* 6]. I went with Mr Lawton to visit one Captain Nichols, in Order to see a parcel of Manuscripts; & must call on the Captain to morrow at 9; and so till the thing can be brought to bear.[1]

6. Mr Gibson came, and we endeavored to agree for the parcel of Printed books sent hither by him long agoe.[2]

7. My Lord sent in two MSS. for me to see.[3]

23 [*sic*] August 1720.

8. I went to see Mr Warburtons MSS. but found no great Rarities among them.[4]

25 August 1720.

9. I went to Captain Nichols; who said his Friend had now Changed his Mind: but should call on me.[5]

10. Mr Gibson agreed to take £50 for the last Parcel left by him; & £40 for that dd the 1st. of June last.[6]

11. Mr Chapman brought the last parcel deliver'd unto him, & received another to bind.

26 August 1720.

12. A Gentleman left his Proposals here with me, for Printing some unpublished English Historians, & writers relating to the Church of Peterburgh, at a very dear Price. He left not his Name, being in much hast[e].[7]

13. M^r O Sullevane brought two small Prints as a Present to my Lord.

27 August 1720.

14. Mr Thomas Harley brought Mr Baron Scrope to see the Codex Aureus, &c.

15. Mr Warner came to speak with my Lord.

16. Mr Sparke Register to the Church of Peterburgh (the forward Gentleman mentioned above at n°. 12) came again to teaze, & rub himself upon me.

17. My Lord sent in a parcel of old Bulls & some other Deeds, mostly relating to

[1] Cf. 25 Aug. 1720, item 9.
[2] See 7 June 1720, item 5, and footnote.
[3] No further ref. to these.
[4] Cf. 3 Aug. 1720, item 3. Wanley's visit was apparently in response to Warburton's letter of 22 Aug. 1720 (in Welbeck Wanleyana).
[5] Cf. 24 Aug. 1720, item 5, and footnote. Nothing further is heard of this transaction.
[6] See 1 June 1720, item 4, and footnote; 'the last parcel' had been sent on 7 June 1720 (item 5).
[7] Cf. 27 Aug. 1720, item 16, for identification of the 'gentleman' (Joseph Sparke); and for subsequent visits connected with the publication of his *Historiae Anglicanae Scriptores Varii* (1723) see 15 Sept. 1720, item 6; 6 Nov. 1722, item 14; 12 Nov. 1722, item 8 (part of subscription paid); 24 May 1723, item 3 (book of the lesser paper sent in); 25 May 1723, item 7 (binding of book); 6 Apr. 1725, item 16 (large paper ed.).

Rufford-Abbey; brought from Welbeck [*This item was inserted after that of 29 August 1720 had been written and the nos. 18 and 19 changed from 17 and 18.*][1]

29 August 1720.

18. I pack'd up 3 Cases of Printed Books, with 4 fine MSS. to be sent to my Lord to morrow.

19. Mr Thomas Harley sent in 54 Printed books.

30 August 1720.

20. The Three Cases of Books were putt into the Waggon.

21. I went to Sir Andrew Fountain & took a Cursory View of his Rarities. /[2]

31 August 1720.

1. I brought the Entire Catalogue of Hohendorffs Library from Mr Moetjens; & perceived that almost half of what was affirmed to be therein, is imbezeled.[3]

2. I went to observe the beginning of Mr Hay's Auction of Pictures & Antiquities.[4] And agreed with him, for the Seguierian MSS.[5]

p. 57
(f. 30a)

1 September 1720.

3. I putt up a Box full of Rarities to be sent to my Lord by the Higler; although Mr Pownhale came not to assist me.

4. Mr Elliot brought a small parcel my Lord had given him to Bind.

5. Dr Smith came about the Cameo he left with me; & we agreed as to the Price.[6]

2 September 1720.

6. I went to attend the Auction of Mr Hays Antiquities, &c.[7]

3 September 1720.

7. I inspected Sir Andrew Fountains coins of the Great Brass.[8]

4 September 1720.

8. I agreed with Mr Noel for 3 MSS. lately brought from Flanders.[9]

5. September 1720.

9. I sent in all the Seguierian MSS. from Mr George Hay; and expressly agreed with him that when ever the MS. Livy, & K. Henry IVth. of France's Letters

---

[1] In Addenda, Lansdowne 771, f. 77b (at p. 197 of the present work) Wanley has entered the present item under 17 Aug. 1720: this is probably the correct date since Harl. charters corresponding in subject-matter to this description are all endorsed by Wanley 17 Aug. 1720, viz. Harl. Ch. III. A. 2–5, 7–15, 17, 18, 20, 22–27, 29–36; III. C. 21. For a full list of Bulls, Charters, &c., relating to Rufford Abbey, in the Harl. Coll., see *Index to the Charters and Rolls in the Dept. of MSS. British Museum*, ed. H. J. Ellis, ii (1912), pp. 639–41.

[2] Cf. 3, 6, 7, 9, and 10 Sept. 1720.   [3] Cf. 11 Jan. 1719/20, item 7, and footnote.

[4] This is the sale of the antiquities, &c. from the Valetta Coll. (cf. 25 July 1720, item 6, and footnote). The Andrew Hay sale cat. has not been identified.

[5] For lists see 1 June (item 5 and footnotes) and 5 Sept. (item 9 and footnote) 1720.

[6] On 17 Aug. 1720; he was paid £8. 8s. od.; it had belonged to Dr. Fuller (Welbeck Wanleyana, Misc. no. 50).   [7] Cf. 31 Aug. 1720, item 2.

[8] Cf. 30 Aug. 1720, item 21, and footnote.

[9] See 12 Sept. 1720, item 1, for list and identifications, where Wanley erroneously refers back to 8th instead of to this date.

shall appear, they shall be deliver'd up as part of the same Parcel, without further Price. The short List I took of them is among the Library Papers.[1]

10. M[r] O Sullevane came, & I shewed him an old Irish Relique; & delivered to him a Gratuity from my Lord.[2]

11. M[r] Sliford came to transcribe for M[r] Bridges.

6 September 1720.

12. I inspected Sir Andrew Fountains Roman Coins of the Midle Brass.[3]

7. September 1720.

13. I inspected Part of S[r]. Andrew Fountains Consular & Imperial Silver Coins.[3]

8 September 1720.

14. Esq Bateman came about the Parchm[ts]. mentioned p. 56, 2. he being the owner; and they being but Fragments, I returned them back.[4]

15. I paid D[r]. Smith for the Cameo, above-mentioned at n°. 5.

9 September 1720.

16. M[r] O Sullevan came to view the old Irish Relique of Antiquity, I borrowed of Sir Andrew Fountaine.[5]

10 September 1720.

p. 58
(f. 30b)

17. I called on Sir And. Fountaine, who shewed me divers other pieces of Antiquity found in Ireland; among them is / a large Brasen Lamp with 5 Sockets. On the Top is a Man on Horseback putting the fore-finger of his Right Hand to his Nose. On his Back & Breast he ha's a ✠. The Work is rude like that of the Bass-Empire; & the Tradition that went with the Lamp, was that it was S[t]. Patric's. Sir Andrew ha's also the Shafts of some small Brasen Columns Fluted; two Brasen Horns, thought to be Danish, &c.[6] This day I returned the old Irish Hand, Scepter, or Mace, which I borrowed of him.[7]

---

[1] Cf. 1 June 1720, item 5, and footnote. The Harl. MSS. from the Séguier Coll. and *bearing the date of this day* are as follows (items specially noted by Wanley on his first examination of the catalogue and mentioned by him under 1 June, item 5, are (so far as they can be identified) asterisked): *2477, *2503, *2508, *2699, *2735, *2759, 2940, 2978, 3127, 3128, 3129, 3144, 3199 (*arts. 4 and 5), *3251, 3254, 3345, *3396, 3450, 3496 (ff. 1–78, 154–95), 3536. A (ff. 39–110), *3539, 3546 (ff. 117–24), 3569 (ff. 295–327), 3570 (ff. 1–73), 3576, 3585, 3587, 3588, 3635, *3664, 3679 (ff. 128–50), 3687, 3695, 3705 (Pt. II), 3727, 3728, *3767, *3799–*3809, 3834, 3857, *3974, *3979, 4114, 4357–60, *4362, 4363, *4365–70, 4394–6, *4400, *4405, 4407, 4420, 4422, 4423, 4426, 4435–43, 4445–7, 4449, 4451–*62, 4463, 4465–72. B, 4479, 4480, 4483, 4486 (ff. 1–67), 4489–96, *4498, 4500, 4502–4, 4513–19, 4522, 4524, 4555, 4736 (ff. 1–57), *4938, 5080, 5124, 5302, 5418 (ff. 83–105), 5446, 5452, 5464. (Harl. 4448 bears no date by Wanley, but internal evidence points to its being a Séguier MS.) Several of these MSS. have Séguier's arms on the covers (with or without the Chancellor's baton): a few have his monogram (PS) and that of his wife, Madeleine Fabri (MF), viz. Harl. 3635, 3979, 4363, 4407, 4422, 5302. A number of MSS. *not* endorsed by Wanley '5 Sept. 1720' have on the spine 'E COLL SEGUIER', however, viz.
  (a) 4450, 4525–34, 4536–40, 4542, 4543, 4545–51, 4559. (These MSS. bear no date at all by Wanley.)
  (b) 4501 (dated by Wanley 13 Aug. 1724; this came through Noel).
  (c) 4507, 4508, 4510–12, 5297 (all dated by Wanley 23 Feb. 1719/20; these came through Noel).
[2] Cf. 9 and 10 Sept. 1720.   [3] Cf. 30 Aug. 1720, item 21.
[4] Cf. 20 Aug. (item 13, and footnote) and 22 Aug. (item 2) 1720.   [5] Cf. 5 Sept. 1720, item 10.
[6] Not traced. But on Fountaine and his colls. see J. Nichols, *Literary Anecdotes*, v (1812), pp. 253–55, and for contemporary references see *Vertue Note Books* (Walpole Soc.), *passim*. For a reference to a cabinet for medals bought of Fountaine by Harley see 26 May 1720, item 14, and footnote.
[7] For this 'relique' cf. 5 Sept. (item 10) and 9 Sept. 1720.

12 September 1720.

1. I brought the 3 MSS. I mentioned before, at the 8 Instant.[1] They are,
   Johannis Lectoris Summa Confessorum, cum alijs tractatibus, folio mag. perg.[2]
   D. Augustini Homiliæ super Evangelium D. Joannis. fol. membr.[3]
   Horæ B. Mariæ secundum Usum Ecclesiæ Tornacensis. Illum. membr. 8ᵛᵒ.[4]

14 September 1720.

2. I sent a Letter to Mr Chapman requiring him to send the new Books he is Binding for my Lord, down to Wympole this Week.

15 September 1720.

3. I recd a Letter from Mr Warburton Somerset Herald, about his MSS. & returned him a cool Answer.[5]

4. I putt up my Lords English, Scots & Irish Coins; together with five pieces of Gold bought yesterday of Mr Barret, into the Box to be sent for Wympole to morrow.

5. Mr David Humphreys came to look into the Greek MS. Catena of Nicetas Serron, upon the Psalms.[6]

6. Mr Sparke came with his New Proposals for Printing more English Historians; & want's me to be active in promoting his Work, & Interest.[7]

17 September 1720.

7. Mr Oliver Marton came for the Keys of my Lords Evidence-Room here; & brought the same back.

20 September 1720.

8. Mr More came from Mr Oliver Marton for the Keys of the Evidence-Room, & brought them back.

9. A Letter sent to Mr Chapman, hastening my Lords New Books now in his Hands.[8]

21 Septr. 1720.

10. A Letter recd from Mr Warburton desiring [me] to call on him again, & see his Things.[9]

22 September 1720.

11. I looked out certain of the Seguierian MSS. & put them up, in Order to send them to my Lord at Wymple.

[1] Cf. 4 Sept. 1720 (*not* 8th as Wanley says and put in each of the MSS.).
[2] Harl. 3162.   [3] Harl. 3171.   [4] Harl. 2433.
[5] Cf. 3 Aug. 1720, item 3, and footnote. Warburton's letter, dated 14 Sept. 1720 (in Welbeck Wanleyana), intimates that he has given away 'the old Cronicle'.
[6] Harl. 5791. Cf. 21 Mar. 1719/20, and footnote.
[7] See 26 Aug. 1720, item 12, and footnote.
[8] Chapman was apparently slow: cf. Harley's letter to Wanley, dated 26 Sept. 1720 (in Welbeck Wanleyana): 'Keep Chapman employed allways if there is work for him because he is but slow . . .'; an injunction with which Wanley complied (cf. Diary, 29 Sept. 1720, item 10).
[9] Cf. 15 Sept. 1720, item 3, and footnote. A Warburton letter, undated, but endorsed by Wanley 'Recd. 21 Sept. 1720', is in Welbeck Wanleyana with Warburton's letters of 30 Sept. and 5 Oct. 1720.

12. Mr Chapman brought back the Parcel last deliver'd to him, excepting the New Books which he sent to my Lord.

13. I sent a Letter to Mr Pownhale about the Case to my Lords Crystal-Vase.[1]

14. I sent a cooling Answer to Mr Warburton. /[2]

p. 59
(f. 31*a*)

23 September 1720.

1. I received a Letter from Mr Henry Hoare, desiring to borrow a Book not here in my Custody; and sent him an Answer.[3]

2. Mr Warner the Goldsmith called here, being desirous of seeing Curiosities of any kind; and was attended by me a long time.

24 September 1720.

3. Mr Vertue came to peruse the Book 59.A.11.[4] and wanting to look upon divers Rarities I had mentioned to him was attended by me almost as long as Mr Warner.

27 September 1720.

4. I sent Letters to Mr Bowyer, Mr Hazard, & Mr Chapman the Binder.

5. Mr George Hay brought two Scots Gentlemen to see the Library.

28 September 1720.

6. I filled a New Case with the Books sent for by my Lord; and others to fill up.

7. Mr Herring came hither to enquire for his Crest, (if he ha's one.) I found the Armes which he says he own's, borne by the Family of HEARING, and a Crest above the Escocheon. He would have given me a Guinea for my Trouble, but I refused it, as I have always hitherto done, all presents of that kind, from the Beginning, Thanking him for his Kindness, but saying I would, by no means, sell my Lords Favor.

8. Mr Hugh Thomas being Deceased; my Book of Notes, & others of my Library-papers to be enquired for.[5]

29 September 1720.

9. I brought the Missale Ordinis Cisterciensis, *Par.* 1529. fol. hither.[6]

10. Mr Chapman the Binder came; was paid for the last Parcel; & received another to Bind.

30 September 1720.

11. Mr Bowyer sent hither the Dr Claggets Sermons,[7] &c. which I sent forthwith to Mr Chapman the Binder, & a Letter desiring him to go about them out of hand, that they may be sent to my Lord the next Week.

---

[1] This is Peter Pownall: his reply, dated 29 Sept. 1720, is in Welbeck Wanleyana.

[2] Cf. 21 Sept. 1720.

[3] Henry Hoare's letter, dated 22 Sept. 1720 (in Welbeck Wanleyana), discloses that the book he wished to borrow was 'a book of Mr Fitzherbert writt on' husbandry, which he had been informed was 'in a Collection of Books on Husbandry' . . . 'bought lately' by Lord Harley.

[4] i.e. Harl. 675.   [5] Cf. 19 Oct. 1720, and footnote.

[6] Several Missals of Cistercian Use printed at Paris, 1529, are recorded in Weale and Bohatta, *Bibliographia Liturgica: Catalogus Missalium*, 1928 (see nos. 1762–5).

[7] Presumably William Clagett's *Sermons on the following subjects. viz. Concerning Christ's not appearing to all the people after his resurrection . . . now first published from the originals by N. Clagett*, London, 1720, 2 vols.

1 October 1720.

12. A Letter recd. from Mr Warburton, with a Catalogue of his MSS. &c. inclosed.[1]

4 October 1720.

13. I sent a Letter to Mr Warburton, in Order to gain some more time of him.

5 October 1720.

14. Mr Hazard came for my Lords Crystal Swan to send to Wympole, which I deliver'd unto him. /

p. 60
(f. 31*b*)

6 October 1720.

1. An Angry Letter Recd from Mr Warburton, falsely affirming that the Heraldical MS. I desired him to add to the Parcel he designed to sell my Lord bring's him in half his Livelyhood.[2]

2. I putt up the Great Book of Prints & Drawings (long since bought of John Kemp) which my Lord Order's to be sent down to Wympole.[3]

7 October 1720.

3. The said book was delivered to the Waggoner.

8 October 1720.

4. Mr Robert Cuningham brough[t] an 8vo. book, sealed up, to be sent to my Lord.

10 October 1720.

5. I sent an Answer to Mr Warburtons last Letter.[4]

6. Mr Slyford came.

11 October 1720.

7. I wrote to Mr Gregory to make up 3 or 4 Cases forthwith, in Order to the Sending down the Printed Books in the two Closets, to my Lord this week.[5]

12 October 1720.

8. Mr Slyford came to transcribe for Mr Bridges.

13 October 1720.

9. Mr Slyford came to transcribe for Mr Bridges.

[1] See 3 Aug. 1720, item 3, and footnote. Warburton's letter, dated 30 Sept. 1720, and accompanying cat. of MSS. are in Welbeck Wanleyana.

[2] Cf. 3 Aug. 1720, item 3. The angry letter from Warburton, dated 5 Oct. 1720 (in Welbeck Wanleyana), concludes with a threat that 'as every thing that I can shew you is trash without it [the heraldical book] [I] shall put them into their old places again and trouble myself no more about Collecting MSS.' No more is heard in the Diary of these MSS., but as late as 2 Feb. 1725/6 Warburton was offering a large parcel of old charters and, when Wanley went to see them on 9 Feb., showed him a few MS. books also.

[3] For previous refs. to Kemp's Colls. see 28 Jan. 1719/20, item 9, and footnote. For Harley's directions for sending to Wimpole the 'great book of prints and drawings' see his letter to Wanley dated 27 Sept. 1720 (in Welbeck Wanleyana). Its receipt at Wimpole was acknowledged by Harley 9 Oct. 1720 (Welbeck Wanleyana).

[4] Cf. 6 Oct. 1720, item 1.

[5] In response to Harley's order to Wanley in his letter of 9 Oct. 1720 (in Welbeck Wanleyana).

14 October 1720.

10. All the Printed books in both the Library-Closets (except those of M[r] Alex[r]. Cuningham) went for Wimple.[1]

11. M[r] Slyford came to transcribe for M[r] Bridges.

12. William Thomas sent in 3 of the four MSS. of Chaucer borrowed lately by him, being 67.C.3. 34.B.18. and that which is yet unmarked.[2]

15 October 1720.

13. M[r] Slyford came to transcribe for M[r] Bridges.

17 October 1720.

14. M[r] Slyford came to transcribe for M[r] Bridges.
I went after M[r] Hugh Thomas's Widow; but found her not.[3]

18 October 1720.

15. M[r]. Slyford came to transcribe for M[r] Bridges.

16. M[r] Dale came to peruse some of the Heraldical MSS.

19 October 1720.

17. I found M[r] Hugh Thomas's Widow, & inspecting the parcel of MSS. Parchments & Papers bequeathed by him to my Lord Oxford; I found some of my own Heraldical References to the MSS. in this Library, which were many years agoe / privately taken out of this Library-Desk, when I had left it safely Locked up.[4]

p. 61
(f. 32a)

20 October 1720.

1. I met M[r] Hugh Thomas's Widow, and rec'd most part of her Husbands MS. Books, Papers, & Parchments (being but a small parcel in the whole:) the remainder, at her Request, were delivered to M[r] Green Blew-mantle, to the End that he may Extract some Notes from them, relating to the Family of Bruges, Chandos, &c; which being done, in a little time, they are to be brought into this Library.[5]

2. M[r] Slyford came to transcribe for M[r] Bridges.

3. M[r] Bridges came to look into M[r] Slyfords Performance.[6]

---

[1] Cf. 11 Oct. 1720, and footnote.   [2] See 17 Aug. 1720, item 7, and footnote.

[3] See 19 Oct. 1720, and footnote.

[4] Cf. 28 Sept. (item 8), 17 Oct. (item 1), and 15 Nov. 1720; 9 Feb. (item 4), 14 Feb. (item 13), and 20 Feb. (item 4) 1720/1. The Harl. MSS. noted by Wanley as having been bequeathed to Robert Harley are Harl. 2218, 2288, 2289, 2291, 2299, 2300, 3325, 3538, 4181. Wanley's 'own Heraldical References' may be his Index of Heraldical MSS. in the Harl. Coll. (undated) now BM Add. 6052. In addition the following Charters are endorsed by Wanley 'Bequeathed by Mr. Hugh Thomas': Harl. Ch. 111. B. 17-45; 111. D. 3, 37; 111. E. 2, 31, 32; 111. F. 49, 55; 111. G. 36, 42; 112. A. 20, 27, 33; 112. B. 4, 46, 56; 112. C. 5, 11, 36; 112. D. 28, 36, 43; 112. E. 27b; 112. F. 8, 13, 25. Cotton Ch. XXVI. 6 also bears the same endorsement by Wanley.

[5] Cf. 19 Oct. 1720 and footnote. The papers delivered to Mr. Greene were brought into the Library 15 Nov. 1720. Harley's instructions to Wanley are in his letters of 20 and 25 Oct. 1720 in Welbeck Wanleyana.

[6] The 'Performance' relates to Slyford's transcripts from Hutton's Papers (cf. 30 June (item 6) and 18 July (item 1) 1720).

4. I sent a new Edition of Bibliotheca Hohendorffiana, lately received from Mr Noel; that my Lord may compare it at Wympole with one which I sent down some time ago. This Book of Noels, is to be returned, because, if he buy's what now remain's of the Library, the Things must be Examined by it.[1]

5. Mr Chapman brought hither the last Parcel deliver'd to Him for Binding.

22. October 1720.

6. Mr Slyford came to transcribe for Mr Bridges.

27 October 1720.

7. Mr Slyford came to Transcribe for Mr Bridges.

8. Mr Bowyer came & Shewed a Catalogue of Books he lately Bought; which contained likewise the Titles of others Bought out of the same Study before him. He also offer'd to present me with a Parcel of Original Letters of K. Charles II: The Earl of Sandwich, &c. Upon my desire, he promised to send the said Catalogue, Letters, & the last Edition of Heylyn's Help to History, down to my Lord, by the next Higler.[2]

28 October 1720.

9. A Letter sent to Mr Chapman, desiring him to call here to morrow.

29 October 1720.

10. Mr Chapman came, & when I desired him to consider what he would have to go down to Wimple, & to Bind & Letter there for my Lord; he promised to Bring me an Answer the next Tuesday.[3]

11. Mr Dale came to peruse the Heraldical Visitations of Devonshire.

12. Mr George Hay came; & said he would indeavor to induce the Lord Widdrington to present a parcel of old MSS. to my Lord. /[4]

31 October 1720.

p. 62
(f. 32b)

1. Mr Hutchinson of Bury came for the MS. he lent me from the Schole-Library of Bury; & received it.[5]

[1] Cf. 11 Jan. 1719/20, item 7, and footnote. The BM *General Cat.* records only one ed. of the *Bibliotheca Hohendorfiana* (cf. also Archer Taylor, *Book Catalogues*, Chicago, 1957, p. 246).

[2] Cf. 1 Nov. 1720, item 2. Harley had received these at Wimpole by 30 Oct. 1720: see his letter in *Welbeck Wanleyana* endorsed by Wanley 30 Oct. 1720, in which also Wanley is instructed to convey to Bowyer Harley's thanks. According to Harley they had belonged to Prince Rupert. Bowyer gave another parcel of original letters, &c. relating to Prince Rupert on 1 Sept. 1722. The Heylyn vol. is Peter Heylyn's 'Ηρωολογια Anglorum: or an help to English History containing a succession of all Kings of England, &c., first pubd. 1641; the last ed. before the Diary date was that of 1709.

[3] Cf. 1 Nov. 1720, item 4. A letter from Harley, dated 25 Oct. 1720, relating to this project is in *Welbeck Wanleyana*. Cf. also 1 and 2 Dec. 1724.

[4] Nothing further is heard of this in the Diary, but in the Harl. Coll. is a large number of MSS., mostly of Durham provenance, which were, according to inscriptions in them, in the possession of Sir Thomas Tempest, Bart. (i.e. presumably Sir Thomas Tempest, 4th Bart., of Stella, co. Durham, who died 1692). He was succeeded by his son, Sir Francis Tempest, who died unmarried at Montpellier 1698 when all the Tempest estates went to his sister and sole heir Jane. It was she who became the wife of William, the 4th and last Baron Widdrington (the 'Lord Widdrington' referred to here), and thus brought Tempest possessions into Widdrington hands. All the Tempest/Durham books may therefore very well have been in Widdrington's ownership and a memorandum by Edward Harley in one of them (Harl. 5289), 'This MS. was given me By my Lord Withrington in 1731. Oxford. B.H.', suggests that they may have come in *en bloc* in that year through Widdrington himself. The Harl. MSS. bearing Tempest inscriptions are 13 in number: Harl. 3858, 3860, 3864, 3946, 4657, 4664, 4688, 4703, 4725, 4894, 5234, 5289, 5751.   [5] See 23 June 1720, item 8, and footnote.

1 November 1720.

2. Mr Bowyer had my Lords Thanks for the fine parcel of Original Letters he sent my Lord the last Week; & was desired to enquire for more.[1] Mr Bowyer told me that he shall yet have the remains of the late learned Mr Archdeacon Batteley's Library.[2]

3. Mr Iñys the Bookseller promised to serve my Lord with Books, as cheap as any man.

4. Mr Chapman gave me his Answer as to the Terms whereupon he is willing to Bind or Letter for my Lord at Wympole.[3]

4 November 1720.

5. Mr Slyford came to transcribe for Mr Bridges.

5 November 1720.

6. D^r. Sherard gave me a smal List of books he is willing to dispose of to my Lord:[4] and said he has bought for my Lord a Sett of the Books Printed by the Greeks at Jassi & Buchorest:[5] and that he is willing to serve my Lord in Case he shall be willing to buy Greek MSS. in Turkey.[6]

7 November 1720.

7. Mr Gibson shewed me a smal parcel of Books lately come from Italy. He say's he ha's actuall[y] bought & paid for Plinij Hist. Nat. printed at Rome by the Maxim, A.D. 1469; and Lactantius printed at Venice by Joan. Spira A.D. 1468; both which my Lord may have at Reasonable price.[7] Also he deliver'd me a Letter from Mr Smith Merchant in Venice, with a Printed Catalogue of his MSS. which he is willing to sell to my Lord; but ask's a price for them horribly extravagant.[8]

---

[1] Cf. 27 Oct. 1720, item 8, and footnote.
[2] See 11 Jan. 1719/20, item 3, and footnote.
[3] Cf. 29 Oct. 1720, item 10, and footnote.
[4] Cf. 8 Nov. 1720, item 9, and footnote.
[5] On the Jassy and Bucharest books see 18 Jan. 1719/20, item 4, and footnote 10.
[6] One of these was a MS. of the Greek Gospels at Nemenia mentioned by Lisle 18 Jan. 1719/20, item 5. Sherard's offer to secure Greek MSS. in Turkey was accepted by Harley (see Harley's letter, 10 Nov. 1720, to Wanley in Welbeck Wanleyana). For subsequent developments (involving Bernard Mould also) see below, especially 17 Nov. (item 9 and footnote), 21 Nov., 29 Nov. (item 15), 5 Dec. (item 5), 7 and 17 Dec. 1720; 17 Apr. (item 8) and 4 May (item 16) 1721; 18 May and 8 Oct. (item 13) 1722; 28 July 1725. Mould returned to England early in 1725 and the list of Hebrew and Greek MSS. received from him is under 6 Aug. 1725.
[7] The 'parcel of Books' is probably that referred to later under 31 Jan. (item 1) and again 9 Mar. (item 6) 1720/1; 14 Apr. (item 3), 25 Apr. (item 24) 1721; cf. also 27 Apr. (item 6) 1721 for list and price (£20) of these *printed* books. There is no further ref. to this Pliny. As regards the Lactantius the only one mentioned in 27 Apr. 1721 list is that of 1478 (printed Venice). Actually there seems to be some transposition of the details of the 2 printed works referred to. There is a Pliny's *Natural History* pubd. at Venice by Johannes de Spira in 1469 (= *BMC* v. 153; Stillwell P 716; Hain 13087), this being the *editio princeps*. (Harley acquired this ed. later from Noel: see 17 Apr. 1722, item 8.) Lactantius's *Opera* was pubd. by Sweynheym and Pannartz at Rome in 1468 (= *BMC* iv. 4; Stillwell L 2; Hain 9807).
[8] The letter from Smith to Gibson (dated 11 Oct. 1720) is in BM Lansdowne 841, ff. 98–99; in it Smith offered his coll. to Harley for £1,500. Harley's comments are in a letter to Wanley, dated 14 Nov. 1720 (Welbeck Wanleyana); in it he says: 'I think they dont come up to what my expectations was raised to. the number of Greek is not great, nor is the whole number so great as might be expected. 121 MSS. is not so great considering the number of years it is said they were collecting nor the place where they were collected. I should be glad to give £500 for them but no more. . . .' Cf. also 17 Dec. 1720 (for reported sale by Smith to the Earl of Sunderland for £1,500), but see 31 Jan. 1720/1, item 1, and 6 Feb. 1722/3, item 7. No cat. of Smith's MSS. has been traced for this date (Smith's extant cats. are: c. 1735, 1737, 1755, and 1773).

8 November 1720.

8. I went to Mr Bowyer, & gave him a List of Books to send down to my Lord. Mr Bowyer said that he yet hope's to purchase the remaining part of A.D. Batteley's Library before Christmass.[1]

9. I wrote to Dr Sherard to send down a small parcel of his Books to my Lord.[2]

9 November 1720.

10. My Lord having returned the Catalogue sent him by Mr Bowyer; I sent the same to him accordingly.[3]

10 November 1720.

11. Mr Bateman the Bookseller called here. /

p. 63
(f. 33a)

11 November 1720

1. Mr Slyford came to write for Mr Bridges: and said that Mr Browne Willis is said to be willing to part with his MS. Collections.[4]

12 November 1720.

2. I wrote to Dr. Sherard, desiring to conferre with him upon my Lords business.

14 November 1720.

3. Mr Slyford came to Transcribe for Mr Bridges.

15. November 1720.

4. Mr Slyford came to Transcribe for Mr Bridges: & brought with him those Papers & Parchments lately belonging to Mr Hugh Thomas, which I delivered to Mr Greene.[5]

16 November 1720.

5. Mr Great of Colchester came, & enquired after the Coins & other Antiquities (found at Colchester) which he left here with me about an year & an half since. They were produced to him, & I promised to take his Matter into speedy Consideration, & by representing it duely to my Lord, to procure him such Satisfaction as will be to his Encouragement.[6]

17 November 1720.

6. Another Letter sent to Dr Sherard, desiring him to meet me.

7. Mr Noel came, & say's he expect[s] a Bill of Lading for his Books in Holland, by the next Post.[7]

[1] See 11 Jan. 1719/20, item 3, and footnote.
[2] Cf. 5 Nov. 1720. Harley in a letter to Wanley, dated 14 Nov. 1720 (Welbeck Wanleyana), observed of these books: 'I like them very well without all doubt he [Sherard] must have very curious books.'
[3] Cf. 27 Oct. 1720.
[4] William Slyford was amanuensis to Browne Willis (as well as to Bridges) (cf. refs. to him in J. G. Jenkins's *The Dragon of Whaddon*, 1953). Browne Willis gave MSS. (*SC* 27652–61) in 1720 to the Bodleian Library, Oxford, to which he also left his MS. colls. (see Macray, pp. 258–60, and Jenkins, op. cit., pp. 225–33, for Willis's will). Cf. 13 Dec. 1725, item 19, for record of an unsatisfactory interview with Wanley. [5] Cf. 20 Oct. 1720, item 1, and footnote.
[6] Cf. 19 May (item 9), 20 May (item 12), and 22 May (item 15) 1721 (when the coins were taken away).
[7] Cf. 22 Dec. 1720, item 7; 2 Jan. (item 10), 9 and 16 Jan. (item 5) 1720/1 (for list).

8. Mr Slyford came to transcribe for Mr Bridges.

9. D^r. Sherard came, & we had much discourse about getting the Greek MSS. now remaining in the Monastery of Nemenia at Scio.¹

18 November 1720.

10. Mr Slyford came to transcribe for Mr Bridges.

21 November 1720.

11. I drew up a Draught of a Commission or Instructions for D^r. Sherard; in Order to his Procuring the Greek MSS. at Nemenia in Scio, &c. to be first transmitted to my Lord for his Approbation.¹

23 November 1720.

12. M^r. Ludlam came to see the Library.

28 November 1720.

13. Grævius & Gronovius's Collections of Roman & Greek Antiquities were brought down, to be sent to Wympole.²

29 November 1720.

14. I packed them up. And, by my Lords Order, took out the MS. of John Fordun 59.C.18. to send to Dr Stratford of Christchurch.³

15. D^r. Sherard came for his Instructions about getting the Greek MSS. at Nemenia, which Instructions my Lord ha's approved of, but not yet Returned.⁴ He said, that the Duke of Devonshire cannot part with S^t. Æthelwolds Benedictionale. /⁵

p. 64
(f. 33b)

30 November 1720.

1. I sent a Letter to Mr Innys Desiring him to send the Frensh Edition of young Thevenots Travels, as he promised.⁶

2. I began to look into D^r. Covels Catalogue of his Rarities, by my Lords Order.⁷

¹ Cf. 5 Nov. 1720, and footnote. Several searches for Greek MSS. in the Levant had been made late in the 17th cent. (e.g. by Covel). The library at the Monastery of Nemenia (Nea Moni) in Scio (Chios) had been the subject of admiration by Johann Michael Wansleben (b. 1635), who had been commissioned by Colbert to search for Greek MSS. and was at Chios 1673-4 (cf. P. P. Argenti, *Chios*, 1941, pp. 44-45). For another 17th-cent. mission sent out by Colbert, that of Monceaux and Laisne in 1667, see L. Delisle, *Le Cabinet des MSS.*, i (1868), pp. 275-6; several missions were sent in the 18th cent. also, for example, Paul Lucas reported to Louis XIV in 1708 the acquisition of Arabic, Persian, Turkish, Greek, and Hebrew MSS. and a second voyage made on instructions dated 25 Apr. 1714 produced further MSS. (cf. Delisle, op. cit., i, pp. 332-3).
² J. G. Graevius and J. Gronovius, *Thesaurus Antiquitatum Graecarum Romanarumque Italiae, Siciliae, &c.*, pubd. 1694 onwards. (For details of the rare complete set see Sotheby's sale-cat. (Signet Library, pt. iv), 11-12 Apr. 1960, lot 1196.)
³ i.e. Harl. 712. Acknowledged by Stratford 6 Dec. 1720. Wanley had been instructed by Harley in a letter, dated 27 Nov. 1720 (in Welbeck Wanleyana), to send it to Stratford. In an earlier letter of 30 Oct. 1720 Harley comments that he thinks it had belonged to a Bp. of Scotland and was bought with Stillingfleet's MSS.
⁴ Cf. 21 Nov. 1720, and footnote.
⁵ Cf. 18 Jan. 1719/20, item 4, and footnote 7.
⁶ Jean de Thévenot, *Relation d'un Voyage fait au Levant*, Paris, 3 pts., 1664-84 (later French eds. before 1720 were 1665-84 (3 pts.) and 1689 (5 vols.)). An English ed. had appeared in London, 1687.
⁷ See 18 Jan. 1719/20, item 4, and footnote 2.

1 December 1720.

3. Mʳ Sanderson came, & (by my Lords Order) borrowed the MS. 90.C.16. (Restored, 7 January following.)¹

2 December 1720.

4. Mʳ Robert Cuningham brought some Papers to go to my Lord by the next Weeks Higler.

5 December 1720.

5. I brought a Copie of the Instructions for Dʳ. Sherard to buy the Greek MSS. remaining in the Monastery of Nemenia in Scio: & elsewhere.²

6. I Sett Mʳ. Virtue the Engraver to Copie a Picture in the MS. of Sᵗ. Æthelwald's Benedictionale; since it will not be parted with to my Lord.³

7. I transcribed a Letter to Mʳ Sam. Palmer Merchant in Cyprus, which I lately drew up: putting him in Mind of procuring for my Lord the Old Greek MS. Bible in Capitals, belonging to the Cathedral Church at Teflis in Gjorgia, a Printed Gjorgian Bible, & other MSS.⁴

6 December 1720.

8. I recᵈ a Letter from Dʳ Stratford, owning the Receipt of the MS. of John Fordun's Scotichronicon.⁵

7 December 1720.

9. Dʳ. Sherard not calling here these Three days; I sent a Letter to him by a special Messenger, together with his Instructions about the MSS. in Scio,⁶ & my Letter to Mʳ Palmer in Cyprus.⁷

9 December 1720.

10. Mʳ Reading of Sion-College sent in a Copie of his Edition of Eusebius of the large Paper, at 5 Guineas. And I sent him a Letter owning the Receipt of it.⁸

---

¹ i.e. Harl. 1584.   ² See 21 Nov. 1720, and footnote.

³ Cf. 29 Nov. 1720; for subsequent visits of Vertue for this purpose cf. 10 and 24 Dec. 1720; and 19 Jan. 1720/1, item 10. The drawing is in Harley Coll. of Prints at Soc. of Ant., vol. ii, f. 85.

⁴ Cf. 7 Dec., 13 Dec. (item 14), and 17 Dec. 1720. The draft of an earlier commission to Palmer, 22 June 1718, is in Welbeck Wanleyana, Misc. 71. We are indebted to Mr. T. C. Skeat for the following note: 'The Biblical MS. in Greek uncials rumoured to exist at Tiflis early in the 18th century cannot apparently be identified with any MS. now extant. Two such MSS. are known from this part of the world. The first is the Koridethi Gospels (numbered 038 or, alternatively, Θ in the agreed enumeration of Greek New Testament MSS.), a MS. of the Gospels written in a *very* peculiar and ungainly uncial script, probably in the 8th cent., and now Cod. Gr. 993 in the Georgian Museum, Tiflis. According to G. Beerman and C. R. Gregory, *Die Koridethi Evangelien*, Leipzig, 1913, the MS. remained at Kala in the Caucasus continuously from c. 1300 to 1869, and was not brought to Tiflis until 1901. The second MS. is also a MS. of the Gospels written in uncials of more conventional type, probably in the 9th cent. It is now Tiflis, Georgian Museum Cod. Gr. 206 (0211 in the standard numeration of New Testament MSS.). According to W. H. P. Hatch, *The Principal Uncial Manuscripts of the New Testament*, Chicago, 1939, text to pl. lv, the MS. was formerly in Bassiani, a district of Turkey on the boundary between Georgia and Armenia, where there are many orthodox Armenians. Later it was bought by one Michael Kafafov, who describes himself as a chief priest. In 1849 the codex was in St. George's Church in Leninakan (formerly Alexandropol), and thence it was taken to the Georgian Museum in Tiflis.'

⁵ Cf. 29 Nov. 1720, item 14. The only letter from Stratford in Welbeck Wanleyana, dated 4 Dec. 1720, acknowledges receipt of a box apparently of MSS., but does not appear to relate specifically to the Fordun MS.

⁶ Cf. 21 Nov. 1720, and footnote.   ⁷ Cf. 5 Dec. 1720, item 7, and footnote.

⁸ Cf. 13 Dec. 1720, item 13, and footnote. Reading's ed. of Eusebius was pubd. at Cambridge, 1720.

10 December 1720.

11. Mr Virtue came about his Drawing from S^t. Æthelwald's book.[1]

12 December 1720.

12. Mr Warner came to see my Lords Proof of the Common-wealths Great Seal, engraven by Tho. Symon.[2]

13. December 1720.

13. I sent back Mr Reading's Eusebius, my Lord being already furnished; with a Letter to him.[3]

14. I sent a Letter to Dr Sherard, desiring to know whether he received the Instructions I sent him with the Letter to Mr Sam. Palmer; & whether he hath sent them away, as I desired? /[4]

p. 65   1. Mr Kingsley came to enquire after some things relating to his Family, which he
(f. 34ª)   says are in Holmes's books.

14 December 1720.

2. I received a Letter from D^r. Charlet Master of University College in Oxford, desiring that I would visit D^r. George Clarke, & consult with him about the best way of securing the Great Collection of Pamphlets made during the time of the Civil Wars, in Case my Lord will not purchase them; the University being unwilling that so useful a parcel should be distracted, & torn in pieces.[5]

3. Mr John Frank came to peruse the MS. 33.A.3.[6]

15 December 1720.

4. I brought hither the 23 old Charters which Mr Sanderson gave me yesterday.[7]

17 December 1720.

5. I received a Letter from Dr Sherard, acquainting me that Mr Smith of Venice ha's actually sold his MSS. (during his Treaty with my Lord, about them,) to the Earl of Sunderland for £1500, & ha's received part of the Money.[8] That

---

  [1] Cf. 5 Dec. 1720, item 6, and footnote.
  [2] A reference to this proof impression (that of the 2nd Great Seal of the Commonwealth, 1651) in Harley's possession is made by Vertue in his *Note Books* (Walpole Soc.), v, 48, and in his work, *Medals, Coins, Great Seals, Impressions, From the Elaborate Works of Thomas Simon*, 1753 (see Plates VI, VII for engravings, dated 1744, of Harley's proof impression in wax). Thomas Simon was a medallist and seal engraver (1623–65). On the Commonwealth Great Seals see A. B. and A. Wyon, *The Great Seals of England*, 1887, pp. 90–94.
  [3] Cf. 9 Dec. 1720. Harley had bought a copy at Cambridge 'some time ago', not being satisfied at Reading's not having sent the copy for him promptly (see Harley's letter to Wanley, dated 11 Dec. 1720, in Welbeck Wanleyana).
  [4] Cf. 7 Dec. 1720.
  [5] Charlett's letter is Harl. 3778, f. 63. The ref. is to the Thomason Tracts (acquired by the British Museum in 1762): see A. Esdaile, *The British Museum Library*, 1946, p. 182. On the subject of Harley's projected purchase and the University of Oxford negotiations see S. G. Gillam, 'The Thomason Tracts', *BLR* ii, no. 27 (Aug. 1948), pp. 221–5. Cf. also 15 Jan. 1723/4, item 10, and footnote.
  [6] i.e. Harl. 3.
  [7] Harl. Charters endorsed by Wanley '15 Dec. 1720' are: III. C. 37; III. D. 10, 25, 59; III. E. 3; III. F. 47; III. G. 10, 34; 112. A. 35; 112. B. 12, 23, 49, 50; 112. C. 23; 112. D. 47; 112. F. 18.
  [8] Cf. 7 Nov. 1720, and footnote. Sherard's letter, dated 17 Dec. 1720, is Harl. 3781, f. 56; it was forwarded to Harley at Wimpole (see address on f. 57 in Wanley's hand). Wanley visited the Earl of Sunderland's (to look at MSS. bought of Smith of Venice) on 6 Feb. 1722/3 (item 7).

he (the D^r.) has sent away my Letter to Mr Sam. Palmer in Cyprus;[1] and ha's actually written to Turkey, in Order to procure for my Lord the Greek MSS. at at [*sic*] Nemenia;[2] the Books printed by the Greeks at Jassi, Buchorest, &c.[3] The old Marble Inscriptions which he ha's caused lately to be brought to Smyrna, the MS. Octateuch, Catena upon the Bible, &c.[4]

21 December 1720.

6. Being in the City, I laid aside (for my Lords Inspection) several Books in Mr Bowyers Ware-house;[5] and some others in Mr Bateman's Shop.[6]

22 December 1720.

7. Mr Noel came to me, & said that some of his Cases are actually deliver'd into the Custom-house.[7]

8. M^r. Hay gave me a List of Books & MSS. which Mr Andrew Hay ha's lately bought in Italy.[8] Mr Hay further said that the Chief Porter of the Custom-house ha's undertaken to bring up his Things from onboard the Martha, which ha's now performed almost Three Quarantines.[9]

24 December 1720.

9. Mr Virtue came to finish his Drawing from S^t. Æthelwold's Benedictionale: but could not.[10]

2 January 1720/I.

10. The 26th past I went to Mr Noels, and went through with [him] all his **Cases** lately arrived, separating those which I thought might probably be for my Lords turn, from the rest; and afterwards, disposed that parcel so reserved for my Lord, into some sort of Order; and employed the four following days in taking a Catalogue of them for my Lords Perusal. /[11]

1. The 31 past, I went to Mr Bowyer, and in his Ware-house, laid aside many more of his old books for my Lord, in Case he shall please to like them.[12] p. 66
(f. 34*b*)

3 January 1720/I.

2. Mr Baron Price enquiring if here may be any old Writings concerning the Manors of Blaen Kuney, Dina, & Mera, in Com Brecon I made some Search.

---

[1] Cf. 13 Dec. 1720, item 14.   [2] Cf. 21 Nov. 1720, and footnote.
[3] Cf. 18 Jan. 1719/20, item 4, and footnote 10.
[4] For the marble inscriptions cf. 3 Feb. 1724/5, for the Octateuch cf. 4 May 1721, item 16; the Catena was subsequently Harl. 5677 (cf. 6 Aug. 1725, no. 1 in list of Greek MSS.).
[5] Cf. 2 Jan. (item 1), 11 Jan. (item 9), 13 Jan. (item 12), and 16 Jan. (item 4) 1720/1.
[6] Cf. 13 Jan. 1720/1, item 12.   [7] Cf. 17 Nov. 1720, item 7, and footnote.
[8] Cf. 26 Apr. 1720, item 18, and footnote, for commission to Andrew Hay to acquire MSS. for Harley in France and Italy.
[9] 'His Things' probably refers to the 'Ritratti' sent by Andrew Hay from Italy; cf. 26 Jan. (item 4), 8 Feb. (item 3), 20 Feb. (item 5), and 3 Mar. (item 1) 1720/1 (when they were returned to George Hay). Padre Orlandi is presumably Pellegrino Antonio Orlandi (1660–1727), Bolognese author of works related to the history of engraving and printing and of *L'Abecedario Pittorico*, 1719, &c. For an account of Orlandi see Hoefer, *Nouvelle Biographie Générale*, xxxvii (1862), pp. 798–9. We are indebted to Mr. Croft Murray for this information.   [10] Cf. 5 Dec. 1720, item 6, and footnote.
[11] Cf. 17 Nov. 1720, item 7, and footnote.   [12] Cf. 21 Dec. 1720, and footnote.

3. Mr Jeremy o Connor came, saying that he is an Antiquary, & skilful in the old Irish Language, & hearing that here are old MSS. in the Irish Language, was very desirous of perusing some of them. I brought him that marked 39.B.17.[1]

4 January 1720
1.

4. M^r O Connor came again: & I shewed him the Cartulary of a Chantry founded within the Cathedral Church of Waterford.[2]

5 January 1720
1.

5. Mr Christ. Bateman came.

7 January 1720
1.

6. M^r. Sanderson returned the MS.[3] he borrowed the 1 of December last. and told me what is bidden for Mr Mickleton's MSS. & what price they are held up at.[4]

9 January 1720
1.

7. My Lord went to Mr Noel's & inspected his Books lately brought from Germany; and selected a parcel from among them, which being afterward consider'd by Mr Noel, he sett a price upon.[5]

11 January 1720
1.

8. M^r. Sanderson (with my Lords Permission) borrowed the MS. 90.C.15.[6]

9. Mr Bowyer came, desiring my Lord to look into his Ware-house soon.[7] And sayd he was going to treat again about the remainder of A.D. Batteleys Library.[8]

12 January 1720
1.

10. I compared a parcel of Books of Sculpture, sent in by Mr Noel, with others here before.

13 January 1720
21.

11. I brought the Printed Catalogue of Hohendorffs Library, which the Widow sent to him, at the same time as She was about selling the same to his Imperial Majesty.[9] Mr Noel present's it to my Lord.

12. My Lord sent me to S^t. Pauls Coffee-house to look upon the late Earl of Stamfords books:[10] and his Lordship look'd upon some others with Mr Bateman[11] & Mr Bowyer.[11]

---

[1] Cf. 4 Jan. 1720/1, item 4, and 4 June 1722, item 6. The MS. is Harl. 432.
[2] i.e. Harl. 3765. (Cf. 3 Jan. 1720/1, item 3.) [3] i.e. Harl. 1584.
[4] Cf. 25 Feb. 1719/20, item 14, and footnote. [5] Cf. 17 Nov. 1720, item 7, and footnote.
[6] i.e. Harl. 1583 (returned 23 Mar. 1720/1). [7] Cf. 21 Dec. 1720, and footnote.
[8] Cf. 11 Jan. 1719/20, item 3, and footnote.
[9] i.e. the Emperor Charles VI (see the footnote to 11 Jan. 1719/20, item 7).
[10] Cf. item 13 below, and footnote. [11] Cf. 21 Dec. 1720, and footnote.

13. My Lord directed me to ask Mr Hill the Painter to buy those few Books of the Earl of Stamfords Library which he wants, at the approaching Auction. /[1]

14 January 1720

I.

p. 67
(f. 35a)

1. Dr. Fiddes came to see things relating to Cardinal Wolsey.[2]
2. Mr Harbin came; & I shewed him the Codex Aureus, and other curious MSS.

16 January 1720

I.

3. I again Visited the late Earl of Stamfords Books; and having made the necessary Remarks, I visited Mr Hill the Painter, & deliver'd the Catalogue to him, that he may bid for my Lord, at the approaching Auction.[3]

4. My Lord sent in a small Parcel of books which he lately bought of Mr Bowyer.[4]

5. Mr Noel sent in the Parcel of Printed Books & MSS. which my Lord lately laid aside at his house.[5] The MSS. are

    1. Biblia SS. ex traductione D. Hieronymi. Voll. 2 grandioris molis. membr. antiq.[6]
    3. Passionale, 3 Voluminibus grandioribus. membr. antiq.[7]
    6. S. Ambrosius de Officijs. Idem, de Resurrectione Domini. Idem, de Poenitentia. Ejusdem Hexaemeron. Idem de Paradyso. membr. fol. mag. antiq.[8]
    7. S. Gregorij Papæ I. Moralia in Librum Job. Voll. 3. fol. membr. antiq.[9]
    10. Excerpta de quibusdam Opusculis S. Augustini. fol. membr. antiq.[10]
    11. S. Gregorij Papæ I, Homiliæ in Ezechielem. fol. membr. antiq.[11]
    12. Joannis Cassiani Collationes. fol. membr. antiq.[12]
    13. D. Augustini Sermones in Evangelium Joannis. Ejusdem Homiliæ in Epistolam I. D. Johannis. fol. membr. antiq.[13]
    14. Hesychij Presbyteri in Leviticum, Libri VII. fol. min. crass. membr. exemplar vetustissimum.[14]
    15. Explanationes Servij in Vergilium. 4to. ampl. membr. Codex valde antiquus & optimæ notæ.[15]
    16. Glosa et Interpretatio nominum Hebræorum, quæ sunt in Libris Divinis. Collectio Glose Novi & Veteris Testamenti. 4to. ampl. membr. antiq.[16]
    17. Lectiones Evangeliorum, ad usum Ecclesiæ Archiepiscopalis Meymdeburgensis, ut videtur. 4to. membr. opt. script.[17]
    18. S. Gregorij Magni Dialogorum Liber. 4to. membr. antiq.[18]
    19. Beda super Canonicas Epistolas. 4to. membr. antiq.[19]
    20. Officia pro Infirmis Defunctis, atq[ue] Sepeliendis 4to. membr.[20]

---

[1] The auction took place 16 Jan. 1720/1, at T. Ballard, Paul's Coffee-House. Cf. also item 12 above, and 16 Jan. (item 3) and 19 Jan. (items 5 and 8) 1720/1. For books kept out of the auction by the Countess of Stamford see 19 Jan. 1720/1, item 8, and footnote.
[2] Cf. 15 Jan. 1719/20, item 5, and footnote.   [3] Cf. 13 Jan. 1720/1, item 13, and footnote.
[4] Cf. 21 Dec. 1720, and footnote.   [5] Cf. 9 Jan. 1720/1.
[6] Harl. 2798, 2799.   [7] Harl. 2800–2.   [8] Harl. 3042.   [9] Harl. 3052–4.
[10] Harl. 3050.   [11] Harl. 3055.   [12] Harl. 3101.   [13] Harl. 3114.
[14] Harl. 3032.   [15] Harl. 2782.   [16] Harl. 3058.
[17] Harl. 2898. (The 'Use' is derived apparently from the colophon on f. 43.)
[18] Harl. 3076.   [19] Harl. 3075.   [20] Harl. 2963.

21. Codex chartaceus & squalidus. Turcice. 4ᵗᵒ.[1]
22. Horæ B. V. Mariæ. 4ᵗᵒ. Illum. membr.[2]
23. Iterum. 4ᵗᵒ. min. Codex egregie Illum.[3]
24. Rursus. 4ᵗᵒ. min. Codex mutilatus. membr.[4]
25. Adhuc. 8ᵛᵒ. member. [sic] Codex ἀκέφαλος. /[5]

p. 68
(f. 35b)

17 January 1720
I.

1. I wrote to Mr Chapman to come hither to morrow.

18. January 1720
I.

2. My Lord sent in 2 MSS. viz.
   1. Cæsaris Calandrini Vindex Feri & Ruperti. fol. min. The Original Licensed for the Press.[6]
   2. James Mab's Observations Touching some of the more Solemne Tymes, &c. fol. min. the Original.[7]

3. I compared the Books lately sent in by Mr Noel; & found all right.[8]

4. Mr Chapman came; & I deliver'd 20 MSS. to him to be Bound.

19 January 1720
I.

5. My Lord sent in an old MS. Greek Psalter, which formerly belonged to a Monastery on Mount Olivet and was bought at the Present Auction of the late Earl of Stamfords Books.[9]

6. My Lord directed me to let Mr Sanderson know that he is willing to buy Mr Mickleton's MSS. &c at the price now sett upon them by his Relations.[10]

7. My Lord Order'd me to lett Mr Roger Gale know that he is willing to grant his Request as to Conan Earl of Britain's 3 Charters, & the Series of the Archdeacons of Richmond; And I wrote accordingly.[11]

8. My Lord is willing that I shall Inspect the MSS. which the Lady Stamford kept out of the Auction.[12]

9. Dr. Sherard came, & said that although the Archbishop of Canterbury ha's offer'd to treat with him for those old Coins which still remain in his Possession; (he having sold many already to the D. of Devonshire, & the Earl of

[1] Harl. 5522.   [2] Harl. 2917.   [3] Harl. 2865.
[4] Harl. 2947 (ff. 14, 15 mutilated).   [5] Harl. 2932 (text beginning imperfect on f. 8).
[6] Harl. 5096. (The licence itself, signed by Thomas Goad, dated 1 Mar. 1625/[26], is on f. 1.)
[7] Harl. 5077.   [8] Cf. 16 Jan. 1720/1, item 5.
[9] Harl. 5571. (The Greek note of ownership on f. 1* is of the monastery of S. Maria 'in Organo' (al. 'in Organio') at Verona, originally a Benedictine, but from 1444 onwards an Olivetan, house (see G. Cappelletti, *Le Chiese d'Italia*, x. 810–11). We are indebted to Mr. T. C. Skeat for the identification of the monastery. (With ref. to the sale of the Earl of Stamford's books cf. inscription in the MS. at f. 1*.) The auction had been held 16 Jan. 1720/1; cf. also 13 Jan. 1720/1, item 13, and footnote.
[10] Cf. 7 Jan. 1720/1 and see 25 Feb. 1719/20, item 14, and footnote.
[11] See 12 Jan. 1719/20, item 3, and footnote; and cf. 25 Jan. 1720/1.
[12] i.e. out of the auction of the Earl of Stamford's books referred to above (item 5) and 13 Jan. (item 13) 1720/1. These MSS. are subsequently referred to under 2 Feb. (item 6) and 17 Mar. 1720/1; 1, 3, 4, and 5 Apr., 19 May (item 8), 27 Nov. (item 8), and 28 Nov. (item 9) 1721.

Penbroke [*sic*]) my Lord may have them if he please's at his own Price; & any book he ha's.[1]

10. M[r]. Virtue came to finish his Drawing;[2] & brought a Latin MS. Bible to be sold, which was thought too dear.

20 January 1720
——
I.

11. My Lord sent in 9 Spanish Volumes in folio from the Rev[d]. D[r]. Colebatch of Trinity-College in Cambridge.

23 January 1720
——
I.

12. M[r]. White of Warwick came to see the Library; & I shewed him some of the fine Books. He ha's promised me to speak to M[r] Fish of Warwick to sell his old Deeds & Rolls to my Lord;[3] and will send up to my Lord one of the Great Round Stones which were shot against Kenilworth-Castle in the Seige thereof by the Army of K. Henry III: my Lord paying the Charges.

24 January 1720
——
I.

13. I deliver'd 23 Books, with their Titles, to M[r] Elliot the Binder.

14. A Letter sent to M[r] Chapman the Binder, with the Title of a MS. which he left behind.

15. A Letter sent to M[r] Gregory the Joyner, directing him to bring in 3 Strong & New Cases for Books. /

25 January 1720
——
21.

p. 69
(f. 36a)

1. M[r] Roger Gale came with his Amanuensis, (M[r] Proby) & transcribed a Series of the Richmond-Archdeacons from D[r]. Hutton's Papers.[4] He received Three

---

[1] Cf. 6 Feb. 1720/1, item 11. The Abp. of Canterbury was William Wake. On Abp. Wake's interest in coins and medals see N. Sykes, *William Wake, Archbishop of Canterbury, 1657–1737*, ii (1957), pp. 252–3. The coll. went with his MSS. to Christ Church, Oxford, and is now on loan to the Ashmolean Museum. On the Earl of Pembroke's other interests cf. 22 Jan. 1719/20, item 12, and 15 July 1720, item 5, and footnotes.   [2] i.e. from the Benedictional of St. Ethelwold (cf. 5 Dec. 1720, item 6, and footnote).
[3] Wanley's knowledge of the deeds and rolls of 'Mr. Fish of Warwick' dates from his early days at Coventry, since we know from Harl. 7505 that in 1691 (when he was 19) Wanley was making facsimile copies of a number of charters that were then in the custody of 'Mr. James Fish of Warwick'. This was James Fish I who died in May 1702: he had been a schoolmaster and was parish clerk and Keeper of the Beauchamp Chapel, and much interested in records: his cat. of the Chapel muniments (now Bodl. Rawlinson D. 868) was completed in 1694, and Wanley himself had compiled the cat. of the MSS. of St. Mary's Church, Warwick, which was printed in 1697 in *CMA* ii, nos. 6683–6715. (His acquaintance with James Fish Senior is illustrated by Wanley's allusion to him under no. 6711: 'Mr. Fish tells me that the rest of this Book and many other antient writings of his, are at Mr. Lucie's of Charlecote now'; and cf. Wanley's letter from Coventry to Charlett, 15 Oct. 1694 [Bodl. Ballard MS. 13, f. 55].) The owner at the time of the Diary entry must be James Fish II, his son, who was a surveyor. The probability is that the deeds in question related to St. Mary's and especially to the Beauchamp Chapel and had been removed by James Fish I into his own 'custody'; this would explain their escaping the disastrous Warwick fire of 1694, but their present whereabouts are not known. On James Fish I see *The Restoration of the Beauchamp Chapel at St. Mary's Collegiate Church, Warwick, 1674–1742*, ed. Sir William Dugdale, Bart., F.S.A. (Roxburghe Club, 1956). 'Mr. White of Warwick' has not been identified: it may be worth noting that Mary, the eldest daughter of Sir William Dugdale the antiquary (1605–86), married a Daniel White. Other Fish documents copied by H. W. in 1694, are Harl. 6466, ff. 33–34[b], and 37–37[b].
[4] i.e. Harl. 6950–85 and 7519–21.

83

Charters of Conan Earl of Richmond. (marked 48.G.40, 42, & 43) for which he gave me his Note:[1] and he saw a great Number of rare Manuscripts & Charters. And he promised not only, upon his next return from the Countrey, to give to the Library some Original Letters of learned Foreigners written to his Father the late Dean of York;[2] but to serve my Lord in any other Matter; particularly with relation to M[r] Warburton's MSS.[3] He likewise desire's to borrow the MSS. 61.C.1. & 36.C.19, with the Charter 48.G.41. for a few days.[4]

26 January 1720
21.

2. M[r] Creak Fellow of 'S[t]. Johns in' ['' *deleted in MS.*] King's College brought a Fellow of S[t]. Johns in Cambridge to see the Library; & I shewed them many fine books, &c. M[r] Creak left with me a MS. whose owner offer's it for what my Lord will give. M[r] Creak also said that M[r]. Hawes Chaplain to the Earl of Winchelsea, being about to go to East-well & reside there having a Study of good Books, is taking a Catalogue of them, in Order to dispose of some of them; and that he will bring me the said Catalogue, in a few days.[5]

3. A Letter sent to M[r] Cowse the Bookseller, desiring him to send M[r] Strype's new Edition of Stow's Survey of London to my Lord.[6]

4. M[r] George Hay came, & said that he hopes the great Collection of Ritratti which his Brother lately sent from Italy, may be putt into the Custom-house-Warehouse to morrow.[7]

27 January 1720
21.

5. M[r] Gale sent back the 3 Charters he lately borrowed.[8]

6. M[r]. Rosengrave came, & received from me the Music which he lent to D[r]. Tudway.

7. The L[d]. Bishop of Chester brought the MSS. which my Lord lent to him from those of Seguiers.[9]

28 January 1720
I.

8. M[r] Noel came, & deliver'd to me a late Letter he received from M[r]. Suttie, with another Catalogue of Curious & Fine Books which he ha's lately bought abroad.[10]

---

[1] Cf. 19 Jan. 1720/1, item 7. For the return of the charters cf. 27 Jan. 1720/1, item 5, and his further study of them 18 May 1721, item 3.

[2] i.e. Thomas Gale (c. 1635–1702: Dean of York), whose MSS. with those collected by his eldest son, Roger, were given by the latter to Trinity College, Cambridge, in 1737 (see M. R. James, *Cat. of Western MSS. in the Library of Trinity College, Cambridge*, iii, 1902). The letters to his father from learned correspondents abroad were given to Harley 22 May 1722 (item 7) (= Harl. 7011, ff. 144–6, 148, 150–64).   [3] Cf. 3 Aug. 1720, item 3, and footnote.

[4] The MSS. are Harl. 793 and 236. They were borrowed 1 Feb. 1720/1 (item 4) and returned 24 Feb. 1720/1 (item 2).

[5] i.e. Eastwell Park, Kent, the seat of the Earl of Winchilsea, who at this time was Heneage Finch, 5th Earl (c. 1656–1726). For further refs. to MSS. from Hawes cf. 2 Mar. (item 13), 6 Mar. (items 10 and 13), and 7 Mar. (item 15) 1720/1 (for list).

[6] This refers to the ed. pubd. in 2 folio vols. in 1720 under the title, *A Survey of the Cities of London and Westminster . . . brought down from the Year 1633 . . . to the present year by John Strype*.

[7] Cf. 22 Dec. 1720, item 8, and footnote 9.   [8] Cf. 25 Jan. 1720/1, and footnote.

[9] The Bp. of Chester was Francis Gastrell. There is no previous ref. to this loan.

[10] The last cat. referred to by Wanley as coming from Suttie is under 4 Feb. 1719/20, item 2; no Suttie list, or extracts from one, of about this date has been traced.

31 January 1720
1.

9. I went to Mr George Hay, & look'd out some books for my Lord which lately came from Italy; & he sent them hither, for my Lords Inspection soon after. /[1]

1. Mr Gibson came with a Letter from Mr Smith of Venice, dated 17 January p. 70 last, N.S. who will not abate anything of the Price he Sett upon his MSS. and (f. 36b) consequently, will not accept the Sum which my Lord offer'd him for them.[2] Mr Gibson further said, that he has some few Books on board a Ship now performing Quarantine. And that he has about 15 or 16 good MSS. in a ship now upon the Seas, bound for London.[3] And that he will send hither a Smal parcel for my Lords Inspection, which I some time since laid aside, at his Lodgings.[4]

2. Mr Rowley came and saw some of my Lords fine Books.

1 February, 1720
1.

3. My Lord sent in a transcript of the Works of Michael Servetus; made A.D. 1667.[5]

4. Mr Roger Gale sent his Note for the Charter 48.C.41, & the MSS. 36.C.19, & 61.C.1. which were deliver'd to his Amanuensis accordingly.[6]

2 February 1720
1.

5. Mr Bowyer sent the Catalogue of a Study of Books which he lately bought. I perused it, & marked some.[7]

6. I went to the Countess of Stamford's & Saw the MSS. which were kept out of the present Auction of her late Lords Books. But they being sett in Confusion, she said she would lett me know when I may come & putt them in Order, & take a Catalogue of them.[8]

7. A Letter written to Mr Wyat the Bookseller to attend upon Mr Prior.

3 February 1720
21.

8. I went to Mr Bowyer, & laid aside a parcel of Books for my Lords inspection.[9]

4 February 1720
21.

9. Mr Noel came with a Letter & Catalogue lately received from Mr Suttie.[10]

---

[1] Cf. 7 Feb. 1720/1, item 15, for completion of transaction.
[2] Cf. 7 Nov. 1720, and footnote.
[3] Cf. 9 Mar. (item 6) and 20 Mar. (item 7) 1720/1; 18 May (item 6), 26 May (item 18), 3 June (item 3), 16 June (item 6), 17 June (item 12, for list), and 20 June (item 5) 1721.
[4] 'Some time since' = 7 Nov. 1720. Cf. 9 Mar. 1720/1, item 6; 14 Apr. (item 3), 25 Apr. (item 24), 27 Apr. (item 6) 1721 (for list and price).
[5] Not identified.
[6] Cf. 25 Jan. 1720/1, and footnote. The charter ref. is a slip for the 48. G. 41 given under 25 Jan. 1720/1.
[7] Cf. 9 May 1721, item 10, and footnote.   [8] Cf. 19 Jan. 1720/1, item 8.
[9] Cf. 9 May 1721, item 10, and footnote.   [10] Not traced.

85

6 February 1720
—
21.

10. The B^p. of Peterburgh came to peruse D^r. Hutton's Collections made from the Registers of the See of Lincoln.[1]

11. D^r. Sherard came, & I spake to him about his Coins.[2]

12. Mr Will. Thomas came.

13. My Lord of Peterburgh, borrowed of my Lord five Volumes of D^r. Huttons Collections.[3]

7 February 1720
—
21.

14. Mr Sanderson told me, last night, that Mr Mickleton's MSS. are sold to Mr Spearman.[4]

15. Mr Hay came, & I agreed with him for a small Number of his Printed books, with a Paper MS. in 4to. of Ovids Amatoria;[5] & I sent to his House the remainder, being refused by my Lord. /

p. 71
(f. 37a)

8 February 1720
—
21.

1. Mr Noel came, & left with me Mr Sutties Letter n°. 10, with a Catalogue of books lately bought by him.[6]

2. M^r. James Hill came to see the CODEX AVREVS.

3. Mr Hay brought a Egyptian Scarabæus of Jasper, with Hieroglyphics engraven on the Bottom. He said that he expect's the Ship up to morrow, which will then have performed four Quarantines; and that he will gett out the Ritratti bought in Italy for my Lord, as soon as he possibly can.[7]

9 February 1720
—
21.

4. Mr William Thomas came, and looked into the Papers & MSS. left by Hugh Thomas deceased; & thinks he misse's a Book relating to Glamorganshire.[8]

5. Young Mr Varenne came with a Catalogue of Books about to be sold by Auction.[9] He is the Owner of four Illuminated MSS. of Hours, which my Lord sent down to be looked into.[10]

10 February 1720
—
21.

6. Mr Virtue came to look into Mr John Norden's fine MS. of the Honor of Windsor.[11]

---

[1] i.e. Harl. 6950–54. The Bp. of Peterborough was White Kennett.
[2] Cf. 19 Jan. 1720/1, item 9, and footnote.   [3] Cf. 22 May 1721, item 1, for return of these 5 vols.
[4] Cf. 25 Feb. 1719/20, item 14, and footnote.
[5] Harl. 2537. Cf. 31 Jan. 1720/1, item 9.   [6] Not traced.
[7] Cf. 22 Dec. 1720, item 8, and footnote 9.   [8] Cf. 19 Oct. 1720, and footnote.
[9] Presumably this is the auction referred to under 13, 14, and 15 Feb. 1720/1, and footnote; cf. also 6 Mar. 1720/1, item 7, for ref. to priced cat.
[10] Cf. 27 Feb. (item 4), 1 Mar. (item 7 and footnote for identification of MSS.), and 6 Mar. (item 7, for payment) 1720/1. The price was £21 (Welbeck Wanleyana, Misc. no. 50).   [11] i.e. Harl. 3749.

7. A Letter sent to Mr Chapman the Binder.

8. Mr Gibson came to inform my Lord how to get the Milan-Tully of 1498, in Case he had it not. I told him that my Lord ha's already a very fine Exemplar of it.[1]

13 February 1720
———
21.

9. Mr Chapman the Binder came with the Parcel last deliver'd to him, & recd another to Bind; & did some other work in the Library.

10. Mr Rowley & Mr Bridgeman Came.

11. Mr Varenne brought three Books to shew to my Lord, which were brought hither to me.[2]

14 February 1720
———
21.

12. Mr Varenne took back the Books he left with me yesterday; he not having power to sell them out of the approaching Auction.[2]

13. Mr William Thomas looked again into the late Mr Hugh Thomas's MSS. and is of Opinion that here are not all that were left by the Deceased.[3]

14. Mr Bowyer came, desiring to know when my Lord will call to see those books I laid by.[4]

15 February 1720
———
21.

15. A Letter written to Mr Noel, to attend my Lord to morrow but he came hither before I sent it, and promised to serve my Lord at the Approaching Auction of a foreign Booksellers Books, in Conjunction with other Booksellers here; they intending to hinder Dutch-men, &c. from coming & taking away their Trade twice a year, as they design to do. /[5]

16 February 1720
———
21.

p. 72
(f. 37b)

1. Mr Noel came; having had some discourse with my Lord about taking a Voiage abroad soon, in Order to buy Books.

2. My Lord sent in an antient Gold Ring found at Newbury in Berkshire, which the Lord Bathurst gave him yesterday. There are some Runic Letters discernable upon it.[6]

---

[1] 'the Milan-Tully of 1498' is the 4-vol. ed. of Cicero's works ed. by Alex. Minutianus and printed by Guillaume Le Signerre at Milan, 1498–9. This was the *editio princeps* of Cicero's Works. (*BMC* vi. 790; Hain 5056; GW 6708.)

[2] Cf. 9 Feb. 1720/1, item 5, and footnote.   [3] Cf. 9 Feb. 1720/1, item 4, and footnote.

[4] Cf. 3 Feb. 1720/1, item 8, and footnote.

[5] This refers to T. Ballard's sale at Paul's Coffee House 20 Feb. 1720/1, at which Harley purchased the MSS. of N. J. Foucault (d. 7 Feb. 1720/1) which are dated by Wanley 23 Feb. 1720/1. Cf. also 18, 21, 22, and 23 Feb. (items 10 and 11, with list) and 24 Feb. 1720/1; 2 Mar. (items 10 and 14 (list)), 4 Mar. (item 4), and 16 Mar. (item 17, for a stray MS.) 1720/1. Cf. Wanley's remarks under 26 Mar. 1723 (item 15) about some Dutch booksellers in London. The MSS. bought through Bacon were paid for 3 May 1721 (item 13).

[6] This ring has not been traced. The donor was Allen Bathurst (1684–1775), Baron Bathurst 1712, and 1st Earl Bathurst 1772: he was distinguished for his taste and learning and was a friend of Pope.

18 February 1720/21.

3. I inspected the MSS. which are to be sold in the approaching Auction; & found some fit to be bought.[1]

20 February 1720/21.

4. My Lord sent in four Rolls, or parcels of Written Papers, recover'd from the Brother of Hugh Thomas deceased.[2]

5. My Lord sent in a Parcel of Prints of Heads, or Ritratti, being in Number about 2420, collected by Padre Orlandi, & bought for his Lordship in Italy, by Mr Andrew Hay.[3]

21 February 1720/21.

6. Mr Morley brought some of his Friends to see the Library.

7. Mr Noel came & shewed me that some Books were bought for my Lord in the present Auction, cheap.[4]

8. Mr Bacon came, & said that he having bought some MSS. cheap, at the present Auction, he is willing to lett my Lord have them.[4]

22 February 1720/21.

9. A Letter sent to Mr Bacon for those MSS. which he soon after sent by his own Servant.[4]

23 February 1720/21.

10. M^r. Noel brought some more MSS. & 3 Printed books bought very cheap in the Present Auction.[4]

11. M^r. Hay sent in a few old Printed Books, which I laid aside, this Day, at his House: some of which my Lord kept at a Price agreed upon.[5] NB. Most of the MSS. which my Lord thought fit to have from the present Auction,[6] being now brought in, I here specifie their Titles, 'leaving room for those which remain; & shall' ['‘ *deleted in MS.*] and shall putt this day at the Head of each of them. vid. infra pag. 74, & 76. The MSS. bought by Mr Bacon.
  1. Libri, Thobie, Judith, & Sapientie, Glossati. Eleganti & vetusta manu. 4to.[7]
  2. Recueil des Litanies de plusieurs Saints & Saintes. 4to. chart. manu recent.[8]
  3. Breviarium Ecclesiæ (*Cathedralis?*) Parisiensis. 8vo. crass. membr.[9]
  4. Manuale Precum, in usum cujusdam Prælati, ut videtur nitide descriptum & illum. 8vo. oblong.[10]

---

[1] Cf. 15 Feb. 1720/1, and footnote.   [2] Cf. 19 Oct. 1720, and footnote.
[3] See 22 Dec. 1720, item 8, and footnote 9. They were returned 3 Mar. 1720/1 (item 1).
[4] Cf. 15 Feb. 1720/1, and footnote. For lists see 23 Feb. (item 11), 2 Mar. (item 14), and 16 Mar. (item 17, for a stray MS.) 1720/1, and footnotes thereto for identifications.
[5] Cf. 27 Feb. (item 5) and 2 Mar. 1720/1.
[6] Cf. 15 Feb. 1720/1, and footnote.   [7] Harl. 4985 = Ballard Sale-Cat., p. 2, lot 16.
[8] Harl. 2995 = Ballard Sale-Cat., p. 3, lot 17.
[9] Harl. 2927 = Ballard Sale-Cat., p. 4, lot 13.   [10] Harl. 2924 = Ballard Sale-Cat., p. 4, lot 6.

Quibus addi possunt,

5. Heures; imprimees a Paris, 1504, par Ant. Verard, sur Velin. 4to. illum.[1]
6. A Chinese Case of Books, being Eight in Number. /

Books bought for my Lord, by Mr Noel.

p. 73
(f. 38a)

1. Rabani Mauri Expositio super Matthæum. fol. vetust.[2]
2. Lectionarium Ecclesiæ Moissiacensis manu vestust. 4to. mag.[3]
3. Missale Ecclesiæ Moissiacensis. man. vetust. 4to. crass.[4]
4. Livre de Faulconerie, par Jehan de Francyeres, fol. min. membr. illum.[5]
5. Traitté du Droit Ecclesiastique & Seculier translaté en François, par Mestre Silvestre Guerin, l'an 1477. chart. fol. min. vetust.[6]
6. Decisiones Novæ Rotæ Romanæ, factæ per Doct Wilhelmum Horborch, &c. A.D. 1376. fol. min. chart.[7]
7. Les Voiages de Jehan de Mandeville Chivaler. } Un Traitte Chronologique. Imperf. } membr. 4to. quadrato.[8]
8. Heures al Usaige de Paris, imprimées l'an 1498. 4to. chart.[9]
9. Livre des Prouffitz Champestres & Ruraulx, compilé par Pierre des Crescens, & translaté en Françoys. Imprimé a Paris, par Jehan Bonhomme, 1486. fol. min. avec. fig.[10]
10. Smaragdi Diadema Monachorum. 4to. manu vet.[11]
11. Liber Statutorum pro Aulicis Plessæis, a Simone Bigoto restauratorum, A.D. 1571. 4to perg.[12]
12. Confessio Generale de Languedoc. (Manuale Precum, &c. lingua Occitana) 8vo. membr. illum.[13]
13. Devises pour les Tapisseries du Roy, ou sont representez les quatre Elemens, et les quatre Saisons de l'Année. Peintes en Mignature par J. Bailly, Peintre du Roy en son Academie Royale de Peinture & Sculpture, à Paris, 1669. fol.

This was the Kings Book, & ha's the Royal Binding. This Painter ha's gotten the Prints purposely wrought-off for him, without the Words, which are added, for Magnificence-sake, by a fine Pen: and ha's performed his part upon the said Prints, extremely well.[14]

24 February 1720
21.

1. M^r. Noel brought a printed Book which he bought for my Lord at the present Auction.[15]

[1] Probably Bohatta (1924), no. 791 = Ballard Sale-Cat., p. 3, lot 24(?).
[2] Harl. 3104 = Ballard Sale-Cat., p. 1, lot 8.   [3] Harl. 2914 = Ballard Sale-Cat., p. 1, lot 11.
[4] Harl. 2893 = Ballard Sale-Cat., p. 1, lot 10.
[5] Harl. 4497 = Ballard Sale-Cat., p. 9, lot 60 (£1. 1s. 6d.).
[6] Harl. 4475 = Ballard Sale-Cat., p. 5, lot 24 (2s. 6d.).
[7] Harl. 3769 = Ballard Sale-Cat., p. 5, lot 25 (6s. 6d.).
[8] Harl. 3940 = Ballard Sale-Cat., p. 7, lot 39 (8s. 8d.).
[9] Unidentifiable: Bohatta (1924) gives nearly 30 eds. in this year.
[10] Printed Jean Bonhomme, Paris, 1486 (GW 7830) = Ballard Sale-Cat., p. 8, lot 51 (18s. 6d.).
[11] Harl. 3078 = Ballard Sale-Cat., p. 3, lot 15.
[12] Harl. 5391 = Ballard Sale-Cat., p. 11, lot 64 (2s. 6d.).
[13] Harl. 3183 = Ballard Sale-Cat., p. 4, lot 12.
[14] Harl. 4377 = Ballard Sale-Cat., p. 15, lot 68. (A similar MS. of designs by Bailly, from Colbert's library, is Harl. 4861, which was acquired 21 Dec. 1723.)
[15] Cf. 15 Feb. 1720/1, and footnote.

2. Mr Gale sent back the 2 MSS. & the Deed which he lately borrowed; & I burnt the Note he gave for them.[1]

3. Mr Hay sent in some Books relating to Painting, &c. for my Lord to see.[2]

27 February 1720
——
21.

4. Mr Varenne came about the 4 MSS. he left with me, & I offer'd him a Price for them.[3]

5. Mr Hay came desiring to know my Lords pleasure relating to the Printed Books he sent in some days agoe. / [4]

p. 74
(f. 38b)

28 February 1720
——
21.

1. Dr. Fiddis came to Study in the Library.

2. A Letter to Mr Cowse; desiring him to send my Lord two New-printed Books.

3. Mr Noel brought two fresh Letters, & two Catalogues lately received from Mr Suttie now in Italy.[5]

4. Dr. Astry [Archer *written first and deleted*] came desiring to peruse some of Dr. Hutton's Papers.[6]

5. Mr Garnier came, & look'd into some Oriental MSS.

1 March 1720
——
I.

6. Mr. Roger Gale came, & look'd into some of the Chartularies of Edmund-bury-Abbey.[7]

7. Mr Varenne came about the 4 MSS. Prayer-books: & we agreed for them.[8]

8. Mr Woodman sent in a few printed Books I laid by at his Shop.

9. Mr Cowse sent in the two Books as desired.

2 March 1720
——
I.

10. Mr. Noel came, & after him his Porter brought a Parcel of Books & MSS. bought at the present Auction; but most of them without my Lords Commission.[9]

11. Mr Hay came, & took with him those books of his last Parcels which my Lord did not like.[10]

---

[1] i.e. Harl. 793 and 236 and Harl. Ch. 48. G. 41 (borrowed on 1 Feb. 1720/1 (item 4)).
[2] Cf. 2 Mar. (item 11), 3 Mar. (item 1), 6 Mar. (item 12), and 7 Mar. (item 14) 1720/1.
[3] Cf. 9 Feb. 1720/1, item 5, and footnote 10.   [4] Cf. 23 Feb. 1720/1, item 11, and footnote 5.
[5] Not traced.   [6] i.e. Harl. 6950–85, 7519–21.
[7] For details of Bury St. Edmunds Cartularies in the Library about this date see footnote to 23 June 1720, item 8. Cf. 8 Apr. (item 15), 11 Apr. (item 19), and 17 Apr. (item 7) 1721.
[8] The MSS. were given this day's date by Wanley and three so identified are as follows: Harl. 2863, 2936, 2969. Cf. 9 Feb. 1720/1, item 5, and footnote 10.
[9] Cf. 15 Feb. 1720/1, and footnote. For list of those bought without commission see item 14 below.
[10] Previous parcels sent in by Hay are mentioned under 23 Feb. (item 11) and 24 Feb. (item 3) 1720/1.

12. M[r] Elliot came & took away part of a parcel he is to Bind for my Lord.

13. M[r] Creake came, about some MSS. which M[r] Hawes Chaplain to the Earl of Winchelsea ha's to dispose of.[1] And M[r] Creake look'd into some of my Lords MSS.

14. The MSS. bought by M[r] Noel at the Present Auction[2] (mostly) without Commission, are:

    A Decad of Livy, in old French, fol. velum. imperf. at both Ends.[3]

    An Old French Romance of Galehan. fol. Velum.[4]

    Le Roman du Roi Marc, fils du Roi Felis. fol. min. Velum; impf at the End, but considerable for the old Pictures.*[5]

    L'Estrif & Debat de Vertu & Fortune par Martin le Franc. 4to. mag. pap.[6]

    Rolland, Aymery, & other Romances in old French Verse. 4to. Velum. Imperf. at beg.[7]

    Roman de Florimont par Aymez de Chastillon in French Verse, 4to. written A.D. 1285.*[8]

    Pauli Æmilij de Gestis Francorum libri IV & V. 4to. membr. nit. script.[9]

    Another copy of Florimon written A.D. 1323. A History [Chronicle *written first and deleted*] of the Holy War, in old French Prose. 4to. membr.[10]

    Psalterium cum Canticis Sacris, Litania, & Precibus. 8vo. mag. nit. script. membr.[11]

    Mariale; seu Sermones de B. V. Maria. 8vo. membr. man antiq.[12]

    Boece de Consolacion, en Francoys par Jean de Meun. 8vo. membr.[13]

    Les 6, 7, 8, 9, & 10 Livres de Vie de Crist. 8vo. crass. membr. illum[14]

    Psalterium; cum Magnificat. 12mo. membr. nit. script.[15]

    Breviarium Cænomanense. 16to. membr. crass.*[16]

    Breviarium secundum Consuetudinem Curie Romane. vol. pusillo membr. /[17]

3 March 1720
———
I.

p. 75
(f. 39*a*)

1. Mr Hay came, & agreed to receive back padre Orlandi's 12 Volumes of Ritratti; which I sent away accordingly.[18] He also desired me to take for him a List of those books about Painting, &c. which my Lord is willing to buy.[19]

---

[1] Cf. 26 Jan. 1720/1, item 2, and footnote.

[2] Cf. item 10 above and see 15 Feb. 1720/1, and footnote. Another MS. bought without commission at Ballard's auction was Harl. 4386 (cf. 16 Mar. 1720/1, item 17).

[3] Harl. 4427 = Ballard Sale-Cat., p. 31, lot 176 (11*s*.).

[4] Harl. 4419 = Ballard Sale-Cat., p. 35, lot 236.

[5] Harl. 4389 = Ballard Sale-Cat., p. 35, lot 237.

[6] Harl. 4474 = Ballard Sale-Cat., p. 9, lot 65 (3*s*. 6*d*.).

[7] Harl. 1321 = Ballard Sale-Cat., p. 32, lot 192 (8*s*. 6*d*.).

[8] Harl. 4487 = Ballard Sale-Cat., p. 50, lot 303.

[9] Harl. 3711 = Ballard Sale-Cat., p. 38, lot 176.

[10] Harl. 3983 = Ballard Sale-Cat., p. 55, lot 338.   [11] Harl. 2949 = Ballard Sale-Cat., p. 4, lot 5.

[12] Harl. 3176 = Ballard Sale-Cat., p. 3, lot 26(?).

[13] Harl. 4330 = Ballard Sale-Cat., p. 8, lot 52 (15*s*. 6*d*.).

[14] Harl. 4328 = Ballard Sale-Cat., p. 4, lot 8.

[15] Harl. 2879 (the Magnificat is at f. 269) = Ballard Sale-Cat., p. 4, lot 4(?).

[16] Harl. 2450 (although not dated by Wanley this is the only Le Mans Breviary (Breviarium Cenomanense) in Harl. Coll.; it answers Wanley's description as to size and is a Foucault MS.) = Ballard Sale-Cat., p. 4, lot 15.

[17] Harl. 2852 (perhaps but not certainly). Not identified in Ballard Sale-Cat.

[18] These had been sent in on 20 Feb. 1720/1. Cf. 22 Dec. 1720, item 8, and footnote 9.

[19] Cf. 24 Feb. 1720/1, item 3.

2. A Letter sent to Mr Hesketh, desiring Mr Clayton of Penwortham's Direction.[1]
3. Mr Elliot came, & took away more books to bind.

4 March 1720
I.

4. Mr Noel came, & made up, with me, the Accompt relating to the Books bought for my Lord in the late [present *written first and deleted*] Auction.[2]
5. M^r. Harbyn came, & perused some of my Lords MSS. & desired to borrow one, which my Lord readily granted.[3]
6. My Lord sent in an Old Deed of Hugo de Nevilla, in the seal whereof he is represented fighting with a Lion, as mentioned by Matthew Paris in his History.[4]

6 March 1720
I.

7. M^r. Varenne came & recd his Money for the 4 Primers he left here. He also gave me a prized [*i.e.* priced] Catalogue of the last Auction.[5]
8. Mr William Thomas came to look more into the late Hugh Thomas's Papers.[6]
9. Mr Chapman brought the parcel last deliver'd to him; & received another larger.
10. M^r. Creak came, & [I] went with him to Mr Hawes, whose Study I saw, & cheapened 3 MSS. & an old English Primer printed on Velum.[7]
11. A letter sent to Mr Anstis, acquainting him that my Lord will lend him the Gallia Purpurata.[8]
12. M^r. Hay came, & received from me a List of the Books in his last parcel, which my Lord laid by.[9]
13. I went with Mr Creake to M^r. Hawes, and saw his 4 MSS. & a Primer printed on Velum, in English.[10]

7 March 1720
I.

14. Mr Hay came, & brought me that List, with the Prices of each of the books.[11]

[1] Cf. 10 Mar. 1720/1, item 11, and footnote.
[2] Cf. 15 Feb. 1720/1, and footnote. The lists of books bought by Noel at this auction are under 23 Feb. and 2 Mar. 1720/1. [3] Returned 11 Apr. 1721, item 21.
[4] Harl. Ch. 112. B. 48 is endorsed by Wanley with date 4 Mar. 1720/1: the seal of green wax tallies with Wanley's description; the Hugo de Nevilla is Hugh de Neville of Essex, d. 1235 (on him see *DNB*). For the Matthew Paris ref. see Paris's *Chron. Majora*, ed. H. R. Luard, vi (R.S. 57 (6), 1882), p. 475, and op. cit. iii (R.S. 57 (3), 1876), p. 71, for origin of the scene. Another seal depicting the same subject is attached to Harl. Ch. 54. B. 14, which is not endorsed by Wanley.
[5] Cf. 9 Feb. 1720/1, item 5, and footnote. Three of Varenne's four MSS. are identified in footnote 8 to 1 Mar. 1720/1. [6] See 14 Feb. 1720/1, and footnote 3.
[7] Cf. 26 Jan. 1720/1, item 2, and footnote; for list of MSS. see 7 Mar. 1720/1, item 15.
[8] i.e. Pierre Frizon, *Gallia Purpurata Qua cum Summorum Pontificum, tum Omnium Galliae Cardinalium, qui hactenus Vixere Res Praeclare Gesta continentur, adjectae sunt parmae et earundem Descriptiones*. Paris, 1638. Harley's copy is no. 2050 in Wanley's Cat. of the printed books in the Library at Wimpole, and had the press-mark, VIII. A. 11 (BM Lansdowne 816, f. 44), and is recorded in Minshull's Cat., BM Add. 19749, f. 22; it was in Harley's possession by 14 June 1717 when Wanley's Cat. was completed. Cf. also 7 Mar. 1720/1, item 1; 19 Apr. 1721 (when it was returned).
[9] Cf. 3 Mar. 1720/1, item 1. [10] Cf. item 10 above.
[11] Cf. 6 Mar. 1720/1, item 12.

15. I went to Mr Hawes & bought the MSS. &c. for my Lord.[1] The MSS. are.

    1. S. Ambrosius de Fide. Idem, de Spiritu Sancto. Idem, de Incarnatione Domini. Ejusdem Epistolæ. Ejusdem, Epistola ad Ecclesiam Vercellensem, de Pastore eligendo. Ejusdem, tractatulus super illo Salomonis, ubi dicit Tria esse sibi impossibilia, Quartus penitus ignorare. Explanatio S. Ieronimi super Epistolam Pauli ad Titum. Ejusdem brevis Explanatio super Apocalipsim. Expositio Abbatis Joachim super Apocalipsim. Libellus Ysidori de Significatione nominum Veteris Legis et Evangelij. Tractatus Magri Petri Cardinalis Cameracensis de Potestate Pape, et Concilij Generalis. Questio Francisci de Maironis de Dominio Apostolorum. Questio Magri Walteri Hunt Carmelite, de eo. Quid est Ecclesia. Questio ejusdem de Preeminentia Petri super alios Apostolos. Liber Ysidori de Ortu & Obitu Sanctorum Patrum. Liber Provincialis, de Sedibus Archiepiscopalibus, et Episcopalibus Mundi. fol.[2]

    2. Vincentij Belluacensis Speculi Historialis Libri 16 priores. fol.[3]

    3. Hugo de S. Victore de Sacramentis Christianæ Fidei. 4to exemplar Vet.[4]

    4. Tractatus cujusdam Neoterici de Sacramentis, De Purgatorio, et de Maleficio. 4to. chart. /[5]

1. M^r. Anstis sent for the Gallia Purpurata, which I dd to his Servant.[6]   p. 76 (f. 39b)

2. Mr Cook the Painter came to inform my Lord of a Wonderful fine Silver Tea-Pot, which is to be Sold.

[December *written first and deleted*] 8 March 1720

1.

3. A Letter sent to Mr Chapman, desiring him to come & take his money for Binding the last Parcel.

4. Mr Cook and another Gentleman came with the fine Tea-pot, & saw some of my Lords fine books.

5. D^r. Astry [Archer *again written first and then deleted*] came to peruse D^r. Hutton's papers.[7]

9 March 1720

21.

6. Mr Gibson sent a Letter with a small Parcell of Books which I laid aside at his Lodgings;[8] & write's that his MSS. & fine old Editions are expected here from Italy very soon.[9]

7. Mr Hay came & said that he hopes to have Mr Fotherbies Books & MSS. soon from the Custom-house.[10]

8. Mr Chapman came, & I paid him off for the last Parcel.

---

[1] See 26 Jan. 1720/1, item 2, and footnote. The price was £4. 4s. 0d. (Welbeck Wanleyana, Misc. no. 50).   [2] Harl. 3049.
[3] Harl. 3689.   [4] Harl. 3847.   [5] Harl. 3119.
[6] Cf. 6 Mar. 1720/1, item 11, and footnote.   [7] i.e. Harl. 6950–85, 7519–21.
[8] Probably the parcel referred to 31 Jan. 1720/1, item 1. Gibson's letter has not been traced.
[9] Cf. 31 Jan. 1720/1, item 1, and footnote 3.   [10] Cf. 28 Apr. 1721, item 11, and footnote.

10 March 1720
1.

9. D^r. Astry [Archer *again written first and deleted*] came to peruse D^r. Huttons papers.[1]

10. M^r. Drake of St. John's in Cambridge came, to know if my Lord will subscribe to his new Edition of A.B. Parkers Antiquitates.[2]

11. A Letter to Mr Clayton of Penwortham, (in answer to one from him) about the Chartularies of Evesham & Penwortham,[3] & his Collection of Greek & Roman Coins.[4]

12. Mr Dunbar brought another Clergy-man to see the Library.

13. Mr Bridges came to see the Books my Lord bought lately. I shewed him a Case full of Manuscripts.

11 March 1720
21.

14. D^r. Fiddis brought a Volume belonging to the Earl of Sussex's Library, for me to put Dates to some of Cardinal Wolsey's Letters, from this Library: which I did.[5]

13. March 1720
21.

15. M^r. Granger came to see some of my Lords fine Books, & tarried here long.

15 March 1720
21.

16. D^r. Sherard came with a Subscription-paper for M^r. De la Motraye's Travels; which I sayd my Lord will Subscribe for.[6] He said, that through the Indiscretion of the last English Minister at the Porte, the Turks are grown into such an Opinion of the Boustrophedon-Inscription, that they will not suffer it to come away by any Means whatsoever.[7]

[1] i.e. Harl. 6950–85, 7519–21.

[2] i.e. Samuel Drake's ed. of Matthew Parker, *De Antiquitate Britannicae Ecclesiae*, pubd. 1729. The proposals for it were issued in 1720. For Harley's subscription cf. 15 May^b and 23 May 1721.

[3] Clayton's letter is apparently that dated 10 Feb. 1720/[21], in Harl. 3778, f. 77; Wanley's letter was acknowledged by Clayton 14 Mar. 1720/1 (see Harl. 3778, f. 78). The Evesham Cartulary is Harl. 3763 (= Davis, no. 382). The owner in fact was Henry Fleetwood of Penwortham, Lancs. Cf. also 18 Mar. (item 3), 31 Mar. (item 8), 9 May (item 9), 18 May (item 4), 21 June (item 7) 1721 (when 'recompense' was paid). The Evesham Cartulary bears the date 21 June 1721; see also footnote to 17 June 1721, item 9, for further conditions.

[4] Cf. 18 Mar. 1720/1, item 3, and footnote.

[5] i.e. from the library of Talbot Yelverton, Viscount Longueville, cr. 1717 Earl of Sussex (d. 1731). The volume is one of the 'Yelverton MSS.' acquired by the British Museum in 1953 (Add. 48000–196: see B. Schofield, 'The Yelverton MSS.', *BMQ* xix (1954), pp. 3–9). The MS. loaned by Fiddes to Wanley is Yelverton MS. 50 (BM Add. 48045, transcripts of letters and instructions from Henry VIII and Wolsey to ambassadors abroad), which still bears in Wanley's autogr. the dates, &c. which he added where these are lacking in the transcripts (viz. ff. 270^b, 283^b, 288^b, 298^b, 300^b, 324^b, 345^b): Wanley at the same time inserted tiny slips to mark the places and these also still remain. The MS. in the Harleian Library used by Wanley for this purpose is Harl. 297. Fiddes was then preparing his Life of Wolsey, cf. 15 Jan. 1719/20, item 5, and footnote. The Yelverton MS. was returned by Wanley 29 Mar. 1721.

[6] Aubry de la Mottraye, *Travels through Europe*, &c. 1723–32. Cf. also 9 Feb. 1721/2, item 16.

[7] Cf. 3 Feb. 1724/5. The 'Minister' was Edward Wortley Montagu (1716–18). The inscription, subsequently given by the Sultan to Lord Elgin, is now BM Greek Inscr. no. 1002.

16 March 1720
$\overline{21.}$

17. I brought in the remaining MS. which Mr Noel bought at the last Auction, without Commission.¹ It is,
A fair Exemplar of John de Soushame's [*sic*] Horologium Sapientiae translated into old French. fol. min. membr.²

18. Mr Jones came to acquaint my Lord that he had bought divers things of John Kemp before his Decease; & that Will. Kemp had more, which were kept from me when I inspected that Collection upon John Kemps Death. Mr Jones brought with him a Book wherein are several models of the Busto's of Princes of the Houses of Saxony, Lunenbourg &c. made by Albert Durer as it seem's to Cast Medals from; which I told him I think not worth my Lords buying, nor his Pictures neither. Will. Kemp, it seem's has a Box of Parmigiani's Copies of Coins: but none of all these things mentioned by Mr Jones, did belong to, or were a part of John Kemps Antiquity-Collection. /³

1. Mr Garnier came, offering his Service, in Case my Lord shall have any thing ^{p. 77}_{(f. 40a)} to transcribe in Oxford.

17 March 1720
$\overline{21.}$

2. I went to Mr Foot the Countess of Stamford's Agent, in Order to bring on a Treaty for those MSS. which were kept out of the late Auction of her Husbands Books.⁴

18 March 1720
$\overline{21.}$

3. I had a Letter from Mr Clayton of Penwortham, who will send up Mr Fleetwoods Chartulary of Eovesham [*sic*],⁵ & a Catalogue of his Coins.⁶

4. I brought the book of old Tracts which Mr Davis left at my Lodgings.

20 March 1720
$\overline{21.}$

5. Mr Tonson sent in some more Sheets of the New Edit. of the Athenæ Oxonienses.⁷

6. Dr Astry [Archer *again written first and deleted*] came to peruse D^r. Huttons Papers.⁸

7. M^r. Gibson came, & said that he ha's about 16 good MSS. coming hither from Italy; among which, one is an Exemplar of the Historiæ Augustæ Scriptores.⁹

---

¹ Cf. 2 Mar. 1720/1, item 14, and footnote.   ² Harl. 4386 = Ballard Sale-Cat., p. 9, lot 66 (7s. 6d.).
³ Cf. 28 Jan. 1719/20, item 9, and footnote.
⁴ Cf. 2 Feb. 1720/1, item 6; for details of the auction cf. 13 Jan. 1720/1, items 12 and 13.
⁵ Cf. 10 Mar. 1720/1, item 11, and footnote. The Cartulary (Harl. 3763) was sent by Fleetwood 31 Mar. 1721 (item 8).
⁶ The cat. of Clayton's coins is in Harl. 6941, ff. 36–39 (see Wanley's endorsement on f. 39ᵇ). Cf. 31 Mar. 1724, item 2.
⁷ This refers to the 2nd ed. (1721) of Anthony Wood, *Athenae Oxonienses*, pubd. in 2 vols. by B. Knoplock, D. Midwinter, and J. Tonson, London, 1721.
⁸ i.e. Harl. 6950–85, 7519–21.
⁹ Cf. 31 Jan. 1720/1, item 1, and footnote 3. The MS. referred to became Harl. 2658 (cf. 17 June 1721, no. 2 of list).

21 March 1720
—
21.

8. Dʳ Astry [Archer *again written first and deleted*] came to peruse Dʳ. Hutton's Papers.¹

22 March 1720
—
21.

9. Mʳ Du Mont came to see some of my Lords fine MSS.

23 March 1720
—
21.

10. Mʳ Sanderson sent in the MS. he borrowed last, & I returned the Note he left with me for it.²

24 March, 1720
—
21.

11. I called upon Mʳ Woodman the Bookseller, who shewed me a parcel of MS[S]. formerly belonging to the Lord Keeper Roberts Lord Radnor. They are about 80 in Number, several of them Rubbish, but the greatest part of them, are of very good Use & Value. I order'd them to be laid by untill my Lord see's them.³

12. Dʳ. Astry [Archer *again written first and deleted*] came to Study in the Library.

25 March 1721.

13. Dʳ. Astry [Archer *again written first and deleted*] came to Study in the Library.

14. Mʳ Du Hamel came to see some of my Lords fine Books.

15. Dʳ. Tanner came to look into some of my Lords Books, & MSS.

16. One Mʳ John Ayres came to sell to [*sic*] MSS. which proved not worth the buying.

17. A Letter recd from Mʳ Boothe; & an Answer sent to him by the Penny post, with a Desire that he will procure my Lord the old Deeds & Rolls formerly in the possession of Randle Holme of Chester, deceased.⁴

18. Mʳ. Dale came to peruse some Heraldical MSS.

27 March 1721.

19. This Morning I went to Mʳ Hill, and gave him a discretionary Commission for buying some more Antiquities at the present Auction of John Kemps Collection. / ⁵

¹ i.e. Harl. 6950–85, 7519–21. ² i.e. Harl. 1583 (borrowed 11 Jan. 1720/1, item 8).
³ The date of the Earl of Radnor Sale was 2 May 1721 at Woodman's shop in Covent Garden. The MSS. purchased by Harley bear the date 4 May 1721. Cf. 17 Apr. (item 9), 26 Apr. (item 2), 29 Apr. (item 3), and 1, 2, 3, and 4 May 1721 (for list see footnote to last date).
⁴ Cf. 23 Jan. 1719/20, item 5, and footnote. Nathaniel Boothe's letter (of 23 Mar. 1720/1) was merely an inquiry relating to a printed book, which Wanley used as an opportunity to raise once again the question of the Randle Holme deeds and rolls.
⁵ Cf. 28 Jan. 1719/20, item 9, and footnote for earlier dealings. Wanley's visit was in accordance with Harley's letter to him of 23 Mar. 1720/1 (in Welbeck Wanleyana): 'I should be glad to have a few of Kemp's things as the Vase wᶜʰ is in your picture, the Lamp, and a few more things I cannot name without a catalogue . . .' (i.e. Hill's portrait of Wanley, dated 18 Dec. 1711, now at Soc. of Ant.).

28 March 1721.

1. Dʳ. Astry [Archer *again written first and deleted*] came to peruse Dʳ. Huttons Papers.[1]

2. Mʳ Gibson came, & said that a Correspondent of his in Italy ha's lately procured some choice MSS. for him; among which one being an old Book, very large & fair, is of Plinies Natural History: but is valued at an high price.[2]

29 March 1721.

3. Dʳ. Fiddis brought a Workman hither to delineate Cardinal Wolseys Armes from the MS. 67.A.1. and I deliver'd to him that MS. of the Earl of Sussex which he left with me.[3]

30 March 1721.

4. Dʳ. Astry came to peruse Dʳ. Huttons Papers.[4]

31 March 1721.

5. Mʳ Bowyer brought a Modern MS. desiring to have my Opinion if it be proper to be printed; & left it.[5]

6. Mʳ O Sullevane came to look upon some old Spanish & Punic Coins.

7. Mʳ Green came to borrow my Lord Oxfords Book of the Statutes of the Garter. I desired him to call again on Monday. 'the book was dd to him on Tuesday the 4ᵗʰ. April' [' 'written in between items 7 and 8 afterwards*].[6]

8. Mʳ Fleetwood of Lancashire sent hither a valuable Register-book of Eavesham- [*sic*] Abbey, for me to peruse.[7]

1 April, 1721.

9. I went to Lady Stamfords, and putt her MSS. into some sort of Order.[8]

3, 4, 5 April, 1721.

10. I took a short List of the Lady Stamford's MSS.[8]

6 April, 1721.

11. Mʳ Noel came, & communicated to me another Letter & Catalogue from Mʳ Suttie, nᵒ. 17.[9]

---

[1] i.e. Harl. 6950–85, 7519–21.
[2] Cf. 3 July 1721, item 3, where ref. is made to the MS. of Pliny being 'shipped of[f] from Leghorn': and cf. 9 Nov. 1721, item 1 (and list there). An older MS. of Pliny's Natural History was subsequently reported by Gibson 11 Feb. 1722/3, item 7 (cf. no. 1 in list under 4 Apr. 1723, item 17).
[3] i.e. for his projected Life of Wolsey (cf. 15 Jan. 1719/20, item 5, and footnote). 67. A. 1 = Harl. 1197; Wolsey's arms are on f. 402. The Earl of Sussex's MS. had been left with Wanley 11 Mar. 1720/1; see footnote to that date.
[4] i.e. Harl. 6950–85, 7519–21.
[5] Cf. 21 Apr. (item 17), and 7 June (item 10) 1721.
[6] i.e. Harl. 4607. Green's letter acknowledging receipt of the MS., dated 8 Apr. 1721, is in Welbeck Wanleyana. The MS. was returned 17 Apr. 1721 (item 10).
[7] Cf. 10 Mar. 1720/1, item 11, and footnote. Finally settled for 21 June 1721, item 7.
[8] Cf. 2 Feb. 1720/1, item 6, and footnote.   [9] Not traced.

12. D[r]. Fiddis came to enquire after a Greek MS. which I borrowed out of Lincoln-College Library, and restored to D[r]. Adam the Rector thereof, long before his Decease.[1]

7 April 1721.

13. M[r] Rowley came; & I shewed him two [one *written first and deleted*] of my Lords fine books.

8 April 1721.

14. A Letter sent to M[r] Green, desiring him to send the certain day when the next Installment will be at Windsor.[2]

15. Another to M[r] Roger Gale, desiring him to call here in the Holy days, to see a Leiger-book, & an old Chronicle of Bury-Abbey.[3]

16. M[r] Davies the Bookseller Brought a small parcel of books, which I bad him lay by for my Lord to see.[4]

17. M[r] Christian came to see one of my Lords fine books.

10 April 1721.

18. A Letter sent to M[r] Innys, desiring him to attend my Lord to morrow.

11 April 1721.

19. M[r] Roger Gale came, & borrowed the Leiger-book of St. Edmunds-bury which my Lord brought up from Wympole for him.[5]

20. M[r] Gwyn & his Son came.

21. M[r] Harbin brought the MS. he borrowed, & took up his Note. /[6]

p. 79
(f. 41a)
12 April, 1721.

1. M[r]. Garter Anstis came to look into some Chronicles MSS. and wrote to D[r]. Thorpe about some MSS. formerly belonging to M[r] William Lambard.[7]

13 April 1721.

2. The Bishop of Chester[8] came, to look into certain MSS.

14 April 1721.

3. M[r] Gibson came to adjust the Price of a small parcel of Books he left with me for my Lord.[9]

---

[1] Cf. 3 June 1723, item 19, for its recovery. The borrowed MS. was Lincoln College, Oxford, Greek MS. XXXV (see H. O. Coxe, *Catalogus Codicum MSS. . . . in Collegiis Aulisque Oxoniensibus . . .*, part i, 1852, *Cat. Cod. MSS. Coll. Lincolniensis*, pp. 18–19): Wanley's transcript made in Apr. 1715 is Harl. 6505.
[2] Green's reply (in Welbeck Wanleyana), dated from the 'Heralds' Office' the same day, notified Wanley that the date fixed for the Installation was Tuesday, the 25th inst.
[3] Cf. 1 Mar. 1720/1, item 6, and footnote. Roger Gale's reply (in Welbeck Wanleyana) is dated the same day: he thanks Wanley for procuring MSS. for him (cf. 11 Apr. 1721, item 19).
[4] Cf. 18 May 1721, item 13, and footnote.
[5] Cf. 8 Apr. 1721, item 15, and footnote.
[6] Borrowed 4 Mar. 1720/1, item 5.
[7] Cf. 23 June 1721, item 14. William Lambard, 1536–1601, was Keeper of the Records in the Tower: part of his coll. of MSS. was sold 3 Dec. 1723 by C. Davis (cf. 23 Nov. 1723, item 10, and footnote) but MSS. relating particularly to Kent remained at the family seat at Sevenoaks until 19 June 1924, when they were sold at Hodgson's, of Chancery Lane, London. Anstis's letter (with PS. by Wanley) is Soc. of Ant. MS. 202, f. 5.
[8] i.e. Francis Gastrell.
[9] Cf. 31 Jan. 1720/1, item 1, and footnote 4.

4. Mr Christian came.

5. Mr James Hill came to look into a Visitation-book of Hereford-shire:[1] & đđ a small Picture of Cartesius to me for my Lord.[2]

6. D^r. Astry came to peruse D^r. Huttons papers.[3]

17 April 1721.

7. Mr Gale sent back the Leiger-book of Bury,[4] & I sent him his Note per Penny-post.

8. D^r. Sherard brought a Letter from Mr Mould Chaplain at Smyrna, who will go to Salonica & Scio, to buy up Greek MSS. but seem's to be preingaged for the MS. of the Greek Gospels in Capitals.[5] The D^r. will send him to Mount Athos.

9. Mr Davis came, & say's Mr Woodman is about to Print a Catalogue of his MSS.[6]

10. Mr Green brought the Statutes of the Garter, which my Lord lent him.[7]

11. Mr George Hay came, and appointed the next Friday for me to see Mr Cook of Norfolk's Library.[8]

18 April 1721.

12. I went to Mr Noel & laid aside such of Sir Joseph Hodges's Books as seemed most for my Lords purpose.[9]

19 April 1721.

13. Mr Anstis returned the Gallia Purpurata which my Lord lent him.[10]

20 April 1721.

14. Mr Elliot sent for Mr Prior's Poems which he is to Bind for Mr Garwood.

15. Mr Vertue came to inspect the Pocket-books of Mr Richard Simonds, being in the Box 63.[11]

21 April 1721.

16. I call'd early upon Mr Hay that he might take me to Mr Cook of Norfolk; & was again disappointed, as is usuall.[12]

---

[1] For Hill's purpose in looking at this MS. see 9 Apr. 1720, item 15, and footnote.

[2] i.e. René Descartes (1596–1650), the philosopher. 'A small Head of Renatus des Cartes, 1640' was in the sale of Edward Harley's pictures, 12 Mar. 1741–2 (sale cat., p. 13).

[3] i.e. Harl. 6950–85, 7519–21.

[4] Borrowed 11 Apr. 1721, item 19.

[5] Cf. 18 Jan. 1719/20, item 5, and footnote for this Greek Gospels and the question of purchasing Greek MSS. in Scio. For purchases made by Mould see list under 6 Aug. 1725.

[6] Cf. 24 Mar. 1720/1, item 11, and footnote.

[7] Cf. 31 Mar. 1721, item 7, and footnote.

[8] See 21 Apr. 1721, item 16, and cf. 21 Jan. 1719/20 (item 7, and footnote), when Andrew Hay suggested that Coke might be prepared to part with his MSS. Wanley eventually saw them 18 May 1721, item 12.

[9] Cf. 5 May 1721, item 2.

[10] Borrowed 7 Mar. 1720/1 (item 1); cf. 6 Mar. 1720/1, item 11, and footnote.

[11] Cf. also 15 May (item 5), 18 May (item 2), and 1 July (item 19) 1721, for other visits by Vertue *for this purpose.* Vertue in his *Note Books* (Walpole Soc.), i. 71, 72, 77, refers to his seeing 63. C. 1, 2, and 28 (i.e. Harl. 964, 965, and 991).

[12] Cf. 17 Apr. 1721, item 11, and footnote. Wanley finally saw the MSS. on Downes's introduction 18 May 1721 (item 12).

17. Mr Bowyer came to know my Lords Opinion of the MS. he left with me.[1]

18. Mr Chapman brought the last Parcel he had to Bind; & recd another.

22 April 1721.

19. Dr. Astry came to peruse Dr. Huttons Papers.[2]

20. Mr Cart of Leicesters Eldest Son came to enquire after some Papers of Arch-Bishop Sancroft, which were lent to Mr Morley by Mr Sancroft.[3]

21. Mr Elliot brought the Parcel of Books he ha's had so long to Bind.

25 April 1721.

22. Mr Noel brought Sir Joseph Hodges to see some of my Lords fine books.

23. Mr Bridges came to look into some of Dr. Huttons Papers.[4]

24. Mr Gibson came, desiring to know if my Lord will have all that small Parcel of books he left here, or not. /[5]

p. 80
(f. 41b)

26 April 1721.

1. Dr. Astrey came to inspect Dr. Huttons Papers.[6]

2. Mr Davis came with a knavish Catalogue of Books as of Hugh Thomas's Books;[7] & also of the Earl of Radnors MSS. which Mr. Woodman has now caused to be printed for Sale.[8]

3. Mr Hill came to see some of my Lords fine MSS.

4. Mr Booth [*substituted for* Gibson *deleted*] came desiring me to write to Mr Baker of Cambridge about the Author of a Treatise entituled A Description of a Counsellor of State;[9] and promised to serve my Lord in procuring the late Randle Holme's of Chesters original old Deeds & Rolls.[10]

27 April 1721.

5. Mr Alderman Ludlam of Leicester came.

6. My Lord consented to give Mr Gibson £20, for the parcel of Books he left here.[11] vizt.

> Tullius de Officijs, &c. *Mediol.* 1478. 4to. mag.[12]
> P. Merulæ Enarrationes in Juvenalem, &c. *Venet.* 1478. fol. min.[13]
> Lactantij Institutiones, &c. *Venet.* 1478. fol. min.[14]

---

[1] Cf. 31 Mar. 1721, item 5, and footnote.   [2] i.e. Harl. 6950–85, 7519–21.
[3] Cf. 28 June 1721, item 8. Perhaps the Sancroft Papers subsequently included in Harl. 3783–98.
[4] i.e. Harl. 6950–85, 7519–21.
[5] Cf. 9 Mar. 1720/1, item 6, and footnote, and also 27 Apr. 1721, item 6, for list.
[6] i.e. Harl. 6950–85, 7519–21.
[7] Hugh Thomas's *Books* were sold 2 May 1721; some of his MSS. and papers were bequeathed to Robert Harley (cf. 19 Oct. 1720 and footnote for identification).
[8] See 24 Mar. 1720/1, item 11, and footnote, and 4 May 1721, item 14, and footnote for list.
[9] The book would seem to be Philippe de Béthune's *The Counsellor of Estate*. Translated by E. G. [Edward Grimstone], London, 1634. (*STC* 1977.)
[10] This matter of the Randle Holme deeds was first raised 23 Jan. 1719/20, item 5; see footnote to that date.
[11] Cf. 31 Jan. 1720/1, item 1, and footnote 4.
[12] GW 6940.   [13] Hain–Copinger 11090; Stillwell M. 430.; *BMC* v. 202.
[14] For identification see footnote 9 under 18 Mar. 1719/20.

Aristidis Orationes Gr. *Florent.* 1517. fol. min.[1]
Terentius cum Donato. *Venet.* 1490. fol. min.[2]
Vasi antichi di Vetro. 4to mag.[3]
Ben. Averanij Opera. fol. *4 Voll.*[4]
Lodi di Ant. Magliabechi. fol. min. ten.[5]
B. Gregorius in Jobum. *Romæ,* 1475. fol. med.[6]
Luciani Dialogi Græcè. *Florent.* 1496. fol. med.[7]

These being now at the Binders.
Lucanus cum Commento Joh. Britannici. *Venet.* 1492. fol.[8]
Justini Historia. L. Florus.—fol. ten.[9]
Athenæi Deipnosophistæ, Græcè. *Basil.* 1535. fol.[10]
Isocrates, Alcidamas, Gorgias, Aristides, Græcè, *Ven. in aed. Aldi.* 1513. fol.[11]
Ruinarti Vita Joan. Mabillonij. *Patav.* 1714. 8vo.[12]
Poesie Toscane da Vincenzio Filicaia. *in Firenze,* 1707. 4to.[13]

28 April 1721.

7. Miles Davis's Widow came with some of her Husbands Works which my Lord had not bought before.[14]

8. Mr Elliot brought a small book he lately bound; & received another to bind.

9. A Letter was Written to Mr Andrew Hay at Rome, reminding him of the Commission my Lord gave him about a year ago, for Buying MSS. in France, Savoy, Italy, & Sicily; & desiring him to putt it in Execution.[15]

10. D^r. Astrey came to peruse D^r. Huttons Papers.[16]

11. My Lord having lately bought a small Parcel of Books of Mr Hay (among which was one small Primer in MS. à l'Usage de Paris)[17] order'd some to be bound, & the rest to be laid up. /

29 April, 1721.

1. D^r. Astrey came to peruse D^r. Hutton's papers.[18]

2. Mr Moses Williams came to inspect Hugh Thomas's MSS.[19]

p. 81
(f. 42a)

---

[1] Printed by Filippo Giunta; this is the *editio princeps.*   [2] Probably Stillwell T. 72.
[3] *Osservazioni sopra alcuni Framenti di Vasi Antichi di Vetro,* Florence 1716 (= Osborne, iii, 1744, no. 2980).   [4] Florence, 1717; only ed. in BM *General Catalogue* is in 3 vols.
[5] Probably A. M. Salvini, *Delle lodi di Antonio Magliabecchi, orazione funerale,* Florence, 1715.
[6] Stillwell G. 388; *BMC* iv. 64.   [7] Stillwell L. 286; *BMC* vi. 667.   [8] Stillwell L. 272.
[9] Unidentified: but presumably eds. of M. J. Justinus, *Epitomae in Trogi Pompeii historias* and L. A. Florus, *Epitomae Rerum Romanarum.*
[10] i.e. Ἀθηναίου Δειπνοσοφιστῶν βιβλία πεντεκαίδεκα. [Ed. by J. Bedrotus.] Apud I. Valderum. Baisileae, 1535, fol.
[11] i.e. Λογοι τουτωνι των ῥητορων . . ., ed. by Aldus Pius Manutius. In aedibus Aldi et Andreae Soceri. Venetiis, 1513. 3 vols. fol.
[12] i.e. the life of Mabillon written by Thierry Ruinart.
[13] i.e. Vincenzio da Filicaja, *Poesie Toscane.* Florence, 1707. 4°.
[14] Cf. 3 May 1721, item 12; 23 Jan. 1721/2, item 5. On Miles Davis's writings see Biogr. Index.
[15] See 26 Apr. 1720 (and footnote); the Commission had been given to Hay on 3 May 1720 (item 17).
[16] i.e. Harl. 6950–85, 7519–21.
[17] Possibly Fotherbie's books and MSS. alluded to 9 Mar. 1720/1, item 7. Cf. also Wanley's Addenda, Lansdowne 771, f. 78, under 28 Apr. 1721 (p. 198 of the present work), where it is recorded that Harley had paid Hay for this parcel on 23 Apr. 1721. The MS. Primer is Harl. 2929 (which bears in Wanley's hand the date 28 Apr. 1721).
[18] i.e. Harl. 6950–85, 7519–21.
[19] i.e. Hugh Thomas's MSS. referred to under 19 Oct. 1720, item 17, and footnote.

3. Charles Davis came and wanted to Treat with me about His & Woodman's MSS. but I said I believed my Lord would not have them, because the[y] had broken their Words with me, & Printed the Titles of them for all the Town.[1]

4. A Letter Sent desiring Mr Chapman to call here on Monday.

5. Mr Harbin came to wait upon my Lord.

1 May 1721.

6. Charles Davis came to know my Lords ultimate Resolution touching Mr Woodmans MSS. and was told that my Lord would have nothing to do with Woodman or his MSS. since Woodman brake his Word by shewing the Things to every Customer, & printed a Catalogue of them in order to bring in other buyers.[1]

7. Mr Elliot the Binder came, & was paid off to 1 Septr. 1719.

8. Mr Chapman came, mended two books; & was paid off, in full.

2 May 1721.

9. Mr Bacon came, & promised that my Lord should have the Inscriptions he bought at Kemps Auction.[2] And that Woodman the Bookseller had Offered him to sell him his MSS. at a cheap price: and upon Discourse, he went from me saying that he would go instantly, & buy them for my Lord.[3]

10. Mr Bridgeman came to see some of my Lords fine Books.

3 May 1721.

11. Mr William Thomas came.

12. Miles Davis's Widow brought, 3 more of her Husbands books, which my Lord bought of her.[4]

13. Mr Bacon came, and my Lord paid him for the MSS. he bought & sent in from a late Auction;[5] for 3 Inscriptions he bought at Kemps Auction;[6] and the Lord Roberts's MSS. he bought yesterday of Woodman ye Bookseller.[7]

4 May 1721.

14. I went to Mr Bacon, & sent hither the MSS. he bought of Woodman (being lately in the Possession of the Earl of Radnor) & Three old Inscriptions he bought at Kemps Auction. I took likewise a List of some other Pieces of Antiquity he bought at the same Auction, & of the Prices he gave for them: which I since find my Lord is Willing to have at the same Rate. Upon all the said MSS. I have putt the Date of this day; and Catalogue them not here, but refer to that printed by Woodman.[8]

---

[1] Cf. 24 Mar. 1720/1, item 11, and footnote.
[2] On Kemp's auction see 28 Jan. 1719/20, item 9, and footnote.
[3] Cf. 24 Mar. 1720/1, item 11, and footnote: and see footnote to 4 May 1721, item 14, for list.
[4] Cf. 28 Apr. 1721, item 7, and footnote.
[5] Cf. 23 Feb. 1720/1, item 11, for list, and footnotes for identifications.
[6] Cf. 2 May 1721, item 9, and footnote.
[7] Cf. item 9 above, and footnote, and item 14 and footnote below for list.
[8] For Kemp's antiquities cf. 28 Jan. 1719/20, item 9, and footnote, and Addenda, Lansdowne 771, f. 78, under 4 May 1721 (at p. 198 of the present work). For Radnor Sale see footnote to 24 Mar. 1720/1, item 11; Harl. MSS. bearing this day's date are: 2185, 2197, 2224, 2231, 2233, 2235, 2237, 2238, 2241, 2243, 2246, 2290, 2294, 2308, 2325, 2428, 3265, 3358, 3683, 3755, 4176, 4177, 4182, 4183, 4186, 4193, 4194, 4207–16, 4231, 4237, 4250, 4261, 4263, 4265, 4268, 4276, 4279, 4281, 4297, 4315, 5078, 5091–5, 5208, 6335, 6779, 6841 (ff. 1–18), 6947 (ff. 298–317), 7174, 7200, 7384.

15. Mr Bateman & Mr Murray came.

16. Dr. Sherard brought a second Letter from Mr Bern. Mould at Smyrna, Dated 20 Febr. 1720. which enclosed an account of the Octateuch remaining in the Metropolitical [*sic*] Church there: Which Account, & a Copie of the Letter, will be found among the Library-papers.[1]

17. A Letter written to Mr Bacon desiring him to send to my Lord the other pieces of Antiquity he bought at Kemps Auction, & my Lord will pay what they cost him. /[2]

5 May 1721.

1. Mr. Bacon sent in the remaining pieces of Antiquity he bought at the Auction of John Kemps things.[2]

2. Mr Noel sent in a Parcel of Books, which my Lord selected from those he bought of Sir Joseph Hodges.[3]

6 May 1721.

3. I 'thought to have' [*portion ' ' added above line over an omission mark*] sent away the Sack wherein Mr. Bacon sent Woodmans MSS. & Mr Corbets Pedegree: but my Lord forbad it.

4. Dr. Bentley came to inspect my Lords Codex Aureus of the Gospels: which he did with some other valuable MSS. and desiring to borrow the Codex Aureus, and another old MS. Gospels belonging formerly (as it is thought) to St. Hilary's Church of Poitiers, my Lord Orderd me to carry them to him on Thursday-morning next.[4]

5. Dr. Astry came to peruse Dr. Hutton's Papers.[5]

6. Mr Dale came: & Mr O Sullevane came.

8 May 1721.

7. I sent away Woodmans Sack; Mr Noels 3 Sacks, with a Letter desiring him to meet me to morrow in the Evening & make up the Accompt; & Mr Corbets Pedegree.

9 May 1721.

8. I went to the Custome house in Order to clear-off the Parcel of Marocco-Goat-skins which my Lord lately bought abroad; & were sent by Mr Beaver from Gibraltar.[6]

---

[1] For Mould's first letter see 17 Apr. 1721, item 8. For other references to the Octateuch MS. affair (which came to nothing) cf. 17 Dec. 1720, item 5; 13 May 1721, item 16; cf. also generally the footnote to 5 Nov. 1720. The account and copy of the letter referred to by Wanley have not been traced.
  [2] Cf. 2 May 1721, item 9, and footnote.   [3] Cf. 18 Apr. 1721.
  [4] The Codex Aureus is Harl. 2788. The second MS. referred to by Wanley is Harl. 2826; the statement that it belonged as 'it is thought' to the church of St. Hilary at Poitiers is due probably to a misunderstanding or hasty reading of the entry on f. 11[b]; it belonged to the monastery of Eller near Cochem on the Moselle and is described in the *Cat. of Ancient MSS. in BM.*, pt. ii, Latin, 1884, pp. 32–33. The MSS. were taken by Wanley to Bentley 11 May 1721; Wanley's account of both MSS. is given under 10 May 1721; they were returned by Bentley 26 May 1721 (item 16).
  [5] i.e. Harl. 6950–85, 7519–21.
  [6] Harley's letter of 18 Sept. 1720 to Wanley (in Welbeck Wanleyana) had accepted the offer of John Beaver (Wanley's stepson-in-law) to get morocco skins: Beaver's efforts to obtain these are described in his letter to Wanley from Gibraltar of 18 Nov. 1720 (in Welbeck Wanleyana). Beaver was able to secure suitable skins only from Fez, 'the cream of the country' (see his letter to Wanley in Harl. 3777, f. 179, dated 22 Jan. 1720/1).

9. Mr Fleetwood of Penwortham came, being so kind as to bring me a Letter from Mr Clayton: and seem's disposed to oblige my Lord with his old Chartulary of Evesham.[1]

10. Mr Bowyer sent in the Parcel of old Books my Lord bought lately of him.[2] My Lord lent the Statutes of Exeter, to the Lord Bishop of Exeter: viz. 63.E.4.[3]

10 May 1721.

11. My Lord having condescended to lend D^r. Bentley the CODEX AVREVS of the Gospels, & that other antient Exemplar which formerly belonged to S^t. Hilary's Church: by his command I take the following short Account of them.[4]
   In the *Codex Aureus*, are

Hieronymi Epistola ad Damasum. NOVVM OPVS.   .
Prologus quattuor Evangeliorum. PLVRES FVISSE.   .
Eusebij Epistola ad Carpianum. AMMONIVS QVIDEM.   .
HIERONIMVS DAMASO PAPE. SCIENDVM ETIAM.   .   .   } folia 5. pag. 1.
Argumentum secundum Mattheum. MATTHEVS ex iudaea.   .   .   .   .   .   .
Breviarium ejusdem. Natiuitas x̄pi.   .   .   .

Canones.   .   .   .   . folia 5. pag. 1.
Titulus Codicis.   .   .   .   .   .   . 1.
D. Matthæi Imago.   .   .   .   .   .   . 1.
D. Matthæi Evangelium. .   .   .   .   . folijs 54. pag. 1. col. 1.
Prologus. MARCVS EVANGELISTA DĪ.   }
Breviarium. DE JOHANNE BAPTISTA.   } .   .   .   .   2.   col. 2.
D. Marci Imago.   .   .   .   .   .   . pag. 1.
Evangelium sec. Marcum.   .   .   .   . folijs 31.

101.   col. 3/

p. 83
(f. 43 a)
Argumentum Evang. sec. Lucam. LUCAS SYRUS. .
Capitula. ZacharIAs uiso.   .   .   .   . } fol. 5. pag. 1.
Imago D. Lucæ.   .   .   .   .   .   . pag. 1.
Evangelium secd. Lucam .   .   .   .   . fol. 50.   ½ Col.
Argumentum (*Johannis*) HIC EST IOHANNES   .
Breviarum. PHARISAEORUM LEUITAE.   . } fol. 1. pag. 1. Col. 1½.
Imago D. Johannis.   .   .   .   .   . fol. 1.
Evangelium secundum Johannem   .   .   . fol. 37.
Capitulare Evangeliorum.   .   .   .   . fol. 10.

106.
101.   col. 3.

207.   col. 3.
Telling the Number of Written & painted Leaves all along, they amount to 208.

besides one vacant.
& 4 makes a leaf.

[1] i.e. Harl. 3763. Cf. 31 Mar. 1721 (item 8) when the Cartulary had been sent in.
[2] This parcel had been bought on 5 May 1721, cf. Wanley's Addenda, Lansdowne 771, f. 78, under that date (at p. 199 of the present work). It was probably derived from the coll. mentioned under 2 Feb. 1720/1, item 5. Cf. also 3 and 14 Feb. 1720/1, item 14.
[3] i.e. Harl. 1027 (returned 13 June 1721 (item 4)). The Bp. of Exeter was Lancelot Blackburne.
[4] Cf. 6 May 1721, item 4, and footnote.

In S^t. Hilarys Gospels, are

Before S^t. Matthew's Gospel . . .	Leaves 11.
S^t. Matthew contain's . . .	Leaves, 34 & 3 lines.
Before S^t. Mark	Leaves 2 wanting 3 lines.
S^t. Mark contain's	Leaves 21 & ½ Page.
Before S^t. Luke, are . . .	Leaves 4 abating that ½ page.
S^t. Luke contain's	Leaves 36 wanting half a Page.
Before S^t. John are	Leaves 2 and that half Page.
S^t. John contain's	Leaves 26 & ¾
After St John, are	Leaves 13 & ¼
	150

Telling over these Leaves together, they amounted to 150.

1. D^r. Astry came, desiring to borrow some of D^r. Huttons papers.[1]

11 May 1721.

2. By my Lords Order, I carried the two MSS. of the Gospels above mentioned to D^r. Bentley & took his Note for them:[2] and then went in the Cotton-Library to use some old MSS. there.[3]

3. I was told that Mr Parry of Reading Sir John Chardins Executor, thinks that he may have a Georgian Bible.[4]

12 May 1721.

4. Mr Bateman came, with M^r. Motte.

5. D^r. Astry came, & borrowed [*blank space*] Books of D^r. Huttons Notes.[5]

6. Mr Davis brought a few Books to shew my Lord.[6]

7. The Bishop of Chester[7] & D^r. Terry came, & look'd into some MSS.

13 May 1721.

8. I went this Morning to D^r. Sherard, and deliver'd to him a Letter to be forwarded to Mr Mould at Smyrna;[8] and I brought from him an Ibis, as it now remain's, being embalmed by the old Egyptians. /

15 May 1721.

p. 84
(f. 43*b*)

1. Mr Drake of S^t. Johns in Cambridge came, & left with me a Receipt for my Lords first Payment of the Subscription-money towards his Book.[9]

2. D^r. Stukeley brough[t] one of his Books (or Account of a Roman Temple, &c.) as a present to my Lord.[10]

---

[1] i.e. Harl. 6950–85, 7519–21. He borrowed them 12 May 1721 (item 5) and returned them 15 May 1721 (item 7), and borrowed 4 more which were returned 18 May 1721 (item 1).
[2] Cf. 6 May 1721, item 4, and footnote.
[3] The Cotton Library was still at Cotton House (and remained there until 1722, when it was transferred to Essex House).
[4] Nothing more is heard of this Georgian Bible. [5] Returned 15 May 1721 (item 7).
[6] Cf. 18 May 1721, item 13, and footnote. [7] The Bp. of Chester was Francis Gastrell.
[8] Presumably about the Octateuch: cf. 4 May 1721, item 16.
[9] Cf. 10 Mar. 1720/1, item 10, and footnote.
[10] Stukeley's *Account of a Roman Temple and other Antiquities near Graham's-Dyke in Scotland*, 1720 (see Stuart Piggott, *William Stukeley*, p. 60, footnote 1).

3. My Lord sent a Pedegree of Savage Written & painted on a Roll of Velum.¹

4. Mr Christian came, enquiring for the Armes of Valence.

5. Mr Virtue came, to peruse some of Mr Rich. Simons's MSS.²

6. Daniel Cohen de Alzevedo a Jewish Rabbin came, offering some modern Hebrew MSS. about the Cabbala, to Sale: but I told him my Lord had no great Value for them.

7. Dr. Astry brought the two Vollumes of Dr. Huttons Collections he borrowed before; & now borrowed four other Volumes.³

8. Mr Slyford came from Mr Bridges, to look into Dr. Hutton's Papers.⁴

16 May 1721.

9. A Letter received from Dr. Sherard, who promise's to call here to morrow, & ha's sent away my Letter to Mr Mould.⁵ He write's likewise, that Mr March the Turkey-Merchant will forward any Letter from me into Turkey.

10. A Letter sent to Mr Downes to tarry for me 'till between 10 & 11, to morrow.

11. Mr O Sullevane called here as he went by, to see me.

18 May 1721.

11 [sic]. Dr. Sherard being about to go to France & so to Holland, I drew up a Commission for him to Execute there.⁶ And he coming hither, I deliver'd to him a Sett of Mr [for my] Lords prints of his Lamp,⁷ Mr. Priors Letter, & My own for Bernard Montfaucon.⁸ The Doctor went also to the Duke of Devonshire about St. Æthelwalds Benedictional, which he carried to his Grace from hence, & spake to Him to give it to my Lord in Exchange for other Books. His Grace replied that he had those books already; That he was yet of Opinion that he could not in honor part with it, without General Comptons Leave, who gave

¹ No pedigree of Savage written and painted on a roll of vellum has been traced in the Harl. Coll. but two such pedigrees are in BM Lansdowne Rolls 7 and 8, and in view of the fact that several items in the Lansdowne Coll. derive from James West (one of Edward Harley's executors) it is possible that one of these rolls is that referred to by Wanley.

² Cf. 20 Apr. 1721, item 15, and footnote.

³ Cf. 12 May 1721, item 5; and 18 May 1721, item 1, for return of the 4 vols.

⁴ i.e. Harl. 6950-85, 7519-21.

⁵ Cf. 13 May 1721. Sherard's letter of 15 May 1721 is in Welbeck Wanleyana.

⁶ For Sherard's projected visit to France and Holland and his interview with Aymon cf. below item 14 (for the items required from Aymon) and 22 May (item 14), 24 May (item 11), 25 May (item 13), 27 Nov. (item 6), and 29 Nov. (item 12) 1721; see the last date for the identification of 2 MSS. bought by Sherard under this Commission. For a full note on Aymon and his MSS. see 2 Mar. 1714/15, item 4, and footnote.

⁷ i.e. presumably of the object in Edward Harley's Coll. described in the Diary and the sale cat. of his colls. (Cock's, Covent Garden, 10 Mar. 1741/2, p. 10, lot 30) as a 'Lamp' but as an 'Urn' by Bernard de Montfaucon, L'Antiquité expliquée et représentée en figures, Supplément, 2nd ed., vol. i, 1724, where it is described and illustrated at pp. 139-41 and pls. 50-52. (Cf. also the English trans. by D. Humphreys, Antiquity Explained, vol. i, 1725, bk. iv, chap. iii, pp. 75-77 and pls. 18, 19): Montfaucon notes, however, that it was described by some as a 'Lamp'. It had been in Colbert's coll. and was given to Harley by Prior. The 'prints' were by Vertue (see Harley Coll. of Prints in Soc. of Ant. vol. i, ff. 10-12).

⁸ Matthew Prior's letter of introduction to Montfaucon for Sherard, dated 12 May 1721, is printed by E. de Broglie, La Société de l'Abbaye de Saint-Germain-des-Prés au dix-huitième siècle; Bernard de Montfaucon et les Bernardins, 1715-1750, i (1891), pp. 138-9 (from Bibl. nat. fonds français 17711, ff. 142-3). Wanley's letter, 12 May, is ibid., ff. 144-5ᵇ, and Montfaucon's reply (7 July 1721) is Harl. 3780, f. 167. Sherard in a letter to Wanley dated from Paris 11 July 1721 (Harl. 3781, f. 58) describes his search in Paris for books and reports Montfaucon as having said he knew of no Greek, Coptic, or Syriac MSS. for sale in Paris.

it Him; That he would ask him, & if he gave his Consent, he would send it to my Lord forthwith.[1]

12. Mr Downes took me yesterday to Mr. Cook of Norfolk, who shewed me part of his MSS. with much humanity for above 3 hours together, & will send to me to see the Rest, as soon as he can have Leasure.[2] He has bought all the MSS. of the Family of Giustiniani at Venice; and the Case wherein the Greek MSS. were, was first open'd Yesterday. He ha's also assurance of 300 MSS. more, to be sent to him soon.[3]

13. Mr Charles Davis brought a List of the Books he ha's left here for my Lord; desiring no more than the Common prices my Lord pay's to Mr Noel; excepting two dear books he bought at the late Auctions.[4]

14. Memorandum that the Things which Dr. Sherard is to demand of Monsr. Aymon at the Hague, are
    The Original Letters of Cardinal Visconti, about the Council of Trent; which he hath Printed.
    Translation of Confucius's Works, in two Volumes, fol.
    Maps of China, in 8vo.
    Letters & Memoirs of Don Herefado de Mendoza. /
And instead of a MS. about the Mahometan Theologie, which Mr Aymon p. 85 cannot now come at; Mr Aymon will give (f. 44a)
    A fine Arabian MS. containing the Prayers & Rites used by the Turks in their Mosques; and 4 quiers (or books) printed by the Chinese, & containing their Mathematics.
    For these the Dr. is to give £25 Sterling; i.e. 250 Florins or Dutch Gilders. The Doctor is also to buy a fine old Latin Bible, in a small Volume, which Aymon ha's; & perhaps other Things.[5]

1. Dr. Astry came, & restored those Volumes of Dr. Hutton's Collections he borrowed the 15th. instant.

2. Mr. Vertue came to peruse Mr. Rich. Symmonds's Collections.[6]

3. Mr R. Gale came, to peruse the 3 Charters of Conan heretofore lent to him.[7] Upon my desire that he would lett my Lord have the Register of the Ambry of Durham, (formerly Mr Mickleton's book) at the price it cost him: He immediately consented, & I am to fetch it from him.[8]

---

[1] For previous attempts to secure the Benedictional see 18 Jan. 1719/20, item 4, and footnote 7; cf. also 23 June 1720, item 9, when an *editio princeps* of Cicero's Letters to Atticus had been offered in exchange and refused. The General had obtained the MS. as executor of Bp. Compton (cf. *BMQ* xxvii (1963), pp. 3–5).

[2] Cf. 21 Jan. 1719/20 for Wanley's first interest in these MSS. and footnote for details of Coke's Coll.

[3] i.e. MSS. of Giustiniani which Joseph Smith of Venice had reported that they would not part with (cf. 18 Jan. 1719/20, item 4).

[4] Cf. 8 Apr. (item 16) and 12 May (item 6) 1721; cf. also 23 May 1721, item 4. Davis's bill was paid 12 June 1721.

[5] Cf. 18 May 1721, item 11, and footnote 6. For the only MSS. actually bought see 29 Nov. 1721, item 12, and footnote. (One of these was the vol. of Letters of Cardinal Visconti mentioned here.)

[6] Cf. 20 Apr. 1721, item 15, and footnote.

[7] The 3 Charters of Conan, Earl of Richmond, are Harl. 48. G. 40, 42, and 43. They had been lent to him 25 Jan. 1720/1.

[8] The MS. is wrongly described here; cf. 3 July 1721, item 4, for its correct description by Wanley, from which it appears that it was an interleaved printed ed. of John Davies of Kidwelly's book on the Church of Durham, i.e. *The Ancient Rites, and Monuments of the Monastical Cathedral Church of Durham. Collected out of Ancient Manuscripts, about the time of the Suppression*, publd. by J. D. [John Davies],

4. Mr Fleetwood & Mr Hesketh came. Mr Fleetwood wants a Transcript of a Charter from his Chartulary of Evesham; and is willing that this valuable MS. do remain to my Lord, provided that he may borrow it when he shall have occasion, and that a Note to that purpose be written in the Book: and he will accept of any present from my Lord in Exchange.[1]

5. I transcrib'd the Charter Mr Fleetwood wanted, & sent it in a Letter to him.[1]

6. Mr Gibson came, & said that the Ship wherein his Books & MSS. are, has actually perform'd Quarantine; so that he hope[s] soon to bring them to my Lord.[2]

19 May 1721.

7. Mr Noel came.

8. A Letter written to Mr Abney, about Lady Stamford's MSS. to know what they will propose.[3]

9. Mr Great of Colchester came, & desire's that the Matter about his Coins & other Antiquities may be brought to some Issue.[4]

20 May 1721.

10. A Letter written to Mr. A.D. Stubs, to attend my Lord on Thursday next.

11. Mr Noel came.

12. Mr Great came, and asking an exorbitant price for his Things, I bad him come again on Monday, when my Lord would give him a Gratuity, & he might take them away.[4]

13. A Letter written to Mr Gale, desiring him not to expect my waiting on him until Wednesday evening.

22 May 1721.

14. A Letter written to Mr A.D. Stubs, for his Letter of Credence to Mr Aymon for Dr. Sherard; & to summon him to Dine with my Lord the next Thursday.[5]

15. Mr Great came & took away his Coins, but left the Tiles & earthen fragments; and my Lord being gone out, I could not give him the Gratuity: whereupon he conceive's himself ill used. /[6]

p. 86 (f. 44b) 1. The Bp. of Peterburgh brought the MSS. he borrowed; & gave me a fresh Note for 7 other Volls. of Dr. Huttons Collections, which he will send for to Morrow, with my Lords permission. He also gave some Syriac & Arabic Papers.[7]

W. Hensman: London, 1672. The copy acquired by Harley is now in the University Library, Durham (MS. 942. 81 D 2 M 5): it has on a fly-leaf a note by Gale dated 23 Nov. 1719. (We are indebted to Mr. A. I. Doyle for this information.)

[1] This Cartulary of Evesham (Harl. 3763) was sent in for Wanley to peruse 31 Mar. 1721 (item 8). For details cf. footnote to 10 Mar. 1720/1, item 11. A memorandum to the desired effect was written on f. 2 of the MS. by Wanley, dated 2 Mar. 1721/2 (see below under this date). Further conditions are set out in the footnote to 17 June 1721, item 9.

[2] Cf. 31 Jan. 1720/1, item 1, where they are reported to be 'in a ship now upon the seas bound for London'; see also footnote 3 to that date.

[3] See footnote to 19 Jan. 1720/1, item 8.   [4] Cf. 16 Nov. 1720, and footnote.

[5] Cf. 18 May 1721, item 11, and footnote. Earlier commissions to Stubbs to deal with Aymon are in Welbeck Wanleyana (Miscellanea).   [6] Cf. 16 Nov. 1720, and footnote.

[7] The Bp. of Peterborough was White Kennett. For borrowings cf. 6 Feb. 1720/1, item 13. Those now borrowed were returned 27 Feb. 1721/2, item 14. The Syriac and Arabic papers (of which Harl. 7013, f. 111, is one) were titled by Negri, cf. 22 June 1721, item 12.

2. Mr Fleetwood desiring to borrow the Register of Evesham,[1] My Lord Order'd me to send it to him; which I did with two Books a present to Mr Clayton.

3. Mr Chapman brought back the books he last had to bind, & took away another parcel.

23 May, 1721.

4. Mr Davies came; I told him I believed that my Lord would allow him for Books the same Rate, as he doe's to Mr Noel.[2]

5. Mr Hasard came; and, by my Lords Order, took away ten of the Lares bought at Kemps Auction, to make new Pedestals for them.[3]

6. I deliver'd 7 Volls of D^r. Hutton's Collections, to the Bishop of Peterburgh's Servant.[4]

7. Mr Drake of Cambridge came, & recd from my Lord his Subscription-mon[e]y towards his Book.[5]

8. Mr Chapman came & divided some Books of Tracts.

24, May 1721.

9. A Letter sent to Mr Fleetwood desiring him to attend my Lord to morrow.

10. Our young Lady Margareta[6] brought two of her Cousins, my Lord & Lady Kinouls Daughters to see some fine Books.

11. I recd a L̄r̄e to Monsr. Aymon from A.D. Stubs, which I sent with my Lords Commission to D^r. Sherard, at his brothers house.[7]

25. May 1721.

12. Mr Charles Davis called here.

13. D^r. Sherard came for my Lords Commission, which I had sent yesterday to his Brothers.[8]

14. Mr Fleetwood came, & desired that I would transcribe an Instrument for him from the Register of Evesham.[9]

15. Mr A.D. [? Stubs] came, & look'd into some Books.

26 May 1721.

16. D^r. Bentley sent the two MSS. Books of the Gospels which he Borrowed, & I returned his Note.[10]

17. D^r. Bentley came himself, & tarried long, looking into many MSS.

18. Mr Gibson came, & brought a Latin MS. with him, which he left.[11] He said that although the Quarantine of the Ship wherein his Books & MSS. are, ha's been

---

[1] i.e. Harl. 3763; cf. 18 May 1721, item 4, and footnote relating to the conditions of gift. The MS. was not actually borrowed until 2 June 1721 (returned 2 Mar. 1721/2 (item 1)). The 2 books sent to Clayton as a present are referred to in Fleetwood's letter to Wanley, 17 June 1721, in Harl. 3778, f. 232.
[2] Cf. 18 May 1721, item 13.   [3] For Kemp's auction cf. footnote to 28 Jan. 1719/20, item 9.
[4] Cf. 22 May 1721, item 1, and footnote.   [5] Cf. 15 May 1721, item 1, and footnote.
[6] i.e. Lady Margaret Harley, Edward Harley's daughter.
[7] Cf. 22 May 1721, item 14, and footnote.   [8] Cf. 24 May 1721, item 11, and footnote.
[9] Cf. 18 May 1721, item 4, and footnote.
[10] These had been borrowed 11 May 1721 (item 2). On these MSS. cf. 6 May 1721, item 4, and footnote.
[11] For the Latin MS. (now Harl. 3306) cf. 7 June 1721, item 11.

performed these Ten Days, he yet cannot get them, nor is she cleared off, or come up.[1]

27. May 1721.

19. Dr. Stukeley came to look into one of Hugh Thomas's MSS.[2] And upon my motion, he promised to ask Dr. Mead to give my Lord his old MS. of the Latin Gospels in Capitals, in Exchange for my Lords MSS. of Avicenna.[3]

20. Mr William Akeman came to know if my Lord will have the books he laid aside for him.[4]

1 June [31 May *deleted*] 1721.

21. Mr Noel brought a Letter & Catalogue from Mr Suttie, No. 24, (saying that he hath not yet recd No. 18, nor 23.)[5] He also shewed me a Letter from his Friend in Flanders, who is expected hither Speedily, in Order to conduct him to a Monastery there, where is a great Library of MSS. & old Printed Books.[6]

22. Mr Dale came to look into an Heraldical MS.

2 June 1721.

23. Mr Harbyn came to look into some MSS. /

p. 87 (f. 45a)   1. Mr. Fleetwood sent to borrow the Register of Evesham, which I sent accordingly, notwithstanding my Lords absence.[7]

3 June 1721.

2. Mr Will. Thomas sent in the MS. 93.B.2. which he had borrowed; & I sent him his Note.[8]

3. Mr Gibson came, & said that his Correspondent in Italy ha's found out an antient Copie of Homer in Greek, written in two folios of Velum; but that the Owners ask a great Price for it.[9] And that he Hope's to get his Books & MSS. which have performed their Quarantine, within a few days.[10]

4. Mr Harbin came; & look'd into MS. 34.B.2.[11]

5 June 1721.

5. Mr Beaver came. Mr Charles Davis came.

---

[1] Cf. 31 Jan. 1720/1, item 1, and footnote 3.
[2] For Hugh Thomas's MSS. see footnote to 19 Oct. 1720.
[3] Nothing further is heard of this projected exchange, except that Sherard on 4 Nov. 1725, item 2, promised to promote this business. There are several Avicenna MSS. in the Harl. Coll.; Mead's library was sold 18 Nov. 1754–7 Apr. 1755 but no such MS. appears in the Mead sale cats.
[4] Cf. 5 June (item 6), 7 June (item 9), 10 June (item 18) (for list of MSS.), 16 June (item 7), 17 June (item 10), and 19 June (item 1) 1721 (for list of printed books).
[5] Not traced.
[6] Cf. 30 June 1721, item 14, from which it appears that the monastery in question was that of the Bernardines at Bruges. On the monastic houses in and near Bruges a little later (1731) see *Gallia Christiana*, v (1731), pp. 260–301; the ref. is probably to Les Dunes (which was a Cistercian house), whose library was notable (cf. Martène and Durand, *Voiage Littéraire*, 1717, ii, pp. 191–2).
[7] Cf. 18 May 1721, item 4, and footnote. Fleetwood's letter is now inserted (f. 1) in Harl. 3763.
[8] i.e. Harl. 1758. (Borrowed 17 Aug. 1720 (item 7); see footnote to that date.)
[9] Cf. 3 July 1721, item 3; 8 May (item 7), 10 Sept. (item 1, for list including this MS., which is Harl. 5600), and 13 Sept. (item 2) 1722 (for settlement).
[10] Cf. 26 May 1721, item 18, and footnote 1.
[11] i.e. Harl. 62.

6. M[r] Ak[e]man desired to know my Lords pleasure about the books he had marked: and said that he will send them in to his Lordship this day.[1]

7. M[r]. Gibson sent hither 5 books in folio, & 4 in 4[to]. at a price.[2]

6 June 1721.

8. M[r] Noel came.

7 June 1721.

9. M[r] Akeman sent in the smal parcel of Books & MSS. my Lord had marked. (except one left behind by mistake)[3]

10. M[r] Bowyer came, & took away the MS. he left here some time agoe.[4]

11. Mr Gibson came, & I told him that my Lord is willing to give him his price for the little parcel he sent in last; provided that he throws in the MS. he brought the 26th. ult. to which he agreed. This MS. is, Nicolai Leoniceni Versio Trium Librorum Harmonicorum Cl. Ptolemæi, in membranis exarata A.D. 1499. fol. min. ten. Peculium Franchini Gafurij. (*vid. infra. pag. 89.*)[5]

8 June 1721.

12. A Letter sent to Mr Noel, desiring attendance on my Lord to morrow-morning.

13. Mr Bogdani brought a Russian Psalter [Liturgy *deleted*] with the New Testament in the same Language, printed A.D. 1692, in 4[to].

14. M[r] Akeman & M[r] Gibson came.

9 June 1721.

15. M[r] Noel brought a Catalogue from M[r] Suttie n[o]. 25; from which I made an Extract.[6]

16. A foreign Gentleman brought a Printed Catalogue of his Books, to be Sold by Auction the 14 Instant.[7]

10 June 1721.

17. M[r] Christian came to take off Impressions of my Lords Seals, & putt them in Order.

18. M[r] Akeman & I agreed for those few of his Books which my Lord liked; among which are these MSS. (vid. pag. 89, 1[).][8]

1. Petrus de Ebano de Venenis.	⎫ Membr. Cod.
Christofori de Honestis Problemata de Venenis. . .	⎬ script. A.D. 1412.
	⎭ 4[to]. mag.[9]

---

[1] Cf. 27 May 1721, item 20, and footnote.

[2] Cf. 7 June 1721, item 11. The list of these books is given under 17 June 1721, after list of MSS.; they were paid for 20 June 1721 (item 5).

[3] Cf. 27 May 1721, item 20, and footnote.   [4] Cf. 31 Mar. 1721, item 5.

[5] For the little parcel sent in last cf. 5 June 1721, item 7, and footnote. The MS. is Harl. 3306: date referred to by Wanley is at f. 46 of MS. and note of ownership is at f. 42.

[6] Not traced.

[7] A ref. possibly to the sale at T. Ballard's [14] June 1721 under title, 'Libri Selecti: being a curious collection of scarce and valuable books in Latin and Italian' (see *CSC*, p. 35).

[8] Cf. 27 May 1721, item 20, and footnote.   [9] Harl. 3659.

2. Jac. Bracellei Liber de Hispaniensi bello. membr. 4to. codex in fine truncatus.[1]

3. J. Solinus de Mirabilibus mundi. chart. 4to. /[2]

p. 88
(f. 45*b*)

4. Cicero de Oratore. Cod. scriptus A.D. 1462. 4to. chart. Deest folium primum.[3]

5. Tullij Orationes pro M. Marcello, &c. chart. 4to. min.[4]

1. Mr Noel came.

12 June 1721.

2. Mr Charles Davis came & Offer'd a book to be sold, which my Lord rejected. I paid him his Bill; & gave him Mr Woodman's Money [Receipt *deleted*]; (which he paid the same day.)[5]

13 June 1721.

3. Mr Sanderson came to peruse a MS. relating to the Chancery; and said that Caxton's Book of Chesse-play cannot be found among the late Lord Somers's Printed Books.[6] I desired him to speak to the Master of the Rolls to lett my Lord have Secretary Thurloe's Papers now in his Possession; saying that my Lord will give any Reasonable Price for them; & to himself a Gratuity & the Use of them. Mr Sanderson undertook to speak to S^r. Joseph, & to send me an Answer.[7]

4. The Bishop of Exeter sent the MS. 63.E.4. which he had borrowed; & I returned his Note by the Bearer.[8]

14 June 1721.

5. Mr Beaver came to Study in the Library.

16 June, 1721.

6. Mr Gibson came, & said that the Ship being now Entred at the Custom-house, he hope's to have his bookes out of her to morrow.[9]

7. Mr Akeman came, & promised to send for those of his Books which my Lord rejected.[10]

17 June 1721.

8. Mr Noel Came & shewed me a Catalogue of Mr Suttie, n°. 26; from which I made an Extract.[11]

---

[1] Harl. 3715.   [2] Harl. 2604.   [3] Harl. 2592.
[4] Harl. 2545.   [5] Cf. 18 May 1721, item 13, and footnote.
[6] i.e. Jacobus de Cessolis, *The Game and Playe of the Chesse*, translated by Caxton from Jehan de Vignay's French version, 1st ed., printed 1475. S. de Ricci, *A Census of Caxtons*, Bibl. Soc., 1909, under no. 1 records no copy as having been in the possession of Lord Somers (or Joseph Sparke, cf. 21 Dec. 1722, item 2). Harley's copy = Osborne, iii, no. 4048, and v, no. 1762 (probably same copy). Wanley had already raised the question of Lord Somers's Saxon Charters, which could not be traced either (cf. 28 Jan. 1719/20, item 4).
[7] On the history of Thurloe's papers now in the Bodleian Library see *DNB*, lvi. 344, and Macray, p. 236. 'Sr Joseph' is of course Sir Joseph Jekyll, Master of the Rolls. Cf. also 14 Feb. 1721/2; 27 June and 14 Nov. (item 9) 1722. Nothing further is heard of this.
[8] Harl. 1027 (borrowed 9 May 1721). The Bp. of Exeter was Lancelot Blackburne.
[9] Cf. 3 June 1721, item 3, and footnote 10.
[10] Cf. 27 May 1721, item 20, and footnote.   [11] Not traced.

9. M[r] Fleetwood Sent me a Letter about taking the Register of Evesham into the Countrey, & causing such parts of it as relate to his Estate to be transcribed there. I returned him an Answer.[1]

10. M[r] Akeman sent for his Books, & they were deliver'd accordingly.[2]

11. A Letter sent to M[r] Elliott, desiring him to call here on Monday to Bind the Volume of Catalogue which I finished to day.[3]

12. I went to M[r] Gibson, and found him sitting upon the Books he had newly received from Italy. The Manuscripts proved to be but fifteen, and not sixteen as he said, and he offer'd me his Letter from his Agent in Italy, wherein no more than fifteen were specified. But I refused to look into the Letter, the Mistake being easie. He sent the said MSS. and some printed Books, upon my request, to my Lord forthwith.[4] Their Titles are,

    1. S. Augustinus de Civitate Dei. MS. fol. membr. man. Ital. rotund. illum.[5]

    2. Historiæ Augustæ Scriptores. MS. fol. membr. man. Ital. rotund. illum. Codex rarus.[6]

    3. Leonardi Aretini Versio Politicorum Aristotelis; cum duabus Epistolis. membr. fol. min. illum. man. Ital. rotund.[7]

    4. Tabula, (cum Capitulorum Titulis) super librum S. Augustini de Civitate Dei. 4to. mag. seu fol. min. membr. man. Ital. quadr. minut.[8]

    5. C. Plinij Epistolæ. scriptæ A.D. 1463. man. Ital. rotund. crass. illum. membr. 4to.[9]

    6. Terentius. man. Ital. fere quadrat. membr. illum. 4to.[10]

    7. Justini Historia. membr. Codex scriptus man. Ital. quadrat. minut. A.D. 1451. 4to. membr.[11]

    8. Boethius de consolatione Philosophiæ. 4to. membr. man. Ital. quadrata illum. /[12]

    9. Qu. Curtius. membr. man. Ital. rotund. 4to. illum.[13]

    10. Virgilius, membr. man. Ital. rotund. illum. 4to.[14]

    11. Corn. Nepos. chart. man. Ital. rotund. cursiv. 4to.[15]

    12. Sallustius. membr. man. Ital. rotund. 4to. illum.[16]

    13. Regula B. Augustini cum expositione *Italica*, per B. Ugonem de S. Victore.—Ordo ad recipiendum Novitium ad Professionem.—Benedictio Vestium regularium. membr. man. Ital. rotund. 4[to].[17]

p. 89
(f. 46a)

---

[1] Cf. 2 June 1721, item 1. Fleetwood's letter, dated 17 June 1721, is Harl. 3778, f. 232: it is important in that it stipulates one condition on which the MS. might pass into Harley's possession. This condition was that Fleetwood might have the use of it in any dispute which might arise (including the production of it in court), a condition embodied in Wanley's memorandum, dated 2 Mar. 1721/2, on f. 2 of Harl. 3763 (the MS. in question). See also footnotes to 10 Mar. 1720/1, item 11, and 18 May 1721, item 4.

[2] Cf. 16 June 1721, item 7, and footnote.

[3] i.e. vol. vi (95. A. 1–98. A. 24) [= Harl. 1920–2184] of Wanley's 'Catalogus Brevior' (now BM Add. 45706), on f. 407 of which is the note: 'Ended, 17 June 1721, by H. Wanley.' Cf. also 21 June 1721, item 9 (for binding).

[4] These are the MSS. referred to frequently above as clearing quarantine, &c. They are those first mentioned 31 Jan. 1720/1, item 1, as '15 or 16 good MSS. in a ship now upon the seas bound for London'.

[5] Harl. 6339.   [6] Harl. 2658.

[7] Harl. 4883.   [8] Harl. 3088.

[9] Harl. 2780 (Wanley's statement as to date is derived from colophon, f. 177[b]).

[10] Harl. 2751.

[11] Harl. 2740 (Wanley's statement as to date is derived from colophon, f. 84). (No date of acquisition by Wanley in MS.)

[12] Harl. 2517.   [13] Harl. 2757.   [14] Harl. 2761.

[15] Harl. 2601.   [16] Harl. 2597.   [17] Harl. 3392.

14. Hesiodi carmen Georgicum—Calphurnij Bucolicon.—Nemisiani Bucolicon.—Petrarchæ Bucolicon.—Theocriti Bucolicon.—Virgilij Bucolicon.—Ejusdem Priapeium.—Ausonij Fragmenta—Probæ Falconiæ Centones—P. Greg. Tiferni Epigramata et Eplæ. chart. man. Ital. cursiva.[1]

15. Demosthenis Oratio περὶ Στεφάνου. membr. 4ᵗᵒ Gr.[2]
Lactantij Institutiones Romæ, per Sweynheym & Pannarts, 1468. fol.[3]
Durandi Rationale. *Romæ, per Udal. Gallum. 1473. fol.*[4]

NB. The Printed Books which my Lord bought of Mʳ Gibson the 7ᵗʰ. Instant, are

1. Plinij Hist. Naturalis. Ven. 1483. fol. min.[5]
2. Virgilij Opera. Mediol. 1481. fol. min.[6]
3. J. Cæsaris Commentarij. Parmæ, 1480. fol. min.[7]
4. Oct. Boldonij Theatrum Temporaneum. Mediol. 1636. fol. min.[8]
5. Aristotelis Organum. Gr. Venet. ap. Ald. 1495. fol. min.[9]
6. Silv. Antoniani Vita per Jos. Castalionem. Rom. 1610. 4ᵗᵒ.[10]
7. Romuli Amassæi Orationes. Bononiæ, 1564. 4ᵗᵒ.[11]
8. Lettioni dell' Estatico Insensato. In Perugia. 1588. 4ᵗᵒ.[12]
9. B(ernardus) à M(alinkroot) de Natura & Usu Literarum. Monast. 1638. 4ᵗᵒ.[13]

19 June 1721.

1. Mʳ. Ackman came, and he was paid for the small parcel of books lately bought of him,[14] the printed books are (*vid. pag. 87, 18*).

   1. B. Hieronymi Epistolarum Liber IIᵈᵘˢ. Romæ ap. Maximos. 1470. fol. mag.[15]
   2. S. Biblia Vulgata, cum Scholijs Isidori Clarij. Venet. ap. Pet. Schœffer 1542. fol. min.[16]
   3. Caeremoniale de Electione Romani Pontificis. Romæ. 1622. 4ᵗᵒ.[17]
   4. Index Librorum prohibitorum, usq ad finem Martij 1717. Romæ, 1717, 8ᵛᵒ.[18]
   5. Historia di Maria Stuarda Regina, di Nicolò Causino, in Bologna, 1646. 24ᵗᵒ.[19]

---

[1] Harl. 2578.   [2] Harl. 6311 A.   [3] Stillwell L. 2; *BMC* iv. 4.
[4] Stillwell D. 331; GW 9104; *BMC* iv. 23.   [5] Stillwell P. 723; *BMC* iv. 257.
[6] Stillwell V. 145; *BMC* vi. 750.
[7] There was no ed. of Caesar printed at Parma in 1480. Presumably GW 5868 is meant. This was printed at Treviso, but probably Wanley thought Parma, the imprint being 'Michael Manzolinus Parmensis librariorum . . . fieri curavit'. Michele Manzolo, the printer at Treviso, was a native of Parma.
[8] *Theatrum temporaneum aeternitati Caesaris Montii Cardinalis et Archiep. Mediolanen. Sacrum*, by Ottavio Boldoni, Bp. of Teano, Milan, 1636, fol.   [9] First part of GW 2334; the *editio princeps*.
[10] No copy in BM *General Catalogue of Printed Books*.   [11] Printed Giovanni Rossi.
[12] 'L'Estatico Insensato' was Filippo Massini.
[13] No copy in BM *General Catalogue of Printed Books*.   [14] Cf. 10 June 1721, item 18.
[15] *BMC* iv. 10. (Part of IC. 17155), i.e. printed by Sweynheym and Pannartz.
[16] Copy in BM *General Catalogue of Printed Books* (press-mark 469. c. 4).
[17] Probably *Caeremoniale continens ritus electionis Romani Pontificis. Cui praefiguntur Constitutiones Pontificiae & Conciliorum Decreta ad eam rem pertinentia.* [Ed. F. Ingoli.] Rome, 1622, 4°. Harley already had a copy of this at Wimpole according to Wanley's cat. of printed books there (1716–17), in which it was 2785 (X. B. 8) (BM Lansdowne 816, f. 60).
[18] Presumably the *Index Librorum Prohibitorum usque ad totum mensem Martii 1716, regnante Clemente XI*, Rome, 1716, 8°. (The next ed. appears to have been 1726.)
[19] Nicolas Caussin, *Historia di Maria Stuarda, Regina di Francia, e di Scotia . . . Portata del Francese nell' Italiano dal Padre Carlo Antonio Berardi.* BM *General Catalogue of Printed Books* records only a Bologna ed. of [1690?] in 12° and an earlier ed. of [1650?] from Venice.

2. Mʳ Peck came; my Lord paid him 1 Guinea as the first Payment towards one of his Books in the Large Paper;[1] & he copied a Letter of Thomas Cecil Earl of Exeter in 38.C.2.[2]

3. Mʳ Noel came with Mʳ Almeyda the Jew & another Gentleman who had an high prized, wrought Ivory Tankard to Sell.

4. Mʳ. Gibson came and we had much talk about his MSS. & the Printed books which my Lord is willing to have; but could not (after long discourse) agree about the Price.[3] So he is to wait upon my Lord to morrow. /

20 June 172L

p. 90
(f. 46b)

1. Mʳ Gibson came.

2. Mʳ Bowyer came.

3. The Gentleman mentioned yesterday at nᵒ. 3 cam[e].

4. A Letter Recd from Mʳ Fleetwood who ha's sent the Register of Evesham into Lancashire in order to be produced at the next Assizes, if there shall be Occasion. He is willing to know what my Lord intend's to allow him for it. I wrote to him by the bearer.[4]

5. My Lord agreed with Mʳ Gibson for the 15 MSS. & two Printed Books; & paid him for them, and the parcell brought in the 7th. instant; bein[g] in full of all his Demands.[5]

21, June 1721.

6. I brought (being left by Mʳ Bogdani at my Lodgings) some Leaves of an old MS. Missal, presented by an old Lord Lovell to the Cath. Church of Saꝛ [*i.e.* Sarum], wherein are the Armes of his Family, with those of Holand, &c. These Leaves came A.D. 1600 into the Hands of Joseph Holand the famous Antiquary: but my Lord declined the buying them, the whole being but a fragment, & the Pictures & Armes belonging to Families not of his Kindred.[6]

7. My Lord sent me to Mʳ Fleetwood, to whom I delivered his Lordships Recompense for his old Register of Evesham-Abbey; which proved to his full Satisfaction & Content. I took no Receipt, it being by way of Gift.[7]

---

[1] Possibly Francis Peck, *Academia Tertia Anglicana*, 1727, in the List of Subscribers to which Harley's name appears as a subscriber to a copy in the large paper (see p. xv).

[2] i.e. Harl. 374 (the letter referred to is at f. 32).

[3] See 17 June 1721, item 12 for list, and footnotes for identifications; cf. also 20 June 1721, item 5.

[4] Fleetwood's letter, dated 20 June 1721, is in Welbeck Wanleyana. The Register of Evesham is Harl. 3763. Cf. 17 June (item 9, and footnote) and 21 June (item 7) 1721 (relating to 'recompense'). The MS. was returned 2 Mar. 1721/2 (item 1).

[5] See 17 June 1721, item 12 (for list), and footnotes for identifications.

[6] The leaves were taken away by Bogdani 28 June 1721 (item 7); Anstis had been invited to come and see them 22 June 1721 (item 11) and on 23 June 1721 (item 14) did so. The MS. in question is now Harl. 7026, the 'Lovel Lectionary', the fragment of a lectionary executed for John, 5th Lord Lovel of Tishmersh (d. 1408) as a gift to Salisbury Cathedral. It was acquired by Harley at the sale of the library of Thomas Granger of the East India House (T. Ballard, sale of 9 Oct. 1732 [postponed to 15 Jan. 1733], p. 100, lot 407): the price paid by Harley was £3. 11s. (see BM Lansdowne 825, f. 30ᵇ). According to inscriptions in the MS. (ff. 1, 3, 4) it had been acquired by Joseph Holland, the antiquary, 5 June 1600. Other notes by Holland occur *passim* (and the pedigree of the Hollands by him is at ff. 2ᵇ–3). Holland and Lovel arms occur at ff. 5, 6, 7ᵇ, 10, 11.

[7] Cf. 20 June 1721, item 4, and footnote, and for full note see 10 Mar. 1720/1, item 11, and footnote 3. For Fleetwood's comments on the original choice of wine as the recompense, see his letter to Wanley, 20 June 1721, in Welbeck Wanleyana. The MS. is Harl. 3763.

8. M^r. Gibson sending for those of his Books which my Lord rejected; they were d̄d̄ to his messenger.

9. Mr Elliot came yesterday & to day to Bind the Sixth Volume of Catalogue.¹

22 June 1721.

10. I finished the Copie of my Lords Catalogue of his old Latin Books, in order to Mr Elliots binding.²

11. A Letter sent to Mr Anstis, wishing him to call here, & see Mr Bogdani's old Leaves.³

12. Mr Negri came & gave the Titles of the papers given lately by the Bishop of Peterburgh;⁴ & left three of his Proposals for Printing the Psalter & New Testament in Arabic,⁵ & 3 Specimens of the Character; two for my Lord & one for my Self.

13. Mr Beaver came to Study. & Mr Mattaire came.

23 June 1721.

14. Mr Anstis came to whom I shewed the old Leaves of Parchment.⁶ He look'd into the Lord Radnors MSS. & Seguiers MSS.⁷ He say's that he ha's no MSS. from Mr Fleetwood of Missenden.⁸ That he ha's not heard from D^r. Thorpe.⁹

15. Mr Noel Came with a Catalogue from Mr Suttie N°. 27.¹⁰

16. Mr Ackman brought a Catalogue of Books & MSS. to be sold by Auction the next Wednesday, &c.¹¹

26. June 1721.

17. Mr Beaver came to study.

27. June 1721.

18. Mr Noel came.

19. A Letter sent to Mr Bogdani a Letter for him to attend my Lord to morrow. /

p. 91 (f. 47a)

1. D^r. Bentley came to thank my Lord for his Favor in Lending to him the CODEX AVREVS, & to Borrow the Greek MS of the Gospels here, inscribed 93.D.6; which was d̄d̄ to him, & I took his Note for it.¹²

2. Mr Elliot begun to work about the CODEX AVREVS, in Order to the New Binding of it, the Cover it had in the Second Binding of it perhaps about 90 years ago, being worn out, and the whole sewing gone to decay.

¹ Cf. 17 June 1721, item 11, and footnote.
² i.e. Harl. 7627 A, 7627 B, the latter of which bears on the paste-down of the upper cover the date by Wanley '20 die Junij, 1721': on the fly-leaf of the former MS. is the date '13 Febr. 1720/21'.
³ Cf. 21 June 1721, item 6, and footnote.
⁴ Cf. 22 May 1721, item 1, and footnote, for the Oriental papers given by Bp. of Peterborough.
⁵ Salomon Negri's ed. of the New Testament in Arabic was eventually pubd. in 1727.
⁶ i.e. of the Lovel Lectionary referred to at 21 June 1721, item 6 (see footnote to that date).
⁷ The Earl of Radnor's MSS. were acquired at sale of 2 May 1721 (for list see footnote to 4 May 1721), and the Séguier MSS. were acquired 5 Sept. 1720 (for list see footnote to that date).
⁸ Cf. 18 Jan. 1719/20, item 4, and footnote 6 for the Missenden Library.
⁹ Anstis had written to John Thorpe, the antiquary, on 12 Apr. 1721 (item 1) about MSS. formerly belonging to William Lambard (see footnote to that date).   ¹⁰ Not traced.
¹¹ i.e. 28 June 1721, when a sale of books and MSS. by Ballard took place.
¹² The Codex Aureus (Harl. 2788) had been lent to Bentley 11 May 1721 (item 2), and returned 26 May 1721 (item 16). The Greek Gospels MS. is Harl. 1810; it was returned by Bentley 5 July 1721 (item 11).

3. Mr Bowyer came, & talked about an Exchange of his Book of Sr. Henry Saviles Chrysostom for my Lords.[1]

4. Mr. Lion sent in a little parcel of old Editions & other Curious books.[2]

28 June 1721.

5. A Letter sent to Mr Noel, about a time when he is to wait upon my Lord.

6. Mr Charles Davis brought a MS. mostly Hebrew, written by a Christian, and partly Latin; being upon the Subject of Conjuration. I rejected it now; as I remember I did before about 7 or 8 years agoe.

7. Mr. Bogdani came, & took away the old Leaves he left with me.[3]

8. Mr Cart came, enquiring about Mr Morley & A Bp. Sancrofts Papers.[4]

9. Mr Bacon came, & told me that he had lately seen in a Booksellers Hands, one part of a Septi-partite Indenture between King Henry VII, and others, dated 16 July, anno regni 19, which is to be sold. But that the Seal & Bosses are taken off. I desired him to buy it for my Lord as cheap as he can; & he promised to do so.[5]

29 June 1721.

10. Mr Bowyer sent in his Saviles Chrysostome.[6]

11. Mr. Beaver came to Study.

12. Mr Gale & his Brother Sam. came.

13. A Letter sent to Mr Abbott keeper of the Swan-Inne at Chelsea, to attend my Lord some Morning.[7]

30 June 1721.

14. Mr Noel came & said that he shall go speedily to Bridges [*i.e.* Bruges] in Flanders, where 'in the Convent of the Bernardins` [there *deleted and* '` *written above the line*] is a very large Library of Books both Printed & MSS. and that the Religious there have Offer'd him to pick & chuse at his pleasure, provided he lay's out a good Sum with them; which, at this time they much want.[8] Item, that he verily believe's that Mr Suttie ha's procured an Exemplar of the Latin Psalter printed at Mentz A.D. 1457. being the oldest Date to any printed book now known.[9]

15. A Letter written to Mr Anstis, desiring him to send all the Volumes of Dr. Natth. Johnston's History of the Family of Talbot (my Lord Weymouth's Book) to my Lord, who desire's to peruse them.[10]

[1] This refers to Sir Henry Savile's ed. of Chrysostom pubd. in 1610. Cf. 29 June 1721, item 10.
[2] No further ref. is made to this parcel.
[3] i.e. of the Lovel Lectionary referred to at 21 June 1721, item 6 (see footnote to that date).
[4] Cf. 22 Apr. 1721, item 20, and footnote.
[5] No further ref. is made to this. The well-known Henry VII septipartite indenture was already in the Harl. Coll. (Harl. 1498) and had been given by Sir Thomas Hoby.
[6] Cf. 27 June 1721, item 3, and footnote.
[7] For services rendered by Abbott cf. 8 July 1721, item 18.
[8] Cf. 1 June 1721, and footnote.
[9] For 1457 Mainz Psalter see Sir Irvine Masson, *The Mainz Psalters and Canon Missae, 1457–59*, Bibliographical Soc. 1954. Cf. also 24 Apr. 1722, item 13 and footnote.
[10] i.e. Nathaniel Johnston, M.D. (1627–1705), antiquary, &c. (see *DNB*). Johnston's compilations relating to the family of Talbot were made in 1693/4 and a copy in 4 folio vols. transcribed by George Clifford about 1704 in the library of Lord Weymouth early in the 18th cent. is recorded, *HMC* 3rd

16. A Letter to Mr Greene, to attend my Lord to morrow morning.

17. A Porter brought in a small parcel of Books from Mr Innys.[1]

18. M^r. William Thomas came; & desired to look into the MS. of Thom. Hoccleve.[2]

1 July 1721.

19. M^r. Virtue came to peruse some more of Rich. Symmonds's MSS.[3]

20. M^r. William Thomas came to peruse the MS. of Hoccleve.[4]

21. M^r. Downes came.

3 July 1721.

22. Mr Chapman brought the last Parcel that was deliver'd to him; and was paid off, in full; & took another large Parcell.

23. Mr Beaver came to Study. /

p. 92
(f. 47b)

1. Mr Noel came.

2. M^r. Abbott of Chelsea brought in his Bill.[5]

3. Mr Gibson came, & talked about sending in a smal parcel of Books 'which he sent soon after` ['` *added afterwards*][6] He say's that his Florentine Monk raise's up the Price of his Velum-MS. of Homer in Greek,[7] yet higher; & care's not to part with it. That the MS. of Pliny is Shipped of[f] from Leghorn;[8] and that an Italian Abbat is willing to sell a most curious MS. of the Hebrew Bible in several large Volumes in fol. (which the Undertakers of our Polyglott Bible formerly offered largely for, but were refused:) but that the price will be great.[9]

4. I went to Mr Roger Gale, who deliver'd to me that book relating to Durham which my Lord lately bought of him, and was heretofore in the Possession of Mr Mickleton. It proved not to be the Registrum Eleemosynariæ Dunelmensis Ecclesiæ, as I was told it was; but John Davies of Kidwellies Printed book about that Church, Interleav'd & amplified with many written Notes.[10]

4 July 1721.

5. A Letter sent to Mr Gale about the word Tacamentum.

6. D^r. Fotheringhay came, enquiring after the old Liturgical Books of the Church of England; and having a large Collection of his own, he invited me to come to him & see it; which I told him I would when I had Time.[11]

Report, 1872, Appendix (Marquess of Bath MSS.), p. 198. (Cf. also BM Add. 18446.) The originals from which Johnston made his own compilations (= *CMA* ii (1697), p. 101, nos. 3848–54) were presented to the College of Arms by Henry, Duke of Norfolk, 1677 (see A. R. Wagner, *Records and Collections of the College of Arms*, 1952, p. 32).

[1] No further ref. to this parcel.

[2] Possibly in connexion with Urry's posthumous ed. of Chaucer's Works, for the supervision of which William Thomas was responsible. And the Occleve MS. therefore may be that containing the portrait of Chaucer, i.e. Harl. 4866. Cf. 17 Aug. 1720, item 7, and footnote.

[3] Cf. 20 Apr. 1721, item 15, and footnote.   [4] Cf. 30 June 1721, item 18, and footnote.

[5] Abbott was employed in varnishing and numbering the presses (cf. 8 July (item 18) and 29 June (item 13) 1721).   [6] Cf. 8 July (item 16) and 9 Nov. (item 9) 1721.

[7] Cf. 3 June 1721, item 3, and footnote.

[8] Cf. 28 Mar. 1721, item 2, and footnote.

[9] For other refs. to this Hebrew Bible cf. 8 May (item 7) and 23 Oct. (item 6) 1722. The *Biblia Sacra Polyglotta* was pubd. in 1657 in 6 vols. (Darlow and Moule, no. 1446).

[10] See 18 May 1721, item 3, and footnote.   [11] No further ref. to him or his coll.

7. M[r] Jenkyn-Thomas Philips came, enquiring after something Curious, that he might print it. I showed him the Gr. MS. given by D[r]. Sherard, being the Vindication of the Greeks Doctrines against those of the Romanists, by Elias Mignati a late Bishop in the Morea.[1]

8. M[r] Le Neve came.

9. M[r] Will. Thomas came to look into the MS. of Hoccleve.[2]

10. M[r] Greene came, and we had some Discourse together about a Course to be taken, in Order to my Lords procuring Copies of all the modern Heraldical Visitation-books which are wanting in this Library. His opinion was that Application should be made to the Duke of Norfolk, or to his Deputy Earl-Marshall.[3]

5 July 1721.

11. D[r]. Bentley came with my Lords Greek MS. of the Gospels, (93.D.6.) the Correctness of which, (as also its Antiquity; which notwithstanding, I know not to be great) he exceedingly extolled.[4] He also brought with him the Lichfield Book of the Gospells commonly called the Textus S. Ceaddæ, and left it here for my Lord to see.[5]

12. M[r] O Sullevane came, to know when I am to go to Oxford.[6]

13. Mr Thomas came & look'd into the Textus S. Ceaddæ, & the MS. of Chaucers Tales.[7]

6 July 1721.

14. Mr Knowles came to know how much my Lord will give him for his two Quarto-books wherein are Impressions taken from the Leaves of Plants, without their Names; and for a Latin Poem he intends to make in praise of them.[8]

15. Mr Bridgeman came & promised to send me another dosen of Black-Lead-Pencills; but they came not.

8 July 1721.

16. M[r] Gibson came, & sett his Price upon four 4[to] books he had sent in.[9]

17. M[r] Knowles took away his two Books he left here.[10]

18. M[r] Abbott came, & said that he will come about Tuesday to Varnish & number some of the Presses.[11]

19. M[r] Roger Gale came to Study. /

[1] Cf. 21 Mar. 1719/20, item 11, and footnote. The MS. is Harl. 5729. Chishull had already proposed to print it in English (cf. 18 Jan. 1719/20, item 4, and footnote). Jenkyn Thomas Philipps came in again to consult it 20 Apr. 1723, borrowed it 21 June 1723 (under item 13), and returned it 10 Aug. 1723.
[2] Cf. 30 June 1721, item 18, and footnote.
[3] Both Robert and Edward Harley had a particular interest in heraldic material, and Visitation Books form a very large portion of the present Harl. Coll. Nothing further is heard of this project.
[4] i.e. Harl. 1810, which Bentley had borrowed on 27 June 1721 (item 1).
[5] Cf. 2 Mar. 1714/15, item 1, and footnote.
[6] Cf. 13 July (item 5) and 28 Oct. 1721.
[7] For 'Textus S. Ceaddæ' cf. item 11 above and footnote. The Chaucer MS. was presumably wanted in connexion with his ed. of Urry's Chaucer. Cf. 17 Aug. 1720, item 7, and footnote.
[8] Cf. item 17. This was later pubd. as *Materia Medica Botanica*, 1723.
[9] Cf. 3 July 1721, item 3. [10] Cf. item 14. [11] Cf. 29 June 1721, item 13.

11 July 1721.

1. By my Lords Order, I took out MS. 40.D.13. for Mr Wise of the Public Library in Oxford.[1]

2. Mr Ainsworth came, and desired Materials from hence, toward the setting out a new Edition of Dugdales Warwickshire, by one of his friends.[2] I told him that here are but few things relating to that County; and that they will soon be sent down into the Countrey; and that I am also about to go down to Oxford for 3 or 4 Months.

3. An Answer sent to D^r. Wilkins at Lambeth, who inquired what MSS. my Lord ha's of Mr Seldens Composition.[3]

13 July 1721.

4. M^r. Denison Fellow of University College in Oxford, & Chaplain to the Duke of Beaufort, came; partly to see the Library; but Principally to have my Opinion touching two Receipts each for £100, & having the Name of the late Duke of Beaufort sett to them. One of them had some words very industriously blotted out, which words might have been *Principle money wth interest*: and otherwise look's like a true Receipt. The other looks like a Forgery; some of the Marks of which are these; The Money is made received from the same person as the former; yet the Hand is plainly different, by far Stiffer, & much labor'd. The first Line so very close to the top, as if cutt off from some Letter which he had written or Subscribed with his Name at a Distance. False English & uncouth manner of writing unworthy of Him who wrote the other: and moreover the Dukes subscribed Name interfering with some of the Writing above; that seem's to have been written upon his Name, & not his Name upon the Receipt which would have been more proper. There are also remaining parts of two Letters belonging to Writing which had been above.

5. Mr Elliot having clothed the CODEX AVREVS in My Lords Marocco-Leather, took the same from hence this day, in Order to work upon it with his Best Tools; which he say's he can do with much more Conveniency at his house than here. This is particularly noted here, because of my speedy Journey to Oxford, in Case any ill Accident should happen.

28 October 1721.

6. I called here, after my return from Oxford, for the Catalogue of my Lords Latin Books of old Editions, but found it not;[4] as also for the List of the Books last delivered to Mr Chapman the Binder, to the End that they may be compared at his House, & so sent to Wympole without being brought hither.

---

[1] i.e. Harl. 563 (returned 27 Nov. 1722 (item 6) through Innys the bookseller). The MS. (Stow's colls., including continuation of Nicholas Trivet's annals) was presumably obtained by Wise on behalf of Anthony Hall for the latter's *N. Triveti Annalium Continuatio*, pubd. late in 1722. Hall used for his text of the Trivet continuation the Royal MS. (15 C. xii) and makes no ref. to a Harl. MS. Harley subscribed to Hall's book (see 27 Nov. 1722 (item 6)).

[2] This may possibly refer to work on the 2nd ed. of Dugdale's *Antiquities of Warwickshire* which was pubd. in 1730 under the editorship of William Thomas; this was the only ed. pubd. between 1656 (the original ed.) and 1765.

[3] For further query from Wilkins on Selden cf. 4 May 1723, item 17. Wilkins was responsible for editing the complete Works of John Selden, which were pubd. in 1726.

[4] Cf. 22 June 1721, item 10, and footnote.

9 November 1721.

7. I called here again. Having by the last Higler, sent down to my Lord some more of the late John Kemp's Antiquities, wch. my Lord bought lately.[1]

8. The Parcel đđ to Mr Chapman the Binder, being all done; were sent down to my Lord the last week.

9. NB. the four 4to Books mentioned in the preceeding page, n°. 16. are not yet paid for to Mr Gibson. /[2]

1. The 7th. Instant I agreed with M^r. Gibson, for his 8 MSS. lately arrived from p. 94 Italy; & gave them to the Binder the same day: but not dated on their first (f. 48b) Pages, lest any inquisitive person coming in, should thereby perceive how lately they were bought.[3] They are,

    C. Plinij Historia Naturalis. membr. fol. mag. man. Ital. nitidissime script. & inlum. cum Insig. Medicæorum.[4]

    Sallustius.—Justinus, 1442.—L. Florus. membr. fol. man. Ital. script. & inlum.[5]

    Lactantij Institutiones—De Ira Dei—De Opificio Hominis—Epitome. membr. fol. man. Ital. nit. inlum.[6]

    Ciceronis Orator.—Brutus. membr. fol. min. man. Ital.[7]

    Tullius de Officijs. script. manu Blasij de Acereto Cancellarij Januensis A.D. 1433.—De Senectute. De Amicitia. Paradoxa. Somnium Scipionis. membr. 4to. min. man. Ital.[8]

    Lucretius. manu Ital. cursiva. 4to. min. chart.[9]

    Ἐπιτομὴ τῶν ὀκτω μερῶν τοῦ λόγου, καὶ ἀλλῶν τινῶν ἀναγκαίων, συντη-θεισα παρὰ Κωνσταντίνου τοῦ Λασκαρέως τοῦ Βυζαντίου. chart. 4to. min.[10]

    Ciceronis Rhetorica, scripta c. A.D. 1433.—Rhetorica Nova ad Herennium. membr. 4to. min. man. Ital. nitid.[11]

18 November 1721.

2. I went to Mr Wilcox the Bookseller, & paid him for 21 MSS. which I had before agreed with him for;[12] being, those of the Study of Robert Paynell of Belaughe Esq in Com. Norff. in his Time an eminent Lawyer of Grayes Inne. They are these Law-Books following.

    1. The Queenes (*Elizabeth*) Prerogative in the Salt-Shores.—That to Marrie or Contract without the Consent of the Parents, is not Lawfull.— Concerning Corporations.—Divers good Cases & their Reasons.—

---

[1] Cf. 3 and 4 May 1721 for inscriptions bought previously at Kemp's auction; the present ref. is to the commission given to Hill on 27 Mar. 1720/1 (cf. that date and footnote). No less than 7 boxes of statuary were sent to Wimpole (cf. Harley's letters to Wanley of 29 and 31 Oct. and 5 Nov. 1721 in Welbeck Wanleyana).

[2] Cf. 8 July 1721, item 16.   [3] Cf. 28 Mar. 1721, item 2, and footnote.

[4] Cf. 11 Feb. 1722/3, item 7, for ref. to purchase of this Pliny. Probably Harl. 2677, which has at foot of f. 1, however, arms *not* of Medici but Piccolomini; it has no date of acquisition by Wanley.

[5] Harl. 2657 (the second item of which bears (f. 137^b) the date 1442, as noted by Wanley).

[6] Harl. 3110.

[7] Probably Harl. 2771. (All other Harl. MSS. of Cicero's Orator and Brutus bear dates of acquisition by Wanley and are accordingly identified under those dates.)

[8] Harl. 2628 (Wanley's statement as to date and scribe is derived from the inscription, f. 1).

[9] Harl. 2554.   [10] Harl. 5741.

[11] Harl. 3925. (Wanley's statement as to date is derived from the inscription on f. 94, which refers to the XXXI year of Pope Eugenius IV (elected 1401): the MS. belonged to a Guicciardini (see f. 94)).

[12] No earlier ref. *N.B.* Letters in square brackets in list below are Wanley's.

Chester-Case of the Fine, notablie argued; with the Record of that Case.—The Case towching the little Abbeys suppressed by Cardinal Wolsey.—Le Joyners Case, touchant le Prerogative le Roy.—Cases sur le stat de 1 E.6. de Chaunteries, Priests, Obbitts, &c.—The Act of Dissolution of Chaunteries, Colledges, &c. 1 Eliz. Other Cases upon the Statute of Chaunteries.—A good Case touching the Aucthoritie of a Deane & Chapter. Bushopp a Lieutenant to the Deane, &c. *with some other Tracts. fol.*¹

2. Relationes Placitorum super Brevibus de Recto: tempore R. Edwardi II, ut videtur.—Relations sur Avowre; dans le mesme temps.—Annales Juridici, de termino Michaelis, anni ejusdem Regis 13; déq terminis Hillar & Paschæ insequentibus—Fragmentum aliud annalium Juridicorum; scil. de termin. Michaelis, anni 18 Ejusdem Regis.—Annales Juridici pro annis 4, 5, 7, (Assise apud Norhamptone coram Rogero de Bakewelle, anno [*blank space*]) 11, 14, 15 & 16 R. Edwardi III. fol. membr.²

3. Relationes Placitorum, annis 10, 11 & 12, Jacobi Regis. [G.R.] fol.³

4. Relationes Placitorum, annis 9, 10, 11, 12 & 13 Caroli Regis. fol. [S.R.]⁴

5. Relationes Placitorum, annis 29, 30, 31, 32 & 33 Elizabethæ Reginæ. fol. [F.R.] /⁵

6. Les Reports de Sʳ. Edm. Anderson Sñr Cheife Justice de Coṁon Banc. Et aussi de Justice Warburton de mesme le Banc. fol. [A.R.]⁶

7. Reports des ans 5, 6, 7, 8, & 9, Caroli Regis *in Scaccario*, per R̄oƀt Paynell. fol. [I.R.]⁷

8. Miscellany Reports, temp. R R. Elizabethe & Jacobi. fol. [M.R.]⁸

9. La douzieme part des Reports de Sʳ. Edw. Coke, Chivalier, &c. ne unques publie in Printe.—fol. 88. Reports & Notes by other persons; very Curious. fol.⁹

10. Les Reportes de tres-reverend Judge Sʳ. Richard Hutton; accordant al Coppy escryt oue sa mayne proper. fol.¹⁰

11. Reports, of several Years of Q. Eliz. Reign. fol. [E.R.]¹¹

12. Relationes ex libro Francisci Moore Militis, Servientis ad Legem, scripto propria manu ipsius fol. [R.M.]¹²

13. Statutes from 1 Edw. III, to 18 Hen. VI. in English. fol. antient.¹³

14. Relationes Tho. Fleming, uti fertur. de anno 39 Eliz.—Relationes, de annis 15 & 16 Jacobi Regis fol.¹⁴

15. The Reading of John Stone of Grayes Inne Esq upon the Statute of 13 Eliz. Cap. 7. touching Bankrupts learnedly & amply explayned. fol.¹⁵

16. Year-book of part of K. Henry VIˢ Reign; comprehending the years, 11, 12 (but part of it cut out.) 13, 14, 15, 18, 19, 21, 22. fol. min. old, & fairly written. At the beg. Mʳ Paynell hath Noted that the 13ᵗʰ. & 15ᵗʰ. Years were not in Print.¹⁶

17. Statutes, in French, from 1 Edw. III. to 20 Henr. VI. 4ᵗᵒ. mag. perg.¹⁷

18. Magna Carta of K. Edw. I, with other Statutes, & antient Law-Tracts perg. 4ᵗᵒ. Exemplar optimæ notæ.¹⁸

¹ Harl. 4717.   ² Harl. 5012.   ³ Harl. 4948.   ⁴ Harl. 4811.
⁵ Harl. 4812.   ⁶ Harl. 4817.   ⁷ Harl. 4816.   ⁸ Harl. 4814.
⁹ Harl. 4815.   ¹⁰ Harl. 4813.   ¹¹ Harl. 4552.
¹² Harl. 4585. (Wanley's note of ownership is derived from f. 1.)
¹³ Harl. 4999.   ¹⁴ Harl. 4558.   ¹⁵ Harl. 4506.   ¹⁶ Harl. 4557.
¹⁷ Harl. 4871.   ¹⁸ Harl. 5290.

19. Brettone.—Juramenta Justiciariorum, Vicecomitum, Majorum & Ballivorum. 4to. perg.[1]
20. Reports of Common Pleas, temp. Caroli & Jacobi Regum. 4to.[2]
21. Magna Carta of Edw. I. with other Statutes, & Law Tracts. The last is, Summa que vocatur Curia Baronis Rimée, i.e. in old French Verse. 4to. perg.[3]

20 November 1721.

1. I began to get the pieces of Antiquity which are in the Closet together; & sent for Mr Gregory to make Boxes for them, that they may sent down to Wympole.[4]

21 November 1721.

2. Mr Gregory came, & promised to bring the Boxes next Thursday morning.
3. Mr Talman came & tarried long here. He wants to Sell his Collection of Drawings.[5]

22 November 1721.

23 November 1721.

4. Mr Gregory came, & we Packed up divers pieces of Antiquity into Six Boxes, to be sent down to Wympole to morrow, either by the Higler, or by the Royston-Carrier. And some few others yet remaining, he promises to / send two more Boxes on Saturday, & an half-Case for MSS. p. 96 (f. 49*b*)

24 November 1721.

1. Mr Beaver came to Study.
2. M^r [*blank space*] Smith came to look after a particular Case in one of my Lords Journals of Parliament: but I could not find the Key.

25 November 1721.

3. Mr Gregory brought 3 Boxes; one for MSS. the others for Antiquities to be sent to Wympole. vizt. N°. 1. MSS. some Printed Books. 2. A Roman Brick from Colchester; two Stones with Runic Letters, and another with the Armes of Courtney, found by Mr Auditor Harley in the Church of [*blank space*] in Northamptonshire, in an heap of Rubbish. It. a Coat or Shirt of Mail, old. N°. 2 [*sic, for 3?*]. A Roman Gutter-tile, broken with two other Fragments from Colchester. It. the laced Band of K. Charles I. Item. the Shash [*sic*] of A.B^p Laude. It. a Point Cravat. It. four little parcels of Casts, &c. had from M^r. Sanderson & S^r. Simonds d'Ewes.[6]

27 November 1721.

4. D^r. Astry came & borrowed 6 Volumes of D^r. Huttons Collections; & I took his Note for them.[7]

[1] Harl. 5134.   [2] Harl. 5131.   [3] Harl. 5213.
[4] For inventory of items sent cf. 25 Nov. 1721. They were sent to Wimpole on Harley's instructions to Wanley, dated 16 Nov. 1721 (Welbeck Wanleyana). (The 'closet' was, according to Harley's letter, 'the bookbinders' closet'.)
[5] Cf. 11 Jan. 1719/20, item 12, and footnote.   [6] Cf. 20 Nov. 1721, and footnote.
[7] i.e. Harl. 6950–85, 7519–21. The 6 vols. were returned 15 Jan. 1721/2 (item 15).

5. A Letter written to Mᴿ Granger to hasten his sending Mᴿ Maddisons Tract about the English Coins, which he promised to me for my Lord.[1]

6. Another to Dᴿ. Sherard, about the Books he lately bought for my Lord, but hath not yet deliver'd in; although he be already paid for them.[2]

7. I putt up some MSS. with four Printed Books, to be sent down to Wympole this week.

8. A Letter recd from Tho. Bacon Esq, desiring me to look over the List of Lady Stamfords MSS. which I took from them some time since (& which he also sent) [( ) *inserted later*] & to lett him know what I would advise [my Lord *deleted and* Mᴿ. Prothonotary *substituted*] Mᴿ Prothonotary Foley to give for them.[3] He sent likewise a List of a small parcel of MSS. (of little value) which are now to be sold in the Strand.[4]

28 November 1721.

9. I waited on Mᴿ Bacon about Lady Stamfords MSS. & gave my Opinion.[5] I also desired him to serve my Lord in the buying of some few Books, at Mᴿ Fairbarne's Auction which will begin on Friday next, & he promised to do so.[6]

10. Mᴿ Beaver, at my desire, bought F. Geronimo de la Conception's Cadiz illustrada, at an easy price.[7]

29 November 1721.

11. I brought hither the book last above-mentioned.

12. Dᴿ. Sherard sent in the Parcel I paid him for on the 18th. Instant: among which are two MSS.[8]

    1. The Book of Card. Visconti's Letters relating to the Council of Trent, being the Original from which / Mᴿ Aymon translated & lately printed the same in Holland; who also crave's some Gratuity for it.[9]

    2. The Genealogy of the Kings of France to K. Lewis XIII. by Angoulesme-Herald.[10]

Both these Books go to my Lord on Friday, in Box. Nᵒ. 1.

1. Dᴿ. Sherard acquainted me that he ha's Liberty to dispose of the Egyptian Antiquities lately given to him by Consul Faringdon: and that he can now serve my Lord in procuring of Greek, Coptic, & other MSS. by the Means of Mᴿ Philip Wheake who is gone Consul to Grand Cairo; as also in getting of other

p. 97
(f. 50a)

---

[1] Maddison's tract on English coins is Harl. 6941, ff. 31–35 (note Wanley's endorsement, f. 31). For Maddison's coins see 28 Jan. 1719/20, item 5, and footnote.

[2] Cf. 29 Nov. 1721, item 12, and footnote. (Sherard had been paid for them 18 Nov. 1721.)

[3] Cf. 3, 4, 5 Apr. 1721—dates on which Wanley made a list of the Countess of Stamford's books; cf. also 19 Jan. 1720/1, item 8, and footnote.

[4] Presumably not 'Mr. Fairbarne's auction' referred to under the following items which was held at Paul's Coffee-house; no further references.

[5] Cf. item 8 above, and footnote 3.

[6] Refers to sale of 30 Nov. 1721 at Ballard's; cf. 4 Dec. 1721 for details of this auction.

[7] Fr. Jeronimo de la Concepción, *Emporio del Orbe, Cádiz ilustrada*. Amsterdam, 1690 (= no. 58772 in A. Palau y Dulcet, *Manual del Librero Hispano-Americano*, 1951).

[8] Cf. 27 Nov. 1721, item 6, and also 18 May 1721, item 11, and footnote.

[9] Harl. 3479 (included at f. 2 is an engraved portrait of Jean Aymon). Aymon's ed. of Cardinal Visconti's letters on the Council of Trent is *Lettres, anecdotes et mémoires historiques du Nonce Visconti. . . . Mises au jour, en italien et en français, par M. Aymon*. 1719.

[10] Harl. 4355.

Egyptian Antiquities, the French Consul there (who was a Curious man & a great Collector) being departed from thence.[1]

2. Mr Bacon sent for my List of Lady Stamfords MSS. & I deliver'd it to his Servant.[2]

4 December 1721.

3. The Auction of Mr Freebairnes Books being over, M[r] Bacon on Saturday-last deliver'd to me my Catalogue, and also his own wherein are the Prices that the Books went at. Hereupon I take Leave to observe, for the Information of Posterity, That although the Current Prices of Books are much advanced during these late Years,

That the books, in generall, went at low, or rather at Vile Rates; through a Combination of the Booksellers against the Sale.[3]

Yet some Books went for unaccountably-high Prices, which were bought by Mr Vaillant the Bookseller, who had an unlimited Commission from the Earl of Sunderland, being

Virgilij Æneis. MS. 4to. scriptus circa A.D. 1450. manu Ital. in
membr.[4] . . . . 11. 5. –
Virgilij Opera, impressa (per Ant. Zarottum) circa A.D. 1472.
fol. liber nitidiss. & illuminat.[5] . . . . . . 46. –. –
Columella de Re Rustica. MS. in perg. manu Ital.[6] . . . 40. –. –
Vitruvius. MS. in perg. man. Ital.[7] . . . . . 16. –. –
Dav. Nicetæ Comment. in Gregorij Nazianzeni Carmina, Gr.
MS. in chart. Bombycin. fol. min.[8] . . . . . 33. –. –

It was noted, that when Mr Vaillant had bought the printed Virgil above mentioned at £46, that he huzza'd out aloud, & threw-up his Hat for Joy, that he had bought it so Cheap.

The Booksellers, upon this Sale, intend to raise the Prices of Philological Books of the first Editions, and indeed of all Old Editions accordingly. Thus M[r] Noel told me yesterday, that he ha's actually agreed to sell the said Earl of Sunderland, six duplicate Printed Books, (now coming up the River toward the Custom-house) for fifty Pounds per Book: although my Lord give's no such Prices.[9] They are,

The Clementines, with the Gloss. Mogunt. per Fust & Schoyffer. 1460. fol. velum.[10]

[1] See 13 Feb. 1721/2, and footnote.   [2] Cf. 27 Nov. 1721, item 8, and footnote.

[3] This refers to the sale of 30 Nov. 1721 at Ballard's, entitled 'A Small Parcel of scarce Valuable Books and Manuscripts Lately imported from Italy'; and cf. 28 Nov. 1721, item 9, and 15 Feb. 1721/2, item 5.

[4] Probably lot 50 in the cat. of sale referred to above.

[5] Probably lot 51; it is to be noted that the sale cat. describes this ed. of Vergil's works as 'absque loci aut Typographi nomine', and '(per Ant. Zarottum)' is therefore interpolated by Wanley; also the sale cat. prints the date as 'MCCCCLXII'. It is not clear why Wanley should have inserted the words 'per Ant. Zarottum' in the description of an unsigned Vergil. It is true that Zarottus began to print in Milan in 1472 (see *BMC*, vi. 708), but he did not produce an ed. of Vergil until 25 July 1475 (Stillwell V. 141) and this is a very rare book. The only undated Vergil which could be described as 'circa 1472' seems to be Stillwell V. 137, Printer of Ausonius, Venice (copy in BM., IB. 20036), and perhaps it is this ed. to which Wanley is referring.

[6] This is apparently to be identified with lot 65 which is described in the sale cat. merely as 'Rei Rusticae Scriptores, Codex MS. in Pergamena'.   [7] This was lot 110.   [8] This was lot 60.

[9] Cf. 19 Apr. 1722, item 3, for Wanley's remarks (at the time of the Earl of Sunderland's death) on the Earl's influence on prices at book-sales.

[10] As regards 'The Clementines' to be sold by Noel to Sunderland cf. 14 Apr. 1722, item 2, where Noel allowed Wanley to cut out 2 pages from it to supply 2 wanting in Harley's copy. The book is the Constitutiones of Clement V, printed by Fust and Schoeffer, Mainz, 1460. See *BMC* i. 20 (= IC. 82); GW 7077.

Lactantius. in Monasterio Sublacensi, per Maximos, 1465. fol.[1]
The Virgil printed at Rome, by the Maximi.[2]

18 December 1721.

4. Mr Noel came, & said that he expect's his Bill of Lading for his four Cases yet expected, by this Post. /[3]

21 December 1721.

1. Mr Bowles the Proto-bibliothecarius Bodleianus having sent up the Complutensian Bibles, (being a Duplicate in that Library, & bought at the last Meeting of the Curators thereof:[)]][4] I brought the same hither this Morning, & packed them up (with Oriental & other MSS, &c.) in Order to be sent down to my Lord to morrow.

2. Mr Gibson came hither, & held me long in Discourse about books, at home & abroad: & d̄d̄ to me a piece of Chinese Gold, which belong's to a Lady who would have 3 Guineas for it.[5]

22 December 1721.

3. Mr Bowles the Bodleian Library-keeper came; & I spent most of the time in Shewing him some of the Rarities here, to his great Wonder & Satisfaction.

23. December 1721.

4. Mr Harbyn came to look upon some of D^r. Huttons papers.[6]

5. Mr Harby[n] borrowed one of D^r. Hutton's Volumes for a few days.[7]

28 December 1721.

6. Mr Bowles came, & saw more of the Rarities here.

29 December, 1721.

7. Mr Bowles came again & saw yet more of the Curious Books, Papers & Parchments here.

30 December 1721.

8. Mr Bowles came again & saw yet more of the like Rarities.

---

[1] Printed by Sweynheym and Pannartz at Subiaco. *BMC* iv. 2; Stillwell L. 1.
[2] Printed by Sweynheym and Pannartz [1469] = Stillwell V. 133.
[3] Cf. 22 Feb. (item 4), 2 Mar. (item 2) 1721/2; and 9, 10, 11, 12 Apr. 1722; and see 17 Apr. 1722 and footnote (for lists of MSS. contained in these 4 cases and marked ⊕ being the balance of those bought on 20 Jan. 1721/2).
[4] Harley had written to Wanley 16 Nov. 1721 (Welbeck Wanleyana) to inquire whether Wanley 'had heard anything from Mr. Bowles about the duplicates in the Bodleian Library': Wanley wrote 21 Nov. 1721 accordingly (Bodl. Library MS. Add. C. 78, f. 22). Bowles's reply signifying the Curators' agreement is dated 9 Dec. 1721 (see letter in Welbeck Wanleyana). The Curators' Meeting had been on 8 Nov., but the Bodleian has no information about the purchase of the Complutensian Polyglot. (We are indebted for this information to Mr. L. W. Hanson and Mr. I. G. Philip.) The Complutensian Bible is the first Polyglot bible printed in 6 vols. at Alcalá de Henares by Arnaldo Guillen de Brocar between 1514 and 1517.
[5] Cf. 13 Jan. 1721/2, item 10.
[6] i.e. Harl. 6950–85, 7519–21.   [7] Returned 3 Feb. 1721/2 (item 6).

2 January 1721

$\frac{}{2}$.

9. I wrote a Letter to Mr Wilcox, upon his not bringing in the two old English Bibles I bought of him, which were sent in accordingly afterwards, & paid for.[1]

13 January 1721

$\frac{}{2}$.

10. My Lord rejected the Chinese piece of gold left here by Mr Gibson the 21st. Instant.[2]
11. Mr Bowles came & perused the Registre of Shaftesbury.[3]

15 January 1721

$\frac{}{2}$.

12. A Letter was sent to Mr Noel about my Lords Calling upon him in a few days.
13. Mr Bateman came.
14. Mr Christian came, & saw some of my Lords Coins.
15. D^r. Astry brought back those books of D^r. Hutton, which he borrowed last;[4] having brought them several times before during my Absence, partly by reason of the late Holy days; & partly occasioned by my late grievous Calamity.[5] And he borrowed 7 other books of Dr Hutton, by vertue of another Note under his Hand.[6]

16 January 1721

$\frac{}{2}$.

16. Mr Beaver came; & renewed his Promise of making my Lord a Present (in some time to come) of all the Letters & Papers relating to the Earl of Portmores last Expedition into Spain./[7]
1. I brought in, by Virtue of an Agreement I made with Mr Charles Davis, two p. 99 Books, viz. 1. Ivonis Carnotensis Excerptiones Ecclesiasticarum Regularum. (f. 51a) MS. antiq. fol. min.[8]
   2. Delle Nozze di Carlo II Rè delle Spagne con Maria-Luisa Borbone, *di Giuseppe Castaldi, in Napoli, — fol. con figg.*[9]

---

[1] No earlier mention of these but cf. Wanley's Addenda, Lansdowne 771, f. 78^b, under 3 Jan. 1721/2 (at p. 199 of the present work) which dates them as of 1551.
[2] Cf. 21 Dec. 1721, item 2 (*not* Jan. as stated by Wanley).
[3] i.e. Harl. 61 (= Davis no. 85).
[4] Borrowed 27 Nov. 1721 (item 4).
[5] Wanley's first wife, Anna (the widow of Martin Berenclow whom Wanley had married 1 May 1705 at St. Swithin's, London Stone), died 3 Jan. 1721/2, and was buried in St. Paul's, Covent Garden, 5 Jan.
[6] Returned 20 Jan. 1721/2 (item 11).
[7] Beaver went with Lord Portmore as his secretary (cf. his letters to Wanley in Welbeck Wanleyana). This Lord Portmore was David Colyear, cr. 1st Earl of Portmore, 1703: he served in Portugal 1703–4 and was Governor of Gibraltar 1713. He died 2 Jan. 1729/30.
[8] Harl. 3090.
[9] Giuseppe Castaldo, *Tributi Obsequiosi della Città di Napoli per gl' Applausi Festive delle Nozze Reali del Carlo Secondo Re delle Spagne con la Duchessa d' Orleans Sotto la Direttione dell' Eccelentiss. Signor Marchese de los Velez Visere di Napoli*, Naples, 1680. (Cf. Minshull's Cat. of Printed Books at Wimpole, BM. Add. 19750, f. 100.)

17. January 1721
2.

2. Letters written to Mr Noel, apprising him of the time when my Lord will call upon him to see to see [*sic*] his Books last arrived from Holland:¹ and to Mr Anstis, desiring him to attend his Lordship upon Occasion of a curious parcel of Books said to be remaining in Yorkshire.²

3. Mr Vander-Meer a Painter of Landskips brought two Dutch-pieces on Copper for my Lord to see.

18 January 1721
2.

4. Mr Vander-Meer came & took away his two Pictures.

5. Came Mr Christian, Mr Gibson, & M^r O Sullevane.

19 January 1721
2.

6. My Lord went to Mr Noel's and look'd over the great parcel of Books which I had selected some time agoe; and from them did make choice of some, which will be found marked in the Lists dated the 8th, 11th, & 12th. of December, 1721. His Lordship did likewise inspect the 47 MSS. whose Titles are Specified in the List dated 13 December 1721. And, the same day Mr Noel deliver'd unto me his Proposal for the sale of the same under his Hand; which I having explain'd, He Signed, & I attested. vid. infra, 106, 7.³

20 January 1721
2.

7. My Lord agreed to Mr Noels Proposal; so that the Things are now Bought, & hourly expected.³

8. Mr Chapman came, & received 3 Books for present Binding. And, upon his Request, I deliver'd (by Order) Six Marocco-Skins to be used in my Lords Service (all which, by mistake, he left behind him.) [( ) *added afterwards*]. He desire's to have them at a cheap price, & to Bind as before. I say, that my Lord will not turn Leather-Seller; & therefore he must on Wednesday morning next bring hither his Proposals for Binding with my Lords Marocco-Skins; otherwise, his Lordship will appoint some other Binder to do so.

9. Mr Noel sent in the Things above-mentioned; and afterward, came himself.³

10. Mr Hazard came & putt on a new Lock to my Lords Cabinet for Coins.

11. D^r. Astry brought in all the books he had lately borrowed from D^r. Hutton's Collection; & gave me his Note for five more. /⁴

---

¹ Cf. 19 Jan. and 20 Jan. (items 7 and 9) 1721/2; and 17 Apr. 1722, item 7 and footnote (for list of items other than ⊕).

² See 25 Jan. 1721/2, item 12, and footnote.

³ See 17 Jan. 1721/2, item 2, and footnote.

⁴ They were borrowed 15 Jan. 1721/2 (item 15). The 5 now borrowed were returned 1 Feb. 1722.

128

22 January 1721
22.

1. Mr Bateman came.

2. D^r. Covel the Master of Christs in Cambridge came; & look'd, a little, into some of my Lords MSS.

3. D^r. Stratford came.

23 January 1721
22.

4. Mr Tim. Thomas came.

5. M^{rs}. Davies brought a few MSS. said to have been her Husbands, which [appear] not to be worth one farthing.[1]

6. D^r. Keith came.

7. Mr Noel came.

8. Mr Gibson came.

24 January 1721
2.

9. Mr Chapman gave in his Proposal for Binding in my Lords own Marocco-Leather; but my Lord being willing to consider upon it, Order'd that he should take a parcel of Books with him, & the Six Skins he left behind him the last time he was here, & set upon the Binding forthwith; and in some time His Lordship will come to a Resolution.

25 January 1721
22.

10. A Letter sent to Mr. Andrew Hay, desiring him to send to my Lord the MS. of Theodore's Greek Grammar, & the Abridgement of Anselm. . . . . . the first Bishop of San Domingo's Travels, which he laid by for my Lord at my Request.[2]

11. Another to Mr Elliot, desiring him to call here to morrow, between one & two.

12. Another to Mr Anstis Garter: in answer to one last received from him.[3]

13. Mr. Noel came.

14. Mr Dale came to peruse some Heraldical MSS.

15. Mr Mattaire came, & I shewed him two Rolls.

26 January 1721
2.

16. A Letter sent to Mr Noel for him to attend my Lord on Monday-morning next.

17. Mr Elliot came, and I discoursed with him upon a Method of Binding for my Lord with his own Marocco-Leather; and desired him to bring in his Proposals to morrow, for that End.

---

[1] Cf. 28 Apr. 1721, item 7.
[2] See 17 Apr. 1722, item 6, and footnotes for identification of these MSS.
[3] Probably in answer to Anstis's letter of 24 Jan. 1721/2 (Harl. 3777, f. 25), which refers to the Jewel House records secured by Layton. (On this subject cf. Ralph Thoresby's letter to Anstis 5 Dec. 1720 in BM Stowe 749, f. 133.) Cf. also 17 Jan. 1721/2, item 2.

27 January 1721
—
22.

18. Mr Lion came to see the Library.

19. Mr Hazard brought a new Frame for my Lords Cabinet of Coins here; & He with his Servant spent much time in mending the said Cabinet.

20. Mr Elliot brought in his Proposal about Binding with my Lords own Marocco-Leather, which not agreeing with the Method I desired him to proceed by; he rated another which I drew up, & signed the same. I also deliver'd unto him a Parcel of Books to Bind, which he promised to bring back this day 3 weeks.

30 [*substituted for* 29] January 1721
—
22.

21. I went to Mr Warburton, & received from him 9 Quaternios fragmentary, being part of the Remainder of a MS. relating to Waltham-Abbey; which was bought of him, some time Ago.[1] He ha's yet more MSS. & Antiquities. /

p. 101
(f. 52a)

31 January 1721
—
22.

1. Mr Warburton sent in for my Lord his Maps of Northumberland & Yorkshire.[2]

2. Mr Gibson came: as also Mr Noel.

1 February 1721
—
2.

3. Mr Moses Williams & Mr William Thomas came.

4. Dr. Astry brought the 5 Volumes of Dr. Huttons Collections which he borrowed last: and gave his Note for the little Bound Book in the same Box.[3]

3 February 1721
—
2.

5. Mr Noel came, & my Lord made up his Accompt.

6. Mr Harbyn came, and perused some MSS. & likewise restored the Book he borrowed last, & took up his Note.[4]

7. I brought in the remaining fragments of the Red book (I call it so) of Waltham-Abbey.[5]

5 February, 1721
—
2.

8. Mr William Thomas came.

[1] Harl. 3766: on the relationship of this MS. to Harl. 3776 (acquired 16 July 1720, no. 7 of list) see E. G. Millar, 'A MS. from Waltham Abbey in the Harleian Collection', *BMQ* vii (1933), pp. 112–18. Cf. 3 Feb. 1721/2, item 7 also.
[2] John Warburton's *Map of the County of Northumberland* was pubd. in 1716 and his *A New and Correct Map of the County of York* . . . in [1720]; his notes relating to the preparation of the Yorkshire map are in BM Lansdowne 911–13, and the List of Subscribers is in BM Lansdowne 916.
[3] Borrowed 20 Jan. 1721/2 (item 11). 'The little Bound Book' was returned 5 Feb. 1721/2 (item 10).
[4] Borrowed 23 Dec. 1721 (item 5).
[5] See 30 Jan. 1721/2, and footnote.

9. M^r [*blank space*] Justice brought a few MSS. to sell.[1]

10. D^r. Astry brought the little Book he borrowed last, & took up his Note.[2]

6 February, 1721/2.

11. Mr Gibson came.

12. Mr Slyford came; & said that Mr Willis's Antiquities of Buckingham-shire are nown [*sic*] in Town; and that my Lord may see the Book & take a Copie of it.[3] He also perused the Chartulary of Dunstaple.[4]

7 February 1721/2.

13. M^r. Justice came, & took away his Things; not accepting what my Lord offer'd for one of his Books.[5]

8 February 1721/22.

14. A Letter sent to Mr Gibson, acquainting him that my Lord will see him after next Monday.

9 February 1721/22.

15. Mr Christian came to look into my Lords Silver Coins.

16. A Letter sent to D^r. Sherard to know when Monsr. de la Mottrayes Book will come out;[6] and when I may receive from him the Egyptian Antiquities given him by Consul Faringdon who lately brought them from Gran-Cairo.[7]

10 February 1721/22.

17. Mr Timothy Thomas came; & said that he had brought up for my Lord from Mr Crynes of Oxford, the Hierom (or Rufinus) upon the Creed printed at Oxford A.D. 1468: which is bound up with 3 other antient & valuable Tracts.[8]

12 February 1721/22.

18. M^r. Hanbury brought Mr Schumacker who is Library-keeper to the Emperor of Russia, to see this Library. He deliver'd to me a Letter in his Recomendation from Mr Bowles of Oxford.[9] I shewed him some few things, & desired him

---

[1] Cf. 7 Feb. 1721/2.   [2] Borrowed 1 Feb. 1721/2 (item 4).

[3] i.e. Bodl. Lib., Willis MS. 6 (*SC* 16299), one of the vols. in Browne Willis's Colls. for a history of Buckinghamshire, which occupied his leisure moments all his life (on the project see J. G. Jenkins's *The Dragon of Whaddon*, 1952, pp. 128–31). Browne Willis's papers were bequeathed by him to the Bodleian in 1760 and are now *SC* 16294–403, of which a very considerable number are devoted to Buckinghamshire.

[4] Harl. 1885. It had once belonged to Wanley himself, from whom it had been bought by Harley.

[5] Cf. 5 Feb. 1721/2, item 9.

[6] See 15 Mar. 1720/1 and footnote, and 20 July 1724.   [7] See 13 Feb. 1721/2, and footnote.

[8] Duff 234. The true date of printing is 1478, 1468 being a misprint in the book itself. Cf. also 10 Dec. 1723.

[9] The letter of recommendation, dated 10 Feb. 1721/2, is Harl. 3777, f. 220. A further letter on Schumacher's character, dated 19 Feb. 1721/2, is at f. 224.

to call again 'the next week' ['` added afterwards], & then I will (God willing) shew him more.

13 February 1721
——
22.

19. I went to D^r. Sherard, & received from him the parcel of Egyptian Antiquities brought from Cairo by Mr Consul Faringdon, / and brought them into this Library.[1]

p. 102
(f. 52b)

14 February 1721
——
22.

1. Mr Sanderson putt into my Hands a Turkish Silver Inkhorn, for my Lord to see. It is said to have been taken from the Grand Viziers Secretary at the late Battel of Belgrade, & weigh's 14½ Ounces. Mr Sanderson also said that he shall soon begin to inspect Secretary Thurloes Papers.[2]

15 February 1721
——
22.

2. A Letter came from Mr Bowles[3] desiring to answer certain Queries about Books, & to make enquiries for him among the Booksellers; which I shall not have time enough to do.

3. Another from Mr Tristram of Pembroke-College, with a Letter & the first part of his Vida for my Lord; & requesting the favor of his Lordship to furnish him with certain Heads for his Second Part, in case they are to be found at Wympole.[4]

4. Yesterday my Lord received a parcel of Printed Books, bought at Mr Woodmans last Sale.[5]

5. Mr Bacon brought in two MSS. the one is Entituled Commentum & Expositio Zoni Florentini super toto Lucano. 4to. mag. chart.[6] which he lately bought at Freebairn's Auction.[7] The other is entituled Πέτρου τοῦ Βέμβου πρὸς Ἐνέτας περὶ τοῦ βοηθεῖν τοῖς τῶν Ἑλλήνων λόγοις. 4to ten. chart. which he gave.[8]

6. Mr Noel brought a Book of Caxtons Printing, & a fair MS. of Wycliffes New Testament; but my Lord rejected them both, as have [sic] them already.

7. Mr Gibson came.

16 February 1721
——
22.

8. Mr Moses Williams came, desiring me to meet him at the Cottonian Library to morrow-morning.

---

[1] Cf. 29 Nov. 1721, item 1, and 9 Feb. 1721/2, item 16, for earlier refs. to Egyptian antiquities. Harley's coll. of antiquities (including Egyptian items) was dispersed 8–23 Mar. 1741/2 by Cock of Covent Garden. Nothing is known of a coll. of Egyptian antiquities made by Faringdon.
[2] See 13 June 1721, item 3, and footnote.
[3] Bowles's letter of 13 Feb. 1721/2 is Harl. 3777, ff. 222, 223.
[4] Tristram's letter dated 7 Feb. 1721/2 is Harl. 3782, f. 22. The first vol. of Thomas Tristram's ed. of Vida's poems was pubd. Clarendon Press, Oxford, 1722, 8°. (*M. H. Vidae ... Poematum ... pars prima.*) Cf. 8 Apr. 1723, item 6, for ref. to 'new edition': the second vol. followed in 1723, and the List of Subscribers includes Harley's name (p. 116).
[5] This probably refers to the sale of the library of John Vaughan, 1st Viscount Lisburne, which took place at Woodman's shop 13 Feb. 1721/2.
[6] Harl. 2479 (this was lot 73 in Ballard's auction of 30 Nov. 1721).
[7] i.e. Ballard's auction of 30 Nov. 1721; see 4 Dec. 1721, and footnote.
[8] Harl. 5628.

132

17 February 1721
———
22.

9. Mr Beaver came.

10. Mr Timothy Thomas having left a parcel of Coins, &c. with me, I selected all those from them, which I thought might, any way, turn to my Lords use. Mr Harbyn borrowed 81.B.12. of my Lord, without a Note.[1]

19 February 1721
———
22.

11. Mr Elliot came for some [of] my Lords Marocco Leather for Binding.

12. A Letter sent to Mr Chapman, desiring him to bring in my Lords Books with all speed.

13. Mr Gibson came.

20 February 1721
———
22.

14. M^r Le Neve Norroy came & is desirous of borrowing the Registre of Castel-Acre.[2]

15. Mr Gibson came, & I paid him in full; & besides, a Gratuity from my Lord.[3]

21 February 1721
———
22.

16. M^r O Sullivane came to Study in the MS. History of the Irish Monastery at Ratisbon.[4] /

1. Mr Harbin sent his note for the book 81.B.12.[5]

2. Mr Hanbury brought Mr Schumacker, to whom I shewed many Rarities in this Library, to his great Delight & Satisfaction. Mr Timothy Thomas came soon after them, as [*sic*] saw the same things.

3. Mr Bridges came; & tarried long.

p. 103
(f. 53*a*)

22 February 1721
———
22.

4. Mr Noel came & said that He is informed that the Venetian Galley being safely

[1] i.e. Harl. 1396: he sent his receipt for it on 21 Feb. 1721/2 and returned the MS. on 21 Apr. 1722.
[2] i.e. Harl. 2110: it was handed over to Le Neve on 27 Feb. 1721/2 (item 15), and returned 22 Mar. 1722/3 (item 6).
[3] The last parcel of MSS. had been acquired from Gibson on 9 Nov. 1721, where it is noted that the 4 books acquired on 8 July 1721 are not yet paid for.
[4] Harl. 3973. The famous 13th-cent. MS. of the 'Libellus de fundatione ecclesie consecrati petri quod vulgariter dicitur Weihsantpeter tractans de hybernia et sanctis hyberniensibus quorum corpora ibi requiescunt', which had been acquired 20 Jan. 1721/2. (Cf. 17 Apr. 1722, item 7 and footnote.) The Weih St. Peter, the Priory of Irish Benedictines at Ratisbon of which Marianus Scotus was Abbot, was founded in 1060 and was incorporated in 1215 in the Abbey of St. James the Great, also an abbey of Irish Benedictines: it was suppressed in 1862 by Pope Pius IX (for bibliography see L. H. Cottineau, *Répertoire Topo-Bibliographique des Abbayes et Prieurés*, 1937, ii, cols. 2408, 2409). Dibdin made a visit to this Abbey of St. James in search of books during his stay at Ratisbon in 1818 (see T. F. Dibdin, *A Bibliographical Antiquarian and Picturesque Tour in France and Germany*, iii (1821), pp. iv–xiii). The *library* of the Irish monastery at Ratisbon had already been the subject of conversation between O'Sullivan and Wanley on 10 Aug. 1720, item 11 (see footnote to that date).
[5] Cf. 17 Feb. 1721/2, item 10.

arrived at Amsterdam is gone for Rot[t]erdam; & will be soon here, the Weather permitting.[1]

5. Mr Harbyn came & perused some Heraldical MSS.

6. Mr Gibson came.

23 February 1721/22.

7. Mr Cowse came with the Proposals for printing all Mr Seldens works.[2]

8. Mr O Sullevane came to Study.

9. Mr. Chapman sent one of my Lords books.

24 February 1721/22.

10. Mr. Harbyn came & looked into some Heraldical MSS.

26 February 1721/22.

11. Mr Chapman brought in Ten more of my Lords books, & recd from me Six of my Lords marocco Skins.

12. Mr Beaver came.

27 February 1721/22.

13. Mr Charles Davis brought a Book to Sell; but my Lord ha's it already.

14. The Bishop of Peterburgh brought those Books of Dr. Huttons Collections which he had borrowed;[3] & borrowed Six other Volumes of the same Collections, and also the Visitation of Northampton-shire inscribed 65.C.6. which last he promised soon to return.[4] His Lordship also brought & gave a Court-Roll of the Manor of Cleygate. (in Com. Essex?)[5]

15. Mr Le Neve came, & I deliver'd to him the Registre of Castel-Acre, by my Lords Order.[6]

28 February 1721/22.

16. Mr Boothe came, & said that soon he shall go down to Chester, & will then serve my Lord in procuring for him the old Deeds & Rolls lately belonging to the Holmes Collection there.[7] And he desires that he may cause to be Copied from Holmes's Books, such matters as relate to the Knights of St. John of Jerusalem in that County.

---

[1] Probably the boat carrying the 4 cases reported 18 Dec. 1721, and arriving 9 Apr. 1722 (see 18 Dec. 1721 and footnote).

[2] A ref. probably to the ed. of Selden's Works pubd. with Preface and Indexes, by David Wilkins, 3 vols. in 6, in 1725.

[3] Borrowed 22 May 1721 (item 1).

[4] MSS. now borrowed were returned 23 May 1722 (item 8). The Northamptonshire Visitation is Harl. 1094.

[5] Harl. Roll T. 17; it comprises views of frankpledge with Courts Baron of Cleygate Manor, Surrey, 28 May 31 Hen. VIII [1539]–24 Sept. 35 Eliz. [1593]; it consists of 14 skins. It is endorsed by Wanley '27 die Februarij, A.D. 1721/22' but not with donor's name.

[6] See 20 Feb. 1721/2 and footnote.   [7] See 23 June 1719/20, item 5, and footnote.

$$\text{1 March } \frac{1721}{22}.$$

17. Mr Vertue came.

18. Mr Hanbury came from Mr Schumacker, whom I desired might again call here on Tuesday-next, to see some more things. /

$$\text{2 March } \frac{1721}{22}.$$

1. Mr Hesketh brought in my Lords Chartulary of Evesham lately sent up by Mr Fleetwood.[1]

2. Mr Noel came; & said, that he expect's a Bill of Lading for his four Cases, by this or the next Post.[2]

$$\text{4 March } \frac{1721}{22}.$$

3. Mr Elliot sent in most of the Books of the last Parcel which he was to have brought in on the 17th. of the last Month, and in looking upon them, I approve not either of the Leather or Workmanship of several of them.

$$\text{5 March } \frac{1721}{22}.$$

4. Young Mr Varenne brought a modern MS. to sell to my Lord, who is now at Wympole.[3]

$$\text{7 March } \frac{1721}{22}.$$

5. Mr Hanbury brought Mr Schumacker, & I shewed him some more Rarities, to his great Satisfaction.

$$\text{8 March } \frac{1721}{22}.$$

6. Mr Benj. Motte sent in two Copies of his Vindication against Mr Jones.[4] I put his Letter & my Lords Copie into a Case which I shall send for Wympole to-morrow.

7. Mr William Thomas came.

$$\text{10 March } \frac{1721}{22}.$$

8. I went to Mr Schumacker, by my Lords Order; and offer'd to accompany him down in his Journey to Cambridge & Wympole. He was very thankful to my Lord for his great favor; & promised to be ready to take Coach upon any day that my Lord will please to appoint.[5]

[1] i.e. Harl. 3763. Wanley's memorandum at f. 2 of the MS. bears this date. (Cf. 20 June 1721, item 4.)
[2] See 18 Dec. 1721, and footnote.   [3] Cf. 12 Apr. 1722, item 13.
[4] i.e. *A Reply to the prefaces published by Mr. H. Jones with his abridgement of the Philosophical Transactions,* &c. [By B. M.], London, 1722.
[5] Apropos of this visit see Harley's letters to Wanley of 8, 11, and 18 Mar. 1721/2 in Welbeck Wanleyana. Schumacher was accompanied by Wanley himself.

9. A Letter written to Chapman the Binder, expostulating with him upon the account of his great Neglect toward my Lord; & requiring him to bring in such of my Lords Books as now remain in his Hands, on Tuesday next by 12 of the Clock, upon pain of my Lords Displeasure, & loss of his Business.

10. Another to Elliot the Binder; requiring him to bring in a book of the last Parcel which yet remains in his Hands, on Monday next at 12; but promising then to deliver to him another parcel.

12 March 1721.

11. M[r]. Chapman brought home the remaining Books of the last Parcel, well done. Part of his Excuse for their long detention, was his late Illness. That he ha's not been out of the House, these Ten days until now; & that he will be more punctual for the future. I Order'd him to call here to morrow for another Parcel.

12. M[r]. Charles Davis brought the 4 MSS. which I lately saw at M[r] Woodmans Lodgings, at a Price. As also a small parcel of Books of his own. I have taken them in, for my Lords inspection.[1]

13. M[r] Elliot brought the book I wrote for; & took away the Parcel I reserved for him. /

p. 105
(f. 54a)

13 March 1721
22.

1. M[r] Chapman came, & I deliver'd to him a large Parcel of Books & MSS. to bind; as also 18 of my Lords Marocco Skins, which he promised to husband to the best advantage.

2. Having done with him; I go to Bishop-gate-street to take places in the Cambridge-Coach, for M[r] Schumacker & my Self. (which I soon after did for Friday next.)

3. M[r] Beaver came, desiring to use a French printed book upon Le Poinct d'Honeur; but I being in hast, lent him the same for two days; he having heretofore done my Lord service.

14 March 1721
22.

4. M[r] Schumacker having Notice from me, promised to be ready on Friday morning next.

5. I having discover'd an Error in M[r] Chapmans last titling one of my Lords books, am obliged to send it to him, that it may be rectified, (which can easily be done) & so sent down to his Lordship by the next Higler.

15 March 1721
22.

6. M[r] Shelton called here, & staying saw several of the Rarities here.

9 April 1722.

7. I being returned from Wympole, M[r] Noel came to me yesterday, & certified me that his so long expected four Cases were come safe, & were in his Ware-

---

[1] Cf. 29 Oct. 1722, item 3, for list of both Woodman's and Davis's MSS. and settlement for books and MSS.

house: whereupon I went to him (by my Lords Order) this Day; & having looked upon them all, I sent up all those that I thought might be for my Lords Turn.[1]

10 April 1722.

8. I putt the said Books in Order, ready for my Lords Inspection; and compared the MSS. with Mr Sutties List of them, and that the books he meant are now all arrived, & some more which Mr Noel threw in.[1]

11 April 1722.

9. Mr Varenne left here yesterday one MS. & one thin Tract printed upon Velum.[2]

10. I waited on my Lord to Mr. Noels where his Lordship Selected such Books as he found most for his purpose, & left me behind, that I might bring him to-morrow, Mr Noels Valuation of them.[3]

11. Mr Elliot sent in some more of the Books deliver'd to him the 12 of March last.

12 April 1722.

12. Mr Noel having putt into my Hands many of Mr Sutties last Catalogues of Books, MSS. & Coins, now lying at Calice ready to be sent over: I made some Extracts from them.[4] Mr Noel sent in the Printed books Selected by my Lord;[5] & also the Manuscripts lately come in, which are mentioned in Mr Sutties list of 13 December 1721; & were bought the 19th. of January 1721.[6]

13. Mr Varenne [*substituted for* Vaillant *deleted*] brought another MS. and putt a price upon the whole little parcel.[7]

14. One Mr. [*blank space*] Greenway an Hampshire Clergy-man came to look into the Chartulary of Hyde.[8]

13 April 1722.

15. Mr Elliot brought in 3 more Books of the last Parcell; and took away one to Title afresh. /

14 April 1722.

1. Mr Virtue came, and saw divers old MSS. &c.

2. Mr Noel came; and we collated my Lords book of the Clementines of 1460, printed upon Velum, with his like Book[9] which is Imperfect; and from thence, with his Consent, I cutt out one leaf towards the Midle being wanting in my Lords Book; and one other Leaf at the End, after the Date, being also wanting in my Lords Copie. It contains the Constitution Execrabilis of Pope

---

[1] See 18 Dec. 1721, and footnote.   [2] Cf. 12 Apr. 1722, item 13.   [3] See items 7 and 8 above.

[4] Wanley's extracts from Suttie's cats. bearing this date (12 Apr. 1722) are in Welbeck Wanleyana, Misc. no. 8 (they cover 14 lists and Suttie's cat. no. 31).

[5] i.e. the printed books selected on 11 Apr. 1722, item 10.

[6] See footnote to 18 Dec. 1721, and lists in footnote to 17 Apr. 1722, item 7.

[7] Cf. 5 Mar. 1721/2; 11 Apr. 1722, item 9, for make-up of parcel; and 17 May 1722, item 6. They were agreed for 24 Oct. 1722 (item 9); see that date for list. The money was paid over to Varenne 27 Oct. 1722 (item 14).

[8] i.e. Harl. 1761 (= Davis no. 1048).   [9] i.e. the copy for Sunderland (see 4 Dec. 1721).

John XXII.[1] I think it not improper here to Note that both these Books do want yet another Leaf; but whether it was blank, or printed upon, I cannot say as yet; not knowing of any third Exemplar of the same in England. It may be likewise remembred, that my Lords Book is Noted by the Hand of the Learned Cardinal Nicolaus Cûs [*sic*] or Cusanus; who first introduced the then wonderful Art of Printing into Italy, from Germany.

3. Mr Christian came, & saw some more of my Lords fine old Books.

4. Mr Harbyn came, & saw the same.

17 April 1722.

5. Mr Chapman brought in the last Parcel, & was paid his whole Accompt. I likewise deliver'd to him another parcel with two books whose Titles were faulty.

6. A Letter was sent to Mr Andrew Hay, desiring him to return my Lords Commission for buying MSS. abroad, he having done nothing therein.[2] Here it may be remembred that in February last my Lord bought of him 3 MSS.[3]

    1. The Four Gospels in the Valachian Language & Character. 4to. paper. /[4]

    2. Salust, in Italian. 4to. mag. Velum.[5]

    3. Part of the Voyage of Anselmo [*blank space*] the first Bishop of San Domingo, translated into Italian by [*blank space*].[6]

7. It may be remembred, that the 19th. of January last, my Lord bought of Mr Noel a large Parcel of MSS. those that were ready are marked thus 20 Januarij 1721, being the day when they were brought hither.[7] The remainder of them, $\overline{22}$

came hither the 12th. Instant and are thus marked ⊕ 20 die Januarij 1721.[8]
$$\overline{22}$$

The Titles of all being sett down in Mr Sutties Paper of the 13th. of December 1721,[9] I think need not be repeated here.

8. It may also be further remembred [*sic*], that when my Lord bought the last parcel of Mr Noel, that Mr Noel deliver'd up to my Lord
Plinij Historia Naturalis Venetijs, 1469. fol. mag. illum.[10]
Les Vies de Plutarque. à Paris *chez* Michel de Vascosan, 1565. fol. crass.[11]

---

[1] See Osborne, ii, 1743, no. 10191.

[2] The Commission referred to was dated 26 Apr. 1720 and delivered to Hay 3 May 1720 (see footnote to 26 Apr. 1720 for details). It was returned 20 Apr. 1722 (item 6).

[3] Cf. 25 Jan. 1721/2, item 10.   [4] Harl. 6311 B.

[5] Unidentified. The only Sallust *in Italian* in the Harl. Coll. is Harl. 3289, which is not that referred to here.

[6] Harl. 3566.

[7] The Harl. MSS. bearing the date 20 Jan. 1721/2 are: 2468, 2494, 2623, 2662, 2703, 2739, 2816, 2829, 2843, 2890, 2908, 2930, 2941, 2953, 2966, 3001, 3012, 3014, 3240, 3322, 3456, 3498, 3569 (ff. 105–293b), 3583, 3633, 3646, 3668, 3676, 3685, 3701, 3736, 3751, 3752, 3753, 3771, 3844, 3971, 3973, 4986, 5491, 7013 (ff. 44, 45, 46, 127). BM Add. 8160 also bears this date.

[8] The Harl. MSS. bearing the mark and date ⊕ 20 Jan. 1721/2 are: 2457, 2472, 2484, 2498, 2501, 2514, 2516, 2529, 2582, 2587, 2590, 2591, 2599, 2606, 2613, 2625, 2627, 2629, 2631, 2638, 2640, 2641, 2646, 2649, 2654, 2663, 2671, 2696, 2698, 2708, 2722, 2723, 2741, 2743, 2776, 2783, 2853, 3393, 3415, 3442, 3478, 3536 A (ff. 19–38), 3557, 3582, 3649, 3893, 4088, 4090, 4165, 4974, 5603, 5611, 5625, 5651, 5652, 5790, 6305.

[9] Not traced.

[10] Hain 13087; *BMC* v. 153; Stillwell P. 716. *Editio princeps*, printed by Johannes de Spira, 1469.

[11] *Les Vies des Hommes Illustres.* Transl. J. Amyot, printed by M. de Vascosan, Paris, fol.

Cicero de Finibus. Venet. 1471, p[er] Joan. ex [*substituted for* de *deleted*] Colonia Agrippinensi, 4to. ampl.[1]

Johannis de Sacrobusto [*sic*] Spera Mundi. 4to.[2]

for which his Lordship hath promised to send up to M^r. Nowel [*sic*] other Copies of the same Books.[3]

9. Mr Will. Clayton's Friend sent in the old Registre of Holm-cultram, for which I paid the money yesterday.[4]

18 April, 1722.

10. Mr Bateman came; & soon after, Mr Noel.

11. Mr Elliot came & rec'd from me another parcel of Books to bind.

19 April, 1722.

12. I being at Mr Vaillant's this Morning, saw with him a little Paper-MS. containing some pieces of the Works of Virgil, & other Latin Poets. And desiring him to present it to my Lord, he consented, & I brought it away with me. /[5]

1. A letter sent to Mr Noel acquainting him that my Lord cannot conveniently see him untill Monday morning.

p. 107
(f. 55*a*)

2. Doctor Colbatch of Cambridge called in here; but tarried not.

3. This day, about 3 in the afternoon, died Robert Spenser Earl of Sunderland; which I the rather Note here, because I believe that by Reason of his Decease, some benefit may accrue to this Library, even in Case his Relations will part with none of his Books. I mean, by his raising the Price of Books no higher now; So that, in Probability, this Commodity may fall in the Market; and any Gentleman be permitted to buy an uncommon old Book for less than fourty or fifty Pounds.[6]

20 April 1722.

4. M^r. Ch. Davis came, & having rec'd from me such of his Books which my Lord will not have, sett his prices upon the Remainder, that I may shew the same to my Lord: & will call again about this day Sevenight.[7]

5. Mr Noel came, & brought a new Letter & Catalogue from Mr Suttie: who loiter's & buye's trifling or useless things.[8]

6. Mr Andrew Hay sent me back the Commission I wrote to him for; together with a Civil Letter.[9]

7. D^r. Sherard came, and tarried pretty long; discour[s]ing about the old Syriac MS, lying near Herborne, & other Library-businesses, in all which he is as ready to do my Lord Service, as before.[10]

---

[1] GW 6885; BMC v. 157.   [2] Ed. unidentifiable.

[3] See 13 Sept. 1722, item 1.

[4] 'Will. Clayton's Friend' may be Fleetwood or Hesketh (cf. 3 Mar. 1720/1). The Holm-Cultram Register is Harl. 3891 = Davis no. 494.   [5] Harl. 2695.

[6] Wanley is in error in the christian name: Robert Spencer, 2nd Earl, had died in 1702. The bibliophile was Charles Spencer, 3rd Earl. Cf. 4 Dec. 1721, for Wanley's comment on the Fairbairne auction and the Earl of Sunderland's bids.

[7] See 29 Oct. 1722, item 3, for settlement: they had been sent in 12 Mar. 1721/2, item 12.

[8] This Suttie cat. not traced. Wanley's extracts from recent Suttie cats. are in Welbeck Wanleyana, Misc. no. 8.

[9] Cf. 17 Apr. 1722, item 6, and footnote. Hay's *letter* has not been traced.

[10] Cf. 19 Nov. 1722, item 8, and footnote.

21 April 1722.

8. Mr Mattaire came, & I shewed him some of my Lords fine old Books here, to his great Delight & Satisfaction.

9. Mr Harbyn brought back the MS. 81,B.12. which he had borrowed.[1] And gave to my Lord 3 Original Letters of Peireskius, with two antient & Valuable Charters.[2]

23 April 1722.

10. Mr Noel came, & staid long.

24 April 1722.

11. A Letter was sent to Mr Wyat, to know whether he will accompany me to visit Mr Strype of Low Leighton.[3]
He not being within I could not receive a sudden Answer.

12. Mr Barret the Goldsmith came, & staid long in looking into some Heraldical MSS.

13. This Evening being with Mr Schumacker, he told me that he saw a Prayer-book in German, printed by Fust & Schoiffer upon Paper, at Mentz, A.D. 1457, with divers other Books of the Infancy of Printing (on one Side) in the Possession of M^r. Zacharias Uffenbach a Senator of Franckfort on the Main; who hath also a good Collection of MSS.[4] Mr Schumacker being about to return into Muscovy soon, is willing to serve my Lord in the buying of two antient Greek MSS. of the four Gospels, written all in Capitals; which are now in the Possession of D^r. Wolfius Professor of Hebrew at Hamburgh.[5]

25 April 1722.

14. Mr Chapman brought the Books last delivered to him; rec^d another Parcel, and Six more of my Lords Marocco-Leather-Skins.

15. A Letter rec^d from Mr Wyat who will write to Mr Strype, to know when we may Visit him. /[6]

---

[1] i.e. Harl. 1396 (borrowed 17 Feb. 1721/2 (item 10)).

[2] This is Nicholas Fabri de Peiresc: the 3 letters are Harl. 7002, ff. 411, 446, and Harl. 7011, f. 118. The charters are Harl. Ch. 111. B. 49 and 111. C. 25.

[3] For Harley's interest in Strype's papers see 30 Mar. 1720, item 6, and footnote. For present exchange of letters cf. 25 Apr. (item 15), 27 Apr. (item 7 and footnote), 3 May (item 6), and 4 May (item 9) 1722 (when the papers were sent in). Cf. also 7 July 1722, item 3.

[4] Cf. 1 May 1722, item 14. On Zacharias von Uffenbach (1683-1734) and his library see J. E. B. Mayor, *Cambridge under Queen Anne*, 1911, pp. 341-7. As regards the Prayer-Book the only known book of 1457 with Fust and Schoeffer's name is a Psalter in *Latin* completed 14 Aug. in that year (cf. p. 117, fn. 9).

[5] For a full account of Johann Christoph Wolf's life (1683-1739), writings, and library see Zedler, *Universal Lexicon*, lviii (1748), cols. 751-63. Cf. 1 May (item 14), 29 May (item 5), and 24 July (item 11) 1722; Schumacher was unsuccessful, but see 11 Mar. 1723/4, item 3, when a report by Walker is recorded that the MSS. were likely to be sold. On 2 Sept. 1731 Sloane wrote to Harley *re* a MS. of the Greek Gospels being offered in London *having been sent from Hamburg* (cf. *HMC Portland Papers*, vi. 40); Harley replied 6 Sept. 1731, stating that if Sloane 'did not design to have it' he would 'be [ver]y glad to have it' (BM Sloane 4052, f. 9). Harley did secure it: the MS. is now Harl. 5684, a late 10th-cent. MS. in late uncials similar to those in the Harley Evangeliarium (Harl. 5598) dated 995 (cf. *Pal. Soc.* i. 26, 27: Maunde Thompson, *Intro. to Greek and Latin Paleography*, pp. 214-16): the MS. is imperfect at the beginning, commencing with Matthew vi. 6, and is Evan. G in Scrivener (*Intro. to Criticism of the New Testament*, 2nd ed., pp. 121-2). The MS. was brought from the East by Andrew Erasmus Seidel, purchased by La Croze, and presented by him to J. C. Wolf.

[6] Cf. 24 Apr. 1722, item 11.

1. D[r]. [*substituted for* M[r] *deleted*] Savage a Clergy-man came to enquire after some p. 108 books he had sent hither the 23 of September last, as he said; and they were (f. 55b) found immediatly.[1]

2. M[r]. William Thomas brought the Bill of the Freight [*substituted for* Lading *deleted*] of my Lords Marocco-Leather, which through one Accident or other happen's not yet to be paid. Hereupon, I went to M[r] Alberto Croce, gave him the Money, & desired him to pay the same to the Husband of that Vessel, who is now in Town: because the Captain is now out upon a Voyage.

26 April 1722.

3. M[r] Christian came.

27 April 1722.

4. M[r]. Schumacker came, & I shewed him more of my Lords fine MSS. Printed books & Coins; & my Lord was pleased to shew him many of his fine Pictures in Great, & Little, & Enameled; with many Gems Engraven by M[r] Christian, &c. Moreover, my Lord presented him with one of the Duke of New-Castles Books of Horsemanship, & with two Sets of the Prints of his old Lamp.[2]

5. M[r] Varenne came about the four books he left with me some time ago; I bad him call here again to morrow.[3]

6. M[r] Charles Davis brought a parcel of curious old & other Books & Pamphlets.[4]

7. Letters were received, one from M[r] Wyat Senior; another from M[r] Strype to him; relating to the Papers which my Lord desires M[r] Strype to Lend him.[5]

8. M[r]. Mattaire came.

28 April 1722.

9. M[r] Harbyn came; & look'd into many Original Letters of foreign Learned Men.

30 April 1722.

10. M[r] Collins came to peruse one of Coles MSS. of the Offices post Mortem.[6]

1 May 1722.

11. M[r] Collins [*substituted for* Geo. Holmes *deleted*] came to peruse the 2 Volume of Coles Collections.[7]

12. M[r] Geo. Holmes came to look into some of my Lords Coins, & fine MSS.

13. M[r] Gibson came, & acquainted me that he ha's now gotten a small parcel of good MSS. lately come from Florence,[8] and that more are coming, among

[1] No previous ref. to this (they had been sent in during Wanley's absence at Oxford).
[2] On prints of the lamp see footnote 7 to 18 May 1721, item 11. Several works on horsemanship were produced by William Cavendish, Duke of Newcastle, the first and most famous being *La Méthode et invention nouvelle de dresser les chevaux*, Antwerp, 1657.
[3] See footnote to 12 Apr. 1722, item 13.   [4] Settled for on 29 Oct. 1722 (item 3 and footnote).
[5] See footnote to 30 Mar. 1720, item 6, for Harley's interest in Strype's papers. A letter from John Wyat, senior, bookseller, dated 27 Apr. 1722, forwarding one which he had received from John Strype, dated 26 Apr. 1722, is in Welbeck Wanleyana (cf. 25 Apr. 1722, item 15); for present exchange of letters see footnote to 24 Apr. 1722, item 11.
[6] Harl. 756.   [7] Harl. 757.
[8] Cf. 4 May (item 8) and 5 May (item 1) 1722 for list of these. See also footnote to 10 Sept. 1722, item 1, for further list and for price paid for the whole parcel.

which are two Volumes of the Works of Homer in Greek, finely written & illuminated upon Velum, about the time of the first Cosmo de Medicis.[1] I am to go to see these that are come, on the fourth instant before 9 in the Morning.

14. Mr Schoemacker having certified me that he must sett out for Muscow to Morrow, or the next Day; I therefore must draw up a Sort of an Order for him to buy the two MSS. in Greek Capitals of D^r. Wolfius at Hamburgh,[2] to serve my Lord with M^r. Zacharias Uffenbach [bach *written over* heim *deleted*] at Frankfort, who ha's a small German Prayer-book Printed by Fust & Schoiffer at / Mentz A.D. 1457, with other Books of the Infancy of Printing;[2] & to buy a few Modern Bibles for my Lord at Amsterdam. And I have promised to draw up for him a little Account of my Lords noble Library.

p. 109 (f. 56a)

1. Mr Charles Davis came, & took away such of the Books in his larst [*sic*] Parcel, as my Lord would not have.[3]

2. Mr Schumacker took me to the House of M^r. [*blank space*] Stirling a Merchant in Billeter-Square, where Mr Stirling read the Order I gave to the former, & I promised punctual Payment, according as he should draw upon me.[4]

2 May 1722.

3. Mr Collins came, & perused the Third Volume of Coles Collections, & a Visitation of Sussex.[5]

3 May 1722.

4. M^r. Collins came & perused the Fourth Volume of Coles Collections, & the said Visitation.[6]

5. Dr Sherard came, & talked about his approaching Journey to France in Order to buy a great Collection of Natural Curiositit[*sic*]ies, & is willing to serve my Lord there in any thing that may Occurre. He also shewed me a List of the late Mr Vossius's MSS. all which I have rejected, as being only the Remains of a great Collection, now in the Hands of those Dutch-Men, who know very well how to Keep or dispose of the Valuable Things, and how to Sett a great Price upon the Worst. These MSS. are but 32 in Number, all in 8vo. or in 4to. They seem to be

    1. Printed Books collated with MSS: or

    2. Tracts or Indigested notes of Isaac Vossius, which have not been thought fit for the Press, or

    3. Recent Transcripts from some older MSS.[7]

6. A Letter received from Mr Strype, who hath found two of the Papers which my Lord desires to see, and will send the other two as soon as they come to hand.[8]

7. Mr Beaver came, & began to peruse the Laws of the Kingdome of Cyprus.[9]

---

[1] The vellum MS. in 2 vols. of Homer is presumably that referred to 3 June 1721, item 3, and 3 July 1721, item 3, and is to be identified as Harl. 5600 in list under 10 Sept. 1722, item 1.
[2] See 24 Apr. 1722, item 13, and footnote.
[3] See 20 Apr. 1722, item 4, and footnote.   [4] Cf. item 14 above.
[5] Vol. iii of Cole's Colls. is Harl. 758; there are several Visitations of Sussex in the Harl. Coll.
[6] Vol. iv of Cole's Colls. is Harl. 759.
[7] Cf. 2 Mar. 1714/15, item 5, and footnote.
[8] This further letter from Strype has not been traced: for rest of correspondence see footnote to 24 Apr. 1722, item 11.   [9] Not identified; cf. also 7 May 1722, item 4.

4 May 1722.

8. I went to Mr Gibson and saw a small parcel of MSS. and a parcel of old Printed Books divers of which I selected for my Lords View. And I desired Mr Gibson to send them hither soon, that they may be ready for my Lord.[1]

9. I went to Mr Wyat and received Mr Strypes Papers abovementioned; which, indeed, prove to be but one, although Mr Strype in his History of A.B^p. Grindals Life, does divide it, & represent's it as if it were two.[2]

10. Being come hither, I shewed the Library to a Noble Person whom Mr Beaver brought, called [*substituted for* named *deleted*] Le Count de Brandebourg. He is said to be a Switzer, & to have formerly been a Monk.

11. In the Evening of this day Mr Noel came to me, & communicated to me a Letter & Catalogue from Mr Suttie, dated from Coblentz the 2 May, N.S.[3] and also a Catalogue of the Library late of Mr Williams the Kings Printer, whom I remember to have been a Curious Collector. /[4]

5 May 1722.

1. M^r. Gibson sent in the Parcel I saw yesterday at his Lodgings.[5] They are,

Codices MSS.

1. D. Hieronymus adversus Jovinianum hæreticum. — Epistola Damasi Pape ad Jeronimum super tribus quæstionibus libri Genesis, cum Jeronimi Responsione; et alijs ejusdem ac D. Augustini Epistolis. fol. min. membr. man. Ital. imperf.[6]

2. Æneæ-Silvij Picolominei, seu Pij Papæ II, Cosmographiæ liber primus ut videtur. quondam Auctoris peculium; cujus etiam Effigies cernitur in principali littera. fol. min. membr.[7]

3. Senecæ Tragoediæ. chart. fol. min. imperf. Codex scriptus videtur Perusiæ, A.D. 1428.[8]

4. Homeri Odyssëa, Græce, cum Scholijs quibusdam. chart. 4to. mag.[9]

5. Sermones Giliberti super Cantica Canticorum. membr. fol. min. manu Italica minutiori. deest una aut altera quaternio.[10]

6. A. Gelij exemplar nitidissimum, olim ut dicitur peculium Pij II. Pont. max. man. Ital. rotund. membr. 4to. mag.[11]

7. Statuta cujusdam Fraternitatis Laicorum (ut videtur) Florentiæ, B.V. Mariæ dicatæ. Codex Authenticus. membr. 4to. mag. illum.[12]

8. Terentij Exemplar nitidissimum. 4to. membr. manu Italica rotund.[13]

9. Seneca de Beneficijs Italicè. 4to. min. chart.[14]

10. Ciceronis Tusculanæ quæstiones. 4to. min. chart. man. Ital.[15]

---

[1] Cf. 1 May 1722, item 13, and footnote.

[2] Cf. 3 May 1722, item 6, and footnote. John Strype's *History of the Life and Actions of Edmund Grindal, Archbishop of Canterbury*, had been pubd. London, 1710. The papers and other MSS. bought of Strype are now in Harl. 416–35 and Harl. Ch. 83. A. 15, 16 (see footnote to 30 Mar. 1720, item 6); many of the State Papers belonged to John Foxe the martyrologist, to whom the Grindal letters in Harl. 417 are addressed.

[3] Not traced.   [4] See 23 May 1720, item 5, and footnote.

[5] Cf. 1 May 1722, item 13, and footnote.   [6] Harl. 3105.   [7] Harl. 3976.

[8] Harl. 2486 (Wanley's statement of provenance is derived from the colophon, f. 182^b, 'ex Perusia').

[9] Harl. 5673.   [10] Harl. 3150.   [11] Harl. 2768.   [12] Harl. 3547.

[13] Harl. 2721.   [14] Harl. 2616.   [15] Harl. 2546.

11. Poemata quædam Franc. Petrarchæ, Italicè. nitide scripta, A.D. 1465. in membranis, 4to. illum.[1]

Libri impressi.

1. D. Hieronymi Epistolarum Volumen I. Rome in domo nobilis viri Petri de Maximis, presidente magistro Arnoldo Pannartz, Anno. 1476, die vero 28 Martij. fol. mag.[2]

2. ———— Volumen II. Rome per uenerabilem uirum magistrum Georgium Laur de Herbipoli; sub anno dñi, 1479, die uero Lune, quinta mensis Aprilis. fol. mag. (ijsdem Typis.)[3]

3. Lactantius. *Romæ, apud Maximos*, 1470. chart. mag.[4]

4. Chronica Donati Bossij Civis Mediolanensis. Mediol. p[er] Ant. Zarotum, 1492. calendis Martijs. fol.[5]

5. Poemata Dantis Alleghieri, cum Comment. Imolæ Benevenuti. Impressa per Vendelinum Spiram, 1477. fol. (dicitur hunc librum pluries, et quidem multa cum laude citari ab Academicis della Crusca.)[6]

6. B. Leonis Magni Papæ, Sermones. sine Dat. Edit. pervetusta & nitid.[7]

7. S. Athanasius in D. Pauli Epistolas. Latinè, per Cristoforum de Persona. Rome per Vdalricum Gallum alias Han Alamanum, 1477, die vero 25 mensis Januarij. fol.[8]

8. Homeri Ilias Latine, per Laur. Vallensem. Brixiæ, 8 kł Decembr. 1474, p[er] Henr. Coloniensem & Statium Gallicum.[9]

9. Omnibonus Vincentinus in Lucanum Venetijs 1475, 12 Kalendas Augusti. fol. min. /[10]

p. III
(f. 57a)

10. Opus Doctoris Samuel contra Judæos, Latinè. Mantue, per Johannem Schall Artium Doctorem,1475. fol. min. litt. German.deest fol. primum.[11]

11. Horatius cum Christoph. Landini Interpretationibus. Venet. per Joann. de Forliuio & socios, 1483. fol. min.[12]

12. Sallustius. Florentiæ, apud S. Jacobum de Ripoli. 1478. 4to. mag.[13]

13. Chronicon Eusebij, Hieronymi, Prosperi, & Matth. Palmerij. sine Data (per Phil. Lavaniam.) 4to. mag.[14]

14. Francesco Petrarcha degli Imperadori & Pontefici. Florentiae apud S. Jacobum de Ripoli, 1478. 4to. mag.[15]

15. Probæ Centones e Virgilio, cum alijs; sine Data. 4to. ten.[16]

16. Nicolaus Perottus de Metris Horatij atque Boethij. Bononiæ, 1471. 4to.[17]

17. Omniboni Leoniceni Grammatica. (*Venetijs*) per Jacobum Gallicum, 1473, 4to. min.[18]

18. Guarinus Veronensis de Diphthongis, sine loco or [*sic*] anno 1474. 4to. folijs 7.[19]

[1] Harl. 3411.   [2] Stillwell H. 154; *BMC* iv. 62 (IC 17929).
[3] Stillwell H. 155; *BMC* iv. 40 (IC 17525).
[4] Stillwell L. 3; *BMC* iv. 10 (IB 17157). The vol. was printed by Sweynheym and Pannartz.
[5] Stillwell B. 925; *BMC* vi. 722 (IB 26067); GW 4952.
[6] Stillwell D. 21; *BMC* v. 248 (IB 20577); GW 7964.
[7] This could be one of half a dozen eds. of Pope Leo I's Sermons.
[8] *BMC* iv. 25 (IB 17343).   [9] *BMC* vii. 964 (IB 31023).
[10] *BMC* v. 219 (IB 20128).   [11] Second part of *BMC* vii. 933 (IB 30652).
[12] *BMC* v. 339 (IB 20941).   [13] *BMC* vi. 622 (IB 27049).
[14] *BMC* vi. 703–4 (IB 26129). Printed at Milan.   [15] *BMC* vi. 623 (IB 27046. a).
[16] There were eds. of Proba Falconia, Vergilii Centones, printed without place or date mentioned, at Basle c. 1474, Leipzig c. 1490, Salamanca c. 1492, Paris not before 1494, Poitiers c. 1500, and Burgos c. 1500. See Stillwell P. 901–8.   [17] *BMC* vi. 798–9 (IA 28509).   [18] *BMC* v. 213 (IA 20062).
[19] Presumably the ed. ascribable to Augustinus Carnerius at Ferrara. *BMC* vi. 606 (IA 25634), but it is 8° not 4°.

7 May 1722.

1. Mr Green came to peruse some Heraldical MSS. relating to Cheshire.

2. Mr Chapman brought the parcel last deliver'd to him, and received another to bind.

3. Mr Elliot brought in the parcel last deliver'd to him, but not at his day. I bad him call again to morrow.

4. Mr Beaver came to peruse the Statute-book of Cyprus.[1]

5. This Evening Mr Noel told me that he is about agreeing for the late Mr Williams's Library, from whence if he buye's it my Lord may have anything that he pleases at the Price it cost; and the Remainder he will keep close till the next Winter.[2]

8 May 1722.

6. Mr Elliot the Binder came & took with him another Parcel to Bind.

7. Mr Gibson came, & said that he ha's recieved [*sic*] the Bill of Lading for another Parcel of Books from Italy, among which is the Homers Works in Greek written by John Rossus the Cretan (who also wrote my Lords fine Gospels) An. Dñi. 1465, in so Elegant a manner, & the whole is so richly Illuminated, that Mr Gibsons Agent calls the two Volumes *una raccolta veramente Reale*.[3] Mr Gibson also again mention'd to me, the old Hebrew Bible, in four vast Volumes, for which the Editors of our English Polyglott formerly offer'd 1000 Ducats, & were rejected.[4] This Book is now to be Sold. Mr Gibson ha's also coming, the Comment of Proclus upon Plato's Parmenides, in *Six* Books; which is supposed not yet to be Printed.[5]

11 May 1722.

8. Mr Collins came to peruse the 4th. & 5th. Volumes of Cole's Collections.[6]

9. Mr Harbyn came to look into some Heraldical MSS.

10. Mr Salomon Negri came to assist me about the Titles of some Oriental MSS. And brought with him a Psalter in Arabic, all written fairly by his own hand./[7]

16 May 1722.

p. 112
(f. 57b)

1. Mr. O Sullevan came, & said that he ha's some prospect of going into Germany this Somer with a foreign Minister; and in that Case if he doe's not get the great Collection of Irish MSS. there, for his Nation; or in case he shall not make this Voiage; he will discover to me the place wherein the said MSS. do

---

[1] Not identified; cf. 3 May 1722, item 7.

[2] Cf. 4 May 1722, item 11, and footnote. In Wanley's letter to Harley (Welbeck Wanleyana) written the next day (8 May) the library is said to consist 'of above 3000 Books, all in fine condition; & is said to be a very valuable collection'.

[3] Cf. 3 June 1721, item 3, and footnote. The MS. is Harl. 5600 (cf. list under 10 Sept. 1722, item 1).

[4] See 3 July 1721, item 3, and footnote.

[5] The MS. is Harl. 5671; and cf. list under 10 Sept. 1722, item 1.

[6] i.e. Harl. 759 and 760.

[7] Negri had a project of publishing the Psalter in Arabic (cf. 22 June 1721, item 12), which came to fruition in 1725. The Psalter in Arabic written by himself is Harl. 5476; for payment for it cf. 14 Nov. 1722, item 12.

lie, to the End that my Lord may get them hither; and his Opinion is that they will come Cheap.[1]

2. Mr Bowyer came, & said that now Mr Batteley of Westminster is deceased, he will renew his Endeavors to b[u]y the remaining part of Mr A.D. Batteley's Library.[2]

3. Mr Gibson came, & said that he hopes soon to have in his Possession the Cargo now Coming; whose Bill of Lading is dated 7 weeks ago.[3]

4. D^r. Sherard came, & said that he sett's forward for Paris on Monday next, & offer'd to serve my Lord there.

5. Mr Timothy Thomas came.

17 May 1722.

6. Mr Varenne came, & took away two of his Books which my Lord doe's not like; & left with me the price of other books lately by him deliver'd to my Lord.[4]

7. Mr Harbyn came and perused some Heraldical MSS. relating to the Lord Weymouths Pedegree.

18. May 1722.

8. M^r. L'Isle came, & brought some Oriental MSS. sent by Mr Bernard Mould from Smyrna to his Sister here in Town, whom (by agreement) my Lord is to pay for them.[5] M^r L'Isle & I had much talk about Mr Moulds unsuccessful Journey the last year to Scio, and of the Reason why it proved so. And we agreed that it was owing to some little prejudices which he (upon slight Reports) took against Signior Paulo, who [is] a Greek by Nation, Druggerman to all the English there, a Man of Understanding & Honesty, and of the greatest Credit with the Greek Ecclesiastics both in Smyrna & at Scio; and by Reason of his Authority can procure those books which my Lord want's from thence, which no other man can do. The Scheme Mr Lisle propose's for my Lords service is this. A new Consul is about to go to Smyrna, one M^r. Boddington, and he say's that Sig^r. Paulo being Druggerman there, will undoubtedly be desirous of living well with the Consul. Mr Bodington owe's his Preferment to Mr Dunstar who is Deputy-Governor [*substituted for* Secretary *deleted*] to the Turkey Company; & M^r Li[s]le is intimate with M^r. Dunstar. So Mr Lisle promises to take me with him, some time the next week, to Mr Dunstar; & I must, in the mean time prepare a List of those MSS. my Lord want's most from thence; because they will not part with all. / [6]

p. 113
(f. 58a)

19 May 1722.

1. Mr Collins came & perused the 5th. book of Coles Collections. as also the 6th. & 7th.[7]

---

[1] 'The place wherein the said MSS. do lie' is claimed later to be Meissen (cf. 29 May 1722, item 2); O'Sullivan associated the coll. of 'Irish' MSS. (on which cf. R. Flower, *op. cit.* iii, p. 17) in the first place with Ratisbon (see 10 Aug. 1720, item 11 and footnote, for details); cf. also 20 Oct. and 1 Nov. 1722; and 27 Feb. 1722/3, item 4.   [2] See footnote to 11 Jan. 1719/20, item 3.
[3] Cf. 8 May 1722, item 7.   [4] See 12 Apr. 1722, item 13, and footnote.
[5] These were 5 Turkish MSS., now Harl. 5450, 5457, 5489, 5493, 5494. Cf. also 20 Feb. 1722/3, item 7.
[6] Cf. 17 Apr. 1721, item 8 and footnote, for proposal that Mould should go to Scio.
[7] Vol. v of Cole's Colls. is Harl. 760; vols. vi and vii are Harl. 410 and 411 (the two latter had been given by Matthew Hutton).

2. Mr Harbyn came to peruse the Wiltshire & Dorsetshire Visitations.

3. D^r. Savage came.

21 May 1722.

4. Mr Chapman brought in 19 books of the Parcel last đđ to him; but could not bring in the rest, because he was not sufficiently furnished with my Lords Marocco Leather.

22 May 1722.

5. Mr Collins came to revise some of his Papers by the 1st. & 5th. book of Coles Collections.[1]

6. The Bishop of Peterburgh came & borrowed 6 small Volumes of D^r. Huttons Collections; & promised to send his servant to morrow morn, with the others which he borrowed last.[2]

7. Mr Roger Gale came to peruse the first Volume of Extracts from Roger Dods-worths Collections,[3] & some old Deeds. He gave to the Library 17 Original Letters written to his Father (the late Dean of York) by so many of his Learned Correspondents beyond the Seas, and one of the Deans own Hand.[4]

23 May, 1722.

8. The Bishop of Peterburgh sent in the Books he borrowed the 27 of February last; & I deliver'd up the Note he left with me for them.

9. Mr Collins came to peruse the MS. 37.B.13.[5]

24 May 1722.

10. Mr Collins came to peruse the MS. 37.B.13.[6]

11. Mr Salomon Negri came, & I shewed him the Oriental MSS. left here by Mr Lisle.[7]

12. Mr Gibson came, & acquainted me that the Ship, wherein his Manuscripts of Homer, Proclus, &c. do lie, is arived, and doe's now abide the Quarentine.[8]

13. Mr Elliot brought in the Parcel last đđ to him to be Bound, 5 days before the Time by him appointed; but then by setting his Servants about them, divers Books are not so well Lettered as they might have been.

25 May 1722.

14. Mr Elliot came; I blamed him for employing his Men about my Lords Work; yet promised to lett him have another Parcel to morrow.

26 May 1722.

15. Mr Eliott came, & I deliver'd to him the Parcel I promised, & he promise's to do it better than the last, *if He can.* |

[1] i.e. Harl. 756 and 760.
[2] The MSS. now borrowed were returned 25 June 1722 (item 5); those previously borrowed on 27 Feb. 1721/2 (item 14) were returned 23 May 1722.
[3] The extracts from the colls. of Roger Dodsworth, the antiquary (1585–1654), are Harl. 793–805.
[4] For the gift of original letters of learned foreigners, see also 25 Jan. 1720/1, and footnote. They are now Harl. 7011, ff. 144–66 (all are endorsed by Wanley with the date 22 May 1722 and the name of the donor), but the one in the Dean's own hand has not been identified.
[5] i.e. Harl. 294.
[6] Cf. item 9 above.
[7] See 18 May 1722, item 8, and footnote.
[8] Cf. 8 May 1722, item 7.

28 May 1722.

1. Mr Beaver came to consult a MS. of Hen. Huntingdonensis.[1]

29. May 1722.

2. M^r O Sullevane came, & said that his Journey to Germany is now Stopped. And after some time, to[ld] me that the great Parcel of old Irish MSS. of which we have had so much talk for many years, are in the Cathedral-Library of *Nessen* which he say's is an Episcopal See in Upper-Saxony, within 10 German Miles of Prague: and that when the Things are Bought, they may be sent dow[n] the Elbe to Hamburgh, & so brought hither without much Expence or Trouble. But he insisted upon two Conditions: First, that when the Things shall be brought hither, my Lord shall make him some Present for his Service; and Secondly, that if among these books there shall be any Tracts discovering the History or Antiquities of His or other Nations; he shall, with my Lords good Leave, have the Benefit of making them Public. To both these I consented: but doubting of this Place NESSEN, I asked if it may not be MEISSEN? which is indeed a great Bishops See. He said, he would look into his Paper, and call here again within 3 days, & then give me a more certain account.[2]

3. Mr Gibson came, and desired that I would shew the Library to Count Simoneta of Milan, who is a curious man, this Afternoon he being to go for Italy to morrow.

4. I came, with Mr Christian this afternoon, & he looked upon the Coins, a Drawer full of which he flung down, by mischance.

5. I found a Letter for me from Mr Schumacker, with another inclosed, from his Correspondent at Hamburg; who write's that Dr. Wolfius there thinks his two old Greek MSS. to be a great Treasure, & therefore will not part with them; but Mr Schumacker will try what he can do in propria persona.[3]

6. Count Simoneta came, accompanied by 4 Gentlemen all curious, and I shewed them for above 2 hours together as well printed Books as Manuscripts, to their great Satisfaction.

31 May 1722.

7. Mr Virtue came to look into some MSS. for Mr Tristram of Pembroke-College.

1 June. 1722.

8. M^r O Sullevane came, and said that the Place he mentioned is MEISSEN, and is also called NEISSEN.[4]

9. Mr Morley came, and talked about an old printed book some friend of his hath. He know's not the Title, but said that his friend affirmed that it was Printed A.D. 1460. (Perhaps it may be the Catholicon.) /

[1] i.e. Harl. 64 (acquired with Sir Symonds D'Ewes's MSS., 1705).
[2] Cf. 16 May 1722, item 1, and footnote, and see also footnote to 10 Aug. 1720, item 11.
[3] The letter from Schumacher dated 5 June 1722 [N.S.] (endorsed by Wanley as received 29 May) is in Welbeck Wanleyana: the letter enclosed (dated 2 June 1722) is from Daniel Bene of Hamburg, Schumacher's correspondent (see Wanley's letter 31 May 1722 to Schumacher, now preserved in the archives of the Academy of Sciences at Moscow). Cf. Ruth C. Wright, 'Letters from Humfrey Wanley...', *DUJ*, N.S. i (1940), pp. 196–7. On Wolf's MSS. see 24 Apr. 1722, item 13, and footnote.
[4] Cf. 29 May 1722, item 2, and footnote.

1. The Bp. of Peterburgh brought a Catalogue of his old Printed Books, which p. 115 (as I understand) he ha's a Mind to dispose of,) & left the same with me.[1] He (f. 59a) borrowed 4 more of Dr. Huttons Pocket-books.[2]

2. Mr William Thomas came, & desired that Dr. Desmasaux may peruse one of the Duke of Buckinghams Papers relating to Mr Chillingworth.[3]

2 June 1722.

3. Mr Tim. Thomas came, inquiring if my Lord ha's Rich. Hulets Dictionary.[4]

4. Dr. Desmaizeaux came to look for a Letter about Mr Chillingworth, in the Duke of Buckingham's Papers.[5]

5. Mr William Thomas came, & said that my Lord order's that the MSS. of Howel Dha's Laws in this Libra[r]y, be lent to Mr Moses Williams.[6]

4 June 1722.

6. Mr Kingsley brought with him Mr Connor, who sett's up for an Irish Antiquary; & who had been here with me before, which Mr Kingsley knew not. This Mr Connor, & another young Irish-man who came now with them, seem to have assurance enough.[7]

7. Mr Noel came, & shewed me a Letter from Mr Suttie who ha's not yet received any part of the 400 pounds remitted to him, & ha's therefore stood still a Month; but ha's gotten together Six Cases of Books almost full.[8]

6 June 1722.

8. A Letter sent to Mr Elliot desiring him to come hither to Morrow to bind a New Sort of Catalogue of my Lords old Printed Books which I finished here this Morning:[9] and to fix in the 2 loose Leaves into my Lords Clementine of 1460.[10]

7 June 1722.

9. Mr Elliot came, fixed in the 2 leaves above mentioned; and sett upon binding the Catalogue.

8 June 1722.

10. Mr Holman having by Letter requested my help upon an Occasion fallen in his Studies; I began to look into the Registre of Waltham, & divers other MSS. relating to Essex.[11]

---

[1] Returned 25 June 1722 (item 5). [2] Returned 25 June 1722 (item 5).

[3] Peter des Maiseaux's inquiry was presumably in connexion with the preparation of *An Historical and Critical Account of the Life and Writings of William Chillingworth*, London, 1725, which contains, however, no document by the Duke of Buckingham relating to Chillingworth.

[4] A ref. either to Richard Huloet's *Abecedarium Anglico-Latinum, pro Tyrunculis*, London, W. Riddell, 1552 (*STC* 13940), or more probably to *Huloet's Dictionarie, newelye corrected by J. Higgins*, London, T. Marshall, 1572 (*STC* 13941). [5] Cf. 1 June 1722, item 2.

[6] For MSS. of Howel Dha's Laws borrowed see 12 June 1722, item 7, and footnote.

[7] Cf. 3 and 4 Jan. 1720/1. [8] Suttie's letter not traced.

[9] This cat. is Harl. 3886, an alphabetical index of early printed books, &c., in Wanley's autogr.; it was begun on 26 Apr. 1722 (see f. 1) and finished (as Wanley says here) 6 June 1722 (see f. 191). Wanley describes the book in his letter to Harley, dated 12 June 1722, in Welbeck Wanleyana.

[10] See 14 Apr. 1722, item 2, and footnote.

[11] Holman's letter is Harl. 3779, f. 278. A copy of Wanley's answer, dated 11 June 1722, to Holman is BM Lansdowne 814, ff. 62–63b.

11. Dr Des Maizeaux brought Six Original Letters of the first Duke of Ormonde to Lieutent. General Massy, which he gave to the Library; & promised to bring in two more speedily.[1]

9 June 1722.

12. I went forward with Mr Holman's Business; & wrote part of an Answer to him, but had not time to finish it.[2]

11 June 1722.

13. Mr Booth came, & said that he had done all he could to gett Randle Holme's Collection of old Deeds for my Lord; but that Mr. Bassano an Herald-Painter, the Owner is obstinately bent not to part with them. /[3]

p. 116 (f. 59b)

1. Mr Timothy Thomas came.

2. Mr Boothe also enquired about Matters relating to the Preceptory of Iveley in Cheshire; & desired that Mr Greene may transcribe for him.[4]

3. Mr Kinnersley brought one Mr Bedel to look into Bp. Bedels Papers.[5]

4. Mr Gibson came, & said that his MSS. are still performing Quarantine.[6]

5. Mr Elliot came at Noon (as he did on Thursday last,) to finish the Binding of the Catalogue.[7]

6. Mr Newman came (Secretary to the Society for Propagating X̄p̄īā̄n̄ Knowledge) and (being before desired by Mr L'Isle) I entrusted him with the Persian MS. 40.B.2. for a few days; & took his Note for the same.[8]

12 June 1722.

7. Mr Moses Williams came & borrowed the MSS. 63.B.20, & 93.C.23. to be consulted in printing of Dr. Wotton's intended Edition of Howel Dha's Laws.[9]

8. Mr Christian & Mr Tim. Thomas Came, & staid long in looking into divers books.

13 June 1722.

9. The Dean of Cloyne brought another Gentleman with Him; & desired to see Irish MSS. or others relating to Ireland; & I shewed him some of both kinds.

10. Mr Christian came.

---

[1] *Five* original letters from the 1st Duke of Ormonde to Massey are Harl. 7001, ff. 207, 220, 222, 224, 264, all of which are endorsed by Wanley as gifts from Des Maiseaux, 8 June 1722. Des Maiseaux brought in 5 more letters on 3 Feb. 1724/5 (item 1), 2 of which were from the Duke of Ormonde.

[2] See 8 June 1722, item 10, and footnote.

[3] See 23 Jan. 1719/20, item 5, and footnote.

[4] This preceptory appears to be apocryphal, but in Wanley's own copy of Tanner's *Notitia Monastica*, 1695 ed. (BM Add. 47842), at p. 29, is the following addition in Wanley's autogr.: 'Ivelie in Cheshire. A Preceptory of Templars, (as it may seem) which came to the Hospitalars. Rentale Terrarum, &c. in Bibl. Harl. 95. C. 9. fol. 18. A. [Harl. 1999]: 96. C. 14. fol. 183b [Harl. 2074].'

[5] i.e. papers of William Bedell (1571–1622), Bp. of Kilmore and Ardagh (see *DNB*). A MS. life of him (containing copies of letters and documents) is in Harl. 6400.

[6] Cf. 8 May 1722, item 7.   [7] i.e. Harl. 3886: see 6 June 1722 and footnote.

[8] i.e. Harl. 496 (returned 22 June 1722).

[9] i.e. Harl. 958 and 1796. Moses Williams's receipt of this date for these 2 MSS. is BM Lansdowne 1039, f. 42. The Wotton in question is William Wotton, D.D. His ed. of the laws of Howel Dha was pubd. in 1730 (*Cyfreithjeu Hywel Dda ac eraill, seu Leges Wallicae . . . Hoeli Boni et aliorum Walliae Principum, quas ex variis codicibus manuscriptis eruit, etc.*).

14 June 1722.

11. Mr. Saml. Palmer came, & detained me long.

12. The Earl of Winchelsea came to see the Library; but it being late, he said he would call here some Morning when he could stay longer.

15 June 1722.

13. Mr Leibe Library-keeper to the Duke of Saxe-Gotha came to see the Library; and having seen many Things, said that he would call at Wympole & see more there, when he shall be at Cambridge.

18 June 1722.

14. Mr Elliot the Binder brought a person who offer'd to Sell to my Lord the Dies of about 30 Medals, mostly of Foreign Princes: I said that I looked upon things of that kind to be out of my Lords way of Buying.

15. Mr. Elliot brought back the Parcel I last deliver'd to him for binding: but both the Boards & the Leather, besides the Lettering, seem to be inferior to what he last promised unto me.

16. Mr Beaver came.

19 June 1722.

17. Mr O Sullevan came. /

1. The Earl of Winchelsea came, & saw many Things for above four hours together. p. 117 (f. 60a)

21 June 1722.

2. Mr Varenne sent for a Printed Book which he had sent for my Lord to see, the last Holidays. I know nothing of it.

3. Mr Elliot came, & I again blamed him for doing my Lords Work so sorrily as he ha's done, contrary to his promise. Yet, upon a fresh Promise of doing better, I entrusted him with another Parcel.

22 June 1722.

4. I recd safe the MS.40.B.2. which Mr Newman borrowed the 11th. Instant.[1]

25 June 1722.

5. The Bishop of Peterburgh sent his Chaplain with all the MSS. of Dr. Hutton which he had borrowed; & desired that his two Cautionary Notes, & the Catalogue of his out of Course Books might be returned; which was done accordingly.[2]

6. Mr Gerdes Library-keeper to the Landgrave of Hesse-Darmstadt came, recommended from Oxford, to see the Library; I shewed him many Rarities for above 3 Hours together, he proving to be a young Gentleman of Good Nature, Parts, & Experience; and was willing that he shall call here again.

7. My Lord the Earl of Kinnoul came.

---

[1] i.e. Harl. 496. [2] Cf. 1 June (item 1) and 22 May (item 6) 1722.

26 June 1722.

8. I being at M^r. Noels busied in looking into the Books lately belonging to Mr Williams deceased;[1]

9. Mr Elliot brought the two Greek MSS. last deliver'd to him; better done than many former books.

10. A Stranger left 2 MSS. Heur[e]s; both are damaged; but if they had been in their first Beauty, they would not have been worthy my Lords buying.[2]

27 June 1722.

11. A Letter sent to Mr Sanderson, reminding him of Thurloes Papers, the Saxon Charters, & Caxton's Chesse-play, which he promised to procure for my Lord from the Master of the Rolls; the Parcel of Old Deeds, which he promised to give me, and the 3 last Volumes of Rymers Fœdera, which my Lord Kinnoul wants to buy.[3]

28 June 1722.

12. D^r. Sherard came, and we talked over the several Library-matters depending upon him, &c.

2 July 1722.

13. Mr Gerdes came to look into the letters I lately shewed him, written by several Princes of the Hessen Family: and, at his Desire, I suffer'd him to transcribe two of them.

14. Mr Skelton came from Mr Midleton of Chirk-Castle, desiring to be instructed as to the Manner of Disposition of my Lords Presses here; Mr Midleton designing to build himsel[f] a Library soon.

5 July 1723. [*sic*]

15. Mr William Thomas came about my Lords Writings; & with a Message to me from the B^p. of Chester. /

p. 118
(f. 60b)

6 July 1722.

1. M^r. Sanderson sent to let me know that he has (of the 3 Volls demanded) but only the last Volume of Rymers Foedera, which my Lord Kinnoul may have if he please's at the price of £10.

7 July 1722.

2. A Letter was sent to Mr Noel, according to my Lords Order.

3. Mr Clayton of the Temple came, in the Name of the B^p. of Chester about the four Papers his Lordship want's from Mr Strype. Whereupon I deliver'd to him Mr Strype's last Letter to me, & two Papers relating to Dispensations by A.B. Grindal; all which Mr Clayton promised to return to me safely.[4]

4. Mr Gibson came, & said that he hope's soon to have his Books from the Ship, & will then give me Notice.[5]

[1] Cf. 7 May 1722, item 5, and footnote. (Wanley had been shown by Noel a cat. of this library 4 May 1722 (item 11).)   [2] Cf. 12 July 1722.
[3] Cf. 14 Feb. 1721/2, and see footnote to 13 June 1721, item 3.
[4] Presumably the letter received from Strype on 3 May 1722 (see footnote). For Grindal papers see 4 May 1722, item 9, and footnote.   [5] Cf. 8 May 1722, item 7.

10 July 1722.

5. Mʳ Charles Bridgeman came; & I shewed him some Rarities.

6. Mʳ Walker of Cambridge came, being newly arrived from France. He tarried long & saw many Rarities; and at length owned that he has a parcel of MSS. & old printed Books to dispose of. He goe's for France the latter End of this Week; and will leave his MSS. a List of them, and his Price, with a Friend who will call & see me here some Morning.¹

11 July 1722.

7. Mʳ Elliot sent in the last parcel I deliver'd to him; but not yet so well done, as might have been.

12 July 1722.

8. Mʳ Bowyer came, and left a price upon two old MSS. of Heures he had left here before.²

13 July 1722.

9. Mʳ Elliot came, & I bad him call on Tuesday-next for another parcel to Bind.

14 July 1722.

10. Dʳ. Midleton Head-Library-keeper to the University of Cambridge came; and I shewed him Books almost the whole morning together, to his great Satisfaction; & the next Week he is to come & see more. He left with me a Catalogue of all the old Editions in Bᴘ. Mores Library; and for as much as the University is loaded with many Duplicates, which will be sold; we have agreed, that my Lord shall have what he wants from thence; & that by way of Trade, for his Duplicates.³

11. 'Mʳ Hill the Painter came, & . . . with Orders to be careful of It & to let Nobody see it.' [*whole entry ' ' deleted*]⁴

18 July, 1722.

12. I lett Mʳ Tim. Thomas carry 2 Hebrew MSS. to his Chamber; which he promise's to bring back before I go away. (And did so.)

13. A Letter came from Dʳ. Midleton signifying that Dʳ. Ferrari being out of town, he defer's his coming hither until his return from Canterbury; & desiring his Catalogue; which I sent accordingly by his Messenger. /⁵

---

¹ Wanley inspected these 7 Sept. 1722 at Casley's. For subsequent negotiations covering these MSS. and printed books see 17, 19, and 26 Feb. 1723/4; 7 Mar. (item 12) and 11 Mar. (item 5) 1723/4 (purchase agreed); and 1 Apr. 1724, item 10. A further lot of printed books (collated with MSS.) was discussed 27 Feb. (item 4), 5 Mar., 8 Mar. (item 9), 11 Mar., 12 Mar. (item 8), 13 Mar. (item 11) 1724–5. Walker's colls. made for Bentley went to Trinity College, Cambridge.

² Possibly the two MS. Hours left on 26 June 1722.

³ The library (printed books and MSS.) of John Moore (1646–1714), Bp. of Norwich and afterwards of Ely, was bought by George I and presented to the University of Cambridge (see de Ricci, pp. 34, 35, and works cited p. 35, n. 1, and J. C. T. Oates, *A Catalogue of the Fifteenth-Century Printed Books in the University Library*, Cambridge, 1954, pp. 14–16). The cat. referred to was returned 18 July 1722, item 13. Nothing further is heard of the proposed exchange of duplicates. A sale of C.U.L. duplicates took place 29 Mar. 1742 (see C. Sayle, *Annals of Cambridge University Library*, 1916, p. 99): a cat. of these duplicates was printed.

⁴ The clue to this is to be found under 25 July 1722, item 2.

⁵ Cf. 14 July 1722, item 10. Middleton's letter is Harl. 3780, f. 143.

19 July 1722.

1. Mr Lieve the German came, Offerring his Service to me when he is in France, towards which he intend's to sett forwards on Saturday next. I shewed him some more things, & invited him to Sup with me this Evening, he being a Candid & good-natur'd Man. He has been lately at Cambridge to see the Libraries there, & thence took a Turn to Wympole in Order to see my Lords Library there, but could not be admitted by reason of his Lordships absence.

20 July 1722.

2. Mr Tim. Thomas came.

3. Mr Cook the Painter came.

21. July 1722.

4. This day it pleased the most Illustrious & High-born Lady, the Lady Henrietta-Cavendish Holles Harley, to add to her former Bounties to me, particularly to a large Silver Tea-pot formerly given to me by her Noble Ladyship; by sending hither (to this Library) Her Silversmith with a fine & large Silver Tea-Kettle, Lamp & Plate, & a neat Wooden Stand, all of Her Ladiships free Gift; for which great Favor, as in all Duty & Gratitude bound, I shall never cease from praying Almighty God to Bless Her & all this Noble Family with all Blessings Temporal & Eternal.

5. Mr Roger Gale came to see an old Charter; & also borrowed the MS. 61.C.1. for a few days.[1]

6. Mr Tim. Thomas came to look into the MS.67.A.8. and Copied from thence the Translation of a remarkable Inscription written by a Jew.[2]

23. July, 1722.

7. Mr Tim. Thomas brought a Note, enquiring for two old Deeds lent by Mr Hereford of Sutton to Mr Hugh Thomas. Upon search, I found one of the said Deeds, but not the other.[3]

8. Mr Harbyn came, & tarried long.

9. Mr Gibson came, & acquainted me that his Cargo is now in his Lodgings. I am to inspect it this afternoon.

10. Mr Christian came.

24 July 1722.

11. A Letter rec^d from Mr Schumacker, dated from Hamburg 17 June last; certifying that Mr Wolfius there will not part with his two $Tετραναγγέλια$ written in Greek Capitals, for any price whatsoever.[4]

12. Yesterday-afternoon I visited Mr Gibson & his Cargoe of old Books, & found the Printed ones to be but indifferent. The MSS. are 25 in Number, & as to the Main, are very curious, 11 of them being in Greek.[5]

13. A Letter sent to Mr Chapman desiring him to call here to morrow morning. /

---

[1] The MS. borrowed is Harl. 793 (returned 25 July 1722 (item 3)).
[2] i.e. Harl. 1204. The translation is probably the Latin one made by Simon Ockley (see *Harl. Cat.* (1759)). [3] Cf. 22 Dec. 1722.
[4] Schumacher's letter 17 June 1722 has not been traced. On Wolf's MSS. see 24 Apr. 1722, item 13, and footnote. [5] Cf. 8 May 1722, item 7, and footnote; and see 10 Sept. 1722, item 1, for list.

25 July 1722.

1. Mr Chapman came & I d̄d̄ to him a good parcel of MSS. to be bound in Calf.

2. Mr Hill brought back safe the κοντάκιον of the Empress Eudocia Ducœna.[1]

3. Mr Gale brought back the Book he lately borrowed, took up his Note, & look'd into some MSS.[2]

28 July 1722.

4. Mr Harbyn came.

5. Mr Elliot brought back some of the Books of the Parcel last d̄d̄ to him.

30 July 1722.

6. Mr Elliot brought the Remainder of the said parcel; but some not done to my Mind.

31 July 1722.

7. M^r. Elliot came; I caused him to take some of the Books back again to amend; & would give him no other parcel now.

1 August 1722.

8. I went to Mr Noels, at his Desire, and inspected 11 Sacks of books he bought lately; & laid some of them by for my Lord to see.[3]

2 August 1722.

9. Mr Elliot brought the Books he took last away to rectifie; and I deliver'd to him another parcel to Bind.

4 August 1722.

10. Mr Woodman brought two of Clan-ricards Memoirs for my Lord, being Subscribed for.[4]

5 August, 1722.

11. Mr Tim. Thomas came: to whom I lent the Hebrew MS. 94.A.16. he to bring back the same before I go from hence. Which he did.[5]

12. Mr Cook the Painter came.

7 August, 1722.

13. Mr Morley sent me a modern MS. in 4to. seeming to have been written or copied by some young Spaniard; in Order to know the Value of it. It contains some Tracts de Beneficijs, de Vectigalibus, &c. compiled by Canon &

---

[1] Cf. 14 July 1722, item 11. A κοντάκιον is generally a roll or scroll and hence official writing of any kind (but in the Ritual means a short hymn related to a church festival): the former is probably the meaning here. Eudocia Ducoena was the wife of Constantine X Ducas, who was Emperor 1059–67. The κοντάκιον has not been traced.

[2] i.e. Harl. 793 (borrowed 21 July 1722 (item 5)).

[3] Harley inspected them 11 Sept. 1722 (item 4).

[4] A third copy (bound) was presented to Wanley himself 'for kindness done in looking over the preface': this proved to be a present from O'Sullivan. (Cf. Wanley's letter to Harley, 9 Aug. 1722, in Welbeck Wanleyana.)

[5] i.e. Harl. 1861.

Civil Lawyers. I think it worth not much more than so much wast Paper. Sometime after, Mr Morley came, & said that he gave a Shilling for it. In respect to him I accepted of it for my Lord, & so laid it aside.[1]

8 August 1722.

14. Yesterday in the Evening Mr Downes brought to me at my Lodging a pocket-Book, consisting of two old Almanacs, for A.D. 1645, &c. in the former of which the Learned Gentleman & Antiquary Mr Gervas Holles with his own Hand, had sett down Notes of the Births, Christenings, Marriages, Funerals, &c. of many illustrious persons of this Noble Family. This Book Dr. Ferrari seeing lately as it lay upon a Stall, bought for 2d. and concieving [*sic*] that it would not be unacceptable to my most noble Lady, humbly presented the same; & I deliver'd it to Mr. Morley accordingly.[2]

9 August 1722.

15. Mr O Sullevane came to peruse a MS. but it is đđ out to be Bound. /

10 August 1722.

1. Mr Bridgeman came.

2. Mr. Tim. Thomas came.

11 August 1722.

3. Yesterday in the Evening Mr Elliot brought in the MSS. I last deliver'd him to be Bound, pretty well done except as to the Lettering, about which he will still employ his Men notwithstanding all that I have been able to say.

4. The Earl of Kinnoul came.

14. August, 1722.

5. Mr Bridgeman came.

15. August 1722.

6. Mr Tim. Thomas came.

7. Mr Chapman brought the Parcel last đđ to him; & I đđ to him another.

8. Mr Copeland & Mr Skelton came to look into the finely-written MS. 94.B.18. which they did to their full satisfaction.[3]

20 August 1722.

9. Mr Salomon Negri came.

10. Mr Collins came to look in to the MS. 61.A.13.[4]

---

[1] Harl. 5241.

[2] Not traced: Gervase Holles wrote in 1658 a history of his family which is preserved in two MSS., one at Welbeck and one at Longleat, but this cannot be the 'pocket-Book' referred to by Wanley. (On Holles's history see the ed. by A. C. Wood, *Memorials of the Holles Family 1493–1656*, Camden 3rd ser., lv, 1937.) Holles's work was used by Arthur Collins for his *Historical Collections of Noble Families*, 1752. In the Harl. Coll. is, however, Holles's vol. of Lincolnshire Church Notes (Harl. 6829) (pubd. Lincoln Record Soc., 1911). On Holles see R. W. Goulding, 'Gervase Holles', *Trans. of the Thoroton Soc.*, 1922, pp. 36–70.

[3] i.e. Harl. 1892.   [4] i.e. Harl. 757.

21 August 1722.

11. Mr Gregory came, & sett to rights the doors of one of the Presses, which raked too much.

25 August 1722.

12. Mr Christian came.

13. Mr Granger brought his Brother-in-Law D^r. Goodall to see the Library.

27 August 1722.

14. Mr O Sullevane came to Study.

28 August 1722.

15. Mr Cooke the Painter came.

29 August 1722.

16. Mr Morley came.

31 August 1722.

17. Mr William Thomas came.

1 September 1722.

18. Mr Bowyer came, & brought with him a Small parcel of Original Letters, & other Papers, chiefly relating to Prince Rupert, which he gave to the Library, & I indorsed them with his name accordingly.[1]

19. Mr Morley brought a Gentleman to see two or three of my Lords fine Books.

20. Mr Harbyn came. My Lord sent-in four MSS. which he brought-up from Bramton-Castle.[2]

3 September 1722.

21. I coming hither, met Mr Innys the Bookseller, and bringing him along with me, shewed him many of my Lords fine Books here, as well printed as Manuscript, to his great Satisfaction & Information: he, [(] although an eminent Bookseller) never having seen such things before. /

1. Mr Varenne came; I bad him call here again this day sennight.

2. Mr Charles Davies brought with him the Book called the *Dictes of the Phylo-sophers*, printed by Caxton, A.D. 1477:[3] I bad him leave it, & call here again, about Saturday next.

3. My Lord sent-in a little Box wherein are five old Deeds, all relating to his own Noble Family.[4]

p. 122
(f. 62b)

---

[1] Harl. 6845, ff. 162–85, 196–8; Harl. 7001, f. 202; Harl. 7011, f. 143. Earlier letters belonging to Prince Rupert were presented by Bowyer 27 Oct. 1720 (cf. that date and footnote).

[2] Harl. 2659, 3257, 3326, and 3586, ff. 68–145. For list of these cf. Wanley's Addenda, Lansdowne 771, f. 78^b, under 1 Sept. 1722 (at p. 200 of the present work), and footnotes.

[3] No further reference is made to this Caxton book (*STC* 6826 or 6827).

[4] The 5 charters endorsed by Wanley 'Brought in by my Lord Harley' followed by this date are now in the *Cotton* Charters, viz. XXII. 6; XXIV. 13, 14; XXVI. 3, 4. The 3 more mentioned 10 Sept. 1722, item 2, are also now in the *Cotton* Charters, viz. XXIV. 48; XXVII. 92; XXX. 8.

4 September 1722.

4. Mr O'Sullevane came to Study in an Old MS. concerning his Nation.

5. Yesterday my Lord sent in the MS. of Fordon (59.C.18.) which had been lent to Mr Hearne of Oxford, the 20 of November 1720.[1]

6. Mr Casley came, and told me that Mr Walker of Trinitie's MSS. are in his Custody; and that I may come to see them when I please, if my Lord be willing to buy them.[2]

5 September 1722.

7. Mr Gibson came, and in discourse about the curious parcel of MSS. & Printed books now in his Possession he promised to send them hither before my Lords Dinner-time. (And he did so.)[3]

6 September 1722.

8. Sir George Ludlam came.

9. Dr. Fiddis came to look into the MS. 67.A.1.[4]

10. Mr Mattaire came, & I shewed him some few of my Lords curious Books.

7 September 1722.

11. By my Lords Order, I went to Mr Casley, and inspecting Mr Walkers MSS. in his Custody, I putt a Valuation upon each of them as I went on. I also found the lowest Price that Mr Walker intends to sell them for. I borrowed Mr Walkers Catalogue of these MSS. and of some old Printed books which he ha's to dispose of; as also his List of the several Tracts bound up together in two Volumes of his Manuscripts; which must be returned, if my Lord is not pleased to Buy.[5]

8 September 1722.

12. Mr Collins came to peruse the 3d & 4th. Volumes of Cole's Collections.[6]

13. Mr Gibson came, & we began to talk about the Price of the two parcels of Books of his, lying here in my Custody: and not having all his Papers with him, & Mr Collins being here, he will call again on Monday, when (God Willing) we shall agree upon a price for the whole.[7]

14. Mr Harbyn came.

15. Mr Noel brought a Letter [from] Mr Suttie, no. 20; which he left with me.[8]

10 September 1722.

16. Dr. Fiddis came.

17. Mr Davis came, & I bad him call again on Wednesday.

---

[1] i.e. Harl. 712. Hearne pubd. an ed. of Fordun's Chronicle in 1722 (*Joannis de Fordun Scotichronicon genuinum . . .*).

[2] See 10 July 1722, item 6, and footnote.

[3] Cf. 8 Sept. 1722, item 13. This seems on evidence of list under 10 Sept. 1722 to be the parcel referred to under 1 and 8 May 1722 which contained the Homer and Proclus there mentioned.

[4] i.e. Harl. 1197. Fiddes's interest was probably in the last item (art. 24).

[5] See 10 July 1722, item 6, and footnote.   [6] i.e. Harl. 758 and 759.

[7] Cf. 5 Sept. 1722, and 5 May and 10 Sept. 1722, item 1, for lists.

[8] Suttie's letter has not been traced.

18. Mr Varenne came, about [*substituted for* wanting *deleted*] two books he left with Mr Crump for my Lord, long since.

19. Mr Chapman the Binder brought-in the Parcel last deliver'd to him; but took-back one of the books to amend a Blunder in the Lettering. I deliver'd to him Six of my Lords Marocco-Skins; and he promise's to Cover my Lords Books still in his Hands, & bring them in this day Fourtnight. /

1. Mr Gibson came, and shewed me his List & Valuation of the several MSS. and Printed Books contained in the two last Parcels sent in by him; of which, a List of the former, may be seen above at pag. 110, of this Journal: and a List of the lat[t]er here follows.[1]   p. 123 (f. 63*a*)

Codices MSS.

Homeri Ilias, Græcè. script. Florentiæ A.D. 1466. manu Joannis Rossi Cretensis. fol. membr. Illum.[2]

Ejusdem Odysséa. Græcè; eadem manu, 4to. mag. membr. Illum.[3]

Proclus in Parmenidem Platonis, Libris VII. Græcè, manu festinante Nic. Turriani Cretensis. fol. min. chart. Opus ineditū.[4]

Joannis Stobæi Ecloge, Græcè. fol. min. chart.[5]

Psalterium (sine Odis Sacris addi solitis) Græcè, Latine, & Arabicè. membr. fol. min. Codex scriptus videtur A.D. 1153.[6]

Σχολία σὺν θεῷ εἰς τὸν τοῦ Πλάτωνος Γοργίαν, ἀπὸ φωνῆς Ὀλυμπϊοδώρου τοῦ μεγάλου φιλοσόφου. 4to. chart. Opus dicitur esse adhuc ineditum.[7]

Ejusdem Philosophi Scholia in Platonis Phædonem, Græcè. fol. min. seu chart. mag.[8]

Maximi Planudis versio Græca Operis S. Augustini de SS. Trinitate. 4to. chart. Codex scriptus Florentiæ, A.D. 1609.[9]

Proclus in Alcibiadem Platonis, Græcè. 4to. mag. chart.[10]

Galeni Aphorismorum Libri Tres, Hebraicè; scripti manu Bar Chaia filij Salamonis Maimonidis. Liber tertius Canonis Avicennæ, de Infirmitatibus particularibus contingentibus cuilibet membro Hominis. 4to. mag. chart.[11]

Titi Livij Decas III. fol. min. membr. manu Ital. rotunda.[12]

Commentarij F. Dionysij de Burgo in Val. Maximum. fol. min. membr. manu invenustâ.[13]

Lucanus; maxima ex parte Chartaceus. 4to. oblongo; manu Ital. rot.[14]

Vitruvius. 4to. manu Ital. quadrata. membr.[15]

Menologij Hymnorum, &c. Græcorum, pars; pro mense scil. Novembre. 4to. membr.[16]

Ovidius de Ponto; 4to. chart. manu Ital. currente, A.D. 1472.[17]

Juvenalis, 4to. chart. manu Ital. cursivà.[18]

[1] For list of former parcel see 5 May 1722, item 1, and footnotes for identifications. For later parcel (listed here) cf. footnote to 5 Sept. 1722. These parcels were agreed for at £350 on 13 Sept. 1722 (item 2). But on 15 Nov. 1722 (item 14) Gibson was asked to throw in a further parcel of printed books which he had sent in 9 Oct. 1722: this was finally agreed 26 Dec. 1722, item 7 (with list).
[2] Harl. 5600.   [3] Harl. 6325.
[4] Presumably Harl. 5671 (though it is not dated by Wanley 13 Sept. 1722 as the other MSS. in the list are).
[5] Harl. 6318.   [6] Harl. 5786.   [7] Harl. 5668.   [8] Harl. 5667.
[9] Harl. 5687.   [10] Harl. 5696.   [11] Harl. 5680.   [12] Harl. 2684.
[13] Harl. 2661.   [14] Harl. 2478.   [15] Harl. 2760.   [16] Harl. 5581.
[17] Harl. 2607 (Wanley's dating is derived from the colophon, f. 59^b).
[18] Harl. 2576.

Epła D. Hieronymi de Officijs Liberorum erga Parentes. Guarinus Veronensis de Liberis educandis. De ingenuis moribus. Franc. Barbarus de Re
Uxoria. Poggij Epła ad Guarinum. 8ᵛᵒ. membr. manu Ital.[1]

Sallustius. 8ᵛᵒ. chart. manu Ital. fest.[2]

Marij Philelfi Laurentiados Libri omnes, ut videtur; priori folio solum desi-
derato. Auctoris autographon. 4ᵗᵒ. manu Ital. membr.[3]

Discorso di Nicolo Machiavegli sopra la prima Decade di Tito Livio. 8ᵛᵒ.
chart.[4]

Tractatus de Contractibus & Usuris, sec. Frat. Bernardinum de Senis,
Ordinis Minorum. 4ᵗᵒ. min. membr. manu Ital. minutiore quadr.[5]

Petrarchæ Triumphorum Liber Italicè. 4ᵗᵒ. membr. manu Ital.[6]

Italian Poetry, badly written. 24ᵗᵒ. paper.[7]

Psalterium cum Odis Sacris, &c. Græcè: scriptum manu Andreæ Hamar-
tolie Civitate Brundusij, A.D. 1283. 24ᵗᵒ. membr. /[8]

p. 124
(f. 63b)

Libri Impressi.

Platonis Opera Latine, per Marsilium Ficinum. Florentie, per Laur. Vene-
tum—fol. min. litt. Germ. Voll. 2.[9]

L. Florus, et T. Livius. Per Mich. Manzolinum Parmensem, 1480. fol. min.[10]

Vita & Epistole de Sancto Hieronimo in Volgare. Ferrara, per Lorenzo di
Rossi da Valenza, 1497. fol. min.[11]

T. Livius, et L. Florus, Venet. in æd. Aldi, 1520 & 1521.[12]

Polybius Lat. per Nic. Perottum, *Ibid.* 1521. fol. min. litt. Rom.[13]

Plutarchi Vitæ, Latinè; & Æmilius Probus. Brixiae, per Herc. Girlandum,
1524. fol.[14]

Petrarcha de remedijs utriusq[ue] fortunæ. Cremonæ, per Bernardinum de
Misintis, ac Cæsarem Parmensem, 1492. fol.[15]

Senecæ Philosophi Opera. Venetijs, per Bernardinum de Coris de Cremona.
fol. min.[16]

As to the Price of these two said Parcels, we had much talk, and he made
very Considerable Abatements of his first Demand. At the last, I told him
that I would make a Report of what he had said, to my Lord: and having done
so, my Lord was willing to keep the Books.

1. Mʳ. Salomon Negri came, & I shewed him an old Stamp, wherein certain Cufic
Characters appear, wrought out in Relieva. Mʳ Negri, looking upon it as made
Backwards, think's it to be only the Name of a Man, *David ben Yemnoch*, i.e.
David filius dexterae tuae: but when I shall shew him an Impression taken from
the same on Wax, he will speak more certainly.[17]

---

[1] Harl. 4150. [2] Harl. 2540.
[3] Harl. 2522 ('auctoris autographon' is derived from inscription, f. 245ᵇ). [4] Harl. 3533.
[5] Harl. 3841. [6] Harl. 3385. [7] Harl. 3355. [8] Harl. 5535.
[9] Stillwell P. 702; BMC vi. 666. [10] Presumably Stillwell L. 214. Pubd. at Treviso.
[11] BMC vi. 614 (IB. 25759).
[12] and [13] These are in fact parts of the same work which was printed by Aldus and Andreas Manutius,
Venice, 1520, 1521, under the editorship of F. Asulanus, and which contained Livy, Florus, and Polybius
(in the Perottus translation).
[14] 'Brixiae, per Herc. Girlandum, 1524, fol.' Hercules Girlandus was not a printer but editor and
translator. There was very little printing at Brescia at this date and the Plutarch is not in the BM. It is
not known who printed it but it may possibly have been G. B. Pederzano. H. Girlandus translated
Theodore of Gaza and edited Isocrates but both were printed at Venice in 1527.
[15] Stillwell P. 363; BMC vii. 956.
[16] Stillwell S. 335 (1490) or S. 336 (1492). [17] See 14 Nov. 1722, item 12.

2. My Lord đđ to me 3 old Deeds, relating to his own Family, or to Wigmore, lately brought from Herefordshire; & I laid them, in the Press or Box n°. 104, by the 5 others mentioned pag. 122, 3.

3. My Lord đđ to me a Printed Catalogue of a Parcel of MSS. now to be sold by the Brother of Mr Smith of Venice.[1]

11 September 1722.

4. My lord went to Mr Noel's & there look'd over those Books of Mr Williams, &c. which I had laid by for his Lordships Inspection; & his Lordship Selected a parcel to be bought, & some few to be changed.[2]

12 September 1722.

5. Mr Varenne came, & I đđ to him his Anthologia printed with Greek Capitals. And he leave's with me untill his return from France, 2 MSS. and a thin Tract printed upon Velum, at the price of 5 Guineas.[3]

6. Mr Elliot came for some Books to Bind; & I bad him call here to-morrow.

7. A letter sent to Mr Casley, acquainting him with my Lords departure into the Countrey, and that he may either recieve from me, or leave with me Mr Walkers Catalogues as he shall think fit.[4]

8. Another to Mr Gibson, that his Lordship hath given a Satisfactory Answer to his Demands for his two Parcels of MSS. & Printed books.[5]

9. Mr Charles Davis came, & gave me an Acct. as to those Books of His, which lie here in my Custody.[6]

10. This Afternoon I went to Mr Noel, in Order to agree with him for the parcel which my Lord laid aside yesterday;[7] He agreed to send down to Wympole those which my Lord desired should be Exchanged for; and that the others, MSS. as well as Printed books should go at Common Prices: and then he reckoned the whole number to be thus, / 35 Folios; 89 Quartos: & 93 Octavos. p. 125 In this Calculation, he reckoned three thin folio-Tracts as three Books; & (f. 64a) would not make any allowance for books smaller than Octavos: saying that he loose's too much by this Parcel without that, &c.

13 September 1722.

1. Mr Noel sent-in the parcel above-mentioned, contrary to my Order; who desired him to keep it untill my Lords pleasure concerning the same shall be fully known.[7] And by his Servant, I returned to him the two Duplicates my

[1] On early printed cats. of Smith's books see de Ricci, p. 55, n. 1. For further refs. to negotiations relating to Smith's books cf. 5 Oct., 12 Oct. (item 8), 13 Oct., 24 Oct. (item 8), 15 Nov. (item 1), 21 Nov. (item 2) 1722; 5 Mar. 1722/3, item 16; 3 Apr. 1723, item 13; 9 Jan. (item 5) and 20 Feb. (item 5) 1723/4; 26 July, 1 Sept. 1725; and 24 Jan. 1725/6. A sale of Smith's MSS. to Sunderland is recorded 17 Dec. 1720, and Wanley visited Sunderland's (to see MSS. bought from Smith) on 6 Feb. 1722/3 (item 7).

[2] Cf. 1 Aug. 1722, and for Wanley's comment on Williams's library see 7 May 1722, item 5, and footnote. For subsequent action cf. 12 and 13 Sept. 1722 and footnotes.

[3] The Anthology 'printed with Greek Capitals' is presumably the Greek Anthology printed at Florence in 1494 under the direction of Joannes Lascaris, by Lorenzo, the son of Francesco di Alopa, a Venetian. The book is typographically of great importance (see R. Proctor, *The Printing of Greek*, Bibl. Soc., 1900, pp. 78–79). For the 2 MSS. and 'thin tract' see list at 24 Oct. 1722, item 9, and footnote to 12 Apr. 1722, item 13.   [4] Cf. 7 Sept. 1722, and see footnote to 10 July 1722, item 6.

[5] Cf. 10 Sept. 1722, item 1, and footnote.

[6] i.e. those sent in 12 Mar. 1721/2 (item 12) and 27 Apr. 1722 (item 6). For settlement see 29 Oct. 1722, item 3.   [7] See 11 Sept. 1722, and footnote. For list of some of these MSS. see 27 Dec. 1722.

Lord lately sent up,[1] being Plinij Historia Naturalis, Venet. per Joan. Spiram, 1469. fol. mag.

Tullius de Finibus. Venet. per Joan. de Colonia 1471. fol. min.

This is done in pursuit of §. 8. of 17 April last, in this Journal. The other books not yet come up for him, are

Les Vies de Plutarque; à Paris chez Michel de Vascosan, 1565. fol. crass.

Johannis de Sacro-busto [sic] Spera Mundi. 4to.

2. Mr Gibson came, & we finally agreed about his MSS. & Printed Books, the Titles whereof are herein to be seen at pagg. 110, & 123 of this Journal; so that now they belong to my Lord, at his price of £.350.[2]

3. Mr Skelton came.

14 September, 1722.

4. Mr. Sam. Palmer Senior came; & I deliver'd to him a Book & a Staff which my Lord left with me for him.

5. Mr Elliot came; and I dd to him a Parcel to be Bound, & two of my Lords Marocco-Skins.

19 September 1722.

6. Mr Elliot's Servant came for a new Title to a book of the last Parcel, instead of that which he had from me.

7. Mr Gregory came to speak with me.

8. Mr Noel brought another Letter & Catalogue from Mr Suttie.[3]

20 September 1722.

9. The Ld. Bishop of London-derry having desired that I would call at his Lodging this morning, I did so; and he came with Me hither to see Irish MSS, or MSS. relating to Ireland, & I waited on him as long as he pleased to stay.[4]

10. Mr Bridgeman called in.

11. Mr Vaillant came.

12. Mr Salomon Negri came.

21 September 1722.

13. Mr Elliots Servant came for a new Title of another book (of the last Parcel,) which he ha's lost.

24 September 1722.

14. Mr Chapman having recd more of my Lords Marocco-Skins (10 Sept) brought in the Books remaining in his Hands, all well done. I hereupon deliver'd to him another parcel all to be bound in Marocco, and Six more Skins; which he judging to be too few for this Service, reckoning also the two Skins & part of a Skin now in his Custody: I bad him try how far they will go, & when he want's more, to send to me for it. /

25 September 1722.

p. 126
(f. 64b) 1. Mr Bowyer came.

[1] For identifications see under 17 Apr. 1722, item 8, and footnotes thereto.
[2] See footnotes to 5 May and 10 Sept. 1722, item 1, for identifications.   [3] Not traced.
[4] i.e. William Nicolson, Bp. of Carlisle 1702–18, when he was translated to See of Derry.

26 September 1722.

2. The Bishop of London-Derry came, and I attended him almost the whole time in shewing him Things, to his very great Satisfaction.[1]

29 September 1722.

3. Mʳ Elliot the Binder brought-in only 8 of the Greek MSS. I last dd unto him; all these without mid[d]le Pieces, & some of them otherwise not so well done as I expected.

2 October 1722.

4. Mʳ Robert Cuningham came.

4 October 1722.

5. Dʳ. Sherard came hither to speak with me; but being told I was gone home, he followed me thither.

5 October 1722.

6. This day (according to agreement) I went to Mʳ Gibson, and took the Titles of some few books which I found to be in my Lords Way;[2] and I brought with me a pretty MS. entituled *P. Cornelij, C.q[ue] Flaminij de vera Nobilitate Altercatio pulchra*; being his Gift.[3] Then Mʳ Gibson & I went to Mʳ Smith in Cornhill, brother to Mʳ Smith the Merchant in Venice; where I inspected 101 Manuscripts lately arrived; compared them with the Printed Catalogue; and made proper Observations upon the same, especially touching their Age, Hands, & Value, according to the present State of the Market.[4]

6 October 1722.

7. I recieved a Letter from Mʳˢ. De: Mould, about some old Marbles & a book she has recieved from her Brother Mʳ Bernard Mould Chaplain at Smyrna; and I wrote to her, desiring her to send them in, with her first Convenience: or otherwise, I would attend her my self & bring them with me.[5]

8. Mʳ O Sullevane came; & I shewed him the Marquis of Ormondes Memoirs.[6]

9. Mʳ Noel came, & left with me (after Dinner at my Lodging) another Catalogue from Mʳ Suttie.[7]

10. Mʳ Elliot sent in the remaining books of the parcel last deliver'd to him, excepting one; of which here remains a perfect Copie in Sheets. He must therefore be spoken to & asked whether he took with him such a book or not, for I have charged him with such a book.

8 October 1722.

11. Mʳ William Thomas came.

12. Mʳ. Chapman coming for 3 more Skins of my Lords Marocco Leather: I dd to him Six Skins, there being more books that require to be Bound therein.

---

[1] Cf. 20 Sept. 1722 and footnote.
[2] Cf. 9 Oct. (item 2), 15 Nov. (item 14), and 26 Dec. 1722, and footnote, for final agreement and list.
[3] Harl. 3332.
[4] See 10 Sept. 1722, item 3, and footnote.
[5] See 8 Oct. 1722, item 13, and footnote.
[6] Unidentified.
[7] Not traced.

13. Mrs. Mould sent-in by her Porter a Box lately come from her Brother wherein was a Fragment of an old Greek Inscription, having been an Epitaph: a small figure of Cybele Sitting; the upper part of the Body of a Silenus, whose Nose is beat off; the Head of a Woman with a Hood on, as a Faustina, much batter'd & abused; a little Head, perhaps of some Philosopher; a very small Head of a Woman with a Sort of Modius upon it. The Book is in folio, and looks like a good Manuscript of St. Chrysostom's Homilies upon the Acts of the Apostles, about 500 years old; but, it is imperfect, being mangled at both Ends, & in some other parts of it. /[1]

9 October 1722.

p. 127
(f. 65a)

1. Mr O Sullevane came to peruse the Marquis of Ormonde's Memoirs.[2]

2. Mr Gibson sent in those few Printed books I saw last at his Lodging.[3]

11 October 1722.

3. Mr Tim. Thomas came.

4. Yesternight my Lord having seen the Czar's Code of his Sea-Laws, printed at St. Petersburg A.D. 1720, in Russian & Low-Dutch: he Order'd it to be paid for.[4]

12 October 1722.

5. Mr Charles Davis came; about the Books of his which lie here.[5]

6. Mr Salomon Negri came, about his MS. of the Psa[l]ter in Arabic.[6]

7. Mr Noel brought another Catalogue from Mr Suttie.[7]

8. Mr John Smith['s] Letter recd; desiring me to lett him know when my Lord will come & see his Brothers MSS.[8]

9. Mr William Thomas came, enquiring after a complete Transcript of Domesdei-book; I said there is no such thing here.

10. Mr Nasofs came, & I paid him 15s. for his Book of the Russian Sea-Laws.[9]

13 October 1722.

11. A Letter sent to Mr Smith, acquainting him that my Lord cannot conveniently go to see the MSS. at this time; but when he shall have recieved the lowest price of them, his Lordship will either go himself, or Send me to Agree for them.[10]

---

[1] Cf. 6 Oct. 1722, item 7, and see 20 Feb. 1722/3, item 7. Harley's antiquities were dispersed 8–13 Mar. 1741/2 (e.g. a Cybele was sold 13 Mar., sale cat. p. 16). The MS. is Harl. 5602.

[2] Cf. 6 Oct. 1722, item 8.

[3] i.e. 5 Oct. 1722 (and footnote).

[4] i.e. Книга уставъ морскои о всемъ что касается доброму управленïю, въ быітности флота на морѣ... На россïискомъ и галанскомъ языкѣ. 1720, 8o. (See P. Pekarski, Наука м литература въ Россïи при Пертрѣ Великомъ, том. 2, 1862, p. 485, no. 439.) See 12 Oct. 1722, item 10, for vendor and payment.

[5] i.e. those sent in 12 Mar. 1721/2 (item 12) and 27 Apr. 1722 (item 6). They were settled for 29 Oct. 1722 (item 3).   [7] Not traced.

[6] Cf. 11 May 1722, item 10, and footnote.

[8] John Smith's letter, dated 12 Oct. [1722], is in Welbeck Wanleyana; see also 10 Sept. 1722, item 3, and footnote.

[9] Cf. 11 Oct. 1722, item 4.   [10] Cf. 12 Oct. 1722, item 8, and footnote.

15 October 1722.

12. Mr Chapman brought back the Parcel last đđ to him, very well done in the main. He say's he ha's four of my Lords Skins remaining by him. I delivered to him another Parcel, & then he asking for Six more of the same Skins, I đđ to him four; & bad him send for more when he find's he want's them.

13. The Bishop of London-Derry came to peruse more Things relating to Ireland.[1]

16 October 1722.

14. Mr Elliot the Binder came & I đđ to him another Parcel. He own's he ha's about the quantity of one Skin of my Lords Marocco-Leather left. I deliver'd also to him two more Skins, & a good piece of a Skin remaining of that wherein he Bound the CODEX AUREUS, as he say's.[2]

15. Mr William Thomas & Mr Alban Thomas came.

17 October 1722.

16. Mr Bridgeman came.

17. Mr Charles Davis came.

18 October, 1722.

18. Mr Vertue came to peruse Sir Simonds D'ewes's Life.[3]

19. Mr Varenne came.

20. Mr Noel came.

21. Mr Harbyn came, & look'd into the Cartulary of Evesham.[4]

19 October 1722.

22. Mr O Sullevane came to peruse the History of the Irish Monastery of Ratisbon.[5]

23. Mr Casley came about Mr Walkers MSS.[6] And I shewed him many fine Manuscripts here. /

1. Mr Charles Bridgeman came.

p. 128
(f. 65b)

20 October 1722.

2. Mr O Sullevane came to peruse the MS. mentioned yesterday. Upon Discourse about the Irish MSS. remaining in the Cathedral Library at Meissen: Mr O Sullevane declared himself very willing to Serve my Lord in the purchasing of them; and to that End will be ready to sett forward for Hamburgh in the beginning of the next Spring.[7]

3. Mr Moses Williams came, and borrowed the Carnarvon-Record, 59.C.1.[8]

23 October 1722.

4. My Lord sent-in Mr Dickenson to look upon the two Antique Heads of

---

[1] Cf. footnote to 20 Sept. 1722, item 9.
[2] Harl. 2788. For binding of Codex Aureus by Elliot cf. 27 June (item 2) and 13 July (item 5) 1721.
[3] Harl. 646.   [4] Harl. 3763.
[5] Harl. 3973; cf. 21 Feb. 1721/2, item 16, and footnote.   [6] See 7 Sept. 1722, and footnote.
[7] See 16 May 1722, item 1, and footnote.
[8] i.e. Harl. 696 (returned 14 June 1723 (item 3)).

Hadrian, &c. of Brass,[1] to which he must put new Shoulders & Pedestals. M[r] Dickenson said that he will call for them this Afternoon.

5. M[r] Beaver came.

6. M[r] Gibson called upon me, at my new Dinner-time, & discoursed with me a great while upon the present State of the Trade of buying old Books & Manuscripts in Tuscany; many of which, by the means of Him & others, are happily reposed in this Library. He mentioned the fine Greek MS. of Plato's Works, which is not yet bought, he says; but will come dear.[2] He also mentioned the MS. Hebrew Bible written in the largest Characters in five grand Folios:—and after much arguing & fencing about it, saying that the Compilers of our Polyglot offer'd one Thousand Roman Ducats for it, and were rejected; and that the present Abbat say's he will not take less now, than ha's been so long ago bidden for it: and I still holding-off, as I have long done with relation to this Book: He turned about, and said that he was very desirous of serving my Lord with relation to this Bible, which is one of the most Antient as well as the finest Copie in the World; and that therefore, if my Lord is willing to have it, he will endeavor to procure it, and be no Gainer, and then asked me if my Lord will allow 500 Roman Ducats or £100 Sterling for the whole five Volumes, in Case the Abbat can be beaten down so Low? I demurred hereupon; and advised him to address himself to his Lordship.[3] [hereupon *deleted*] He further said, that the Abbat above-mentioned keep's a Copie of the four Gospels in Greek, in a fine Case; fancying it to be very old & very Valuable, and ha's hitherto refused to part with it.[4]

7. M[r] [*blank space*] van Hoeck, a Dutch man, who Sell's Books in the Strand, brought to my Lord a small parcel of modern Manuscripts with a List & their lowest Prices; which proved so abominably wicked that he was sent away with them immediatly; and without any part of the Animadversion which he deserved.[5]

24 October 1722.

8. My Lord order'd me to write to M[r] Smith who has sett an unreasonable price upon his Brothers MSS. that he cannot medle with them at that Rate; that if he buy's the Whole, it must be at a more moderate Valuation, so as that the Goods may be worth his Money; but that he had rather take those only which he shal find the most fit for his purpose. Such a Letter was sent accordingly.[6]

9. M[r] Varenne came, and sett the price of 5 Guineas upon the three Books he left here, & my Lord gave me the money / for him.[7] They are,

p. 129
(f. 66a)

    1. The Authentic Book of the Statutes & Armes of the Society or Gild called The Round Table, which was begun at Bourges A.D. 1486. 4[to]. Velum, finely Illuminated. MS.[8]

---

[1] One of these 'Antique Heads of Hadrian' is represented in Hill's portrait of Wanley now in the Students' Room of the Dept. of MSS. in the British Museum (see Wanley's letter to Schumacher printed Ruth C. Wright, 'Letters from Humfrey Wanley . . .', *D.U.J.*, N.S. i (1940), p. 196).

[2] This Greek MS. of Plato's works was not bought—see 11 Feb. 1722/3, item 7; its value is referred to 9 Nov. 1722, item 6. But see 3 Sept. 1725, item 7 and footnote.

[3] For the earliest ref. to this Hebrew Bible cf. 3 July 1721, item 3, and footnote.

[4] This MS. is not referred to again.   [5] Cf. 24 Oct. 1722, item 1.

[6] See 10 Sept. 1722, item 3, and footnote.

[7] See 12 Apr. 1722, item 13, and footnote.   [8] Harl. 5301.

2. The Commission of S[r]. Francesco Barbarigo to be Captain Governor of Feltri, by Leonardo Lauredano Doge of Venice, A.D. 1515. 4to. thin, Velum. MS. authentic. with a fine Illuminated Frontispiece, wherein is his Effigies kneeling.[1]

3. Vincentij Pimpinelli Archiēpi Rossan̄ Oratio Augustæ habita 12 Kal. Julij 1530. 4to. a very thin Tract, printed upon Velum.[2]

1. Mr Varenne told me that the Dutch-man mentioned yesterday, bought that parcel of MSS. and as many others as make them up above 100, for £60; 20 pounds of which he paid down, & gave his Note for the £40, to be paid a year hence. Further, that the said Fellow had offer'd Him that whole parcel for 80[li].[3]

2. M[r] Christian came.

3. M[r] O Sullevane brought one M[r] Smith a young Gentleman to see the Library.

25 October 1722.

4. M[r]. Charles Davis came, with 3 MSS. to sell, or to be advised about; but having shewed them before to others, and of no great Value in themselves; I would not medle with them.

5. M[r] Dickinson came for my Lords two Antique Heads of Brass; and I deliver'd them unto him, taking his Note for the same.

6. M[r] Noel came.

7. M[r] Cook the Painter came, & said that he had left his Picture of the Sacrifice to Ceres, by Reubens,[4] at my Lodging; for my Lord to see at his Leasure.

8. M[r] Casley came inquiring after what MSS. my Lord ha's of Lucan, here or at Wympole? I shewed him two Lucan's and Zonus's Com̄ent upon him, here.[5]

9. M[r]. O Sullevane came to study in the MS. before mentioned.[6]

26 October 1722.

10. A Letter sent to M[r] Hugh Howard, desiring him to return my Lords Copie of A.B[p]. Sharpes Work upon the Coins of England.[7]

11. Another to M[r] Cooke the Painter, certifying that my Lord having seen his Picture, like's it not so much as to buy it.[8]

12. M[r] O Sullevane came to Study, in the MS. before-mentioned.[9]

27 October, 1722.

13. I brought M[r] William Day to see the Library.

14. M[r] Varenne came & I paid him 5 Guineas for the Books he had left with me.[10] He said, that he shall go soon to Paris; & I bad him, if he happen's to light upon any Rarities, to lett me see them first upon his Return, which he promised to do.[11]

---

[1] Harl. 3403.
[2] Printed at Augsburg in 1530. This vol. is entered by Wanley under this date in his vol. of notes on printed books (Harl. 3886, f. 189[b]).
[3] Cf. 23 Oct. 1722, item 7. For Wanley's further experiences of Van der Hoeck and Gronewegen see 26 Mar. 1723, item 15.   [4] This was subsequently refused (see 26 Oct. 1722, item 11).
[5] Cf. 29 Oct. 1722, item 1, and footnote. Zoni's commentary is Harl. 2479.
[6] Harl. 3973. Cf. 19 Oct. 1722, item 22.   [7] Harl. 4119 (returned 27 Oct. 1722 (item 16)).
[8] Cf. 25 Oct. 1722, item 7.   [9] Harl. 3973. Cf. 19 Oct. 1722, item 22.
[10] i.e. for those books listed under 24 Oct. 1722, item 9.
[11] See 28 Jan. 1722/3, item 9, and footnote.

15. Mr Harbyn came, & look'd into the Leiger-book of Shaftesbury.[1]

16. Mr Hugh Howard sent-in my Lords book, as was desired.[2]

29 October 1722.

17. Mr Elliot brought in the Parcel last dd to him; and I deliver'd to him another parcel, and seven more of my Lords Marocco-Skins. He was likewise Order[ed] to make Three Port-folios, each 3 Inches thick; which he promised to do, & to bring them in, by the next Saturday. /

p. 130
(f. 66b)

1. Mr Casley bringing a Letter from Dr. Bentley to my Lord, who desire's to borrow what MSS. he ha's of Lucan: His Lordship Order'd me to deliver to him such as are here, (since those that are at Wympole cannot now be brought up;) taking his Note for the same: and I delivered to him four MSS. accordingly.[3]

2. A Letter sent to Mr Elliot, upon Occasion of his Neglect in not putting-in Midle-pieces into the Covers of such Books as he Binds for my Lord in Marocco: and likewise for taking away many of the Dates I putt at the beginning of MSS. which shew the Times when they were Bought.

3. Mr Charles Davis came, and my Lord having inspected his Bill of Prices as to the Books & MSS. he had left here, 4 of which MSS. were said to belong to his Friend Mr Woodman: my Lord Order'd me to pay-off the said Bill, which I did accordingly, & took his Receipt in full.[4] The Manuscripts are,

Woodman's,
1. Compotus Manualis.
   Kalendarium Lincolniensis.
   Algorismus.
   Tractatus de Spera Magri Johannis de Sacro Bosco.
   Compotus Johannis de Sacro Bosco.
   De Compositione et Utilitate Quadrantis, secundum Modernos: i.e. circa A.D. 1292.
   Messehaläth de Astrolabio.
   Practica Astrolabij.
   De Gnomonis Officio; et post, de Umbra attitudinis. (videtur pars superioris Tractatus.)
   Theorica Planetarum; et post Motus Solis, Circuli ejus.
   Liber Tebith ben Corat de Motu octave Spere.
   Tebith de hijs que indigent Exposicione antequam legatur Almagestum.
   Tebith de Ymaginacione Spere, et Circulorum ejusdem.
   Tebith de Quantitatibus Stellarum & Planetarum.
   Canones Arzachelis in motibus co[e]lestium Corporum; cum Tabulis Toletanis.
   De Eclipsi Lune.
   Libellus cum Tabulis. Humeni Egyptij super Annos Egiptiorum; quas Arzachelus Grecorum Philosophus de Annis Egiptiorum ad annos Alexandri Magni mutavit.

[1] Harl. 61 (= Davis, no 885).   [2] Cf. 26 Oct. 1722, item 10.
[3] Bentley's letter to Harley of this date is printed *HMC Portland Papers*, v. 633. (Cf. also 25 Oct. 1722, item 8.) The 4 MSS. were returned 22 Nov. 1722 (under item 11). Another Lucan MS. which did not come into the library until 3 June 1723 was also lent to Bentley 17–22 June 1723.
[4] These had been sent in 12 Mar. 1721/2 (item 12) and 27 Apr. 1722 (item 6).

De inveniendis veris Locis omnium Planetarum. (membr. 4to. manu Belgicâ.)[1]

Woodman,

2. Poggius de vera Nobilitate.
Ejusdem Epistola ad Gregorium Corrarium super eodem Tractatu.
Karoli Aretini ad Poggium, de Nobilitate, Carmen.
Guarini Veronensis (*seu* Leonardi Aretini) Ysagogicum ad Moralitatem.
Guar. Veronensis de Assentatoris et Amici Differentia, ex Plutarcho.
De claris Virginibus.
Collectio Inscriptionum. (partim membr. partim chart. manu Ital. rotund. festin.)[2]

Woodman,

3. Joannis Joviani Pontani ad Marinum Tomacellum Libri duo Hendeca-syllaborum. membr. 4to. min. ten. man. rot. Ital.[3]

Woodman,

4. Abrege des Armes, ou Blasons, &c. with some French Cutts of Armes, &c. Printed. 12mo. paper.[4]
5. The Registre-book of the Courts-Letes & Courts-Baron holden for the Bishops of Ely at Ely-Barton, from 6 April 1619, to 2 October 1637. fol. /[5]
6. The Ambassadors Idœa, by T. Rogers. 4to. the Original. (to Jerosme Earl of Portland.)[6]

p. 131
(f. 67a)

7. Epistola Mag̅r̅i Vincencij Beluacensis de morte Amici, consolatoria ad Ludovicum Regem Francorum. 4to. min. chart.[7]
8. The Life of S. Margaret in Italian Verse, 300 years old; with Pictures very good for that time. 16to. membr.[8]

1. My Lord sent in two MSS. 'for me to see what they are:' [*Words between* ' ' *obliterated*] viz.
A Registre of the Deeds belonging to the Lands, &c. of Edmund Bohun in Fresyngefeld in Com Suff. temp. R. Edw. IV. fol.[9]
A Copie of the Grant of K. Henry VIII of the Site of the College of St Mary in Campis near Norwich, with some others of its Possessions to Milo Spencer D^r. of Laws, (who was the last Dean thereof[)]. fol. ten.[10]

30 October 1722.

2. Mr Gibson came, & I told him my Lord would send for him some day this Week.
3. Mr Christian brought with him Mr White the Engraver of Mezzo Tinto.

31 October 1722.

4. Mr Noel brought another of Mr Sutties Catalogues.[11]
5. Mr J. Hill came, just at 11, desiring me to shew the Library to 4 of his Ac-quaintance.

[1] Harl. 3647.   [2] Harl. 2571.   [3] Harl. 3331.
[4] Harl. 4326. (Sheets of *printed* shields of arms at ff. 89–99 are folded in the MS., which bears the date 1658.)
[5] Harl. 2239.   [6] Harl. 3365.   [7] Harl. 2423.   [8] Harl. 5347.
[9] Harl. 2201 (= Davis no. 1200).   [10] Harl. 7555, ff. 65–77.   [11] Not traced.

6. Mr Casley caught me at my Lodging, having made a Blundering Lie to his Master, as if here were yet more Manuscripts of Lucan; when as he had carried them all away the other day.[1]

1 November 1722.

7. Mr O Sullevane came, to study in the MS. before-mentioned.[2] He wishe's that my Lord would find out some way of having the Cathedral-Library of Meissen inspected, that he may be sure of the Quantity of Irish MSS. remaining there.[3]

2 November 1722.

8. Mr O Sullevane came to stud[y] in the said. MS.[4]

9. Mr Gosling the Bookseller brought the new printed book of the Honor of Richmond.[5]

3 November 1722.

10. Mr Chapman sending for two more Marocco-Skins; I deliver'd Three to his Servant. He having also, by accident, disorder[ed] a Collection of old Tracts which were to be bound together: I sett them again to rights.

5 November 1722.

11. A Letter sent to Mr Gosling desiring him to send my Lord a copie of Mr Gales Book of the Honor of Richmond, of the lesser Paper, sewed, in Boards with a blue-paper-Cover.[6]

12. Mr Noel came.

13. Mr Negri came, about my Lords recompense for his Copie of the Pentateuch;[7] I bad him call again the next Week.

6 November 1722.

14. Mr Sparke came, desiring to speake with my Lord, & that his Lordship would subscribe to his Book; but afterward, left his Specimens, & Rates with me.[8]

15. Dr. Sherard came & promised to send my Lord quickly, a parcel of Cones which he had caused to be gathered from about the Cedars of Lebanon.

16. Mr Bridges came, & I shewed him some Notes of references to Charters relating to Northamptonshire. /

p. 132
(f. 67b)

7 November 1722.

1. Mr Morley came.

2. Mr Bridgeman came.

[1] Cf. 29 Oct. 1722, item 1.
[2] Harl. 3973. Cf. 19 Oct. 1722, item 22.
[3] Cf. 16 May 1722, item 1, and footnote.
[4] Harl. 3973. Cf. 19 Oct. 1722, item 22.
[5] Cf. 5 Nov. 1722, item 11, and footnote.
[6] Roger Gale, *Registrum Honoris de Richmond Exhibens Terrarum & Villarum quae quondam fuerunt Edwini Comitis infra Richmundshire Descriptionem*, R. Gosling, London, 1722. Harley is entered in the List of Subscribers in the vol. as subscribing to a Large Paper copy. Cf. footnote to 8 Nov. 1722.
[7] Perhaps a slip on Wanley's part for the *Psalter* Negri had copied and brought in 11 May 1722 (item 10). He was paid for this 14 Nov. 1722 (item 12).
[8] Joseph Sparke, *Historiae Anglicanae Scriptores Varii e Codicibus manuscriptis nunc primum editi*, William Bowyer, London, 1723, 2 vols., fol. Cf. 9 Nov. 1722, item 5, and footnote; but for full details see footnote to 26 Aug. 1720, item 12.

3. Mr Sparke came, about my Lords Subscription to his Books; and for his Specimens.[1]

8 November 1722.

4. A Letter sent to Mr Gosling (who sent a Copie of Mr Gale's Book, according to Order) desiring him to bring or Send-in his Bill to my Lord, that he may be paid.[2]

9 November 1722.

5. Mr Sparke came for his Specimens, & recieved the same; & my Lord said that he would have two Copies, one of the best, the other of the least Paper.[3] And He declaring that he has several MSS. by him, & desiring me to come & see them, I promised to do so.[4] 'And this day I paid to him' [*words between ' ' deleted.*]

6. Mr Gibson came, & said that his Correspondent write's that the owner of the Greek MS. of Plato's Works, written about the beginning of the 11th. Century, value's it at 60 pounds Sterling.[5] Also that he ha's sent another Parcel of Books for England; among which is a good MS. Copie of Demosthenes his Orations in Greek.[6]

10 November 1722.

7. Mr O Sullevane came; & promised to write some Remarks upon Mr Baxters Glossary.[7]

12 November 1722.

8. I visited Mr Sparke yesterday; & paid him 6 Guineas being my Lords first payment towards his Books.[8] I saw with him some valuable Manuscripts, the best of which is now Printing, & may be an Unique as to a great part of it. It now belong's to the Earl Fitz-Williams; & if Mr Sparke can get the property of it, it will go to the Library at Peterburgh, with his other Things relating to that Place, there to remain for ever. Mr Spark[e] is not unwilling to oblige my Lord with his other Things either Written or Printed; & said that he had rather take Duplicates in way of Exchange than Money.[9]

9. Among other Matters, Mr Sparke said that Mr Bridges ha's gotten the fine MS. Primer formerly belonging to K. Henry VII:[10] and while we were talking

---

[1] Cf. 6 Nov. 1722, item 14, and footnote.

[2] See 5 Nov. 1722, item 11, and footnote. Gosling's bill, dated 8 Nov. 1722, for £2. 17s. 6d., is in Welbeck Harley Papers (Edw. Harley Book Bills); the bill was settled the same day.

[3] Cf. 6 Nov. 1722, item 14. A copy of the lesser paper was sent in (in sheets) 24 May 1723 (item 3) but a copy of the large paper was still being requested 6 Apr. 1725. Harley's first subscription was paid 12 Nov. 1722 (item 8).

[4] Cf. 12 Nov. 1722, item 8.

[5] Cf. 23 Oct. 1722, item 6, and 11 Feb. 1722/3, item 7.

[6] i.e. no. 15 of list under 4 Apr. 1723, item 17 (i.e. Harl. 5670).

[7] William Baxter, *Glossarium Antiquitatum Britannicarum sive Syllabus Etymologicus antiquitatum veteris Britanniae atque Bernice temporibus Romanorum.* W. Bowyer, London, 1719.

[8] Cf. 9. Nov. 1722, item 5, and footnote.

[9] The 'Earl Fitz-Williams' MS. (referred to again under 18 Feb. 1722/3, item 1) is the Walter of Whitlesey Chronicle (which was one of the Peterborough MSS. printed by Sparke (at pp. 125–237) and one page of which (f. 20) was engraved for Sparke's work); it comprises a chronicle, rental, cartulary, &c., c. 1322–9, and is now BM Add. 39758 (= Davis no. 758): it remained in the Fitzwilliam family until 1918, when it was lot 255 in Sotheby's sale, 30 Apr. of that year. The Lords Fitzwilliam had owned at one time or another no less than four Peterborough registers (Davis nos. 755, 758, 761, 770).

[10] For details of the Primer and what happened to Bridges's library and the MSS. in it see footnote to 24 Mar. 1725/6.

of it Mr Bridges came in. Upon my speaking to him about it, he said that Mr Sparke should not have made mention of it; that he had it, in the South-Sea time of Mr Graham for a Debt; that he ha's divers other fine books of that Kind; That his Edge for Purchasing of Books is much abated, & now wear's off; and that it is possible that he may oblige my Lord with that Capital Book, if he disposes of the others to him at the same time; and that he is Determined to Order in his Will, that his whole Library be sold, after his Decease.[1] Here-upon, I immediately desired, that in such Case, he would Charge his Executors that my Lord may have the Pre-emption of what He may then want, without being putt off to the Sale: This Mr Bridges promised, but afterwards added a Condition, which was thus, *Provided that my Lord doth not prejudice the Sale thereby*. This should be explained.

10. Mr Elliot sent or brought-in last Saturday-Evening soñe [*sic*] of the Books last deliver'd to him. In the Lettering of one of them is a Blunder in the Date; and the Midle-pieces of the Marocco-work are all too small. /

p. 133
(f. 68a)

1. Mr Chapman brought-in the last Parcel deliver'd to him, well done; excepting 3 Blunders in the Lettering: so that I bad him take 3 books back to amend; which he did.

2. Mr Elliot brought-in the remainder of the Books of the last Parcel, & recieved from me another Parcel, & three more of my Lords Marocco-Skins, according to his Desire.

3. Mr Newton of S^t. John's in Cambridge came, with a Letter from Dr Tudway to my Lord; wherein (he said) there is a Note [*substituted for* Letter *deleted*] from Mr Baker, specifying that an intire Copie of the first Edition of King Edward VIth's Liturgy printed by Grafton is now found; and that his Lordship may have it for five Guineas. For that which M^r. Baker presented to my Lord, want's the Title-page.[2]

4. My Lord sent in a Japonese or Chinese Book printed with Blue Ink; which came up from Welbeck.

13 November 1722.

5. A Letter sent to Mr Gibson, desiring him to call upon my Lord next Thursday-morning.

6. Mr Reading Library-keeper to Sion-College came, & I shewed him many Rarities here.

7. Mr Hawkins late Minister of the Tower came to me at Noon, & presented to my Lord Six Denarij of Constantius & Julianus apostata, with a small Silver-Ring; all found, as he said about Ten or more Years agoe, in repairing of Eden-bourg-Castle, among the Rubbish of an old Roman Wall there.

8. M^r O Sullevane came to Study in the MS. before mentioned.[3]

---

[1] See footnote 10, p. 171; for relevant extract from Bridges's Will (dated 8 Aug. 1723) see BM Lansdowne 1056, f. 36.

[2] There were at least 7 eds. or variations of the First Prayer Book of King Edward VI in 1549 but the one usually held to be the first ed. is that printed at London 8th day of Mar. in the 3rd year of Edward VI by Richard Grafton entitled *The Booke of Common Praier and Administracion of the Sacramentes*. The letters referred to have not been traced but in Welbeck Wanleyana is a letter from Baker to Wanley, dated 29 Nov. 1722, in which he notifies Wanley that Dr. Massey expects 5 guineas for the Book of Common Prayer and asks Wanley to write direct to Massey on the subject as he [Baker] relinquishes all claim to the book, for which he would have offered 2 guineas.   [3] Harl. 3973. Cf. 19 Oct. 1722, item 22.

14 November 1722.

9. Mr Sanderson came to my Lodging and told me that he is now Inspecting Oliver Cromwell Secretary Thurloe's Papers now in the Possession of S^r. Joseph Jekyll Master of the Rolls; and upon a new Desire from me, promised to take a proper Opportunity of putting his Master in Mind of Letting my Lord have them for an Equivalent.[1] Mr Sanderson also enquired for the remainder of the Money (about 15^s. 6^d.) which he yet claim's as due to him, about the Diamond-Buckle, & Pocket-Glass of Q. Anne: He likewise touched upon the Medal of the two Kings of Denmark, which he presented to my Lord by me; and hearing me again averre this, he acquiesced; and acknowledged that it might be, & was so.

10. Mr William Thomas came about the Writings in the little Closet.

11. M^r. Harbyn came to look into the Copies of, or Extracts from, the Libri Niger & Rubeus Scaccarij.[2]

12. Mr Salomon Negri came, & I paid him my Lords 6 Guineas for his Copie of the Psalter in Arabic; which he says, come's from the Greek & not from the Syriac; if [*sic*] of a different Version from that in the Polyglot-Bible; and also much better Language.[3] I also took-off an Impression in Wax from the Arabic Seal above mentioned in page 124, 1. and then M^r. Negri looking carefully upon it, the Letters appearing in their proper Shapes, he Read it thus, *Lawi ben Dawoud*, i.e. *Levi filius Davidis*; adding that he is sure of the two last Words, & believe's that the first is right.[4]

15 November 1722.

13. M^r O Sullevane came to look into the MS. abovementioned.[5]

14. Mr Gibson came, and talked very much with my Lord, & afterward with me about the last Bargain of MSS. &c. which he Sold to my Lord; and being told that they are very dear, & therefore desired to throw-in his last little parcel of printed Books, thereto, to make the said Bargain the Easier: He did not agree to this proposal positively, but leave's the matter to my Lord. / [6]

1. In discoursing with Mr Gibson about Mr Smith of Venice's MSS. lately Arrived;[7] p. 134 to my Quere, Whether he be concerned in them as a partner, or Seller, he (f. 68b) utterly denie's it: but say's, that as Mr Smith ha's Sett a Price upon them, he Expects to know what my Lord will bid for them; if reasonably, (that is, to Mr Smith's mind) his Lordship may have them; if not, they will be disposed of elsewhere.[8]

---

[1] See 13 June 1721, item 3, and footnote.

[2] The 'Liber Niger' MS. referred to here is Harl. 95 (a D'Ewes transcript of the original now in the P.R.O.): it was subsequently borrowed by Harbin 19 Nov. 1722. The extracts from 'Rubeus Scaccarii' are in Harl. 313 (cf. 1 Dec. 1722 under item 9).

[3] See 11 May 1722, item 10, and footnote. The MS. is Harl. 5476; a memorandum by Negri in the MS. contains the information quoted by Wanley.

[4] Cf. 10 Sept. 1722, item 1 (the Negri item).

[5] Harl. 3973. Cf. 19 Oct. 1722, item 22.

[6] For details of this bargain of MSS. see lists at 5 May and 10 Sept. 1722, and for agreement on price 13 Sept. 1722, item 2. For the 'last little parcel of printed books' see 26 Dec. 1722 for list of titles. Gibson valued the latter at £30 (see 13 Feb. 1723/4, item 6, for general settlement with Gibson).

[7] Wanley had inspected these 5 Oct. 1722.

[8] See 10 Sept. 1722, item 3, and footnote.

16 November 1722.

2. M^r O Sullevane came, to peruse the MS. above-mentioned.[1]

3. Mr Virtue came to look into the Life of old S^r. Simonds D'ewes.[2]

4. Mr Holman was brought by Mr Morley; but I being extraordinarily busied, putt (for the first time) into his Hands the MS.42.B.3, it relating to his County; and afterwards, other things.[3]

5. Mr Harbyn came, when it was late.

17 November 1722.

6. Mr Sparke brought a proof-Map of the Fens, as lately surveyed by Dr Stukeley; with desire that my Lord would Subscribe for Six, at the Rate of Half a Guinea.[4]

19 November 1722.

7. Mr Harbyn came, & borrowed the MS.34.C.13.[5]

8. D^r. Sherard brought 60 Cones of the Cedars of Libanus, a Present to my Lord. He say's that this Tree is the hardiest of any in the World, for no Frosts or Coldest Winds will hurt it. It is the best Wood for any Sort of Work, is most lasting, & when young will make the best Sort of Hedge, Piramids, &c. for Gardens. He left this direction for the Sowing, that it be done early in the Spring, when Pines, &c. are Sown; that the Gardiner do not cutt the Cone with a Knife, because he will cutt the Seeds, which are scarce, so as not easily to be had again. Each Cone will yield about one hundred Seeds. When the Gardener intend's to Sow, lett him putt only so many of the Cones as he intend's to use, into Water Luke-warm, and in about 2 Hours, they will open, & he may gett the Seeds, which must then be soon Sown, otherwise they will dry up, & be good for nothing. The Doctor further said, that his Friend ha's been at Herborn and enquired after Professor Lents Son, who ha's the most antient Syriac MS. of the Historical part of the Old Testament, by which Masius corrected his Greek Text of Joshua: that, he can learn no more of him, but that he ha's been gone from thence many years, but whither, it was not known.[6]

20 November, 1722.

9. By my Lords Order, Froissard's History in 2 Volls. fol.[7] with the second Volume of Du Fresne's Latin Glossary,[8] were sent to my Lord Oxford.

[1] Harl. 3973. Cf. 19 Oct. 1722, item 22.   [2] Harl. 646.

[3] i.e. Harl. 640, a D'Ewes vol. of transcripts of records relating to Essex. Both Morley and Holman came from Halstead in Essex.

[4] Probably *A Map of the Levels in Lincoln Shire commonly called Holland. Described by Wm. Stukeley*, 1723. (It is no. 91 in E. Lynam's list of Fenland maps in *VCH Huntingdonshire*, iii (1936), p. 305.)

[5] i.e. Harl. 95 (cf. also 14 Nov. 1722, item 11): the MS. was returned 16 Feb. 1722/3 (item 14).

[6] This matter of the Syriac MS. was first raised with Sherard 20 Apr. 1722 (item 7). As far back as 27 Apr. 1714 Wanley had drawn up a commission for Thomas Harley, Envoy at Hanover, to buy for Robert Harley this Syriac MS. in the possession of Professor Lentz (Harl. 7526, ff. 150, 151). The Masius book referred to is *Josuae Imperatoris Historia Illustrata atque Explicata ab A[ndreas] Masio*, &c. Hebrew, Greek, and Latin, 1574, fol. (his collation with a Syriac MS. is referred to in the dedicatory epistle). There was a Johannes A. Lent who pubd. Jewish theological works in the 1690's.

[7] Presumably Harl. 4379, 4380.

[8] A ref. to the *Glossarium ad Scriptores Mediae et Infimae Latinitatis*, &c., of Charles Dufresne, Seigneur Du Cange (usually referred to loosely as 'Du Cange'); first pubd. at Paris in 3 vols. 1678, secondly at Frankfurt in 1681, and in a third ed. also at Frankfurt and in 3 vols. in 1710.

10. Mr Holman came, & I shewed him (with Mr Morley) some Rarities; and attended on him, with many things in his way.

11. Mr O Sullevane came, to peruse the MS. abovementioned.[1]

21 November 1722.

12. I brought in 46 Deeds & 3 Rolls, as a Free-will Offering to the Library. /[2]

1. Mr Holman came to peruse some more of my Lords MSS.

p. 135
(f. 69a)

2. Mr Smith came to know what my Lord will give for that parcel of his Brothers MSS. which I lately saw. I told him my Lord will not bid anything untill he know's his Brothers lowest Price.[3]

3. Mr Collins came. I bad him call again after the next Week is over, because I want the whole Room for sorting of Charters.[4]

4. Mr Bateman came; & I shewed him some Rarities.

P.M.

5. Sr. James Thornhill brought Mr Norton of Southwick & Mr Chichley, to see some of the Rarities of this Place, and after my long attendance, went away extremely well satisfied.

6. Mr O Sullevane came, to peruse the above-mentioned MS.[5]

7. Mr Will. Thomas came & Borrowed the MS. of Chaucer inscribed 93.B.2.[6]

22 November 1722.[7]

8. A Letter sent to Mr Vertue desiring him to Attend my Lord about Sir Hugh Midelton's Picture.[8]

9. Mr William Thomas came.

10. Mr Rob. Cuningham came.

11. Dr. Bentley sent Mr Casley with the four MSS. of Lucan which he had borrowed; & I deliver'd up his Note.[9]

23 November 1723 [*sic*].

12. Mr William Thomas came, about the Writings in the Closet.[10]

13. Mr O Sullevane came still to peruse the MS. above-mentioned.[11]

---

[1] Harl. 3973. Cf. 19 Oct. 1722, item 22.

[2] The following deeds bear Wanley's endorsement of 21 Nov. 1722 or (possibly by error) 22 Nov. 1722: Harl. Ch. III. B. 60; III. C. 7, 12, 57; III. E. 48; III. G. 16, 33, 57, 58; III. H. 24 a, 33, 36; 112. A. 6, 7, 8, 13; 112. C. 10; 112. E. 21, 22, 26, 42 a, b. Two more bearing the same date are in Welbeck Wanleyana, Misc. nos. 65 and 66.

[3] Cf. 5 Oct. 1722. For note on Smith transaction see footnote to 10 Sept. 1722, item 3.

[4] Cf. 23 Nov. 1722, item 14.

[5] Harl. 3973. Cf. 19 Oct. 1722, item 22.

[6] i.e. Harl. 1758.

[7] Harl. 6986 (ff. 9–10) is endorsed by Wanley with this date, but see 22 Nov. 1725, item 13.

[8] For the portrait of Sir Hugh Middleton (1560–1631, the projector of the New River Scheme) in Harley's possession see *Vertue Note Books* (Walpole Soc.), i. 3 and 73: for reference to engraving see 8 Dec. 1722 and 17 Sept. 1723, item 8. Sir Hugh Middleton's picture was not disposed of after Edward Harley's death, presumably because it was treated as one of the family portraits, Robert Harley having married as his second wife Sarah Middleton. It is now in the possession of the Duke of Portland. For description and details of Vertue's engraving and the inscription see R. W. Goulding, *Catalogue of the Pictures belonging to His Grace the Duke of Portland, K.G.*, Cambridge, 1936, no. 99.

[9] These had been borrowed 29 Oct. 1722.

[10] Harl. 7003, f. 172, is endorsed by Wanley as having been given by *Timothy* Thomas on this date.

[11] Harl. 3973. Cf. 19 Oct. 1722, item 22.

14. I being now about to replenish the Press 111, 112 with Charters or Instruments of all Kinds, do here notify (for future Observation,) that the Charters which fill the Boxes 43, 44: 45, 46: 47, 48: 49, 50: 51, 52: 53, 54: 55, 56: 57, 58: were all bought together of Sir Simonds D'Ewes, with his Books, Manuscripts & Printed.[1] Besides which Charters, remained some of later Dates, & less Value as Leases, &c. which were laid aside, as not then thought worthy of another Press. Since then, some Thousands more have come-in, viz. those from 75.A.1, to 75.D.25 inclusive, by the Gift of the Right Honorable Thomas, now Lord Mansell,[2] those from 83.A.21 to 83.C.9 inclusive, by the Gift of the late Reverend D[r]. Matthew Hutton of Aynho in Com Northampt.[3] Those from 83.C.10, to 84.B.61 inclusive (excepting a few perhaps in 83.B.8.) [sic] by the Gift of John Anstis Esq. now Garter King of Armes.[4] And some others have been brought in by my noble Lord Harley. The Rest, preserved in the Boxes 84; 85; 86; 111, & 112 (excepting some of Sir Simonds D'ewes's abovementioned, which are very easily discerned & known,) were Bought of me, (so far as I can now remember) if they be not Indorsed to the contrary. /[5]

24 November 1722.

1. M[r] Harbyn came to Study; & gave one Letter of M[r] John Muddyman, which is Endorsed.[6]

2. M[r] O Sullevane came, as usual.

26 November 1722.

3. A Letter sent to M[r] Innys desiring him to send hither the MS. 40.D.13. which M[r] Wise of Oxford sent up to him, to be returned hither.[7]

4. M[r]. Sparke came, to see some Books; I being very busy, shewed him but few.

5. M[r] Gibson came.

27 November 1722.

6. M[r] John Innys brought hither the MS. last mentioned, which I putt into its place & burnt M[r] Wise's Note; & I paid him 14[s]. being my Lords Subscription-money to D[r]. Halls Edition of the Continuation to Nic. Triveth.[7]

7. My Lord Brought-in a thin MS. viz. Oracio habita in tradicione Garterij ad X̄pianissimum Franciscum Galliarum Regem, Parisijs, 10 Nov. 1527 Joh̄e Taylero Vice-cancellario pronunciante.[8]

---

[1] The library of Sir Symonds D'Ewes (1602–50), the antiquary, was purchased by Robert Harley in 1705 for £450: the purchase had been negotiated by Wanley.

[2] The donor was Thomas Mansell, of Margam, Glamorganshire, cr. 1st Baron Mansell of Margam 1 Jan. 1711/12: he died in 1723 at Margam. It is interesting to note that nearly all of this very considerable group of Charters (75. A. 1–75. D. 25) relate to the Cistercian abbey of Margam. Lord Mansell was one of the bidders for Edward Lhwyd's things (see earlier in the Diary, under 26 Apr. 1715).

[3] Harl. Ch. 83. A. 21–83. C. 9, Dr. Hutton's gift, have no endorsements by Wanley, but cf. 30 June 1720, item 6.

[4] As regards the Anstis gift cf. 18 July 1716 when Anstis gave a 'second parcel' of old deeds amounting to 363 in number, all dated according to Wanley with that date. For other refs. to Anstis's gift of deeds at this date cf. 24 Dec. 1722 and 20 Feb. 1722/3, item 6.

[5] A recent gift of deeds and rolls by Wanley is noted 21 Nov. 1722, item 12. See footnote to that date for identifications.

[6] Not identified.

[7] i.e. Harl. 563: it had been taken out for Wise 11 July 1721 (see footnote to that date).

[8] Harl. 5287.

1 December 1722.

8. Mr Boothe came, and said that he intend's to be in Cheshire about 2 Month's hence, and then (if my Lord please's) he will again endeavor to purchase the Original Deeds, &c. lately in the Possession of the last Randle Holme;[1] and said that he ha's about 40 or 50 Volumes in Folio relating to the Estates of Royalists Sold by Order of Oliver Cromwell, &c. And desiring that I would transcribe for him 3 Notes which I have inserted in the Notitia Monastica; I promised to do it.[2]

9. Mr Harbyn came & look'd into the MS. 37.C.16.[3] & said that he had brought a Patent of K. Edw. III.[4] and certain Original Letters of Wilmot Earl of Rochester, Mr Henry Savile &c; to Present to my Lord: and did so.[5]

10. A Letter Sent to Mr Elliot, for him to come hither on Monday morning.

11. Mr Elliot sent back only part of the last Parcel; & half of them are too badly Letter'd.

3 December 1722.

12. Mr Elliot came, but not according to my Summons; he brought some more books of the last Parcel with him; but I made him take back five of the Books in Order to amend their Vicious Lettering. These he will amend & bring back this day Señight. I also deliver'd unto him Seven Parcels of Original Warants from the Signet to the Privy Seal de temp. Annæ Reginæ; & another Parcel of the times of K. Charles I, & K. Charles II. with Instruction to fasten with Strong Past (wherein Rosin is mingled) all the Seals that are loose, or have come off, by Reason of the Parchments Greasiness. /[6]

4 December 1722.

1. Mr Warburton the Heralds Brother came Enquiring after a Grant of Armes to some Family;[7] but I being busie, desired him to call again, the next week.

6 December 1722.

2. Mr Collins came to peruse some Heraldical MSS.

7 December 1722.

3. M^r O Sullevane came & perused the above-mentioned old MS.[8] Mr Bateman came.

8 December 1722.

4. Mr Virtue came about the Engraving of the Inscription to the Print of Sir Hugh Midelton.[9]

---

[1] See 23 Jan. 1719/20, item 5, and footnote.
[2] A ref. presumably to Wanley's own annotated copy of Tanner's *Notitia Monastica* (1695 ed.), now BM Add. 47842.
[3] i.e. Harl. 313.　　　　　　　　　　　　　　　　　　　[4] Not identified.
[5] No letters presented by Harbin are endorsed by Wanley with this date.
[6] The 8 parcels in all of Privy Seal Warrants handed over to Elliot are probably Harl. 7344–51 (see descriptions in *Harl. Cat.* (1759)). Cf. 27 Aug. 1723.
[7] Cf. 12 Dec. 1722, item 7. The arms were those of the family of Lewis.
[8] Harl. 3973. Cf. 19 Oct. 1722, item 22.　　　　[9] Cf. 22 Nov. 1722, item 8, and footnote.

10 December 1722.

5. Mr Bateman came.

12 December 1722.

6. Mr Morley brought 14 Old Deeds being presented by Mr Holman of Halsted.[1]

7. Mr Warburton's Brother came again Searching after certain Armes born by a family of the Name of Lewis.

8. Mr Beaver came to look into some old Articles of War.

9. Mr Elliot came to conferre with me about the manner wherein he should Bind the Parcel of Parchments last deliver'd to him.[2]

13 December 1722.

10. Mr Beaver came again to Study.

14 December 1722.

11. Mr Gibson came.

12. Mr Elliot came again, as he did the other Day.

15 December 1722.

13. Mr Moses Williams brought Mr Clarke Fellow of St. Johns in Cambridge to see the Library, & I attended them about two hours.

14. Mr Gibson came to wait upon my Lord.

17 December 1722.

15. My Lord Brought Mr Hazard, & bespoke 3 Presses of him.

16. Dr. Fiddis came to look into an Original Letter of Cardinal Wolsey.[3]

17. Mr Beaver came to Study.

18 December 1722.

19 [*sic*]. Mr Bowyer came & acquainted me that Mr. Jones is dead, & ha's left a great Cargo of uncommon Books, & other Things behind him, which may now perhaps be come-at-able. I answer'd, that I believe he had few Things left worthy the looking after, I having already bought all of him that I thought worth the having.[4]

19 December 1722.

20. A Letter sent to Mr Elliot with Orders for Binding the Warants to the Privy Seals. /[5]

December 21, 1722.

p. 138
(f. 70b)

1. I having packed up two Cases with Printed Books bound in Marocco, sent them away for Wimpole.

[1] These are now in the *Cotton* Charters, where the following are endorsed by Wanley with this date, viz. XXI. 6, 8, 23, 27, 40; XXIX. 44, 77.

[2] i.e. on 3 Dec. 1722.

[3] Fiddes was preparing a life of Cardinal Wolsey, cf. 15 Jan. 1719/20, item 5 and footnote.

[4] Wanley's purchase of a parcel of MSS. from Jones is noted under 15 Aug. 1715. Jones had also bought items at John Kemp's sale (cf. 16 Mar. 1720/1, item 18).

[5] Cf. 3 Dec. 1722, and footnote for identification.

2. Mr Sparke came to looke upon two MSS. I talked to him about the first Edition of K. Edw. VI^ths. Liturgy;[1] and he promised to bring up his Caxton's Chesse-play,[2] upon his first going into the Countrey.

3. Mr Charles Davis came and talked with me about the Books he lately bought of Mr Lion; and looking over the Catalogue of them, I desired that some of them might be brought hither this afternoon.[3]

4. Mr Davis brought the said Books, together with divers others. Part of them I rejected; the others are left with me in Order to my transmitting to my Lord an Account of them by the next Post.[4]

22 December, 1722.

5. Mr Walwyn Shepherd sent for the Deed which Mr Hugh Thomas borrowed of Mr Hereford; and I deliver'd it to his Messenger, according to my Lords Order.[5]

24 December, 1722.

6. My Lord having sent up from Wimpole, I this day recieved a parcel of old Charters which Mr Anstis gave to the Library the 18th. of July 1716: which Date, God willing, will be putt on the Back of each of them, wherby they will be known & distinguished.[6]

26 December, 1722.

7. It is not too late to note here, that on Thursday-night last, my Lord was pleas'd to tell me that Mr Gibson's last little Parcel of Printed Books, mention'd in the Minutes of the 9 of October & 15th. of November last, are all his own, as being gained into the two last Parcels of MSS. bought of him.[7] I being now about to give their Titles to the Book-binder, do give the following List of them.

   1. Suetonius de XII Cæsaribus; Æl. Spartianus, Jul. Capitolinus, Æl. Lampridius, Treb. Pollio, Fl. Vopiscus, Eutropius, Paul. Diaconus de Regg. & Impp. Romanis. Mediol. per Phil. Lavagniam, 1475. fol. min. Chart. mag.[8]

   2. Psalterium Hebræum, Græcum, Arabicum, & Chaldæum, cum 3 Latinis Interpretationibus & Glossis per Aug. Justinianum. Genuæ, 1516. fol. min.[9]

   3. D. Cypriani Opera. Romæ, apud Paul Manutium, 1563. fol. min.[10]

---

[1] Conversation over the first ed. of K. Edward VI's Liturgy arose probably as the result of Baker's offer of a copy as recorded under 12 Nov. 1722, item 3 (see footnote to that date).

[2] No further ref. to this Caxton (for a note on *The Game and Playe of the Chesse* see footnote to 13 June 1721, item 3).

[3] Cf. item 4 below and 24 Jan. 1722/3, item 6 (for list).

[4] Cf. item 3 above and footnote.

[5] Cf. 23 July 1722 (item 7) when it had been borrowed.

[6] See 23 Nov. 1722, item 14, and footnote. Cf. also 20 Feb. 1722/3, item 6, for another parcel of those formerly given by Anstis.

[7] For details see footnote to 15 Nov. 1722, item 14. The printed books listed here are referred to again on 10 Feb. 1723/4, item 5, and were taken account of in general settlement under 13 Feb. 1723/4. Gibson valued them at £30.

[8] Hain *14561; *BMC* vi. 702 (IB 26112).

[9] *Psalterium Hebreum, Grecū, Arabicū, & Chaldeū, cū glossis.* [Ed. by Agostino Giustiniani.] 1516, fol.

[10] *Divi Caecilii Cypriani . . . Opera . . .* Paul Manutius, Rome, 1563, fol.

4. Hermolai Barbari Plinianæ Castigationes; Castigationes Plinianæ Secundæ; Emendatio in Pomp. Melam. In Plinium Glossema, Romæ, per Eucharium Argenteum, 1493. fol. min.[1]

5. Agathias de Bello Gotthorum, &c. Lat. per Christ. Personam. Rom. ap. Jac. Mazochium, 1516. 4to. ampliss.[2]

6. Paul. Orosij Historia. Basileco, per Leornardum ——— 4to. ampliss.[3]

7. Papiæ Elementarium. Venet. per Andr. de Bonetis, 1485. fol. min.[4]

8. Terentius. Taurini, per Joh. Fabri, 1578. 4to. ampliss. sed impf. & lutulent.[5]

9. Pompeius Festus. ——— 1477, Litt. Germ. fol. minim.[6]

10. Terentius, cum Donato et Eugraphio, edente Fr. Lindenbruchio. Parisijs, 1602. 4to. /[7]

p. 139 (f. 71a)

11. Plautus; edente Georgio-Merula Alexandrino [*substituted for* Eusebio Scutario *deleted*]. Venet. ——— 1495. 4to.[8]

1. Mr Thomas Hill came.

27 December 1722.

2. I being about to make up a Parcel of MSS. for Mr Chapman to Bind, some of them will be part of those which Mr Noel sent-in, without Order, 13 September last. These lay long in his Sacks, with the Printed Books, untill that at length my Lord sent for the said Sacks to him; and keeping the Printed Books, and some of the MSS. he sent down to me these only whose Titles do here follow.[9]

1. Formulæ Instrumentorum in Curia Episcopali Bristoliensi. fol. min. chart.[10]

2. [Liber Consuetudinarius Abbatiæ S. Edi *deleted*] Pars libri II. de Sacramentis, per Hugonem de S. Victore. 4to. membr.[11]

3. Rodbertus in Cantica Canticorum, cum alijs. 4to. membr. (*Hunc autorem haud agnoscit D. Guil. Cave.*)[12]

4. Tractatus varij de Lapide Philosophico. 4to. chart.[13]

5. Homiliæ D. Joan. Chrysostomi XXX, Latinè, ad Editiones Græcas perfidendas fortè non inutiles. Sermo de Celebratione Dierum Fratrum defunctorum. Isidorus Hispalensis de Differentijs. Beda de Naturis Rerum. Anselmus de libero Arbitrio. 4to. membr.[14]

6. Medicinal Reciepts. 4to. chart.[15]

7. Ma. Achardi Sermones. 4to. med. membr. (Annon extarent hi, dubitavit D. Guil. Cave.)[16]

[1] BMC iv. 113–14 (IB 18955); Hain 2421; GW 3340.
[2] *Agathyus de Bello Gotthorum et aliis peregrinis historiis per Christopherum Persona . . . e Graeco in Latinum traductus*, Rome, 1516.
[3] This may be a copy of the undated ed. printed at Vicenza (without mentioning the name of the place) by Leonardus (Achates) de Basilia about 1480; BMC vii. 1032 (IB 31720), but this is fol. not 4°.
[4] BMC v. 361 (IB 22093).
[5] This should read 1478 *not* 1578. It is Hain 15379 (no copy in BM, no copy in America, and no copy at Cambridge). Very rare. ? Osborne sale, i, no. *3574.
[6] Hain 7040; *Indice Generale* 3852 [Bartholomeus Guldinbeck, Rome]. No copy in BM; 6 copies in Italy.
[7] i.e. *Publii Terentii, . . . Comoediae Ñ. VI Etineas: AElii Donati VC. Oratoris Urbis Romae, et Eugraphii Veteris Grammatici Commentaria. Fr. Lindenbruchius collatis MSS. veteribusque exemplaribus ecensuit. . . .* H. Périer, Paris, 1602. Presumably Osborne, i, no. *3590.
[8] Stillwell P. 712; BMC v. 486 (IA 22775). Presumably Osborne, i, no. *3558.
[9] See 11 Sept. 1722 and footnote.   [10] Harl. 4305.
[11] Harl. 3137.   [12] Harl. 3006.   [13] Harl. 3703.   [14] Harl. 3015.
[15] See footnote to item 23 in this list for books of medicinal receipts bearing this date.
[16] Harl. 3122.

8. A Collection of Italian Phrases, shewing the Propriety of that Language, to English Learners: by B. S. A.D. 1686. fol.[1]
9. Traitté de la Geometrie Pratique. fol.[2]
10. Rental of the Bishoprick of Gloucester, A.D. 1608. fol. very thin.[3]
11. A Collection of Precedents used by Common Lawyers; as it seem's, by some Practitioner in Coventre. fol.[4]
12. Instrumentorum Formulæ nonnullæ, in Curijs Episcopalibus usurpatæ. fol. min. ten.[5]
13. Exemplar authenticum Litterarum Patentium R. Henrici VIII. quibus fundavit Episcopatum Gloucestriensem. fol. min. ten & paullum a muribus corrosum.[6]
14. A Good book of Reciepts in Cookery & Pharmacy. fol. min. *Init.* To boyle a Carpe.[7]
15. Four oblong Books of Tracts relating to Physic or Chirurgery.[8]
16. Fabrica Horologial universal, por Andres de Vega; año 1627. 4to. corio Russico.[9]
17. Medicinal Reciepts. 1587. 4to. *Init.* To eate the Filme or Hawe in the Eye of anny beast.[10]
18. Georgij Smithi Loci Communes. 4to.[11]
19. Memoranda de Causis litigatis coram Johanne Archbold in Curia Episcopi Wigorniensis, a nono die Octobris A.D. 1612, usque ad 15 diem Julij 1613, inclusive. 4to.[12]
20. Formulæ Instrumentorum in Curia Episcopali Gloucestr. 4to.[13]
21. Memoranda de Causis ventilatis in Curia Consistoriali Wigorn coram Radulfo Willett, a 27 die Septembris 1615, usque ad 3 diem Julij A.D. 1617. 4to.[14]
21 [*sic*]. Memoranda de Causis conclusis coram Johe Seman in Curia Consistoriali Gloucestr. a 4 die Aprilis A.D. 1609, usq. ad 26 diem Septembris 1611. 4to.[15]
22. Peter Smart's Book about Logarithms. A.D. 1685. 8vo. (little written in it.)[16]
23. Several other Books or Tracts of Medicinal Rec^{ts}. in English or Latin; some of which perhaps may be good for something. /[17]
24. Historical & Geographical Notes taken A.D. 1622, from sundry Printed books, 16to.[18]

p. 140 (f. 71b)

25. Horæ B. Mariæ Virginis sec. usum Saꝛ. Desunt pictæ Tabulæ Sanctorum majores: quin et folia quamplurima Bibliopegi oscitantiâ transponuntur. 4to. Corio Turcico. membr.[19]
26. Horæ B. V. Mariæ Belgicè. (Codex videtur inluminatus A.D. 1486. 4to. membr. Corio Turcico.[)]][20]

---

[1] Harl. 3492.　　[2] Harl. 4356.　　[3] Not identified.　　[4] Not identified.
[5] Not identified.　　[6] Not identified.　　[7] Not identified.
[8] e.g. Harl. 4096 (which bears this date).　　[9] Harl. 3394.　　[10] Not identified.
[11] Harl. 4085.　　[12] Harl. 4064, ff. 95–191 (dated 12 Sept. 1722 by Wanley on f. 95).
[13] Harl. 6679.　　[14] Harl. 6668.
[15] Harl. 4064, ff. 2–94 (dated 12 Sept. 1722 by Wanley on f. 1).
[16] Harl. 5031 (answers to Wanley's description precisely but bears no date by him on the fly-leaf).
[17] e.g. Harl. 2389, 4720, 5354, 6042, 6812 (ff. 328–46, 347–51), 6937, 7360 (and cf. item 6 in this list above), all of which bear this date by Wanley.
[18] Harl. 2334 (the date 1622 is at the end of the Contents List, f. 2★).
[19] Harl. 2976.　　[20] Harl. 2943.

27. Horarum Liber, cum Rubricis Gallicè conscriptis. Desiderantur passim Sanctorum Imagines, &c. 4to. min. Corio Turcico.[1]

28. Officium B. V. Mariæ cum alijs Precibus tam Gallicè quam Latinè. Codex satis eleganter inluminatus; plurimæ tamen e venustioribus Pictoris jam desiderantur. 4to. Corio Turcico. membr.[2]

29. Horæ B. V. Mariæ secundum usum Angliæ. Codex haud invenustè tenuissimis Membranis cum scriptus tum inluminatus. Volumine pusillo, cum oporculo è Corio Turcico.[3]

1. Mr Moses Williams came.

29 December 1722.

2. Mr Charles Davis came; and I sent him to my noble Lord Oxford, who want's somebody to serve him in the way of out-of-course Books, as John Bagford used to do.

3. Mr Gregory came, and I order'd him to make up some more Cases, to be ready upon occasion.

1 January 1722/3.

4. A Letter sent to Mr Elliot for those books which he took back in Order to amend their Lettering.

2 January 1722/3.

5. Mr Beaver came, and borrowed the Printed Book of the Czars Sea-Laws for a few days.[4]

6. Mr Elliot (in the Evening) sent-in the books demanded of him yesterday.

3 January 1722/3.

7. A Letter Sent to Mr Gregory to come here and make-up a Lid for a Box to go to Wimple with Books.

8 January 1722/3.

8. D^r. Sherard came.

9 January 1722/3.

9. Mr Boothe came, and talked about his willingness to procure the original Deeds lately belonging to old Randle Holme, for my Lord.[5] And then wanting some Notices about part of his Estate in the City & County Palatine of Chester, he employed me some Time; and yield's to my Desire of sending some Clerk to do the remaining part of the Service for him.

[1] Harl. 2948. [2] Harl. 2944. [3] Harl. 2846.
[4] Cf. 11 Oct. 1722, and footnote. [5] Cf. 1 Dec. 1722, item 8 and footnote.

10. Mr Elliot came, & after much Conversation about the best way of getting out the Cockles risen in my Lords Virgil, & Tullies Epistles, both Printed upon Velum: I deliver'd them to him, & he thinks they may be both done in about Six Weeks time; and promise's to use all possible Care about them.[1]

10 January 1722/3.

11. Mr Woodman sent hither a large Printed Catalogue of the Books he pretend's to have lately bought in France; and intend's to Expose to Sale the 22 Instant.[2] In running it over, I observe he ha's not left-off his old Custom of Lying. /

11 January 1722/3.

p. 141 (f. 72a)

1. I sent away a large Box full of Printed Books, to my Lord at Wimpole.

12 January 1722/3.

2. Mr Moses Williams came.

3. Mr Bateman came & stayed long.

14 January 1722/3.

4. M^r O Sullevane came.

15 January 1722/3.

5. Mr Bateman brought Mr Alexander; to whom I shewed some of the Rarities of this Place.

6. This Afternoon I went to Mr Elliot in Order to give Titles to the several Volumes of Warants to the Privy Seal[3] now remaining with Him, and did so; although they lie in Boards, without Covers, through want of the largest Calve-skins, which must be found & dressed purposely for this Service. This done, I returned hither.

16 January 1722/3.

7. M^r. Hazard came for a New Key to that Presse which my Lord sent-in last, & recieved it; in order to make divers new Locks to it.

17 January 1722/3.

8. Mr Elliot sent for a small parcel of Old Books to Bind; which I refused to deliver but to himself.

9. Mr Charles Davis came.

[1] See 18 Mar. 1722/3, item 18, 21 May 1723, and 9 and 10 July 1723.
[2] i.e. the sale of the library of Mons. Anctil, librarian to the Archbishop of Rheims, 22 Jan. 1722/3, at Woodman's shop. Cf. 22 Jan. 1722/3, item 1, and footnote. [3] Harl. 7344-51.

10. M^r Du Mont brought, for my Lord to See, an Original Picture in Miniature of the late Duchess of Cleaveland, by the old Cowper, as 'tis said.[1]

18 January 1722/3.

11. Mr Dickinson sent-in the two antique Brasen Heads he had from hence some time ago; they being now fixed upon Pedestals.

12. M^r O Sullevane came.

13. Mr Bateman came.

19 January 1722/3.

14. Mr Barett came, to look after a Suffolk-Pedigree. He also said that he ha's some Curious Coins to shew my Lord.

22 January 1722/3.

15. M^r O Sullevane came.

16. A Letter sent to Mr Barret, desiring him to bring his Coins to my Lord some Morning.

17. Mr Bridges came. /

p. 142 (f. 72b)   1. Mr Woodman sent-in a little parcel of Books bought at his present Sale.[2] But not all that my Lord had Marked, he having before promised some of them to others. But those he promise's to procure for my Lord at his next Journey to France. But omitting those which have come-in rightly, though at too dear rates, I observe in his printed Catalogue.

Pag. 28.   n°. 28. Rich. Smithei Flores Historiæ Ecclesiast. Gentis Anglorum. Par. 1654. fol. chart. mag. *wanting*.

8.   171. Festiva ad Capita Annulumque Decursio, a Rege Lud. XIV, &c. Par. e Typ. Reg. 1662. fol. 'The Galleria Farnesiana was sent in instead of it.' [*Portion between ' ' deleted.*] Sent back, & the Festiva brought-in.

9.   202. Le Ceremonial François, par Godefroy. Paris, 1649. fol. chart. mag. 2 Voll. Here should be 3 Volumes.

10.   216. Histoire de Bearne, par Pierre de Marca. a Paris 1640. fol. chart. mag.

20.   421. Vita S. Thomæ Cantuariensis. Paris. 1495. 4to.[3]

423. Certamen Seraphicum Provinciæ Angliæ. Duaci, 1649. 4to.

23.   512. { Balnearum quæ Neapoli, &c. extant, Virtutes, &c. Jul. Cæs. Capacio autore. Neap. 1604, 4to. Puteolana Historica, ab eodem. *Ibid.*

---

[1] Returned to Du Mont by Wanley 22 Jan. 1722/3, item 3. A number of miniatures stated to be of the Duchess of Cleveland by Samuel Cooper are still extant.

[2] Cf. footnote to 10 Jan. 1722/3 for identity of library. The bill for this parcel was sent in 28 Feb. 1722/3 (item 6); 2 books from this sale did not come in until 17 Apr. 1723 (see item 15), i.e. nos. 779 and 797 of Woodman's Cat. listed below.   [3] *BMC* viii. 148 (IB 40476a); Hain 15510.

27.   590. 'Recueil des Traitez, &c. par Leonard. a Paris, 1693. 4to. 6 Volls. My Lord did not desire this book.' [*Portion ' '* *deleted*.] It was returned.

29.   627. L'Historia Ecclesiastica della Revoluzion d'Inghilterra, da Girolamo Pollini. Rom. 1594. 4$^{[t]o}$.

33.   711. Letters intercepted by Coll. Milton near Ruthyn. Lond. 1645. 4$^{[t]o}$.

36.   779. Tres Thomæ: authore Tho. Stapletono. Col. Agr. 1612. 8vo.

37.   797. Brevis Explicatio Martyrij [Vitæ *deleted*] S. Ursulæ & 11000 Virginum. per *Rich. Vitum Basinstochium.* Duaci, 1610. 8$^{[v]o}$.

41.   937. Yvonis Duchatis Tærensis de Bello Sacro, Narrationes IV Græcè. Par. 1620. 8vo.

44.   999. L'Heritiere de Guienne. Rot. 1691. 8vo.

46.   1064. Marguerites de la Marguerite des Princesses. à Lyon, 1547. 8$^{[v]o}$.

50.   1153. Unkind Deserter of Loyal Men. 1676. 8$^{[v]o}$.

          1154. Baillies Offspring, &c. of our Scottish Calvinian Gospel. 1636. 8vo.

          1156. 'His Life of B^{p}. Fisher, 1650. 8vo.' [' ' *deleted*] This was sent-in afterward.

37.   795. Pinax Rerum Naturalium Britannicarum, per Christ. Merrett. Lond. 1667. 8vo.

2. Mr Barett came, to look into the Suffolk Visitations: not knowing that I had written to him.

3. M^{r} Du Mont came; & I restored to him the Picture he left for my Lord to see.[1]

23 January, 1722/3.

4. A Letter sent by a Porter to Mr Woodman, with the Galleria Farnesiana & the Leornards Treaties;[2] & desiring him to send by the Bearer n°. 171 of his Catalogue;[3] & the MS. of the Marquiss of Clanricardes [Antrims *deleted*] Memoirs.[4] Which he did.

24 January, 1722/3.

5. M^{r} O Sullevane came.

6. Mr Davis the Bookseller came, and my Lord having seen the Books which he had last left here with me[5] and [was *deleted*] pleased to chuse out of them such as he best liked; I returned the rest back to Mr Davis, who left with me a Bill of the remainder, which [are] /

---

[1] See 17 Jan. 1722/3, item 10.

[2] For these 2 items see list under 22 Jan. 1722/3, item 1, and Wanley's comments.

[3] i.e. under 22 Jan. 1722/3, item 1.

[4] See R. Flower, 'A Lost MS. of the Clanricarde Memoirs', *BMQ* v (1930–1), pp. 24–25. James Woodman was, in fact, the publisher in 1722 of *Memoirs of the Rt. Hon. the Marquis of Clanricarde, Lord Deputy General of Ireland . . . Pubd. from his Lordship's Original MSS. To which is prefix'd a Dissertation* [by Thomas O'Sullivan] *wherein some passages of these Memoirs are illustrated with a digression . . . concerning the Antiquities of Ireland.*

[5] Presumably those bought by Charles Davis from Lion (cf. 21 Dec. 1722, items 3 and 4).

Eight folios, and Seven Quartos at Common Prices.

Two Quartos at Higher Prices, and Eight Volumes in Manuscript, which are

1. Five Books of Valerius Maximus as translated (with Additions) into French at the Command of the French King Charles V, by Symon de Hesdin Master in Theologie, a Religieux of the Order of S[t]. John of Jerusalem. very large. fol. Velum. Illuminated; *but the last Leaf Renewed.*[1]

2. The four last Books of the same Work; whereof the 9th, 8th, & part of the Seventh were done by Nicolas Gomesse Master in Theologie, &c. by the Command of The Duke of Berry & Auvergne, &c. whose Armes are extant before the First Book. This Volume is agreable to the former; *but the first Leaf is Renewed.*[1]

3. Certain Epistles & Orations of Louis Lassere Provisor of the College of Navarre in the University of Paris. A.D. 1510; Being the Present-Book to Vedast Brioys Dean of S[t]. Martins of Tours. 4to. fine Velum; elegantly Illuminated.[2]

4. Boethius de Consolatione Philosophiæ, translated by Jehan de Mehun for K. Philip the IVth. of France. 4to. This seem's not to have [been] John's Original Book, but a fine Copie of it done for one of the succeeding Kings, upon very fine Velum, and very splendidly illuminated. Now Bound in five Volumes.[3]

1. M[r] O Sullevane came.

25 January 1722
——
3.

2. M[r] Barett came to look into some Heraldical Books.

3. M[r] Bateman came.

4. M[r]. Ashfield came, about Selling my Lord two Books, one Printed viz. Janssonius's Atlass, where he says, (what I don't believe[)] that the Maps are the Originals drawn by Hand, & very finely Painted.[4] The other a German MS. of Alchymy; with exceeding fine Paintings as he say's.[5]

26 January 1722
——
3.

5. D[r]. Savage came for a superfluous quire he left in one of my Lords Books; and promised to bring-in the Quire wanted.[6]

6. M[r] Bridgeman came.

28 January 1722
——
3.

7. M[r] O Sullevane came.

8. M[r] Noel having putt into my hand, yesterday M[r] Sutties Catalogue n[o]. 29. I made an Extract from it here.[7]

---

[1] Harl. 4372–5.   [2] Harl. 2536.   [3] Harl. 4335–9.
[4] On Jan Jansson see R. V. Tooley, *Maps and Map-Makers*, 1949, pp. 33, 35.
[5] Unidentified, but cf. footnote to 30 May 1723, item 14.
[6] The wanted part was brought in by Savage 19 Mar. 1722/3.
[7] No extract from this cat. traced.

9. Mr Varenne came & told me that he ha's brought [*substituted for* gotten *deleted*] from France some very fine books,[1] which he is desirous that I should see: I promised to call on him next Wednesday in the Afternoon.

29 January 1722/3.

10. Mr Vertue came.

11. Mr O Sullevane came to Study.

31 January 1722/3.

12. Mr Bateman came.

13. Dr. Stratford brought Mr Drummond. /

1 February 1722/3.

p. 144
f. 73b)

1. I brought my Nephew George Browne here; to see some of my Lords fine Books.

2 February, 1722/3.

2. Mr Bateman came.

4 February 1722/3.

3. Yesterday Mr. Noel communicated to me part of Mr. Sutties last Letter, & his Catalogue no. 30.[2] from which I have now made an Extract for my Lord.

4. Mr. Davis Brought two Catalogues of his Books which will be Sold at an approaching Sale[3] [*substituted for* Auction *deleted*]; that my Lord may be Secure of having such as he shall think fitt to mark.

5 February 1722/3.

5. Mr. Davis came, for my Lords Commissions.[4]

6. February 1722/3.

6. I left my Lords Commissions for Mr Davis.[4]

7. I went to the Earl of Sunderlands to look into the MSS. his Lordship bought of Mr Smith of Venice, & to take some account of his Greek MSS:[5] and tarried there until twelve o'Clock.

[1] Cf. 27 Oct. 1722, item 14, and 9 Feb. 1722/3, item 4; Varenne held an auction in Dec. 1723 (see 21 Dec. 1723 for extracts from his cat. and identification of MSS. bought by Harley).
[2] No extract from this cat. traced.
[3] i.e. that of the Library of Henry Stanley, M.D. at Dick's Coffee House, Covent Garden, 12 Feb. Cf. 12 Feb. 1722/3, item 9, when books were bought (for the price, £23. 2s. 6d., see Charles Davis's bill under that date in Welbeck Harley Papers (Edw. Harley Misc. 1)).
[4] Cf. 4 Feb. 1722/3, item 4, and footnote.
[5] Cf. 17 Dec. 1720, and footnote, for a sale of Smith's MSS. to Sunderland. For a full note on the final dispersal of Smith's MSS. see footnote to 10 Sept. 1722, item 3.

8. Mr Bowyer the Bookseller came to my Lodgings, intreating me to instruct him touching the Prices of Old Editions, and of other Rare & Valuable Books; pretending that thereby he should be the better able to bid for them: but, as I rather suppose, to be the better able to Exact of Gentlemen. I pleaded utter Inexperience in this Matter; & without a Quarell, in my Mind rejected this ridiculous Attempt with the Scorn it deserved. This may be a fresh Instance of the Truth of Tullies Paradox, that All Fools are Mad. Then he ran-on exceedingly in Commendation of certain Books he was about to buy; and I bad him send 5 of them hither for me to see. Which he did; but above four hours after the time by himself appointed.[1]

7 February 1722
3.

9. I went again to the Earl of Sunderlands, and finished what I had to do, soon after Eleaven.[2]

10. I look'd again upon Mr Bowyers Books; & found that my Lord ha's the best Three of them; and that the other two are in too bad a Condition for him to buy. I therefore sent him the same back, with a Letter.[3]

11. Mr Tim. Thomas came.

12. Mr Morley came.

8 February 1722
3.

13. My Lord sent-in a Greek Inscription which he lately bought of Mr Andrew Hay; being sett-up by Kasia to the Memory of her Husband Caius Julius Karacouttius. Mr Tim. Thomas brought Mr Edward Harley.

14. M^r [*blank space*] Wright a Scots Gent. brought a small parcel of MSS. & old Printed books to Sell. /[4]

p. 145
(f. 74*a*)

9 February 1722
3.

1. A Letter was Sent to Mr Noel according to my Lords Order.

2. I went to Mr Andrew Hay, & took a short Catalogue of a little Parcel of MSS. lately brought out of Italy by Mr Andrew Hay: the Price whereof he say's he will intirely leave to me.[5] And I brought away, as a Present to my Lord, an Antique Circular Medalion or Plate of Brass above 6¼ Inches in Diameter, which seem's by the Figure theron (in Mezzo-Relievo[)], the Inscription, & Signs of the Sun upon Taurus, & the Moon upon Libra to have some Astrological or Talismanical Signification relating to ANTIOCH, but whether this was any one of the Cities so called, or a Woman viderint Docti.

3. Mr Davis came about the books he had sent-in; took-away some that were

---

[1] Cf. 7 Feb. 1722/3, item 10.   [2] Cf. 6 Feb. 1722/3, item 7, and footnote.
[3] Cf. 6 Feb. 1722/3, item 8.
[4] Cf. 12 Feb. (item 8), 19 Feb. (when printed books were removed) and 12 Mar. 1722/3; MSS. were finally bought 24 June 1723. List in Wanley's Addenda, Lansdowne 772, ff. 73, 73^b (at pp. 416–18 of the present work), and (priced) in Welbeck Wanleyana, Misc. no. 27, with receipt for £97.
[5] Cf. 18 Mar. 1722/3, item 20, and 7 June and 13 July 1723 (item 7, and footnote, for list of MSS.).

wrong; & left with me the Prices of the Remainder; promising to send-in the rest this Evening: which he performed.[1]

4. I went to Mr Varenne's to see the MSS. he lately brought from France; but he was not at Home.[2]

11 February 1722
—
3.

5. Mr Davis came; and I bad him to call again the latter End of this Week.

6. Mr Noel came; and said that he Expect's his Things lately bought in Italy soon: being in hopes that they are on their Way hither.[3]

7. Mr Gibson came to me at home, & said that he ha's some MS[S]. now coming from Italy.[4] Among them are Demosthenes's Orations in Greek;[5] & Plinies Natural History;[6] being an older Copie than that which he sold to my Lord.[7] As to the Antient Greek MS. of Plato, it is not bought, the Owners holding it up at too high a price.[8]

12 February 1722
—
3.

8. Mr Wright came, & gave me a Paper of the Prices of his Books & MSS.[9] but upon my Remonstrance of the Excess of his Demand, he promised to abate; when my Lord shall appear to be willing to buy them.

9. M^r [*written for* My] Lord looked into the Books bought at Mr Davis's Sale,[10] and will keep them. Among them, is one MS. of the Provincial Constitutions of the Arch-Bishops of Canterbury.[11]

13 February 1722
—
3.

10. Mr Bowyer came.

14. February 1722
—
3.

11. Mr Noel came, & left with me another Catalogue lately rec'd from Mr Suttie.[12]

12. Mr Sparke came to peruse the MS. 59.B.8.[13]

16 February 1722
—
3.

13. Mr Charles Davis came.

---

[1] Presumably relates to transaction 4 Feb. 1722/3, item 4. Cf. 5 and 6 Feb. 1722/3 and see 12 Feb. 1722/3, item 9, for books bought.

[2] See 28 Jan. 1722/3, item 9, and footnote.

[3] These books eventually arrived and were inspected by Wanley 1 June 1723; list follows under 3 June 1723.

[4] Cf. 22 Mar. 1722/3, item 5 (for first parcel, where provenance is also disclosed), and 4 Apr. 1723, item 17, for list of the 2 batches of books, of which the first was inspected 21 Mar. 1722/3, and the second 2 Apr. 1723. Cf. also 13 Feb. 1723/4 for agreement on their price.

[5] i.e. no. 15 of list under 4 Apr. 1723, item 17 (Harl. 5670).

[6] i.e. no. 1 of list under 4 Apr. 1723, item 17 (possibly Harl. 2676).

[7] See 9 Nov. 1721, item 1, for ref. to this earlier Pliny MS. (Harl. 2677).

[8] Cf. 23 Oct. (item 6) and footnote 2, and 9 Nov. (item 6) 1722.

[9] See footnote to 8 Feb. 1722/3, item 14.   [10] Cf. 4 Feb. 1722/3, item 4, and footnote.

[11] Harl. 3705, pt. 1.   [12] Not traced.   [13] i.e. Harl. 691.

14. Mr Harbyn brought-back the MS. he borrowed last;[1] & look'd into the Visitation of Suffolk. /[2]

p. 146
(f. 74b)

18 February 1722
—
3.

1. Mr Sparke came to peruse the MS. 36.B.17.[3] He told me formerly that his chief MS. relating to Peterburgh-Abbey, doe's belong to the Lord Fitz-Williams.[4] He said now, that the Lord Griffin of Dingley of Northampton-shire ha's a great number of MSS. which he Believe's must soon be disposed of.[5] Also, that Sir [blank space] Cave of Stamford in Northamptonshire ha's likewise a great Number of MSS. the Titles whereof are unknown.[6] Also that the Earl of Cardigan hath another great Parcel.[7] He say's that he will give me Notice where things lie; and that he will exchange some of his old Printed books with my Lord for Duplicates of Historians or Classical Authors.[8]

2. My Lord sent in 3 fine Manuscripts, which are
   Tullies Orations written upon Velum in a Square-hand A.D. 1483, & finely Illuminated. fol.[9]
   The Bible translated out of Latin into French by . . . afterward Dean of St. Peter of Air within the Arch-bishopric of Trement, being finished A.D. 1294: finely written, and Illuminated, with many Historical Pictures, setting forth the Habits, &c. of those Times, in two Volumes in large folio.[10] This Bible belonged to John Duke of Berry Son to the King of France; & to other Princes of that Royal House.

19 February 1722
—
3.

3. Mr Wright came, & I shewed him that my Lord will not have any of his Printed Books; and that he think's the Prices of his MSS. too high. He therefore somewhat lower'd the Prices of the said MSS. & took the Printed books away with him.[11]

4. Mr Noel came.

[1] Harl. 95 (borrowed 19 Nov. 1722).
[2] There are at least 8 MSS. of Suffolk Visitations in the Harl. Coll.
[3] i.e. Harl. 215.
[4] Sparke gave Wanley this information 12 Nov. 1722 (see footnote to item 8).
[5] Edward Griffin, Baron Griffin of Braybrooke, d. 1742 at Dingley, Northants, when the barony became extinct: his father had been a Roman Catholic but he conformed. He left his estates in trust to his illegitimate son, Edward. Dingley Hall was the family seat built on the site of the famous Preceptory of the Hospitallers.
[6] i.e. Sir Verney Cave, 4th Bart., of Stanford (upon-Avon) Hall, on the Leicestershire–Northamptonshire border (b. 1705; d. 1734). The next Baronet, the 5th, Sir Thomas Cave (d. 1778), was a well-known collector of MSS.
[7] i.e. George Brudenell, 3rd Earl of Cardigan, d. 1732. Joseph Sparke was for a time his librarian and in a letter to Maurice Johnson from Stukeley, Sparke is mentioned in 1719 as having lately arranged on a new method Lord Cardigan's library at Deene (see Joan Wake, *The Brudenells of Deene*, 1953, p. 239).
[8] Cf. 12 Nov. 1722, item 8, and footnote.
[9] Harl. 2681. (Wanley's date is derived from the inscription on f. 305.)
[10] Harl. 4381, 4382. This is a Bible History in French, translated by Guiart des Moulins, 1291–4, from Petrus Comestor's Historia Scholastica; the MSS. were executed c. 1400 and certainly belonged to Jean, Duc de Berry, the brother of Charles V of France, and a great patron.
[11] See footnote to 8 Feb. 1722/3, item 14.

20 February 1722

$\overline{3}$.

5. M.ʳ O Sullevane came; & desires to borrow D.ʳ. Davies's Welsh Dictionary.¹

6. My Lord sent-in a small Parcel of Old Deeds, some given by my Lord Oxford; the Remain[d]er, (I believe, long since) given by Mʳ Anstis.²

7. I recḋ a very kind Letter from the Revᵈ. Mʳ Bernard Mould dated a[t] Smyrna 4 December 1722;³ Shewing that the Greek MS of S.ᵗ. Chrysostom on the Acts, with the old Marbles which came along with it, are his present to my Lord. vid. supra, 126, 13.⁴ But as to the 5 Turkish MSS. which M.ʳ. Mould sent to his Sister, & D.ʳ. Lisle brought hither (vid. pag. 112,8.) my Lord is to gratifie her.⁵

22 February 1722

$\overline{3}$.

8. One Sign.ʳ. Stanglini came with a Parchment desiring my Lord would putt his Hand to it as a Subscription for printing a New Edition of Veneroni's Italian Dictionary.⁶ But I told him I believed that His Lordship would not be willing to do it.

9. D.ʳ. Massey of Wisbich came, & told me that he ha's a great Number of MSS. Deeds, & curious Books Printed; and, I believe, will be willing to part with any of them to my Lord, at reasonable price.⁷

23 February 1722

$\overline{3}$.

10. Mʳ Davis the Bookseller came.

26 Febr[u]ary 1722

$\overline{3}$.

11. Mʳ Baret came; to look upon some Visitations of Wiltshire, Somerset & Dorsetshire. /

1. Mʳ Gibson came; and said that he hope's that the Ship wherein he is concern'd, is now in the River.

p. 147 (f. 75a)

2. D.ʳ. Sorell of Cambridge came, & brought me a Letter from D.ʳ. Tudway, about the late D.ʳ. Covell's Things.⁸

27 February 1722

$\overline{3}$.

3. One Mʳ John King a German came, desiring that my Lord would subscribe to the Printing his German Grammar in English. I sent him away, re infectâ.

---

¹ i.e. John Davies, *Antiquae linguae Britannicae, nunc vulgo dictae Cambro-Britannicae . . . dictionarium duplex*, London, 1632 (*STC* 6347). It was lent to O'Sullivan 28 Mar. 1723, item 1.

² For those endorsed by Wanley with date 19 Feb. 1722/3 among the *Cotton* Charters see footnote Addenda, Lansdowne 771, f. 79, under 19 Feb. 1722/3 (at p. 201 of the present work). On the sources of the charters in the Harl. Coll. see 23 Nov. 1722, item 14; for the gift of Anstis charters see 18 July 1716 (cf. also 24 Dec. 1722). ³ Mould's letter of 4 Dec. 1722 has not been traced.

⁴ On the Chrysostom MS. cf. 8 Oct. 1722, item 13 (and footnote).

⁵ See 18 May 1722, item 8, and footnote for identification of MSS.

⁶ G. Veneroni, *Dictionnaire Italien et Français*, London, 1723.

⁷ For Massey's gift to the Bodleian Library in 1710 see Macray, pp. 178–9.

⁸ Tudway's letter is dated 20 Feb. 1722/3 (in Welbeck Wanleyana). See also footnote to 8 Mar. 1722/3.

4. M^r. O Sullevane came, & talked about the Irish MSS. yet remaining at Meissen;[1] about the MSS. of the Duke of Chandos;[2] and of some few other MSS. in the possession of Sir Gervase Clifton,[3] which he think's may be procured.

5. Mr Davis the Bookseller came.

28. February 1722/3.

6. Mr Woodman brought-in his Bill for the Books last bought of him.[4]

7. My Lord sent-in a Specimen of Mr John Dundasses Writing & Flourishing, being done for my Lord Oxford A.D. 1703. And a little print of B^p. Ken's Head with much Flourishing, Engraven from the same Mr Dundasses Copie.[5]

2 March 1722/3.

7. [sic] Mr Charles Bridgeman came.

8. Mr Bowyer came & told me that M^r. Batteley is now willing to sell the remainder of the late A.D. Batteleys books & MSS. and brought me the Catalogue of those Printed, which he desire's me to peruse & consider of.[6]

9. D^r. Me[a]de borrowed the MS. of Robert of Gloucester, 36.B.3.[7]

10. M^r O Sullevane gave a thin MS. in small Fol. being Sir Francis Bacon's Collections touching Præmunire, Treason, &c.[8]

4 March 1722/3.

11. Mr Noel came, & left with me a small Catalogue lately received from Mr Suttie, being N°. 32.[9]

12. Mr Sparke came, & Borrowed the MS. of Walter de Hemingford, 59.B.8. according to my Lords Order.[10]

5 March 1722/3.

13. Mr Bowyer came, and I returned him him [sic] the Catalogue he left with me, with this Answer that I believed my Lord would be willing to take all the MSS. and that I believe that many among the Printed books are for his Turn.[11]

---

[1] See footnote to 16 May 1722, item 1.

[2] i.e. James Brydges, 1st Duke of Chandos; his library was sold 12 Mar. 1747. (On it see C. H. Collins Baker and M. I. Baker, *James Brydges, First Duke of Chandos*, 1949, chap. iv; and A. N. L. Munby's review of the same in *Cambridge Review*, 19 Nov. 1949, p. 162.)

[3] On the Cliftons and MSS. cf. 24 Nov. 1724, item 11; 27 Jan. 1724/5, item 16; 15 Oct. 1725, item 13; 31 Jan. 1725/6, item 15. On this last date they gave the 'Leiger-book of Blythe' (i.e. the cartulary of Blyth Priory, Notts., Harl. 3759 = Davis no. 58).

[4] Presumably those sent in 22 Jan. 1722/3 (item 1).

[5] On John Dundas, father and son (fl. 1700), see Sir Ambrose Heal, *The English Writing Masters and their Copy-Books, 1570–1800*, Cambridge, 1931, p. 47. An engraved example of Dundas's work is Harl. 5949, no. 296. For the portrait of Bp. Ken (i.e. Thomas Ken, Bp. of Bath and Wells, d. 1711), engraved by Dundas, see F. O'Donoghue, *Cat. of Engraved British Portraits in British Museum*, ii (1910), p. 684.

[6] See footnote to 11 Jan. 1719/20, item 3. The cat. was returned 5 Mar. 1722/3 (item 13).

[7] i.e. Harl. 201.   [8] Harl. 6688.   [9] Not traced.

[10] i.e. Harl. 691. The return of the MS. was demanded by Wanley 6 Apr. 1725 (item 16).

[11] Cf. 2 Mar. 1722/3, item 8. Wanley finally agreed with Batteley for the remainder of MSS. and printed books 5 and 6 Nov. 1723 (see footnote to those dates for list of MSS.).

14. D^r. Sherard brought Monsr. le Duke a young French Physician to see the Library; and I shewed them Manuscripts for above an hour, to great Satisfaction. M^r. le Duke was born in Constantinople, is about to return thither; and will willingly do my Lord Service there.

15. Mr Taylor of Oxford came, and I had (at my Lodging) some Conference with him touching the Library of Dr Charlet deceased.[1]

16. Mr John Smith came to my Lodging, and read to me part of a Letter he ha's lately rec^d from his Brother, to do what he shall find reasonable with the Parcel of MSS. now in his Custody; and therefore said that he had rather sell to my Lord than to any other, and will accept of any reasonable Price for them, Not understanding their Value. I said I would speak to my Lord about this Matter; and believe I shall treat with him. /[2]

[*Daily entries and Wanley's pagination for Vol. I end here*]

Books brought in.[3]

(f. 76*a*)

Russian MS. p. 6. 1.
English Shorthand. Ib. 6.
S^r. Francis Bacon's Tracts. 7.
Speculum Humanæ Salvationis Illuminated: The Lord North's Primer. 9. 1.
About the Earls of Essex, Northampton, Somerset, &c. temp. Jac. I. Ibid.
Dr Beaumonts Determinations. 10. 1.
Old Postills. 11, 4.
Old Primer, small. 12. 5.
Three small MSS. 13, 2.
Sign Manual of K. Charles I. 13, 4.
——————————— Henry VII. 13, 5.
Lords Prayer in Hungarian, & Latin. *Ibid.*
Late Elector Palatin's Letter to Qu. Anne. 13, 6.
Abstract of the Emperor of Morocco's Letter to Qu. Anne. *Ibid.*
Princess of Holstein's Letter to Qu. Anne. 13, 7.
King of Sicily's Letter to the Earl of Oxford. 13, 8.
Qu. Anne's Letter to the Duke of Wirtenberg. 13, 9.
The fine Persian MS. & two Liturgical MSS. 13, 10.
Smal Theological MSS. in Old English. 14, 1.
S^r. Edward Cokes Law-MSS. & S^r. William Stroud's Notes. 14, 7.
A Parcel of MSS. bought of Mr Jones. 15, 1.
A small Parcel sold by me. 15, 3.
A Parcel of Printed books from Mr Noel. 19, 4.
The Rouen-Primer printed on Velum. 19, 8.
Joan. Cocceij Lexicon. 19, 7.
Duplicates for Mr Noel. 19, 9. Rev^d. M^r. Sam. Lisle's MSS. 20, 5.
Two worn Copper Coins, brought in by my Lord. 21, 4.

---

[1] Arthur Charlett, Master of University College, d. 18 Nov. 1722. For ref. to a cat. of part of Charlett's library see 10 Feb. 1723/4, item 3. According to Thomas Hearne Charlett's library was sold to Wilmot, a London bookseller, for 500 guineas (*Remarks and Collections*, Ox. Hist. Soc. viii (1907), p. 142); cf. also *DNB*. For his coll. of MSS. see S. G. Gillam, 'Arthur Charlett's Letters and Manuscripts', *BLR* iv (1952–3), pp. 105–14.   [2] For Smith's MSS. see footnote to 10 Sept. 1722, item 3.

[3] *Note*—the page refs. given by Wanley in this list (called 'Addenda' throughout the footnotes) refer of course to Wanley's own pagination (i.e. page numbers in the margins). The entries are for the most part short notes for material in the body of the diary. Ref. should always be made back to the date cited.

23 MSS. sent in by Mr Gibson, with 2 printed Books. 22, 4.

MS. Copie of Le Romant de la Rose, sent in by My Lord. 24, 7: (but sent back to the owner, 4 Febr. 1719 he asking 30^{lib} for it[.)]

$$20$$

My Lord sent in an Exemplification of an old Fine.

pag. 28, 1. The Books bought of Mr John Gibson, are.[1]

Libri Impressi.

    1. D. Augustinus de Civitate Dei. Ven. ap. Windel. Spiram, 1470. fol. chart. mag.[2]

    2. SS. Biblia Vulgata. Ven. ap. Franc. de Hailbrun, &c. 1476, 4to. mag. litt. colorat. /[3]

(f. 76b) Codices MSS.^{ti} Compacti.

    3. Servius in Virgilium. fol. membr. (Codex fuit dono datus A.D. 1478.)[4]

    4. Sicconis Polentoni Epithoma in Vitas Scriptorum illustrium Latinæ Linguæ. (Dicitur hunc librum Sicconis esse ineditum.) fol. chart. script. A.D. 1438. Illuminat.[5]

    5. Lucanus. fol. chart. (Codex fuit donatus A.D. 1467.)[6]

    6. Alanus (de Insulis) de Conquestione Nature contra hominem.
Bernardi Sylvestris Macrocosmus,et Microcosmus.
Ovidius de Ponto, libris 3.
Liber de Vitis Philosophorum *veterum*
          } script. in chartis antiquioribus, fol. min. fuit liber Joannis Marchanovæ A.D. 1440.[7]

    7. Boccatius de Casibus Virorum illustrium
Albertini Muxati Tragedia Ecorinis.
       } 4to. mag. in membranis, illum. liber quondam
                                       Sicconis Polentoni.[8]

    8. Boccacij Bucolicum, in 16 Eglogas distinctum: cum intentionibus earundem. script. Florentiæ A.D. 1408. in membranis. 4. (hunc itidem Librum aiunt esse ineditum.)[9]

    9. Ciceronis Orator. manu Italica minutiore, 4to. membr. illum.[10]

    10. Jacobi Lucensis Cardinalis Papiensis, de Pontificis & Sacri Senatus Officio, Libellus.
Idem de Morte Cardinalis Theanensis. Dat. 1492.
Idem, ut videtur, de Institutione Principis.
Marsilij Ficini Dialogus, inter Deum et Animam.
Ejusdem Epistola de Platonis Legibus a se Latine redditis.
Idem de Divino Furore.
         } Libellus perpulchre scriptus, (manu Italica) membranulis tenuioribus; nec non egregie illuminatus.[11]

Codices MSS. incompacti.

    11. L'Inferno, Purgatorio, e Paradiso, di Dante. fol. script. in chart. A.D. 1469. (cum rudioribus picturis.)[12]

---

[1] Cf. 20 Jan. 1719/20, item 4.   [2] *BMC* v. 153 (IC 19510); Hain 2048; GW 2877.
[3] *BMC* v. 193 (IB 19849); Hain 3063; GW 4223.
[4] Harl. 2680 (for date see f. 192).
[5] Harl. 4769 (for date see f. 263^b).   [6] Harl. 2507 (for date see f. 132).
[7] Harl. 3234 (for ownership and date see f. 1).
[8] Harl. 3565.   [9] Harl. 5421 (for date see f. 57^b).   [10] Harl. 3932.
[11] Harl. 5335 (Art. 2 is dated in MS. 1482 *not* 1492 as stated by Wanley).
[12] Harl. 3460 (for date see f. 86).

12. Lactantij quædam, eleganter scripta in membranis. fol. min.[1]
13. Commentarius in 8 Plauti Commœdias. fol. min. chart. (liber dono datus A.D. 1478.)[2]
14. Polybij Libri V. Latine, per. Nic. Perottum. fol. min. membr. Illuminat.[3]
15. Plauti Comœdiae. fol. min. chart.[4]
16. Plutarchi Apophthegmata, Latine, per Franc. Philelphum. 4to. chart.[5]
17. Tullius de Officijs. 4to. chart.[6]
18. Sallustius. scriptus A.D. 1469. ——
    Aurispe V. CL. Epistolarum Hippocratis translatio. cum alijs } 4to. chart.[7]
19. L. Florus. ——
    Alexij Scintillarium Poeticum. } 4to. chart.[8]
    Grammaticalia. ——
20. Macer de Viribus Herbarum. script. in membranis A.D. 1448. 4to. illum. /[9]
21. Juvenalis, in Membranis, eleganter et scriptus & illuminatus, A.D. 1410. 4to.[10] (f. 77a)
22. Persius, festinanter scriptus in Membranis. 4to.[11]
23. Horatius. emendatus manu Angeli Politiani. illum. in 4to.[12]
24. Virgilius, scriptus Panormi A.D. 1454. 4to. chart.[13]
25. Juvenalis & Persius. membr. 8vo. medio.[14]
26. Emanuelis Chrysoloræ Erotemata. Graecè. membr. 8vo.[15]

18. February, 1719/20.

Mr Sanderson of the Rolls gave the tatter'd Theological MS. in Old English, which he before left here.

19 February, 1719/20.

My Lord sent in a Parcel of Papers relating to the Endowment & State of many of our English Benefices.[16]

23 February 1719/20.

My Lord bought of Mr Noel a Parcel of Printed Books; with 6 MSS. viz.[17]

Tullius de Oratore, manu antiquâ: imperf. 4to. quadrato.[18]
IV Evangelia, manu antiqua. 4to.[19]
Jac. Palmerius de Temporibus. *fol. min. membr. illum.*[20]
History of Venice, in Italian; large *fol.*[21]
Series of the Doges of Venice, with the Armes painted, thin fol.[22]
Gasparini Pergamensis Institutiones Epistolicæ. Ciceronis Paradoxa. fol. min. chart.[23]

---

[1] Harl. 3056. [2] Harl. 2454 (for date see f. 85b). [3] Harl. 3293. [4] Harl. 2476.
[5] Harl. 3398. [6] Harl. 2544. [7] Harl. 2541 (for date see f. 100). [8] Harl. 2557.
[9] Harl. 2651 (for date see f. 44). [10] Harl. 2648 (for date see f. 77b). [11] Harl. 2588.
[12] Harl. 2642 [13] Harl. 3518 (for date see f. 201b).
[14] Harl. 3896. [15] Harl. 5569.
[16] These items were acquired from Bowyer (see item 6 of date cited).
[17] Cf. 20 Feb. 1719/20, items 8 and 9.
[18] Harl. 2736. [19] Harl. 2826. [20] Harl. 3677.
[21] Not identifiable with certainty, but probably Harl. 5020, which is large folio. It has no date of acquisition by Wanley but the old fly-leaf has been mutilated, only part remaining, and the date may therefore have been destroyed. [22] Harl. 4820. [23] Harl. 2594.

Mʳ Noel also deliver'd his Oriental & other MSS.
He also sent in those of Dʳ. Alix, in Exchange for an Aldus's Horace.[1]

26. February 17$\frac{19}{20}$.

The Original MS. of K. Edw. VI's Latin Catechism bought.

10. March. 17$\frac{19}{20}$.   Two of Dʳ Whincopps MSS. (had of Mʳ Noel) were laid up.[2]

21. March 17$\frac{19}{20}$.

Elias Meniati's Gr. MS. Entituled πετρα σκανδαλου brought in.

23. March 17$\frac{19}{20}$.

Mʳ Bowyer sold me a MS. Chronicle of England for my Lord.

1 April 1720.

Mʳ Bowyer sent in a MS. Latin Prayer-book: bought 5 April. /

(f. 77ᵇ)   1720.

April 5. Mʳ Vaillant sent in a MS. having sent in another before.

    11. I agreed with him for those MSS. one being Codex Justinianeus, the other Q. Curtius.

    23. Mʳ Gibson sent hither the following MSS. my Lord having left their Price to me. viz.[3]

        1. Virgilij exemplar chartaceum; (script. A.D. 1465.) sed non absolutum. fol. min.[4]

        2. Senecæ Tragoediae Exemplar perpulchrum in membranis. fol. min.[5]

        3. Nonius Marcellus. Exemplar pulchrum, in chartis. fol. min.[6]

        4. Ovidij Metamorphosis. Exemplar nitidum et membranaceum. fol. min.[7]

        5. Tullius de Amicitia. Paradoxa. De Creatione Coeli & Terræ. De Officijs. Senecæ quædam chart. fol. min.[8]

        6. Summa de Grammatica. membr. 4ᵗᵒ. ampliori.[9]

        7. Prosperi Aquitanici Epigrammata quædam. membr. 4ᵗᵒ. ten.[10]

[1] The oriental Harl. MSS. bearing the date 20 Feb. 1719/20 are: 3279, 3446, 5449, 5451, 5455 (belonged to John Covel), 5465, 5466, 5470, 5479, 5488, 5490, 5492, 5505, 5510, 5513, 5524, 5527, 5528, 5529, 5532, 5585. The three following MSS. though Oriental bear the date 23 Feb. 1719/20: 3418, 4634, 6529. Apart from the above Oriental MSS. there is now no means of distinguishing in all cases between Noel's 'other MSS.' and 'those of Dr. Alix', all of which bear the date 20 or 23 Feb. 1719/20 and are as follows: 2302, 3260, 3263, 3307, 3427, 3428, 3430, 3536. B (ff. 1–33), 3563 (ff. 101–307), 3663, 3810 (pt. 2), 3947, 3948, 4364, 4378, 4507–12 (Séguier MSS.), 4566, 4584, 4787, 4823, 4836, 4837, 4876, 4877, 5081, 5133, 5136, 5283, 5297 (a Séguier MS.), 5397, 6610, 6665, 6880. Harl. 2403 is endorsed on f. 1 by Wanley 'Mr. Noel (from Dr. Whincop) Febr. 1719/20'.

[2] For refs. to Whincopp's books see footnote to 11 Jan. 1719/20, item 6.

[3] For further details see 18 Mar. 1719/20, item 8, and footnotes.

[4] Harl. 2502 (for date see f. 46). [5] Harl. 2669. [6] Harl. 2451.

[7] Harl. 2769. [8] Harl. 2469. [9] Harl. 2464. [10] Harl. 3069.

8. Flore de Virtú, e de Costumi. membr. 4to. cum picturis.¹
9. Ordo Breviarij secundum Consuetudinem Curie Romane. Codex pulcher in membranis. 4to.²
10. Poetria Magri Gualfredi Anglici. Antonij Astensis Poemata. Epistolæ quædam. De Rhetorica. chart. 4to.³

May 7. My Lord bought the two fine MSS. formerly belonging to Thomas Howard Earl of Arundel & Surrey.⁴

24. My Lord bought some Printed Books, & [*blank space*] MSS. of Mr Bateman.⁵

26. The Collection of Coins & Medals, with some Antiquities, lately belonging to the Rev^d. M^r. [*blank space*] Maddison (a Scots Nonjuring Clergyman) deceased; were this day bought of Mr Robert Sanderson of the Rolls, his Executor: and for the most part, actually brought in.
My Lord bought a Cabinet for Medals.

27. The MSS. & Printed Books bought of Mr Bateman, came in.

June. 1. Mr Gibson sent in a small parcel of MSS. & Printed Books. vid. 46, 4.

2. My Lord sent in a Parcel of Printed Books.

7. Mr Harbin gave 4 Papers.

11. A small parcel of books sent in by Mr Bateman.

16. The heavy pieces of Antiquity, bought of Mr Sanderson (as above) were brought in.

27. The CODEX AVREVS was deliver'd into my Custody; &

29. Actually brought into the Library.

July 12. A small Parcel brought into the Library.

15. Mr Hesket Windsor-Herald, give's a Chinese Sheet.

16. Mr Warburton's MSS. & two Pictures brought into the Library. (The Antiquities I rec^d 2 August following, & they are brought in.)

Aug. 6. I brought in a Printed Breviarium Prædicatorum Paris, 1655 4to. with some written Corrections.

10. M^r O Sullevane brought in his Copie & Latin Versions of the Irish Poem in 93.C.29. *fol. 9,b.*

12. A Printed book given by Mr George Hay.

16. K. Henry VI's fine MS. of the Lives of S. Edmund & S^t. Fremund, bought.⁶

17. My Lord sent in a Parcel of Bulls & other Deeds, mostly relating to Rufford-Abbey.

20. Mr Tho. Harley gave certain old Coins found in Hereford-shire.

22. My Lord sent in a fine MS. of Franc. Patricius de Institutione Rei Politicæ, given by M^r. Vaillant. /

1720. (f. 78*a*)

August 29. Mr Thomas Harley sent in 54 Books.

Septr. 5. I sent hither the Seguierian MSS. lately bought.⁷

12. Three old MSS. brought in.

---

¹ Harl. 3448. ² Harl. 2986. ³ Harl. 2586.
⁴ See item 3 under date cited and 4 May 1720, item 2, and footnote.
⁵ For list of the MSS. see 26 May 1720, item 15, and footnotes.
⁶ Cf. also 12 Aug. 1720, item 14.
⁷ For list see footnote to 5 Sept. 1720, and also 1 June 1720, item 5.

Sept. 29. I brought in the Missale Cisterciensium, *Paris.* 1529.[1] & sent it for Wympole.

30. I brought in the Helvici Chronologia.[2]

Oct. 20. I brought in the greatest part of the MSS. Papers & Parchments bequeathed by M[r] Hugh Thomas to my Lord Oxford, (vid. pag. 63, 4.[)]

Dec. 15. I brought in 23 old Charters given by M[r]. Sanderson.

1720

I.

Jan. 16. A small parcel of Printed books brought in from M[r] Bowyer.
M[r] Noel sends in a larger Parcel of Printed Books & MSS. which my Lord had chosen at his house.

18. My Lord send's in two Modern MSS.

19. My Lord send's in an old MS. Greek Psalter.

20. My Lord send's in 9 Spanish Books.

Febr. 1. My Lord sent in a transcript of Mich. Servetus's Works.

7. Ovids Amatoria, MS. in 4[to]. Paper; bought of M[r]. Hay: together with a small parcel of Printed Books.

20. More of Hugh Thomas's Papers Recovered.
Padre Orlandi's Ritratti brought in: (and being disliked they were all returned.)

22. M[r]. Bacon send's in some MSS. bought in the present Auction. (Paid for them & other Things 3 May 1721.)

23. M[r] Noel bring's more; which with the former, and those to be Bought, will be Noted with this Day.
M[r] Hay sends in a small parcel of old Printed Books.

March 1. I agreed with M[r] Varenne for 4 fine old MSS. Primers.

4. My Lord sent in an Original Deed of Hugo de Nevilla.

7. Four MSS. bought of M[r] Hawes, & brought in.

April 26. My Lord agree's for a parcel of M[r] Gibsons books.[3]

28. My Lord gives Orders about a small parcel of books, for which he paid M[r] Hay the 23[d] instant.

May 4. Three old Inscriptions, & the Lord Radnors MSS. sent in by M[r]. Bacon, (who was paid for them, Yesterday:) NB. The Inscriptions were John Kemps; as were four others, two fine Vases, & a figure of a Woman without Armes, being bought for my Lord by M[r] Hill, at the same Auction, & are in my Lords Possession.

5. M[r] Bacon sent in the other pieces of Antiquity he bought at Kemps Auction.[4]
My Lord bought a parcel of Books of M[r]. Noel (who sent them in Accordingly) consisting of 42 [33 *deleted*] Folios, 49 [50 *deleted*] Quartos, & 54 [55 *deleted*] Octavos, &c.

---

[1] See footnote to this date in the main text of the diary.
[2] This item is not mentioned in the main text under this date: it is Christopherus Helvicus, *Theatrum Historicum sive Chronologiae Systema Novum*, 1st pubd. Giessae Hessorum, 1609: later eds. were pubd. at Marburg, 1629, 1638 and at Oxford 1651, 1662.
[3] See 27 Apr. 1721, item 6.   [4] For prices see Welbeck Wanleyana, Misc. no. 8, p. 14.

At the same time His Lordship bought another Parcel of Mr. Bowyer, which he sent in the 9th. It consists of Folios 15: Quartos 47. Octavos & Lesser Books, 234. MSS. 5. Pamphlets about 45.[1]

13. The Bird Ibis, being Embalmed by the old Egyptians, brought in.
15. My Lord send's in a Pedegree of Savage.
26. My Lord sent in a smal Parcel of old Printed books.[2]

June 7. My Lord buys a small parcell of Mr Gibson.
19. My Lord buy's a small parcell of MSS. & printed Books of Mr Ackman.
20. My Lord buy's 15 MSS. & 2 printed Books of Mr Gibson.

Nov. 9. Mr Gibson leaves 4 quarto-books.[3]
7. Eight MSS. bought of Mr Gibson.[4]
18. 21 MSS. bought of Mr Wilcox the Bookseller.
29. I brought a book bought by Mr Beaver:[5] and Dr. Sherard sent in his Parcel, wherein were 2 MSS. /

1721.   (f. 78b)
Dec. 21. The Complutensian Bible come's hither from Oxford.
Jan. 3. Two Bibles of 1551 brought in.[6]
16. Two Books brought in.
20. Mr Noel sent in a large parcel of curious Books & MSS.

1721
—
2.

Febr. 3. The remaining fragments of the Red-book of Waltham Abbey brought in.
10. The Hierome upon the Creed, Oxon, 1468, being the first book Printed in England, brought in; together with 3 other antient & valuable Tracts.
13. My Lord bought a Curious parcel of Egyptian Antiquities of Dr. Sherard.
14. A Parcel of Printed books bought at Mr Woodman's last Sale.[7]
15. Mr. Bacon brought a MS. he bought for my Lord; & another which he gave.
27. The Bp. of Peterburgh gives a Court Roll of Cleygate.
   Some time this Month, my Lord bought 3 MSS. of Mr Andrew Hay. see pag. 106, 6.

1722.
April 12. Came-in the Remainder of the MSS. bought of Mr. Noel the 19th. of January last: as also a parcel of Printed Books wch my Lord selected yesterday. See pag. 106; 7, 8.
17. An old Chartulary of Holmcultram, was b[r]ought-in.
19. Mr Vaillant having a little Paper-MS. I brought it into the Library.
21. Mr. Harbyn gives 3 Original Letters of Peireskius, & 2 valuable old Deeds.

May 22. Roger Gale Esq gives 18 Original Letters of so many Learned Men.

---

[1] For Bowyer parcel cf. 9 May 1721, item 10.
[2] This item is not mentioned in main text under this date.
[3] Cf. also 8 July 1721, item 16.   [4] Entered in main text under 9 Nov. 1721, item 1.
[5] For the book bought of Beaver see 28 Nov. 1721.   [6] See 2 Jan. 1721/2.
[7] Cf. 15 Feb. 1721/2, item 4.

Septr. 1. Mr Bowyer give's a small parcel of Original & other Papers.

My Lord send's in four MSS. which he lately brought up from Bramton-Castle. They are,

Proverbia Senecæ. Idem de remedijs fortuitorum. Epistolæ Senecæ ad Paulum, & Pauli ad Senecam. Epistolæ ejusdem ad Lucilium. fol. Exemplar 600 annorum.[1]

Secunda et Tertia pars Operis dicti Pan-theologus, per Petrum Ecclesiæ S. Trinitatis Londoniæ Canonicum compilati. fol. Exemplar 500 Annorum.[2]

Regest[r]um Cartarum Monasterij de Wormesley in agro Herefordensi. fol. min. in membranis.[3]

The Names, Armes, & Precedencies of all the Knight-Baronets created by K. James I, since Anno 1611. 4[to]. parchm[t].[4]

3. My Lord sent-in 5 old Deeds, all belonging to his own Noble Family.

10. My Lord send's in 3 other Old Deeds.

13. M[r] Noel send's-in (without Orders) a parcel of Books & MSS.

A List of the MSS. therein, is given above, at pag. 139.

M[r] Gibsons two last parcels Agreed for.

Oct. 5. M[r] Gibson give's a pretty Latin MS.

8. M[rs]. Mould sends-in from her brother Six Greek Marbles, & a Greek MS. of S[t]. Chrysostom upon the Acts. Impf.

11. My Lord orders the Russian Sea-Laws to be bought.

24. My Lord buys two MSS. & a Tract printed upon Velum, of M[r] Varenne.

29. My Lord buys a small parcel of Printed Books, & 8 Manuscripts of M[r] Charles Davis the Bookseller.

My Lord sends in two MSS. more.

Nov. 12. My Lord send's in a Japanese or Chinese Printed Book.

21. I gave 46 Charters & 3 Rolls.

27. My Lord bring's in a MS.

1 Dec[r]. M[r] Harbyn gives to my Lord an old Patent, & a parcel of very Valuable Letters.

12. M[r] Holman give's 14 old Charters.

20. M[r] William Thomas gave a folio-Welsh Bible, finely printed at Oxford A.D. 1690, on the large Paper; in 2 Volumes.[5]

26. List of the Printed books added to his[6] two last Parcels of MSS. without enhancing the Price.

---

[1] Harl. 2659.   [2] Harl. 3257.

[3] Wormesley Cartulary is Harl. 3586, ff. 68–145 (formerly numbered 1–77) (= Davis no. 1081) with (at f. 67) half leaf of contents and followed at ff. 146–50 by letters of Thomas Blount (11 Dec. 1676) and Thomas Good (26 Oct. 1676), &c. addressed to Sir Edward Harley at Brampton Bryan. (On Dugdale's request for the loan of this MS. see T. Blount to Sir E. Harley, 1 June 1671, *HMC Portland Papers*, iii. 323.) This Wormesley Cartulary was presumably therefore either the first or only item in the MS. when Wanley made the entry in the Diary; Wanley's inscription written on a small slip of paper now mounted on f. 1 of the MS. is presumably not in its original position, viz. 'Hunc Codicem in Bibliotheca quae est in Castro Bramtoniensi repertum, secum advexit Dominus meus, mense Augusti, A.D. 1722.' The first part of the MS. (ff. 2–66) is now a cartulary of St. Martin's at Battle (= Davis no. 34).

[4] Harl. 3326.

[5] This item is not mentioned in the main text of the Diary. (On this Bible see Ifano Jones, *The Bible in Wales*, 1906.)

[6] i.e. Gibson's.

Jan. 21. My Lord buyes a Small Parcel at Mr Woodmans Sale.[1]

    23. Mr Woodman Send's in the Original MS. of the Marquis of Clanri-
cardes Memoirs. /

24 Jan. 1722/3. Mr Charles Davies give's a Bill of the Parcel now bought of him. (f. 79a)
[at foot
of page]

Febr. 8. My Lord send's in a Greek Inscription fairly engraven in Marble.

    9. A kind of Talismanical Plate, Greek; beg'd of Mr Andrew Hay.

    12. My Lord will keep the Books bought at Mr Davis's Sale; among which,
is one MS.

    18. My Lord send's-in 3 fine MSS.

    19. My Lord send's-in a small parcel of old Deeds.[2]

    28. My Lord send's-in a Specimen of Mr Dundasses Writing; & a Print
Engraven after one of his Performances.

March 2. M^r. O Sullevane give's a thin MS.

---

[1] Cf. 22 Jan. 1722/3, item 1.

[2] These are now among the *Cotton* Charters; the following are endorsed by Wanley with the date
19 Feb. 1722/3, viz. XXI. 30–39; XXIII. 6, 7; XXVI. 13, 18; XXVII. 159; XXIX. 62. Cf. also 20 Feb.
1722/3, item 6.

PRINTED IN GREAT BRITAIN
AT THE UNIVERSITY PRESS, OXFORD
BY VIVIAN RIDLER
PRINTER TO THE UNIVERSITY